"A Fit Representation of Pandemonium"

MERCER
UNIVERSITY PRESS

Endowed by
TOM WATSON BROWN
and
THE WATSON-BROWN FOUNDATION, INC.

"A Fit Representation of Pandemonium"

EAST TENNESSEE CONFEDERATE SOLDIERS IN THE CAMPAIGN FOR VICKSBURG

William D. Taylor

MERCER UNIVERSITY PRESS
MACON, GEORGIA

MUP/H712

Books published by Mercer University Press are printed
on acid free paper that meets the requirements of
American National Standard for Information
Sciences—Permanence of Paper for Printed Library
Materials.

Library of Congress Cataloging-in-Publication Data

†Taylor, William D., 1948-2007.
A fit representation of pandemonium : East Tennessee Confederate soldiers
in the campaign for Vicksburg / William D. Taylor. -- 1st ed.
p. cm.
Includes bibliographical references and index.
ISBN-13: 978-0-88146-034-6 (hardcover : alk. paper)
ISBN-10: 0-88146-034-6 (hardcover.)
1. Vicksburg (Miss.)—History—Siege, 1863. 2. Vicksburg (Miss.)—History—Siege,
1863—Personal narratives, Confederate. 3. Vicksburg (Miss.)—History—Siege,
1863—Social aspects. 4. Soldiers—Tennessee, East—Biography. 5. Soldiers—
Confederate States of America—Biography. 6. Tennessee, East—Biography.
7. Confederate States of America.—Army--Military life. 8. Tennessee,
East—History—Civil War, 1861-1865—Social aspects. 9. United
States—History—Civil War, 1861-1865—Social aspects. 10. United
States—History—Civil War, 1861-1865—Personal narratives, Confederate.
I. Title.
E475.27.T39 2007
973.7'62—dc22
2007022568

Contents

vi

For the days shall come upon thee, that thine enemies shall cast a trench about thee, and compass thee round, and keep thee in on every side.

(Luke 19:43; KJV)

"My 95-year old cousin Dock Kite, who still lives alone at the old Kite homestead on Dodson Creek in Hawkins County [Tennessee], knew 'Uncle Jimmy' Everhart very well. When he was up in years, Uncle Jimmy married 'Aunt Susan' Grigsby, the widow of Confederate soldier Samuel Grigsby. She was formerly a Kite and related to Dock and me. Dock once told me about walking along the road with his father when Dock was a little boy, seeing Uncle Jimmy and Aunt Susan coming toward them in a buggy on their wedding day. Dock marveled how Uncle Jimmy could drive his team with only one arm."
—Donahue Bible, 22 July 2002, Mohawk, TN

Note: "Uncle Jimmy" left the other arm, many years before, at the 4th Brigade Hospital, Vicksburg, Mississippi, on 24 June 1863.

Acknowledgments

Though most readers will probably bypass the Acknowledgment pages, I know that without the names listed here, there would be precious little to be presented in the following pages. Credited here are the individuals and institutions that graciously allowed their materials, expertise, and photographic images to be used so that this story could be presented in as complete a manner as possible. Thoroughness in remembering everyone is always a major concern and never satisfactorily achieved.

For the wonderful anecdote about Tennessee Confederate soldiers operating around Vicksburg, I am grateful to the Louisiana State University Press.

For the hand-drawn map of the vicinity around Vicksburg, I wish to express my gratitude to the Museum of the Confederacy in Richmond, Virginia. For my own "cartographer," I am "beholden," as the mountain man might say, to Mary Ann Kolpak, a graphic arts major at Carson-Newman College.

In regard to primary materials, I want to acknowledge the kind assistance of the authors and the University of Tennessee Press for excerpts from Dr. Willene Clark's book *Valleys of the Shadow: Diary of Capt. Reuben G. Clark of the 59th Tennessee Infantry* and from Charles Northen's book *All Right, Let Them Come: Diary of an East Tennessee Confederate Soldier*. I also appreciate the permission of Mr. Glenn A. Chattin for the use of the diary of William Raleigh Clack, and for the images of Clack and his brother Micajah.

For the use of material from his book *A Smith in Service: Diaries of Calvin M. Smith*, I am most earnestly thankful to Mr. Leland L. Smith of Friendswood, Texas. It is most difficult to imagine the completion of my book without the inclusion of Lieutenant Calvin Smith's vivid observations. I also appreciate the kind words and support from Mrs. Emily Woodall-Ivey of Broaddus, Texas, concerning the material in the book relating to one of its most interesting characters, Benjamin C. Giddens of the 3rd Tennessee.

Steve Cotham and Sally Polhemus of the McClung Historical Collection of the Knoxville Public Libraries have been extremely gracious with their time and expertise on this and other projects. Specific to this work, they provided access to the letters, diary, image, and sketch of Sergeant John Thomas Moffitt of Lynch's Battery, as well as the various letters from the Hall-Stakely papers written by several insightful soldiers from Madisonville, Monroe County. In addition, I was able to rely on Cotham and Polhemus for letters written by Sergeant Stuart Nelson. The entire staff of "the McClung Room" has ever been ready with leads and assistance. I would also like to thank Norma Myers and Ed Speers of the Archives of East Tennessee State University for help in accessing the Alfred and Richard Bowman letters. Thanks are also due the Bicentennial Library of Chattanooga for providing access to the image of Colonel William M. Bradford and letters and image of Lieutenant Colonel David M. Key.

I wish to acknowledge the kind assistance of the Cleveland City Library for permission to use material from the diary of Sergeant Isaac J. Stamper. His observations are also key to understanding the experiences of East Tennessee Confederate soldiers at Vicksburg.

At Vicksburg, I am eternally grateful to Terrence Winchell, a historian at the Vicksburg National Military Park, for leads on Lynch's Battery, Battery "Tennessee," and the James Darr diary. Also, I appreciate the leads provided by Jeff Giambrone, a historian at the Old Courthouse Museum in Vicksburg, particularly related to the letters of Benjamin Giddens, William Harr, William Morton, and the autobiography of Sergeant Robert Bachman of the 60th Tennessee. I appreciate the assistance of Nick Wyman of the Special Collections, the University of Tennessee, for the letters and image of J. C. M. Bogle.

For kind permission to use various photographs, I want to thank Terry McGinnis, the Robert McFarland Jones family, Donahue Bible, Bill Tucker and Mike Miner, and Chris Propst and Dale Wiseman. I also wish to thank Al Lang, the archivist at Carson-Newman College, and the Rose Cultural and Arts Center, Morristown.

I wish to acknowledge the kind cooperation of the Tennessee State Archives and Museum for the diary of Lieutenant John J. Blair, the letters of Newton J. Lillard and John C. Vaughn.

I would like to thank Dr. Charles G. "Bubba" Moffat, professor of history at Carson-Newman College, for reading the manuscript in an early draft and for his always wise and thoughtful suggestions for improvement. My friend Carl Jenkins has also provided information on the flag of the 59th Tennessee, and Claude Pennebacker, owner of much of the land on which the Battle of the Big Black River was waged, has been helpful in showing me the various locations important to understanding that action there.

Lastly, I would like to thank sincerely my wife, Darby, and my daughters, Ashley and Shelby, for attempting to help me make the manuscript more "readable," and my compatriots in the Colonel William M. Bradford–Colonel James G. Rose Camp, Sons of Confederate Veterans, Morristown, Tennessee, who kept pushing and encouraging me by asking the poignant philosophical question: "Haven't you finished that thing yet?"

W. D. T.

INTRODUCTION

"A Purer Political Atmosphere Removed from Present Associations"

During the 1880s, the University of the South's most famous professor, ex-Confederate general Edmund Kirby-Smith, often rode through the 10,000-acre highland wood at Sewanee, Tennessee. Sitting astride his charger "George," "so erect, every inch a soldier, with his long white beard blowing in the wind," he looked like a Confederate Tolstoy. Often in the company of his young privileged scholars, Kirby-Smith was preoccupied with his favorite past time: botanical investigation. Sometimes he was slow and deliberate with the fauna he studied, and at other times, it was a quick glance, after which he spurred George on to the next item of interest. The younger men were responsible for keeping up with General Kirby-Smith because, as one of his former students attested, he "waited for no one, and would soon be out of their sight in the pathless forest through which they rode."[1]

Kirby-Smith, a dedicated communicant of the Episcopal Church, came to Sewanee as a professor of mathematics soon after the Civil War, along with a number of other former Confederate officers. Indeed, the faculty and the administration of most Southern colleges that had been closed during the War Between the States were well-populated by the South's former officer gentry.

General Kirby-Smith's primary service to the late Confederacy had been as commander of the Department of the Trans-Mississippi, and indeed, he was one of the last to surrender his forces at the war's conclusion. In 1862, however, he had had another assignment, which caused him much frustration and often tried his limited patience: as commander of the Department of East Tennessee headquartered in Knoxville.

The region seethed in constant unrest, with unionist sentiment always at loggerheads with what Kirby-Smith sought to do. Insurrection was often threatened and displayed, and many in the citizenry constantly looked for

---

[1] Rene Lynch, *Rebel's Rest Remembers: Sewanee Summers When We Were Very Young* (Sewanee TN: Proctor Hall Press, 1998) 50.

Federal army intervention into the valleys in which they dwelled. There were, of course, the other residents who expected protection from these "Tories," bushwhackers, and bridge-burners, and who were impatient with the Confederate authority's soft dealing with those whom they perceived as "traitors" to the state and the new Confederacy.

Kirby-Smith and those under his command who were not native to that section of the Confederacy were always suspicious of both groups. Rarely did these authorities think either group's sympathy was far from the other, nor did the authorities believe that most East Tennesseans could be trusted or relied upon even when they professed loyalty. Confederate authorities had developed a low regard for troops from that third of the state, particularly those who served in or near their home section. Such a reputation was fed by poor performances by native East Tennesseans at the Battle of Mill Springs and smaller clashes occurring late in 1861 and early 1862. Frequent absences without leave by some of these troops strained their superiors' patience, coupled with a propensity to readily give aid and succor to the interests of unionist neighbors.

There was perhaps no greater example of this untoward and unseemly empathy fueling Kirby-Smith's distrust of native East Tennesseans called to serve in their home region than the mysterious circumstances surrounding the ill-fated 36th Tennessee Infantry. This regiment had been organized in Knoxville December 1861 and January 1862 with its muster rolls made up of volunteers mainly from Marion, Hamilton, and Bradley Counties in southeastern Tennessee. Under the command of Colonel Robert J. Morgan, its first duty was at Cumberland Gap, where almost immediately telegrams warning of its suspected disloyalty were sent to Knoxville. Federal reports noted that men from the 36th Tennessee were deserting "constantly," which caused the garrison commander, General Carter Stevenson, to order that the regiment be removed from the post and sent out of the Department of East Tennessee altogether.[2] As departmental commander, General Kirby-Smith, on 28 April 1862, directed that part of the 36th Tennessee to escort Yankee prisoners from East Tennessee to the military prison at Milledgeville, Georgia. Two weeks later, he sent Colonel Morgan the following letter, which was pointed in its implication:

---

[2] Tennessee Civil War Centennial Commission, *Tennesseans in the Civil War: A Military History of Confederate and Union Units with Available Rosters of Personnel*, 2 vols. (Nashville TN: Civil War Centennial Commission, 1965) 1: 252.

Owing to the peculiar circumstances [which are apparently lost to history] under which your regiment was organized and the evil influences surrounding it, some unfaithful members have been received into it. Removed from the disloyal element of East Tennessee and to a purer political atmosphere, no longer arrayed against relations who have joined the Federal Army in Kentucky and with examples of true patriotism about them, these men will become good and loyal soldiers.

For these reasons, your regiment is ordered to Savannah, Ga.[3]

With the passage of the Conscript Act a few weeks later, all Confederate regiments were "re-organized" to allow the election of new officers voted on by members of the commands. The Act also required these twelve-month volunteers to extend their obligation of service to three years, or the duration of the war. Colonel Morgan's papers indicated that there had been so many desertions in his command that it could not be re-organized, and it was apparently disbanded. Whether the termination of the command was official or unofficial has never been determined. Ironically, some of the men on its rolls wound up serving again with the 43rd Tennessee under Carter Stevenson at Vicksburg.

Kirby-Smith sent a dispatch to Adjutant General Samuel Cooper in Richmond with his recommendation on what he thought should be done with the East Tennessee troops. It echoed many points in his earlier letter to Colonel Morgan: "Would it not be well to remove such of the East Tennessee troops as are suspected [of disloyalty] to a different section of the Confederacy, where a purer political atmosphere and removed from their present associations they can do little or no harm and become loyal and good soldiers?"[4]

Within eight months, that "purer political atmosphere" was determined to be around the threatened Gateway to the West: "Vicksburg, Mississippi. As the last Confederate stronghold left on the Mississippi, Vicksburg was a vital link with the Trans-Mississippi Confederacy from which came supplies and forces from Arkansas, Louisiana and Texas. Jefferson Davis himself metaphorically termed the city to be "the nail-head that holds the South's two halves together."[5]

---

[3] Gen. Edmund Kirby-Smith to Col. Robert J. Morgan, 11 May 1862, *Official Records*, ser. 1, vol. 10, pt. 2, p. 511–12.

[4] Gen. Edmund Kirby-Smith to Gen. Samuel Cooper, 13 March 1862, *Official Records*, ser. 1, vol. 10, pt. 2, p. 321.

[5] Quoted in Shelby Foote, *The Civil War: A Narrative (Fredericksburg to Meridian)*, vol. 2 (New York: Random House, 1963) 346.

"Fortress Vicksburg" also proved to be quite a symbol of Southern resolve, and one which Lincoln had an obsession to remove. General Ulysses S. Grant proved to be the man for the job, just as he had and would continue to be for many such difficult assignments during the War Between the States. Vicksburg would prove, however, to be much more tedious, aggravating, and costly than ever imagined by the Washington strategists. Still, Grant would be the man to see it through.

In response to Kirby-Smith's suggestion, Gen. John C. Vaughn's newly-formed East Tennessee brigade was the first to go, leaving the first and second weeks of December: the 79th Tennessee "aboard cattle and freight cars" from Haynesville (now Johnson City), the 80th Tennessee from the depot at Sweetwater, Monroe County, and the 81st Tennessee from Henderson's Depot in Greene County. The trains carried these farm boys through places they otherwise would probably never have seen: Chattanooga, Atlanta, Montgomery, Pollard, and Mobile (where they were carried across the bay in ferry boats), then back on the train to Meridian and Jackson. From Jackson, Vaughn's Brigade was sent after a time a hundred miles north to Grenada on the Mississippi Central Railroad, where General John C. Pemberton was assembling forces to meet Ulysses S. Grant's expected advance from North Mississippi.

Vaughn's new regiments had been formed in East Tennessee after the passing of the Conscript Act in May 1862 and were composed of "volunteer" conscripts—that is, men who had not joined before because they thought that they would not be compelled to serve. Such sentiment would always make them suspect. Their commander, General Vaughn, was a remarkably adaptable individual who was sheriff of Monroe County, and who had been an invited guest of the State of South Carolina to witness to the bombardment of Fort Sumter the year before. Though Confederate authorities never questioned his allegiance, his capabilities as a brigadier often were inconsistent.

Vaughn had raised the 3rd Tennessee Infantry 29 May 1861 before the state had seceded 8 June 1861, making it the first Confederate regiment in service from East Tennessee. It was called immediately to Virginia and was on the field of battle at the war's first major engagement, the Battle of First Manassas, where Vaughn's men, during McDowell's retreat to Washington, captured a battery of Yankee artillery.

The 3rd Tennessee soon thereafter found itself back in East Tennessee, where its troops thought they would be used to defend their native soil. Colonel Vaughn instead found himself promoted to brigadier general and given command of the new brigade composed of the 79th, 80th, and 81st Tennessee. These men were not to remain long in their home section.

Vaughn's old regiment, the 3rd Tennessee, was now brigaded together with the 31st Tennessee, the 43rd Tennessee, and the 59th Tennessee under the command of Colonel Alexander W. Reynolds of Virginia. Because Reynolds was not from Tennessee, was only a colonel, and was apparently given to frequent intoxication, his men never respected him or liked him, although often during the Vicksburg campaign he led them well.

After Braxton Bragg's ill-fated invasion of Kentucky during the summer and fall of 1821, the approach of winter found Reynolds's men being gathered around Lenoir Station for their deployment in the same section of Mississippi. Their route southwest was to be the same as their sister brigade's, but their departure was two weeks later and more direct because they went straight to Vicksburg.

Thus, at Vicksburg these East Tennesseans found themselves arriving at different intervals during December 1862 and January 1863. Literally within days of climbing from the boxcars, Vaughn's East Tennessee Confederates were marched at the double-quick to the battlefield at Chickasaw Bluffs north of the city. His raw and undisciplined men encountered the concentrated musketry and cannon fire of an enemy whose numbers, according to a Mississippi state historical marker on the field, were nearly four times that of the Confederate defenders. Some of Vaughn's brigade was called to man the rifle pits along the base of the ridge that overlooked the field of approach and were protected by huge felled trees whose gnarled, entangled limbs faced toward the flat mostly swampy ground through which Sherman's men would be forced to advance.

On the right flank, the 80th Tennessee, during the three-days' action, accorded themselves in such a manner that General John Pemberton, commander of forces at Vicksburg, permitted it as only one of four regiments out of dozens engaged to paint the battle honor "Vicksburg" on the white bar of its first national regimental flag. The 80th Tennessee had helped man the rifle pits farthest in advance of the ridge against which came the most severe Federal assaults, often in a heavy rainstorm and in "mud up to our knees," as one participant described it. The gallantry of 80th (62nd) Tennessee led General Pemberton himself to note that the 80th "behaved with distinguished coolness and courage," and General Stephen D. Lee remarked that, though their position was heavily assaulted time after time, the 80th Tennessee's fire into the

Yankee attackers was "terrific."[6] This resolve came from "fresh fish" who two months before had probably never seen an Enfield musket.

Other singular experiences of Tennesseans worthy of special mention include the 22 February service of volunteers from the 31st Tennessee and 79th Tennessee aboard the gunboats *Queen of the West* and *William H. Webb*, which sank the powerful ironclad gunboat *Indianola*, prompting Colonel Bradford of the 31st Tennessee to proclaim for these East Tennesseans: "The capture and surrender of the boat [the *Indianola*], after the desperate defense of a well-drilled and disciplined foe, entitle[s] you to the highest honors of veterans." Major M. S. Brent, over-all commander of the operation, told the detachment of 31st Tennessee "sailors" and their officers: "To you and to your men I accord the honors of this victory, and to you belong the spoils."[7]

And when David Farragut's sloop-of-war *Hartford* attacked the small earthen fort at Warrenton, Mississippi, on 25 March 1863, the riflemen from the 59th Tennessee traded .577 caliber Enfield rounds with the Federal warship's heavy naval guns, while the fort was literally pounded to rubble over their heads. General Stevenson wrote in his report afterwards that "the *Hartford* approached so near that our musketry drove her gunners from their guns, causing her to withdraw back down river."[8]

And not all drama resulted from action with the enemy. On the night of 28 March 1863 a tornado blew through the camps of John Vaughn on the north side of Vicksburg, killing a number of his men in the 79th and 81st Tennessee, as well as some Georgians camped next to them. "Cabins were smashed to atoms in the dead of night before many would fairly escape," wrote Captain Allen Wash of the 79th Tennessee, causing "six men to be killed outright in one tent, and ten others injured in various parts of the regiment."[9]

Two days later, a squad of men from the 3rd Tennessee under the "command" of Private William Ellison volunteered to take a skiff down river and set ablaze the *City of Vicksburg*, a Confederate transport that had broken free of the Vicksburg wharf and drifted onto the federally-controlled shores of

---

[6] Report of Gen. Stephen D. Lee, *Official Records*, ser. 1, vol. 17, pt. 1, p. 683.

[7] John M. Carson, "Capture of the *Indianola*," *Confederate Veteran* 32/8 (August 1924): 383.

[8] Report of Gen. Carter L. Stevenson, *Official Recordss*, ser. 1, vol. 24, pt. 1, p. 480.

[9] William A. Wash, *Camp, Field and Prison Life: Containing Sketches of Service in the South, and the Experience, Incidents and Observations Connected with Almost Two Years' Imprisonment at Johnson's Island Ohio Where All Confederate Officers Were Confined* (St. Louis: Southwestern Book and Publishing Co., 1870) 19–20.

Louisiana across the channel. Their mission was accomplished right under the Yankees' noses, earning for them a 90–day furlough.

The incredible story of Reynolds' Brigade serving as guard to Pemberton's immense supply train during the Battle of Baker's Creek on May 16 is noteworthy, as these East Tennesseans protected it on narrow roads from countless Union advances and raiders, finally getting the whole bulky concern back safely into the lines at Vicksburg. Also, the 61st Tennessee at the Battle of the Big Black River the next day showed some grit for the briefest of moments, returning some effective fire when the full thrust of the Yankee assault struck its position in the lines.

After the siege of Vicksburg commenced, the ironclad *Cincinnati* was sunk by John Lynch's East Tennessee gunners on 27 May. "It is generally allowed we did it," Sergeant Jacob Alexander noted: "it was a shot from the banded 62–pounder on the hill below the Water Batteries."[10] An artilleryman serving with a neighboring battery down the river indicated that he felt "safe in saying that Capt. Lynch is entitled to the honor of sinking the *Cincinnati*. Lynch's was a splendid company."[11]

The bravery of the 43rd Tennessee was continuously displayed during the siege. As Colonel Reynolds's reserve, it was called on numerous occasions to help support weak or overwhelmed points in General Stevenson's line against Union attacks, notably on 22 May, 21 and 22 June, when it suffered significant casualties. After the 22 June sortie in which a Yankee colonel and a number of his sharpshooters were captured or killed, a Louisiana infantryman in the center of the works indicated, "this little episode of the siege caused much excitement and enthusiasm along the whole line."[12]

Two days before the surrender of Vicksburg on 4 July 1863, in response to Pemberton's question about the condition of his troops to fight their way out of the siege, Reynolds wrote: "The spirits of my men are good, and I believe that almost to a man they would be willing to make vigorous efforts to strike a blow for freedom; but, I regret to say that two-thirds of my men are unable to endure a march of ten miles."[13] The end was a foregone conclusion: "The Yankies came along our company and inquired who it was wore a red shirt," a Confederate

---

[10] Jacob Alexander to John T. Moffitt, 30 March 1863, John T. Moffitt Papers, McClung Archives, Knoxville Public Libraries, Knoxville TN.

[11] W. L. Kidd to W. T. Rigby, 27 June 1903, W. T. Rigby Correspondence, National Military Park, Vicksburg MS.

[12] William H. Tunnard, *A Southern Record: the History of the Third Regiment Louisiana Infantry* (Baton Rouge LA: privately printed, 1866) 225.

[13] Report of Col. A. W. Reynolds, *Official Records*, ser. 1, vol. 24, pt. 2, p. 348–49.

officer with the 31st Tennessee reported after the surrender. They offered $40 for the man's musket, saying that the Hawkins County sharpshooter had "killed four men at one of their port holes, and scarcely ever missed it."[14]

A paroled lieutenant with the 31st Tennessee awaiting orders to leave Vicksburg indicated that he was anxious to be gone, since the boys no longer had any role in the defense of the city. In summing up his experience, he declared: "I wouldn't take the world for the trip." Except for these and a few other deviations from the normal, however, the East Tennessee Confederate soldier at Vicksburg endured a hellish routine common to most of the Confederate defenders there right up to its surrender on the 4th of July 1863.

Unfortunately, a number of recent historians have sought to minimize the East Tennessee Confederate soldiers' six months of sacrifice and perseverance at Vicksburg because of one panicky morning when a number of them either ran for their lives toward the Big Black Bridge, or in meekness laid down their arms there because many lost their nerve. There will be no offering here of the overused, tiresome, and unsupportable conclusion that they were less than loyal Confederate soldiers because of the section of Tennessee from which they came. Men with such proclivities by this time were still hiding back in the mountains, or skulking through dark to gaps at unionist Camp Dick Robinson in Kentucky. The uniqueness of the East Tennessee Confederate soldier's Vicksburg story is that at no other point during the Civil War would two brigades totaling nearly 4,000 men made up entirely of men from that section of Tennessee (a land Bedford Forrest himself labeled "the God-forsaken") serve in the field in a Confederate army.[15]

A stroll through the Tennessee Section of "Soldier's Rest" at Vicksburg's Cedar Hill Cemetery, where nearly 400 men from the eastern section of the state were interred, provides graphic proof that many of them (fully ten percent of their total placement) never left Vicksburg alive. Many died as a result of exposure to a myriad of diseases imposed by natural conditions. Others succumbed to horrific man-made conditions that were administered with

---

[14] Leland Smith, ed., *A Smith in Service: Diaries of Calvin Morgan Smith, 1847–1864* (Rogersville TN: Hawkins County Genealogical and Historical Society, 2000) 66.

[15] With the exception of Andrew Jackson's 1st Tennessee Heavy Artillery Regiment, to which Lynch's East Tennessee Battery had been assigned, all the soldiers from the state within Pemberton's lines once the siege commenced were East Tennesseans. Several Tennessee regiments were detached from the Army of Tennessee and served with Joseph Johnston, but their only Vicksburg combat experience would come before the first of the year at the Chickasaw Bluff battles. For the rest of the campaign, these regiments were attached to Johnston's "Army of the Relief."

awesome efficiency by Grant's relentless hordes, including an unending contribution of tons of government-issued iron and lead flung and zipped into the Confederate works almost continuously for forty-seven days and nights.

A note here must be added regarding Company C (detached) of the Colonel James Carter's 1st Tennessee Cavalry Regiment (recruited in McMinn and Monroe Counties, East Tennessee), which served during the Vicksburg campaign with Pemberton's horse soldiers. There is precious little recorded of their activity there, and no veterans' remembrances are included in the present work, though their duties included escort and body-guard duty for General Carter Stevenson. Indeed, little has been written concerning the activities of Pemberton's cavalry during the Vicksburg campaign. One of the few memorials to the service of this East Tennessee cavalry company is in the Tennessee Section, "Soldier's Rest," of Cedar Hill Cemetery, Vicksburg, where two of their dead lie buried among their other Tennessee comrades.

The experiences related in this work come from many East Tennesseans who withstood the ordeal at Vicksburg, and from those who observed their actions. Much of the history of this crucial campaign will not be found in these pages unless it deals directly with these men. This work is a micro-study of the macro-campaign of Vicksburg—or as Sam Watkins put it in the subtitle of his book *Company Aytch*, "a side-show of the big show." For an exhaustive record of the complexities of the campaign as a whole, see volumes 17 and 24 of *The Official Records* or Ed Bearss's excellent *The Vicksburg Campaign*. What lies ahead in these pages is instead a story drawn from some of the recollections of a segment involved in the Campaign for Vicksburg that has never had a collected voice: the East Tennessee Confederate soldier—unnoticed, unhonored and unsung.[16]

---

[16] Smith, *A Smith in Service*, 66.

Prologue

"The Gaunt, Sallow-Faced [East] Tennesseans." Sergeant Robert Patrick of the 4th Louisiana kept a diary that chronicled his experiences during the War Between the States. Usually laden with sardonic wit, his reminiscences spared few with whom he came in contract, including, as luck would have it, some impressions Patrick had of the East Tennessee boys serving in Mississippi with the Confederate brigades of John C. Vaughn and Alexander W. Reynolds during the first half of 1863, an assignment that would culminate in the awful siege and subsequent surrender of Vicksburg. In the following anecdote, Patrick seemed to describe the very cousins of Sut Lovingood himself:

> I called at the house of a citizen to see if I could get my shirts made. I found a homely girl and her mother at the house. In answer to my inquiry as to whether they could make my shirts, the old lady said I could get them in a few days, if I would leave the cloth, and give her the measure of the shirts. This I did.
>
> While here, I saw a fair instance of how the Tennessee boys work their way in with the citizens. It has always been a mystery to our regiment how the Tennesseans managed to procure such a quantity of fresh vegetables, milk, butter, and everything else, while we were starving for them, and offering any price. When our boys went about the citizens they seemed surly and unaccommodating and showed no disposition to grant us any favors, for which I could not blame them because the soldiers I know to be a great nuisance.
>
> When I went in, I found a gaunt, sallow-faced Tennessean sitting in the little parlor. He looked like he had been reared from infancy on goobers, green apples, persimmons and dirt. His eyes looked like two minie balls set in a pile of clay. He was occupying a chair near the center of the room, with his hands stuffed into his pockets, and his feet crowded into a pair of number eleven government brogans.
>
> After I had been there for a short time, I ascertained that the object of his visit was to purchase a chicken. The lady said she had a few—but that she wished to keep them for her own use—as it was an impossibility to purchase them through the country, and besides, that some of her

children were sick and she needed what few she had and could not think of selling them. This would have been enough for me, but it wasn't half enough for my Tennessee friend.

"Well," said Tennessee, who spoke in a drawling tone, "we'uns (Tennesseans nearly all say we'uns and you'uns)[1] we'uns haint got nothin' to eat hardly, and the feller that stays with me is sorter sick, and I want to buy a chicken for him."

"I would like very much to accommodate you," replies the lady, "but as I informed you just now I haven't one to spare."

"Well, but you know how it is with us poor soldiers in camp—we can't get nothin'," whined Tennessee.

The lady repeated what she had already said, but Tennessee begged until she was almost forced to let him have it, and finding that it was impossible to get rid of him, she had one caught though I know at the same time she wished him to the devil.

He took the chicken and commenced again: "Well, hain't you got ary buttermilk?"

"Yes," she replied with an air of resignation, "I have some but I expect to reserve it for dinner."

"Well," drawled Tennessee, once more lengthening his countenance, which had almost resumed its natural appearance after receiving the chicken. "I haint been very well, and I have the heartburn mighty bad, and

---

[1] The East Tennesseans were apparently not the only Southern soldiers whose language drew the attention of the Louisianans. Will Tunnard noted that while his 3rd Louisiana Regiment was camped near Saltillo, Mississippi, their near neighbors were some Arkansas troops. While addressing the issue of deserters, Tunnard stated that "the usual morning greeting was—'Hillo, Arkansas! Did the "owls" (a term the soldiers used in reference to desertion) catch any of you'ens last night? We'ens is all here.' Their reply generally showed that some one had disappeared." Will Tunnard, *A Southern Record: The History of the 3rd Louisiana Infantry* (Baton Rouge LA: privately printed, 1866) 151. The Arkansans and Tennesseans were not the only soldiers singled out for their rustic speech. A Union soldier noted in his diary that after the surrender of the Vicksburg garrison, he was walking among the Alabamians of Stephen D. Lee's brigade when he encountered "some of the greenest specimens of humanity there," he observed. "…Their ignorance being a little less than that of the slave they despise, with as imperfect a dialect." He added the fiction that "they all wished they could come back into the old Union again." Jenkins Lloyd Jones, *An Artilleryman's Diary* (Madison WI: Wisconsin History Commission, 1914) 79. In order to provide the reader with a fairly realistic flavor of the rich language of the letters, reminiscences, and diaries, and to provide as unobtrusive a narrative as possible, the grammar and spelling of the referenced material have not been altered.

ever'body says buttermilk is a mighty good thing for the heartburn, and I think you ort to let me have some. Now, can't you let me have a little?"

Tennessee went out to get his milk and I left, thoroughly disgusted with his pertinacity, with him, and with his whole tribe in general.

This is the way that the citizens around Vicksburg are annoyed by the soldiers, and for this reason, I dislike to enter the house of a citizen for any purpose whatsoever. The Tennesseans are very annoying in this way; more so I think, than the troops from any other state. They are great peddlers and speculators on a small scale. They will sell anything in the world they possess and think that everyone else will do the same.

They will come around our mess fire and want to trade for the dinner that's cooking.

The other day as I was riding from town with a small bundle on my arm, I met a great many Tennesseans and everyone would ask me what I had to sell. I met one fellow by himself, pulling along in the hot sun, with the sand about shoe mouth deep, and the perspiration pouring from his face.

"What you got to sell, Mister?" said he, stopping and wiping the streams of sweat from his face.

"Nothing," I answered.

"Well, did you see anything up yonder that looked like it was fit to eat?"

"Yes."

"What was it?" said he, apparently much interested.

"I saw a pair of old pants hanging on the fence that I would think might make a good soup."

"Kiss my —— and go to hell, —— damn you," said Tennessee, very much incensed. I rode on.[2]

While there were undoubtedly hundreds of Tennesseans at Vicksburg who fit this stereotype, probably few of them were literate. What follows is the story left by some of defenders of the Vicksburg from East Tennessee who write about their experiences.

---

[2] F. Jay Taylor, ed., *The Reluctant Rebel: The Secret Diary of Robert Patrick, 1861–1865* (Baton Rouge LA: LSU Press, 1959) 124–26. Used by permission.

CHAPTER 1

"Till My Country Is Freed from the Darkee Lords of Lincoln" November–December 1862

The Second Winter of the War, East Tennessee. First Lieutenant Calvin Morgan Smith, a Mexican War veteran and a native of Persia, Hawkins County, East Tennessee, had been home since late October 1862, having been detailed to bring back members of his company absent without leave. He was second in command of Company D, 31st Tennessee Infantry Regiment, C. S. A., recruited in that vicinity. His regiment, as part of A. W. Reynolds's Brigade, had returned to its home section after Braxton Bragg and Edmund Kirby-Smith's unsuccessful invasion of Kentucky, culminating in the Battle of Perryville. Some of the boys felt that they had earned a leave to check on their homes and loved ones, whether they had a furlough or not. Smith was dispatched to bring them back. As the winter months approached, he found it his unpleasant duty to brave extreme weather conditions with his reluctant volunteers ambling before him on a snowy late November morning, as they trudged southward toward the winter camps of his command. They probably boarded a train down at Rogersville Junction (now known as Bulls Gap), a mile and a half from the village.

Smith wrote in his journal that he and eight or ten absentees "set out in snow 9 inches deep," bound for Lenoir Station and Loudon.[1] This second winter of the war left many of these boys wondering, during this season of Thanksgiving, what sort of gratitude was required of them. They had come to the realization there was apparently no end in sight to the war. Just as many were curious about what the new winter and the subsequent new year might bring. There had been numerous rumors.

As weather was beginning to turn its face toward winter, some of Smith's comrades down in what was then Roane County were trying to make their camps as comfortable as possible. At least during the first two years of the

---

[1] Smith, *A Smith in Service*, 37.

conflict, this had been a war in which little active campaigning was attempted during the cold months. During this Thanksgiving season of 1862, the East Tennessee brigade of Alexander W. Reynolds was still in its home country. Three of Reynolds's regiments (the 31st Tennessee, the 43rd Tennessee and the 59th Tennessee) were in camps around Lenoir Station along the railroad line. Their service for the past year had been mainly as protectors of the railroad lines in East Tennessee, guards of the Cumberland Gap, and peripheral support to the "invasion" of Kentucky during the late summer and autumn just past. The fourth regiment in the brigade, "the old 3rd Tennessee" as it was often referred to due to its seniority, had moved on Saturday, 22 November, to nearby Loudon.[2] What this foretold few huddled around the smoky campfires could imagine.

"The old 3rd Tennessee" was Colonel John C. Vaughn's own creation, assembled by the ex-sheriff of Monroe County, and mustered before the state had even entered into a military alliance with the Southern Confederacy. The 3rd Tennessee had been hustled off northeast to Virginia, and arrived in time to take a part in the first great battle of the war at First Manassas. It had, therefore, been in active service for a year and a half.

Vaughn and his regiment were brought back to Tennessee that fall, and he was promoted to brigadier general and given his own brigade, made up of three new regiments then in formation at Haynesville (now Johnson City) in Washington County, Henderson's Depot (now Afton) in Greene County, and in Vaughn's own home county of Monroe near Sweetwater. These regiments would initially be numbered as the 79th Tennessee (out of Haynesville), the 81st Tennessee (out of Henderson's Depot) and the 80th Tennessee from Sweetwater. At some point in March 1863, the regiments' order of muster were re-adjusted, and they were assigned lower unit designations by the War Department: the 79th Tennessee became the 60th Tennessee, the 81st Tennessee became the 61st Tennessee, and the 80th Tennessee became the 62nd Tennessee. Vaughn's regiments were also often referred to during the Vicksburg campaign by the names of their commanding officers: Crawford's regiment, Pitts's regiment, or Rowan's regiment.

"I volunteered in the 60th [79th] Tennessee Regiment," Sergeant Robert Bachman of Kingsport, Sullivan County wrote, "and joined Company 'G,' of

[2] Isaac J. Stamper, "Travels of the 43rd Regiment, Tennessee Volunteers: Diary of I. J. Stamper" (unpublished manuscript), Cleveland Public Library, Cleveland TN, 15.

which my brother Johnnie was captain."[3] Their colonel was John Crawford of Haynesville. This regiment like the other two was mustered in during the first weeks of November and composed mainly of "volunteer" conscripts. Once the Confederate government had initiated the first Conscript Act the previous spring, the Confederate Congress, with Senator Landon C. Haynes of Tennessee as an important proponent, afforded the three regiments' commanding officers the time to complete their commands. Many of the men composing the commands now saw that there would be no allowance for them to escape military service and chose to enlist in these regiments from their home sections to serve with friends, relations, and neighbors. Their other options would have been to serve in other East Tennessee regiments then assigned to the Army of Tennessee, service in a cavalry command (provided they had their own horse), hide out in the mountains, or take flight to federal lines in Kentucky.

"For some time we were in camp near what is now Johnson City," Bachman of the 79th (60th) Tennessee reported.[4] The regimental campground was in the swale between the present-day Veterans Hospital and East Tennessee State University along the East Tennessee & Virginia railroad line running by the whistle-stop often referred to as "Johnson's Tank." The village nearby was known during the war as Haynesville, in honor of Senator Haynes, a native of nearby Carter County. Southward past Knoxville, the railroad's name changed to the East Tennessee & Georgia railroad. This was where the 81st (61st) Tennessee of Colonel John A. Rowan of Vaughn's Brigade practiced military science in its mustering camp near its colonel's home in Sweetwater. The 80th (62nd) Tennessee Regiment, commanded by Colonel Fountain E. Pitts, a former Methodist minister, drilled near Henderson's Mills in Greene County.

Comparatively, Reynolds's Brigade of East Tennesseans was composed of veterans. Isaac N. Stamper of Cleveland, Bradley County, served with the 43rd Tennessee as a fifer in its regimental band. His regiment, as part of Reynolds's Brigade in camps at Lenoir, had been involved in the Kentucky campaign during the fall, though it missed out on much of the action during the battles

---

[3] Robert Luckey Bachman, "Reminiscences of Childhood and the Civil War" (unpublished manuscript), Old Courthouse Museum Archives, Vicksburg MS, 16.
[4] Ibid.

there.[5] He and his fellow soldiers from their camps observed the continual movement of the troop trains north and south.

"The express train in the evening brought up Fain's Regiment," Stamper wrote in his diary on 24 November 1862, when he was able to see and visit with a number of his friends and acquaintances. Their impression was that this regiment, the 63rd Tennessee (another recently formed East Tennessee command), was on its way northward to Knoxville, where it was destined "to join some brigade." Stamper also reported that the boys soon thereafter observed a second train filled with another East Tennessee regiment, "the old 26th Tennessee," as it traveled west-bound for Murfreesboro on the well-used line.[6] It had been surrendered in February at Fort Donelson to General Ulysses S. Grant. Weak Confederate leadership caused this garrison to be shamefully sacrificed. Such a misfortune would be repeated. The 26th Tennessee was exchanged in time to be heavily involved at the bloody Battle of Murfreesboro, where it suffered heavy casualties.

From their camps along the railroad, the men of the 31st Regiment constantly observed trains traveling both east (heading north) and west (heading south). Calvin Smith of the 31st Tennessee now back in his camps nearby the 43rd Tennessee, reported that it was common to see four long trains with sixteen to twenty cars pass down the line by the camps every day "full of soldiers."[7]

Vaughn's Men Start South. On 25 November, Stamper of the 43rd Tennessee noted in his diary that "Croff's" [Crawford's 79th Tennessee] Regiment passed their station headed for Mobile.[8] Their initial training had

---

[5] Stamper, "Travels of the 43rd Tennessee," 4. Stamper noted that "we thought we would get a chance to try our pluck [at Duck River, KY], but this was another *flash.*" Capt. William L. Ritter of the 3rd Maryland Battery, CSA, attached to Reynolds's Brigade both on the Kentucky campaign and during the siege of Vicksburg, recalled that as a part of that command, "we marched to within four miles of Cincinnati, OH." William L. Ritter, "Capt. William L. Ritter of Maryland," *The Confederate Veteran* 40/22 (April 1914): 172.

[6] Stamper, "Travels of the 43rd Tennessee," 15–16. The 63rd Tennessee would join Gen. Archibald Gracie's brigade. After valorous service at the Battle of Chickamauga and being involved in Longstreet's East Tennessee campaign, the 63rd was transferred as a part of Gen. Bushrod Johnson's Tennessee brigade to Lee's Army of Northern Virginia. The 26th Tennessee, after the Battle of Murfreesboro, in which it took a violent part, would serve in all the campaigns and battles of the Army of Tennessee until the end of the war.

[7] Smith, *A Smith in Service*, 37.

[8] Stamper, "Travels of the 43rd Tennessee," 16.

been compressed into only a month and a half, but it could not be helped. They were needed elsewhere. Lieutenant James T. Earnest, a native of Chucky, Greene County, and serving as quartermaster for the 79th Tennessee, indicated that from 18 November on, he was engaged in gathering rations for his regiment's trip. Rather than displaying any reluctance to leave their home area, most of the men seemed excited to be off. "The boys all seem anxious to go," Earnest wrote in his diary, and "I feel a little of the same anxiety myself." By next morning, the regiment struck camp at Camp Crawford near Haynesville and "bid adieu to her crystal streams and beautiful groves."[9] Bachman of the 79th Tennessee indicated that their transfer occurred during "the latter part of December," when "we went aboard freight and cattle cars and started for Vicksburg, Mississippi."[10] Little did the boys in the 43rd Tennessee realize what relation to their own future this train huffing and inching its way southward foretold. "I was pleased to meet my old friend Estes, who did not get his transfer," Stamper noted, so "consequently, he did not relish the trip."[11]

Lieutenant John J. Blair of Philadelphia, McMinn County, and the 80th (62nd) Tennessee, wrote in his diary on 26 November that, on this date, he and Colonel John A. Rowan's Regiment left Sweetwater, Monroe County, bound for Mobile, Alabama.[12] While Vaughn's Brigade was being dispatched southward toward points beyond Mobile not yet fixed, Reynolds's men, under no similar orders yet, continued to make themselves at home in their camps at Lenoir Station, believing that they would remain there for the winter. One of those men, Isaac Stamper of the 43rd Tennessee, spent his day "visiting the boys" and, as their sergeant, inspected the work they had done constructing fireplaces for their "shebangs." The pleasing results in drawing off smoke convinced him to build his own.[13]

Stamper and John, his brother and tent-mate, decided to collect bricks from a nearby mill that had burned sometime before, and "in a short time," Stamper noted, "we had a sufficient number [of them] to do our work." Little construction was accomplished on this day, however, because it took them all day to "lay in our material." Stamper added that he forgot to record that his brother had been home for a time and had just returned with "two bushels of

---

[9] Charles Swift Northen, ed., *All Right, Let Them Come: The Civil War Diary of an East Tennessee Confederate* (Knoxville TN: University of Tennessee Press, 2003) 36–37.

[10] Bachman, "Reminiscences of Childhood," 16.

[11] Stamper, "Travels of the 43rd Tennessee," 16.

[12] John J. Blair, "Diary of John J. Blair" (unpublished manuscript), Tennessee Library and Archives, Nashville TN, 1.

[13] Stamper, "Travels of the 43rd Tennessee," 17.

nice dried apples." The next day, 29 November, found work on the Stamper brothers' chimney progressing quite nicely, in that they had it completed by noon. They were pleased with the work the chimney did drawing the smoke from their tent, though Stamper admitted that they had a nagging fear that now being so well situated, it would surprise none of them to receive orders to leave at any time. This foreboding was even more troublesome, he noted, because "Vaughn's old regiment [the 3rd Tennessee] left for Knoxville" today.[14] Being dispatched to Knoxville was often the precursor to deployment north or south on the railroad. "Our fear was," he stated, "we would be next."[15]

Quartermaster Earnest of the 79th Tennessee claimed that by the time his regiment had arrived at Knoxville, "all the boys [were] hoarse from exercising their lungs too freely."[16] Every town on the route was alerted by their cheers that they were passing through. In relatively short order and under trying travel conditions, Vaughn's men were well on their way through Alabama. On 29 November 1862, E. D. Parker of the 79th (60th) Tennessee, wrote his wife back in Fordtown, Sullivan County, during a stopover in Montgomery, Alabama. He informed her that his health was good at present, and that they were only staying in the capital city of Alabama a brief time before moving on: "I don't know wher."[17]

"I expect we will go to Mobeal," Parker guessed, adding, "we have more to eat hear than we did when we was stationed in Tenn." He told his wife, "I am getting as fat as a bare" because he had been eating plenty of "beef bacon flour and sugar, and we have got plenty of sweet potatoes as large as my arm" and were available for a dollar a bushel. He considered apples high at a quarter apiece, and he had even seen single ones costing as much as a half dollar. Once the Tennesseans arrived at their final destination in Mississippi, apples (and in most cases peaches) could not be had for any price. "I would rather stay hear for good fare than in" Tennessee, Parker confessed, but "I would be glad to be at home with you and bill if I could be there in piece but if not, I will fight for you bill and my country til I die or til peace."[18]

Like many of the East Tennessee boys, Parker did not expect the war to continue much longer. Ever mindful of his investment opportunities back home, which he based on the markets he saw in his travels, Parker instructed his

---

[14] Ibid.

[15] Ibid.

[16] Northen, *All Right, Let Them Come*, 37.

[17] E. D. Parker to his wife Susan, 29 November 1862, in E. D. Parker Letters, "King History," Jonh S. Mosby Camp Archives, SCV, Kingsport TN.

[18] Ibid.

wife to "bacon your hogs if you can get salt for your beef and pork both." If she failed to acquire enough of the precious preservative, she was to sell "too of them on foot." As though to enlighten his wife on the market value of their holdings, Parker informed her "pork is worth 40 cts. per lbs." "I want you if you sell them [the hogs] to have the highest price," he insisted. She was also to save "[as much] as possible of my corn." Parker also wanted his wife to write him about their stock: "how they look."[19] There can be little doubt that he was a man who expected to be coming home soon.

With business matters taken care of, Parker wanted to know whether his cousin Samuel Childress, a private in the 19th Tennessee, had returned to the regiment serving with the Army of Tennessee near Murfreesboro. He also requested information on all the Childress family, and asked Sam write him "as often as he can when he gets in [the] service." Parker noted that their neighbor and friend Samuel King, who served in Parker's company, "is in better health now than he was when he was at home." Parker closed his letter by asking his wife to write him often, and he told her to continue to direct her letters to him at Montgomery in care of "Col. Crofford's 79 Tnn. in car of Capt. Sams Co. 'C.'"[20]

Another member of Parker's regiment was having a more difficult time with the trip as the brigade left Montgomery for Mobile. "We went to Mobile, and [I] was taken sick and became unconscious," Private John Gray, also of the 79th (60th) Tennessee, later wrote in response to the Confederate Veterans' of Tennessee questionnaire. "I fell out of a [train] window and [was] crippled for life. I was in the hospital at Mobile, and was treated very well. I went before the examining board and was sent home—my company was sent on to Vicksburg and was there at the surrender."[21]

Meanwhile, on the last day of November, a Sunday, Reynolds's men back in East Tennessee found it to be a lazy one about camps. Stamper of the 43rd Tennessee recorded that because the "chaplain was away, we had no preaching." The only duty required of the regiment was when it was called to fall in for an inspection at 10 a.m.[22]

The Alarm is Raised in Mississippi. On 1 December, while at Mobile with his men awaiting his superiors' pleasure, General Vaughn received from Major

---

[19] Ibid.

[20] Ibid.

[21] *Civil War Veterans' Questionnaires*, eds. Gustavus Dyer and John Trotwood Moore, 6 vols. (Easley SC: Southern Historical Press, 1985) 3: 944–45.

[22] Stamper, "Travels of the 43rd Tennessee," 18.

General John H. Forney, commander of the District of the Gulf, orders to proceed with his brigade without delay to Meridian, Mississippi, where he was to report to Lieutenant General John C. Pemberton, commanding the Department of Mississippi and East Louisiana.[23] Pemberton was a Pennsylvania native who had married a Virginia woman, and, during their life together, found himself converted heart and soul to the Southern way of life. Like many officers in the hierarchy of the Confederate command, he was a graduate of West Point, knew many officers on both sides, and was forced to choose between his adopted state and the Union. A friend of President Davis and an artilleryman by training, Pemberton rose quickly through the ranks to his current command.

In Jackson, Mississippi, Pemberton awaited the arrival of other reinforcements in the department in addition to the brigade of John Vaughn. With the loss of most of West Tennessee and portions of northern Mississippi and Alabama after the Battle of Shiloh on 6–7 April 1862, Grant's advance toward Jackson and Vicksburg was long expected. With naval support from Commodore David G. Farragut's fleet dispatched from occupied New Orleans, and Admiral David Porter's fleet from occupied Memphis, Grant's aim was ultimately to converge on Vicksburg. The city was not only a powerful symbol of Southern resolve; it was also a strategic link for supplies and troops from the Trans-Mississippi and the eastern Confederacy. With the fall of Memphis and New Orleans, the city was the last junction with the West left on the Mississippi River. As President Davis himself stated, Vicksburg was "the nail-head that held the South's two halves together."[24]

General Forney sent the following communication to Pemberton at the same time Vaughn was receiving his orders: "I am directed by General [Braxton] Bragg so soon as the Tennessee regiments (Brigadier General John C. Vaughn's command) arrive to send a strong brigade of infantry to Meridian subject to your orders, but to be recalled whenever we are threatened here [Mobile]. I have directed General Vaughn to proceed without stopping to Meridian with his command agreeably to these instructions." Forney added that

---

[23] Gen. John H. Forney to Gen. John C. Vaughn, 1 December 1862, *War of the Rebellion: A Compilation of the Official Records of the Union and Confederate Armies*, 70 vols. (Washington, DC: Government Printing Office, 1880–1901) ser. 1, vol. 15, p. 885. These are the orders that initiated the ultimate move of East Tennessee troops to Vicksburg.

[24] Quoted in Shelby Foote, *The Civil War: A Narrative (Fredericksburg to Meridian)*, vol 2 (New York: Random House, 1963) 346.

"[Vaughn's] command consists of three regiments of infantry,"[25] but he failed to mention the brigade was made up of raw and untested troops.

Back in East Tennessee in the camps of Alexander W. Reynolds's Brigade, Isaac Stamper of the 43rd Tennessee wrote that a rumor festered, which predicted "we are to move." Such talk irked the men of the regiment, he noted, because "we had just completed our chimneys."[26]

Lieutenant Blair, of the 80th (62nd) Tennessee, noted in his 2 December entry that Rowan's regiment stopped over in Montgomery, Alabama, and then continued on to Mobile, where he remembered being compelled to "sleep in a filthy stable."[27] There would be little in these new environs that would meet the approval of Blair during the days ahead. Lieutenant Earnest of the 79th (60th) Tennessee was a bit more positive in outlook, noting in his diary that "the ladies of Montgomery are not so beautiful as our East Tennessee mountain girls or the bonnie belles of Georgia, but they still possess a kind of languishing charm all their own."[28]

Back in Reynolds's camps at Lenoir, Stamper of the 43rd Tennessee wrote that 2 December had been wet and cold, and that the regiment had done no military duty during the previous twenty-four hours. Another rumor working its way through the tents stated that Gillespie's men may not be called on to move to Kingston, Tennessee, after all. Stamper reported that Parson Archibald Brooks and J. W. Talley had returned to camp after passes home.[29] These days of service in their home section found the boys often gifted with liberal leaves of absence.

Nearby in an adjoining camp in the brigade, William S. Brown of Madisonville, Monroe County, and the 59th Tennessee informed his friend Carrie Stakely back home that "we are here yet, and I expect doomed to a worse place." The murmuring circulated that they would be moved toward Big Creek Gap near Kingston, where the federals were expected to sweep down from Kentucky in great force that very night. Brown hoped that, in the midst of the mountain winter, the boys would be headed instead a bit "further south in Dixie." Little did he realize how soon his wish would be granted. Brown declared the area in which they were encamped to be a "broken country," and that the terrain was rough on the wagons to which he and others were assigned.

---

[25] Gen. John H. Forney to Gen. John C. Pemberton, *Official Records*, ser. 1 vol. 38, pt. 2, p. 773.

[26] Stamper, "Travels of the 43rd Tennessee," 18.

[27] Blair, "Diary," 1.

[28] Northen, *All Right, Let Them Come*, 40.

[29] Stamper, "Travels of the 43rd Tennessee," 18.

"Whenever we arrived here," he noted, the site "was a beautiful grove of oaks. There was no place to park wagons only in the road, but it's quite different now." All the trees had been cut down, Brown observed, and "it is no problem to turn a wagon now in any direction." He informed Carrie that the companies of the 59th Tennessee had drawn tents, and like Stamper's 43rd Tennessee, most of the boys were busy fitting chimneys to keep them warm. Captain John R. Stradly had a tent with a brick chimney, he mused, "making it the nicest in the camp."[30]

Brown recorded that his mother had just sent him a nice box of apples, from which the boys all had a nice serving of dumplings. The taste of a bite of apple would be a simple luxury they would soon forgo for over six months. Brown regretted the fact he had been unable to get home to see his mother. When he had been able to get off "on the march" to see Carrie's father, he found himself required to double-quick it back to camp at Lenoir's for fear the regiment would be called up any moment toward some unknown destination.[31]

A mutual friend, Jimmy Caldwell of the regiment, had told Brown that Carrie's sister Margaret ("Maggie") had been on the train to Knoxville, where she was to meet her and Carrie's brother, staff officer Captain Sam Stakely of the 59th Tennessee. Brown hoped that Maggie would not forget him while she was in the big city. With the conclusion of Bragg's unsuccessful Kentucky invasion in the fall, Brown remarked that the army was now in possession of neither the bluegrass state "nor the North Pole."[32]

"The yanks drove us before them like we drove cattle before us," he reflected, and "it seems to have given them some encouragement for they are advancing on us at every point that is heard from." Brown hoped that the enemy would not drive the boys out of their comfortable shebangs while the winter

---

[30] William S. Brown to Carrie Stakely, 2 December 1862, Hall-Stakely Papers, McClung Historical Collection, Knoxville Public Libraries, Knoxville TN.

[31] Ibid.

[32] Ibid. Reynolds's Brigade, composed of the 3rd, 31st, 43rd, and 59th Tennessee, had been marginally involved with Gen. Edmund Kirby-Smith's force during Gen. Braxton Bragg's Kentucky campaign. Some units of the command were left to guard the Cumberland Gap, and at least elements of the 43rd and 59th Tennessee accompanied Kirby-Smith's Department of East Tennessee force supporting the Army of Tennesseeinto the heart of the Bluegrass state. The 43rd Tennessee, while on the advance, received its first national regimental flag from the ladies of Mt. Sterling, KY. Once the invasion ended, Reynolds's men returned to East Tennessee and went into winter camps at Lenoir Station (now Lenoir City), Roane County (now Loudon County). From the depot there, they would embark for Vicksburg sometime in December.

weather was worsening, though fanciful reports warned that there were 15,000 federals poised to pour through the Big Creek Gap within four miles of Kingston. If they came, Brown predicted they would not find anything of value because there was precious little in the present country by way of either forage or provision.[33]

As always the case with any soldier during this war, the hope for a good meal was ever on his mind. "We anticipate tomorrow a good dinner," Brown told Carrie, because "Mr. Caffee has sent to the boys in his mess two fat chickens, 'nicely dressed.'" Brown compared Carrie's sister "Martha" having "flown the coop," possibly in marriage, to the hens presently in the soldiers' custody. He predicted the chickens would not have so lucky an escape. With the approaching darkness, Brown stated that he had to stop writing because "candles [were] very scarce."[34]

In response to the departure of his command pursuant to the orders of General Forney, Blair of the 80th (62nd) Tennessee noted in his diary that "we left on this date [3 December] for Jackson, Mississippi," where the regiment remained for the next two weeks.[35] From there, they were dispatched northward toward Grenada, some 100 miles distant, where an expected Union army advance from Northeast Mississippi was anticipated. Grant, following up his successes in that sector, was pressing his advantage toward Grenada with 30,000 men by way of Holly Springs and then Oxford, roughly along the route of the Mississippi Central Railroad. Another 110 miles due south of Grenada would bring Grant right to the city limits of Jackson, allowing him to swing west toward his ultimate prize, Vicksburg. Pemberton had assembled a comparable force and sought to check the Federals by digging in on the southern bank of the Yalobusha River at Grenada. Vaughn's men were being directed to reinforce to these defenses.

Also on 3 December, Reynolds's men, for the time being untouched by these strategic maneuvers in Mississippi, were content with executing regimental drills prior to and just after noon near their camps at Lenoir. Stamper of the 43rd Tennessee noted in his diary that camp routine was their comfortable order of the day. "Bruce came from home with a bushel of dried peaches," he recorded, "so you may guess we had something good at our house." On 6 December, Stamper indicated "those of us who had work to do pitched in early." With no military duties required of them, he indicated that

---

[33] Ibid.
[34] Ibid.
[35] Blair, "Diary," 1.

the boys set about making improvements on their living quarters. "We raised our tents, put up our beds, finished our chimney and cleaned generally," he wrote. Once these tasks were accomplished, all felt their winter quarters were complete. Still, the nagging questions occupied their chatter. "Would we have to move?" he wondered. "Or will we get to enjoy our [new] quarters?" These were questions they had to risk, he decided, and added: "I still felt we would 'get our money back' as we were not long building." The task left to them about camps now was to lay in wood for the Sabbath, and after that, Stamper reported, "Talley ... baked some cracklin' bread, which, with butter and fruit, made our supper," which the men ate "heartily."[36]

In a campsite nearby, another acquaintance of Carrie Stakely was Private Jimmy Caldwell with the 59th Tennessee, who penned her a letter on 7 December and prefaced it with the realization he would not be hearing from her until he wrote her first. "I have nothing of special interest to write," he noted, "except we have received orders to march in the direction of Kingston tomorrow morning at 8 o'clock." These long dreaded orders were the reason he wrote on the Sabbath, he explained. "I believe the three regiments [the 31st Tennessee, the 43rd Tennessee in addition to the 59th Tennessee] which are here," Caldwell wrote, "have the same orders." The whereabouts of the fourth regiment (the 3rd Tennessee) was unknown to him, though it had left camps at Lenoir Station "about a week ago." This regiment had been ordered to Knoxville. The 31st Tennessee was at Loudon, he noted, and the thought was that it would remain there for some time. He was not happy with the thought of leaving the camps at Lenoirs, he complained, since "we are just getting ready to live like we were at home." Some days previous, his acting company commander "Captain Sam" Stakely, Carrie's brother, had returned from Knoxville, where he "drew some very comfortable tents." Caldwell was pleased to admit that he drew one of them. Work commenced immediately toward the construction of the all-important chimney attachment, as well as the assembly of a bed frame, in which ample piles of straw for a mattress was placed.[37] Such simple improvements like these made a tent into a "shebang."

"I had done the necessary work about the tent to make it comfortable," Caldwell lamented, "and had sat down before the fire to enjoy the benefits of my work, [when] the order came to cook two days' rations and be ready to march by morning." He attempted to put a devil-may-care attitude toward this familiar preliminary to moving out, when he noted that "we are in the *wars* now

---

[36] Stamper, "Travels of the 43rd Tennessee," 19.

[37] Jimmy Caldwell to Carrie Stakely, 7 December 1862, Hall-Stakely Papers.

and have to obey Jeff and all his officers while it lasts." Caldwell reported that the previous night had been bitterly cold, and the next night was probably going to be worse. He blamed frigid temperature on the snow and sleet that had fallen "the other day," but was grateful the boys had just recently drawn extra blankets and clothing to help block the chill. Perhaps due to their exposure to the cold, all the field officers except for Captain James Pryor Brown were then on sick furlough recuperating. Captain Brown of his Madisonville Company was in command of the regiment during the field officers' absence. Caldwell stated that, since he had written the preceding information, he had just returned from brigade headquarters, where he learned that "we are to remain at Kingston for some length of time and have our mail brought there from Loudon" on Mondays, Wednesdays, and Fridays. With that report, Caldwell indicated that it was getting late and "tattoo is beating," directing all soldiers to bed down for the night. His closing request to Carrie was on behalf of a Private "Nachy," who requested knifes from home, should any of their mutual acquaintances make the rounds up to Roane County in the next day or two. Apparently Nachy had lost his knife and fork while campaigning in Kentucky during the fall, and needed replacements.[38]

Stamper, in the 43rd Tennessee' camps nearby, echoed the observation that 7 December was bitterly cold. It was so cold that the usual Saturday inspection had been cancelled. Then around noon came the dreaded orders of which Caldwell had foretold. "We received orders to cook two days' rations,"

---

[38] Ibid. In this letter, Caldwell mentioned an interesting comrade referred to only as "Nachy." Any reference to him in this and subsequent letters was always accompanied by a humorous anecdote with Nachy as the central focus. Nachy, who was apparently preparing rations for the march, called for water with which to cook. The sound of his voice made Caldwell recall an occurrence the week before when in the middle of the night, most of the boys in camp were awakened by the loud singing of the old hymn "Happy Land of Canaan." The rendition originated in Nachy's tent. Caldwell said that he was mystified at first, not knowing if Nachy was tired of sleeping and was attempting to while away the time in song, although Caldweel thought that the night was too late and too cold for such a frivolous pastime. After a while, the singing ceased, and quiet returned to the 59th Tennessee's camp. Caldwell reported that the next morning, after building his own fire, he went about visiting some of the boys to see how they had spent the night. Stopping at Nachy's tent, Caldwell learned about Nachy's dream. Nachy had dreamed that he, Caldwell, Carrie, her sister Maggie, and various other young people of their community were on Fork Creek in the upper end of Monroe County at an old-time singing, and all were singing at the tops of their voices. In reality, Nachy's voice was the only one performing. He denied having sung the previous night and stated that if he had, it was part of a dream. All the boys around Nachy's tent informed him that he had indeed been singing, and very nicely too.

Stamper acknowledged, "on which we were to march to Kingston." All the preparation of winter camps was to be for naught. The boys murmured, not only because they had to leave their cozy digs, but also because they believed that they were going to be ordered on a winter campaign replete with rain, mud, and snow. "We sat around our snug little firesides [after supper] and discussed this 'wrong,' in moving us from our extremely comfortable quarters," Stamper observed. But after some reflection, he noted, the boys reluctantly agreed that "soldiering was a pretty rough living anyway." "We should respond cheerfully to every call," they all decided, "animated by the hope of our Southern independence."[39]

Around 10 o'clock on the morning of 8 December, Stamper stated that his regiment and the 59th Tennessee of A. W. Reynolds's Brigade, both of which still remained at Lenoir, tore "down their tents and packed up and in a short time were on the march for Kingston." Along the way, the 31st Tennessee fell in with them as they passed through Loudon, and three-quarters of Reynolds's East Tennessee Brigade marched the 12 miles into Kingston, where, he noted, "the boys [took] up for the night." In a short time, Stamper observed, "we had our fires built, our tents stretched, and all quietly seated around our log fire." Despite leaving some wonderful quarters back at Lenoir Station, "some of the boys remarked that we had here a pretty good situation." Unaccustomed to marching such a distance, the men were exhausted and went to their blankets early, where they slept well, "although we were in the woods and far from home."[40]

In Mississippi on 8 December, Grant had headquartered in Oxford and was considering his plan of advance southward. He had ordered his favorite subordinate, Major General William T. Sherman, to march his command to Memphis, where a new division of federal recruits was being amassed under the command of Grant's least favorite subordinate, Major General John A. McClernand. Grant worried that McClernand, a general with considerable political connections, would be permitted unfettered discretion to move on Vicksburg on his own, thus thwarting the implementation of any of the plans set in place previously. Grant, seeking to suppress McClernand's impulsiveness, ordered Sherman to assume overall command of this new division at Memphis in addition to his own. Sherman was to then to load his men on transports and sail downriver to Vicksburg, where they would meet up with and be supported by Admiral David Porter's gunboat fleet. Grant's strategy was designed to force

---

[39] Stamper, "Travels of the 43rd Tennessee," 20–21.
[40] Ibid., 21. Colonel Newton J. Lillard's 3rd Tennessee was still in Knoxville.

Pemberton at Grenada to choose between returning to the fortifications to defend Vicksburg, or remain on the Yalobusha River and check the advance of the Union Army of the Tennessee.

Early on the morning of 9 December, Reynolds's Brigade in East Tennessee was once again on the move and by 1 p.m. had marched through the town of Kingston. Apparently the boys were not impressed with its rustic charm. "This is, as everyone knows," Stamper proclaimed, "a very ugly place and with very little to attract the attention of anyone." Perhaps as result of this affront to their sensibilities, the brigade moved through without stopping and camped a mile beyond the town limits. Conditions indicated that the command would remain there for a while. A day later, Stamper recorded that the brigade was still in its camps outside Kingston, and the boys had been working feverishly in the construction of new chimneys for yet other set of winter quarters. After more chopping and planning layouts, he noted with some exasperation, orders came from on high about noon that they were to cease their building. "We assumed that another move [was] in sight," he reported, "but just at dark, we [were] told to go on with our work." There was an inferred probability that the brigade would remain in camps there for the duration of the winter. And though Kingston was an "ugly" place, the boys went eagerly into their construction work, according to Stamper, "like they were at an old-fashioned wood chopping and quilting, where a big party was expected when the work was done."[41]

Sergeant John T. "Tom" Moffitt of New Market, Jefferson County, and of Captain John Peyton Lynch's Company of Light Artillery, wrote his wife, Sallie McDowell, on 12 December from Knoxville, informing her that he had been ordered by Colonel M. Blake, commander of the large conscript camp there, to the "upper counties" of East Tennessee to recruit for his unit. Moffitt admitted that he was frustrated with the duty, given the poor results he had realized thus far, since most citizens of that section had by now already gone to their chosen organizations or "had run off." The remaining men were of the poorest quality, he felt. Moffitt was sincerely considering returning to his battery's camp at Columbus, Mississippi, where he knew he would be perceived as having failed as a recruiter. "I would scarcely have earned the train fare home," Moffitt admitted. In a matter of days, his command would no longer be at Columbus,

---

[41] Ibid.

for Lynch's artillerymen were being drawn by the great suction of all available area troops in the direction of Vicksburg.[42]

By 14 December, Vaughn's brigade had been in Mississippi for several days, first at Jackson and then up at Grenada, where Pemberton expected Grant's legions to make their first strike. Two weeks after his last letter to his wife, Private E. D. Parker of the 79th (60th) Tennessee was apparently in the vicinity of Jackson, with the other regiments of Vaughn's Brigade. While there, Parker wrote "his 'dear wif'" again, informing her about his health. "I weight 4 lbs. more than I did when we took camps," he reported proudly and stated that their fare "ranges," in variety and quality though there is "plenty of corn dodgers poor beef bacon sugar molasses, &c." He described the considerable sickness that plagued his friends and comrades in the 79th (60th) Tennessee, and he indicated that the change in locale had been physically taxing on Vaughn's East Tennessee boys. He provided his own diagnoses for friends and neighbors: Private Sige Brown had the measles, and G. L. McCullys "[was] down with his brest." Their neighbor Samuel King "[had] the sore eyes, or reather a blindness and misery in the head." King wanted Parker's wife to tell his spouse that "he [was] not as well as he was when he was at home[;] his eyes and hed [were] in a pretty bad fix."[43] Concerning the long and grueling train travel to Jackson from Haynesville, Parker wrote that the boys had a long and tiresome "march," but he "stood it fine."[44]

On 14 December, Parker told his wife that "We have very bad water[;] it is pond water and muddy at that." The weather, however, in this section of the country was a marvel to him. Even though it was December, "the wether [was]

[42] John T. ("Tom") Moffitt to Sallie McDowell, 12 December 1862, Thomas J. Moffitt Papers, McClung Historical Collection, Knoxville TN.

[43] E. D. Parker to his wife Susan, 14 December 1862, Parker Letters. King's diagnosis was probably measles that had, as the boys might have said, "gone into his eyes."

[44] Ibid. The boys rode mainly on boxcars to Mississippi, with many riding on top. Sometimes they were on flat cars as well, and there were incidents of trains going off the tracks, with serious injuries. Reuban Justus, a citizen of Cocke County and a member of the 79th Tennessee, apparently while on route, fell or jumped off a flatcar and "landed on his stomach and a stob penetrated my right side." His injury was severe enough that he was discharged from the service. Edward Walker, III, ed., "Eyewitness and military Accounts," Tales from the Civil War (Newport TN: self-published, 1983) 26. Note also J. C. M. Bogle's letter dated 23 April 1863, Saffell Family Papers, University of Tennessee Archives, Knoxville TN. It was generally acknowledged that Mississippi had some of the worst-maintained railroads in the Confederacy. Arthur J. L Fremantle, Three Months in the Southern States, April-June 1863 (Rprt, Boston: Little, Brown and Co., 1864) 127.

very warm hear I have planted corn at home when the wether was cooler than it is hear at present." The 79th (60th) Tennessee and Vaughn's brigade "are to leave hear," but he admitted, "I don't know when we will go" or where.[45]

Parker then informed his wife that he had been "sent to preaching today, and heard a fine surmant." He added that he would meditate on it "til I hear an other." He told his wife that he had quit "hard swearing" and was "determined to live more sober than I ever did before." Such news undoubtedly must have comforted Mrs. Parker. He indicated, "a soldiers lif is a hard won but I will bare it as patiently as any other til my country is freed from the Darkee Lords of Lincoln." Parker promised that "[when] our homes are restored to peace I will come home just as soon as I can."[46]

Parker told his wife, "I think of you and bill often I want you to kiss bill for me and tell him his papy wants to see him very bad." He made her promise to write him if either she or their son, Bill, got sick. He then provided her with the prices of goods in Jackson: corn was $25 a barrel; flour, $75 or $80 a barrel; bacon, $1 a lb.; pork, from 62¢ to 75¢ cents a lb. "I wrote two letter sin I got any answer," he said in admonition, and he wanted his uncle Bill Childress and family to write him as well as to his cousin Sam in the 19th Tennessee. When she did write, he suggested that she send the letter without paying the postage and "it will come quicker & corrector."[47] Probably any letters she addressed to him were sent along behind the 79th (60th) Tennessee toward Parker's new address: Vicksburg, Mississippi.

Another member of Parker's regiment was Stuart Nelson, a son of the influential Unionist turned Confederate lawyer and politician T. A. R. Nelson. Stuart Nelson served as a sergeant with the 79th (60th) Tennessee. He wrote a letter from Jackson dated 15 December addressed to his parents in Jonesborough, Washington County, while his regiment and brigade awaited orders. In the letter, which he might have begun the previous Sunday, he stated that he was just off some hard drilling the week just passed, and he took this "holy sabath" to sit and write a few lines. The 79th (60th) Tennessee, he noted, was now encamped about two miles northwest of Jackson in "a low swampy place."[48]

[45] Parker to his wife Susan, 14 December 1862.
[46] Ibid.
[47] Ibid.
[48] Stuart Nelson to mother and father, 15 December 1862, in T. A. R. Nelson Papers, McClung Historical Archives, Knoxville Public Libraries, Knoxville TN.

"The fare we get hear is very good," Nelson wrote, "and I am enjoying fine health." As he scribbled his few lines, he imagined that he could see his father and mother back in their comfortable home on the road between Jonesborough and Haynesville "in the sitting room surrounded by Charlie, Tom, Anne and all the children." He visualized the children in his mind's eye reciting the catechism, and "Lizzie in Anna's lap repeating her little verses." Although he professed himself to be good health, Nelson, like Parker, reported that "our men are taking sick very fast. We had 75 men when we left Jonesboro & now we have only 57 fit for duty." He was at a loss to explain his own continued good health, given that "we have been exposed to every sort of weather," yet he believed that his vitality must be due to the grace of God. He hoped that his family would write him soon, "if they [had] the time," and he noted in an aside that "Jackson [was] a very poor place to be the capital of a state." The army, Nelson recorded, was storing ammunition, cannon, and clothes in the city, as though in preparation for some great campaign ahead. He also informed everyone that Captain Mark M. Prichal (Pritchett) of Company D, Boone's Creek, Washington County, "died very sudden the other day from congestive chills." As he wrote, Sergeant Nelson recorded that the weather was so warm that he found himself "writing in my tent with my coat and hat off." He asked his father to let everyone at home know he loved them, and he hoped they would soon correspond with him. They were to send their letters to Jackson, Mississippi, and address them to the "79th Regt. Tenn. Vols., in care of Captain Francis R. Blair."[49]

On or about the date of the previous letter, Nelson penned another one to his brother, noting that "the warter hear is very muddy and about as warm as our river warter in the summer time." He repeated that he was sitting in his tent without a hat or coat, and added he was "sweating like I had been hard at work." "I am enjoying very good health my self," Nelson repeated, "and so is Saml Gammon [commanding a company of Hawkins County men in the 79th Tennessee] & the rest of my men." Nelson noted that the boys had plenty to eat "of molasses, corn meal, sweet potato, dried beans, rice and shugar." He informed his brother that the letter he had received from home had done him much good, and if the folks knew what a positive influence it had on his spirits, they would write to him more often. He remarked that he was glad to hear

---

[49] Ibid. Parker noted that he had gained four pounds since he had been in camps, and Nelson indicated that the food was excellent. Unfortunately for the Vicksburg army, these happy conditions would not last.

"Dave" was getting along as well as common, and Nelson hoped that Dave would be allowed to go to work in "Sam's Ironworks" before he was eighteen.[50]

Concerning area military matters, Nelson joked that one of the soldiers in the company named Hal Broyles "swears a private's life is a dogs life & he intends to hire him a substitute if it costs him a thousand dollars—a good idea." Nelson repeated that the 79th (60th) Tennessee was "camped now at the edge of a low flat swampy place," and that there had been several cases of small pox in the brigade diagnosed in Pitt's regiment, the 81st (61st) Tennessee. As for the state capital of Mississippi, Nelson repeated to his brother the widely-held belief that "Jackson is the most contemptible place I ever saw for the capital of a State."[51]

Nelson's stay with Vaughn's Brigade in "contemptible" Jackson continued for only one more day. On 16 December, General Martin Luther Smith, under whose command Vaughn's men had been assigned, sent a dispatch to General Pemberton at Grenada indicating that he did not believe that there was any danger of an immediate attack on the Capital. Therefore, Smith ordered Vaughn's Brigade to Pemberton, stating, "they will leave [here] early in the morning [of the 17th]."[52] Vaughn's boys were on their way a little over 100 miles north to Grenada, where danger was anticipated from two divisions of Ulysses S. Grant's approaching Army of the Tennessee. He moved southward with uncharacteristic caution and deliberation, rebuilding the railroad and bridges in his rear to insure his lines of supply and communication.

The next day at Grenada, General Pemberton issued orders indicating that "the brigade of Brigadier General Vaughn [has] just arrived at this point." Pemberton assigned it to the command of Major General Dabney H. Maury, Second Corps, and directed the Tennessee general to "report accordingly."[53] Earnest of the 79th (60th) Tennessee recorded in his journal that the brigade arrived at Grenada on 16 or 17 December. He found the works along the Yalobusha River to be "well fortified and naturally strong." By 20 December, everyone in the regiment believed that they were destined for immediate action since the brigade was ordered at the double-quick to the rifle pits along the

[50] Stuart Nelson to an unnamed brother, 15 December 1862, T. A. R. Nelson Papers. An unnamed recipient fragment exists of this letter exists.

[51] Ibid. Small pox would continue to plague not only the 81st (61st) Tennessee in Vaughn's Brigade, but also Reynolds's 43rd Tennessee.

[52] Gen. Martin L. Smith to Gen. John C. Pemberton, 16 December 1862, *Official Records*, ser. 1, vol. 17, pt. 2, p. 797.

[53] Gen. John C. Pemberton to Gen. Dabney H. Maury, 17 December 1862, *Official Records*, ser. 1, vol. 17, pt. 2, p. 799.

river, which, Earnest proudly proclaimed, "the boys did without any hesitation."[54] The alert proved to be a false alarm.

Reynolds Follows Vaughn to Mississippi. Vaughn's old regiment and Reynolds's "orphaned" one (Colonel Newton J. Lillard's 3rd Tennessee) also received orders on 17 December from General Edmund Kirby-Smith, commanding the Department of East Tennessee at Knoxville. The regiment had been positioned at Big Creek Gap, where a Yankee incursion was believed imminent, but never materialized. Lillard was directed back to Knoxville to reunite with the Reynolds's Brigade in its preparations for the move to Jackson, Mississippi. "The regiment will move with its ammunition, tents and camp equipage," Kirby-Smith's orders read. "When the Regt. starts to this place, you will dispatch information of the fact to the Dept. Headquarters, so transportation may be provided upon its arrival."[55] The 3rd Tennessee, Reynolds's senior regiment, was in the vanguard leading the brigade's transfer to Pemberton's growing army assembling to confront Grant. Due to additional duties it was assigned, the regiment would travel with the 43rd Tennessee, one of the last to arrive.

Others in Reynolds's command were also getting the alert at this time. While at home on a brief furlough in Cleveland, Isaac Stamper of the 43rd Tennessee reported that Reynolds's Brigade received orders "to start to Jackson, Mississippi." Again, the boys were required to dismantle their comfortable campsites and be prepared to move. The anxiety and excitement associated with this change of location, however, were considerably more dramatic than moving the twelve miles from Lenoir Station to Kingston. On 19 December, Stamper of the 43rd Tennessee recorded that he left for Kingston from his home in Cleveland, but learning that his regiment was "coming on the [rail]road," he stopped at Lenoir to await their arrival. Gillespie's men did not get loaded up and out of town as quickly as they had expected, however, and Stamper indicated that the train did not arrive there until after dark. By then, it was decided to try again in the morning. Stamper indicated that "we occupied our old quarters at Lenoirs" for one last night's sleep on the old campgrounds.[56]

While Reynolds's brigade lingered in East Tennessee, matters in West Tennessee and North Mississippi suddenly seemed to be playing against Grant. General Bedford Forrest and his cavalry were operating at will in that section,

---

[54] Northen, *All Right, Let Them Come*, 45–46.

[55] Gen. Edmund Kirby-Smith to Col. Newton J. Lillard, 17 December 1862, Newton J. Lillard Papers, Tennessee State Library and Archives, Nashville TN.

[56] Stamper, "Travels of the 43rd Tennessee," 22.

destroying much of the railroad, tearing down telegraph lines, collecting great numbers of federal horses and weapons as spoil, and recruiting for his command scores of additional troopers behind the lines. To make Grant's situation even worse, Major General Earl Van Dorn and a sizeable Confederate cavalry force rode into Grant's huge supply depot at Holly Springs on 20 December and burned or carried off all the stores of food, forage, ammunition, and other supplies being amassed for the campaign ahead. Grant had had enough. The next day he pulled out of Oxford and fell back to Memphis. The lead battalions of Sherman's two divisions composed of 30,000 men had already begun boarding fifty-nine transports at Memphis on 20 December before finally sailing for Vicksburg. Although Sherman had been notified of the disaster at Holly Springs, matters were too far along for him to change his plans.

At Grenada, while a nervous General John Pemberton watched anxiously for the Yankees' approach, he received a dispatch on the same day Grant was leaving Oxford alerting him of "a large fleet of gunboats and transports moving down the Mississippi River for the supposed purpose of attacking Vicksburg." This development caused "the Lieut.-General commanding," as Pemberton often referred to himself, to order immediately John C. Vaughn and his East Tennesseans "to that point."[57]

Reynolds's Brigade was still back in East Tennessee, though its days there for the first half of the war were drawing to a close. Stamper of the 43rd Tennessee recorded on 20 December that the entire command was ordered to prepare two days of rations. "The day was spent in cooking," he noted, "and fitting out for our trip south."[58] The Record of Events for Company C, 31st Tennessee indicated that on this date the regiment "started for Charleston [Bradley County], and reached by rail Vicksburg, Mississippi, arriving at Jackson 31 December after being crowded into freight cars for 10 days and nights without respite."[59]

Young Private George Crosby, in another of Reynolds's regiments (the 59th Tennessee), wrote in his reminiscence sketch that at Lenoir's Station, "we had to load the box cars with all the equipage that was common for an army to have." "So, when we were ready to leave," he added, "the old men, ladies and the rest of the folk came to see the last sight of friends leaving for a distant

---

[57] Report of Gen. John C. Pemberton, 17 December 1862, *Official Records*, ser. 1, vol. 17, pt. 2, p. 799.

[58] Stamper, "Travels of the 43rd Tennessee," 22.

[59] Record of Events, 31st Tennessee Infantry, *Compiled Service Records of Confederate Soldiers Who Served from the State of Tennessee, RG 109*, National Archives, Washington, DC.

country, [some] never to see friends nor home again." Crosby recalled that "Farewell" was the watchword for grieving mothers and wives. For the soldiers, however, he believed that the excitement of the impending adventure on the "long railroad trip was the big thing."[60]

Crosby's regiment boarded cattle cars around 10 a.m., Stamper of the 43rd Tennessee noted in his daily entry.[61] Private Benjamin Giddens of the 3rd Tennessee wrote his brother James, who was still in Cleveland, on 22 December and described what the train ride looked like coming through lower McMinn and upper Bradley Counties: "your company [Company F] was some mad when the cars run through Calhoun and Charleston like lightning[;] it was done a purpose." The impression given was that the officers did not want the boys from any of the East Tennessee communities along the railroad line jumping off the train as it neared their hometowns, causing them to miss their transportation to Mississippi. "You ought to hear the boys talk about the cars running I was tickled at Lucker Haze you can guess what he said," Giddens added, much amused.[62] Almost a month earlier, Earnest of the 79th (60th) Tennessee reported that when his regiment was on its way south, it arrived just below Haynesville at Jonesboro, "where the ladies [were] out to see us pass with numerous delicacies." All the men on the train were indignant when "the engineer ran by without even checking up."[63]

Undoubtedly, the trains bearing the East Tennessee Brigade of A. W. Reynolds carried a number of boys from the mountains and valleys who during their young lives had never had cause to set foot outside their communities. Lieutenant Calvin M. Smith of the 31st Tennessee, a veteran of the Mexican War, was not one of these awe-stuck lads. Still, the changes in the country through which they traveled attracted his keen eye. Commenting on the new terrains he was witness to early in the journey south, he noted in his journal that "from Loudon to Dalton the land seem[ed] good and large crops of hay and grains of all kinds [were] raised."[64]

At dusk on 23 December, Stamper of the 43rd Tennessee indicated that his train rolled into Dalton, Georgia, where the boys were told to "sleep in, on, and about the cars." He believed that they tried their best. Early the next

[60] Shirley C. Hodges, *The Crosby Collection: "For Love of Family"* (Morristown TN: self-published, 1998) 412.

[61] Stamper, "Travels of the 43rd Tennessee," 22.

[62] Benjamin C. Giddens to James Giddens, 1 January 1863, Benjamin C. Giddens Letters, Old Courthouse Museum Archives, Vicksburg MS.

[63] Northen, *All Right, Let Them Come*, 37.

[64] Smith, *A Smith in Service*, 37.

morning, the gray-clad nomads were awakened before daylight when the air was at its coldest, shivering with their blankets wrapped around their shoulders, yawning, and stretching in their make-shift camps. They complied with orders to prepare rations for two more days.[65]

Down in Mississippi, General Pemberton had begun to rush his forces at Grenada toward the anticipated crisis at Vicksburg. He directed that Vaughn's Brigade be relieved from duty with General D. H. Maury's division and "proceed with all dispatch to report to Major-General [Martin L.] Smith."[66] Colonel John A. Rowan's 80th (62nd) Tennessee was near Grenada on 23 December as Vaughn's Brigade prepared "with all dispatch" to tear down and load up camp equipment for yet another march. Amid the chaos of yelling sergeants and officers, and of flustered and hustling privates struggling with the loading of the regiments' goods, Rowan had, as privilege of his rank, the time to write his wife back in Sweetwater, Monroe County. His chief aim was to inform her of his whereabouts, since the brigade literally had been "foarced from Post to Pillow & in such quick sucession that it is no telling one day where we will be tomorrow." He reported that his boys were "placing our tricks in the wagons" for the nearly 150 mile trip to Vicksburg via Jackson.[67] The wagons would carry the camp equipment and "tricks" of the regiment to the railroad for the trip down.

"We start forth without delay to Vicsburg," Rowan reported to his wife, "where I think we will be located for the winter." He requested that Mrs. Rowan send his mail to him at Vicksburg, and he let her know that all the boys were "well pleased [to go there], and glad to move [from Grenada]." He

---

[65] Stamper, "Travels of the 43rd Tennessee," 22.

[66] Report of Gen. John C. Pemberton, 23 December 1862, *Official Records*, ser. 1, vol. 17, pt. 2, p. 803.

[67] John Rowan to wife, 23 December 1862, in *Civil War Records of Tennessee*, 3 vols. (Nashville TN: Works Progress Administration, 1939) 2: 198. Next to Newton J. Lillard, Rowan was probably John C. Vaughn's most trusted subordinate. All three men were prominent citizens of Monroe County before the war. (When Rowan was killed in action in East Tennessee in 1864, Vaughn's condolences to Rowan's family appears most heart-felt on a personal as well as a military level. See "Death of Colonel Rowan," *Knoxville Register*, 12 October 1864 [cited in *Civil War Records*, 2: 195]). Of Vaughn's three regimental commanders, Rowan was also the youngest and most fit for the severity of extended military life. Fountain Pitts, who was a Methodist minister, and John Crawford, who was in his fifties at the time his regiment was mustered in, seem to have delegated many of their daily responsibilities to younger subordinates James G. Rose (61st Tennessee) and Nathan Gregg (60th Tennessee) during the Vicksburg campaign.

informed her that his letter "leaves me in good health," and that he was pleased that he had been "kindly treated by all the officials."[68]

"I am proud of my Regt.," Rowan boasted, "and they are as fine a looking set of men as there is in the survis." His letter stressed all his boys were well. Rowan stated his brother, Captain "Bob Crockett" Rowan serving in the commissary department, had reported some 100 cases of measles among his men.[69]

The following day, Christmas Eve, probably brought few thoughts of the approaching holiday celebrating Christ's birth to the minds of most of the men in Isaac Stamper's 43rd Tennessee. Instead, they were again aboard the train that left Dalton around 6 a.m. and arrived in Atlanta just before sunset.[70] "From Dalton to Atlanta," Lieutenant Smith of the 31st Tennessee observed, "the country is generally poor and hilly, some land extremely poor. Large crops of wheat are sowed and looked tolerably well. Poor looking hogs." As for Atlanta itself, Smith described it as being a "large town with fine large buildings, large machine shops and other large houses of large dimensions." He was in awe of the city's many railroad yards, with long trains and many engines "whistling in every direction."[71]

"The ladies have a committee who feed all the soldiers that come through," Smith noted, and the people there all seemed "kind and obliging." Before boarding and resuming their long trip, Smith remembered that his colonel, William M. Bradford, "called on us for a 'Dixie.'" He said that he and several others got together and sung one "the best we could," which pleased all the officers and the citizens gathered around the train.[72] Stamper of the 43rd Tennessee had less romantic remembrances of the stop and stated that as soon as the boys were given an opportunity to stretch and take care of other bodily functions, the train was again on its way toward West Point, Georgia, where it pulled into the depot at 3 a.m. Christmas morning.[73]

Yankee Gunboats Enter the Yazoo. In the Cotton State, Christmas Eve arrived with the unwelcomed news that enemy gunboats had begun to appear again at the confluence of the Yazoo and Mississippi Rivers. The warships were lying at a point known as "Young's Point" in the Mississippi River six miles north of Vicksburg, and Pemberton knew that the large contingent of

---

[68] Rowan to wife, *Civil War Records*, 2:198.
[69] Ibid.
[70] Stamper, "Travels of the 43rd Tennessee," 22.
[71] Smith, *A Smith in Service*, 37.
[72] Ibid.
[73] Stamper, "Travels of the 43rd Tennessee," 22.

Sherman's transports filled with troops and supplies could not be far behind. The troop conveyances arrived at Milliken's Bend on Christmas Eve and were moored at the wharves for the night.

Pemberton immediately dispatched the brigade of General John Gregg composed of one Texas and four middle Tennessee regiments to Chickasaw Bluffs to keep an eye on developments.[74] Colonel James G. Rose of the 81st (61st) Tennessee recalled the arrival of the vanguard of Sherman's command, which ultimately threatened Vicksburg with "a large force of gunboats and troops on board the transports." After Vaughn's Brigade had arrived at the Grenada depot from their camp and loaded their equipment aboard the train, Rose wrote that they were ordered to Vicksburg by railway through Jackson.[75] Lieutenant John J. Blair of the 80th (62nd) Tennessee wrote in his diary that he saw Vaughn's Brigade again in Jackson on Christmas Eve. Upon arriving at the Mississippi capitol, he noted, "we slept on the ground."[76]

Early Christmas morning, Vaughn's brigade was soon off again toward the "Gibraltar of the West." Lieutenant Earnest of the 79th (60th) Tennessee noted that the boys had their tents loaded aboard the train at the Jackson Depot the day before, in anticipation of the short trip to the Hill City. "Being Christmas eve," he reported, "the boys were sending up rockets all along the road, and everything seemed in unusually good spirits."[77]

Sergeant Robert Bachman of Sullivan County and the 79th (60th) Tennessee, indicated in his journal that Vaughn's Brigade arrived at their destination later in the morning, the forty-five miles by rail being traversed rather quickly. "One of the first things I did," he declared, "was go down to the Mississippi River [which was nearby the depot] and wash my hands and face. I'd had no water for such purpose since leaving Tennessee."[78] Considering the time they had spent in Grenada and Jackson (not to mention Montgomery, Mobile and Atlanta), this grievance does not sound credible, though Earnest of Bachman's regiment made the same claim, indicating that he also sought the river to wash his face. "I had heard so much about the great Mississippi that I

---

[74] Report of Gen. John C. Pemberton, February 1863, *Official Records*, ser. 1, vol. 17, pt. 1, p. 666.

[75] James G. Rose, "Sixty-First Tennessee," in *The Military Annals of Tennessee (Confederate) 1st Series Embracing a Review of Military Operations, with Regimental Histories and Memorial Rolls, Compiled from Original and Official Sources*, ed. John B. Lindsley (Nashville TN: J. M. Lindsley & Co., 1886) 2: 574.

[76] Blair, "Diary," 1.

[77] Northen, *All Right, Let Them Come*, 47.

[78] Bachman, "Reminiscences of Childhood," 16.

felt a thrill of satisfaction as I gazed on her broad waters," Earnest wrote. The city of Vicksburg itself seemed to him to be composed of old dusky buildings, "with an occasional tower reared on some rugged steep that stands up far above those below." Earnest found the Hill City's streets thronged with the military.[79]

Bachman remembered that, after stepping from the train, Vaughn's Brigade was marched about two miles northeast of town, "and there established camp."[80] Blair in the 80th (62nd) Tennessee indicated that "we left Jackson on Christmas morning at 7 o'clock" and arrived at Vicksburg by noon. He echoed Bachman's assertion that the brigade was hustled two miles north of town to make its camps hastily along the Mint Springs Bayou.[81] Colonel Rose of the 81st (61st) Tennessee recalled that, after "arriving on the Vicksburg bluffs 24 December [actually Christmas Day], ... the regiment first saw the enemy." And within twenty-four hours, he recorded that active operations commenced along the line of defenses "from the Vicksburg bluffs northward to Haynes Bluff, a distance of twelve miles."[82] General Pemberton, himself not far behind, indicated in his official report that he left Grenada on Christmas Day, probably after all of his troops were away, and arrived in Vicksburg around midnight.[83]

Meanwhile, Reynolds's Brigade persisted in its slow journey west as well. Calvin Smith of the 31st Tennessee continued recording his observations of sites along their travels, remarking that from Atlanta to Montgomery, "we passed through some fine country with fine houses. The land between West Point and Montgomery is generally level."[84] Just before entering Alabama, Isaac Stamper of 43rd Tennessee noted that Reynolds's Brigade found itself on Christmas morning in West Point, Georgia. His regiment was treated to a holiday celebration, Stamper declared, and his commanding officer picked up the tab. "The Colonel [Gillespie] treated the boys [to Christmas spirits]," he wrote, "and some of them got a little too much." Consequently, some of the men "got pretty tight," and Stamper found them to be "quite funny" all day.[85]

Gillespie's regiment was not only the regiment to get "pretty tight." George Crosby of Morristown and the 59th Tennessee indicated that his

---

[79] Northen, *All Right, Let Them Come*, 47.

[80] Bachman, "Reminiscences of Childhood," 16.

[81] Blair, "Diary," 1.

[82] Rose, "Sixty-First Tennessee," in Lindsley, *The Military Annals of Tennessee (Confederate)*, 2: 574.

[83] Report of Gen. John C. Pemberton, February 1863, *Official Records*, ser. 1, vol. 17, pt. 1, p. 666.

[84] Smith, *A Smith in Service*, 37.

[85] Stamper, "Travels of the 43rd Tennessee," 22.

regiment also was able to procure whiskey at West Point. "Here [he incorrectly called the city, Marietta] some of the boys got whiskey and started out over the town and ran every Negro out that could be found." A fellow native of Morristown in Crosby's company, Private John Southern, also confirmed the drinking at the stopover, but not the other activity.[86]

After a while, with the spirited regiments finally back aboard, the train left West Point about noon, and arrived at Montgomery, Alabama, around eleven that night. Though the inebriated soldiers perhaps did not feel up to it, they were obliged to change cars there. Stamper mentioned that "the teamsters drove up their drays and we soon had our baggage all packed and ready for the move." The 43rd Tennessee marched across town to the Mobile road, and after loading their "tricks," remained in that vicinity all morning awaiting orders. After some delay, Stamper wrote that the regiment was again on the move toward Mobile, and to get there traveled the entire day and night of 26 December.[87]

Captain Reuben G. Clark of the 59th Tennessee summarized the long train ride through Tennessee, Georgia, Alabama and Mississippi: "Our journey to Vicksburg was a succession of ovations all the way. We were greeted all along the route with cheers, smiles, bouquets and good things generally." He suspected that much of the appreciation stemmed from the fact that the Yankees were approaching from the west, which "excite[d] the people, who were now thoroughly aroused."[88]

"The best farms I saw in Georgia or Alabama was after we left Montgomery," Smith of the 31st Tennessee reported. "You pass[ed] through some beautiful little towns." He noted that the country around the Tensaw River north of Mobile was a dense swampy country, "where the cypress trees grow in abundance." The river itself was around a mile wide, and seemed deep and swirling with eddies. "We went on a steam boat about dusk, was quite cool—slept some, got up and saw [the] lights [of Mobile] ahead," he continued. Smith observed the stakes or row of pilings set up in the river to show pilots the

---

[86] Hodges, *The Crosby Collection*, 412. Word regarding the readily availability of liquor in West Point must have been a poorly guarded secret among the troops passing through. When the 79th (60th) Tennessee came through earlier, Lieutenant Earnest recorded that his train had a layover. The East Tennesseans poured out of the cattle cars, he reported, "looking for brandy." They found plenty, "and of course the regiment all got drunk but a few" (Northen, *All Right, Let Them Come*, 38).

[87] Stamper, "Travels of the 43rd Tennessee," 22.

[88] Willene B. Clark, ed., *Valleys of the Shadow: The Memoir of Confederate Captain Reuben G. Clark* (Knoxville TN: University of Tennessee Press, 1994) 14.

safe channels. Proceeding along the river, he noticed a battery on the river, which was now opening up into a massive bay. "[We saw] several war vessels, [ironclad] rams, and many steamer boats and transports of every form and size," he reported. Some of the steamers were used to land Reynolds's men at the wharf where they put their baggage on wagons that hauled their gear to the eastern-most terminus of the western railroad. After the brief march, Smith noted that the boys started fires and lay down in the streets to rest until daylight. Prior to sleeping however, Smith wrote that he and several other officers had been invited to a place for supper where they were promised fish, oysters, good coffee, cake, and butter. "We sat down to eat," he recorded. "Nothing on the table. Commenced calling, got a little perfumed warm water, sweet potatoes, no meat but promise. Got enough of that. Paid one dollar and left, never to call again."[89]

Another Smith back at Vicksburg was charged during this time period with securing its defenses until "the Lieut.-General Commanding" and reinforcements could arrive. The background of General Martin Luther Smith, West Point class of `42, mirrored in many ways that of Pemberton. He was a "yankee" from New York who married a Southern woman and spent much of his early military career in the Southern states. His sympathies were firmly with that region when the war commenced, and he resigned his U. S. commission 1 April 1861, to join the Confederate army. Because he was trained as a military engineer, Smith was well-suited for planning the defensive preparations in anticipation of Sherman's landing on the southern bank of the Yazoo River just north of Vicksburg. These Federals were mainly mid-westerners from Iowa, Illinois, and Ohio. As they disembarked in this strange country and looked out across the misty fields made swampy with recent rains, they saw the terrain dotted mainly with leafless hardwoods and broken by ponds, large and small. Traversing the landscape were broad creeks the natives called "bayous," and looming in the distance could be seen the imposing ridge running north and south along the floodplain between the Yazoo and Vicksburg. This ridge, known collectively as the Walnut Hills, stretched from the northern city limits of Vicksburg up to Snyder's Mill and Haynes Bluff. Of immediate concern to Sherman, however, was the tactical consideration to his front: the rifle pits and

---

[89] Smith, *A Smith in Service*, 37. Lt. Earnest of the 79th (60th) Tennessee indicated that he and others, on their walk around Mobile, visited the gunboat in progress. As for his "voyage" across Mobile Bay, Earnest wrote that the boys were loaded on the steamer *Planter*, "a first-class passenger boat," for the twenty-two mile passage across the harbor. Northen, *All Right, Let Them Come*, 42–43.

cannon emplacements at the foot of the connected hills known as the Chickasaw Bluffs.

Confederate forces from divergent sections of the mid-South continued to gather at the Hill City, which made the depot down Washington Street near the river a most congested port of entry. Troop trains were often backed up for a mile as they waited their turn to unload defenders. It was Smith's Division to which John Vaughn's newly arriving brigade found itself assigned upon climbing down unsteadily from the cars on Christmas Eve.

"Seeing The Elephant" Along the Chickasaw Bluffs. General Smith, with the learned eye of a surveyor, described the ground the Southerners were to defend in the vicinity of the Chickasaw Bluffs over which so much attention was being lavished during this time by the opposing armies. The land was "a broken ridge of hills touching the Mississippi," he noted, with the city of Vicksburg extending eastward at "a direction of about right angles with the general course of the [Yazoo] River." Twelve miles inland, the Yazoo touched the base of the hills near Snyder's Mill, Smith wrote in his report, and then diverged from them before emptying into the Mississippi six miles north of Vicksburg. The ground in contention, according to Smith, was the triangle between the Yazoo and the hills, "an area of bottom land, densely wooded, intersected with bayous, and low swampy ground." Hugging the ridge from Snyder's Mill almost down to the Mississippi River, was the old bed of the Yazoo, which in these final days of 1862, still contained considerable amounts of standing water and could only be crossed without a bridge at three points: Snyder's Mill itself, Blake's Levee, and along and through the treacherous Chickasaw Bayou.[90] The next few days, the Midwestern invaders would at times find themselves attempting to advance in places while wading in water up to their knees.

"From the terminus of the old [Yazoo River] bed to the Mississippi," Smith continued in his description, "a belt of timber," comprised of thick and tangled branches outward toward the river, had been "felled, forming a natural abatis." This engineering marvel would prove to be an impenetrable natural barrier. It was across this rugged landscape that Major General William T. Sherman sought to overwhelm with his three to one numerical superiority the Southern defenders aligned for the most part along the base of the ridge behind them. Once the Confederates were flushed from these works, the Federals believed that they could file into the upper fortifications of Vicksburg itself.

[90] Report of Gen. Martin L. Smith, January 1863, *Official Records*, ser. 1, vol. 17, pt. 1, p. 671–72.

On the north side of the ridge near Snyder's Mill were fixed fortifications and batteries, General Smith wrote, and on the southern side were the heavy batteries and breastworks around and atop imposing Fort Hill.[91] It was a daunting task with which elements of the corps of Sherman and Major General John A. McClernand were assigned, with the results of its implementation predictable.

Upon arriving in Vicksburg, Pemberton "found the enemy's gunboats engaged in shelling the banks of the Yazoo River up to the vicinity of the first bluffs at Snyder's Mill." From this covering fire, he noted, the Union troops were busy scrambling from the transports. Their deployment for attack was underway. "Snyder's Mill is situated 13 miles north of Vicksburg on a bluff which overlooks the Yazoo River," Pemberton indicated, and at this point Confederate engineers had planted a strong battery, "and the river [was] blockaded by a raft." He agreed with General Smith's assessment of the terrain, noting that swamps, lakes, and bayous ran along the levee nearly at right angles to the River. These natural obstacles, therefore, were also most formidable. Pemberton reported that another approach was about a mile below along the Chickasaw Bayou. A third pass, as stated by General Smith before, was through a dry part of the old lake, opposite an old Choctaw Indian mound, and the fourth approach was by a road leading "from Johnson's [plantation] by the race track." All the approaches, Pemberton was pleased to note after surveying the defenses, were manned by well-positioned troops behind breastworks, supported by batteries at key points. All this preparation was due to the foresight of General Martin Luther Smith.[92] The Confederates who were rushed to the field were under the immediate command of General Stephen D. Lee, a most capable officer who would always give a good account of himself and his command throughout the Vicksburg campaign.

Sherman's legions came ashore in the miserable gloom and fog shrouding the cold morning of 26 December. He planned to launch heavy demonstrations probing for points where a breakthrough might be accomplished along the four approaches at Chickasaw Bayou, Blake's Levee, the Choctaw Indian Mound, and Snyder's Mill. Skirmishing began soon after Colonel John F. DeCourcy's Brigade had solid ground under its feet and began to reconnoiter cautiously along the road toward the Widow Lake's house. DeCourcy's infantrymen were deployed in a large field near her house when they were fired upon by the 26th

---

[91] Ibid, 672.
[92] Report of Gen. John C. Pemberton, February 1862, *Official Records*, ser. 1, vol. 17, pt. 1, p. 666.

Louisiana and two companies of the 46th Mississippi posted in the woods bordering the Chickasaw Bayou. Pemberton recalled that the fire "resulted in driving in the Federals' advanced parties from Mrs. Lake's plantation into the swamps bordering the river." Throughout the evening and even after darkness closed this short winter's day, the brigades of Generals Vaughn, Gregg, and Barton arrived from Grenada.[93] General Smith declared that the eight regiments of Tennesseans (three of which were Vaughn's), the five regiments of Georgians, and the one regiment of Texans "add[ed] greatly to our strength and confidence." Before daylight on 27 December these reinforcements had all been rushed at the double-quick into position, with Vaughn's East Tennesseans placed on the left of the line at the Race Track, a mile up the Long Lake Road. Gregg's men were held briefly in reserve before being moved quickly into position to protect the sparsely defended gap in the center between Vaughn's and Barton's lines at the foot of Walnut Hills.[94]

"The position assigned me was the extreme left of the line in front of the trenches covering the abatis on the lake road," General Vaughn noted in his report. He deployed Fountain Pitts' 81st (61st) Tennessee as skirmishers in the line of woods before the felled trees extending from the riverbank to the left of the line. Their right flank rested against Seth Barton's skirmish line. Colonel John Crawford's 79th Tennessee and John Rowan's 80th Tennessee were to be held in reserve during the first day's fight.[95] Having never experienced combat, the men of these regiments hunkered low at their posts, trembling with cold, fear, and excitement. Rowan's regiment, John J. Blair of the 80th (62nd) Tennessee wrote later to his wife, was "double-quicked one mile to the ditches" where the boys were required to stand at the ready "all night in the rain and mud." He further indicated that the fight on the Yazoo began around dark under the most miserable conditions imaginable.[96] His regiment would soon be in the thickest part of the battle. The plan for the defense was each brigade draw reinforcements from the one immediately to the left, General Smith explained, with "the left itself [Vaughn's Brigade] to be re-enforced by fresh arrivals from the interior [Vicksburg] or from the reserve."[97] Some of the men

---

[93] Ibid.

[94] Report of Gen. Martin L. Smith, January 1862, *Official Records*, ser. 1, vol. 17, pt. 1, p. 673.

[95] Report of Gen. John C. Vaughn, 10 January 1863, *Official Records*, ser. 1, vol. 17, pt. 1, p. 678–79.

[96] Blair, "Diary," 1.

[97] Report, Gen. Martin L. Smith, January 1863, *Official Records*, ser. 1, vol. 17, pt. 1, p. 673.

who were expected to stand in the gap were in the first cars bringing in A. W. Reynolds's East Tennessee Brigade, led by the 31st Tennessee. Colonel Bradford noted that "about 23 December 1863, our brigade and [Stevenson's] division were ordered to Vicksburg, Miss., and reached there about the 27th. We participated in a little skirmishing around the city for a few hours after our arrival, the Federals being in the act of abandoning their efforts to land at Chickasaw Bayou above the city."[98] Concerning the situation on 27 December along the Chickasaw Bayou, Bradford's prediction was not necessarily grounded in fact. Perhaps a few of Bradford's men were with him on this date, if indeed he has the correct date, though it is likely some of the regimental commanders reached the depot in Vicksburg before their men did.

Indeed, Calvin Smith of the 31st Tennessee, which was Bradford's own regiment, noted that on 27 December he and the men were still on the trains and not even arrived at Meridian, almost ninety miles due east of Vicksburg. Oblivious to matters unfolding on the Chickasaw Bayou while serenely on their way to Meridian, Smith wrote that their train progressed through some extensive pine barrens and "across some large level tracts of prairie-looking country." Upon arriving in the Lauderdale County town, the regiment impressed another train and reshipped their baggage to Jackson. Continuing west again, the boys passed "beautiful little towns and large farms" that Smith noticed had been cultivated in corn the previous year. Their stopover in Jackson, according to Smith, was brief and rainy. While there, the soldiers that heard President Davis, General Joseph E. Johnston, and other dignitaries were in town. The regiment slept in its cars until morning, when they drew cooked beef and bread.[99] They continued on at their leisurely pace with no apparent alarm over the military emergency awaiting them at Vicksburg.

Even with the slow rail travel toward Vicksburg, Bradford's 31st Tennessee was most likely ahead of the other regiments of Reynolds's command. Colonel James Gillespie's 43rd Tennessee was still some considerable distance behind most of the brigade in Mobile on 27 December. Sergeant Isaac Stamper of that regiment recorded at daylight, "we came to Tensaw wharf and took the [ferry] boat, leaving that point about noon." An hour later, the 43rd Tennessee arrived in Mobile. Many of these East Tennesseans were seeing sights they would have never otherwise seen in their lifetime. They were amazed by the wonders of the large coastal city, particularly

---

[98] William M. Bradford and W. T. Toole, "Thirty-First Tennessee," in Lindsley, *The Military Annals*, 1: 463.

[99] Smith, *A Smith in Service*, 38.

its formidable defenses, large vessels, forts, and, further out in the bay where it entered the Gulf of Mexico, the faintly visible masts of the Yankees' blockading squadron. The 43rd Tennessee left Mobile at 7 a.m., on 28 December, and arrived at Meridian, Mississippi, around sunset. As had been the case with the 31st Tennessee, the 43rd Tennessee was compelled to change cars at Meridian "and lay all night."[100]

As the 43rd Tennessee was heading toward Meridian, the Battle of Chickasaw Bayou was now underway in earnest by daylight on the 28th. "I was awakened this morning at 4 a.m. by heavy firing on our right," Lieutenant Earnest of the 79th (60th) Tennessee reported. After a bite of breakfast, he "shouldered a musket and put out to join the boys in the swamps." It was the first time Earnest heard the roar of a battle, which he described as muskets keeping up "a continual crackling…[and] light artillery [creating] one continual roar while far in the distance could be heard at regular intervals the sound of heavy guns from the enemy's fleet and Snider's Bluff."[101]

In keeping with the strategy outlined by General Smith concerning the shift of reinforcements to the upper defensive works, Vaughn was ordered to dispatch two of his three regiments, the 79th (60th) Tennessee and 80th (62nd) Tennessee, at different times during the battle in support of defenders up the line bracing against heavy federal assaults. Colonel Pitts's 81st (61st) Tennessee was the only regiment Vaughn had remaining to defend the extreme left flank just above the upper works of Vicksburg itself.[102] The elevation of this flank, protected in front by nearly impenetrable "abatis" and the Chickasaw Bayou lying at its base, made Pitts's responsibility less dire than might have been supposed. Colonel James G. Rose of Morristown, serving with the 81st (61st) Tennessee, wrote that his regiment's company on the unit's extreme left rested on the bluff of the Mississippi River just above the Vicksburg. Though his men were untested in battle, Rose believed that they displayed almost no unsteadiness due to the natural defenses between them and their foe. These Tennessee riflemen believed correctly, Rose predicted, that "a direct assault on our part of the line was impracticable."[103] With his small brigade divided into three units and scattered across the field of battle, Vaughn remained on the high ground with Pitts's 81st (61st) Tennessee in its assigned position guarding

---

[100] Stamper, "Travels of the 43rd Tennessee," 23.

[101] Northen, *All Right, Let Them Come*, 49–50.

[102] Report of Gen. John C. Vaughn, 10 January 1863, *Official Records*, ser.1, vol. 17, pt. 1, p. 679.

[103] Rose, "Sixty-First Tennessee," in Lindsley, *The Military Annals of Tennessee (Confederate)*, 2: 574.

the left flank. In his report of the battle, Vaughn indicated that "the enemy were in strong force in front of my line of pickets, and made several attempts to drive my forces from the line of abatis and woods."[104]

At noon on 28 December, according to Lieutenant James Earnest, the 79th (60th) Tennessee was startled by the report of musketry on their position from the left. They discovered that the enemy was seeking to cut off Crawford's regiment by flanking it on the left. They fell back a little way, he reported, posting the main body in line behind some large logs of the abatis while the watch extended obliquely backward on each wing. Here they awaited the enemy advance.[105]

About 3 p.m., the enemy moved up a battery near the position occupied by the 79th (60th) Tennessee in the morning and opened fire over the East Tennesseans' heads.[106] Colonel Crawford's regiment drew what seemed a rather choice assignment of standing in reserve behind the main works on the left. Sergeant Robert Bachman noted that the regiment was initially "lying about in a cotton field awaiting orders," when suddenly, the Yankees began to shell their position. "At first," he wrote, "the cannon balls flew far over us, and some of the boys laughed at the poor marksmanship." Perhaps this was nervous laughter, for the regiment and the whole of Vaughn's command were receiving their baptism of fire. Bachman continued: "The first intimation that we were in reach of the enemy's artillery was a shell which passed over us and exploded within five feet of our quartermaster Captain John McClure." Suddenly, there was nothing funny about their situation. The 79th (60th) Tennessee was then ordered to move into the breastworks, just beside their position "for protection." The Union gunners adjusted their range, Bachman reported, causing the "merriment [to] cease, for a shell fell into our company, passed directly through one man, then exploded." He recorded that the shell wounded four men, "one of whom later died on the field." In another account, Bachman stated that the shell had mortally wounded five men. "A fragment from this shell," he added, "knocked the bottom out of a soldier's tin cup, and broke his bayonet in its scabbard."[107] Lynch's Battery soon responded with its two 24–pounders,

---

[104] Report of Gen. John C. Vaughn, 10 January 1863, *Official Records*, ser. 1, vol. 17, pt. 1, p. 679.

[105] Northen, *All Right, Let Them Come*, 50.

[106] Ibid.

[107] Bachman, "Reminiscences of Childhood," 16–17; Robert Bachman, "A Perilous Ride at Chickasaw Bayou," *The Confederate Veteran* 10/9 : 408–409.

according to Earnest of the 79th (60th) Tennessee, silencing the Federal guns, but not until they had killed two men and mortally wounded three others.[108]

From its reserve position, Colonel John Rowan's 80th (62nd) Tennessee initially found itself dispatched from Vaughn's lines as reinforcements for Barton on the extreme right where Sherman's heaviest assaults were underway. Lieutenant Blair recorded that the 80th (62nd) Tennessee was then ordered from this position three miles to the other end of the line to support General Stephen D. Lee's Brigade, then under severe pressure. Blair wrote, "We lay flat on the ground to shelter ourselves from the fire of the enemy," while exchanging minie balls with the attacking bluecoats from three in the afternoon until dark. Blair indicated that they were also under continuous cannon barrage all afternoon.[109] Captain Calvin A. Curley of Company H and of Madisonville, Monroe County, was killed in action, and Private Riley "Vies" [Viar] of Company F and Loudon (then Roane County) was mortally wounded. Blair, who suffered severely with rheumatism during his short stay at Vicksburg, noted that he was permitted to leave the lines and return to camp around midnight.[110]

According to Major J. T. Hogane, who served during the Vicksburg campaign as an engineering officer of the line under Vaughn's division commander Martin L. Smith, "the first man killed in Vicksburg [in the operations begun around Christmas day 1862] was an infantry officer belonging to Vaughn's command." Hogane said Vaughn told him the officer "had crept between the opposing lines to relieve a wounded man, and met with his death." The officer was probably either Captain Calvin Curley of the 80th [62nd] Tennessee or Captain J. Davis of the 79th [60th] Tennessee.[111]

Earnest of the 79th (60th) Tennessee indicated that, throughout the night of 28 December, his company from Washington County was ordered to stand picket at the foot of the Chickasaw Bluffs. "The Yankees continued to shell the woods on the Yazoo," he reported, which required the whole regiment to be in the trenches above the Vicksburg.[112] Indeed, most of the men in the 79th (60th) Tennessee, the pickets Vaughn spoke of in his report, were required to stand duty before the battle line in front of the rifle pits among the felled trees. Bachman reported that three men were assigned to each picket post or watch.

---

[108] Northen, *All Right, Let Them Come*, 50.

[109] Blair, "Diary," 2.

[110] Ibid.

[111] J. T. Hogane, "Reminiscences of the Siege of Vicksburg," *Southern Historical Society Papers* 11/1 (January 1883) 291.

[112] Northen, *All Right, Let Them Come*, 49.

He and his watch, particularly after the day's fight, were nervous because they were stationed in advanced positions between the two armies. "One man stood guard for two hours," he reported, "and then rested for four hours."[113]

"Our surroundings were most doleful," Bachman lamented. "The giant trees lay across each other, twisted and torn. From their immense boughs, the gray southern moss fell in long streamers, giving a funereal aspect to the already gloomy surroundings." He stated that the tension was often increased when "a great swamp owl nearby would break the death-like stillness by his 'ooho, ooho.'"[114]

If the unrelenting anxiety of standing picket between the two opposing forces was not severe enough, the weather added to the soldiers' misery. "A tremendous rain fell," Bachman recorded, and "as I sat by a little tree with my blanket wrapped about me, I could feel the water running down my back and the ground upon which I sat was literally saturated." His first night of real war afforded him little sleep, and all the boys at his picket post "gladly welcomed the dawn of the morning."[115]

On Monday, 29 December, General Sherman's desire to march down the northern avenues into Vicksburg was finally thwarted. His plan was to unleash concentrated strike at the Confederate center. Colonel John DeCourcy's Brigade of Ohio, Kentucky, and Indiana infantry was to advance between Chickasaw Bayou and Thompson's Lake and to be supported on the left by General Frank Blair and on the right by General John Thayer's Brigades. The attack was to advance down the road from the Widow Lake's property, cross Chickasaw Bayou on a corduroy bridge, and storm the Confederate works at the base of Walnut Hills. Simultaneously, General Andrew J. Smith was also to cross Chickasaw Bayou with two divisions and carry the Confederate position at the Indian Mound on the left center of the line.

General Pemberton reported that disaster struck the Federals during their frenzied 11 a.m. attack, "when a whole brigade [closer to three brigades] of 6,000 men emerged from the woods in good order and moved gallantly forward under a heavy fire from our artillery." The Yankees had worked their way through the tangled abatis, and as the assault came within 150 yards of the Confederate rifle pits manned by the 80th (62nd) Tennessee and two of Gregg's middle Tennessee regiments in the center and at the foot of the bluffs,

---

[113] Bachman, "Reminiscences of Childhood," 17.
[114] Ibid.
[115] Ibid.

the Yankees "broke and retreated."[116] Before retreating, however, the Federals, through sheer numbers, had driven Rowan's regiment from their advanced rifle pits and back into the main line along the Vicksburg road. From here, a blistering fire from Gregg's riflemen and the 80th (62nd) Tennessee stalled the Yankee's attack and then threw DeCourcy's men back across the corduroy bridge over the Chickasaw Bayou. General Stephen D. Lee, commanding the center, counterattacked with the 17th and 26th Louisiana capturing twenty-one officers, 311 infantrymen, four regimental colors, and over 500 Enfield muskets. DeCourcy's losses also included forty-eight men killed and 321 wounded. Two of the four Union regiments in the attack, the 54th Indiana and the 16th Ohio, were virtually annihilated.[117]

The assault at the Indian Mound against Barton's men, who were augmented by the 79th (60th) Tennessee, also failed. Lieutenant Earnest of Crawford's regiment reported that "the fight was carried on [only] at intervals raging furiously on the right." His regiment had been sent out to support the 31st Louisiana "and came suddenly under a most galling fire from artillery."[118]

General Vaughn reported that he was ordered during the evening of 29 December to reinforce General Barton, and then Vaughn ordered the 79th (60th) Tennessee to the Georgians' support.[119] Sergeant Bachman recalled incorrectly that they rushed to augment Maury's Brigade (now commanded by Lee), not Barton's Georgians, which was being hard pressed on the left. This was one of the other points where Sherman hoped to force a breakthrough in the center of the Southern line. The Vicksburg road over which the 79th (60th) Tennessee needed to advance "lay at the foot of the range of hills on the right [Walnut Hills of the Chickasaw Bluff], and an open plain, unobstructed, on the left [and across which the Yankees were attempting to advance]." The regiment was ordered to move out at the double-quick, and an enemy battery promptly opened up on them, as well as a bevy of hostile sharp-shooters. "The faster we

---

[116] Report of Gen. John C. Pemberton, February 1863, *Official Records*, ser. 1, vol. 17, pt. 1, p. 667–68.

[117] Report of Gen. John DeCourcy, 27 December 1862, *Official Records*, ser. 1, vol. 17, pt. 1, p. 648–50.

[118] Northen, *All Right, Let Them Come*, 51. Earnest mistakingly said that his regiment had been sent to support the although he called it the 31st Tennessee. Although Earnest indicated that only one man in the 79th Tennessee was mortally wounded, Capt. J. Davis and Pvts. John Everhart and W. Toney, all with Crawford's command, were either killed in the battle or died of their wounds.

[119] Report of Gen. John C. Vaughn, 10 January 1863, *Official Records*, ser. 1, vol. 17, pt. 1, p. 679.

moved, the more rapidly did the enemy fire," Bachman wrote. The closer Colonel Crawford's regiment moved to its assigned place on the left, the more deadly became the Yankee aim. Bachman stated that after marching at the double-quick for nearly a mile and a half in full range and view of the enemy, the boys came to a cut in the road that curled up through the Chickasaw Bluffs. Colonel Crawford ordered his men into this gap, hoping that it would provide some protection from Union artillery and small arms fire.[120]

Crawford also wanted to determine where General Barton's position was. He finally decided, in order to find Barton, it was far more practical to send one man ahead "on the scout" rather than jeopardize the entire regiment. Crawford asked his capable adjutant and his former drill-master, Lieutenant C. S. Newman, to make the hazardous expedition. Newman did not hesitate and urged his horse forward some half a mile or more "under a raking fire," which Bachman described as "fast and thick with the shells and minie balls ... whizzing over and around him."[121]

Newman dismounted when the road curved into a swampy area where the enemy was most likely clustered, and lay down for a moment in a wagon rut to catch his breath and to assess his options. Evidence of General Barton's line was nowhere to be seen. Realizing that he and his horse would soon be killed where they were, "Newman remounted, and, pull[ed] his cap over his face, and lying almost flat on his horse, made the perilous ride back to where the regiment was halted." There he found Colonel Crawford in a very agitated state because his horse had been wounded by the Yankee fire. He ordered Newman back out again, telling Newman not to stop until he found Barton's position, enemy fire be damned. Newman complied and this time succeeded in finding the headquarters atop the ridge. Barton sent Newman back with orders directing Crawford to take his regiment up the ridge and out of harm's way. Again, Newman saddled up and rode off into the gale of Yankee gunfire. Regarding the adjutant's bravery, Bachman emphasized that, "under these perilous conditions," Newman had "passed over a portion of that dangerous road not simply once or twice, but thrice."[122]

The 79th (60th) Tennessee settled toward its position while under fire and was subsequently deployed where needed. While traveling on the bloody Yazoo City Road, Bachman saw "one poor fellow lying ... with both his feet shot

---

[120] Bachman, "A Perilous Ride at Chickasaw Bayou," 10: 408.
[121] Ibid.
[122] Ibid.

off."[123] E. D. Parker, also of the 79th (60th) Tennessee, presented his own unofficial report of the action in a letter to his wife. He was extremely aware of the awesomeness of "seeing the elephant," as the soldiers of this war termed the initial experience of a first battle, and wanted to impress upon her the danger to which he and the boys had been subjected. "Our boys were in line of battle for three days & nights," he indicated, "and it was porring down reign more than half of the time." The regiment was often "in mud up to our knees." "The shells and minny balls fel as thick as hail all around they killed 6 of our regiment," he continued, "but none of our company got hurt but it was a wonder for we was marched up to 400 yards of the canons." Parker told his wife, "I cant tell you half the fights I siegn," but he promised to enlighten her "if ever I live to get home." The magnitude of the engagement was fearsome as well, for "there were several men in with us that had bin in several fights, but [said] none of them was frightening as this one."[124] If he was attempting to calm the fears of his wife back in Sullivan County, Parker probably failed.

Pemberton noted that the 3rd Tennessee, (which was designated as "Clack's" to differentiate it from "Lillard's" 3rd Tennessee), the 30th Tennessee, and John Rowan's 80th (62nd) Tennessee "occupied the rifle pits in front and behaved with distinguished coolness and courage."[125] General Stephen D. Lee added that the 80th (62nd) Tennessee and the two other Tennessee regiments manned "the pits where the enemy made their most formidable attack." Lee characterized the Tennesseans' volleys here as "terrific."[126] Even Pemberton, who never lavished praise except upon his favored officers and commands, praised Rowen's men: "Those to whom I would call particular attention as entitled to the highest distinction are [among others] the 80th Tennessee."[127]

Though he was no longer in the rifle pits with the 80th (62nd) Tennessee, Lieutenant John J. Blair, who had been confined to camp, noted in his diary that his regiment experienced heavy combat from noon until nightfall. He recorded that 423 Yankees had been taken prisoners during the twenty-four-hour period as Sherman's fiasco fizzled into wretched failure before the

---

[123] Bachman, "Reminiscences of Childhood," 17.

[124] E. D. Parker to his wife Susan, 9 January 1863, Parker Letters.

[125] Report of Gen. John C. Pemberton, February 1863, *Official Records*, ser. 1, vol. 17, pt. 1, p. 668.

[126] Report of Gen. Stephen D. Lee, *Official Records*, ser. 1, vol. 17, pt. 1, p. 683.

[127] Report of Gen. John C. Pemberton, February 1863, *Official Records*, ser. 1, vol. 17, pt. 1, p. 668.

Chickasaw Bluffs.[128] Pemberton noted that the left, commanded by Vaughn (and at the conclusion of the battle only represented by Pitts's 81st [61st] Tennessee) remained in "heavy abatis [which] prevented the approach of the enemy except with sharp-shooters." But, for some reason, the Federals continuously fired on the position with artillery and sharpshooters, only to find themselves "met firmly by [Vaughn's] East Tennesseans."[129]

Vaughn's divisional commander, General Martin Luther Smith, also commended the entire brigade at first, but once the 81st (61st) Tennessee was left alone in its position, he singled out Pitts's men for commendation. "The formidable abatis in front of General Vaughn, together with the batteries in position in the line to his rear, seemed to have disheartened the enemy there from the first, rendering his attack uncertain, feeble, and easily repulsed. [The yankee] skirmishers, as they advanced in the fallen timber, were boldly met by our sharp-shooters and their progress arrested. A few well-directed shots from some 12– and 24–pounders drove them back into the woods where they dispersed."[130] As though seeking to garner some of the credit for his men, Colonel Pitts proclaimed, "my Regt., the 81st Tennessee Vols., fought for six days and nights [against] the entire right wing of the enemy's army."[131] His second in command, Lieutenant Colonel James G. Rose, described the operations of the regiment during the Chickasaw Bluffs' battles as being continuously under arms and in their works day and night during the five or six days it lasted, with "rations being cooked and issued to the men in line of battle, but as no vigorous assault was made on its position, the casualties in the regiment were but few."[132]

In praising all of Vaughn's men, General Smith reported that they "showed perfect steadiness and gave evidence of reliability should they be more particularly called upon to show it."[133] Pemberton had faint praise to put in his report concerning the activities of General Vaughn personally during the battle. With reference to both him and General John Gregg, the "Lieutenant-General

---

[128] Blair, "Diary," 2.

[129] Report of Gen. John C. Pemberton, February 1863, *Official Records*, ser. 1, vol. 17, p. 1, p. 666.

[130] Report of Gen. Martin L. Smith, January 1863, *Official Records*, ser. 1, vol. 17, pt. 1, p. 673–74.

[131] 61st Tennessee, *Compiled Service Records*.

[132] Rose, "The Sixty-First Tennessee," in Lindsley, *The Military Annals of Tennessee (Confederate)*, 2: 547.

[133] Report of Gen. Martin L. Smith, January 1863, *Official Records*, ser. 1, vol. 17, pt. 1, p. 673.

Commanding" noted only that the two generals, "though not so prominently involved in the several actions with the enemy, performed their respective duties in an entirely satisfactory manner."[134] John C. Vaughn, in his report, noted with some satisfaction, "the troops of my command, being new and undisciplined, held their position with great steadiness and nerve under a heavy fire at intervals for two days." He believed that his men "showed a willingness and zeal to defend their ground to the last extremity." He recorded that nine of his men had been killed and nine wounded, with "the larger portion of the wounded having since died."[135]

A return of casualties in the Chickasaw Bayou and Chickasaw Bluffs battles, 26–29 December 1862, showed the specific losses in Vaughn's Brigade as follows:

79th Tennessee: 5 enlisted men killed, 1 enlisted man wounded: 6 total casualties.
80th Tennessee: 1 officer killed, 1 enlisted man killed, 2 officers wounded, 4 enlisted men wounded: 8 total casualties.
81st Tennessee: 1 enlisted man killed; 1 enlisted man wounded: 2 total casualties.
Totals for the Brigade: 8 men killed; 8 men wounded.[136]

Colonel Cooke Runs Afoul of General Stevenson. Despite an occasional shot or cannon round still resounding beyond the hills just north of Vicksburg, the Battle of Chickasaw Bluffs had pretty much run its course. Sometime after darkness had fallen, probably during the night of 28 December, one of Reynolds's regiments, the 59th Tennessee, arrived at the depot in Vicksburg in rather surreal and unsettling circumstances. Captain Reuben G. Clark of Rutledge and later Morristown, who commanded of a company of Morristown men, recorded that his regiment's introduction to the streets of Vicksburg transpired during "one of the stormiest nights I have ever experienced."[137] To make matters worse, as the stiff-legged and travel-wearied boys disembarked from their train, they were immediately braced by officers and sergeants with

---

[134] Report of Gen. John C. Pemberton, February 1863, *Official Records*, ser. 1, vol. 17, pt. 1, p. 668.

[135] Report of Gen. John C. Vaughn, 10 January 1863, *Official Records*, ser. 1, vol. 17, pt. 1, p. 679.

[136] Monthly Return of Troops—December 1862, 31 December 1862, *Official Records*, ser. 1, vol. 17, pt. 2, p. 814–15.

[137] Clark, *Valleys of the Shadow*, 14.

great animation and with loud and often conflicting orders, almost without being allowed to catch their breath. George W. Crosby, a high private in Captain Clark's company with the 59th Tennessee, wrote that when the regiment landed at the Vicksburg depot, the command rang out, "All off and out!" quickly followed by the order, "Fall in, Company I," which was his company.[138]

Once they had formed up in columns of four, the boys were force-marched without delay toward the Chickasaw Bluffs as reinforcements from "the interior," where the battle was in progress. "Thence amid darkness, rain and mud," Crosby continued, "we started and traveled toward Snyder's Bluff. So, on we went." And once in the vicinity of the Chickasaw Bluffs, the 59th Tennessee was halted and rested in line of battle the remainder of the night. Word had already swept through the ranks that the Federals had either fallen back or were in the process of doing so. Therefore, Cooke's regiment was ordered to advance toward the Yazoo River, where the enemy was preparing to leave. Crosby noted that the 59th Tennessee remained here a short time.[139]

"We were compelled to march quite a distance through the swamps and thickets [toward the Chickasaw Bluffs], and having no guide furnished us, it was almost impossible to make our way through the dense darkness in the midst of the terrible rainstorm until daylight," Clark remembered. The 59th Tennessee reached the field at sunrise. Immediately, Colonel James Burch Cooke, who was commanding the regiment, found himself unceremoniously placed under arrest for "non-compliance with General [Carter L.] Stephenson's [Stevenson's] orders, and was to be held over for court-martial." He was tardy in reaching the field at Chickasaw Bluffs. His court-martial was held on 29 January 1863, and he was acquitted (Compiled Service Records, 59th Tennessee). Cooke would demand a court-martial to clear his name (which is what later happened), but he would never again command the 59th Tennessee. Once exonerated, he resigned his office and returned home to Chattanooga, as Clark stated, due to this "humiliation that he felt very keenly, for he was a proud man." Lieutenant Colonel William L. Eakin assumed command of the regiment, Clark noted, "but the battle was over."[140] Meanwhile, Sherman had begun withdrawing his

---

[138] Hodges, *The Crosby Collection*, 412.

[139] Ibid.

[140] Clark, *Valleys of the Shadow*, 14. In his formal request dated 28 February 1863, Cooke stated that he resigned because he had been suffering from "diarrhea, jaundice and general prostration" for a two-month period prior to this date. 59th Tennessee, *Compiled Service Records*.

men under the cover of darkness back to the transports on the Yazoo from which they had come ashore.

Aftermath of the Battle of Chickasaw Bluffs. "Although the enemy still occupied his position in front of our lines," Pemberton recorded on 30 December, "the firing was confined to the sharp-shooters on either side."[141] Lieutenant John J. Blair of the 80th (62nd) Tennessee, still in camp "suffering severely with rheumatism," affirmed Pemberton's observation that, though there had been some little fighting along the base of the bluffs on 30 December, there did not seem to be much violence left to the Yankee bluster.[142] While this drama was playing itself out, at least two of Alexander Reynolds's regiments, the 3rd Tennessee and the 43rd Tennessee, were still not yet at Vicksburg. Stamper of the 43rd Tennessee indicated that his command did not leave Meridian until 10 a.m. on 29 December on the Southern Railroad headed toward Jackson. Even with the seriousness of the situation at Vicksburg, the 43rd Tennessee continued to take its time and lay over for the night in Forest, about mid-way between Jackson and Meridian. Stamper wrote in his journal that "it rained all night, but the boys took shelter in the cars and under sheds, spreading their beds on cotton bales." Stamper and his brother W. D. were more fortunate, he claimed, because they set out and found "a lodging place in a good lady's house in a good bed." They implored her to take some money for her hospitality, but she said that she could not charge a soldier. "We did well that time," Stamper noted gladly.[143] All too soon, the local population would become less hospitable and come to feel increasingly the imposition of all the needy soldiers in their midst.

Around 8 a.m. on 30 December, Stamper of the 43rd Tennessee stated that his regiment left Forest for Jackson, where it arrived about four p.m., a distance of only some forty-five miles. The boys set about immediately unloading their baggage, thinking that they would soon be taking another train. Instead, they were ordered to re-board and "go immediately to Vicksburg." In true military fashion, however, the boys were allowed to draw rations and cook them and enough for an extra day. By eight p.m., the regiment was still around the depot and subsequently ordered to retire for the evening. The 43rd Tennessee's departure, as it turned out, was not to be so immediate. The

---

[141] Report of Gen. John C. Pemberton, February 1864, *Official Records*, ser. 1, vol. 17, pt. 1, p. 668.

[142] Blair, "Diary," 2.

[143] Stamper, "Travels of the 43rd Tennessee," 23.

regiment was still there on New Year's Eve. With the furor going on north of Vicksburg, and the flurry of Confederate troops being rushed to the Hill City from all quarters, transportation and coordination through Jackson were proving to be difficult. Each unit must wait its turn. Stamper noted that his regiment's turn would come the following morning.[144]

Much of the crisis at Chickasaw Bluffs had now passed. Sherman had abandoned his hopeless attempts at storming the city from this quarter. Still, for a time the Yankees lingered back in the woods paralleling the Yazoo across the way from the battlefield, and their intentions remained unclear to the Confederate command. Pemberton noted in his report that "the enemy sent a flag of truce asking permission to bury his dead and care for his wounded." The number was now considerable. Permission was granted.[145]

"Some little fighting along the lines," Blair of the 80th (62nd) Tennessee wrote in his journal on the last day of 1862, "but nothing accomplished." New Year's Eve had been "dry cold frosty," according to Blair. He would later add that on this date, the terrible Battle of Murfreesboro was being fought back in Tennessee, where indeed "great was the slaughter."[146]

Sergeant William H. Long of Morristown and the 59th Tennessee recorded that his regiment arrived at Vicksburg during the night of 31 December, and spent New Year's Eve trying to get some sleep in dark and strange surroundings.[147] Long belonged to the same company as his captain, Reuben Clark, so it was likely his memory regarding day of arrival was a bit off.

On 1 January, because of foggy conditions, Sherman cancelled a final plan to assault Snyder's Bluff. His men boarded their transports, steamed down the Yazoo River into the Mississippi, and, for the time, departed the Vicksburg area. The battles at the base of the Chickasaw Bluffs had cost Sherman 1,176 casualties, of whom 208 were killed in action. The Confederate losses had been fifty-seven killed and 130 wounded.

Near the end of the month of December (or soon thereafter), the first bi-monthly company muster rolls at Vicksburg were submitted for Vaughn's and Reynolds's Brigades. Some representative companies' census showed the following:

---

[144] Stamper, "Travels of the 43rd Tennessee," 23.

[145] Report of Gen. John C. Pemberton, February 1863, *Official Records*, ser. 1, vol. 17, pt. 1, p. 668.

[146] Blair, "Diary," 2.

[147] William H. Long, "Autobiography," in *Civil War Records*, 2: 54.

Company I, 59th Tennessee (mustered in at Morristown, Tenn., under the command of Captain William H. Smith): 91 men carried on the rolls; status not stated for 2 others; 81 men listed as present for duty; 10 men were listed as sick in Vicksburg area hospitals; 1 man received a discharge for disability; 1 man was on detached service; 2 men were carried on the rolls as absent without leave (1 stated as serving with Thomas' Legion without permission at Strawberry Plains, Jefferson County).[148]

Company H, 79th [60th] Tennessee (mustered in at Morristown, Tenn., under the command of Captain James C. Hodges): 66 men carried on the rolls; status not stated for 6 others; 54 men were listed as present for duty; 12 men were absent sick in Vicksburg area hospitals; 3 men were carried on the rolls as being absent without leave.[149]

Company I, 80th [62nd] Tennessee (mustered in at Newport, Cocke County, under the command of Captain William R. Smith): 83 men carried on the rolls; status not stated for 8 others; 76 men were listed as present for duty; 4 men were absent sick in Vicksburg area hospitals; 1 man was present sick in camp; 1 man was on detached service; 3 men were carried on the rolls as absent without leave.[150]

In addition to these routine bi-monthly reports, General John Vaughn and the other brigade commanders were ordered to provide for General Pemberton the totals of their command at the end of December 1862. Vaughn indicated that he had 110 officers and 1,508 men present for duty in his three regiments, for a total of 1,730 (with an aggregate total of 2,734 men present or accounted for).[151] Many of the "accounted for" were sick at various hospitals along the route to Vicksburg, or incapacitated in camps in the city.

The year 1862 drew to a close with the invaders leaving the immediate vicinity of Vicksburg, first to Milliken's Bend, and then up to the Arkansas River to create mischief at Fort Hindman, whose existence behind them proved an irritant to the Union forces in the region. The fort's capture gave Sherman

---

[148] 59th Tennessee, *Compiled Service Records.*

[149] 60th Tennessee, ibid.

[150] 62nd Tennessee, *Compiled Service Records.*

[151] Return of Casualties, Confederate forces, Chickasaw Bayou, 26–29 December 1862, *Official Records*, ser. 1, vol. 17, pt. 1, p. 671. Some of those killed (by regiment) were: 79th Tennessee: Capt. J. Davis, Pvt. John Everhart, Pvt. John Goodman, Pvt. W. Toney; 80th Tennessee: Capt. Calvin A. Curley, Pvt. William Harrison, Pvt. Riley Viars; 81st Tennessee: casualties unknown.

and Porter some compensation for the debacle at Chickasaw Bayou. Meanwhile, the growing Confederate army left behind around Vicksburg assumed that the Yankees were abandoning their attempt to take the city. Those who made such rash assumptions, however, did not appreciate nor yet know the tenacity of their enemy's soon-to-arrive field commander, Ulysses S. Grant.

CHAPTER 2

"The Country Is So Poor You Can Hear It Groan at Night" January

Getting Acclimated. "Our command arrived at Vicksburg from East Tennessee on the night of 1 January 1863," remembered Robert Spradling of the 43rd Tennessee, "and moved at once upon the Yazoo River where fighting [at the Battle of Chickasaw Bayou] was in progress." Specifically, he indicated that the regiment left Jackson on New Year's morning at 8 a.m., and arrived at Vicksburg 12 hours later at 8 p.m., "a distance of 45 miles."[1] Sergeant Stamper, also in Spradling's regiment, described the day as a beautiful one, during which "eight companies [of the 43rd Tennessee] left for Vicksburg about 9 o'clock" in the morning. The two other companies did not leave Jackson until about dark. He remembered arriving at Vicksburg at about midnight "in the hindmost train," and discovering that the regiment "had already gone to the battleground, or rather the rifle pits." Stamper's company was ordered to bed down where they stood, and he remembered that the boys had "to lie along side of the railroad ... trying to sleep a little, but the cars kept up such puffing and blowing up and down the road," making rest difficult to come by. The following morning further aggravation surfaced when he and his messmates found that "someone made free to take our skillet without promising to bring it back." He wondered about the perpetrators' "seriousness upon battle occasions," but rather than doubt anyone's patriotism, Stamper's presumed that the borrower must "have wished to prepare rations for the next day or he would not have taken the skillet."[2]

Along the rifle pits at the base of the Chickasaw Bluffs, the danger from Sherman's threat would pass after his fully loaded transports departed. Some of the newly-arrived East Tennesseans were assigned to picket duty, and the rest

---

[1] Robert Spradling to W. T. Rigby, in Robert Spradling, "Diary" (unpublished manuscript), National Military Park Archives, Vicksburg MS.

[2] Stamper, "Travels of the 43rd Tennessee," 23–24.

were directed to set up camps just above the city limits of Vicksburg. On 1 January 1863, Jim Caldwell of the 59th Tennessee took the respite to write a letter to his cousin Carrie Stakely back in Madisonville, predicting that she "would probably like to hear from your friends of the old 59th." Just off picket, he wrote that he was blessed with a couple of hours with nothing much to do, so he vowed to use them to write to her, though he did not know if he had anything to report that she might find interesting. The new day had brought with it a new year, he noted, and "eighteen hundred and sixty-two ha[d] gone with all the horrid scenes, bloody battles and infamous outrages committed all over our lovely land by an invading foe." Caldwell lamented that the new year still had the lingering remembrances of unhappy times, but he entertained hopes that the days ahead would be fraught with a "brightened prospect of the future." Indeed, he felt that the day when peace would reign seemed to be an ever-closer reality. "We hope (and believe we have reason to hope)," he pointed out, "that before another year rolls around—if our lives be spared—we will be permitted to go home in peace and enjoy the pleasure of friends." Some of these friends, he noted with pointed criticism of those avoiding military duty, had not been "allowed or rather compelled to share our hardships in this present wicked war."[3]

Caldwell informed Stakely that the enemy was still "in considerable force" three or four miles from his location along the road to Snyder's Bluff north of the Vicksburg. "Our line of battle is very close to that of the enemy," he noted, and "the pickets fight every day and generally we have a few balls thrown through the day." Such a pattern of co-existence with the enemy was one with which he and his comrades would soon become familiar. Three companies of the 59th Tennessee were on picket at the present time, and he thought that they were within three or four hundred yards of the Yankee pickets. In some places, he thought that the outposts were no more than a couple of hundred yards apart.[4]

As he wrote, Caldwell had no way of knowing that another regiment in the brigade, the 43rd Tennessee, was unloading down at the Vicksburg depot. Thus he mistakenly declared that "General" Reynolds and the other two regiments in the brigade, the 3rd Tennessee and 43rd Tennessee, had not yet arrived. Their arrival was imminent, Caldwell believed, and when they did finally report, "we will have a regular position assigned to us on the line of battle, as we yet have none." The Confederate forces in the Vicksburg vicinity, he indicated, were

---

[3] Jim Caldwell to Carrie Stakely, 1 January 1863, Hall-Stakely Papers.
[4] Ibid.

only half the number of the Federals, but the boys felt no concern and relied on the advantage of their position. Their position caused them to be "perfectly confident of success," according to Caldwell, and Confederate reinforcements were continuing to arrive "slowly." Among others, these reinforcements included Reynolds's men, and Caldwell noted that other East Tennesseans, under General Vaughn's command, were nearby and had been in the section for some time. "Some of General Vaughn's staff have just been here to see us," he reported, including Major M. H. Stephens and another aide or two.[5]

Caldwell wondered about the Christmas festivities back home familiar to Carrie and him. He also welcomed her declaration that she looked forward to "picking his letters to pieces." Her corrections, he promised, would enable him to inscribe his "delicate missives" with more precision to better affect, and her editing would do him more good than "reading a hundred pages of writing on that subject." He requested that Carrie "criticize all my letters, and by the bye this war will bear a great deal of it from which I can see allready." He wished that his cousin would remember him to "Madisonville Sallie," and he was interested in hearing from them about any Christmas activities he and the boys had just missed. "I have not been here long enough to find out much about the city of Vicksburg," he remarked. Caldwell referred to the battles just concluded along the Chickasaw Bluffs and to the brag the foe had made about taking their holiday meals in Vicksburg. He believed that "a great many of them have been sadly disappointed." He also added, with considerable satisfaction regarding the large number of Yankees taken prisoner, "some 400 of them are eating here now." Caldwell stated the next day would find these prisoners "turned over" (paroled) if nothing happened, allowing them to return home "and see how they like that compared to the army."[6]

The news from the great battle of Murfreesboro was beginning to reach the lines in Mississippi, Caldwell reported, and it was all good. He hoped that the proclamation of a great victory was true. At the end of the first day's battle on 31 December 1862, Bragg's Army of Tennessee had indeed given Rosecrans' Army of the Cumberland a rather thorough beating, though both armies still faced each other on the field. Apparently, this news was received at Vicksburg by telegraph and relayed to the soldiers who were still flushed from their victory along the Chickasaw Bluffs. "The boys are all tolerably well," he wrote in

[5] Ibid. Reynolds was often referred as "General" during the campaign, though he was still only a colonel.

[6] Ibid. He is, of course, speaking of the prisoners captured during the engagements at the foot of the Chickasaw Bluffs the last days of December 1862.

conclusion, and he indicated that "S." had gone back to his company for the present, since there were "no wagons for him to 'master.'"[7]

Indeed, most of the brigade's wagons were still many miles to the east in the vicinity of Montgomery, Alabama, from where they were to be driven cross-country to Vicksburg by companies mainly from Colonel Newton Lillard's 3rd Tennessee. "We have been here in Montgomery nearly a week," Private Benjamin Giddens of that regiment wrote to his wife, Melinda ("Linda"), on 1 January, reporting that they would be leaving town in the morning headed west toward Jackson. His company had been detailed to take most the wagons and mules of Reynolds's Brigade in that direction, "though it is about two hundred miles." He warned her that he would not be able to write her for two or three weeks while in route, and was extremely "ankcious" to get away from the capital of Alabama. "I never saw so many strumpets and their audacity and vulgarity is beyond all reason," Giddens declared, adding: "I think that my company has not spent less than 200 dollars after the nasty whores." In his disgust, he concluded that, though he had believed that most of his acquaintances in the company were "decent," they had now "turned from the path of virtue." He was loathed to admit "just now while I am writing, I received an invitation from an officer to go to one of these houses of ill fame." Two of the "strumpets," he added, had been in their camp that day "in their fine carriage and dressed in their silk," and had invited the "whole company" to come to their house that night.[8]

After talking about "bad characters," Giddens again reminded Linda that she would not hear from him until his company reached its destination. He was not quite sure the route they were going to take, he told her, but he knew that the road would be long. "But I can ride in the wagons," he noted with some conciliation.[9]

"We have news from Murfreesboro," Giddens informed his wife, "that our forces whipped the yankies taking four thousand prisoners and two brigadier generals—don't know how true it is." He reported that there had been some fighting at or near Vicksburg, where they are headed, "in which our folks whipped the yanks." And in other pressing matters, Giddens told Linda that he had no idea when he would get paid, but dutiful husband that he was, he would send it home when he got it.[10]

---

[7] Ibid.

[8] Benjamin C. Giddens to Melinda ("Linda") Giddens, 1 January 1863, Giddens Letters.

[9] Ibid.

[10] Ibid.

Some of Giddens's most important news related to his travels concerned the construction of an ironclad ram they had passed by along the Alabama River near Selma. "It is a very formidable weapon of war," Giddens noted, believing it would be done by spring. "It is a very strange looking concern…about 300 feet long about sixty feet wide they are working as fast as they can." He promised Linda that he would write her when he finally got to Jackson, to tell her "what I see and hear." In concluding his letter, he assured his wife that everyone was getting "plenty to eat, for the people are all southern down this away." He signed the letter "yours truly, B. C. Giddens," and added, "your homesick husband."[11]

Back at Vicksburg, where Giddens and his fellow wagon-masters were headed, Lieutenant John J. Blair of the 80th (62nd) Tennessee sat in his tent in the camps occupied by John Vaughn's Brigade. Contrary to many reports, he indicated in his journal that the action with the enemy was not entirely over and continued to be rather lively at his end of the line, though he noted that neither army had advanced toward the other on 1 January. Sherman had taken nearly three days to unload his division and put it into position to attack the Confederates along Chickasaw Bluffs, and it would take him a few days to get them all back aboard the transports and to Milliken's Bend, where the Yazoo and the Mississippi joined. Meanwhile, the 80th (62nd) Tennessee continued its share of picket duty "in the ditches" along the battle line near the Vicksburg road, Blair noted, adding that his rheumatism was some better. He also recorded the news the boys had received concerning the battle in Middle Tennessee involving General Braxton Bragg's Army of Tennessee, though now new reports indicated the Confederates had retreated from Murfreesboro to Tullahoma, leaving the field to Rosecrans after the second day's battle.[12] Repeated Confederate attacks on the east side of Stones River had failed to secure the victory. The Chickasaw Bayou battles were the only good news the Confederate nation could enjoy as the new year began.

The second day of January brought an end to the third attempt by the Union forces to capture the Hill City, according to the report of General Pemberton. The first two failed attempts had transpired the year before. Soon after Admiral David Farragut captured New Orleans in April 1862, he was

---

[11] Ibid. This 271-foot long ram with a beam of sixty-three feet would become the mighty ironclad that would be named after the capital of Giddens's home state, the *Nashville*. Weeks after the surrender of both Lee's and Johnston's armies, she would still be flying the Confederate naval jack and protecting the Tombigbee River until her surrender on 9 May 1865.

[12] Blair, "Diary," 2.

ordered up the Mississippi with his fleet to demand the surrender of the Vicksburg. He believed that the show of force by his grand fleet would be all that was required. The Confederate batteries on the bluffs were little impressed. Thinking perhaps that the warships he had brought with him the first time were not sufficient in numbers to cow the stubborn Rebels, Farragut returned the following month from the lower river and was supplemented by Admiral David Porter's fleet from above. Porter brought his gunboat armada down river from Memphis, which had also been subjugated by the invaders the same month New Orleans fell. After exchanges again with the troublesome river batteries, and some considerable excitement occasioned by the appearance and daring of the Confederate ironclad *Arkansas,* a solely naval attack to capture Vicksburg was abandoned. The Northern press and leadership were becoming increasingly obsessive in their demands that Fortress Vicksburg be eliminated.

Just as the Union navy would be unable to conquer Vicksburg alone, Chickasaw Bluffs proved that Sherman's army was also unable to achieve that goal. Pemberton, surprised perhaps by his successes, stated that the Yankees were at last re-embarking for points unknown, their hopes of easing into Vicksburg by a mythical hole in the northern gate crushed. To hurry Sherman's infantry along, General Stephen D. Lee with five regiments was dispatched across the battlefield toward the Yazoo landing. There must have been considerable looking over shoulders by the boys in blue as they hustled away toward the succor and comfort of their transports and gunboats in the river beyond the reach of the frightful Southern guns of both large and small caliber. The dozen gunboats there, the commanding general reported, fired randomly over their men's heads to cover the infantry's withdrawal toward the Yazoo. The three-day action along the Chickasaw Bayou, according to Pemberton, resulted in Confederate losses of sixty-three killed, 134 wounded, and ten missing. With little inflating, the commanding lieutenant-general noted that he had reason to believe "the enemy's loss in killed, wounded and prisoners, was not less than 2,000."[13] Lieutenant Earnest of the 79th (60th) Tennessee indicated in his journal that on 2 January the last of the smoke from the Yankee warship smokestacks had finally disappeared.[14]

Some of the late arriving East Tennesseans of Reynolds's Brigade were now afforded an opportunity under somewhat more placid conditions of adjusting to their new surroundings. When the men of the two last-arriving

---

[13] Report of Gen. John C. Pemberton, February 1863, *Official Records,* ser. 1, vol. 17, pt. 1, p. 668–69.

[14] Northen, *All Right, Let Them Come,* 54.

companies were awakened the next morning, groggy from fitful sleep from their slumber along the railroad near the Vicksburg depot, Stamper of the 43rd Tennessee noted that they were ordered to leave a considerable collection of their camp equipment. A detail watched the equipment while the rest "struck out to find our regiment." Citizens and other soldiers provided directions that led the boys to the 43rd Tennessee's camp two miles from town, "in a low level place, surrounded by small mounts." Almost before they could unsling their Enfields and drop their bedrolls among their friends, the late arrivals were greeted with the news that these two companies and the rest of the 43rd Tennessee were to relieve the 80th (62nd) Tennessee at the rifle pits six miles away, where Rowan's regiment had done its good work during Sherman's attacks. Prior to moving out, however, Stamper and his comrades learned that the enemy was abandoning the field. "So our regiment did not have to go on duty that day," he reported, no doubt with considerable relief, for the men in Stamper's company were dead on their feet.[15]

Meanwhile back in Montgomery, Benjamin Giddens of the 3rd Tennessee also found himself with a bit more time on his hands because his regiment had not received orders to get its wagons yet underway. He decided to add a few more paragraphs to his letter for his wife, Melinda, since she liked to read long letters. As for military matters in general, he professed that he was satisfied in camps as long as he was writing to her, and despite being "a good ways apart, my affection and esteem for you is as if I was present with you." His awareness that she was praying for him was a comfort, as was her determination to live a religious life while he was forced to be away from her. This led him to confess, "I am not as religious though I ought to be." Giddens also addressed a few words to his daughter, Julia, to be a good girl and to mind her mother and grandparents. He directed his little son, John, to do the same, warning him that he should "stay away from the creek or you might get drowncd." As for his baby son, Anderson, Giddens expressed great concern that the little fellow was so ill and his dad could not do anything about it. Giddens did not know what to say to comfort the boy.[16]

Within the dismal camps along the draws of the Mint Springs Bayou north of Vicksburg, the ground was wet and muddy and the grass worn quickly off where so many men, horses, and wagons continued to pass. Few places existed

---

[15] Stamper, "Travels of the 43rd Tennessee," 24.

[16] Benjamin C. Giddens to Melinda ("Linda") Giddens, 2 January 1863, Giddens Letters. After the war, Giddens was a Methodist minister for most of the remainder of his life.

where a man could squat on his heels in the slick mud to catch his breath. The cool air about them was choked by the thick smoke of damp wood that provided nearly flameless fires coaxed by the fanning and blowing of the members of the various messes attempting to raise enough glow to burn some supper. As darkness approached, so did the showers, "fast and thick," and Stamper and others of the 43rd Tennessee, with their tricks still in route with the brigade wagons, stood chilled and soaked. "We were without shelter," Stamper lamented. Fortunately for them, however, there were some unoccupied tents nearby with the tenants on picket or duty in the field. Therefore, the 43rd Tennessee was given permission to inhabit the tents until the unnamed regiment, probably the 80th (62nd) Tennessee, returned [17]

"About the time we got our fires built," Stamper indicated, "word came to us that the regiment was coming in, and would want their tents." The 43rd Tennessee had to vacate their snug homes and were again cast out into the cold, rainy night. "Fortunately for my crowd," he continued in his diary, "we had selected a tent where but two men stayed, so when they came in, they told us we could stay with them." As for the rest of the regiment, he noted that some went to houses, others to barns, a number to other tents, and "a few stayed on the ground where we first stacked arms, and took the rain all night."[18]

Blair of the 80th (62nd) Tennessee recorded in his diary that adding to the misery of the night was the "heavy firing on the Yazoo [River, north of their fortifications]" where Lee's men were pressuring Sherman's retreat. Thankfully, "the Yankies all left our lines." Sherman's artillery and gunboats were taking precaution that Lee's men were not to get too close to the wharves where the bluecoats were loading. Blair also indicated that his camp was awash in rain and mud, and such conditions aggravated his rheumatism to such an extent that he was "scarcely able to walk."[19] Soldiers were forced to slop about camp with their arms extended for balance, and from time to time their brogans were sucked so firmly by the mud that their feet came up shoeless.

The third of January was just as miserable as the second. "The rain continued all day," according to Stamper. The boys of the 43rd Tennessee were again left homeless and were required "to shift as they had the night before." But even with the rain, lightning, and thunder, Stamper thought that the regiment did "pretty well." Spirits were boosted in Reynolds's regiments

---

[17] Stamper, "Travels of the 43rd Tennessee," 24–25. These tents were probably in Vaughn's camps.
[18] Ibid., 25.
[19] Blair, "Diary," 2

because they were afforded the opportunity of meeting up "with our East Tennessee friends of Vaughn's Brigade."[20] Ironically, both of the commands were seldom in the same proximity during their service around Vicksburg, and even these rare occasions would soon end when Reynolds's Brigade was given its new responsibilities down toward Warrenton, where it would make camp along the Big Bayou six miles south of the Vicksburg.

One member of the East Tennessee fraternity continuing to suffer was John J. Blair of the 80th (62nd) Tennessee, who noted that it "rained all day and night, and I suffered severely with the rheumatism." He noted in his peckish manner that despite the horrible weather, "no accommodations [were] extended to us by the Mississippians."[21]

The weather finally broke on Sunday, 4 January. Around 10 a.m., the 43rd Tennessee was ordered "into camp four miles from town on the Jackson [Southern] railroad," which was in the vicinity of Mt. Albans Church. By sundown, their camp had been established "in a lovely beech grove," Stamper recorded, toward what ultimate purpose he had no idea.[22] Even Blair of the 80th (62nd) Tennessee recorded his appreciation of the beautiful Sabbath day, though he continued to be "very sick." He wrote a letter to wife, Mary, in the afternoon and welcomed the regimental assistant surgeon, Dr. John Abernathy, who visited him and "was very kind."[23]

The next day Stamper commented that "the enemy [was] still out of sight" and that the boys were enjoying the peace. A regimental inspection was conducted in the morning, which led him to conclude that "the 43rd [had] made a nice appearance." The remainder of the day was spent in camp, where the men "rested all day" and recuperated from the long train ride and the unpleasant first few days in Vicksburg.[24] "How ungrateful the citizens of Vicksburg are to the Tennesseans who are defending their firesides for them," Blair complained. He was still mired within the wretched, water-logged, muddy camps north of town, where he continued to feel quite sick until noon and despondent for sometime thereafter.[25]

Captain George Hynds, son of a prominent judge in Dandridge, Jefferson County, and commander of a company in the 31st Tennessee, shared in a letter dated 6 January to his mother, Anne, interesting news and opinions relating to

---

[20] Stamper, "Travels of the 43rd Tennessee," 25.

[21] Blair, "Diary," 2.

[22] Stamper, "Travels of the 43rd Tennessee," 25.

[23] Blair, "Diary," 2.

[24] Stamper, "Travels of the 43rd Tennessee," 25.

[25] Blair, "Diary," 2.

his observations of his present circumstances. He wrote about his journey with his regiment to Vicksburg, the Battle at Chickasaw Bluffs, the terrible thunderstorm referred to by Stamper, acquaintances he had met along the way and upon arriving at Vicksburg, the contribution of Tennessee to the Confederate war effort, and his impressions of conscripts and evaders.

"It would not interest you to know...of our travels to the 'Mississip,'" Hynds told his mother, yet he then described how the boys traveled the nine hundred miles "in [overcrowded] boxcars" before landing at the "celebrated" city of Vicksburg twelve days after leaving Loudon. "Most of the country through which we passed was so poor," he observed, "I could almost hear it groan at night." After referring to the anomaly of ferrying across Mobile Bay in the darkness, which gave him "poor chance to see the sights," Hynds described the regiment's trek though southeast Tennessee, Alabama, and Georgia: "we were greeted everywhere by the ladies and old men, who showered us with their cakes, apples, bouquets and blessings." The scene changed, however, once they crossed into Mississippi: "Soldiers are treated with less respect and more contempt in Miss. than any other state in the Confederacy, and there is no exception to this rule in favor of volunteers from this state, but all are looked upon as tools in the hands of President Davis to work out the salvation of Mississippi with."[26] Because most of the boys knew that the President of the Confederacy and his brother, Joseph, owned a number of plantations in the section to which they were now assigned, they often questioned Davis's motives in his determination to defend Vicksburg to the last drop of their blood. Pemberton would be trapped ultimately in the siege due primarily to his understanding that Davis believed that Vicksburg must be held at all costs, though his superior, General Joseph E. Johnston, indicated that it was more important to save the garrison than the city. But these events and misunderstandings lay ahead.

As for the cool "reception" received by the soldiers in Mississippi, Hynds would not be the only East Tennessee Confederate to record such impressions and experiences. He had been told that the citizens of Vicksburg were decidedly different from others in their state in their treatment of the Defenders of the Gibraltar of the West. Similar to experiences of regiments of Reuben Clark, Stamper, and Spradling, Hynds noted that he and the 31st Tennessee had also been thrust into their totally unfamiliar environment in the dead of night. Unlike the 59th Tennessee and 43rd Tennessee, however, his portion of the regiment was not immediately rushed off at the double-quick toward the sound

---

[26] George Hynds to Ann Hynds, 6 January 1863, in *Civil War Records*, 1: 80.

of heavy gunfire up along the Chickasaw Bayou. "After getting off the cars," he wrote, "[we] marched about two miles and halted for the remainder of the night."[27]

At first light the next morning, Hynds indicated that his half of 31st Tennessee was marched another half mile toward Warrenton, where the rest of the regiment, which had arrived two days earlier, waited. He wrote that "we found their tents in a large cornfield near the river." These tents were mostly empty because this half of the regiment had been rushed out on picket duty. Hynds told his mother, "we soon had our tents up, our rations cooked and the men were ready to go on picket, too." Fortunately, they were never called forward.[28]

Hynds spent the next part of his letter describing the awful thunderstorm which struck on Friday night, 2 January, and continued unabated into Saturday. "About dark, it commenced raining what I thought was a hard shower," he wrote, "but about ten o'clock, I found out that it was a small sprinkle for this country." Lieutenant Newton K. Howell, who shared the tent with Hynds, awoke him to the news that a flood of water was gushing through their quarters. "I jumped up and sure enough, it was about 3 inches deep and still falling in torrents," he observed. "It didn't rain but the water was falling in sheets—the wind was blowing like fury—flashes of lightening followed each other in rapid succession across the heavens and the loud peals of thunder shook the ground." Hynds shared with his mother that all their bedclothes were now covered with mud, and "there was but little sleeping done by us that night." A young private named Bill Inman was sleeping in their tent with them, and Hynds stated that it was the first time he had seen the elephant. "He thought that soldiering was [a] rather hard bargain and that we ought to be home with our families."[29]

The rain continued on 3 January, and Hynds noted that "the mud was so deep that it was almost impossible for one to walk about." He joked that the boys were thankful the "yankees [left] their boats" in their haste to be gone, a reference probably to the pontoons and skiffs they had used as transport in the swampy ground around Chickasaw Bayou.

By Sunday, 7 January, the Confederate hierarchy had concluded that the campground on the Mint Springs Bayou had exceeded its capacity to hold the troops there. Reynolds's entire brigade was ordered to move to another camp four miles below town on the Warrenton Road, as Stamper had reported.

---

[27] Ibid.
[28] Ibid.
[29] Ibid., 1: 80–81.

Perhaps due to its elevation and the fact it had seen little traffic, the camp, Hynds declared, was "a very nice place." He was still compelled, however, to sympathize with the plight of the twelve regiments belonging to General Martin Luther Smith's Division left in the muddy field at Mint Springs Bayou, "including Vaughn's Brigade."[30]

Hynds also wrote to his mother about the recent action at Chickasaw Bayou, where "the loss to the enemy is said to have been between 1,500 and 2,000 men." Confederate loses he estimated at around sixty "in killed and wounded." He described the field of battle to allay her incredulousness concerning the disparity in casualties between the two armies. "Our men were almost entirely concealed while the enemy were exposed," he said, "not only to the fire from the trenches, but from our batteries, too."[31]

The Union gunboats and transports, Hynds was "proud" to report, had left on Sunday, 4 January, and traveled up beyond the mouth of the Yazoo River. He noted that the "grapevine telegraph" suggested that the Yankees were either going to Louisiana to attack Port Hudson, or to "reinforce [William] Rozencranz [Rosecrans] in Tennessee."[32] Undoubtedly, Hynds would have liked to have been among Braxton Bragg's men there in his home state to battle the enemy, should they be headed that way. Sherman and Porter, though, had first gone on 2 January to Milliken's Bend to reorganize under their new commanding officer, Major General John McClernand, as "the Army of the Mississippi." McClernand was a political officer much despised by Grant, but he had date of rank on Sherman and so became his superior. Half of the forces Sherman led at Chickasaw Bluffs were new recruits brought into the Union army by McClernand, and he was miffed that he had not been a part of the operation on the Yazoo. For sometime, Fort Hindman, on the Arkansas River upstream, had been a threat to plans dealing with the campaign against Vicksburg, so McClernand took his new and somewhat bloodied army along with Porter's fleet to remedy that threat. The elimination of Fort Hindman would also provide an opportunity for all the principals either to salvage their reputations or to recover their reputation somewhat after the Chickasaw Bluffs fiasco.

Hynds at the time was unaware of any these events, but he did believe that whatever the Yankee plans were for the army around Vicksburg, and wherever they sought to test the Southerners, "we will meet them." Hynds attempted to

---

[30] Ibid., 1: 81.
[31] Ibid.
[32] Ibid.

paint a verbal picture for his mother regarding "Fortress Vicksburg," as it was often termed in the Southern press: "Our fortifications begin four miles below the City, and run to Snyder's Bluff, eight miles above. Part of the way—if not all—there are around the town already fortified. The country is hilly for miles around the town on this side of the river, except in front of our main line of works [fronting the Sherman's landing area and battlefield of Chickasaw Bayou], which is a swamp and is now knee deep in water."[33] The lines would shift dramatically to four miles below the city in just a few short days.

As captain of his company, Hynds knew that his mother would be expected to relay word from him to neighbors back in Jefferson County concerning the health and well-being of his men. "Tom Jones [of Hynds's Company E] and John Henry [of Company A] are both well and in good spirits," Hynds wrote, as were others of their acquaintance he had met since arriving at Vicksburg. The only sad news he had to relate regarded the death of a Jefferson County boy serving in Colonel Pitts's regiment: Private Alexander Hamilton of the 81st (61st) Tennessee had died of fever on Sunday, 4 January, in a hospital in Jackson. Lillard's 3rd Tennessee, the regiment of Hynds's brother David, had finally made its way into Jackson. "I don't suppose it will come up soon," Hynds wrote, "unless there is some prospects of battle here." He informed his mother that there was another 3rd Tennessee Infantry Regiment, Colonel Clack's out of lower middle Tennessee on loan from Bragg from the Army of Tennessee, in the area, which had been in the Chickasaw Bluffs battles some days before.[34] Should she read about that regiment in the papers, she should not confuse it with the 3rd Tennessee from East Tennessee.

"We have a large army here," Hynds reported, obviously feeling secure in the strength of arms apparent in the forces around Vicksburg. "If the Yankees intend to fight us, we would like for them to come on. There is not another place in the South where we can slaughter them as fast, and with as little loss to ourselves as this one." Overstating somewhat the strategy to be employed by his government, Hynds indicated, "it seems to me that we will have to kill them off before the War will end, for they can't become satisfied that it is impossible to subjugate us." Trumpeting the contribution of his home state, Hynds boasted to his mother: "To show you that Tennessee has done her duty in furnishing soldiers for this war it is only necessary to say that the reports in Gen. [Samuel]

[33] Ibid.
[34] Ibid., 1: 81–82.

Cooper's office at Richmond show that she now has more volunteers in the field than any other state except Virginia."[35]

Hynds believed that twenty-seven regiments of Tennesseans were serving around Vicksburg, and he proclaimed for his homeland: "Proud State: she is still entitled to be called 'the Volunteer State.'" Hynds reacted negatively, however, to the various Conscript Acts that sought to bring "stay-at-homes" into the service. "The enforcement of the Conscript Law in East Tenn. has either been a failure or a farce," he indicated. "[While] it has been the means of putting a few soldiers in the Confederate army, you might as well try to make a Christian of the devil as a good [Southern] soldier out of a Lincolnite." And as for law's effect in Mississippi, Hynds sought to correct a misconception by pointing out: "I had taken up the idea from the newspapers that everybody in the Cotton State has gone into the army, as have to be drafted or stay at home." He admitted that he was wrong because "there are plenty of them left about town who invent as many ways to dodge the Conscript Law as the people of East Tenn. do, except they have no salt peter caves to hide in."[36]

His thoughts on social matters did not end here. Hynds, whose xenophobic attitudes reflected the homogeneous background of the East Tennessee of his day, addressed the military exemption problem plaguing the large cities of the South, which he felt "were cursed with a foreign population." He particularly blamed the Jews, whom he believed had gained exemption from the Conscript Act so that they might spend all their efforts on speculation. "I saw a great deal of sugar and molasses along the [rail]road," he cited as an example, "but most of it belongs to the Jews and they wont sell it except at very extravagant prices."[37]

Hynds apologized for the rambling nature of his letter, because "in camp I always have to write amid noise and confusion, and if I can write one letter without being interrupted a dozen times to answer questions, I am doing very well."[38]

---

[35] Ibid., 1: 82.

[36] Ibid. The number of regiments and batteries included the Tennessee units attached to Joseph Johnston's army operating to the east in and around Jackson. Many of these commands were on loan from the Army of Tennessee then in winter camps around Tullahoma. Except for the 1st Tennessee Heavy Artillery Regiment and some of its attached river batteries, the only Tennessee commands that would remain after the siege began on 18 May would be from East Tennessee.

[37] Ibid.

[38] Ibid.

Up in the Mint Springs Bayou camps and still experiencing illness-induced moodiness, John J. Blair of the 80th (62nd) Tennessee still had duties to perform. One of the more pleasant ones was drawing up re-enlistment bounties of $50 per man for those volunteers in his regiment not conscripted into Confederate service. The duty must have passed quickly because most of the men were considered conscripts. "Disagreeable business" he was required to perform included being the judge advocate of a court-martial.[39]

Despite Captain Hynds's prediction in the letter penned on 6 January concerning the plans for the 3rd Tennessee to remain in Jackson, Stamper of the 43rd Tennessee indicated that Colonel Newton J. Lillard's regiment arrived at Reynolds's camps on 7 January. Lillard's was the final regiment in the brigade to report, and it went into camps at the Big Bayou with the 31st and 59th Tennessee regiments. The 43rd Tennessee was still in its camp east of Vicksburg at Mt. Albans Station, but not for long. In efforts to tidy up and make the grounds presentable and livable, policing of the Mt. Albans camp continued, Stamper wrote, interrupted only by the usual afternoon drill. At sundown came the call nobody wanted to hear: the regiment was to move again. "Tear down and pack our tricks to the railroad," Stamper stated. Thereafter, "the men were detailed to load [the camp equipment] on the cars, and we took it afoot down to Vicksburg, and then five miles down the Mississippi River" with the rest of Reynolds's Brigade.[40]

This relocation of the Brigade Hynds of the 31st Tennessee wrote about on 6 January was already in process by his regiment and the 59th Tennessee. More ground was made available for the impending arrival of the 43rd Tennessee and 3rd Tennessee. The brigade was making its camps along the knobs overlooking the Big Bayou where it bisected the road a couple of miles above Warrenton. Reynolds's men would call that camp home for nearly the next four months, right up until the time when Grant would force his way across the river at Bruinsburg. "We arrived there about ten o'clock," Stamper recorded in his daily entry, "and were led to a rough piece of woods and told to rest until morning." He indicated that the weary boys quickly had their blankets spread on the ground, and all were soon "snugly in bed, where we took a fine night's rest."[41] Their comrades in Vaughn's Brigade were still at the Mint Springs camps above the Vicksburg, and Lieutenant Blair of the 80th (62nd) Tennessee reported that though the day had been a "nice" one, he, Captain

---

[39] Blair, "Diary," 2.
[40] Stamper, "Travels of the 43rd Tennessee," 25.
[41] Ibid.

James G. Blair, and Lieutenant William Douglas ("Doug") Johnson were all sick. Blair's friend and fellow junior officer Lieutenant John Yates Johnston had to conduct the company drill in "the school of the soldier."[42]

On 7 January, Stamper of the 43rd Tennessee wrote, "we arose early not knowing what orders we would receive but under the impression we would march into rifle pits [along the river]." Such orders, however, did not come. Instead, Stamper and Private Bill Hartley set out to find breakfast. "After walking about one and a half miles," Stamper recollected, "we came to a nice house, went in, asked for breakfast, and were told we could get a meal in a few minutes." And they had quite a breakfast consisting of cornbread, fried ham, fried potatoes, butter, and sweet milk.[43]

"You may guess I enjoyed our meal finely," Stamper wrote, "in that we had not had any supper the night before." An offer to pay their hostess was politely refused. He and his friend thanked their hosts and returned to camp. On the return, they passed many soldiers headed their way looking for a meal. "About two o'clock, our commissary came with cooked provisions which were soon issued to our men," Stamper reported. He and Hartley probably did not decline this early supper. He indicated that nothing of a military nature occurred on 8 January except that near sundown the regiment's camp equipment was finally delivered, and in the nick of time. Stamper stated that it had just begun to rain again as they were spreading out their tents for the night.[44] Of course Blair of the 80th (62nd) Tennessee took note of the rain, which, he said, continued all afternoon, though nothing of importance transpired otherwise throughout the day. He was sorry to report several more of the boys in the regiment had taken sick, and the company's orderly sergeant was "quite ill."[45]

The morning of 9 January dawned warm and drizzly, and Stamper of the 43rd Tennessee reported that there was no engagement to report "between us and the Feds," probably because most of the Yankees had vacated the area. Thus the boys spent the day "sporting about camps." Stamper said that as night approached, "we spread out our beds expecting to have a good snooze, when the rain pattered down on our tents." Later in the night while all were deep in slumber, Stamper was rudely awakened when the tent he shared with others came down with a splash, exposing them to a heavy rain that came fast and thick, "as the lightening played athwart our rugged hill camp." Stamper and his

---

[42] Blair, "Diary," 2.
[43] Stamper, "Travels of the 43rd Tennessee," 26.
[44] Ibid.
[45] Blair, "Diary," 2.

tent mates attempted to get their shelter reset, all the while "getting smartly sprinkled and our beds too damp to make them comfortable." "We crawled back to bed and tried to sleep till morning," he wrote, "but little we got having been aroused in the manner just described."[46]This had been the same experience described by Hynds.

Meanwhile, in Vaughn's camps sickness began to make strong inroads into all his regiments. Private E. D. Parker of the 79th (60th) Tennessee wrote a letter to his wife informing her that he was in "moderet" health at the present, though he "had been sick for several days but [was] now on the mend." His malady was "the yellow ganders," and he reported that his lungs were affected. He also noted that several others in the company had been sick "and a great many in the regiment." Parker asked his wife to get word to some of the boys home on furlough due back shortly with the regiment. He wanted her to give some money to "one of the Copass brothers and George Hamiltown" so that they could bring to him when they came. In turn, he promised to send to her $30 by the "wider Hamiltown's" son who "lives at the Acufs Meeting Hous." As usual, he closed his letter by asking his wife to say "howdy" to Uncle Bill and the rest of the family and by promising to "write more the next time."[47] In an adjoining camp nearby, Lieutenant John J. Blair of the 80th (62nd) Tennessee continued to "suffer severely" with his rheumatism in conditions he described as "damp and wet." Being unable to walk at present, he reported lying in bed all day and unable to eat anything.[48]

On 10 January, General Pemberton sent out a request to all his commands for reports on the effective strength of the brigades at Vicksburg. Colonel A. W. Reynolds's Brigade reported totals of 1,960 men in his four regiments, and Vaughn's Brigade reported totals of 1,427 men in his three regiments, for an effective strength of 3,387 East Tennesseans present for duty, which did not include the East Tennesseans assigned to Captain Lynch's Battery, which was assigned to the siege guns along the river.[49] The aggregate number of men accounted for but not on duty due to detached service, furlough, and sickness would have been greater, but it was not asked for nor provided.

The day was warm and blessed with sunshine, according to I. J. Stamper of the 43rd Tennessee, "so we had a general drying out of beds, &c." All continued quiet because the boys in blue had gone, though no one knew what their future

---

[46] Stamper, "Travels of the 43rd Tennessee," 27.

[47] E. D. Parker to his wife Susan, 9 January 1863, Parker Letters.

[48] Blair, "Diary," 3.

[49] Gen. Carter L. Stevenson to Lieut. Col. J. R. Waddy, 10 January 1863, *Official Records*, ser. 1, vol. 17, pt. 2, p. 831.

plans might entail. Stamper described the meaning of "sporting about camp." He wrote, "we spent the day running squirrels which would scale from tree to tree, and in perfect safety," except for the two or three he indicated that the boys caught, "which made a handsome meal."[50] Happy news came from the other end of the line as well, with the usually irritable Blair of the 80th (62nd) Tennessee seeming a bit more cheerful because, he said, "I am better today." He was visited by one of his unnamed neighbors in the regiment just back from furlough in Roane County, from whom Blair was unable to glean any news at all. "He is certainly a strange boy," Blair concluded.[51]

The next few days continued to provide beautiful weather for the boys, and Stamper wrote that the Sabbath, 11 January, was "as warm as a spring day in Tennessee." The regimental chaplain, Archibald Brooks, preached this Lord's Day, and Stamper stated that the large congregation "paid particular attention and seemed to be delighted in the worship of God." He observed that, at least for the time being, his comrades seemed quite content with military life. Around the time of the religious service, the 43rd Tennessee had regimental inspection at 9 a.m., and at 1 p.m. there was a "general inspection" of the entire brigade. With all this activity, Stamper felt that "our Sabbath labor was somewhat complicated." Services did not end at dark. Stamper and a number of his fellow soldiers gathered together after supper and "sang a great many sacred songs." Their slumber thereafter "was undisturbed until morning."[52] Up in Vaughn's camps on the Mint Springs Bayou, Earnest of the 79th (60th) Tennessee spoke of a rousing speech he had heard the evening of 11 January from Colonel Fountain Pitts, commander of the 81st (61st) Tennessee. Earnest described the speech as "a very good war talk."[53] Though he felt that he was getting better and was enjoying as he could this "bright warm Sabbath," Lieutenant John J. Blair of the 80th (62nd) Tennessee complained that he had turned somewhat against the citizens of Vicksburg. To wit, he wrote: "I am denied the privilege of sleeping before their fires because I am a Tennessean."[54]

Stamper of the 43rd Tennessee wrote in his diary that there had been no change in the general situation on Monday, 12 January, and all continued quiet. "We drilled before and after noon," he reported.[55] Blair noted that it was "a beautiful day," though several of the boys in his regiment were still sick, as was

---

[50] Stamper, "Travels of the 43rd Tennessee," 27.

[51] Blair, "Diary," 3.

[52] Stamper, "Travels of the 43rd Tennessee," 27.

[53] Northen, *All Right, Let Them Come*, 54.

[54] Blair, "Diary," 3.

[55] Stamper, "Travels of the 43rd Tennessee," 27.

he. "Done nothing at all [today]," he seemed to say with a sigh.[56] His inability to even move about his camp played on his idle mind. Tuesday, 13 January, was pretty much a copy of the previous days. The regiment was required to perform a military drill before and after noon. Matters continued quiet and serene in their camps on the Warrenton Road. Unfortunately, the rain returned in the evening and continued into the night.[57] Tuesday, however, proved to be a milestone for young Lieutenant John J. Blair of the 80th (62nd) Tennessee, who submitted his letter of resignation to the Secretary of War, which was necessitated by his inability to perform his duties because of his rheumatism. Lieutenant John Y. Johnston helped Blair prepare it.[58]

The chilly Mississippi winter rains resumed on 14 January. Stamper of the 43rd Tennessee reported that the boys had nothing to do all day but "keep fires and guard the camp."[59] From Colonel Eakin's camps nearby on the Warrenton Road near the Big Bayou, William S. Brown of Madisonville and the 59th Tennessee wrote to Carrie Stakely that the news was sparse within the Confederate lines, except for "the war news of this place" and across the Mississippi River to the west. He informed her that he had entered a three-month subscription for her to the Vicksburg *Whig* so that she could learn of the boys' news, courtesy of the local press.[60]

"It will give you more news than I can write," Brown promised Stakely, "since it is a soldier's duty to make news for others to circulate." Their camps, he told her, were four miles down the Warrenton Road from Vicksburg near the river, which itself was clear of Union gunboats unseen now for several days. As for rations, he reported that the boys drew plenty of sugar and molasses, "though flour and bacon are too high for a soldier to eat." Flour was worth more than gold, costing nearly eighty dollars a barrel, and bacon, a favorite soldier's staple, was 75 cents a pound. "We boys prefer bacon and flour," he suggested, over the sugar and molasses, for "Tennesseans like a good deal of *hog*." Contrary to some soldiers, Brown preferred the relatively warm and rainy climate in Mississippi to East Tennessee winter, though he admitted that he and "Jemmy Caldwell" were a bit disappointed that they had not been home for the Christmas holidays. Brown's postscript indicated that he must go, for he was called to picket duty.[61]

---

[56] Blair, "Diary," 3.

[57] Stamper, "Travels of the 43rd Tennessee," 27.

[58] Blair, "Diary," 3.

[59] Stamper, "Travels of the 43rd Tennessee," 28.

[60] William S. Brown to Carrie Stakely, 14 January 1863, Hall-Stakely Papers.

[61] Ibid.

John J. Blair of the 80th (62nd) Tennessee recorded on 14 January that he had received letters from his wife and from an acquaintance, D. W. Siler. With the little duty he was asked to do, he speedily penned replies to both. The effort and memories of home drained him emotionally, and he concluded by admitting in his journal that "I had the blues all afternoon."[62]

More rain welcomed the East Tennesseans on duty at Vicksburg with the daylight on 15 January, though at noon it turned to sleet and snow, which continued all evening. When darkness descended, "it snowed outright."[63] All the boys from Stamper's company went into Vicksburg to look around and see what they might trade for, Blair of the 80th (62nd) Tennessee wrote. The horrible weather caused him to profess that "the boys all want to leave Vicksburg."[64]

Stamper of the 43rd Tennessee indicated that the boys awoke the morning of 16 January to find the ground white with snow. "And it's still snowing," he wrote, which combined with a robust north wind to make life during the morning hours "very disagreeable in camp." Then at noon, he noted, the skies cleared and the sun shined "in all its splendor," melting the snow just as quickly as it had fallen. News of more grave concern in the regiment was that a number of the men had taken sick, and some had been infected with small pox. They were sent off immediately to what the army called the "Pest House" for treatment. Some would recover; some would not. When night fell, Stamper noted that "the ground froze hard, a little after the old style in Tennessee."[65]

"Snow is on the ground and it is very cold and windy," Blair of the 80th (62nd) Tennessee wrote in his diary for 16 January. After days of lying around in a soggy and drafty tent, his circumstances were about to change for the better. "I went to a private house and slept on my blankets before a warm fire," he indicated and then added with considerable contentment, "I enjoyed it very much."[66] Lieutenant Earnest of the 79th (60th) Tennessee measured the depth of the snowfall to be three inches up the Enfield ramrod.[67]

Stamper recorded that 17 January was spent washing and cleaning. It was as though these routine camp tasks helped take from the soldiers' minds disturbing news still other cases of small pox had been discovered in the 43rd Tennessee. Otherwise, all was quiet.[68]

---

[62] Blair, "Diary," 3.
[63] Stamper, "Travels of the 43rd Tennessee," 28.
[64] Blair, "Diary," 3.
[65] Stamper, "Travels of the 43rd Tennessee," 28.
[66] Blair, "Diary," 3.
[67] Northen, *All Right, Let Them Come*, 57.
[68] Stamper, "Travels of the 43rd Tennessee," 28.

Falling back into his customary moodiness, John J. Blair of the 80th (62nd) Tennessee found himself back in camps on 17 January, where he bewailed the fact there was no wood for campfires unless "we carry it one half a mile." The weather of the day continued the trend of the past few, remaining cold and windy. Blair's daily mitigation included two pieces of correspondence: the receipt of a letter from his wife, Mary, and the forwarding of his resignation letter to Richmond aboard the next train east out of the Vicksburg depot.[69]

Though another Sabbath had arrived, Stamper of the 43rd Tennessee wrote in his journal on 18 January that the weather was "too cold and disagreeable to have preaching." The men, he observed, sat about camp during the day reading and writing, and occupying themselves in the other ways soldiers do during times of inactivity. "Another case of small pox was sent to the hospital," according to Stamper, which signaled that the disease had not yet run its course. The boys in the regiment must have been a bit anxious as they considered their own likelihood of being stricken. "During the night, a desperate wind arose," Stamper recounted, "which was followed by a slow but thick rain." Consequently, life continued to be extremely unpleasant in camp.[70]

W. T. Beeler of Grainger County and the 59th Tennessee, probably only a few company streets away from Stamper, wrote a letter home on 18 January in which he also discussed the weather, calling it more changeable than even in East Tennessee. The weather, coupled with the sickness reported all around him and in parts of Reynolds's Brigade, led Beeler to observe: "I am afraid we cannot have our health here as well as we could in Tennessee." He recorded that many of the men were suffering from diarrhea, and that, though some soldiers in the brigade had small pox, no one in the 59th Tennessee had it. The disease was "in the 43rd Tennessee," he reported, "[and] they have sent men off that was suppose to have the pock there was I have been informed 6 or 8 cases." Beeler apparently did not worry about the disease, for "we have all been vaxinated it took no effect on Enoch nor David [his brothers] and did not much take affect on me." The regimental surgeon assured them that since they had been vaccinated, "it [would] not take much effect on any of us anymore." An acquaintance assigned as an attendant to small pox cases in the "Pest House" described for Beeler the symptoms of the disease: "When [the victims] broke out [with the disease], [it] looked very much like a man with the measles with

[69] Blair, "Diary," 3.
[70] Stamper, "Travels of the 43rd Tennessee," 28.

the exception that in the place of being red, he was all over covered with yellow pimples and got so that he could not talk."[71]

Concerning war news, Beeler said that the Federals had not returned since they had been "run off at Chickasaw Bayou," and his regiment had been "for 2 weeks or more [camping and doing duty] 4 or 5 miles below Vicksburg." The circulating rumors of the day, according to Beeler, predicted they were going to be transferred to Texas, but he doubted it. "I would not be disappointed that when we move we would come back towards Tenn.," Beeler admitted, but he added: "I do not know anything about it." He complained that the East Tennesseans had not drawn any soap since they left Kingston almost a month before, causing "our clothing [to get] tolerable dirty." Their rations also left much to be desired. "We draw beefe and meal, sugar and molasses, pies [peas] and rice," he reported, though "the beefe is generaly tolerable pore [and] our water is very bad we get water out of a branch about 3 or 4 hundred yards from our encampment." Beeler expressed concern about an acquaintance, Private J. V. Hill of the 26th Tennessee. This regiment of East Tennessee origin had been hotly involved in the Battle of Murfreesboro. Beeler had learned from his sister Polly's letter of 28 December "that he [Hill] was well at that time and was near Murfreyborough [yet] we have never received but one letter from him that was to Joseph [Beeler] when we was at Lenores before we left Tenn."[72]

Meanwhile in Vaughn's camps, a melancholic Lieutenant John J. Blair, 80th (62nd) Tennessee, wrote in his diary: "how it does rain in this swampy country—mud ten inches deep."[73] The men slept in the mud and ate mud in their food. Other maladies plagued the soldiers at Vicksburg during the rainy season in addition to mud and small pox. Isaac J. Stamper of the 43rd Tennessee thought that the heavy gloom attendant to 19 January was most appropriate. "Was a very damp, cloudy day, suitably adapted to the business in which some of us were engaged," he recorded, "for on the day previous, a member of our company died of typhoid fever and we dug his grave and buried him." The young soldier's name was Asa G. Kincaid, and he was only eighteen years old. "He had enlisted in the cause of the South," Stamper observed, "and soon found a soldier's grave far from his home and parents." He was laid to rest in a "gentle manner," according to Stamper, with head and footboards upon

---

[71] W. T. Beeler to "Beloved Sister", 10 January 1863, W. T. Beeler Letters, David C. Smith Collection, Personal Archive New Market TN. Although he probably would not have used these terms in a letter to his mother, many of the boys referred to diarrhea as the "Tennessee two-step" or the "die-rear."

[72] Ibid.

[73] Blair, "Diary," 3.

which his name was carved so that those passing would know that "his home was in Tennessee."[74]

Describing the misery of his day, Blair wrote, "Done nothing but sit by a fire," from which the smoke "came very near [to] putting my eyes out." Blair had extracted from "Doug" Williams, his tent mate, a pledge to build a chimney for their wall tent the next day.[75] In Vaughn's camps, the improvements involved to convert their modest tent into a "shebang" required that Blair and Williams erect a chimney for their quarters. It made their quarters "very comfortable." The efforts, Blair reported, made them both very tired when night came. "How often a soldier thinks of the pleasures of home," Blair concluded wistfully, "though it be ever so humble."[76]

The good news the following day [20 January] in the camps of the 43rd Tennessee was "no new cases of small pox" had been reported. Therefore, Stamper relieved to report that the daily routine was the usual.[77]

The Return of the Infernal Yankees. "The sun shone so brightly and the air was so mild and pleasant," Stamper recorded on 21 January, that it made everything seem to be in perfect order in their small corner of the war. Out on the Mississippi, however, he observed the ominous signs of the return of a "number of gunboats" that had "puff[ed] in[to] sight of Vicksburg" fifteen miles up river from their base at Milliken's Bend, Louisiana. The grapevine rumor channels clamored to life again, predicting at the very worst that "a fight [was] pending," and at the very least that the infernal Yankees had returned.[78] Fresh from their conquest of Fort Hindman, Sherman, McClernand, and Porter were gathering for a fourth attempt at subjugating Vicksburg.

From his headquarters in the Edwards's house near the Mint Springs Bayou, which was within visual distance of the smoke from the stacks of the Union vessels, Colonel Fountain E. Pitts, commander of the 81st (61st) Tennessee, drafted a letter on 21 January to an unidentified acquaintance, declaring that, despite being fifty-four years old, his "physical and mental powers, [had] not abated." "Camp life rather improves than deters me," he reported. Contemplating his life to this point, Pitts indicated that he had always labored for the public good, noting that, as a preacher of the gospel, he had "taken some 30,000 sinners into the [Methodist] church." Thus he felt that he had made "several friends." One of his friends, the Tennessee Confederate

---

[74] Stamper, "Travels of the 43rd Tennessee," 29.

[75] Blair, "Diary," 3.

[76] Blair, "Diary," 3.

[77] Stamper, "Travels of the 43rd Tennessee," 29.

[78] Stamper, "Travels of the 43rd Tennessee," 29.

senator Gustavus A. Henry, mentioned in an address to an unspecified audience that, as of 1863, Pitts had been a Methodist preacher for forty-five years, and alluding Pitt's's reference to saved souls, Henry expressed his faith that the good reverend would also be able to "take 30,000 yankees prisoner!"[79] As things turned out, however, Pitts proved to be a far better minister than a commanding officer.

For poor John J. Blair of the 80th (62nd) Tennessee, camp life had a far different effect on him than it did on Pitts. His physical maladies continued to multiply, and on 21 January, he reported that he had contracted a troublesome case of "the soldier's complaint": diarrhea. It was, of course, "very bad," and forced him to send "to the country for medicine."[80]

As though to affirm the rumor Stamper reported the day before in his diary, Blair stated, "[at] about eight o'clock [a.m.], we got orders to cook two-days' rations." Such a directive during the war usually indicated that the command was to be shortly on the march in direction of the enemy. The boys all drew this conclusion, but he noted, "we were not called to battle that day," for the Federal infantry had not yet come ashore.[81]

On the Picket Line at Warrenton. The Confederate soldiers expected that the enemy would be landing troops along the Vicksburg waterfront at any moment. The camps of Reynolds's Brigade were near the river, and across on the Louisiana side lay what was known as the DeSoto Peninsula, which was created by a loop of the Mississippi that began on the peninsula's west side three miles southwest of Vicksburg. At this point the river, at what was known as Tuscumbia Bend, swung back north a mile above Vicksburg and then curved around toward the city below Fort Hill, before turning south again past the bluffs and then proceeding toward Warrenton, four miles below. Reynolds's camp was two miles north of this small village, at which an earthen battlement had been constructed by the pioneers (engineers) and styled "Fort Warrenton." General Carter L. Stevenson described the battlement as a casemated structure built of cotton bales, reinforced with logs, and coated with railroad iron. Over the whole structure was packed a deep layer of Mississippi soil. Its battery was composed of two 20–pounder and two 30–pounder Parrott rifles.[82]

---

[79] 61st Tennessee, *Compiled Service Records.*
[80] Blair, "Diary," 3.
[81] Stamper, "Travels of the 43rd Tennessee," 29.
[82] Gen. Carter L. Stevenson to Lieut. Col. J. R. Waddy, *Official Records,* 17(2): 831.

From Vicksburg toward Warrenton, the terrain began to flatten out somewhat, necessitating, years before the war, the building of alarge levee extending several miles upriver to where the bluffs began near Vicksburg. Right up until Grant's landing at Bruinsburg on 30 April, the Confederates often assumed that the Northern army might also attempt to land its troops here. Reynolds's men went on picket duty usually between Warrenton and along the levee that ran between their camp at Big Bayou and the Mississippi. Around the middle of January, the Yankees had begun to scatter out up and down the peninsula, erecting their massive camp there where the pale glow of the canvas of their countless tents painfully glared to the Confederate pickets' eyes in the dull winter sun. Grant's initial plan when he assumed active field command in a week would be incredible and far beyond what any of those rebels watching and waiting could imagine.

From their camps on 22 January, as well as from Warrenton, the boys studied the "smoke of the gunboats with great interest," as though the designs of the invaders could be ascertained through reading something in it. "We were ready at any time," Stamper insisted, "to respond to a call to repel the enemy if they undertook to land their forces."[83] The inability to do much physically and the constant lying about continued to wear on Lieutenant Blair of the 80th (62nd) Tennessee. He spent most of his days in his tent talking to "Dough" Williams. "I am tired of our camping ground," he grumbled, waiting anxiously the news from Richmond concerning his request to be discharged from the army.[84]

The twenty-third of January brought with it a suspicion that the Union forces were at last ready to initiate a landing at Warrenton, according to Stamper. "We, being on alert," he wrote, "were ordered at dark to march down to the river, after the order of the pickets, [namely] one company in a place a half mile from the other company [ahead]." Once in position, "we were ordered to build a large number of fires, thus showing to the enemy as though there was a large force supporting our left to prevent their landing." All involved believed the fire building to be "a singular way of soldiering," and the boys had a grand time in the endeavor. Some of them built "chunk" fires, others made theirs out of cornstalks, and Stamper said that his captain, Sterling Turner, selected "a very large white oak with a very large top of good wood." Being oak, the tree proved to be "awfully hard," which forced the men to work on it in shifts. Once the tree was felled and its branches set ablaze, the men spread out around their

---

[83] Stamper, "Travels of the 43rd Tennessee," 29.
[84] Blair, "Diary," 3.

huge fire to take a "snooze." As was often the case when a rest was undertaken, the rains soon arrived, and the men began to scurry about trying to find whatever shelter they could. Refuge was close by for Stamper, under a large log with a root extending out some length. There, he noted, "I would drop into a kind of a doze, from which I was frequently aroused by someone laughing or talking."[85]

During the night, two large owls, "hallowing at a most alarming rate," awakened Stamper from one of his fitful naps. The owls apparently awoke most of the men, and Captain Turner, to the considerable amusement of his men, began to imitate the sounds. "The Captain was posted between two trees which grew so close together there was just room for him to slide down between them," Stamper wrote. While Turner was in the midst of his owl imitation, "a little flying squirrel which had become frightened by the owls, sailed off a nearby tree and lit on Captain Turner's tree." This unexpected event quite unnerved "the old hero," as Stamper called him, causing Turner to exclaim: "Who is that?" Stamper noted that everyone "had a big laugh and then went to sleep."[86]

Lieutenant John M. Carson, of Mossy Creek, Jefferson County, and the 31st Tennessee, recorded that, during this rainy night, Colonel William "Reshy" Bradford, commander of the regiment, sent Carson's company and two others to Warrenton in order "to strengthen our pickets and watch the [anticipated] movements of General Grant's forces, then preparing to cut a canal across the bend of the Mississippi River [at the base of the DeSoto Peninsula] with a view to landing his army at Warrenton." Carson recalled that "after spending a very hard night in the mud and rain," the three companies [B, C, and I] of the 31st Tennessee at dawn were marched aboard a small steamer that carried them down river to [New] Carthage, Louisiana, where they were directed "to await further orders."[87]

The Yankee gunboats and transports came down the Yazoo River into the Mississippi [at Young's Point] on 23 January, John J. Blair of the 80th (62nd) Tennessee noted in his diary. The gray leafless trees provided little obstruction between his camps and the point, making for Blair an awe-inspiring sight. With the multitude of smoke stacks and masts visible, Blair noted that the scene looked like a city had sprung up at Young's Point overnight. Rather than be dismayed, and in stark contrast to his strong feelings regarding his assignment

---

[85] Stamper, "Travels of the 43rd Tennessee," 30–31.

[86] Ibid., 31.

[87] John M. Carson, "Capture of the *Indianola*," *The Confederate Veteran* 32/8 (August 1924): 380.

to Mississippi, Blair believed, like so many of his comrades who were there against their liking, that "by the help of God we will defeat" the enemy.[88]

About 10 a.m. on 24 January, Stamper and the men of the 43rd Tennessee returned to camp after sitting at arms most of the night waiting for the Yankees to cross and "not knowing whether our trip had been in vain," since the enemy had not come. Once back at their familiar campground, they received the sad news that the small pox in their regiment had claimed the life of one in their own company: Private Thomas Goodwin. "The company deeply mourned the loss of this young fellow soldier," Stamper sadly recorded. Unfortunately, Goodwin's remains were interred at an unspecified location in Vicksburg by persons detailed for such work, causing Stamper to lament, "we were very sorry that we could not bury him ourselves [as was the custom], but his disease was such that we were not permitted to wait upon him."[89] In fact anything young Goodwin had touched after being infected would have been burned.

Blair of the 80th (62nd) Tennessee reported that, on the twenty-fourth, numerous enemy gunboats upriver took several shots at the Confederate transport *City of Vicksburg* moored at the wharf below town, which was under the protective watch of the Confederate water batteries. On 3 February, Admiral Porter would become bolder still, sending the rugged and sturdy gunboat *Queen of the West* past the Vicksburg guns. Blair recorded on 24 January, his company commander, Captain Francis Blair, and a number of other officers were dispatched home to collect conscript replacements for their commands.[90] Undoubtedly, the sick young lieutenant who shared Blair's name would have liked to join Captain Blair on his trip back to Roane County, East Tennessee.

By 25 January, the alternating picket assignments for Reynolds's regiments along the Warrenton levee were becoming commonplace. The 43rd Tennessee was ordered on this date to relieve "Colonel Bradford's regiment," the 31st Tennessee. For those not on guard with their picket post, it was a relaxing duty. "We stacked arms when the required details were made," Stamper noted, and

---

[88] Blair, "Diary," 3.

[89] Stamper, "Travels of the 43rd Tennessee," 31. Like many of his fellow soldiers who died in the camps, Goodwin's remains were disinterred after the war and moved to the Tennessee Section of Soldier's Rest at Cedar Hill Cemetery, Vicksburg.

[90] Blair, "Diary," 3. The steamer *City of Vicksburg* was moored below the city until the night of 2 February when the *Queen of the West* rammed her and set her afire as the gunboat passed the water batteries.

the boys enjoyed the quiet passage of time during which "we were not disturbed by the enemy."[91]

In Vaughn's camps, John J. Blair of the 80th (62nd) Tennessee indicated that there was no preaching on this Sabbath day. "How lonesome I am," he groaned, obviously missing his wife. It helped when Wiley Johnston and his orderly sergeant, whom Blair never identified by name, spent the evening with him in his tent. "If I could get out with the boys," he sighed, "I would feel much better."[92]

The following morning at 10 a.m., Stamper recorded, "we were relieved [from picket] by Colonel Cook[e]'s regiment [the 59th Tennessee]." Back at Camp Reynolds, as their campground was termed in honor of their commanding officer, Stamper wrote that the boys spent the remainder of the day resting, cooking, and eating.[93]

The life of the boys in blue in their camps around Milliken's Bend tried the stamina of the invaders from the beginning. Like the Confederates, the Yankees had to deal with swampy campgrounds, wretched rainy weather, and the same variety of rampant illnesses. Their number of deaths due to disease was staggering, and the resulting disaffection with duty was understandable. On the evening of 26 January, a sizeable number of Union deserters (130 men and a lieutenant colonel) surrendered to Confederate pickets on the upper lines, Blair wrote in his diary. The cheerful news they brought with them, accordingly, was of "great dissatisfaction in the federal camp." The next day, he read the novel titled *Life Among the Upper Tennesseans*. He proclaimed it to be a good one.[94] Down toward Warrenton, Reynolds's Brigade concluded its picket duty assignment, and another brigade in Stevenson's Division assumed it, according to Stamper of the 43rd Tennessee. No other duty was prescribed.[95]

Meanwhile, Ulysses S. Grant, the new commander on the Louisiana side of the river, assumed responsibility for the campaign against Vicksburg on 30 January 1863. No plan, no call for provisions, supplies, or troops would be denied Grant by Washington. For example, his engineers suggested that he resume construction of the DeSoto Peninsula canal begun by the Yankees back in June 1862 during Farragut's second sortie against Vicksburg. At this time, as it had been then, the construction was a bold plan devoid in the long run of success due to considerable physical limitations. The canal was to run north to

---

[91] Stamper, "Travels of the 43rd Tennessee," 31.

[92] Blair, "Diary," 3.

[93] Stamper, "Travels of the 43rd Tennessee," 31.

[94] Blair, "Diary," 3.

[95] Stamper, "Travels of the 43rd Tennessee," 31.

south across the mile-wide neck of the DeSoto Peninsula opposite Warrenton, and if the fickle Mississippi could be convinced to change her course a little and flow through it from the opposite side, the Federals could bypass Vicksburg altogether with their gunboats, troop transports, and supply efforts, and come ashore at Warrenton.

An earthen dam had been constructed on the western side of Grant's ditch to hold out the Mississippi while the lengthy gully was being excavated across the base of the peninsula. Once the impressed slaves charged with the excavation had finished their back-breaking work with their shovels, the dam was to be blown up, and in theory the waters would flood the canal, allowing for steamer traffic free from the danger of the batteries at Vicksburg. General Sherman was given the task of overseeing the work, which he considered to be a massive waste of manpower and doomed from the start. Even if the channel proved capable of drawing the Mississippi through the canal, it would empty out in front of the batteries at Warrenton and the South Fort, which led Sherman to conclude that the first vessel coming through it back into the Mississippi would be immediately "blown out of the water." Still, the work went on. Grant believed that busy Yankees were happy Yankees, and he kept his army perpetually involved in heavy physical labor on one project after another throughout the campaign. As for his ditch, however, with the heavy rains in January and February, Old Man River proved that he had a mind of his own (and possibly Confederate sympathies as well), washing through the dam before the implementers were ready. Instead of neatly filling the canal, the water settled out into the level bottoms, adding to the swampy marshes so prevalent all along the Mississippi Delta.

On 22 January from across the river on the levee, Stamper of the 43rd Tennessee and his comrades had begun watching with some interest the "cutting" of the canal. The racket of the work was accompanied by the continual noise of the army drums, which "could be heard distinctly at all times through the day and night." Stamper reported that there was also enough cannonading during the day to draw attention, "but to no purpose." Actually, the cannonading was designed to discourage the Johnnies from getting too curious. Little could the Southern soldiers appreciate what a terror this indiscriminate shelling would become in the months ahead.

The boys in camp, Stamper wrote, had "nothing much to do."[96] There was, however, good news in Vaughn's camps. "We draw three quarters of a pound of pork today," Blair of the 80th (62nd) Tennessee indicated. "It makes

---

[96] Ibid.

the boys as well as myself rejoice." He noted that it was the first issue of "hog meat" they had had since arriving in Mississippi. "May it come more frequently," he prayed, as if entreating his superiors.[97]

W. T. Beeler of the 59th Tennessee wrote a letter to his sister on 29 January, stating, "we are still five miles below Vicksburg, and we have to go on picket duty very often, sometimes down as far as Warrenton." He noted that the duty was very hard since the Yankees had come back, and everyone believed that "we stand a tolerable good chance of having a fight in a few days." As though he has heard that one before, Beeler added, "though we may not have one at all." Looking across the river, the men saw the growing enemy encampment, and through the grapevine telegraph word came that a Federal lieutenant colonel and eighty men had recently given themselves up to General John Vaughn's men on the upper defenses along the old battlefield. Most of these deserters declared that they would not fight anymore, and were it not for fear of getting killed in the crossing over from the peninsula, others would also make the trip and surrender. Beeler did not know the veracity of this news, but he stated, "I know that 3 did come down near Warrenton and gave themselves up." He reported that one had floated across on a piece of split timber, "and the other two came across on some drift." "They were from Ohio," Beeler wrote, adding that the deserters claimed "that there were a great many that would present [desert] in the spring."[98]

Beeler also described for his sister how the citizens of Vicksburg had dug "holes" in most every hillside, wherein they might "go in time of a fight [so] that they may not be hurt." He also reacted to a letter he had received on 18 January from home that caused him and his brothers at Vicksburg considerable anguish: "Our pore hearts mourn to hear that our neighbors suffered so much in the fight at Murfreysborough." Added to this misery was the news that one of their brothers was missing in action. Beeler trusted that his brother might still be alive and return to his little family "in piece to join them in the lonely walk through this world of trouble." If such was not the Lord's will, however, Beeler said, "we have to be content with our lot and try to meet beyond this vial of tears where parting can never come."

Beeler believed that "we will leave here soon," but he wanted his sister-in-law to write soon and give the Beeler boys all the news. He scolded her because he had written "1, 2 or 3" letters a week since they had been at Vicksburg, with few coming his way in return. Food was expensive there just now, and the boys

---

[97] Blair, "Diary," 3.
[98] W. T. Beeler to "Beloved Sister," 29 January 1863, W. T. Beeler Letters.

could not afford to buy it. "We cannot get anything only what we draw," he reported, and when his brother Enoch was sick, W. T. had bought a dozen small cornbread cakes for a dollar, a pound of butter for the same price, a quart of milk for 25 cents, and a dozen eggs for a dollar. In closing, Beeler said that he had sent his brother Joseph the same news he was sending his family and he promised to write more often. He challenged them all to do the same.[99]

In an adjacent camp, Stamper of the 43rd Tennessee indicated that his regiment was again on picket, "but [we've] had no engagement with the enemy." The Confederate batteries, however, had lobbed a few "bombs" across the river toward the canal, "to no effect."[100]

William H. Tibbs, a Confederate congressman from 3rd District of Tennessee, received a letter written on 29 January from the camps below Vicksburg by Captain James Pryor Brown of the 59th Tennessee. Brown solicited the congressman's aid in forwarding to the Confederate congress his recommendation for promotion to Major. As senior captain of the regiment, Brown felt entitled to fill the vacancy resulting from the death of Major Charles M. Alexander just before the regiment left for Vicksburg. "There has been no fighting here since the Yankees came back," Brown wrote in the letter, "and there are said to be 40,000 strong on the La. shore and seem to be moving down the rail road and keeping out of range of our batteries on this side of the river." He indicated that the Confederates on the Mississippi side of the river moved along parallel with the enemy, but Brown felt that no attack was imminent. He could still see smoke, funnels, and masts of the gunboats above the city, but the boats had made no effort to pass the batteries.[101]

In his 29 January diary entry, Lieutenant John J. Blair of the 80th (62nd) Tennessee recorded that his company had been "very cold" during its picket duty. Becoming resigned to the fact that his discharge might not be granted, he wished that "Jeff [Davis] would send us to another point." He expressed his contempt for conditions in general and for the Cotton State in particular by declaring, "I hate Mississippi."[102] He noted that his ever-dependable wife, Mary, had sent him another letter to which he had immediately responded.

Quartermaster Sergeant John T. "Tom" Moffitt, of New Market, Jefferson County, and Captain John P. Lynch's Company of Light Artillery, were home on 29 January, detached to the Knoxville Conscript Camp of

[99] Ibid.
[100] Stamper, "Travels of the 43rd Tennessee," 32.
[101] 59th Tennessee, *Compiled Service Records*.
[102] Blair, "Diary," 3.

Instruction to bring back replacements for his unit somewhere in Mississippi. He spent two days in Knoxville, Moffitt wrote in his small pocket journal, and netted for the battery 22 conscripts, who were reluctant volunteers at best.[103] On the last day of January, Sergeant Moffitt of Lynch's Battery left with his new collection of gunners from the depot in Knoxville for the long exhausting journey to Vicksburg where the Lynch's command was now posted.[104]

Around noon on the 30th, Stamper of the 43rd Tennessee indicated that his regiment had returned to camp from picket. Around five that evening, after a few hours rest, his company was called out a mile from camp to guard a battery at the South Fort for twenty-four hours. "It is interesting to hear the Yankee drums," he wrote, "which for some several days had been beating on the other side of the river at an awful rate."[105] The boys in John J. Blair's company with the 80th (62nd) Tennessee received much appreciated winter clothing, and he noted that he had "great excitement in issuing it." Blair noted that an officer named "Woods" charged that "there was partiality in distributing it."[106]

"J. Y. Johnston and myself worked all day at our payrolls," John J. Blair of the 80th (62nd) Tennessee wrote in his journal 31 January. This work would be one of his final duties as an officer for the company. This marked the first payday the regiment had had since being mustered in back in November, and each man drew at a rate covering "2 months and six days' service." As a result, the average private was entitled to approximately $24.19. "Poor boys," Blair empathized: "$11 per month is poor pay."[107]

---

[103] John Thomas Moffitt, "Diary" (unpublished manuscript), McClung Historical Collection, Knoxville TN, 1.

[104] Moffitt, "Diary," 1.

[105] Stamper, "Travels of the 43rd Tennessee," 32.

[106] Blair, "Diary," 3.

[107] Blair, "Diary," 3. Artillerymen were paid $12 a month.

CHAPTER 3

"How Ungrateful the Citizens of Vicksburg Are to the Tennesseans Defending Their Firesides for Them:" February

General Henry H. Taylor was from Kentucky and a West Point graduate, V. C. Allen of the 3rd Tennessee remembered, describing him as "a gallant officer with common sense enough to understand Tennessee volunteers." At Vicksburg, Taylor served as a brigade commander and Pemberton's chief of staff, though back in Tennessee he had commanded many of the troops now serving under A. W. Reynolds. Allen recalled being in a barbershop in the Vicksburg sometime during the spring of 1863 while a barber was giving Taylor a shave. One of Allen's friends asked the general which troops were under his command, and Taylor rose up in his chair and exclaimed: "I am in command of four Tennessee regiments who refuse to drill, but they will go at a double-quick all day, sleep on a brush heap when night comes without blankets or rations, and fight the next day like h—l!"[1]

Occasional cannonading across the river coming both ways continued on 1 February, according to Stamper of the 43rd Tennessee. Otherwise, he saw "no change in affairs."[2] Enoch C. Beeler of the 59th Tennessee in a letter home to Grainger County on this day affirmed Stamper's report, noting, "I have heard the report of several guns since I've been writing." Two days before, while some of the boys in his regiment were on picket at or near Fort Warrenton with some other regiments of Stevenson's Division, the Federals suddenly began to shell them from the Louisiana side of the river. "One shot struck a stack of Enfield muskets which belonged the [to] 23rd Alabama [of Stephen D. Lee's Brigade]

---

[1] V. C. Allen, *Rhea and Meigs Counties in the Confederate War* (Dayton TN: self-published, 1908) 98. Actually, Taylor never commanded the brigade at Vicksburg. Some of the brigade had been under his command for a brief time before it participated in the Kentucky campaign.

[2] Stamper, "Travels of the 43rd Tennessee," 32.

and shivered one to pieces," Beeler revealed, "and while the major and some of the men were picking up the pieces, a second shell struck a man about the hips passing nearly through him." Though the shell did not explode, Beeler recorded that the soldier "died in about half an hour." Some of the boys from the 59th Tennessee helped carry the body back to Lee's camps, and Beeler thought that the "shell missed our regiment by something like 400 yards."[3]

The Queen of the West *Tries the Vicksburg Batteries.* The Yankees, again, were beginning to stir. In his letter Beeler addressed the digging of Grant's canal, referencing the noise of the enemy musicians on the peninsula. He considered the music to be a ruse, a perpetration akin to the lighting of fires by the Confederate pickets nights before. "The Yankees keep up a great deal of noise with their drums which makes me believe there is more noise than danger," he surmised. The enemy continued occupying the Louisiana side opposite them, noted Beeler, passing their wagons down on the peninsula where the day before he had observed a regiment of bluecoats on the march. Their gunboats and transports were anchored upriver, he reported, "but they are careful to keep out of the range of our guns."[4]

The "Queen of the West". On the evening of 2 February, Admiral Porter dispatched from his fleet off Young's Point the sturdy but cumbersome cotton-clad gunboat ram *Queen of the West*, under the command of Colonel Charles R. Ellet. The ram was manned by a detachment of army volunteers who were to attempt a run past the fearsome upper batteries of Vicksburg and destroy the transport *City of Vicksburg*, moored at the wharves there. Should he succeed and not be sunk, Ellet was then tasked to proceed down toward the Red River and destroy as many Southern transports headed to supply Vicksburg as he encountered. An important secondary benefit to the Northern cause should Ellet's venture prove fruitful was to prove that the batteries were not beyond evading.

The high gunnels of the *Queen of the West* had been stained with black paint for the night's work. The plan was for her to keep her speed slow and steady as she made her way around the Tuscumbia Bend on the approach to the upper works at Vicksburg in order to limit the racket from her rough-running machinery, and then to slip on down the river. Implementation is always more difficult when measured against the unpredictable. The bulk of the *Queen of the*

---

[3] Enoch Beeler to "Little Sister," 1 February 1863, Enoch Beeler Letters, David C. Smith Collection, Personal Collection, New Market TN.
[4] Ibid.

West, churning along in the river, was hard to hide even in the deep gloom of the night. The Confederate gunners detected her as she made the bend in the river, not only by the racket of her supposedly muffled engines, but also by the sparks spraying from her funnels. John Lynch's pickets in skiffs off the upper water battery raised the alarm. When the *Queen of the West* was fired upon by the big siege guns at the foot and atop Fort Hill, Ellet ordered his engines to full speed and pointed the bow of the tough, old gunboat ram straight toward the transport *City of Vicksburg*, tied at the wharf down the hill from town. To Ellet's advantage, the closer the *Queen of the West* got toward the lower wharves, the more difficult it was for the massive cannon of the city defenses to be depressed to engage her.

Moffitt wrote in his diary, "the ironclad *Conestoga* [*Queen of the West*] ran down the river, and our [Lynch's] Battery struck her seven times." Even though Moffitt and his comrades with Lynch's Battery hoped that she had been sunk out in the dark river, they all believed that at the very least she had been badly damaged. They calculated that she had received a total of thirty hits, seven from Lynch's guns alone. Moffitt indicated in his pocket journal that the crew of gunner Corporal Rufus Caldwell, of New Market, Jefferson County, fired the first shot at the ironclad.[5]

With all audacity, Ellet drove the *Queen of the West*'s reinforced prow into the *City of Vicksburg* at her mooring while his men flung torches of turpentine-soaked cotton onto the Confederate steamer's decks, igniting numerous fires. Thus, despite Moffitt's declaration concerning the damage done to the ram, the *Queen of the West* proved herself capable of absorbing significant punishment that did little to slow her down. Though the well-placed shower of shells of the batteries inflicted some hull damage, she defiantly and deliberately backed out into the main channel to make her way across river to the "friendly" Louisiana side. The transport *DeSoto* was sent out to meet her and provide escort below Fort Warrenton.

Beeler of the 59th Tennessee noted that the *Queen of the West* previously "had made several attempts to pass down the river, but had as often been driven back by our batteries." With the attempt on 2 February, however, the lumbering and ungainly warship had finally succeeded in running the fearsome river defenses. Now, Ellet's daredevil ram found herself in a new predicament, according to Beeler: "hemmed in above and below so that it will hardly make its escape but will likely be destroyed."[6] Indeed, the *Queen of the West*'s trials

---

[5] Moffitt, "Diary," 1.
[6] Beeler to "Little Sister."

against the river batteries were not yet over. The guns at South Fort and Fort
Warrenton down river waited their turn.

Major James P. Brown, Field and Staff, 59th Tennessee, began a letter to
his cousin Carrie Stakely back in Monroe County on 2 February, in which he
reported that he had not been on duty all day. This free time allowed him, he
wrote in jest, to pen just one more letter this morning and it would be to her.
He began by describing the excitement generated at daylight on 3 February by
the *Queen of the West*. "Just at daylight," he reported, "the Batterys at the City
commenced firing which is four miles from our camps above [north]." With the
alarm, Brown rushed to saddle his horse and rode four miles to the Louisiana
batteries at the South Fort to see what was transpiring. What he saw there atop
the high knoll of the fort was the river awash with the glow of the bonfires lit by
the pickets along the banks, and the tremendous hurling of shells from the
batteries at the *Queen of the West*. She was trying to make her way by "very
quietly," though Brown guessed that there were "hundreds of balls being fired
at her." Some hit, he concluded, and some missed. Though he could not
estimate the damage to her, he did not feel like the dash of a single gunboat
posed any real injury to the Confederate cause, with the possible exception that
it might "cut off our communications via the river between this point and Port
Hudson."[7]

Captain Reuben G. Clark, commanding a company of men from
Morristown with the 59th Tennessee, recorded that his company wanted the
whole of Porter's fleet to attempt a run past the river batteries at Vicksburg.
Any movement of the vessels of the fleet filled him with "delight," Clark
professed. Boredom, Yankee feints, and their annoying demonstrations
increased the anticipation of finally confronting the enemy coming ashore from
their transports. The Confederates on the east bank of the Mississippi had a
strong desire for something to happen. Clark wrote that the river before them
was extremely wide from shore to shore ("over a mile"), and as they observed
the *Queen of the West* and the *DeSoto* inching closer to the "friendly" bank of the
peninsula, his Confederate comrades manning Fort Warrenton became
exceedingly animated with the thought of "getting them." Clark reported, "the
rear boat [the *DeSoto*] backed out of the formation and returned up the river
before reaching the range of the river batteries." But the lead vessel, "which
proved to be the *Queen of the West*, went by, hugging the other [Louisiana]
shore with all the speed she could command." He described her as "a black
streak," and indicated that the sharp-eyed Confederate gunners "thunder[ed] on

[7] James P. Brown to Carrie Stakely, 2 February 1863, Hall-Stakely Papers.

her like an avalanche." She completed her run "without loss," Clark stated in amazement, "except for slight damage to her hull."[8]

"There was a gunboat that passed down the river day before yesterday," Giddens of the 3rd Tennessee told his wife in a letter describing the incident, "and [of] all the cannonading that I ever heard it took the lead." He noted that the projectiles striking the river around the *Queen of the West* made the "water fly as high as a house around this old black steamer and to see the balls shot off her whether they injured her or not I could not tell." Indicating his preference, however, Giddens opined, "I would have been glad to see her sink to the bottom of the Mississippi." The nearness of the boys on picket to the action allowed him to observe that the gunboat "did not fire a single shot but her port holes were stopped up so that I could not see a single man."[9] Cheers and yells from the East Tennessee observers were loud and frequent during this relatively safe (for them) action; a whoop from the Johnnies rolled with the smack of every ball and shell against the *Queen of the West*'s cotton-clad and wooden sides.

Vaughn's men, including Lieutenant John Blair's 80th (62nd) Tennessee, were still in their camps a mile and a half north of Vicksburg. Blair made notes concerning the passing of the gunboat ram, including its miraculous escape past the batteries. It "engaged our guns below Vicksburg for an hour," he recorded, "and went on down the river." Blair wrote another letter to his wife, Mary, on 2 February, noting that his fellow officer and friend John Y. Johnston was unwell. Blair complained he had "had nothing to eat today but rice and sugar. Oh, for one good meal from an East Tennessee farmer's table!"[10]

"The Yankees have a large force over on the La. side opposite us," Major Brown of the 59th Tennessee continued in his 2 February letter to Carrie Stakely, but even given that situation, he did not "believe they intend fighting us here though they maybe attempting a landing below." Even should that occur, he boasted, "I have no doubt of our ability to defeat them." The terrain around Vicksburg, Brown described for Carrie, was "very hilly, and ruff—the ravines are so numerous and steep it is impossible to ride over it [except] for where the roads have been made."[11]

"We are all well," Brown declared, providing an interesting contrast to some of the other regiments in the brigade. "The health of the regiment is very

[8] Clark, *Valleys of the Shadow*, 17.
[9] Benjamin C. Giddens to Melinda ("Linda") Giddens, 6 February 1863, Giddens Letters.
[10] Blair, "Diary," 3.
[11] J. P. Brown to Stakely.

good." Even with all sorts of "disagreeable weather" since their arrival, he noted that the general health of the 59th Tennessee was "better than it ever has been."[12]

Everyone on 2–3 February was giving his observations relating to the exciting gunboat sprint. "One gunboat passed Vicksburg at sunup," Stamper of the 43rd Tennessee observed, "amid a number of heavy shots from our batteries." Like Clark, he also concluded that the *Queen of the West* "passed unhurt as far as we could see." Perhaps rationalizing a bit, he reasoned that the Union gunboat made good its run because "she did not pass all of our guns, but took shelter in a secure place," first the near and then along the far bank. The *Queen* remained in that "secure place" most of the day up until evening, according to Stamper, when "she came out and made her escape, passing all of our guns apparently unhurt." The boys spent some time, Stamper reported, arguing over how any boat could have made such a successful pass through such a gauntlet of cannon.[13]

Dirty Work: Laundry, Judge Advocacy, Conscript Duty, and Standing Sentry in Foul Weather. Though the 43rd Tennessee was called to picket duty along the river for next two days, Stamper wrote he did not have to go. This allowed him some time to take care of personal matters. "During the day, I took four pieces of clothing to a neighboring house to get them washed," he wrote. "When I asked what the charge was, I was told 'four bits a garment.'" Stamper said that, though such gouging irked him, he chose not to be insulting, since "she was a woman." She owed him a quarter from a time before, so instead of being rude, he decided to let her wash two pieces, and "we would settle the bill for the war." The brigade was still without a soap allowance, making it impossible for the soldiers to do their laundry. The day and evening had turned cold and windy again, he observed, and the night was very chilly. "I guess the boys shivered while on picket," Stamper concluded, his own personal experience provided a frame of reference.[14]

---

[12] Ibid. Col. Eakin seemed particularly adept at keeping his men and their camps as clean as possible, both before and during the siege. These reports indicating their relative good health stand in contrast to their sister regiments in Vaughn's and Reynolds's Brigades. After the parole, the 59th Tennessee would be the first to make it to Enterprise, Mississippi, for the train passage home, demonstrating the superior physical condition of its men.

[13] Stamper, "Travels of the 43rd Tennessee," 32.

[14] Ibid.

Again on 3 February, John J. Blair of the 80th (62nd) Tennessee (along with his friend J. Y. Johnston) found themselves as judge advocates for men who had been caught a second time deserting from Company H. Results were not indicated. He noted that Hugh Gooden and Jim Pane, two men in his company, had also left camp without permission.[15] Some had perhaps left, but others would be coming.

Sergeant Thomas Moffitt of Lynch's Battery in route from the conscript camp of instruction in Knoxville arrived at the Vicksburg depot on 4 February escorting his cargo of twenty-two East Tennessee conscripts who were soon to be converted into artillerymen.[16] They would be greeted by more inclement weather, Stamper of the 43rd Tennessee wrote, and what began on 4 February as a day of clouds and cold, turned about 10 a.m. into sleet and rain that lasted until around midnight. Undoubtedly grateful for being left behind in camp, Stamper empathized with those from the 43rd Tennessee still out on picket, for it was "the coldest time you ever saw," requiring those in camp "to go to bed to keep from freezing."[17]

"I expected to start for home today," Blair recorded in his diary on 4 February from the camps of the 80th (62nd) Tennessee, with the validation of his disability discharge having been achieved earlier. But as though to vex him yet a day or so longer, he stated, "it rained so that I could not get to the depot." He had no other option but to remain in his chilly tent, where there was no wood to burn in the fire. "We burnt our bed frames to keep warm," he wrote and then indicated that "our company went to the ditches [at the foot of Chickasaw Bluffs] at 4 o'clock." There they had no fires, even if they had had wood or bed frames with which to fuel. This would be Blair's final entry in his diary at Vicksburg, and he would soon be on his way back home toward Philadelphia in McMinn County.[18]

Duty Among the Siege Guns. On the cold morning of 4 February, while Blair was waiting to depart, Moffitt of Lynch's Battery reported with his conscripts to Captain John Lynch. "All were surprised to see me," he declared, "but more surprised to see the men." How bewildered, sullen, or even excited many of those men looked regarding their new surroundings, Moffitt did not say. He was glad to find that his captain was extremely pleased by his recruiting successes, and Moffitt felt he personally had "gained the confidence of my

---

[15] Blair, "Diary," 3.
[16] Moffitt, "Diary," 1.
[17] Stamper, "Travels of the 43rd Tennessee," 33.
[18] Blair, "Diary," 3.

company more fully." He also voiced his pleasure at his showing among the boys. To their myriad of questions concerning conditions back at home, Moffitt decided "not to say anything to persons concerning certain reports."[19]

Later that day, after being assigned to quarters in the hillside bomb-proofed cave of his captain, Moffitt had the time to sit and write two letters home, in which he shared news and observations of his strange, new environment with his father and his wife, Sallie. Much of the information in the letters was repetitious regarding his trip to and observations of Vicksburg. He indicated that he was seated in Captain James Peyton Lynch's tent writing on a "dry goods box used as a table, and is now covered with plates, a coffee pot and other table furnishings." In his letter to his father, Moffitt noted that they had left Knoxville on Saturday morning 31 January, thirty-one members strong, and arrived at Vicksburg the night before 4 February at about 11 o'clock. To Sallie, he reported that they had no trouble along the way, except for the cargo and personal effects they carried, which were "troublesome and required close watching." He informed her that once they got to Athens, McMinn County, Captain Carmack of the Conscript Camp got aboard and rode with them as far down as Benton, Polk County. "He had a new suit," Moffitt mused, "and looked like a Brig. Genl."[20]

Due to some improvements with the railroads, Moffitt's replacements for Lynch's Battery found their route to Vicksburg was different from the one taken earlier by Vaughn's and Reynolds's Brigades. Once at Montgomery, Moffitt stated that they got on a boat on the Alabama River and steamed over to Selma. As they were trying to leave Montgomery, Private Isaac Baker had the misfortune of losing his trunk because of the negligence of the station's baggage master; it "contained his clothing [and] clothing for the Pryor boys and others." Moffitt added in his letter to his father that they had had no problems with the conscripts they were escorting to Vicksburg; since all seemed resigned to the fact "they were in for it." He felt that they would reconcile themselves to the service in time.[21]

From Selma, the would-be gunners boarded a train that carried them to Demopolis, where they boarded another boat on the Tombigbee and sailed four miles down river to where the rail-line resumed westward. Here, they picked up a train that transported them to Meridian. "The route from Demopolis is on a

---

[19] Moffitt, "Diary," 1.
[20] Thoms J. Moffitt to his father W. H. Moffitt, 4 February 1863, Thomas J. Moffitt Papers.
[21] Ibid.

newly made track," he informed his father, "and over a sandy soil. The recent rains softened the earth [making] the track very rough." Eight miles out of Meridian, he recorded, "the track gave way throwing two cars off …creating some confusion …[although] the car we were on remained on the track." Fortunately no one was injured, and the passengers on the two wrecked cars were placed in the baggage car, "and away we went," arriving in Meridian after dark. It was raining there when they detrained, he reported, and "we had to hunt around for two hours after dark trying to find comfortable quarters." Their luck was not good, so they were directed to a "new, unfinished building" and were offered accommodations on the floor. "We built fires, spread blankets, ate supper," he told his wife, "and laid down to dream about those we left behind."[22]

The next morning, Moffitt told Sallie, the train carried them on to Jackson, which they reached by six p.m.. While there, the would-be artillery-men took notice of the army of General Sterling Price, camped about the rail-road, and Moffitt believed that Price's men would soon be going to Vicksburg as well, since "it is thought the enemy will make his big effort at that point." They were back on a train that pulled into the Vicksburg depot by 11 p.m., Moffitt wrote, and the boys were told to just bed down in the cars. Early the next morning, he stated, "we set out for camps 1 1/2 miles up the river." Upon their arrival there, Moffitt indicated that all was glorious, for the boys were "proud" to see him and wished him joy and happiness in his recent marriage to Sallie. He noted that they were all surprised that he was back so soon with such a large haul of replacements. Moffitt felt affirmation in his recruiting results, he told Sallie. He obviously felt resplendent in his new uniform as well, and stated that it fit him "finely, jacket, boots, and the rest." Using his favorite adverb, Moffitt declared after only one day to be enjoying camp life "finely."[23]

Moffitt told his wife and his father that "Vicksburg is a strongly fortified place," which "nature with the assistance of *art* has rendered almost impregnable." Not only did the environment of Fortress Vicksburg cause him great pride, but he also asserted Captain Lynch and his company had "ever a name" because of its reputation for the accuracy of its guns and its gunners were extremely well drilled and efficient. "We, as the upper battery [nearest where the enemy fleet would first appear from up river], occupy the post of honor," Moffitt boasted. He indicated that their assigned siege pieces to be a

[22] Ibid. The Confederate government apparently used this building as a rest stop for troops leaving and entering Mississippi.
[23] Ibid.

32–pounder rifle, a 32–pounder smoothbore and a 24–pounder howitzer. "They will bore a hole when they strike broadside," he told his father. "No fears are entertained by our Genls.," he bragged. Porter's fleet was anchored up at the confluence of the Yazoo and Mississippi Rivers, some five miles distant, he reported, and with no leaves on the trees, the ships were easily seen from the high ground where the battery's camps were. He stated that the enemy base looked like a "floating city," packed in tightly and with men busy at work among material, masts, spars, superstructures, and stacks boiling smoke.[24]

"The boys were by their guns every night, ready to go into action. Tonight being very dark and rainy," Moffitt noted, made matters worthy of "a close watch." He remarked that the river was extremely high and all the ground about was "juicy and sloppy." The air temperature was cool and damp. "Dr. Gillespie's regiment [the 43rd Tennessee] is six miles below us," he told his father, "and Bradford's [the 31st Tennessee] is 10 or 15. Pitts' [the 81st (61st) Tennessee] is just in sight." All the Confederate pickets were keeping a close eye on the river. Moffitt, however, was not one of the constantly vigilant. As his pen began to slow down, he indicated that he expected shortly to be sound asleep in his comfortable quarters while Captain Lynch sat nearby quietly reading his Bible. Ever cognizant of his duty to update neighbors back home, Moffitt asked his father to inform Thomas Childress that he got his box back safely, and to tell Mr. Elmore that his son Alex is doing well and "is reckoned by Captain Lynch to be the *best* soldier in the entire company."[25]

"I find our boys mostly well," Moffitt continued. "Will McFarland and Will Nance are looking finely. The Smiths, Claiborn Cates, Thomas Clark, W.

---

[24] Ibid. The tip of the peninsula at the bend of the river was cleared so that Battery Tennessee (as the 1st Tennessee Heavy Artillery Regiment and its attached batteries were called) would have a clear shot at any of Porter's fleet making a move toward the city from Young's Point. Lynch's Battery was the first gun emplacement aimed at the Tuscumbia Bend in the river; therefore, it had the responsibility of getting off the first rounds at approaching enemy vessels. J. T. Whitehead and H. T. Norman indicated that the northernmost battery along the river was Capt. Lynch's, known also as the Water Battery. It was mounted on a 30–foot knoll above the edge of the Mississippi near where the Mint Springs Bayou entered the Father of Waters. Lynch's Battery was comprised of three 32–pounder rifles, a 32–pounder smoothbore, and later a 10–inch Columbiad. J. T. Whitehead to W. T. Rigby, 7 July 1903, and H. T. Norman to W. T. Rigby, 5 May 1904, William T. Rigby Correspondence, Vicksburg National Parks Archives, Vicksburg MS.

[25] Thoms J. Moffitt to his father W. H. Moffitt. James Gillespie was a physician before and after the war. McFarland was a prominent attorney in Dandridge, Jefferson County, prior to hostilities. Antebellum, he became a distinguished judge in Chattanooga.

C. Margraves, William B. C. Bettis, Isaac Day, Milliken Trogden, David L. Russell were all well." Moffitt indicated he had seen Alex Davis of Greene County and the 81st (61st) Tennessee, young John W. Gass of Mossy Creek, Jefferson County and the 81st (61st) Tennessee and Colonel Hamilton that day, all were well. He believed all the boys "had taken to the country," with the exception of Will Nance, Will McFarland and Joe Kersey. Though increasingly reluctant volunteers, Moffitt supposed they would be held to their service obligation of 12 months and 90 days. "I am performing my duty to my country," Moffitt asserted, "a duty every loyal citizen owes his country and all should be willing to perform." Moffitt closed his two letters by sending greetings to all his acquaintances and family, some of whom were mentioned by name, and by requesting that his father "tell the Darkies howdy, and to remember the advice I gave them."[26]

Though the chilly rain had finally ceased, Stamper of the 43rd Tennessee wrote that it was still cloudy and cold as "whiz" on 5 February. Around noon, the boys in his regiment returned from picket as the weather cleared. News came to the camp that another young soldier from the 43rd Tennessee had died of small pox, and Stamper noted that this was the third death in that regiment from the disease. "The gunboat which passed a few days ago," he wrote, "came back and anchored opposite our camps about three miles distant." Though the *Queen of the West* may have done this to annoy the short-range guns at Fort Warrenton, Stamper recorded that their fire on her this time "crippled" the Union vessel.[27]

At long last, on 5 February, Lieutenant John J. Blair of the 80th (62nd) Tennessee bid adieu to his comrades around the works at Vicksburg. He left around midnight aboard a train toward home, rumbling across the state and rolled into Meridian around seven the next morning.[28]

Also on 5 February, Moffitt noted that he and his First Sergeant Thomas Elmore, also a Jefferson County man, went walking about Vicksburg on this date. They called on Jacob Sweet, having been given a letter of introduction to the gentleman from Dr. Peck back home. Afterwards, Moffitt checked in with Major George Gillespie at the Quartermasters, General Carter L. Stevenson's Division. Gillespie, brother of Colonel James W. Gillespie of the 43rd

[26] Ibid.
[27] Stamper, "Travels of the 43rd Tennessee," 33.
[28] Blair, "Diary," 3.

Tennessee, was assigned there. "Before I left," Moffitt wrote, "George gave me an eggnog."[29]

On 6 February, Benjamin Giddens of the 3rd Tennessee wrote a letter to his wife the next day back in McMinn County, indicating that his health to be good. He hoped that she and all the children were as well as common. "Though I have nothing of any importance to write to you," he admitted, "that I am well I know will be of great words of comfort to you." The yanks were still in their camps across the river, Giddens said, and he saw them every day. "Our position is so strong," he bragged, "that I don't think that they will attack us for if they do, they will get a whipping." Given all that, Giddens admitted that he was more than ready to return to East Tennessee by the spring, "for if we stay at this place I believe we will all have the chills." Illness continued to be on the minds of the men in Reynolds's Brigade, and Giddens wrote that his friend Charley Highbarger was suffering chills. And even worse, Giddens indicated that he felt the unmistakable onset of his own similar symptoms as well.[30]

Perhaps changing the subject so as not worry his wife, Giddens noted that this part of Mississippi was a very poor country "and is farmed for nothing but cotton." He indicated that the old 3rd Tennessee and the rest of Reynolds's Brigade were still in their usual camps four miles below Vicksburg, and that the lines around the fortifications stretched for some twenty miles. "Our regiment goes on picket in the morning," he wrote, "and we will not be relieved for two days" from their watch at Warrenton four miles from camps and eight miles from the outskirts of Vicksburg. Regarding their rations, Giddens stated that though they were getting "lots of old tough hard beef," he was very thankful for it. "We ate it up yesterday," he joked, "and now we are chewing away on buck and will finish him good by dark if nothing happens." Plenty of molasses and sugar supplemented their fare, he added, and they used sugar to make sassafras tea. "You may think that I exaggerate," he explained, "when I tell you that I have seen some sassafras trees here [that] would make forty rails to the tree." he stated that he had seen other unusual herbage such as huge magnolia trees, "lots of cotton[wood] trees," and "bamboo bushes as thick as my leg."[31]

Concerning the prices around Vicksburg, Giddens recorded that a good sized chicken cost $1.50 a pound, flour 50 cents a pound, a dozen sweet potatoes a dollar, a pair of $3 brogans $18, and a pair of boots $50. Giddens noted that he was watching daily for his brother James to arrive at the regiment,

---

[29] Moffitt, "Diary," 1.
[30] Giddens to Giddens, 6 February 1863.
[31] Ibid.

and that his wife should send with the $2 from George Williams Giddens he was owed. Giddens assured that her that when he got his money, he would send her some. He extended his respects to his kinfolks at home and admonished his children to "mind Ma." Giddens asked the baby, Riley, "does you suck yet you ought to be wean?" Giddens closed his letter by commenting on the pleasantness of the weather that day, which looked "like the spring of the year." He wished that he could see his wife and children one more time, realizing that "the fortunes of war and danger to which one is exposed …[prevents one from telling] whether we will ever see each other [again] in this life or not." Interestingly, Giddens, ever theologically skeptical in his letters, confessed that he was not afraid to go into battle even "if there is no hereafter." His only regret for being killed in action would be that his wife and children would not be taken care of. "But, if I can only get through safe I know I will do better," he promised. Tellingly, he showed his heart of hearts to his wife in the closing sentences of the letter as one who really sought after Christ but was clumsy in the attempts. "With all my fears, I have some consolation in knowing that you pray for me often and sometimes in the dead midnight hours I try to pray, but it is very seldom said and appears to me that it does no good."[32]

Stamper of the 43rd Tennessee in his journal on 6 February indicated the bright sun in the clear sky brought some warmth to the chilly countryside, putting "new life into the boys." Glorious also was the news that the regiment was finally drawing a liberal allotment of soap. Stamper suggested to two of his comrades that they pitch in and wash clothes for his entire mess, which consisted of five to ten men who are assigned to cooking and eating together. His only volunteer, however, was a soldier Stamper identified only as "Peter S." They "bundled up" and headed down to the branch, where they built a fire and were "soon into the washing up to our elbows." Stamper reported, "we rubbed and paddled faithfully for some time, but I cannot say I like the business."[33]

Moffitt of Lynch's Battery wrote in his journal that on this date he had visitors at his modest hillside quarters he shared with Captain Lynch and Lieutenant Butler. "Colonel [James W.] Gillespie, Major [Robert] McFarland and George Gillespie called to see me," he recorded, "and they all looked well and healthy."[34]

At nine o'clock that evening, John J. Blair of the 80th (62nd) Tennessee, homeward bound, noted that his train left the Meridian depot and arrived at

---

[32] Ibid.
[33] Stamper, "Travels of the 43rd Tennessee," 33.
[34] Moffitt, "Diary," 1.

Mobile, Alabama, the next morning around eight. "We were put up at the Chester House for the night," he noted. "Lying before a large fire within 200 yards of me, I slept so sound I did not even know it."[35]

Dealing with Deserters, Part I. At three thirty on the afternoon of 7 February, Stamper of the 43rd Tennessee reported on the public punishment against two deserters from his regiment. John Keilen of Company B and William Elkins of Company I were marched out to the front of the regimental formation, their sentences read, and then punishment imposed. Keilen was sentenced to wear a ball and chain for two months and to forfeit two months' wages. He was also assigned to clean-up duty around the entire regimental camp area. Elkins's sentence was more severe, suggesting this was not his first offense. He was tied to a post and had thirty-nine lashes applied to his naked back. The letter "D" was then branded on his left hip as a further manifestation of his shame. With the regimental band playing "Yankee Doodle," Elkins was then drummed out of the service and exiled from camp to make his own way home as best he could. The regimental drum major and Stamper's own brother James administered the lashes. Admitting that this punishment "looked pretty hard," Stamper had no doubt that the prisoners "deserved all of it." Even with that, the men of the regiment returned to camp expressing their disgust with having to witness such humiliating treatment of their comrades, wayward though they may be.[36]

Referring to this demonstration of military justice, Lieutenant Calvin M. Smith of the 31st Tennessee noted that the penalty administered to the two deserters convinced him that, as his friend L. C. White stated, to make a good soldier a man must first be made a perfect gentleman. "The man [Elkins] of the 43rd Tennessee Regt. was charged with stealing a few percussion caps and some money, and forging a furlough," Smith wrote in his journal. These infractions had occurred while Elkins's regiment was still in the Knoxville vicinity. The man's sentence was 37 stripes and to have the letter "D" branded on his left hip. As if these degradations weren't enough, the soldier was then marched in front of his regiment under guard while the fifers and drummers [including the Stamper boys] played "Yankee Doodle" in Elkins' "honor." As a final punishment, the soldier was expelled from camp, "to shift for himself 1000 miles from home." Smith reported that Elkins "hollowed and begged" while he received his lashes with a leather strap, "but all to no purpose."[37]

---

[35] Blair, "Diary," 3.
[36] Stamper, "Travels of the 43rd Tennessee," 33.
[37] Smith, *A Smith in Service*, 35.

"All the colonels and General Reynolds was present" at Elkins's flogging, Smith noted, "along with the three regiments [of the brigade]." Unlike most of the soldiers, who, according Stamper, were disgusted by the punishment, Smith wrote that he was glad that the occurrence happened because it served as "a lesson for us all." Smith indicated that he was writing in a little book he had purchased the day before from a sutler in order to record his observations during his travels since leaving home. Smith believed that the South was fighting to protect its way of life, homes, and hearths. "I consider I was right in enlisting when I did," he noted, "soon to be in the service of my country twelve months as first lieutenant." He indicated that he was often required to serve as the company's commanding officer in the absence of his brother-in-law, the captain. The love and esteem of his company had been earned, he believed, and "every man in the Regt. knows me." Smith indicated that the regimental field officer cadre, consisting of Colonel W. M. Bradford, Colonel Humes, Major Bob McFarland, Adjutant W. Hawkins, and the Sergeant Major J. White, along with Surgeons Corcoran and Toal, all had "the utmost friendly and implicit confidence" in him as an officer and friend. "I find it easier to be dutiful than to attempt to do some disgraceful act that would be a disgrace to" his wife and children, Smith affirmed, with the Elkins's example perhaps fresh in his mind.[38]

"Liet-Colonel [James W.] Humes [of the 31st Tennessee] called to see us today," Moffitt of Lynch's Battery penned in his daily journal entry. He reported that there was, according to Humes, "graet dissatisfaction in the Fed. Army."[39]

John Blair of the 80th (62nd) Tennessee, on his way home, wrote on 7 February that he was aboard the ferry *Mary Jane* at 7 a.m. for a two-hour journey across Mobile Bay. Reaching the shore where the eastern terminus of the railroad began, he boarded the train for Montgomery, arriving there 10 p.m. He and his traveling companions were put up in Montgomery Hall until the next morning.[40] Blair of the 80th (62nd) Tennessee's homeward odyssey continued at 7 a.m. from Montgomery. "Had Willie King for company," Blair noted. "He is a good fellow."[41] Seemingly all was now bright and cheerful in Lieutenant Blair's world as the train carried him away from Mississippi.

Matters on the river back at Vicksburg were quiet, according to Stamper of the 43rd Tennessee, and at 8 a.m. on 8 February, the regiment stood

---

[38] Ibid.
[39] Moffitt, "Diary," 1.
[40] Blair, "Diary," 3.
[41] Blair, "Diary," 3.

inspection.[42] Morale needed an injection of military discipline after the unpleasantness with the deserters the previous day.

An inspection was ordered in Reynolds's camps for 9 a.m. on 9 February, Stamper of the 43rd Tennessee wrote, and there was no activity to report from out on the river. The day held up warm, but was a bit cloudy.[43] Today, as the battery did some gunnery practice, Moffitt noted that Lynch's boys fired their pieces at a floating target in the river. Some of the shots were good, he observed, and the cannon commanded by his fellow artilleryman from New Market, Corporal Rufus Caldwell, "done the best firing." Moffitt later found some time to write another letter to his young wife, Sallie, back in New Market (Greeneville, her home), with the news that Colonel Loyd Bullen of the 29th Tennessee was in Vicksburg to see some of the boys. The colonel was only to be in town for the day, taking the long southern route back to East Tennessee from his duty with the Army of Tennessee. Moffitt was understandably in a rush to complete his letter so that it could be carried home to his wife by Bullen. Moffitt, at the conclusion of his first week at Vicksburg, told Sallie that the weather had been cold and rainy. Suffering recently with a cough and a cold, he was feeling "about right" at this time. He stated that he was enjoying himself then just "finely," and his quarters, which he shared with his superior officers Captain Lynch and Lieutenant Butler and which had been carved out of the hillside and "covered and weather-boarded with plank," proved cozy. The fare continued to be rough, consisting of "poor beef, molasses, cornbread and coffee." Moffitt was glad to report that he still had some ham, sausage, and biscuits his mother prepared for him that would supplement his menu for a short time longer.[44]

Moffitt reported to Sallie that the boys all seemed to be well, though all needed the attention of heavy applications of soap and water. He, however, suffered no shortage of soap because he had brought plenty from his father's store, and the water was provided by the Mississippi River "rolling by my feet." Moffitt indicated that his clothing was satisfactory, including a supply of towels he had brought along; indeed, all the boys seemed well protected against the cold weather. He repeated the news that he had had visits from Colonel Jim and Major George Gillespie, Major Bob McFarland, and Colonel Jim Humes. The Gillespies were Moffitt's cousins and tried to convince him to transfer from the battery and join the 43rd Tennessee. Though Colonel Gillespie promised him a

---

[42] Stamper, "Travels of the 43rd Tennessee," 33.

[43] Stamper, "Travels of the 43rd Tennessee," 33.

[44] Moffitt, "Diary," 1.

promotion to lieutenant, Moffitt indicated that he could not in good faith leave his present company.[45]

"The Feds will probably attack Vicksburg soon," Moffitt recorded in his journal, "though there was no certainty of it." Should they come, he suggested, Lynch's Battery would deliver the first volley at them as they headed around the bend toward the city. He informed his wife that their artillery had guns that weighed 8,000 to 10,000 pounds and that could hurl with considerable velocity cannon balls weighing sixty-four pounds. All the river batteries fell under the command of General Stephen D. Lee, whom Moffitt described as a "brave South Carolinian, not more than 38 years old." The divisional commander was Major General Martin Luther Smith, "a soldierly looking man of about 50 years." Moffitt declared, "today cleared off warm, reminding me of June. The birds are singing merrily, and often I find my thoughts wandering away to my mountain home." Such nostalgia brought Moffitt to encouraged his young wife to believe that he loved her more deeply than ever. He asked her to pray for his safety and requested that, when she sent him packages, not to do so by express train. "Private conveyance is the safe way," he reminded her, though even that was uncertain.[46]

Lieutenant John J. Blair, 80th (62nd) Tennessee (retired), finally arrived home at Philadelphia, McMinn County, on 9 February, where he found "the ground covered with snow." He went immediately "to see Mary."[47]

Colonel Alexander W. Reynolds, commanding the four regiments of East Tennesseans in camp along the Warrenton Road, wrote a letter on 10 February to his sister indicating the month was proving to be a rather dormant period for most military activity around Vicksburg. He repeated the news from other sources regarding Union deserters coming into the Confederate lines, and he predicted that if the enemy attacked, "we will slaughter nearly all of them in the balance." The Federal army across the river confronting them numbered 40,000 men, but even if they had 100,000, Reynolds asserted, "they could not take this place for we are strongly fortified." His East Tennesseans, he declared, were in the best spirits and satisfied they could defeat the enemy, "who [were] very demoralized and won't fight."[48]

---

[45] John T. ("Tom") Moffitt to Sallie McDowell, 9 February 1863, Thomas J. Moffitt Papers.

[46] Moffitt, "Diary," 1.

[47] Blair, "Diary," 3.

[48] Alexander W. Reynolds to his sister, 10 February 1863, Brian Green Collection, Personal Collection, Kernersville NC.

"If we defeat them here," Reynolds insisted, "it will end the war—at least the war in the southwest." Still, General Pemberton was bracing for any contingency once active campaigning resumed with spring weather, and Reynolds noted that the women and children of Vicksburg, though invited to leave the city, "foolishly chose to stay." The leadership cadre all believed that before matters at Vicksburg were concluded, Vicksburg would be "terribly shelled for the Yankees don't mind and will put forth every effort to take this place." Reynolds swore, however, "we are just as determined to hold out." He was also concerned about family matters, indicating that his son Frank, for whom he was praying, had taken command of his regiment serving in Bragg's army at Tullahoma. On an even more personal note, Reynolds addressed problems he was having with his wife, Mary, who was living behind enemy lines. He was fearful that she "had taken advantage of the Federal congress's decree to divorce [him]."[49]

Among Reynolds's men in the camps along the Big Bayou, Stamper of the 43rd Tennessee entered the following in this daily report: "[The tenth of February was] warm and very much like spring." The regiment returned to picket duty the next morning, and the weather continued to be warm and cloudy. "My company and one other were posted near the river," Stamper stated, and while he did not mind the duty, he complained that "the Yankees kept up such a racket with their drums that it was quite annoying." That evening, the clouds lifted, and while Stamper believed it would not rain, he and his fellow pickets constructed as a precaution a "kind of tent with a few rails and our blankets."[50]

In the vicinity of the old Spanish fort just north of the Vicksburg, Moffitt of Lynch's Battery wrote about another visitor from Gillespie's 43rd Tennessee, Private Will McKeldrin, who, like Moffitt, was also from New Market in Jefferson County. McKeldrin told Moffitt that the booms, thuds, and rumbles they were hearing to the north were Confederate batteries at Snyder's Bluff shelling the boys in blue. Afterwards, Moffitt could not help but observe: "Will look[ed] homesick."[51]

Around daylight on 12 February, thunder began to roll in and in a short time, Stamper recorded, the rain started "pattering down." So much for Stamper's accuracy in predicting the weather. The 43rd Tennessee was still on picket. The rain was not as heavy or prolonged as Stamper first feared it would

---

[49] Ibid.
[50] Stamper, "Travels of the 43rd Tennessee," 34.
[51] Moffitt, "Diary," 1.

be, and about noon, he was pleased to report that the weather had begun to clear, leaving "everything refreshed by the good shower." The 59th Tennessee came out the following morning and relieved the 43rd Tennessee from picket duty, he wrote. Back in camp, the regiment spent the day lying around after two days of picket feeling "somewhat fatigued."[52]

A Second Gunboat Passes the Batteries. In clammy darkness masked by a dense fog somewhere out in the river, Lynch's gunners were drawn to their stations about midnight on 12 February to man the cannons of the upper water battery in response to the signal flares fired by Vaughn's pickets. Porter was attempting to run another warship past. Afterward, according to Sergeant Moffitt, the boys discovered that it was the powerful ironclad *Indianola*. The Yankee gunboat was dispatched down the river with a two-fold purpose: to support the *Queen of the West* in savaging Confederate shipping and to disperse and destroy a small Confederate flotilla reported to be gathering on the Red River in the vicinity of New Carthage, Louisiana. "The Battery fired several rounds at it," Moffitt indicated, "but the night was dark and foggy." Lynch's gunners thought that they had hit the phantom and kept up a steady fire at it for three miles. "The excitement was great for a while," he declared, adding: "divers shots were fired, and it is believed a 42-pounder struck her."[53] "I thought I would never get my shoes on," Moffitt confessed, all thumbs in his anxiousness to get dressed and to his gun. He noted that by the time he finally got there, it was only for a brief time because the gunboat had moved quickly downriver.[54]

Life in a Vicksburg Battery. Back in East Tennessee, Sallie McDowell Moffitt's brother Will was seeking a transfer to John Peyton Lynch's Battery and a day after the gunboat action, his brother-in-law John T. ("Tom") Moffitt wrote a letter to him with his advice regarding his intentions. This rather weak council was based on only one week's worth of duty in Warren County, Mississippi. "If you have a good constitution and can eat anything and everything," Moffitt suggested with some hyperbole, "if you can smile in adversity, and drive dull care away, you may be able to live here." A week at Vicksburg, he wrote, had convinced him that though he had believed Corinth, Mississippi, to be the "worst, dirtiest place on earth," he found that Vicksburg more than rivaled it. Moffitt's comparisons were the classic good news–bad news descriptions, and he commenced with the unpleasant aspects first. Though

---

[52] Stamper, "Travels of the 43rd Tennessee," 34.
[53] Moffitt, "Diary," 1.
[54] Ibid.

in other letters Moffitt had convinced the folks at home that his quarters were idyllic, he described his quarters in this letter as "unpleasant, especially in rainy weather." He indicated that his camp was 200 yards above the battery's guns, and the tents used by the men were worn and leaked, though most had plank floors under them and were equipped with chimneys.[55]

"We use the Miss. River water for drinking and cooking," Moffitt continued, though soap needed for cleaning and washing was hard to come by. Women in town washed clothing for the outrageous sum of twenty-five cents per article, and then there was the added risk of it getting "lost" before it could be picked up. He again described the poor menu to which they were subject, consisting of poor beef, cornbread, rice, sugar, molasses, salt, and field peas. "Our guard duty is heavy," Moffitt indicated, "requiring a man to stay at the guns about two-thirds of the time." In their rather exposed position, the boys also were required to carry Enfield muskets while on duty to guard against sudden attacks. As for diseases, he stressed that diarrhea and chronic colds plagued the men of the battery. The river water they used was said to safe, but Moffitt predicted that its quality would degenerate once the weather began to warm. "Some of the boys complain of *silver backs*, alias, body lice," he wrote. He correctly predicted that the infestation would get worse with the arrival of spring and summer heat, which he predicted would be a exasperated by the filth and uncleanliness rampant in the camps.[56]

Moffitt lamented that a number of the boys also suffered from another condition, which he called "hog stealing." He considered this malady to be a predictable reaction to the poor quality of meat they were forced to eat, and to the fact that prices were so high; the boys had no money to buy better. "Twelve dollars a month will not furnish a sufficient amt. of pocket change," he opined.

---

[55] John T. ("Tom") Moffitt to Will P. McDowell, 13 February 1863, John Thomas Moffitt Papers.

[56] Ibid. The need for the men to be armed with Enfields was apparent because, if their battery was attacked, they immediately would have to convert to infantry. A defender serving with the 1st Tennessee Heavy Artillery during the campaign wondered how different the results at Vicksburg would have been had Grant "sent down three or four gunboats to draw our fire, and eight or ten transports with 1000 or 1200 troops to make a dash for the bluff and the City front. [The Yankees] could have been practically out of our range, [and] they could have taken the batteries and City in 30 minutes after landing." Grant could have then "thrown his army into the City" before Pemberton could have gotten a single brigade there to defend it. So great was his respect for the river batteries, however, Grant never attempted any landing of troops from the riverfront at Vicksburg. D. M. Upton to W. T. Rigby, 30 July 1903, William T. Rigby Correspondence.

This dark picture of the artilleryman's life at Vicksburg, Moffitt asserted, was provided so that his brother-in-law would not come to the unit suffering from any illusions. He also wanted McDowell to be aware that Lynch's Battery was probably going to become what the boys termed "a local institution," suggesting that the East Tennesseans were going to remain at Vicksburg for the foreseeable future.[57]

Then, as though to offset his rather bleak portrayal of conditions, Moffitt spent the remainder of his letter describing what he considered the high points of duty among the big guns. The first advantage was the fact there were a number of young gentlemen in the battery who were pleasures to be around. "There are here a good many clever, accommodating kind-hearted fellows," he suggested, "who will be good friends," although he would not categorize them all as "gentlemen." He attributed their failings to the fact that they were simple country boys who "were deficient in the social qualities," but their good, warm hearts were a welcome balance against their "rough manners." Moffitt warned McDowell that the company also had its share of "bad boys."[58]

"One great advantage we have here," Moffitt continued, "is we avoid the long marches, [having to] dig our intrenchments, or having to carry heavy knapsacks any great distance." The food he maligned earlier in the letter, was, he supposed, as good as anywhere in the army. Though Lynch's unit was officially designated "Light Artillery," Moffitt was glad, he told his brother-in-law, the men in the battery did not have to serve in that capacity. "Light artillery [means] moving from point to point in the rain, through mud, frequently without tents," he recollected from his earlier experiences at Corinth and Columbus. Moffitt indicated that the light artilleryman also had to deal with horses and was required ultimately to fight in open fields. "We have heavy works to our front," Moffitt noted, which provided effective security to the gunners during action.[59]

Finally, Moffitt suggested that if McDowell joined them, he should bring the following items with him, as they were in short supply at Vicksburg: plenty of soap, Cook's pills, blue mass, castor oil, and Radway's ready relief. He also believed that McDowell would be wise to bring good black ink with him since it was unobtainable at Vicksburg. A box full of general provisions was also highly recommended.[60] In closing, Moffitt knew that McDowell intended to seek a

---

[57] Moffitt to Will McDowell.
[58] Ibid.
[59] Ibid.
[60] Ibid.

transfer from his undisclosed unit. Rather than fully encourage his plans to join the battery, Moffitt suggested that his brother-in-law instead seek to clerk at the headquarters where he was. But if McDowell were to come to Vicksburg, Moffitt promised to do all in his power to help make his life comfortable.[61]

After completing this letter, Moffitt crafted one to his wife, Sallie. "I date my letter the 14th though this is the evening of the 13th," he wrote, because "I propose writing a Valentine to my sweetheart." He confessed to her that his letter to her brother may have been "colored" a bit since he believed that the true nature of the duty "will be dark enough at best." If, on the contrary, conditions should be better than McDowell expected, so much the better. "I can say nothing to encourage any on entering the army," Moffitt said, ironically as it turned out since on his last trip home, he had spent days on the journey back convincing numbers of conscripts that the artilleryman's life was the one for them. Though this might be considered hypocritical, he said that he would never use such propaganda on his friends or his brother-in-law]. Regarding his own patriotism, Moffitt explained to Sallie that he knew coming into the service as a volunteer would require him to "sacrifice my comfort and ease for the sake of my country." He hoped only to retain his health and life once his military career was over. "I am determined to be brave and strong," he promised, "uncomplaining and contented if I can."[62]

The remainder of Moffitt's letter consisted of praise and instruction to his wife, declaring how much she meant to him, and how she should always look toward taking care of her health during these winter months. Moffitt challenged her to "cultivate" her mind by reading good books, but "not novels." And her letters to him must be positive and hopeful in order to help him keep *his* spirits up. He remained a member of Captain Lynch's mess, a distinct honor for a non-commissioned officer, and his bed was most comfortable. If he only had some good food to eat, Moffitt joked, he would have no complaints at all.[63]

St. Valentine's Day, 1863, saw the weather turn warm again, though the clouds remained indicating the possibility of more showers, Stamper of the 43rd Tennessee wrote. By midnight, the thunder and lightning had built up, and soon the heavy precipitation the boys had grown so accustomed reappeared. The accumulation of water on the tent canvas finally soaked its way through, he recorded, and made Stamper's feverish brother W. D. even more miserable. All

[61] Ibid.
[62] John T. ("Tom") Moffitt to Sallie McDowell, 14 February 1863, John Thomas Moffitt Papers.
[63] Ibid.

their bedding was in short order soaked from the leaks.[64] Moffitt of Lynch's Battery also commented on the storm in his journal calling it "terrific," with the vivid lightning and heavy thunder. He recorded that Major Bob McFarland of the 31st Tennessee had again visited him during the day.[65] Perhaps referring to the attention given to and gotten from the young ladies of the area, Lieutenant James Earnest of the 79th (60th) Tennessee on this Valentine's Day noted that though he had not sent out any valentines himself, he had collected a goodly number for various boys in his regiment during his meanderings through the community.[66]

The "Queen" Tries Fort Warrenton. The following day, 15 February, the *Queen of the West* again attracted the attention of other East Tennessee Confederates down river when she steamed back in the direction of Warrenton after some twelve days of raiding Confederate supply vessels in and around the Red River. The boys believed that she had come back to Warrenton to land troops and they had all been on the alert for some days against this contingency. Instead, subject to the vicissitudes of the conflict, she was soon to become a not only a "prisoner of war," but a productive addition to the Confederate navy operating in the vicinity.

Pertaining to the *Queen of the West's* cautious nighttime approach toward Fort Warrenton, Lieutenant C. M. Smith of the 31st Tennessee affirmed that the Confederate defenders easily observed the sparks and flame from her stacks, and listened to the noisy workings of her boilers, wheels, and machinery as she labored closer and closer. Beneath the low and sagging clouds between the dusk and dawn of 14 and 15 February, it was so dark that the Confederates not see the boat's actual form until the pickets along the levee set the alarm fires. "She came in sight of us and ankered at a Yankie camp on the opposite side above us," Smith reported. He noted that she came down on them at Warrenton like some "dark monster" and acted as if she intended on landing troops. All hands in Fort Warrenton were either manning the "bull pups" or on the alert as sharp-shooters.[67]

Lieutenant John Carson of Talbott Station, Jefferson County, serving with the 31st Tennessee on duty at Fort Warrenton, noted: "we saw the *Queen of the West* within range of our guns at the fort. The river at this point made a curve forming a horseshoe. Captain John Kelso opened fire, which was returned by

[64] Stamper, "Travels of the 43rd Tennessee," 33–34.
[65] Moffitt, "Diary," 1.
[66] Northen, *All Right, Let Them Come,* 59.
[67] Smith, *A Smith in Service,* 34.

the *Queen*. All of these shots were without results.[68] "Soon she fired from the prow," Smith of the 31st Tennessee wrote, "then our cannon let loose with round shot and connicle shells making her sides rattle[;] 8 or 10 cannon firing and the explosions of shells made the *welkin* ring."[69] Seeking the darkness beyond the glow of the picket fires, the *Queen of the West* could not definitely be seen. One of the East Tennessee soldiers ran down the levee just at the bend, Carson reported, where he set afire a large frame building that had been used previously as a hospital for Reynolds's sick men. As the flames caught their breath inside the old structure, the fire lighted up for Carson a brilliant and exciting scene. Quite suddenly and to its crew's dismay, the *Queen* was in full view and quite within range of the guns of the fort. "One well-directed shot from Captain Kelso's battery took effect, cutting through the steam pipe of the *Queen*, and scalding to death [their] engineer," Carson wrote, which "result[ed] in the prompt surrender of the *Queen of the West* and her crew."[70]

Lieutenant Calvin Smith of the 31st Tennessee explained how the union vessel wound up in this predicament. One of the pilots the raiders had captured off a Confederate transport was compelled to guide them in the dark toward Fort Warrenton, according to Smith. Using subterfuge and the attendant darkness, the pilot told his handlers that they were quite some distance from the fort, when, in actuality, they were just across from it. He steered the gunboat ram closer to the Confederate guns, jumped overboard, and swam to safety just as the burning building illuminated the *Queen of the West*'s unfortunate (for it) proximity.[71] Carson reported that "the strong, unwieldy, slow *Queen of the West* was ours in crippled condition. Soon, however, all damages were repaired, and we thus added to our improvised Confederate navy another steamer which had evaded our guns at Vicksburg and pursued us in full hope of making our little detachment prisoners and destroying our new navy."[72]

Stamper of the 43rd Tennessee addressed none of this in his journal, merely stating that a few miles east of this little battle at Camp Reynolds it was just another rainy and dreary day. He borrowed his regimental surgeon's horse and rode out with ambitions of finding quarters where his sick brother William could lodge until his health improved. Stamper's ride took him ten miles in various directions with no success. When he returned to camp that evening, his

---

[68] Carson, "Capture of the *Indianola*," vol. 32, no. 8, p. 381.
[69] Smith, *A Smith in Service*, 35.
[70] Carson, "Capture of the *Indianola*," vol. 32, no. 8, p. 381.
[71] Smith, *A Smith in Service*, 35.
[72] Carson, "Capture of the *Indianola*," vol. 32, no. 8, p. 381.

legs and feet wet and cold, Stamper found that his mess had built a nice fire and that the men had dried themselves and their bedding in hopes of getting a drier night's sleep. The rain, he wrote, was not as heavy that evening.

By daylight on 16 February, however, the rain had intensified, leading Stamper to observe that the steady shower lasted the whole day and night, causing the water to stand at considerable depths in the low ground where their camp was situated. The boys were forced to wade around much of the day in the standing water in their commons area. Stamper expressed sympathy with the men of the 3rd Tennessee and the other unfortunate regiments of Stevenson's Division standing picket at the Fort and along the levee in the deluge.

The rain continued on 17 February, according to Stamper's daily entry, with no appearance of let-up. Dark and heavy clouds hovered and lingered. The bayous, canebrakes and ponds all around them were swollen and overflowing, he wrote. The 3rd Tennessee came in from picket duty around Fort Warrenton and the surrounding riverbanks after carefully working their way through the flooded trails back to camp. They had been relieved by Bradford's 31st Tennessee, Stamper wrote, and "compelled to wade the water like so many horses." He indicated that it was nearly impossible to get around camp and the continuing rain had "everything covered with mud."[73]

Also on 17 February, John T. Moffitt of Lynch's Battery wrote his mother back in Jefferson County on his father's business letterhead imprinted with "W. H. Moffitt & Son, Dealers in Fancy & Dry Goods & Merchandise Generally, New Market, Tenn." He informed her that he had spent the rainy day reading Oliver Goldsmith and, like any good Confederate of Scottish descent, the poetry of Robert Burns. He noted that the miserable weather had kept him indoors for several days, for it had rained most every day he had been at Vicksburg. "I have been comfortable being in a cabin in the hillside," he wrote, "and keep warm and dry." He stated that the boys who stood guard "see a rough time," however. As for Vicksburg itself, he informed his mother that, even though "John Phoenix believed the Washington territory to be the priciest spot on the continent, my experience so far leads me to believe Vicksburg is the priciest place in the Confederacy." Its defense was costly, and its conquest he predicted would come dear. He noted that a steady queue of friends had been to see him: Jim and George Gillespie, Will McKeldrin of the 43rd Tennessee, and Bob McFarland of the 31st Tennessee. Moffitt indicated that they all looked

---

[73] Stamper, "Travels of the 43rd Tennessee," 35.

well, and that he intended to visit them in their camps when the rainy season broke, which, he had been told, occurred sometime in the spring.[74]

Gillespie's 43rd Tennessee and Bradford's 31st Tennessee [as part of Reynolds's Brigade] "are two or three miles below town," Moffitt informed his mother, while the regiments of Pitts, Crawford, and Rowan "lay above us in sight." "They all have sickness," he wrote, "mostly chills and diarrhea." These were minor complaints, perhaps, though more serious were the cases of small pox discovered in the 43rd Tennessee. Those infected were sent immediately to the hospital. The city of Vicksburg, he indicated, was a "rough place in every respect." Moffitt provided his mother with the menu of their fare he had outlined many times before. In quoting some prices for her, he stated the boys had to pay 75¢ a pound for pork, and 75¢ for potato or peach pies. Eggs cost $1 a dozen. Everything was high and scarce, he noted. "I get along very well, sleep soundly, eat heartily and enjoy myself as well as anyone," he stated, despite all the inconveniences. Moffitt informed his mother that two letters from his father had arrived, and one of them referenced the scheduled execution of a young soldier of their acquaintance identified only as Harris. "Sad fate for one so young!" Moffitt agreed. "I feel sorry for his parents. To die the death of a deserter, a spy, or a traitor must be terrible."[75]

Moffitt followed his letter to his mother with another letter to Sallie. He made note of his study of Goldsmith and Burns to her, which he had enjoyed while snacking on parched corn. He was becoming accustomed to camp life, he assured her, indicating that soldiers could enjoy themselves even under great disadvantage. "I enjoy myself finely, can laugh as heartily, joke as freely, eat as much, and smoke as long as any man in the company," he boasted.[76]

"I smoke here because I find company in my pipe," Moffitt said. He confided to Sallie that another reason for smoking was that it soothed his brain and helped him think and dream. He wondered what his wife was doing at home. He could imagine her popping corn, or coming down to supper, or at her piano playing "I'm going home to Dixie." Regarded her playing, he apologized for not being able to find the sheet music she had requested, either in Atlanta, Montgomery, or Selma. Inquiries in Vicksburg had also proved futile. "We had a good time a few nights since," he continued in the letter. "Another gunboat [the *Indianola*] passed us, and we gave her some iron balls to

---

[74] John T. ("Tom") Moffitt to his mother Mrs. W. H. Moffitt, 17 February 1863, John Thomas Moffitt Papers.
[75] Ibid.
[76] Ibid.

carry on her route." Many soldiers believed that a ball from the battery's
32–pounder rifled gun penetrated her stern. General Stephen Lee indicated that
the boat did not pass his position down river causing many to believe she had
been sunk. Even with the fog and darkness, Moffitt noted that a number of men
from the battery and at other placements further down had seen her pass.
"Well, again, if I only had plenty of biscuits and ham and chicken and eggs to
eat," he teased his wife, "I would be perfectly satisfied." He amended his
declaration of satisfaction to note that it would only be perfect if his darling
wife were also present. He apparently had not heard anything from her brother
Will McDowell regarding to his transfer. "If he has it and has not left," Moffitt
suggested, "tell him to remain home until he hears from me. If he can hold his
position in the hospital, I would advise him to do so."[77] His concern was that if
Will came to camps during the rainy season in Mississippi, he would most likely
take a cold and be laid up while his body tried to acclimate itself to the
environment.

Heavy fog had replaced the rain by Wednesday, 18 February, according to
the diary of Isaac Stamper of the 43rd Tennessee. The quartermaster came
down from Vicksburg and paid the men, "for some of the boys had begun to get
uneasy about their pocketbooks." Stamper described the feverish activity that
transpired around camp at such times when the boys floated around from tent
to tent rounding up debts. "This was rather annoying," he wrote, "for before
one could pocket his money, some good creditor would pluck him up and take
him to one side, where he would demand his 'shinplaster.'" But before the
collector made his getaway, Stamper continued, someone else gave *him* a call.
"The poor little bill would pass [through] so many hands," he mused, "that it
would almost become threadbare." In military matters, Stamper noted that the
enemy had shelled Vicksburg with "no effect." One of the boys, identified as
Garry Goins, returned from the city during the day with the sad news of his
mother's death back home in East Tennessee. There was little the young son
could do. The federals continued throwing some shells at them the next day,
but Stamper of the 43rd Tennessee recorded "without much damage." One
civilian in Vicksburg, however, was reported to have had his arm blown off by
an exploding shell, which "caused some little excitement among the citizens,"
he noted.[78]

---

[77] Ibid.
[78] Stamper, "Travels of the 43rd Tennessee," 35–36. "I received … a pair of very nice
janes [jean] pants … from home," Earnest of the 79th (60th) Tennessee recorded on this
date. Northen, *All Right, Let Them Come,* 59. In the latter days of the war, most of what

"Shelling from a mortar boat commenced yesterday [18 February] about 11 o'clock," Moffitt of Lynch's Battery wrote from his quarters at the foot of Fort Hill. The artillerymen called these terrifying annoyances from the river rafts "yank pots." These rafts were anchored on the far side of the peninsula, well out of range or sight, and lobbed their rounds for great distances into the Confederate works. Their fire was kept up at 15–minute intervals and began again at daylight on 19 February.[79] The army around Vicksburg was nonplussed with the increased shelling, Stamper indicated, because they believed that it caused little damage.[80] Despite Stamper's assertion from one far removed from where the projectiles fell, however, Moffitt reported that just before he met Major McFarland in town, a shell exploded near the Dandridge officer. Moffitt wrote that he had seen "several burst in the air," and the resulting consternation caused all the stores in town to close early. Sadly, both the residents and businesses in Vicksburg would, in the months ahead, become much more used to the Grant's unrelenting and endless shelling. Despite the shut down of most of the traditional commerce due to cannonading, the world's oldest profession continued to flourish this day when Moffitt was strolling about town, prompting him to remark, "we saw three or four 'hookers' on the streets."[81]

The 43rd Tennessee went back on picket on 18 February, Stamper wrote, "but as good luck would have it, all the water had dried up and the sun was shining warm and cheerful." Stamper again remained in camp with his sick brother W. D., though he spent a portion of the day in the country on another unsuccessful venture to find a house where his invalid brother might recuperate.[82]

---

these soldiers serving with John Vaughn would wear would be jean-cloth pants and shell jackets made at home by their women-folk. One federal participant noted after the surrender few of the Confederate garrison at Vicksburg wore what he would call uniforms. Their hodgepodge clothing and their rough trials during the siege made them appear to be "hard-looking critters." John C. Pemberton Papers, National Archives, Washington DC.

[79] Moffitt, "Diary," 1. One historian noted that the mortar boats "dropped an average of one 256-pound shell into the City every five minutes for the duration of the siege." The problem with these fearsome projectiles was "they were grossly inaccurate, so neither the Union gunners nor anyone else had any idea where the next shell might land." Warren E. Grabau, *Ninety-Eight Days: A Geographer's View of the Vicksburg Campaign* (Knoxville TN: University of Tennessee Press, 2000) 427.

[80] Stamper, "Travels of the 43rd Tennessee," 33–34.

[81] Moffitt, "Diary," 2.

[82] Stamper, "Travels of the 43rd Tennessee," 34.

The positive effect the invigorating weather had on the men's spirits carried over to the 79th (60th) Tennessee, according to Lieutenant Earnest, who remarked that Lieutenant Colonel Nathan Gregg had gone into Vicksburg and procured a fresh ham and a small bucket of lard "for only $20". "The beef we are issued," Earnest complained, "was literally unfit for use." Until that time, the men of his regiment had been trying to subsist on cornbread alone. "We have plenty of molasses," he noted, "but I didn't dare eat them on account of the diarrhea."[83]

Friday, 20 February, was quiet and the weather was lovely, Stamper of the 43rd Tennessee reported. He felt blessed to listen to Chaplain Brooks' sermon. Then, at dark, it clouded up again and began to rain, which caused Stamper to remark, "this we did not like." The only activity he noted for the day was that rounds from the Southern batteries were thrown toward a Union transport with unknown results.[84] Sergeant Moffitt of Lynch's Battery took advantage of the nice weather to investigate an old graveyard in which the battery was setting up new positions. "Saw several skulls and bones laying around," he reported matter-of-factly. He noted that Colonel Andrew Jackson, Jr., commander of the Tennessee artillery at Vicksburg, told him that "our forces had captured the *Queen of the West* a day or two since." Yankee gunboats and transports were moving about quite actively now on the river, Moffitt recorded, and below Vicksburg heavy firing was heard toward evening. At around 11:30 p.m., he attested, "we were aroused from our sleep" by heavy firing below Vicksburg out on the Mississippi. The alarm rockets were set off calling for all the river batteries to be manned to meet an anticipated federal threat. The boys rushed to their guns, where they remained at the ready for an hour or two before being allowed to go back to bed.[85]

Stamper's 43rd Tennessee returned from picket duty on the next morning of 21 February, according to his diary entry. It had rained some during their duty. W. D. Stamper, his brother, rode out to the Greene family home in hopes of getting convalescence lodging, but was turned away. The regiment's issue of beef from the army's stores was refused because the meat had begun to turn

[83] Northen, *All Right, Let Them Come*, 59–60.
[84] Stamper, "Travels of the 43rd Tennessee," 35.
[85] Moffitt, "Diary," 2. Lynch also had to guard against a dash past the river batteries during the night. Capt. Paul T. Dismukes, commanding Company A, 1st Tennessee Heavy Artillery, indicated that "Captain John P. Lynch was in command of what the boys called 'the Mosquito Fleet,' which was made up by a detail from all the companies and whose duty is was to guard [and] prepare lights for night, should the fleet attempt to pass." Paul Dismukes to W. T. Rigby, 28 July 1903, William T. Rigby Correspondence.

rancid and was too repugnant for even a hungry man to stomach.[86] The day for Lynch's Battery's was quite routine, Sergeant Moffitt wrote, and he awoke early to make the fire for his mess, after which he helped cook breakfast. Then he helped with the dishes, despite not well all day. He was plagued with the Confederate soldier's chronic companion: "diarrhea."[87]

By contrast, the day was a busy one for the boys in the 43rd Tennessee, reported Stamper in his diary. First a regimental inspection occurred at nine a.m., followed by preaching at ten, and around noon, there came a sudden heavy expenditure of shells hurled back and forth by the belligerents from some point miles down the river.[88] Lieutenant Smith of the 31st Tennessee reported that he heard on this Sunday morning a sermon preached by Stamper's regimental chaplain, Parson Archibald Brooks, titled "Why Will Ye Die?" Smith knew Brooks, who preached in Hawkins County before the war. During this particular message, the cannon fire down river seemed to grow louder and more frequent in their discharges, "until it was all that could be heard." Some of the men speculated that battle was being fought on the Mississippi between opposing gunboats, though others suggested that it must have been the Federals firing salutes in honor of George Washington's birthday. Lieutenant Smith scoffed that the enemy must have believed Washington to be "an abolitionist."[89] Though Stamper supposed the Washington celebration probable, the cannon fire was, in fact, a result of contact between the belligerent warships.

East Tennesseans on Gunboat Duty. The naval engagement down river on 22 February was between a patchwork Confederate naval force and the powerful ironclad *Indianola*. John Carson of the 31st Tennessee and his company had been ordered to serve with the "fleet," along with a sizable detachment from his regiment and some other East Tennessee volunteers mainly from Crawford's 79th (60th) Tennessee. They were all called to service this month in what their official records designated as "gunboat duty" aboard a small squadron up the Red River safely out of reach of Farragut's heavier-gunned fleet known to be steaming its way from New Orleans. The Southern gunboats consisted of their prize *Queen of the West*, which had been repaired after her capture near Warrenton and removed up the Red for her own safety. The speedy steam tug

---

[86] Stamper, "Travels of the 43rd Tennessee," 38.
[87] Moffitt, "Diary," 2.
[88] Stamper, "Travels of the 43rd Tennessee," 35.
[89] Smith, *A Smith in Service*, 38.

William H. Webb was anchored nearby and manned mostly by men from the 31st Tennessee.[90]

Carson recorded that others from the East Tennessee detachments were serving aboard the *Queen of the West*, and both vessels were ordered to get up steam in preparation to move. Around noon, Major Joseph L. Brent of Texas arrived from New Orleans aboard the steamer *Dr. Batey* (also spelled "*Beatty*") with some two hundred men who modestly designated themselves "the Desperadoes." Carson described the *Batey* as a "transport of ordinary dimensions." Pursuant to orders, Brent assumed overall command of the pending expedition and gave a stirring speech to the men of the Red River flotilla at Port Hudson, Louisiana, during which he outlined his order of "march" and plan of battle. Because it was the anniversary of George Washington's birthday, he proposed to celebrate by moving out in order to intercept and destroy the strongest gunboat in Admiral Porter's fleet, the *Indianola*, which had passed the Vicksburg batteries some nights before. Thoroughly manned and equipped, the powerful ironclad's original mission had been to join the *Queen of the West* at the mouth of the Red River to blockade the river where it entered the Mississippi, thereby starving the garrison at Port Hudson.[91] With the misfortune that had befallen the old ram, the *Indianola* now had another assignment: destroy the growing Confederate navy assembled in that area.

With a full-rounded salute from all the guns aboard the little Confederate navy and the guns at Port Hudson, the little fleet moved out in the following order: the *Queen of the West*, with a crew made up of Company C, from Dandridge, Jefferson County, and Company K, from Sweetwater, Monroe County, on detached service from the 31st Tennessee. It was also manned by a few volunteers from Vaughn's 79th (60th) Tennessee. Captain Elliott Carnes of Maryville, Blount County, commanded the gunboat. Next in line was the *Dr. Batey*, commanded by Major Brent, accompanied by his 200 desperadoes. These Texans referred to Carson's boys as "copperas breeches Tennesseans," and proclaimed that they "could do no good in the conflict."[92] In other words, these boys of the 31st Tennessee were considered green and untested. The final vessel in the squadron, according to Carson, the "little" *William H. Webb*, with her small crew of around fifty men from the aforementioned companies of the 31st Tennessee, brought up the rear. John Carson and Hampton A. Rice, both

---

[90] Carson, "Capture of the *Indianola*," vol. 32, no. 8, p. 381.
[91] Ibid.
[92] Ibid. "Copperas" is a green-colored sulfate often used in the making of inks.

of Jefferson County, shared command.[93] Small but mighty, the *Webb* had caused Admiral Porter to warn the commander of the *Queen of the West*, when the ram was still a member of the Yankee navy,: "If you get the first crack at her [the *Webb*], you will sink her, and if she gets the first crack at you, she will sink you."[94]

"We steamed down the Red River to its mouth, thence into the 'Father of Waters' to Natchez. Our little *Webb*, small but mighty, could run so much faster than our other steamers that we often, by permission, passed on and made long stops," Carson noted, "gathering information and all the good things we could get from the planters along the way."[95] Their adventure would be continued.

Speculation on a Small Scale. Meanwhile, back in the defenses of Vicksburg, Private E. D. Parker of the 79th (60th) Tennessee, wrote a letter to his wife back in Sullivan County on 22 February, noting that his health was still good, as was the health of a number of their mutual acquaintances serving at Vicksburg. He expressed his futile desire to be home so that he might play with his young son. "I have knowthing knew to rite more than I have rate to you before the yankeys haint left her yet but I think that we will make them git before long," he opined almost apologetically. Though he made passing reference to the cannonading, he saved most of his letter to discuss financial matters. Giving attention to things at home and the idea he will one day return, Parker gave instructions to his wife concerning the sale of a piece of land, reminding her not to take any less than $224 for it, and if she was in doubt, she should consult with "Uncal William Childress," and Parker will be "saddistfied" with his judgment. Parker showed himself to be a bit of a speculator when he dictated his wife to manage what his farm produced during his absence. "I want you to be savang of your corn the reason that I sed for you to be savan of hit was that hit is so skars her corn is worth $15 a busel, wheet is worth $90 to a hundred dollars per Barl and other produce acordan." He closed with his usual "Ill remain [your] husband until deth, E. D. Parker."[96]

---

[93] Ibid.

[94] Adm. David Porter to Col. Charles R. Ellet, 8 February 1863, *Official Records of the Union and Confederate Navies in the War of the Rebellion*, 31 vols. (Washington DC: Government Printing Office, 1895–1926) ser. 1 , vol. 24, p. 374.

[95] Carson, "Capture of the *Indianola*," vol. 32, no. 8, p. 381.

[96] E. D. Parker to his wife Susan, 22 February 1863, Parker Letters.

Reynolds Gives a Pep Talk and Lieutenant Earnest Goes to Church. Isaac Stamper recorded that his Company F of the 43rd Tennessee had gone on picket, though again he was excused from duty. He went uptown and had a new crystal put in his watch, after which he walked up and down the hilly streets of Vicksburg until he "played himself out." Before returning to camp, Stamper indicated he bought himself a little tobacco. Once within sight of the familiar row of tents on the rise above the Big Bayou, he was surprised to find his entire brigade in formation listening to "General" (Colonel) A. W. Reynolds "addressing them at the top of his voice upon the subject of hardships and rough diet." Stamper intimated that the boys did not need that particular speech since it dealt on a topic "with which we were well acquainted."[97]

Another visitor uptown on Sunday morning was Lieutenant James Earnest of the 79th (60th) Tennessee. While strolling about the streets, he was introduced by a mutual acquaintance to Colonel James Gillespie, commander of the 43rd Tennessee. The Greene County quartermaster found Colonel Gillespie to be "quite a clever portly gentleman." Ever curious, Earnest later happened by a Catholic church where services were just beginning. He attended and found them to be "very mysterious." Earnest added that the congregation was mostly "Irish and very rough." Later during his walk back to the Mint Sprints Bayou campsite, he observed from the "top of the giddy heights on our left…the dark outlines of huge collumbiads and the sentinel walking his lonely rounds."[98]

The Sinking of the "Indianola." Meanwhile, Grant's soldiers and his "freedmen" continued dredging and digging on their canal and on yet another project further west that would become known as the Lake Providence route. This second endeavor sought to dig multiple channels off the Mississippi River further north to link up with the Bayou Macon. This channel would progress some twenty-five miles westward and provide a link through that body of water down nearly 150 miles into the Ouachita River. The Ouachita would then provide entry into the Red River, which in turn emptied into the Mississippi near the southwestern corner of the Magnolia State. This grandiose scheme, of course, sought also to allow the invaders a by-pass around Vicksburg. In the end, the city fell before it could be completed, so it proved to be yet another of Grant's elaborate make-work projects to keep his soldiers exercising and busy.

Such behind-the-line diversions allowed matters to remain relatively quiet around Vicksburg, Stamper of the 43rd Tennessee reported, noting the only

---

[97] Stamper, "Travels of the 43rd Tennessee," 38.
[98] Northen, *All Right, Let Them Come,* 60–61.

duty on 24 February his regiment had was standing inspection at 3 p.m. Around 10 p.m., he learned that some of the Confederate warships had attacked a Yankee boat near New Carthage, Louisiana, "damaging her and capturing the boat with over a hundred prisoners." All this was accomplished, he remarked, with a Confederate loss of only two men killed and three wounded. The river to Port Hudson, he wrote, was once again open. Little did he realize that many of the Johnnies involved in the attack were from East Tennessee, and the two men killed were from Blount County.[99]

Lieutenant John Carson, on detached service with his company from the 31st Tennessee, went into somewhat greater detail regarding the amazing naval battle in which he had personal involvement. He stated that the *William H. Webb*, the lightly-armed Confederate warship he co-commanded, reached the city of Natchez two hours ahead of the rest of the "fleet," and he set his men to taking on coal under supervision of the ship's captain, a man named "Pierce," and his unnamed brother, who served as pilot. Both of these mariners were "copperas breeches," Tennessee riverboat-men, "of which they claimed to be proud," Carson wrote. While the refueling progressed, Lieutenants Carson and Rice occupied themselves at "Natchez on the Hill," which Carson indicated, "was our custom." Their object there was to call on the young ladies—"who were always glad to see us"—and, as the news of the "squadron's" arrival spread about town, seemingly the city's entire remaining population turned out, consisting of many lovely, young women. "They lined the hill for many a mile," Carson wrote, "to greet our new navy on arrival."[100]

At a distance appeared the rest of the fleet, the *Queen of the West* and *Dr. Batey* steaming slowly towards the wharf at Natchez, dark strips of soot rising from their smoke stacks, dipping like tails into the muddy water churned up as froth behind their fantails. Carson stated the *Webb* was still tied down at the wharf below. "On the east was the beautiful little city" of Natchez, "almost deserted by her inhabitants, who had come out to look upon a scene so 'grand, gloomy, and peculiar.'" After coaling had been completed, the little navy continued apace up the river, where Carson and his men realized that the terrible ironclad *Indianola* awaited, slowly prowling about like some hungry predator, making its deliberate way downriver towards the makeshift rebel fleet. The sun sank below the clouds where "it shed golden rays" all about the scene

---

[99] Stamper, "Travels of the 43rd Tennessee," 38.
[100] Carson, "Capture of the *Indianola*," vol. 32, no. 8, p. 381. Natchez had declared itself an "open" or "neutral" city. Consequently, it did not experience the miseries of the war.

before Carson and his men. As dusk settled about them, the Confederates soon saw the Yankee monster resembling an enormous flatiron come into view, with curling, heavy black smoke rising from its tall twin stacks, its dull metal catching the final dying rays of the daily sun. At that moment, according to Carson, "we realized we must soon engage in a combat where all chances seemed to be against us."[101]

The *Queen of the West*, according to the orders parlayed by Major Joseph Brent, moved out front with the *Dr. Batey* following next. The *Webb* was directed to follow the others due to its small armament and frail appearance. "At precisely ten o'clock," according to Carson, "Boom! went our guns and the 13–inch mortars from the *Indianola*." The distance had closed quickly until the tough old *Queen* and the mighty *Indianola* were bow to broadside, and with as much speed as she could muster, the *Queen* struck the ironclad and bounced off, "with the loss of two or three brave soldiers, mangled and torn beyond recognition." In what Carson termed "thick darkness," not a ray of light was seen, nor a sound or voice was heard from within the casemate of the huge ironclad in these close quarters. Without further orders and with the gunners and riflemen on his vessel at the ready, the little *Webb* pressed its attack, according to Carson, impervious to the fact "that we all might go down to a watery grave. Our brave Captain Pierce and his brother, our pilot, moved rapidly, till our boat struck a barge in tow by the *Indianola*, sinking it instantly with all its living freight of pigs, ducks, chickens and turkeys." The pitiful sounds of drowning livestock pilfered from area farms and plantations were considerable, Carson stated, until silenced when the sinking barge pulled them all under with it.[102]

Carson related that the Federals responded with their terrible 13-inch mortar, which was fired "in our very faces," lighting up the scene about and succeeding in tearing away parts of the forward gunnels on the little bark. All the while, Carson said that his 31st Tennessee sharpshooters worked furiously at their task, their mouths and teeth black from the tearing of the paper cartridges with which they loaded their Enfield muskets, keeping up a vicious and effective fire into the portholes of the big ironclad. So productive were they at harassing the ironclad's gunners, the one mortar round was the only shot leveled against the *Webb*. Rapidly, things got deadly quiet, and the *Indianola*, critically damaged from the blow delivered by the *Queen of the West*, began

---

[101] Ibid.

[102] Ibid. Two of the men killed were Pvts. J. W. Wright and Garner Edmonds of Company B, 31st Tennessee, which was recruited in Maryville, Blount County.

limping for shore near the plantation of Joseph Davis, brother of President Jefferson Davis. The *Webb* was taken up river for a mile or so, rounded to, and then propelled back toward the Yankee behemoth with all the steam her two efficient low-pressure engines could muster. "With a mighty power, we came back down stream," Carson recalled, "followed around a small tow-head, with volley after volley from our little 12-pounder and riflemen, with not a shot was fired at us."[103]

The "little *Webb*" struck the great ironclad at the base of her wheelhouse with a deadly crash, Carson stated, "tearing splinters and rolling back great bars of iron as if [they were] made of lead." The *William H. Webb*'s forward thrust carried her bow several feet further into the *Indianola*'s side, causing a great inrush of water. The federal ironclad came to rest on the shallow bottom in twelve feet of water up to her casemate and within twenty feet of the shore. Lieutenant Commander George W. Brown, commander of the flooded warship, came out of her hull where all his men had taken refuge atop the casemate, and implored of the Confederates: "For God's sake, men—cease firing! I surrender unconditionally." Carson indicated, "we at once began taking prisoners off the *Indianola* and provided them safety aboard the *Webb*." The *Queen of the West* had been knocked out at the very beginning of the battle, and the *Dr. Batey*, plodding along behind, was not in gunshot range of the fight.

---

[103] Ibid., 32: 381–82. Several accounts of this battle exist, including some contradictory ones left by participants within Col. Bradford's regiment itself. The Company B record of events noted that "Lieut. Carnes and Lieut. Miller with 30 men on board the steamer *Queen of the West* attacked one of the enemy's gunboats on the night of 24 February 1863, and captured her crew of about 123 in number." As almost an aside, the record added: "It is proper here to remark that parts of Companies I and C and a company of Texas artillery were also engaged in the action and did good service on another boat [the *Webb*] principally, the officers and men acted gallantly and bravely on the occasion referred to and deserve much credit." The record of events for Company I, 31st Tennessee, indicated the men "on board the *Webb* on the night of 24 February 1863 … fought gallantly and bravely…. The *Webb* and *Queen of the West* having fought and captured the federal gunboat *Indianola*, Lts. Rice and Carson were in command of the company and the men were for the first time engaged to man the guns on the *Webb* as well as sharp-shooters. All the officers who were engaged in the capture rendered honorable praise to the company for its heroic conduct." The men of Company C, 31st Tennessee, were "ordered to report on 24 January 1863, and at that time were ordered on a boat to defend the river and capture a ferry boat. They were transferred to the Dept. of Louisiana soon thereafter and the majority of the company was [then] at or near Alexandria, Louisiana, on detached service." 31st Tennessee, *Compiled Service Records*. Also, see Report of Major J. L. Brent, 25 February 1863, *Official Records*, ser. 1, vol. 24, pt. 1, p. 364–69 Brent's account indicated that the action was a bit more complex, and that his men deserved their share of the credit for the victory.

Long after the *Indianola* had settled on the bottom, the *Queen of the West* came along side the *Webb*, and Major Brent, in the attempt to come aboard, stepped onto a cotton bale placed as armament on the little war vessel's deck. The bale shifted under his weight and pitched him in the river. Carson stated that he threw Brent a bucket on a rope to grab and brought him up on the deck. Except for a few broken ribs, the rather bombastic Brent was none the worse for the experience. "Gentlemen," Brent told them, "to you and to your men I accord the honors of this victory, and to you belong the spoils."[104]

Lieutenants Rice, Carson, and Handy, along with the detachment of Jefferson County boys belonging Company I, were left in charge of the sunken ironclad. Their assignment was the dubious task of raising the *Indianola*, "if possible." General Carter L. Stevenson, their divisional commander, sent a number of pioneers, equipment, and laborers to work at the futile attempt to raise the ironclad. Brent had left them, taking the ships of the little Confederate navy with the prisoners aboard downriver toward Port Hudson.

The racket of the fight carried up the valley to Warrenton and Vicksburg causing the men in the defenses to be apprehensive and alert. Sergeant Tom Moffitt of Lynch's Battery noted that at "about 10 o'clock [on 24 February] as I lay in bed, Lieut. [William] Butler, who had not retired, called me to get ready" for battle. "We repaired to the battery," he indicated, as all were expecting some sort of general engagement to be soon headed their way. But just as soon as the noise began, it stopped. "We all laid down around our gun," Moffitt wrote, "and took us a little nap." After they awoke, they headed returned to camp and crawled into bed. The unknown commotion way down river had lasted only "a short season," as Moffitt phrased it.[105]

Around 1 a.m. on 25 February, they were again rousted from their sleep, left to grabbing for their shoes and accoutrements in the darkness in response to firing of John Vaughn's infantry pickets nearby. "Rockets from Vaughn's headquarters were sent up," Moffitt reported, "and the upper batteries soon opened up." He and Lieutenant Butler rushed to their gun, and just as they got there, the darkness was ripped by the roar and flash of their piece, discharged under the competent leadership of Corporal Rufus Caldwell.[106] As the 32-

---

[104] Carson, "Capture of the *Indianola*," vol. 32, no.8, p. 381–82.

[105] Moffitt, "Diary," 3.

[106] Ibid. In an interesting aside, related to the aforementioned Lieutenant Butler, Corporal Samuel Brazelton Scott serving with Lynch's Battery and a native of Moffitt's hometown of New Market, Jefferson County, indicated that Butler, from Jackson, West Tennessee, was thought to be "popish, overbearing, [and] a cussing kind of a feller, and

pounder was being reloaded, the soldiers saw something like "a dark body floating" in the river beyond the parapet, which had been illuminated for an instant, when the cannon roared again. With the added light of signal fires and cannon discharges, the soldiers soon determined that the object was nothing more than a coal barge, which had been struck by twenty to thirty rounds. After the grand display of the water batteries at what amounted to a night target practice, Moffitt indicated that the boys all trudged back to their tents and slept until late in the morning.[107]

First Corporal Scott of Lynch's Battery noted the battery's weapons were pointed right over the elevated bank of the Mississippi River, "so close [we] could not depress the guns low enough to reach vessels passing if they were near the east bank."[108] Ironically, the safest route past the Vicksburg batteries was to run as close to the Mississippi shoreline as possible. No better example illustrated the futile work of the gun crews on this particular night than when the gunners discovered that they had depressed one of the barrels so low that "the next morning, we found the balls lying on the parapet in front of the gun." The end result was that the piece had been firing blank cartridges, according to Scott, "and we had a good laugh on the Lieut. and the gunner."[109] Stamper recorded in his diary that the boys watched a small boat pass down the river on 25 February, which was identified as a coal boat sent to supply the ironclad the Confederates had captured. Lynch's men would have been interested to know that, with all the rounds they fired at during the night, they had failed to sink it. That evening, the clouds came in again and the rain commenced, with a heavy storm that blew nearly all night.[110]

John Carson of the 31st Tennessee, at the site where the *Indianola* rested on the shallow bottoms, suggested they all were involved in trying to figure out a way to raise her. The futility of the proposed enterprise soon became apparent, and the naval heroes decided to play upon their newfound celebrity nearby to see if they might be rewarded by a decent meal. "Finding it useless to make any effort to raise the ironclad," Carson wrote, and because we "[had] with us no Elisha who could make iron swim, we spent the day at the home of Mr. Joseph Davis where we found some good things to eat." A number of the

---

was not popular with the boys." (Samuel Scott Brazelton to W. T. Rigby, 3 March 1904, William T. Rigby Correspondence.)

[107] Moffitt, "Diary," 3. This barge was on its way to supply coal for the *Indianola*.

[108] Samuel Scott Brazelton to W. T. Rigby, 26 February 1904, William T. Rigby Correspondence.

[109] Ibid.

[110] Stamper, "Travels of the 43rd Tennessee," 38–39.

boys were left behind with the sunken warship, and they fashioned grab hooks from materials at hand to fish out of the sutler's stores aboard the *Indianola* "many useful articles which were badly needed."[111]

"At nightfall [26 February], we found ourselves completely surrounded by water," Carson stated. "The great bayou across the bend of the 'Father of Waters' was so swollen that the lowlands for miles around were covered with water, leaving us no way of escape." After consultation, those who were there decided to spike the guns and make their way to the Louisiana shore in yawls. Lieutenant Handy was left with one yawl and two or three men to strike the match and make certain of the explosion. Lieutenants Rice and Carson, with their men, started across the channel from the Mississippi shore. Before they reached the island, a terrific explosion occurred, "throwing all around us what seemed to be hundreds of pieces of iron, with great sheets of fire, lighting up the scene for miles around."[112]

"We never returned to know the result, but after a long night of 'pulling for the shore,' at the dawn of another day we landed [and] emptied the yawls," Carson continued. From there, the sailor/soldiers marched via Lake to St. Joseph to Port Gibson, and thence to "Camp Magnolia," another name the boys used for Camp Reynolds. Arriving in camps below Vicksburg, hungry, ragged, and weary, they were "glad to meet our beloved Colonel Bradford and Major [Robert] McFarland, and all our comrades from whom we had long been separated, without a change of clothing or rations issued in the usual manner. The grand ovation given for us, for the moment repaid us for the hard service and many privations during our service in the Confederate navy, but we were glad to quit the navy and rejoin our command on solid earth again."[113]

John Miller, a Morristown native and member of the 79th (60th) Tennessee and who was on detached gunboat duty during this operation, indicated years after the war that he had gone "with a scouting expedition up the Yazoo [Red] River and had a good time and enjoyed the company I was with

---

[111] Carson, "Capture of the *Indianola*," vol. 32, no. 8, p. 382. Joseph Davis was the brother of Jefferson Davis.

[112] Ibid. Much was made in the Northern press and in Grant's and Porter's commands concerning the success of this ruse of the "plywood" gunboat, sent to harass those trying to raise the *Indianola*. On its sides were painted the reminder "Deluded People Cave In." Its appearance was reported to have panicked the Confederates into blowing up their sunken prize. Whatever led to its destruction, the mighty *Indianola* was gone and would never again rise to roam the Mississippi.

[113] Ibid. Apparently Company C of the 31st Tennessee remained in Louisiana for an indefinite period of time.

fine." His service, and that of others from this regiment, was aboard the *Queen of the West*.[114]

Colonel William M. Bradford, commander of the 31st Tennessee, summarized the naval action involving his men as follows:

> Late in February 1863, a detachment of three companies of this regiment was ordered down the Mississippi from Warrenton to watch the movements of the gunboat *Queen of the West*, which had passed our batteries. This detail of three companies was placed on a small steam ferryboat with two small cannon. They proceeded down the Mississippi and up the Red River until they captured the *Queen*. Then, an expedition was fitted out with the *Queen of the West* and the *William H. Webb* and some barge transports, and placed under the command of Major M. S. [J. L.] Brent, who had some other troops besides these three companies. Lieutenant Miller, of this regiment (Company B) and Lieutenants Hampton A. Rice and John M. Carson of Company I, with their two companies and other troops [including some Morristown boys from the 79th (60th) Tennessee], manned the *Queen of the West* and the *Webb*. In ascending the river they met, attacked and captured the ironclad gunboat *Indianola*—a gallant and brilliant achievement by Major Brent and his men.[115]

"The Yankees Are Tired of Being Whipped." Back in the lines along the Mint Springs Bayou, Private Alfred Bowman of Jonesborough, Washington County, and the 79th (60th) Tennessee wrote a letter home to his parents from Vicksburg on 24 February, informing them that he was not in the best of health. "I have a very bad cold and sore throat," he confessed, and "for the last few days [have] been hardly fit for duty—we are exposed so much to the rain and cold that it is a wonder we aren't all sick." He hoped, however, that everyone was well back home, and he noted that the Yankees were still hard by, and word had it they were "making great preparations for a fight." As did so many of the East Tennessee soldiers who wrote home, however, Alfred doubted that the enemy would ever take Vicksburg because "it is so well fortified."[116]

---

[114] *Civil War Veterans Questionnaires*, eds. Dyer and Moore, 4: 1539.

[115] Bradford and Toole, "Thirty-First Tennessee," in Lindsley, *The Military Annals of Tennessee (Confederate)* 1: 465.

[116] Alfred Bowman to his parents, 25 February 1863, Bowman Family Papers, East Tennessee State University Archives, Johnson City TN.

"I think it is impossible for them to land troops at this place on account of the high water," Bowman reported. "They will have to land their transports from 50 to 200 yards of our batterys [which] will sink them as fast as they can land." In regard to the ill-fated missions of the *Queen of the West* and *Indianola*, Bowman indicated that the Federals had tried to run two of their gunboats by Vicksburg, but both were captured and, perhaps referring to the coal barge that was not sunk, the "batterys sank one yesterday 27 miles below Vicksburg." Bowman indicated that a call came to the 79th (60th) Tennessee and other regiments to send volunteers to attempt to raise the *Indianola*. Men in his company who went were Wash Johnson, Henry Crouch and A. V. Fitzgerald. Due to some chicanery on the Northerners' part, and a lack of equipment to lift the heavy vessel, the raising of the *Indianola* was abandoned, and she was, as Carson had reported, blown up. "I was not well enuff to go," Alfred suggested. He added that the two boats sunk were two of the best in the Northern fleet, and he was convinced that "our batterys can sink all of the boats that passes this place." The strategy seemed to be, according to Bowman and others, "to capture a few more of their boats [so] we can fight them on the water."[117]

The New Conscripts Adapt to Life in the Battery. Bowman said that the boys were able to watch across the Mississippi on the Louisiana side, where the enemy had a large force encamped, but as long as they stayed in sight on that side of the river, there was very little worry over what Grant might try. The war was playing in favor of the Confederacy, according to Bowman's limited sphere of observation. "I think the end of the war is close at hand," he wrote, "since the Yankees are getting tired of being whiped so much and not whiping any—they begin to think it is time to stop [since] they know they never can whip the south." Bowman reported that a gaggle of conscripts reported to camps from his home section during the Sunday just passed, courtesy of the efforts of Sergeant Moffitt and Lieutenant Rhoton of Lynch's Battery. "George Stevens, John Emmert, Hendricks, John Bowman, and one of Bill 'Umphries boys are here," Alfred Bowman indicated, "and several others from Washington and Carter County." The newly arrived "volunteers" were said to have admitted that they could no longer evade the conscript officers, so they enrolled with Captain John Lynch's Light Artillery Company occupying gunmounts near Vaughn's camps. Bowman intimated that such an assignment seemed ideal for these stay-at-homes now forced into the service, since they believed that they would not be in

---

[117] Ibid.

as much danger with the batteries as were the boys in the seven East Tennessee infantry regiments.[118]

"[That] is the very place for them," Bowman asserted, "where there is no chance to doge they will have to doo their part in that I don't think they will hollow for old Abe about the time the Yankees batterys turns loos on them." Bowman closed his letter by informing that their son Richard was in "tolerable good health" and that his prospects were good at receiving a disability discharge. Both Bowmans believed that Richard would be sent home in a matter of days. "The health of our army is very bad," Alfred admitted. He asked his parents to notify "Mr. Eden" that his son Mike was well "when he left here to go on a gunboat on the Yazoo [Red] River" one day the week before. Bowman also reported that an acquaintance, Wash Johnson, was well, though James Fulkerson was not. As had most East Tennessee soldiers writing from the area, Bowman reproached those at home for not writing more, and he begged them to ask others to send him mail. "I have received only one letter from you all since I lef home," he stated as a graphic example. They were requested to direct their mail to him "in care of Capt. Bacon, Com. F, 79 Tenn. Vols., Vaughn's Brigade."[119]

Later on 25 February, after the considerable excitement of the prior evening, Moffitt of Lynch's Battery reported to headquarters, where he picked up papers authorizing him to return to East Tennessee to collect more recruits for the artillery company. His good work in developing human resources had not gone unnoticed. While at headquarters, he met with his brother-in-law James Gillespie and Lieutenant Colonel James Humes. By evening, it was raining again, and Moffitt was able to hear sporadic bursts of musketry downriver. "The firing last night proceeded from the gunboats," he reported, resulting in the sinking and capture of the *Indianola*. He also recorded the incredible (and erroneous) news that a Yankee tugboat was thought to have made it all the way through Grant's canal, coming out into the Mississippi across from Warrenton.[120] Such a report, had it been true, would have indicated the Federals were now capable of bypassing the Confederate batteries in accord with Grant's ambition to land his army down river below Vicksburg.

Stamper of the 43rd Tennessee described 26 February as blustery, shaken by thunder, whipped by wind, and pelted by rain. Around 10 p.m., the winds stripped the tents of their flies, tore their shelters from the ground, and exposed

---

[118] Ibid.
[119] Ibid.
[120] Moffitt, "Diary," 4.

"some of the boys to the rain which darkens everything on account of its intensity." Two hours before sun-up, the rain ceased, allowing the boys of the regiment time to cook two days' worth of rations in preparation for their turn at brigade picket duty on the Warrenton levee.[121]

Thomas Moffitt of Lynch's Light Company was again in the process of making preparations to leave camp for East Tennessee to collect conscripts for the battery. Around noon, he indicated in his journal, friends Private Charlie Lide and 1st Sergeant Jacob H. Alexander accompanied him to the depot to catch his train. Prior to his walk down the long hill to Levee Street, he went by General Stevenson's Headquarters to sign out. While there, he heard from Colonel George that "Capt. Edward A. Watkins' company [I, raised at Talbott Station, Jefferson County,] had assisted in the capture of the *Indianola*." He also happened upon his brother-in-law Colonel James Gillespie, commander of the 43rd Tennessee, who told him about a dream he had about his wife, Nan, Moffitt's sister. After good-byes and best wishes were exchanged, Moffitt went on to the depot, and soon his train was on its way to Jackson, where after a short layover, it proceeded on its way eastward, leaving the capital "about dark."[122] Though Moffitt would rejoin his battery after Vicksburg, he would never return to it while it served in Mississippi.

Stamper reported that, as the 43rd Tennessee marched out to the picket posts on 27 February, a thick fog was rolling in, enshrouding everything. Again, he avoided the duty to stay back in camp with his sick brother W. D., who was "still unable to take care of himself." The fog lifted about 10 a.m., and the weather turned and remained warm and pleasant until the evening. During the night, however, the clouds came in again, accompanied by the omnipresent rain. Stamper reported that Private Osteen of Company C died of measles during the night.[123]

On his trip home, Sergeant Moffitt of Lynch's Battery noted, his train entered Meridian about 1:30 p.m. on 27 February, which caused him to complain, "we should have reached that point about 3 o'clock this morning." He recorded that the track from Jackson to Meridian was almost completely under water. When they got to the Chunky River, he saw the graves of the twenty-six victims of an earlier railroad accident and was told that "the bridge there [was] yet unsafe." Once safely in Meridian, he booked passage on to Mobile, where he met an acquaintance whom he called "Little McElroy," a

---

[121] Stamper, "Travels of the 43rd Tennessee," 39.
[122] Moffitt, "Diary," 4.
[123] Stamper, "Travels of the 43rd Tennessee," 39.

husky Confederate staff officer from East Tennessee, and with whom Moffitt had served previously under General Felix Zollicoffer. "He stands over a great deal of ground," Moffitt smirked, "swears like a sailor and smokes very large cigars."[124] And not only did Moffitt have to endure this husky popinjay; he was dismayed to find his train to Mobile was running behind time.

Praise for the 31st Tennessee's Gunboat Detail. From the headquarters tent of the 31st Tennessee on 28 February, Colonel William M. Bradford issued the following Special Order in honor of his men who had been involved in the battle with the *Indianola*:

> The Colonel commanding has received, with emotion of no ordinary gratification, the intelligence of the recent gallantry and bravery of Companies I and B in the attack upon the federal gunboat *Indianola*.
>
> It would be an act of injustice to the officers and privates, as well as violence to my own feelings, to withhold from you the just tribute of praise which your chivalry in that engagement so richly merits. The capture and surrender of the boat, after the desperate defense of a well-drilled and disciplined foe, entitle you to the highest honors of veterans.
>
> I therefore trust that the country will justly appreciate the honors which you have so nobly won and can give you the highest assurance of the warmed gratitude and pride of your officers in thus giving tone and character to the 31st Tennessee regiment.
>
> May the God of battles thus favor your stout arms and serve your generous hearts for all future emergencies of a similar character.[125]

By evening, the clouds had dispersed and the sun sat "in splendor," according to Stamper of the 43rd Tennessee, "while the gentle breeze fanned our low cotton country so pleasantly that we could not refrain from notching the close of another winter."[126]

Far down the railroad line at Meridian, Moffitt of Lynch's Battery had made friends with three traveling soldiers from Virginia, while they all awaited the train to carry them to Mobile. By 9 p.m., they decided that it was not coming, so they found a boxcar loaded with corn, spread their oilcloths and blankets, and settled down to sleep. After they had been so engaged for some

---

[124] Moffitt, "Diary," 39.

[125] Bradford and Toole, "The Thirty-First Tennessee," in Lindsley, *The Military Annals of Tennessee (Confederate)* 1: 465.

[126] Stamper, "Travels of the 43rd Tennessee," 39.

hours, their train pulled into the depot at about 2 a.m. Close to twelve hours later, Moffitt and his Virginia comrades finally arrived in Mobile, where they took rooms at the Battle House, which he described as the "the crack hotel" in town. Rooms there were at a premium, Moffitt wrote in his journal, so he and new friends Virginia acquaintances, whom he described as "clever fellows," were crowded in among others in a second floor room.[127]

Moffitt used his free time to walk around town and did a little shopping for the folks back home. He met the proprietor of a bookstore, who though a native of East Tennessee, had resided in Mobile for over 50 years. As coincidence would have it, this man was also a kinsman of Moffitt's friend Charlie Lide from the battery. Later, Moffitt noted he "took a plate of oysters, and smoked" his pipe, feeling quite contented with himself and matters in general. In fact, he was enjoying himself so much, he decided not to leave Mobile until the next day as he had originally planned, but to continue his investigation of the city, "which was quite a place for business." Additionally, he asserted Mobile was also "a great place for oysters and *officers.*"[128]

The February Muster Rolls. Back in Vicksburg, the first bi-monthly company musters were submitted at the end of February for Vaughn's Brigade, detailing each soldier's service status for the months of January and February. Lieutenant Earnest of the 79th (60th) Tennessee indicated in his journal that he had spent a good portion of his day making out payrolls for his company from Washington County.[129]

For general comparisons as related by the musters submitted, following is the census for six companies of East Tennesseans serving at Vicksburg, two in Reynolds's Brigade and four in Vaughn's Brigade:

> Company C, 59th Tennessee (mustered at Carter County, TN): fifty-three on the rolls; one man left off sick in Montgomery, and died there on 13 January; forty-seven men present for duty; one conscript added to the rolls during the muster period; three men present, sick in camps; two men absent in the hospitals.[130]

---

[127] Moffitt, "Diary," 5. He was probably traveling with fellow artillerymen because the only Virginia command at Vicksburg was the Botetourt Artillery Battery.

[128] Ibid.

[129] Afterwards, he visited some of his sick men at the hospital tents, where he heard that an enemy deserter who had come over that day had reported the the boys in blue were "dying rapidly." (Northen, *All Right, Let Them Come*, 63).

[130] 59th Tennessee, *Complied Service Records.*

Company I, 59th Tennessee (mustered in at Morristown, TN): ninety-four on the rolls; status of one not stated; eighty-three men present for duty; one man absent, on detached service in Vicksburg; nine men absent, sick in hospitals; one man died during the period of unspecified cause; one man carried on the roll as absent without leave.[131]

Company H, 79th (60th) Tennessee (mustered in at Morristown, TN): sixty-seven on the rolls; status of four others not stated; forty-seven men present for duty; thirteen men absent in hospitals, sick; two men died of illness in Vicksburg hospitals; three men absent, on detached service (two on gunboat duty aboard the *Webb* or *Queen of the West*); four men carried on the rolls as absent without leave.[132]

Company I, 79th (60th) Tennessee (mustered in at Newport, Cocke County, TN): eighty-eight on the rolls; status of eight others not stated; seventy-six men present for duty; nine men absent, sick in Vicksburg hospitals; one man absent on detached service; five men carried on the rolls as absent without leave.[133]

Company I, 80th (62nd) Tennessee (mustered in at Newport, Cocke County, TN): eighty-three on the rolls; status of nine other men not stated; seventy-seven men present for duty; three men absent, sick in Vicksburg hospitals; one man present, sick in camp; three men died of disease in Vicksburg hospitals; one officer resigned his office; one man on detached service; three men carried on the rolls as absent without leave (one of whom returned to duty).[134]

Company G, 81st (61st) Tennessee (mustered in at Morristown, TN): seventy on the rolls; status of twelve others not stated; fifty-seven men present for duty; thirteen men absent, sick in Vicksburg hospitals; one man died of disease in Vicksburg hospital; two men carried on the rolls as absent without leave.[135]

Much of Tennesseans' duty now revolved around routines they had settled into in the camps. And as long as they stayed well, had a nice fire to huddle

---

[131] Ibid.

[132] 60th Tennessee, *Compiled Service Records*. Vaughn's inspector Gen., Bob E. Houston, wrote in his review for the muster period concerning Company G, 79th (60th) Tennessee: "I take great pleasure in stating that in discipline, efficiency and military appearance, this company exceeds that of any I have ever seen in the volunteer service."

[133] Ibid.

[134] 62nd Tennessee, *Compiled Service Records*.

[135] 61st Tennessee, ibid.

around, and received edible food on occasion, the East Tennessee defenders of Vicksburg seemed content. They looked anxiously for letters from home, and their excitement came primarily from the safe spectator sport of hoping that the Yankees would occasionally attempt to run their gunboats down the river past the big siege guns.

CHAPTER 4

"Hard Living and Sacrifice Will Not Divert Us from Our Duty"
March

"March 1st was one of the prettiest [mornings] I ever saw," Stamper of the 43rd Tennessee wrote in his diary, which seemed to him to be bringing with it all the glories of approaching spring. The regimental chaplain, Archibald Brooks, preached at ten o'clock, though some undesignated portion of the unit, perhaps half of the ten companies, only came off picket duty around noon. Stamper indicated that the day was relatively quiet, with no demonstrations around Vicksburg. Once roll call was completed that evening, a signal was given for the men to assemble for an evening prayer meeting. Perhaps feeling spiritual with the approach of Easter, coupled with the uncertainty they faced in the days ahead, Stamper noted, "a considerable crowd assembled, and we had an interesting meeting."[1]

On the upper lines near the Mint Springs Bayou where John Vaughn's Brigade was encamped, E. D. Parker of the 79th (60th) Tennessee composed a letter to his wife back in Fordtown, Sullivan County. He told her that he was well, hoped his family was the same, and wished that he was there to help her along. "I would like to see [and talk with] you and Willie one time more," he continued, but he realized that, with times as they were, "I caint but I don't think it will be so long for I think in six months we will all be at home to tend to our business inn pease." Parker said that the grapevine telegraph was spreading the rumor that "old abe is dead," but he doubted it was so. "It is thought that the Yankees is leaving hear and dont intend to attact us," he said, "and well it will be for them iff [they] don't." He concluded his letter by requesting that his wife send a pair of socks with Jerey Cox when he returned to the regiment, and if he was not coming "right soon," she was to send them with Lieutenant James Crawford, who was home on recruiting duty.[2]

---

[1] Stamper, "Travels of the 43rd Tennessee," 39.
[2] E. D. Parker to his wife Susan, 1 March 1863, Parker Letters.

Also on 1 March, in a Vicksburg hospital, Private Nathan Black, also a member of Parker's 79th (60th) Tennessee, succumbed to typhoid fever. He was a widower and left behind five young children back in Cocke County. Four months hence, his children would be placed under the guardianship of Thomas M. Minneford, at which time they were awarded three months' back pay owed to Black and commutation for clothing due. The total amount was $85.83, though three dollars were withheld from the amount owed by Black to the Confederate government, liability not specified.[3] Concerns over other possible fatal diseases found their way into Lieutenant Earnest's diary on this first day of March. He wrote that he had spent the morning lying around the 79th (60th) Tennessee's camp and talking with other soldiers about the prospect of coming down with small pox, since a case had shown up in a neighboring company's tent row.[4]

At the Battle House in Mobile, Moffitt of Lynch's Battery, on his way back to East Tennessee to recruit, indicated that he was able to move upstairs after breakfast, finally securing a room to himself. During the afternoon, he took a stroll around town and stopped at "the Sunday School room," where worship was in progress. He was unable to stay, he noted, since he suddenly felt extremely sick. On his way back to the hotel, he stopped at an apothecary "for medicine to relieve my bowels." He believed that it was the "oysters [that] done the work on me," and added, "I don't want anymore."[5]

A Lieutenant James of the Knoxville Conscript of Instruction met with Moffitt at the hotel. Moffitt indicated that during his walk he saw Colonel Walton of the New Orleans Artillery, whom Moffitt declared to be a fine looking man who appeared every bit the soldier. Still, Moffitt declared that eagle buttons and fine uniforms spooked him somewhat. "I never saw as many officers wearing stars in all my travels," he asserted, "as I have seen at this place."

Moffitt enjoyed his walk around town and commented on the numerous public squares and large buildings, including the hotel where he was staying. "Saw an ironclad ram and two wooden gunboats lying in the river yesterday evening," he recorded. The gunboats were the *Gaines* and *Morgan*; the ram was most likely the *Baltic*. Two other rams, he indicated, arrived from Selma that very day. "We now have a good supply of crafts," he believed, "should the Feds be foolish enough to attack us at this point." Moffitt's evaluation of Mobile was

[3] 60th Tennessee, *Compiled Service Records*.

[4] Northen, *All Right, Let Them Come*, 63.

[5] Moffitt, "Diary," 5–6.

that it was "destined to be a great place someday," though all the commerce seemed to him to be dominated by Jews. "The place is full of foreigners," he concluded, who paid "but little regard to the Sabbath day."[6]

Back at Vicksburg on 2 March, Private Benjamin Giddens of the 3rd Tennessee wrote his wife, Linda (short for Melinda), that the city "[was] a sickly place soldiers are dying and Tennesseans cant stand this climate." The Louisiana soldiers told the boys that the weather and water also affected the poorly acclimated Georgians, who, Giddens noted, "died here last summer like sheep with the rot."[7] Later, after the surrender, General Alfred Cumming, commander of a brigade of Georgians in the same division as Reynolds's men, wrote that the sweltering Vicksburg summer had been "a debilitating climate" for his soldiers.[8]

"We are still camped within four miles of the city [near Warrenton]," Giddens wrote, and he echoed Stamper's declaration that, though "the yanks are still insight of us [across the river on the Louisiana side] every thing is quiet." Giddens thought that in "a few days [the Federals] will break loose" after the Confederate army. And as was typically the case with these East Tennessee Confederates, he loathed the area they were defending, but boasted that if the enemy attacks "us, we will have the advantage of them for this place is strongly fortified." Giddens also noted in his letter that, like Stamper, he had attended religious services the day before, and that the 3rd Tennessee's chaplain, Brother Joseph Pealer, had admonished the boys to quit swearing and playing cards, and to "quit ever thing that was immoral." Giddens, who indicated to his wife in more than one of his letters that he was spiritually skeptical, said, almost teasing her: "I felt a clear conscious, and like King Agrippa when Paul was making his defense, I was almost persuaded to be a Christian."[9]

Giddens informed his wife that Lieutenant John Hightower of the 59th Tennessee, having been cashiered from the regiment for leaving his command in the face of the enemy at the Duck River during Bragg's and Kirby-Smith's Kentucky invasion the previous fall, was now on his way home in humiliation.

---

[6] Ibid., 6. The names of the ironclads to which Moffitt referred are unknown, although the *Huntsville* and *Tuscaloosa*, smaller sisters of the *Tennessee*, were also under construction at the naval yard near Selma and would see service in the waters of South Alabama.

[7] Benjamin C. Giddens to Melinda ("Linda") Giddens, 2 March 1863, Giddens Letters.

[8] Report of Gen. Alfred Cummings, 1 July 1863, *Official Records*, ser. 1, vol. 24, pt. 2, p. 348.

[9] Giddens to Giddens, 2 March 1863.

Giddens had asked Hightower to let him know when he was leaving, but he did not do so. "I reckon he did not want to see me for it is a disgrace to be casherd," Giddens reported. Most likely hoped that the ex-lieutenant would carry some letters home for him to his wife and other family members. "I am in hops we will leave this place," Giddens declared, but he impressed upon his wife the importance of her writing him: "I have never received but two letters from you and I have read them till they are nearly wore out." He reminded her that he had written her ten letters since being sent to Vicksburg, and "I would nearly shout if I was to get a letter" in return at any time. Giddens said his sick brother, Captain James K. Polk Giddens, was a "great deal better [since he] had a negro woman to wait on him he gets good attention the doctor says he is out of danger." However, Giddens supposed that his brother would resign his office before much longer. Finally, he closed his letter by admitting that he missed his wife, telling her that he "would like to see you and kiss them ruby lips of yours."[10]

At 7 a.m. on the morning of 3 March, Moffitt of Lynch's Battery, still on his way home on conscript duty, left Mobile on the steamer *Mary Wilson*, crossing the Tensas River for Pollard, where the railway resumed its way northeast. The sun was radiant, and the sky was completely clear, he wrote. His train arrived at Montgomery at 10 p.m., where Moffitt reported that he stayed at the Exchange Hotel and "slept some." The next morning, Moffitt's train left for Atlanta at 11 a.m., arrived around five that afternoon. In Atlanta, he found several East Tennessee friends and soldier acquaintances. "Met with Parson Alexander, Tom Cruikshanks [of the 43rd Tennessee], George Mays, Will Turley and Sam Boyd," he reported. By 7 o'clock p.m., they had left Atlanta and arrived at Dalton by 4 a.m., "where we had to lay over all day." Moffitt admitted that the layovers were becoming a very wearying routine, though he hoped this one would be brief and they would be able to leave relatively quickly.[11]

On 3 March, Colonel Bradford's 31st Tennessee and Colonel Gillespie's 43rd Tennessee were moved from the vicinity of Camp Reynolds about a mile east, where there was plenty of water, according to the daily entry of Isaac Stamper of the 43rd. "We had pretty hard time packing tents, cooking utensils and everything," he wrote, "but we soon had everything set up in order." After undergoing the rigor of breaking down, marching, and setting up a new camp, Stamper indicated that the boys "were prepared to take a good night's sleep." The following day, camp set-ups for the men of the 31st Tennessee and 43rd

---

[10] Ibid.
[11] Moffitt, "Diary," 6.

Tennessee continued, many busy with the construction of chimneys for their "shebangs." Others hammered together bedsteads for their quarters, Stamper reported, with rope suspensions to get their bedding off the ground. He wrote that his brother, James N. Stamper, "cut his foot getting out timber for his chimney." He did not indicate the seriousness of the injury and stated that for this day at least, there were "no changes in military matters."[12]

Sergeant William Raleigh Clack, also of the 43rd Tennessee, wrote a letter home on 3 March to his sister Amy back in East Tennessee. He informed her that he had perused her recent letter "over and over," and his thoughts were of her and the great distance that separated them. He told Amy that they should not shed tears over this misfortune, and he informed that her an acquaintance had failed in his attempt to get a medical discharge. Though the request was approved all the way up the chain of command to Pemberton himself, Clack noted that Ambroze W. Hodge, a surgeon, suggested that the soldier in question receive treatment in one of the Vicksburg military hospitals. "This killed his hopes," Clack concluded. The dangerous conditions in the wretched military hospitals led Colonel James Gillespie and even Surgeon Hodge to suggest that Clack's friend take his cure in the camps, "where he can do just as well." The individual's ultimate good fortune was to be sent to the Stout's home nearby, and when he got "stouter," Clack joked, he could return to camp.[13]

Clack admitted to Amy that he had no real news, beyond the fact that the Yankees were reinforcing daily. "They sent a flag of truce over the other day," he reported, demanding the Confederates stop shelling the Federal transports attempting to pass Vicksburg. And if the firing was not suspended, they threatened to execute some Southern prisoners captured in the area. "Our reply was to 'go ahead,'" Clack wrote, "and we will retaliate." He believed that there would be a "heavy fight" here in the spring or summer.[14]

For the cakes and sausage they had received, Clack and his brother Micajah extended their sincere thanks, both commenting that the food reminded them of "pleasant scenes of home." He asked Amy to extend their gratitude to Marion and King for their letters, and Clack was pleased to hear that Marion "is excused from service." As for Amy's question whether it was right for a person to go to the army contrary to their will, merely to please

---

[12] Stamper, "Travels of the 43rd Tennessee," 40. The reasons for moving half of Reynolds's regiments were not indicated.

[13] William Raleigh Clack to Amy, 4 March 1863, William Raleigh Clack Letter, Vicksburg National Military Park Archives, Vicksburg MS.

[14] Ibid.

others, Clack responded that one should not do so. "Live according to the Golden Rule if you want to live right and happy," he suggested. Finally, he asked Amy to tell "John" that he would like to have him join their company if he comes into the service. In a postscript, Clack asked his sister to tell "Pappa" that he had been laid up for four days at the Stout home after his hospital stay; his "jaw swelled up over my eye and pained me a great deal." He was at present, however, completely recovered.[15]

"Today [4 March] ends Abraham Lincoln's reign of two years," Calvin Smith of the 31st Tennessee wrote in his daily journal entry. "Two more years to reign as the great dictator, the first of many presidents that has graced the chair of Washington City." Smith supposed that, even though Lincoln had come in like a lion, he was destined to leave office with his "courage low." The enemy, he noted, had done some minor damage the previous day with their random artillery fire across the river into Vicksburg, but some well-placed projectiles from the fearsome water batteries encouraged the Yankee gunners to attend to other duties. As was their want with a new day, however, they had commenced to their mischief. Repeated Confederate rounds into their positions sent them scurrying off again.[16]

"The boys caught some raccoons today," Smith noted, so for some soldiers, rations were augmented with fresh meat. Smith's company was called out on picket during the morning, and would be posted two days and nights. On this date, the prisoners taken on the ironclad *Indianola* were marched by, leading Smith to suppose that the Confederates were now in control of the Mississippi from Vicksburg to a point below Port Hudson, 250 miles away. The growing Confederate navy now consisted of the *Queen of the West*, which Smith indicated was referred to as the *Queen of the South*, and the *Webb*. Other transports and steamers flying the stars and bars of the Confederacy numbered nearly 100, he noted, and were again free to use the waters of the Big Black, Red, and "Washitaw" [Ouachita] Rivers.[17]

At the Mint Springs camps, Lieutenant Earnest of the 79th (60th) Tennessee recorded on 4 March that he was able to do very little since he was

---

[15] Ibid.

[16] Smith, *A Smith in Service*, 39.

[17] Ibid. The Big Black River, emptying into the Mississippi at Grand Gulf, continued to be a major supply artery for the garrison around Vicksburg, with transports steaming up it to unload their provisions for the short over-land journey to the city. The prisoners were probably deserters since Carson indicated in his article the crew of the *Indianola* were taken to Port Hudson. Carson, "Capture of the *Indianola*," vol. 32, no. 8, p. 382

feeling unwell. "Decidedly bilious and very low spirited," was his self-diagnosis, "with an entire aversion to anything eatable except such things as are acid."[18]

Up the railroad line and only a few miles from entering East Tennessee, John Thomas Moffitt of Lynch's Battery indicated that he left Dalton with his friends at 5 p.m. on 4 March. By 10 a.m. on 5 March, they had arrived in Athens, Tennessee, where they laid over until seven the next morning, spending the night at the home of the Bridges, old friends from the peaceful times.[19]

Work continued in the new camps on 5 March outside Warrenton, according to Stamper of the 43rd Tennessee, with ditches built around the base of their tents to drain off abundant spring rainwater. This necessity was taught to them by the torrents rushing through their beds in the dead of night. The soldiers also spent their time cleaning up the debris and clutter attendant with setting up a new military camp.[20]

Finally back in his native valleys between the Cumberland and Great Smoky Mountain ranges, Moffitt of Lynch's Light Artillery Company noted that he was early the next morning aboard the express train bound for Knoxville from Athens. His baggage had been sent on with Colonel Andrew Jackson, who was also on his way to Knoxville. In Athens, Moffitt had met with Captain J. M. Carmack of the Conscript Camp, who gave him a letter authorizing permission to collect conscripts for Lynch's Battery. Moffitt's travels seemed to be progressing nicely until his train ran off the tracks within a few miles of Knoxville. Though the delay was longer than he would have liked, he was not injured and was soon on his way along the East Tennessee and Georgia railroad. "At 3 o'clock," he wrote, "I put on my [sergeant's] stripes and called to see Colonel Blake, commander of the Conscript Camp." Unlike his first recruiting trip home, however, Moffitt was told that prospects for replacements just then were "gloomy." The willing conscripts had just about been tapped out. The New Market artilleryman's last effort of the day with no bearing on military matters was to send a telegraph to wife, Sallie, asking her to meet him at the New Market depot some thirty miles east of Knoxville.[21]

Dealing with Deserters, Part II. Back in the Vicksburg camps, the issue of dealing with deserters was entering a terrible new phase. With a lot of time on their hands, the men in both lines were tiring of the duty. Some left for home as soon as darkness fell; others walked (or rowed) over to the enemy pickets and

---

[18] Northen, *All Right, Let Them Come*, 64.
[19] Moffitt, "Diary," 7.
[20] Stamper, "Travels of the 43rd Tennessee," 40.
[21] Moffitt, "Diary," 7.

surrendered. On 6 March, orders from Pemberton sought to fix the problem by using firing squads, with a number of executions being carried out in the different divisions.

Stamper of the 43rd Tennessee stated that the executions in Reynolds's Brigade occurred around 12 noon when the half of his regiment not on picket. The 3rd Tennessee and 59th Tennessee were required to witness a soldier from their brigade being shot for desertion. "At about two o'clock, the convict arrived in his shroud riding on his coffin," Stamper wrote. "A picture of death was on his countenance. Upon his arrival, a deadly silence reigned all through the [Stevenson's] Division." Within a minute after being tied to a post, the condemned man was shot "dead, dead, dead." "This was a solemn occasion," for the man "was a deserter from our army, and had joined the enemy and had been taken prisoner." Stamper observed philosophically: "we see thus that examples must be made for the good of others."[22]

Benjamin C. Giddens of the 3rd Tennessee also commented on the executions, although he indicated that he witnessed two soldiers shot instead of one. "I saw a man shot for deserting O what a horrible way to die," he reported. "I never want to witness such a sight as long as I live. There were about 6 thousand soldiers present." He stated that the men he saw shot were taken prisoners aboard the *Indianola*.[23]

In Vaughn's Brigade, Captain William A. Wash of the 79th (60th) Tennessee also wrote about two soldiers who died by firing squad the same day in General Martin Luther Smith's Division on the northern end of the lines. "They met their fates like martyrs and said it was just." Their offense, according to Wash, was mutiny.[24] Allen Wash's friend James Earnest, also of the 79th (60th) Tennessee, reported that the deserter executed in front of their brigade was Private Thomas Graham of the 1st Louisiana Heavy Artillery. "Refusing a blind-fold," Earnest wrote, "Graham made a little speech to those soldiers close

---

[22] Stamper, "Travels of the 43rd Tennessee," 40.

[23] Benjamin C. Giddens to Melinda ("Linda") Giddens, 6 March 1863, Giddens Letters. These deserters had the misfortune of being picked up by the big Yankee ironclad off the riverbank as it steamed down the Mississippi. One can imagin their horror at being pulled from the water by their ex-comrades aboard the *Webb* and *Queen of the West* as the *Indianola* was sinking.

[24] William A. Wash, *Camp, Field and Prison Life: Containing Sketches of Service in the South: and the Experience, Incidents and Observations Connected with Almost Two Years Imprisonment at Johnson's Island, Ohio, Where All Confederate Officers were Confined* (St. Louis MO: Southwestern Book and Publishing Co., 1870) 25.

enough to hear, tipped his cap, and announced he was ready."[25] The bodies of
the men executed on 6 March are buried in the Confederate Section of Cedar
Hill Cemetery in Vicksburg, identified only by regiment, date, and as
"Unknown" soldiers.

"We see a very hard time," Giddens wrote, addressing the rations they
received, "for we get but little to eat." He told his wife, Linda, that he was
willing to live on bread if necessary, "if I can get nothing else." He also
complained about the bad water. "Shor is lots of sickness in the army," Giddens
indicated, "but the authoritys of this place are trying to get us some bacon." If
such a happy occurrence resulted, he wrote, "it will be a good idea." He asked
Linda to continue to address her correspondence to him "in care of Captain
[John W.] Fender, 3rd Regt. of Tenn. Vols."[26]

Homecoming for Sergeant Moffitt. Moffitt of Lynch's Battery, home to
gather conscripted replacements for his unit back in Vicksburg, was subject to
none of these unhappy and tragic lessons. He instead was nearly home and
spent the night in Knoxville with an acquaintance, George Parrott. He had his
supper with H. Ault, and there met a Mr. Baker and "a lady from Fla." Moffitt
also had the opportunity of meeting Colonel Blake's wife, whom he adjudged to
be "a fine looking woman, pleasant and agreeable." On the morning of 6 March,
he finally arrived home at New Market, where "Papa was greatly surprised to
see me, as were all the family." Moffitt went to the depot that evening in the
family buggy where he met his "darling, blue-eyed pet," whose love for him
brought her out on this dark and rainy day. His wife had apparently taken the
train down from her parents' home in Greeneville. "At home with those I love!"
Moffitt exclaimed. "The thought is glorious. Friends and kindred met me with a
smile—the joys of heaven are mine. I thank thee, O God!"[27]

The left wing of the 43rd Tennessee went out on picket 7 March along the
levee to keep an eye on the Yankees on the Louisiana shore across from the
Confederate works near Warrenton, according to Stamper. This wing was in
relief of the right.[28]

On the upper lines around the Mint Springs Bayou, Private William G.
Morton, 79th (60th) Tennessee, Vaughn's Brigade, wrote a letter on 7 March to
his cousin May McClain. "We are still encamped near the river there has been a
fight expected here ever since I have been here but there has been no fighting."

---

[25] Northen, *All Right, Let Them Come*, 65.
[26] Giddens to Giddens, 6 March 1863.
[27] Moffitt, "Diary," 41.
[28] Stamper, "Travels of the 43rd Tennessee," 41.

He reported, however, that the heavy guns had resumed their work just the night before, "yet there had been more than a week that there has been no cannonading." He remarked that the firing continued to be heavy in volume, though its purpose and results were unknown. "The yankees still remain in sight of us," he pointed out, and two of their massive camps across the river on the peninsula were visible from the high ground near Vaughn's camps at the base of Fort Hill. "We can see either one plain." Two gunboats, he reported, had run by here since the 79th (60th) Tennessee had arrived, and "we succeeded in capturing one and disstroying the other."[29]

"Times here are tolerable hard, but not much worse than is common in the army," Morton reported. "Those who had not been in the army long think it a hard way of living but if they had been in the army since the beginning of the war, they would have found out the army then was not like being home." He informed his May that his health was still good, and "there is nothing more pleasant than health while so far away from home." He asked her to address his mail to him at "Vicksburg, Mississippi, Co. G, 79th Tennessee Volunteers." He also begged his cousin to tell all the girls "howdy," but more importantly, "the right one you must not forget to tell her my love and best respects."[30]

Colonel Rowan Gets a Letter from Home. From Sweetwater, Monroe County, the wife of Colonel John A. Rowan, commander of the 80th (62nd) Tennessee, wrote a letter to her husband informing him that everyone was well and that she had not intended to write him again "untill I saw you." But a member of his regiment had returned to Sweetwater with Rowan's letter, which caused her to realize that "as you did not say much about comeing home I thought perhaps you thought it doubtful about getting a chance to come soon." Though she told him that she was still hoping for the best, the newspapers told her that the "Feds are receiving reinforcements," and she feared that "the prospects of an engagement will prevent you from comeing soon." From the Memphis *Appeal*, which was published in exile since the fall of the city on 6 June 1862, she learned things that "she would normally not get" concerning war matters from the West. As for conditions at home, Mrs. Rowan reported the sad news that "brother franks wife," who had not recovered from the birth of her child, was not expected to live; however, "the babe is harty nearly two weeks old," though it was suffering with "nursing soar mouth." Her own family's health was

---

[29] William G. Morton to May McClain, 7 March 1863, William Harr and William G. Morton Letters, Old Courthouse Museum Archives, Vicksburg MS. Hereafter cited as Harr-Morton Letters.
[30] Ibid.

"tolerable," though her mother had been sick. John Hightower, one of Rowan's men who had been cashiered from his regiment, was now home—"just landed"—and had made the folks in their neighborhood very happy to hear about the boys in Vicksburg. He asked Mrs. Rowan to pass the word through the colonel to his brother Thomas Hightower that "his health is not any better than when he left camps." (Whether Hightower, in a face-saving manner, was indicating that he was discharged for medical reasons is not clear.) "Mollie rec'd her music & is dancing around like a top," Mrs. Rowan mused, "though she is so hoarse she can't make much noise she sends many thanks for it."[31]

The weather in East Tennessee was also very dreary, according to the Rowan's wife. "It is raining yet we have more rain than I ever saw this time of the year," she wrote. "The creek has been up so for 3 or 4 weeks," she noted, "tom could not cross half the time to haul wood." She closed her letter by thanking her husband for a present he had sent her. "Many thanks dearest for my new pipe," she said: "the girls accuse me of smokeing just to show my new pipe well if I do there is nothing wrong in being proud of as nice a present as that *so I say*."[32]

The Boys Draw Bacon. The next day, 8 March, Stamper of the 43rd Tennessee wrote about a Sunday worship service he probably never forgot. Preaching commenced at the usual time, 10 a.m., but before the parson could complete reading his text, the men heard an Enfield musket fired nearby, and in a minute or two, Stamper declared, "here came a nice fat buck bounding over the hill, right towards where we were seated." Instantly, "the whole crowd was engaged in looking after the fugitive making its way through one camp, dodging first to one side and then the other, trying to evade the boys who were trying to get it." The excitement rendered the delivery of chaplain's message futile. After a short while, the deer had darted through all the camps, and through considerable random gunfire, before it dashed into its natural habitat of "creeks, ponds, hills and hollers," where it safely vanished from sight. Many of the boys continued to run after the animal, anticipating the change of pace venison would make to their pitiful rations, but it was of no use. The buck, this time, had made good its escape.[33]

Disappointed though they were at not getting the deer, the boys found that a good meal was waiting for them at the commissary. "It would be well to

---

[31] Mrs. John Rowan to Col. John A. Rowan, 7 March 1863, in *Civil War Records*, 2: 200.

[32] Ibid.

[33] Stamper, "Travels of the 43rd Tennessee," 41–42.

say here we drew bacon," Stamper reported, "and not necessary to say we were pleased to see it." He reported that the army had been subject to tough, ropey "blue" beef for a month or so, and for the last week or two they had not even had any of that. Needless to say, Stamper affirmed, "there was a great do over 'hog.'" Due to its scarcity and certainly personal preference, bacon was the meat of choice for most Confederate soldiers around Vicksburg, especially when put up against the poor quality evident in the government issue of "cow." On the morning of 9 March, Stamper indicated that his Company F, 43rd Tennessee, was sent to the river lines on picket.[34]

More Letters from Home. Lieutenant Smith of the 31st Tennessee indicated the good news for him on 9 March was the delivery of a letter from home, brought back by Private Thomas Lee, who had been on furlough in Hawkins County. Though most of his family and acquaintances were in good health, Smith was somewhat distressed to learn that his mother was ill and his Grandfather Grigsby was "at the point of death." Smith dispatched Privates John Reynolds and Will Chesnutt to the camps of the 79th (60th) Tennessee on the upper lines where some provisions, also brought back by Lee, waited. These supplies would be gladly received, Smith believed, since rations recently had been light and of poor quality. Their rations consisted of low-quality beef, coarse corn, bread, rice, sugar, and molasses.[35]

The day of 10 March evolved into one shrouded with constant heavy drizzle that muddied and slimed up the camps' fields where the soldiers were huddled chilled and drenched around smoking fires. Conditions caused Stamper of the 43rd Tennessee to conclude that the weather gave "anyone in camp the blues." One of the few distributions the boys received put some life and spirit back in them occurred at 3 o'clock, according to Stamper, "when the Captain-of-the-Day began to pay off the regiment."[36] Thus, every private soldier in the camp received his monthly allowance of $11 from the Confederate government.

In an adjoining camp belonging to the 59th Tennessee, Private William Harr wrote a letter on this date to his cousin May McClain. During the Vicksburg campaign, she also corresponded with Private William G. Morton of the 79th (60th) Tennessee, in Vaughn's camps. The Monroe County general's brigade was between seven to ten miles away from Camp Reynolds. Harr reported that no fighting was occurring that day, though there had been some cannonading the day before. "We have but little to eat," he said, adding, "we

---

[34] Ibid.

[35] Smith, *A Smith in Service*, 39.

[36] Stamper, "Travels of the 43rd Tennessee," 42.

have to buy meat and pay 50 & 60 cts. per pound for pork." There had been a case of small pox diagnosed in the brigade, but he was in good health, "considering the country." As did many of his fellow soldiers, Harr hoped that soon they might be headed back for duty in Tennessee. Also echoing the sentiments of many others, he hoped, "I would rather we could have peace, but I fear it will be some time before peace is made." Despite his assertion earlier in the letter that his health was good, a few lines later he indicated, "I will stay in the company but do no duty atall but cant get a discharge." Harr's letter also contained his admission that he had read two of May's letters out of sequence, which led to the resulting confusion in his replies to "old Sullivan [County]." He concluded by telling May McClain he had sent cousin May Morton a letter home by H. J. Hicks. (It was becoming evident much of the mail delivered back home by the East Tennessee Confederate soldiers at Vicksburg was being hand-carried by friends and officers going home.) Harr also wanted messages delivered to various concerned folks at home regarding the "tolerable health" of cousin William "Billie" Morton.[37]

On the morning of 11 March, Companies F, C, K, and G of Isaac Stamper's 43rd Tennessee were called to picket duty to "the levee near Warrenton." As they marched to their familiar posts, Stamper studied the heavens and concluded that the weather would hold off while on duty. Once spaced along the levee after the posts were set, Stamper reported, "we had nothing to do but sleep, eat and play." Still on picket duty the next day, Stamper of the 43rd Tennessee wrote, "we passed it the same way [as the day before]." The weather continued "fine" and all was quiet.[38] This assignment during these days was often restful and routine, and as long as one of the four designated pickets kept the watch, the rest of the guard were considered "off duty." They entertained themselves as they pleased.

Private Benjamin C. Giddens of the 3rd Tennessee wrote a lengthy letter, with an attached note to his wife, Malinda, on 11 March to his father back in McMinn County. To his wife, Giddens hoped first and foremost that good health was hers and their children's. He boasted of the quantity of his letter writing, noting his father's report that she had received three letters from Giddens in one day. He promised that several more "were on the road." "I have

---

[37] William Harr to May McClain, 10 March 1863, Harr-Morton Letters.
[38] Stamper, "Travels of the 43rd Tennessee," 42.

received three letters from you," he told her, "and I have read them so often that I have nearly got them by heart."[39]

"Our generals are determined to hold Vicksburg," Giddens continued, indicating that many men were positioned around the city. He had heard one colonel say, "we have fifty thousand men [in the vicinity]." He added that, according to the grapevine telegraph, General Sterling Price's army was within twelve miles of the Vicksburg. Giddens noted that he had acquired a new pair of britches and a new shirt, which would allow him to "go see the girls over about Ephraims."[40] The importance of fresh new clothes would not have been lost on any soldier ever garrisoned at Vicksburg, and Giddens's jest of visiting the "girls over about Ephraims" would probably have not been a mystery to his wife.

Giddens reiterated that East Tennesseans at Vicksburg were "tired of the place," and "I would like to see you all but I don't know when I'll get home." The weather was beginning to get extremely warm, he reported, "and we all dread hot weather." He feared that before long they would have only the dirty tepid river water to drink. "The Mississippians will not let a soldier drink water out of their wells or cisterns," he complained. In closing, he shared the news that "the Raper's boys were all well," and that he remained her "husband in love and affection," challenging his wife to write him often, while promising he would continue to write her weekly.[41]

Giddens addressed the remainder of the letter to his father, stating that he and his brother James had read a recent letter from the family, which had encouraged them both. He recorded that James was still sick, though improving, and that he had twice been to see him since James went to recuperate at the Ferguson's home, three miles from camp. "He is on the mend," Giddens stated, "but his health is very unsteady and I do not wish to uneasy you, but it is very evident that James cannot stand the service." Giddens suggested that his father "use his influence" to get James to resign his office, since "if he [James] stays in service and is exposed a few more times he will die." Fortunately, however, James was at a "good house, and has good attention."[42]

"Everything is quiet," Giddens told his father, "and what the Yanks are doing I cannot tell." Once again, showing the East Tennessee Confederate soldier's dichotomous attitude in regard to service at Vicksburg, Giddens stated,

---

[39] Benjamin C. Giddens to his father Riley A. Giddens, Sr., 11 March 1863, Giddens Letters.
[40] Ibid.
[41] Ibid.
[42] Ibid.

"I don't believe [the Federals] will attack this place for it is strongly fortified and we are still fortifying and planting cannons of the largest calebra." The opening fight for the city, he felt, would occur at Port Hudson. Providing a geography lesson, Giddens told his father that Port Hudson was located at the mouth of the Red River, "also a strongly fortified place." The grapevine telegraph was circulating the news that 20,000 Confederates defended Port Hudson, and that "[General Nathaniel] Banks has concentrated at Baton Rush [Rouge] for the purpose of attacking [the place]." Giddens predicted, "if we can hold Vicksburg, Port Hudson, Charleston and Talluhoma, ...I think the north will give up all hopeless subjugation against us." Giddens professed his confidence in General "Lea" in Virginia, and by May, he surmised, "we will know if we are to have a long or short war."[43]

"We are living some better than we did some days ago," Giddens indicated to his father, lamenting the fact many of the boys were disturbing private property around the vicinity of Vicksburg and Warrenton. Since the army was unable to provide sustenance, as it should, he stated that the "killing of hogs and sheep [are a result] of the fact some of our army has drawn no rations for days." Consistent with the patriotism of most of the East Tennessee soldiers who left writings during most of the campaign, Giddens affirmed that "hard living and sacrifice shall not divert us from our duty."[44]

The confidence in the security of Fortress Vicksburg, whether well founded or bravado, continued in the 13 March writings of soldiers. Colonel Newton J. Lillard, commander of the 3rd Tennessee, wrote his wife that it would take a "tremendous force" for the Yankees to accomplish their ends in subjugating Vicksburg, since the city was well fortified. "If we are provisioned we can hold out for a long time," Lillard predicted.[45]

Meanwhile, Stamper, coming in from picket, found "plenty of hog meat cooked" in the camps of the 43rd Tennessee. "While on picket," he stated, "I gathered my haversack full of wild salad which I put in with the meat, making quite a delicious meal." The boys ate well on this day at least, which led Stamper to surmise, "if we could have such a good meal every day, 'we could live and do well.'"[46]

---

[43] Ibid. Tullahoma, Tennessee, was the location of Bragg's Confederate Army of Tennessee, which was still in winter camps facing Rosecrans's Army of the Cumberland wintering in Murfreesboro.
[44] Ibid.
[45] Newton J. Lillard to his wife, 13 March 1863, Newton J. Lillard Papers.
[46] Stamper, "Travels of the 43rd Tennessee," 42.

The East Tennessee Confederate soldier's life was reduced by now to the basic needs of survival, with an adequate meal during this campaign equal to any other reward a man could envision, perhaps secondary only to the receipt of a letter from back home. Alfred Bowman of the 79th (60th) Tennessee indicated in a letter also dated 13 March that he was enjoying good health at present, but that his brother Richard's health was only "tolerable." Like many Confederate soldiers at Vicksburg, Bowman believed that the Federals would not make much of a fight at there in the days ahead because they knew that the city was unconquerable. He referred to the two Union gunboats that passed Vicksburg recently, stating that the boys had managed to capture them both. "Ben Garst was on the *Queen of the West* when they taken the *Indianola*," Bowman reported. "He says they had very hot work for a few minutes." Bowman believed that the Confederates could capture all the Yankee boats, "if they don't do better."[47]

"The prospect of peace is very good at this time," Bowman continued. He seemed to be encouraging himself and those back home who would read his letter by predicting, "we will get home by harvest." His bad news concerned his brother Richard, whom he had predicted in his previous letter would be home on discharge most any day. Now, Alfred reported, "he had been assigned over to the hospital to wait on the sick." Such assignments increased the danger of contacting any number of infectious maladies concentrated in such close and filthy confines; duty there was to be avoided at all costs. "Colonel [Nathan] Gregg and Major [James] Rhea told him to not gow to the hospital," Alfred noted, "[since] they would get him a discharge." He hoped that the folks would tell his children and his wife, Martha, that he loved them, and that they would tell Hanah Johnson that Wash was well. He reminded them that he had been waiting for a letter from them "for a long time."[48]

Stamper of the 43rd Tennessee, on 14 March, wrote in his diary that he and some of the boys went into Vicksburg and "bought a show" of costumes and scenery, which cost him and his partners "one hundred and fifty dollars." Diversion for the Vicksburg soldiers was anywhere they could find it. The day proved rainy and damp, according to Stamper, and "there was but little to do." The next day, beautiful weather had returned. He and his fellow actors tried out their new production on this "Ides of March," taking in about forty dollars in admissions. "The boys were all pleased with our scenery," he indicated in his

---

[47] Alfred Bowman to "Father and Mother", 13 March 1863, Bowman Family Papers.
[48] Ibid.

journal. By evening, the regiment devoted its time to preparing for and standing inspection.[49]

"[We were] four miles below camp on picket," Smith of the 31st Tennessee wrote on 16 March. He recorded that Thomas Lee came down to Camp Reynolds and brought him some butter, a towel, and some sewing thread from his mother-in-law, as well as some biscuits, cake, socks and bread he calculated to be eighteen days old, and though moldy, still good. Smith spent some time in the journal entry discussing the strategy of the two belligerent armies at Vicksburg. His awareness of his enemy's composition was impressive. He confirmed that Admiral David Porter had twenty-nine boats of every description above Vicksburg, carrying nearly 200 cannons. He believed that Porter wanted to approach the back of city through the Yazoo Pass, but he knew that Snyder's and Haynes' Bluff were well defended, and predicted that the Yankees' efforts would be thwarted at that quarter. "The Yankies know very little of the geography of the surrounding country of Vicksburg," Smith indicated, "and if we had provisions here, 20,000 men could hold this place against 100,000 Yankies one month,"[50] which, as it turned out a month and a half later, was true.

Smith did not believe that the Yankees would be foolish enough to attempt a siege, nor did he think that they could be successful in trying to land a force along the waterfront. If they did, Smith predicted that the fearsome water batteries would sink their fine fleet, causing Grant to abandon the campaign for Vicksburg altogether. "There seems to be much dissatisfaction in the mind of the Yankies," Smith wrote, "who are tired of war and are deserting every day and trying to get home." But the Northerners were not the only ones plagued by desertions. Smith noted that three Confederate deserters had been shot on 6 March, but he had not witnessed the executions. While on picket, Smith learned that Colonel Gillespie's 43rd Tennessee and Colonel Lillard's 3rd Tennessee had been ordered to Vicksburg for the next couple of days, but did not know why.[51] Most likely, these regiments were moved in response to the

---

[49] Stamper, "Travels of the 43rd Tennessee," 42.

[50] Smith, *A Smith in Service*, 39.

[51] Ibid. There may have been other reasons for the discontent in the Federal ranks. Referring to the Emancipation Proclamation issued by Lincoln on 1 January 1863, Sgt. Theodore Kellogg of the 13th Illinois Infantry in Sherman's XV Corps remarked, "President Lincoln's proclamation is not very well endured by the [Union] army here. You will hardly find one [federal] soldier in ten who says free the negroes. They rather say keep them slaves at any cost…. We did not come to free slaves and we will not do it. And just on account of the negro question, over 500 men have deserted this army in the

increasing activity of the enemy's naval and infantry around Vicksburg, where a landing was always anticipated.

Stamper of the 43rd Tennessee stated that he that put on his show again, though half the regiment was gone on picket duty. During the evening of the 17 March, "Parson [William H.] Crofford [Crawford] of Pitts' regiment [the 81st (61st) Tennessee] preached to the 31st and 43rd regiments." Stamper described the sermon as "noble" and to "good effect." 18 March developed into an extremely warm day, though with the heat came indications of more rain. Everything was quiet, Stamper wrote, until around 10 p.m., when "one of our batteries threw a few shells over on the yankees." All night, he reported, "one of our guns played on the canal" where Grant's men were working feverishly on the peninsula across the river from Warrenton, though with little success.[52]

Earnest of the 79th (60th) Tennessee recorded on 18 March that Vaughn's Brigade "was occupied with moving our encampment further up into the woods." He remarked that most of the men constructed a nice cabin, complete with bunks, thereby "improving our circumstances considerably."[53] By the end of the month, the move would have disastrous consequences for some of the men in his regiment.

"I heard the report of 20 cannon about Vicksburg," Smith of the 31st Tennessee recorded in his diary. "At 10 o'clock [on 17 March] last night three more of large size made a loud rumbling noise like heavy thunder." At the time, Smith did not know what caused the noise. After relief pickets replaced Smith and his company, they returned to camp, where he learned that the firing was a reaction to the Yankees working on their canal on the opposite side of the river. Lanterns flickered after dark through the newly-leaved trees, leading the officers to suspect the boys in blue were placing a battery there, so the shells were thrown at them, "screaming and howling and scaring them off." Based on his own experience, Smith noted that "shells weighing 100 pounds each [were] a fearful visitor."[54]

Private Richard Bowman of the 79th (60th) Tennessee sent news on 18 March to his father stating that he was "well as common," but he was "sorrow" to report his brother Alfred was sick with a fever and getting "worse all the time." Doctors had predicted that Alfred "[would] have a hard spell of it."

last fifteen days." Theodore Kellogg to Sarah Eastman Draper, 25 January 1863, Theodore Kellogg Letters, unknown private collection. Kellogg was from Chicago and did not use the term "negro"; it has been substituted for the racial slur.

[52] Stamper, "Travels of the 43rd Tennessee," 43.

[53] Northen, *All Right, Let Them Come*, 69–70.

[54] Smith, *A Smith in Service*, 39.

Richard was despondent over a recent letter to Alfred informing him of the death of one of his children, and Richard thought that "it would have been best for [Alfred] if he had not heard of it till he got well."[55] Alfred had small pox and would not survive the month.[56] He was buried at an undisclosed spot in the City Cemetery, not too far from Vaughn's camps. Because the friends of men who died of small pox did not attend to them, the names of these men often would not be recorded properly by those assigned to those duties at the Pest House, where "We are not expecting a fight at this time," Richard suggested. "The yanks are all leaving and I think it is best thing they can do [since] they tried this place one time and we whipped them so bad."[57] His conclusion concerning their departure was based on inaccurate information.

Richard Bowman tried to hold out hope for his parents concerning his discharge, stating that others who had failed to gain permission on their first submission were often successful in later attempts. Meanwhile, he encouraged his father to continue as best he could with the farming, hoping that he might be home soon to help out. The corn had already been out for some days in Mississippi, he reported, and the little stalks already had three or four blades on them. This observation led him to write about their rations. "We get corn bread, molasses, rice and sugar," Bowman noted. They also received some bacon, "which is about half spoilt." The beef they got was so poor, he testified, that when it was boiled, "it [made] a good glue." Bowman asked about A. J. Klepper, who had had a fever "awfully bad." Bowman noted that when Klepper had been with the company and heard the cannon firing, he told the boys that he would shortly be "bedfast" in one of the miserable Vicksburg hospitals if he did not get home soon. "I am sorrow to hear they have took Jasper Cristy away," Bowman indicated, since Cristy was the "only gunsmith they was about there [in Jonesborough]." He affirmed that he had heard about his father and others making "three thousand rails" over the summer, and he suggested that they put out a large corn crop with the spring. Prices were good for speculators. "Flour is worth $130 a barrel," he wrote, "and bacon is selling one dollar a pound." In closing, Bowman complained that the "musketeers getting very numerous." Other East Tennesseans continued to disparage the pests as the warm weather intensified. Echoing Giddens' letter of the 12 March, Bowman

---

[55] Richard Bowman to his father, 18 March 1863, Bowman Family Papers.

[56] Alfred died on 29 March. 60th Tennessee, *Compiled Service Records*. Small pox victims were usually buried quickly to avoid spreading the disease. Their clothing was either buried on them or taken off their bodies and then burned. Once hot weather set in, soldiers dying in camps or hospitals were by necessity buried immediately.

[57] R. Bowman to his father, 18 March 1863.

predicted, "in a little time we will have no running water here." As it was, he concluded "the water [was] getting bad." He hoped that his parents would forgive all his "mistakes and bad writing" in the letter, and he begged them to write him soon "and sooner."[58]

One of the water batteries' cannon continued banging away on the Yankees at work digging their canal on the peninsula across the river from Warrenton, Stamper wrote on 19 March. The 43rd Tennessee came in from picket, where they probably had observed the good work of the enormous siege gun at the South Fort flinging its huge projectiles across the Mississippi.[59]

Jimmy Caldwell of the 59th Tennessee wrote Carrie Stakely informing her that he had received her "very kind but unfinished" letter via his company First Sergeant Edward P. Clark. Caldwell was afraid that she was "going to play quits" in her writing to him. The company had received a contingent of conscripts during the week, he reported, including Robert McClung, John McSpadden, "one of Mr. DeBrusk's sons," and two others. Dr. John W. Stratton had joined one of the 59th Tennessee's other Madisonville companies, of which there were three, under Captain Josiah Wright. Caldwell also reported that another Madisonville native in the brigade, Lieutenant William H. Rudd, had been made captain of Company H, in Vaughn's old 3rd Tennessee, since its captain, Joseph Marr, had resigned. "I think [Rudd] deserves the position," Caldwell noted, "for he has been a good and faithful soldier throughout the war."[60]

Caldwell wrote that he had received from Carrie's sister Mary "three or four letters" in the past four days, "but as I am in the wars, she will have to wait my own turn, for answering them." As for war news, Caldwell reported that some considerable skirmishing on their end of the line between the opposing artillery near Warrenton had occurred, "resulting in our favor generally." He predicted that by the time Carrie received this letter, she would have heard about the "glorious victory at Port Hudson." Caldwell was alluding to the "great naval battle" that had transpired that morning down the river, and he stated, "we had not heard [about] it yet except the long and loud rumbling noise which comes up the river for near half an hour."[61]

It was said "to have been an engagement with the *Monongahela* [actually the *Albatross*] and *Hartford* by our batteries at the Big Black" on the bluffs at

---

[58] Ibid.
[59] Stamper, "Travels of the 43rd Tennessee," 43.
[60] Jim Caldwell to Carrie Stakely, 19 March 1863, Hall-Stakely Papers.
[61] Ibid.

Grand Gulf, he supposed, "with our batteries and our boats the *Webb* and *Queen of the West.*" In actuality, these Confederate vessels were not involved in the brief clash that was a result of Farragut's probe of the resistance his fleet might face if they approached Vicksburg from the south. With the successes the Confederates had had capturing Union warships, Caldwell believed that if the small Southern fleet had captured any more, "we will have a rite formidable fleet on the Miss." A Confederate siege piece near their camps, he added, threw shells night and day into the midst of the impressed slaves and their liberators across the river working on Grant's canal being dug across the base of the DeSoto Peninsula as a bypass route of the Vicksburg batteries. "I think the shells are doing some good," he thought, "as [the yankees] like to stand behind trees very well lately, and the negroes won't 'face the music' [except] at the point of a bayonet."[62] Much of the actual physical labor, then, was not being done by Grant's men but by slaves who had exchanged one kind of bondage for another.

The boys were eating well at the time, Caldwell noted happily, getting "meal, pork, rice, sugar and molasses, beans or peas and fruit everyday if we want them, and coffee for breakfast and supper." Caldwell was fearful, however, that a box of provisions Carrie had sent would not arrive. He concluded his letter the next day by noting that he had learned nothing new about the supposed naval battle down the way. He informed Carrie that the regiment remained in "tolerably good health." "Colonel" Isbill, he wrote, had reported to the regiment escorting his substitute, an option to those wealthy enough to employ when conscripted, though Caldwell believed that this man would not be "received, "compelling Isbill into the service himself.[63]

"I am always glad to hear of boats passing," Lieutenant Calvin Smith of the 31st Tennessee declared on 19 March. "I love to hear the big cannons." Early that day they had heard a heavy cannonade down around Grand Gulf, and since that time word had spread that the Union tars had anchored two of their

---

[62] Ibid. Carter L. Stevenson corrected the misconception concerning the name of the vessel misidentified as the *Monongahela*. It was in fact the *Albatross*. Report of Gen. Carter L. Stevenson, 25 March 1863, *Official Records*, ser. 1, vol. 24, pt. 1, p. 480. Kellogg, in his letter home to his fiancé in Chicago, indicated these "freedmen" employed in this enterprise were "a nuisance to [the Yankee soldiers]," and the practice of employing them was ultimately discontinued. Theodore Kellogg to Sarah Eastman Draper, 28 January 1863, Kellogg Letters.

[63] Ibid. The only "Isbill" in Company E was "William," who, according to the service records, was a private.

gunboats below Warrenton. Smith was glad to know that he and the Southern army at last "had something to do."[64]

At 9 a.m. on 20 March, the 43rd Tennessee stood inspection. That evening, the regimental chaplain, Archibald Brooks, held a prayer meeting in camp, and after a short exhortation, sinners were called to the "mourners" bench to receive the prayers of the saved. Stamper indicated that six soldiers answered the altar call. "This made me happy," he reported, "to see a humble soldier for his country enlisting for the Cause of the Lord." Later that evening, Stamper noted that the lone Confederate siege gun at South Fort opened up again across river in the direction of the canal work, "and this was kept up all night at intervals of one-half hour."[65]

Benjamin Giddens of the 3rd Tennessee reported in a 20 March letter to his wife that his health had gotten in a bad way. "I have got the chills and fever and can scarcely stand on my feet," he wrote. Though he was in no "misery," the night before he had caught a bad "shake," which left his shirt all wet the following morning "as though he had been dipped in the river." Giddens believed that he had suffered a recurrence of "the ague," he told his wife, though the doctors told him that he was in no real danger and was only suffering from the same chills he had previously experienced. Giddens indicated that he was going out to stay in a private house, just as his brother had done when he was sick, and intended on remaining there until he felt better. His overriding fear was that he would retain the malarial chills all summer. The regimental surgeon had given Giddens the usual quinine to combat his symptoms. Giddens said the last time he had heard from his brother Jim, he had been out "squirrel hunting." Not only had Jim not resigned his office as brother Ben had predicted; he appeared to be getting stronger and healthier. "I expect he will be back with the company in a few days," Giddens continued, "as he is getting stout."[66]

As for conditions around Vicksburg, Giddens believed, "there will be a fight above Vicksburg as the Yanky gunboats and transports are gone up the river."[67] Grant had for the better part of the month of March dispatched a third initiative in addition to the Lake Providence and peninsula projects. This third project proceeded from the north along the Yazoo River via Steele's Bayou.

[64] Smith, *A Smith in Service*, 39–40.
[65] Stamper, "Travels of the 43rd Tennessee," 43.
[66] Benjamin C. Giddens to Melinda ("Linda") Giddens, 20 March 1863, Giddens Letters.
[67] Ibid.

This effort was checked at Fort Pemberton by the Confederate batteries, natural conditions, and obstacles sunk in the Yazoo cutting off the advance of transports and gunboats. Like Grant's other efforts to find easy egress to Vicksburg, this one would also prove a failure. Giddens observed the work the Yankees were doing on their canal, indicating that the 3rd Tennessee was back down near Warrenton after spending some time at the upper works above Vicksburg. The conclusion drawn by Giddens and most Confederate onlookers was that the canal work in the final analysis "[would] do them no good." He noted in closing that he "would like to have some money if you or father could send me some,"[68] perhaps with the expectation that he might need it to pay for private care while he recuperated.

Lieutenant Smith of the 31st Tennessee had much "news" to report from other quarters on 20 March. General Earl Van Dorn was said to have captured 2,600 Federal prisoners on a cavalry raid at Franklin, Tennessee. There was also fighting reported along the Yazoo River to their north, and a Yankee gunboat flotilla had attacked Port Hudson resulting in the defeat of their naval force, the sinking of several boats, and the damaging of Farragut's flagship the *Hartford*. An erroneous report contended that an attempted ground assault had been made, resulting in the capture of 3,000 Union infantrymen. However fanciful some of these stories were, it was obvious Grant was still trying to find a way into the rear of Vicksburg, Smith noted. They were finding it a fight all the way. "They will find it a hard road to travel," Smith suggested, "and difficult to find."[69]

The "Albatross" and "Hartford" Try Fort Warrenton. Sometime around midday on 21 March, Stamper of the 43rd Tennessee wrote his regiment was detailed to picket duty about the works at Warrenton. At four p.m., a couple of gunboats, the *Albatross* and Farragut's flagship the sloop-of-war *Hartford*, came up the river and shot some shells into the fort there. "Our men," Stamper reported, "were soon in the fort quite secure." He found sitting inside the fort while the shells were flying overhead to be an unpleasant experience. Some of the shells occasionally struck the earthen casemate, cutting off the rails of the two railroad irons that were part of the covering breastwork.[70]

---

[68] Ibid.

[69] Smith, *A Smith in Service*, 40.

[70] Stamper, "Travels of the 43rd Tennessee," 43–44. These vessels were the mighty *Hartford*, Farragut's flagship, and the *Albatross*, which had passed the batteries at the southern works along Grand Gulf. Their immediate mission was for Farragut to ascertain the strength of the combined defenses at Warrenton.

Just prior to this bit of testing by Farragut's ships, Lieutenant Smith of the 31st Tennessee also found himself and his men out on picket in the vicinity of the Warrenton levy. Once they got to their observation area, they stacked arms. Adjutant Hawkins proceeded to assign details to patrol their watch territory. Smith had volunteered to lead a squad in place of his captain, and they relieved the previous pickets. They could hear Farragut's demonstration against Port Hudson down the river, as well as the heavy cannonade occurring up on the Yazoo. A few shots rang out from one of the South Fort guns positioned across from the canal, making work on Grant's ditch very uncomfortable. Smith noted that he had heard so much heavy gunfire lately that he almost ignored it.[71]

The men could not, however, ignore Farragut's mighty flagship and its escort gunboat lying just below Warrenton, prompting Smith to remark that the masted vessel, the *Hartford*, looked large and capable of transporting seven or eight hundred men. Her escorting gunboat, he reported, made a dash up to Warrenton and fired one harassing shot at the men working on the fort, then floated back down to where the *Hartford* was anchored. There seemed to be no concern that these Union vessels would try to pass up river toward Vicksburg.[72]

On the other end of the line above Vicksburg, both sides were sending up heavy reinforcements toward the Yazoo, Smith noted. There was every indication that that was the direction where a major battle might erupt in the days ahead. And Smith believed that it would have to be soon since the Mississippi was falling along with its tributaries emptying into it. This would confound Grant's timing should Admiral David Porter run elements of his fleet up to Snyder's Bluff on the Yazoo as support since the warships would soon be land-locked by the ebbing water.[73]

Smith indicated that sometime after midnight on 21 March, the Federals set fire to a wharf boat that lay above Warrenton and turned it loose. The burning contraption lit up the dark night. Smith recalled that the glow of the burning boat was as bright as moonlight, and though he was a mile and a half away, it made an unusual and beautiful sight.[74]

Early the next morning, the *Albatross*, which Smith repeatedly misidentified as the *Monongahela*, was now anchored defiantly opposite Warrenton close to the Louisiana shore. She was a twin-masted deep-sea screw

---

[71] Smith, *A Smith in Service*, 40.
[72] Ibid.
[73] Ibid.
[74] Ibid.

steamer with a battery of seven cannon. At sunrise, her stack belched thick black smoke as she inched cautiously across the channel. From a vantage point near midstream, she opened fire whenever she saw a man move along the Confederate works. After a short while, the *Albatross* passed up river to where the burning barge had been released the night before and anchored out of sight of the men at Fort Warrenton. Suspicious that the enemy was trying to land spies there (or worse, troops), Smith reported that Lieutenant John Neil of the 31st Tennessee and some twenty volunteers of his McMinn County company made their way through the woods skirting the river to check on the intentions of the *Albatross*. The Yankee sailors soon observed them. Whenever they saw Neil's men move about in the tree line, the *Albatross* hurtled a shell in their direction. Bored with striking at gnats with sledgehammers, the gunboat floated down river across from Warrenton, firing her three portside guns as she went. Churning up a great wake as she ranged broadside to the current, the *Albatross* labored in a slow turn to retrace her route and get off broadsides from her starboard battery.[75]

The *Albatross'* consort, the sloop-of-war *Hartford*, moved up the river to help antagonize the gunners and riflemen in Fort Warrenton with her massive eight-gun broadsides, slamming what Smith supposed to be 125-pounds shells into fort's earthen breastworks. Often, the two vessels passed in tandem, firing at the fort in an awe-inspiring display that Smith described as "most terrific and sublimely terrible."[76]

Other Confederate troops from East Tennessee occupying Fort Warrenton during this action were Captain Reuben G. Clark of the 59th Tennessee and his men from Morristown. He described Fort Warrenton as a small dirt structure with walls some twenty feet thick covered with railroad iron lying in the flat near the river. Clark "expected to be attacked by" the *Hartford* "any minute." Standing on the parapet watching the ship "move up under a dark cloud of smoke," he saw the first shell whiz past around 7:15 a.m.: "every fellow [was] to get to his post, both for self-protection and to be ready to fire should the enemy attempt to land." The Confederates were convinced that all the attention coming their way was a result of the enemy's plan land troops in the vicinity of Fort Warrenton. Clark was awestruck with the rapidity and volume of shells pouring from the *Hartford*'s broadsides, and as the great Yankee sloop turned in the river to fire, "it was impossible to count the number of shots" she discharged. The Grainger County officer recalled that he and his

[75] Ibid.
[76] Ibid.

men were almost buried alive by the dirt churned up by the impact of the numerous shells. The bombardment, "was terrific."[77] The crew of the *Albatross* had been ordered to fire at every man who might be trying to repair the bulwarks, while the *Hartford* was to continue pounding the fort. Farragut's object was to drive away the repair workers, Lieutenant Smith of the 31st Tennessee declared, which the renegade Tennessee admiral failed to do. "The enemy's cannon broke several bars of iron in two," Smith noted, "which fell in and filled up the port hole that a 32-pounder was to be fired from." This result, he concluded, prevented the siege piece from delivering much more damage to the two enemy vessels.[78]

Stamper of the 43rd Tennessee wrote that the *Albatross* had been sent to do its worst at Fort Warrenton, but neither the fort nor any Confederate soldier suffered serious injury. The *Albatross* and the *Hartford* then moved up the river near the enemy batteries planted across from Warrenton near the canal where the available Confederate guns could not get the range. There, as Smith had reported, the warships anchored. The right wing of the 43rd Tennessee was brought in off picket where it had had to dodge the warships' shells in the woods, but, Stamper declared, "no harm was done."[79]

With the sunrise on 23 March, the enemy's boats continued their shelling of Warrenton "to no effect." It rained all day, he wrote, "making it very disagreeable in camp." The enemy's relentless barrage caused the earth beneath him and his men to shake constantly, and the stately cypress trees the pickets on the levee used as cover trembled as though rocked by a violent thunderstorm. The hands assigned to conduct repairs after the big shells struck, he observed, soon abandoned that stressful line of work and skedaddled away from the river for all they were worth.[80]

Lieutenant Calvin Smith of the 31st Tennessee reported that men on the exposed levee it also found their duty dangerous, though after a few hours the Hawkins County boys were relieved by a company from the 37th (57th) Georgia, Cumming's Brigade. Smith relayed standing orders to three of the Georgia lieutenants, after which they hustled their men to man the three posts Smith's men had occupied prior to being relieved. Smith reported that the *Hartford* took notice of their activity with the Georgia relief and "came down like a floating castle and sent them messengers of iron to warn them to leave."

---

[77] Clark, *Shadows of the Valley*, 18.
[78] Smith, *A Smith in Service*, 41.
[79] Stamper, "Travels of the 43rd Tennessee," 44.
[80] Ibid.

Smith watched as he hurried his men a little distance through the mud toward camp as one heavy round passed over their heads. Behind them the Georgians made it double-quick out of danger, though many projectiles were shot at them."[81]

The rains poured all night, and the roads back in to camp became muddy. Smith and his little Hawkins County army, weary with their struggle through the muck, made it back to their tents by 10 p.m. Along the way, they passed a battery of four long-barreled six-inch rifled cannon being rushed to reinforce Fort Warrenton. Smith suggested that the gunners be sure to get there before daylight because the *Hartford* was positioned just below the fort to discourage any attempts at repairs. During the night, the *Hartford* withdrew back down river and anchored just below the hamlet. Smith noted that some of her volleys, falling fast and thick, came quite close to his men. The big guns of the sloop were within a half mile of one of their posts making the boys there quite nervous.[82]

All was quiet after dark except for a heavy Mississippi Valley spring storm, which pushed rain and hail ahead of the arrival of a bone-chilling wind. "The boys had on their overcoats," Stamper reported, "just like winter had set in again." Lieutenant Cleve Jones of Stamper's regiment returned with his pickets from Warrenton and entertained the boys in camp with a full description of the shelling they had endured in the fort, providing some idea about what his squad had experienced during the heavy pounding from the naval guns of the *Hartford* and the *Albatross*. "Though there were none hurt," Stamper remarked, "it was not pleasant to have those shells whizzing over their heads." Though not a casualty of enemy action, Private John Dennis, Company H, had succumbed to measles. "His friends tried to send his body home," Stamper wrote, "but failed—so his body was buried in Mississippi far from home."[83]

The "Switzerland" and "Lancaster" Try Their Luck. Grant felt that the guns of Ft. Warrenton had to be negated for a couple of strategic reasons. They were an annoyance to his workers on the peninsula, and troops landing there later would have to cross the flats around Warrenton. In order to provide some added firepower to Farragut's two warships, the young daredevil Colonel Charles Ellet, the former commander of the ill-fated *Queen of the West*, was

---

[81] Smith, *A Smith in Service*, 41.

[82] Ibid.

[83] Stamper, "Travels of the 43rd Tennessee," 45. Up to this time, if their families could afford to do so, a number of deceased soldiers' bodies were shipped home on trains.

assigned the task of taking two so-called timberclads, the *Switzerland* and *Lancaster*, past the Vicksburg batteries down river as support. Ellet had made his initial successful run with the *Queen*, and Union war planners hoped that he and his courageous volunteers could repeat the feat, but they failed.

Isaac Stamper of the 43rd Tennessee recorded that the attempt began at daybreak on 25 March, when "two boats attempted to pass Vicksburg and our batteries opened up on them, sinking one [the *Lancaster*] and so damaging the other [the *Switzerland*], that it was unmanageable."[84] Smith of the 31st Tennessee commented in his journal, "This was a grand affair. We had four or five batteries of heavy siege guns, perhaps ten or twelve one-hundred pounders, firing away at a time. The bursting of shells [and] the roar of artillery was a scene not easily described." At the same time eight miles down river, Farragut continued giving the fort at Warrenton another major shelling, but no one had been hurt as far as Smith could ascertain.[85] The East Tennesseans along the Warrenton shore watched the disabled *Switzerland* drift slowly past with the current, Stamper noted, where "she was taken up by the enemy somewhere down the river on the Louisiana side."[86] She was run aground where repairs could be conducted near the Biggs Plantation under the protection of a detachment of the invader's infantry.

Though Stamper indicated that the Yankee boats continued shelling Fort Warrenton, causing some damage to its casemate, the fort was quickly repaired. Debris from Ellet's stricken timberclads continued to be propelled along with the river's swift current, with survivors "clinging to cotton bales, lumber, &c." From the riverbanks at the fort and at Warrenton, Stamper noted, the disabling of one and sinking of the other vessel brought "a yell from the Rebels that made the valley ring."[87]

Farragut's lack of success was not due entirely to the artillery in Fort Warrenton, according to General Carter Stevenson. The *Hartford*'s near approach to the fort allowed Confederate musketry "to [drive] her gunners from their guns [causing] her to withdraw [back down the river]."[88]

Meanwhile, the two gunboats Admiral David Porter had sent past the batteries from his fleet above Vicksburg encountered "less success than before" (the passage made earlier by the *Queen of the West* and later by the *Indianola*).

---

[84] Ibid.

[85] Smith, *A Smith in Service*, 41.

[86] Stamper, "Travels of the 43rd Tennessee," 45.

[87] Ibid.

[88] Report of Gen. Carter L. Stevenson, 25 March 1863, *Official Records*, ser. 1, vol. 24, pt. 1, p. 70, 480.

"One of the boats [the *Switzerland*] was sinking, and gave the alarm of distress," Clark observed. This signal caused the *Hartford* to come to the rescue of the failing gunboat. Clark and his men came out of the fort, "just in time to see the second yankee boat [the *Lancaster*] go down, leaving her smokestack in sight and her men struggling in the water for the shore." The racket brought on by the booming cannon and the cheering of the men seemed shake the very ground, Clark recalled, "And we enjoyed greatly the victory."[89]

Regarding the dawn's excitement, Lieutenant James Earnest of the 79th (60th) Tennessee reported that a signal gun and the drums beating to arms alerted him and sent the boys flying to the rifle pits. At daybreak, he saw the *Lancaster* and *Switzerland* attempting to pass. A half hour later he watched the *Switzerland* begin to sink and her crew abandoned her. "A shout rent the air and was repeated again and again by our boys," he declared. The 79th Tennessee was then ordered back to camp, leaving the young officer from Greene County to proclaim: "A good morning's work, this."[90]

Occupying the same ground as his captain, Private George Washington Crosby of Captain Clark's company in the 59th Tennessee recorded that the men had been on picket duty on the levee of Warrenton for weeks before the attack and, while in the swamps there, had made the acquaintance of "all manner of cottonmouth snakes, alligators, lizards and 'gallinippers' [mosquitoes]." He recalled that about this time the boys were called from the swamps to form into a line of march. "We were ordered down and into Fort Warrenton," he noted, where two Yankee gunboats had made their way down through the canal cut through the peninsula on the far shore, he believed. This was in error in that Grant never completed his canal, and it was never fit for steamer traffic. The gunboats *Lancaster* and *Switzerland* had actually come, as indicated earlier, past the river batteries. "This happened to be our first experience of gunboat fighting," Crosby asserted, "but alas, I happened to be on post above the fort a fourth of a mile away." Even given that distance, he maintained, they could observe the terrific fire from their vessels that slammed into the fortifications. But on this morning, he was privileged to receive the bombardment directly from behind the earthen walls of the fort. "My Company [I from Morristown, Hamblen County] was in the fort when the gunboats came and opened up on it fast and heavy. The boys in the fort behaved nicely, held the fort and all came out safe."[91] Though Crosby indicated that this action was a

---

[89] Clark, *Valleys of the Shadow*, 18–19.
[90] Northen, *All Right, Let Them Come*, 72–73.
[91] Hodges, *The Crosby Collection*, 412–13.

result of the malicious intent of the gunboats coming downriver, it more than likely occurred during the *Hartford*'s and *Albatross*' bombardment since the *Lancaster* and *Switzerland* were in no condition to offer much of a fight.

Routine. On 26 March the 43rd Tennessee was at rest, according to Stamper. He reckoned all to be quiet. A man in Company K of his regiment, Isaac Martin, had died and "was buried at five o'clock with military honors," Stamper wrote. There was a prayer meeting later in the evening after roll call, and "several went to the mourner's bench."[92]

Captain Sam Crawford of the 79th (60th) Tennessee had returned the day before with some conscripts for that regiment, and Lieutenant Earnest indicated that he spent the morning drilling them in the manual of arms. "No very pleasant job," he had to admit.[93]

Though the prospects for active campaigning increased with the dropping of water levels in the Mississippi and each warming day, Captain Jacob Hays of Elizabethton, Carter County, and the 59th Tennessee, still had to attend to mundane routines. On 26 March, he submitted and drew for his company the following from the brigade quartermasters: sixteen hats, six shell jackets, fourteen pair of government brogans, thirty-nine pair of pants, forty-seven cotton shirts, and fifty-nine pair of drawers.[94]

Once again, elements of the 43rd Tennessee were on picket duty during the morning, according to Stamper. A lull had settled into military matters with the day passing quietly, the weather warm and cloudy "with occasional misting rain." At daylight 27 March, however, the enemy again began shelling the fort at Warrenton, where "they threw about twenty-five shells doing no damage." Then, the enemy commenced dropping shells toward the town itself, landing frequently in the old campgrounds where Reynolds's Brigade had its first permanent settlement soon after arriving at Vicksburg.[95] Reynolds's other two regiments, after a brief sojourn north of Vicksburg, had rejoined the 43rd Tennessee and the 31st Tennessee at their new camps a mile to the east.

Nature Ravages Vaughn's Camps. The night of 28 March, however, would not pass as calmly as many others had since the East Tennesseans had arrived. A severe storm blew through the area accompanied by at least one tornado, striking at the heart of the Confederate camps. The storms near Warrenton,

---

[92] Stamper, "Travels of the 43rd Tennessee," 45. The meeting may have been a response to President Davis's call for 27 March 1863 to be set aside as a National Day of Fasting and Prayer across the Confederacy.

[93] Northen, *All Right, Let Them Come,* 72–73.

[94] 59th Tennessee, *Compiled Service Records.*

[95] Stamper, "Travels of the 43rd Tennessee," 45.

according to Stamper, "[tore] up our tents, [and left] us poor Rebels to take shelter the best [we] could." He and his brother Joe succeeded in physically holding their tent to the ground, though their "bed got a good wetting."[96]

Captain William A. Wash of the 79th (60th) Tennessee, commanding a company of Cocke County men camped in the upper end of the line above Vicksburg, stated that his regiment received the principle fury of the storm when the tornado tore though the center of his regimental camps. "About 10 o'clock at night the wind commenced blowing a steady gale and black clouds loomed up," he wrote in his autobiography. "For an hour, it seemed we were only going to have a thunder gust, but the storm increased and the winds howled among the thick foliage of the tall trees. Not one in our camp dreamed of danger till the limbs commenced crashing and the huge poplars were being torn up by their roots in the center of our camp." Wash recounted how his men darted wildly from their cabins, "eagerly seeking a place of safety." Often, he reported, the cabins were "smashed to atoms before the men had fairly escaped." A tent occupied by his brother and five other men was torn to pieces only moments after they safely got out. "Six men were killed outright in one tent," Wash stated, "and ten others injured in various parts of the regiment." "Twas the most pitiable sight imaginable," he wrote, "to see six stalwart men lying side by side, mangled and bruised, in death." The men killed, five of whom were from the Morristown area, were buried side by side on a neighboring hill. The tornado left the camp desolate and gloomy, Wash lamented, and "it required several days to clear up our camping ground so as to make it passable."[97]

Alexander described the terrible storm that had struck on 28 March as having occurred just as they were going to bed that night. It was, he declared, "the most terrific storm of wind and rain that I have ever witnessed." By 11 p.m., only one tent in the entire company was left standing. The boys all

---

[96] Ibid.

[97] Wash, *Camp, Field and Prison Life*, 19–20. Five of the men, all from Capt. James Hodges' Company H, were Jeremiah Miller, John A. Owens, Jackson Pinion, and the brothers Jacob and Thomas Rich from Morristown (now Hamblen) County. All were privates. Bob Houston, Vaughn's inspector general, indicated incorrectly that the men killed were in the "63rd" Tennessee, which never served at Vicksburg. Four of the dead were brothers from Monroe County. Two of these brothers buried at Cedar Hill were identified as A. B. and Harvey Lindsey. Other soldiers buried there who were killed by the tornado had served with the 80th (62nd) Tennessee. These soldiers included Thomas Malone, Robert Smith, and Joseph Stafford, all privates. A number of Georgians camped nearby were also killed by the storm. Houston overestimated the number of storm-related fatalities at sixty.

scampered to carry their things to the cook's houses to get them out of the weather. Since that evening, he stated, the battery had been densely packed by boys gathered around the few good campfires. "But we were small losers compared with some here," he wrote. "Colonel Crawford [79th (60th) Tennessee] lost six men killed and several others wounded. Colonel Rowan [80th (62nd) Tennessee] lost another four men killed, and two wounded." One of the Georgia regiments camped nearby had had five men killed, Alexander noted, and there were perhaps others about whom he had not heard. All the regiments harmed, he recorded, were camped close together in heavy timber, and the dead were victims of massive falling trees.[98]

Stamper of the 43rd Tennessee described the storms of the previous day as "very blustery, like an Easter spell." His regiment came off picket from the river, and the drop in temperatures and the dampness that followed the stormy front had all the boys in camp "huddled around our smoky fires to prevent chilling." His recollection of 29 March was of soldiers with "eyes almost smoked out," hunkered around pitiful campfires in their blankets and overcoats with "the rain water dripping off [their] noses."[99]

Provisions Arrive from Newport. The effects of the tornado on Crawford's regiment and others camped in the vicinity were predictable. Following the gruesome details occasioned by the deaths in his regiment, Captain Wash of the 79th (60th) Tennessee recorded that, back on 1 February, orders had been issued for each company to send selected officers or non-commissioned officers home on recruiting and conscript service. Wash's choice for the duty was his orderly sergeant, R. A. Anderson, "being most suitable because of energy and perseverance." Their company had been raised in Newport, Cocke County. Anderson, on this day after the awful tornado, returned to the company, "with twelve men and no less than thirty boxes of provisions, and some clothing and a host of letters for the boys." His popularity with the company was considerable. Wash wrote, "never was there more joy over the return of a stray child than then."[100]

"The provisions were prized more highly than gold," Wash indicated, "for our rations had for some time been slim, in quality and quantity and besides, they were from the loved ones back home." At roll call that evening, Wash recorded, his men "raised a lively yell, which they had not done before for weeks. The letters were anxiously perused and treasured away in the hearts and

---

[98] Ibid.
[99] Stamper, "Travels of the 43rd Tennessee," 45–46.
[100] Wash, *Camp, Field and Prison Life*, 20–21.

knapsacks of the fortunate recipients." This happy moment perhaps helped the boys put aside the recent loss of six friends to the tornado. Wash, who was originally from Kentucky, indicated that the people back in Cocke County remembered him as well and sent "a new box of staples," a ham, and "no less than fourteen letters." He marveled that, "before the war, I had never known a member of my company or regiment, nor a citizen from where they came: East Tennessee."[101]

3rd Tennessee Volunteers Earn a Furlough. Stamper of the 43rd Tennessee recorded that though things remain quiet around Warrenton on 30 March, "it is still very windy and cold." Private Cornett was discharged from the service and sent home on this day; others would join him. In a display of incredible bravery, Stamper related the story of an unusual offering made by the division commander, Major General Carter L. Stevenson. A ninety-day furlough would be awarded to any men who would take a skiff and run it out to the *City of Vicksburg*, which had broken its moorings the night before at the Vicksburg wharfs and had drifted down river, grounding itself near an anchored Yankee gunboat, probably the *Switzerland*. The *City of Vicksburg* was the same hapless transport set afire by the *Queen of the West* during her run past the river batteries in February. Four privates from Colonel Lillard's 3rd Tennessee, according to Stamper's daily entry, offered to make the attempt. Private Benjamin William Ellison of Company C, "went into the boat, set it on fire, got in his schooner with his crew, and made their escape back to their command at Camp Reynolds." The next day, "these boys were furloughed ninety days."[102] In other words, they would never lay eyes on Vicksburg again.

Quartermaster Sergeant John T. Moffitt of Lynch's Battery was still at home on his recruiting service, and like the aforementioned boys in the 3rd Tennessee, he too would never have to return to Vicksburg. He had spent only three weeks in Vicksburg, the rest of his time being spent in the pursuit of conscript replacements. His fellow New Market comrade and friend Orderly Sergeant J. H. Alexander wrote him a letter on 30 March from the chilly confines of his camp above Vicksburg. Alexander indicated that he had been asleep in his bed when something awoke him. After lighting a candle, he was surprised to discover it was only 3:30 a.m. Rather than going back to bed, Alexander decided to write some letters "before the boys awake, for then there will be little opportunity to write as we crowd around the fire as close as if

---

[101] Ibid., 21.
[102] Stamper, "Travels of the 43rd Tennessee," 46.

winter." The weather was as frigid as it had been any day since they arrived there, he testified.[103]

The cruel change in weather with its heavy rains and cold wind was harder to bear, Alexander noted, because the temperatures had been so spring-like before. "The boys are generally pretty very well," he reported, stating "Seath ____ was improving tho' he was another cast down, failing in his application both for detail and furlough. He tried to get a sick furlough after the detail failed." Thomas Clark and Allen F. Brown, also from New Market, had small pox, "but were getting well." James W. Burgess, who had served with the Battery, died in the hospital at Jackson. Jo Moore, Alexander indicated, was also in the Blind Asylum hospital at Jackson. "He had thought he had secured a substitute for $3,000," he wrote, "but he failed to get him."[104]

Alexander closed his letter by suggesting that Moffitt "stay long enough to get all [the replacements] you need."[105] That fact was, Sergeant Moffitt would never return to his battery at Vicksburg though he would serve with distinction as a part of John Vaughn's Mounted Infantry Brigade once it was exchanged after the surrender of Vicksburg.

Reynolds's Officers Recommend Him for Promotion. On the last day of March, Colonel James W. Gillespie of the 43rd Tennessee and his fellow field officers in the brigade wrote a letter addressed to President Jefferson Davis, in Richmond, on behalf of their brigade commander, Colonel A. W. Reynolds. It read as follows:

> Camps near Vicksburg, Fourth Brigade
> Stevenson's Division, March 31, 1863.
> Sir—We the undersigned field officers of this brigade would respectfully yet urgently recommend and request that our brigade commander, Col. Alex W. Reynolds, be promoted to the rank of Brigadier General.
> It is needless that we should here rehearse the military antecedents of Col. Reynolds. So well known to yourself particularly those connected with our present national struggle, from the very commencement of which his conduct has been meritoriously and devotedly winning the commendation of his superiors and without exception the ardent attachment of his troops.

---

[103] J. H. Alexander to John T. Moffitt, 30 March 1863, Thomas J. Moffitt Papers.
[104] Ibid.
[105] Ibid.

Was but reflected the universal desires of this brigade as far as it is known to us, when we ask that promotion and rank for Col. Reynolds to which we consider him so justly entitled by both his career and characteristics as an officer.

Apart from the consideration of the just claims to promotion which we recognize in Col. Reynolds high merits there are reasons of direct inherent to ourselves in soliciting that he be advanced from the rank of Col. to that of Brigadier General. It is scarcely necessary in this communication to state how much the character of the brigade may oftentimes be affected by the rank and consequent influence of its commander. His position and title are matters of no little pride with his command, and they all soon learn in camps and on the march as well as striving for laurels on the battlefield. How many real advantages daily arise from having a Gen'l instead of a Col. for brigade commander. For nearly 12 months past we have been in the same division as Colonel Reynolds. Since November last, he has been our brigade commander, and we take sincere pleasure after the long association in expressing in this manner our sincere appreciation of his official and personal merit.

The news of Colonel Reynolds' promotion as most respectfully urged in this letter would be received with expressions of genuine hearty satisfaction throughout our entire command.

Most respectfully yours, your Obt. servants,
Jas. W. Gillespie, Col., 43rd Tennessee Vols.
D. M. Key, Lieut. Col., 43rd Tennessee Vols.
S. Guthrie, Major, 43rd Tennessee Vols.
W. M. Bradford, Col. comdg., 31st Tenn. Regt.
Robt. McFarland, Major, 31st Tennessee Regt.
N. J. Lillard, Col., 3rd Tennessee
D. C. Haskins, Lieut. Col., 3rd Tennessee
J. C. Boyd, Major, 3rd Tennessee
W. L. Eakin, Lieut. Col., 59th Tenn. Regt.
J. P. Brown, Major, 59th Tenn. Regt.[106]

The sentiment would be contradicted a few months later once the siege was over, when another letter would be penned by many of the same officers with a decidedly different point of view.[107]

---

[106] 43rd Tennessee, *Compiled Service Records.*

"Clear and pleasant," reported Stamper this last day of the month, with things military being described as "all quiet." Spirits were high in the 43rd Tennessee, as they were in the 79th (60th) Tennessee, since both had been privileged to receive a supply of eggs, butter, candy, and tobacco, courtesy of some recruiting officers returning from home.[108] Regardless of these momentary

---

[107] Ibid. After the brigade entered parole camps, the four regimental commanders sent to Gen. Samuel Cooper, adjutant general for the Confederate States, the following letter, along with Gen. John Vaughn's blessing. The letter was dated 23 August, and the brigade was still two weeks away from being exchanged. Their patience with Col. Reynolds had been exhausted after the long months at Vicksburg, along with their division commander, Carter Stevenson. The letter read as follows:

Sir: We undersigned colonels commanding the respective regiments composing the 4th Tennessee Brigade, desire that some other officer shall be assigned to command the brigade.

Personally we have no unkind feelings toward Col. A. W. Reynolds, but conscientiously believe that it will be preferably and manifestly to the interest of the public service that the change should be made.

The belief prevails among the officers and men of the brigade that we are justly entitled to a brigadier general, having served for a great while under the command of a colonel only, and that for some reason (and perhaps a very good one), the President declines to recommend Col. Reynolds for the position.

The frequent (and as we consider) too free use of ardent spirits on the part of Col. Reynolds renders him inefficient and very objectionable to us, and as we consider equally as much so, the soldiers under our command.

For these, and other reasons, we most earnestly desire to be removed from his command, and another assigned to us, in whose character and habits, these objections are not found.

As but few brigades have been appointed from this division of the state, we think it but an act of justice that we should have one assigned us from our own brigade, or at least from E. Tenn., as this will inspire officers and men with a more general spirit of satisfaction.

We furthermore most earnestly desire to be assigned to the command of another major general as the dissatisfaction as to Genl. Stevenson is very great among men and officers.

Very Respectfully, W. M. Bradford, Col., 31st Tenn. Regt; N. J. Lillard, Col., 3rd Tennessee; Jas. W. Gillespie, Col., 43rd Tennessee; W. L. Eakin, Col., 59th Tenn. Regt."

The following endorsement was attached to the letter:

Headquarters, Parole Camp, Sweetwater, Tenn., Aug. 25th,'63/Genl. S. Cooper:

Sir, I am personally acquainted with all the facts stated & I feel certain that the good of the service demands the change that is desired by the Cols.

Very respectfully, your Obt. Serv., John C. Vaughn, Brig. Gen., CSA." 43rd Tennessee *Compiled Service Records*.

[108] Stamper, "Travels of the 43rd Tennessee," 49.

good tidings, all the East Tennesseans in both brigades had to sense a shift in routine demanded in response to a terrible stirring among the infernal Yankees, who seemed as though they were just beginning to awaken from a long hibernation.

CHAPTER 5

"Our Men Don't Ask the Yanks Any Odds" April

In his diary on "fool's" day 1863, James T. Earnest of the 60th Tennessee wrote that Lieutenant Colonel Nathan Gregg "played off" the junior lieutenant from Greene County and some of his fellow junior officers. "We paid him off in his own coin before the day was out," Earnest bragged.[1]

On or about this date in the campaign, the three regiments of Vaughn's Brigade began using their smaller unit number designations (60th, 61st and 62nd Tennessee). Nothing much happened in a military way, Stamper of the 43rd Tennessee reported this first day of April, and the weather was clear, calm, and pleasant.[2]

Lieutenant Calvin M. Smith of Persia, Hawkins County and the 31st Tennessee, reported that his company was on picket along the levee near Warrenton, across the river from the enemy camps on the Louisiana side. Smith's company commander and brother-in-law, Captain James Spears, was back in camp, and the picket was under the command of Company F's Lieutenant John C. Neil of Mouse Creek in McMinn County. "I shot three beautiful fish yesterday," Smith bragged, so his picket post had "excellent eating." He indicated that he cooked the fish in the mess's frying pan that he always took out on picket should opportunity present itself. Some excitement arose when the Yankees attempted a landing above their picket line. They had crammed themselves into two "yawls," but the company out of Mouse Creek (now Niota) "ran up the levee and scared them off." Way up the river, perhaps as far as on the Yazoo itself, Smith detected the rumbling of distant cannon. Across the river, the continual racket of Union drummers played on his nerves,

---

[1] Northen, *All Right, Let Them Come*, 6. Such camaraderie with Gregg showed the growing respect he earned with many of his men. Col. Crawford was scarcely ever mentioned in any of the men's writings except in a derogatory manner.

[2] Stamper, "Travels of the 43rd Tennessee," 46.

causing him to joke, "they seemed to have a band of music that fights the elements like a roaring storm." He though it strange that so many men should be in such close proximity and occupied in seemingly menial tasks while actually waiting for the opportunity to take another's life.[3]

"While I sit here on the levee, I can hear heavy cannon," Smith wrote. "Bunches of cotton on barrels are floating down the river which shows the uncanny aim of our artillery men. I can hear the explosion of shells." Smith wrote a sloop of war (the *Hartford*), a brig (perhaps the *Albatross*), and another boat (*Switzerland*) which had been firing for several days at Fort Warrenton had finally retired back down the river, allowing work and repairs on the fortifications to resume. "The steamer [the *City of*] *Vicksburg* that had been tied up at the wharf ever since we have been here tore loose and floated down and lodged below Warrenton," he reported, "where she was set on fire and destroyed [by the previously-mentioned volunteers from the 3rd Tennessee]." Smith indicated that the demolition of the doomed transport occurred on the same night as the storm that "blew down some timber and killed several soldiers in Colonel Rowan's and Crawford's regiments."[4]

Always one with an eye for his natural surroundings, Smith observed that though the weather had been extremely cool lately, it was now as warm as the summer sun. The birds were singing all about him, and at night the owls "laughed and hooted." Peach trees had lost their blossoms, revealing young fruit the size of beans. He heard the bark of the fox squirrel and the "chaying" of the red-tailed hawks perched high in the cottonwood or cypress trees. "Thousands of tadpoles and little blue catfish are sporting beneath my feet," he mused, "with myriads of other insects enjoying a state of happiness together. And yet we more intelligent creatures than they, are scattered far from home, and seem ready to shoot each other on first sight." He continued to wax philosophical, indicating that the Creator of all things intended for man to have justice, and showed His mighty hand in war. Smith believed that God permitted wars, pestilence, and famine occur warnings to humanity. "God instituted slavery as He did the languages," Smith declared. "He doubtless changed the color of the skin by His miraculous power. He instituted inequality among men when Noah said unto Ham, 'thy seed shall be servant unto my servants, &c.'"[5]

---

[3] Smith, *A Smith in Service*, 42. Smith must have been an excellent marksman with his pistol. In his journal Earnest of the 60th Tennessee mentioned numerous hunting trips with fellow junior officers seeking out squirrels or rabbits to augment their meager rations.

[4] Ibid.

[5] Ibid.

"We lived hard a while back," Private Enoch C. Beeler of the 59th Tennessee stated on 1 April in letter home to Powder Springs Gap, Grainger County, indicating that the boys had nothing but bread to eat. "I have seen the time that I would have given 50 cents for as much bread as I could eat," he remarked, "or that you throw in the slop at Pap's." However, times were better, and "we have good bread and meat now, and Joseph brought us a heap of good meal and flour." Joseph, his brother, had apparently been home on furlough, or had recently joined the command at Vicksburg. Beeler apologized for being so tardy in his response, but stated that he had had a number of letters to respond to and was doing so in the order they had been received. He thanked his sister for sending the sugar (a commodity, along with rice, for which the Vicksburg boys were never in short supply), and he promised to bring her a nice present in return, as well as "talk with you about a great many things that I have not time to write about." The cannon continued to roar everyday, he stated, but had not hurt much yet. Beeler said that he and his comrades had been under fire while at Fort Warrenton. The weather had a profound effect on him, he stated, and "when it rains, very often we have no shelter and when night comes, we lye on the wet ground and cover with our wet blankets." Enoch trusted that the war would end soon, when all the boys can come home where "we can eat at the table … all the good things we used to when we stayed at Pap's." He wanted his unnamed little sister to continue helping their sister Polly around the house, and told her how happy he was to learn that she had done the dinner when Polly was out in the field working the crop. "If I ever come home," Beeler promised, "I will try to bring you a present."[6] In closing, he promised to write the other children shortly.

Hitching a Ride on a Yankee Gunboat. Earnest of the 60th Tennessee indicated that on the morning of 2 April, Martin L. Smith's Division held a review under the watchful eye of the general himself. "The Second [Vaughn's] Brigade did splendidly," Earnest noted modestly, "especially our regiment."[7] Down river at Fort Warrenton, Smith of the 31st Tennessee reported, "Gabriel Tate was up the river bank and saw some men at a cotton house who came down and gave themselves up to us." These soldiers were deserters who wanted to go home, they told their captors, but Smith and others believed that they were on their way across the river to "yankeedom." Indeed, when the *Indianola*

---

[6] Enoch Beeler to "Little Sister," 1 April 1863, Enoch Beeler Letters. Farmers back in East Tennessee fed "slop," composed of left-overs of the day's meals, corncobs and shucks, and other "edibles, "to the hogs.

[7] Northen, *All Right, Let Them Come,* 76.

had been captured back in February, she had deserters aboard who had managed to get picked up by the ironclad's lifeboats as she passed where they were hiding. These particular deserters the day before had been waving strips of cotton so that the enemy across the river would come over and pick them up. That was the motive, Smith thought, of the Yankee skiffs suspicious activity the day before.[8] Two of the deserters were from Company B, 31st Tennessee and four others were from Company E, 3rd Tennessee, all from Maryville, Blount County.[9] Displaying little honor among cowards, Smith reported that the shirkers were quick to testify two others had actually planned the deed but had lost their nerve and returned to their respective camps before getting caught.[10]

Soon thereafter, Smith said these companies of the 31st Tennessee were relieved by two companies of the 43rd Tennessee, in whose camp preaching was in progress. "Parson [Napoleon B.] Goforth of Green[e] County [actually Sevier County] made one of the power fullest efforts to convince us we were fighting in a just cause and we should be satisfied not only with poor beef, but that were defending our families," Smith wrote. Goforth told the boys that they were "also fighting for the liberties that we had always enjoyed free and equal rights of the South with the entire world; an independence it now has and we have always enjoyed, to rejoice in all time to come."[11]

Parson Goforth declared to the men that the South, unlike the North, did not want a dictator. The South loved the constitution and the rights handed down by the nation's forefathers. Smith believed that Lincoln would lead his people to disaster by following his decrees, and the North's once mighty cities and towns, factories and institutions would fall to ruin. Smith's greatest fear, stated repeatedly in his diaries, was the subjugation of the Southern people and their way of life. "It is hoped that our wives, mothers, children and friends will keep in heart and continue to work and manage affairs of homes and farms while we continue to keep back the foe," Smith proclaimed. "The people of the North are beginning to understand the nature of the great warfare they are engaged in and will desert their armies until they can not even have men to

---

[8] Smith, *A Smith in Service*, 42.

[9] 3rd Tennessee, 31st Tennessee, *Compiled Service Records*.

[10] Smith, *A Smith in Service*, 42.

[11] Ibid. Goforth served with his regiment until its surrender at the war's end. He then returned to serve another term as president of Carson College (now Carson-Newman College), Mossy Creek (now Jefferson City), Tennessee. Later, he and a graduate of that institution, W. A. G. Brown, also a former Confederate soldier, opened a Baptist academy at Riceville, McMinn County. Goforth was a native of Boyd's Creek in Sevier County.

guard a camp. Our armies are in better spirits and health than ever before and will do wonders in every engagement with the enemy." The arms and ammunition of the army at Vicksburg, Smith declared, were sufficient for its defense. He wrote that the boys used to fear the approach of an enemy gunboat, but now they all loved to have one try to pass their formidable works. "The sound of cannon used to make us start and hearts to palpitate," he wrote, "but now it is a joy to our ears, relieves our pent up cares and cheers us powerfully." He predicted if a battle were fought about Vicksburg, the people back home would hear of the valor from these boys had already occurred on other fronts, and he hoped to survive the war so that he might live again with his family in the enjoyment of the rights of the Southern people.[12]

Smith noted that Captain Spears had been detailed on 3 April to return home to recruit for the company. He would be trapped outside the lines after Grant invested the Vicksburg on the 18 May, leaving Smith in command during the siege. Heavy cannonading erupted down the river during the morning, Smith indicated, and at 2 p.m., was still underway. Even then, he believed that the Yankees were destined to leave the scene soon, but he was wrong. "James Tyner will be discharged shortly," Smith observed, "and I will send this book to you [his wife Nancy] which will show some of the scenes and difficulties and duties as well as other important points that I or you may refer to in time to come." Smith concluded his daily entry by noting that another large deer had just come loping through their camp that day and had been shot for its carelessness.[13]

Elsewhere, the often monotonous routine continued. Stamper and the 43rd Tennessee rotated to picket duty again. He wrote that the orderly sergeant in a company of the 31st Tennessee had dropped dead inexplicably at his post. Military activity was nil the next day, 3 April. A memorable incident of the day (to which Smith had alluded), occurred in camp on 3 April. All the soldiers were sitting around as normal, when suddenly a fine stag came bounding through the company streets. The boys scampered after their muskets and fanned out to get to the best spots where they hoped the buck might pass. In a few moments it came dashing along where at least three soldiers were waiting. The three shot at the deer, and one shot crushed the deer's shoulder. Down it went. Stamper noted that he had been set "at the ready" within fifty yards of where the deer was taken down and was one of the first on the scene. "As I did not get a shot at the buck, I was not invited to eat any of him," he said, "but I gave two hundred

[12] Ibid., 42–43.
[13] Stamper, "Travels of the 43rd Tennessee," 42–43.

dollars for the hide to make a head for our bass drum." Stamper wrapped the skin around his musket and returned to his tent.[14]

Meanwhile, his brothers W. D. and James had prepared $2.02 to send home by William Benjamin Ellison, he wrote, but Ellison did not get off as planned, "so we laid away to await his departure."[15] Ellison was the leader of the group of volunteers who had been awarded a lengthy furlough for setting the *City of Vicksburg* afire. The 60th Tennessee continued its drills on the upper lines, according to Lieutenant Earnest. "Colonel Gregg like[d] to have forgotten to stop this evening on battalion drill," Earnest mused. "Some of the men growled a great deal, but I thought it altogether in place."[16]

Recuperating in the Country. A few miles east of the Big Bayou camps, sickly Private Benjamin Giddens of the 3rd Tennessee had found quarters in the home of Mr. Sexton where he could convalesce. In a letter to his wife, Linda, Giddens wrote that, though he had been ill, he was within eight days of being well enough to return to camp. In response to a query she had written him on 16 March, Giddens replied that he was pretty well fixed for clothes, "but I would like to have me a pair of socks." As for his illness, he supposed that "the chills has quit me, and I hope they will never come back." Giddens reported that the surgeon had given him some medicine to treat his "yellow gander."[17]

In regards to a request for a letter from him to a neighbor or relative with whom he had had dealings before, Giddens indicated that "all they want to [do] is misrepresent what I would write and give it the lie a few times I know them like a book." As to the news regarding another acquaintance that had recently been jailed, Giddens insisted, "that is where he ought to be." He also reacted to the news that, sadly, would be all too familiar the longer the war raged, and especially in East Tennessee, where lawlessness would reign years after the conflict concluded. Giddings's desire for these bushwhackers was readily apparent. "Poor Miss Hams had to cry you said that the renegades came down out off the mountain and stole Trimmer's meal and hog," he wrote. "That is just what any boddy would do that wont fight for their own dung hill I hope the last one of them may be caught." Giddens then shared with Linda his good fortune regarding the first day of his stay with the Sextons. "Mrs. Sexton," he told her, "killed a turkey and stuffed it and fried ham and butter and milk and rice and apple butter and molasses and sweet potatoes now I do say it was

---

[14] Ibid., 46.
[15] Ibid., 46–47.
[16] Northen, *All Right, Let Them Come*, 77.
[17] Benjamin Giddens Letters, 4 April 1863.

good." He related that his benefactors were Baptists, and a Baptist preacher also resided with them. Giddens described him as a very young man and looked like one that could just say "Baptidzo and rantidzo." This preacher prayed with the Sextons in the mornings and the evenings. Mrs. Sexton, Giddens would have his wife know, "is very well off she has 20 negroes and 10 milk cows, 3 yoke of oxen, 5 mules, 2 carriage horses, and a fine farm and a fine house." Giddens was also amazed that the Sextons had a piano, but "I never liked the musick of a piano." He believed his host family to be "big quality" people of high society, but, despite that, he told Linda, "I try to be as big as any boddy [here], though [I] make some dreadful blunders." He indicated that the Sextons's daughters were school graduates, having attended a female academy in Nashville.[18]

Giddens occupied a room to himself, with a library, a press, bed tongs, a shovel, washbowl, and a pitcher, and "I liked to have forgot a night pot." He worried about what he might have to pay for such luxurious accommodations, but knew that his compassionate company commander, John W. Fender, who had loaned him $20 in the past, would help again if he needed help. "Captain Fender is a clever man," Giddens stated, "and he will do anything to help us when we was sick in camps and had nothing scarcely to eat he would send the Lieut. to me with a cup of sweeten tea and some biscuits." With some random observations, in reaction to his father's news that the State of Georgia had made appropriations to care for soldiers' wives, Giddens declared: "that is one of the most noble and patriotic acts that the future historian will have to chronicle—all honor to the noble State of Georgia." The oft-mentioned John Hightower (Giddens called him "Hitoe") had gone home and not told Giddens where to reach him. Hightower, who had been cashiered out of service, apparently had no desire to see any of his acquaintances before he left. Giddens did not say why he needed to see Hightower before he left. "I would rather be home with my wife as to be any place on this earth," Giddens insisted. "The boys gets lots to eat at [this] time in Vicksburg," he noted, and "our batteries has tore up four iron steamers [ironclads]."[19]

Easter Day Drill. "Our men don't ask the Yanks any odds," Giddens declared.[20] Among those "asking no odds" was the 43rd Tennessee. No East Tennessee regiment serving in the campaign at Vicksburg suffered greater losses to enemy fire or sickness than it did. In a letter written on 4 April to the Athens (Tennessee) *Post,* his hometown newspaper, the regimental chaplain,

---

[18] Ibid.
[19] Ibid.
[20] Ibid.

Archibald Brooks, stated, "the fell destroyer still continues his ravages among us, bearing away in his icy arms the soldiers of the Forty-Third Tennessee."[21]

Sergeant Isaac Stamper, also of Brooks's regiment, noted that the weather remained clear, though it had turned a bit cooler. The 43rd Tennessee came in off picket to no new tidings. With Easter a day away, Stamper and some of the others of his mess had agreed to celebrate by buying some eggs for their morning meal. "Two dozen eggs made us a fine breakfast," he wrote, but it would be a scarce extravagance all agreed, since they "would not make a business of eating eggs when they cost two dollars per dozen." On Easter morning, more firing was heard down the river near New Carthage, Louisiana, leading the boys to suppose that it was an attack on the boats that had left Warrenton the day before. Parson Brooks preached on this "great getting' up mornin'," and all in attendance, according to Stamper, paid good close attention to the serson, which had "some effect on the congregation." There was also a prayer meeting held that evening at 4 o'clock.[22]

Stamper's company was put through drill beginning at 8 a.m. on 6 April. The 43rd Tennessee went through battalion drill that afternoon, being divided into two separate units for the exercise. Waxing a bit nostalgic for an earlier day in the war, Stamper remembered the time when the regiment had just formed in Charleston, Bradley County, and when it was later assigned to Castlewood, Virginia. There, the regiment was supervised by a drillmaster referred to by the boys as "Old Stonewall." Those days were long gone. Nevertheless, "Our boys did very well," Stamper reported, "not having drilled for some months." His weather that day was quiet and beautiful, though a little cool. Stamper described the following day as clear and just cool enough to be most pleasant. They were put through their paces again at company drill, he reported, followed again by battalion drill at 3 p.m.[23]

Strolling along a steadily elevating roadway for seven or eight miles from his camp, Stamper of the 43rd Tennessee made 8 April a visiting day. He walked up to the Mint Springs Bayou bivouac of John Vaughn's Brigade on the upper reaches of Vicksburg, where he dropped in on his friend and neighbor from back in Bradley County, Private J. W. Talley of the 62nd Tennessee. Talley accompanied him back to Reynolds's camps for a return visit. Stamper also indicated on this date that a "Colonel" Fry connected with the 43rd

---

[21] Rev. Archibald Brooks to the Athens [TN] *Post*, 4 April 1863, McClung Historical Archives, Knoxville Public Libraries, Knoxville TN.

[22] Stamper, "Travels of the 43rd Tennessee," 47.

[23] Ibid.

Tennessee left Vicksburg for home. The regiment sent with him $5.07 for some purpose not specified, in addition to money for "fourteen subscriptions to the Cleveland *Banner*." News within the regiment pertained to officer elections in Company H, which saw A. S. McClaney elevated to the office of 3rd lieutenant, and W. N. Russell and A. S. Casteel elected sergeants. Stamper wandered over to the tents of Company K, where the boys there struck up an old fashioned singing, "making our minds turn back to times of peace at our singing classes," he reported. The soldiers reminisced of those good times back home, which had been taken for granted then, but were now so yearned for under the present circumstances.[24]

Recruiters Returning Home. Friday, 10 April, proved to be a day of some excitement in Reynolds's Brigade as a number of its officers left aboard trains for recruiting detail in their home sections in East Tennessee. According to Sergeant Stamper, some of the officers being detached from the 43rd Tennessee included Captains Joseph Huffmaster of Company E and Rogersville, Hawkins County; John Tonkin of Company A and Polk County; and Lieutenants William Wilson of Company B and Rhea County; John Webb of Company G and Mossy Creek (now Jefferson City), Jefferson County. In their company was the squad of furloughed men from the 3rd Tennessee who braved the guns of the Yankee gunboat to burn the *City of Vicksburg*.[25]

Reynolds's Brigade in a Grand Review. Undoubtedly, these men carried a number of parcels containing letters from many of their soldier friends for the people back home. The envy of the boys left behind in Vicksburg can well be imagined as they watched the train pull out for the east. Soon after the train left, on 10 April, the 43rd Tennessee took its turn out on the picket line along the river at Warrenton, where they kept vigil against any enemy landing. At 9 a.m., those in camp were treated to the military spectacle of the 59th Tennessee and the 31st Tennessee passing in review. Later that afternoon at 4 p.m., the 3rd Tennessee joined her sister regiments of the brigade in another general review, after which "General" Reynolds took personal charge of the brigade drill. Stamper noted, "After several movements, he [Reynolds] rode along the line telling the men to yell with all their might at the word 'march.' He brought them charging with bayonets and commanded, 'Forward—double quick—March!'" As the brigade executed the command, "they raised the yell, keeping it up for a hundred yards, so it was impossible to hear anything but the yelling of the boys." Though Reynolds yelled for them to "halt," Stamper

---

[24] Ibid., 48.
[25] Ibid.

indicated that the brigade continued to charge up an extremely steep hill, "as though Yankees were [there] who would soon be their victims."[26]

Lieutenant Smith of the 31st Tennessee described the spectacle as "a general review" with General Reynolds present. Smith noted that the boys "executed several evolutions, charged bayonettes at quick time, about faced, [and] charged at the double quick time with hollowing and yelling." Smith had a somewhat different opinion of the spirited demonstration than did Stamper, calling the exhibition "laughable."[27]

Morale and fighting spirit were perhaps never greater among these East Tennessee Confederates than it was at that particular moment. Nor was the increased emotion to end on the drill field, Stamper wrote, when some violence occurred in the camps, but not instigated by the enemy. "At one o'clock, a difficulty arose between Elisha Scott and John Barnett of Company F," Stamper recounted, when "Scott struck Barnett on the head with a club, breaking his skull and inflicting a wound out of which came a thimble full of brains."[28] C. M. Smith described the incident this way: "One struck the other with a stick of wood and broke a hole in his skull. Not dead yet. Handcuffed the other." Smith indicated that he had just returned from picket, where the morning before he had heard cannonading down the river. He reported the "musketeers" were very troublesome, the days and nights both being very warm.[29]

While on picket, Smith shot more fish and received a letter from home with locks of hair from his children Laura, George and Tabitha. He wished that he could see them all, and they did not realize how much he loved them. "I'll see them yet," Smith wrote in his journal. He decided to send his journal home by James Tyner. He noted that his brother "Severe" (Sevier) and an unnamed Hawkins County comrade with the 60th Tennessee had spent the previous night with him in Reynolds's camps.[30]

On the Mint Springs Bayou end of the line, Captain William A. Wash of the 60th Tennessee recorded on 11 April that "the enemy was making moves which we could not exactly comprehend, and evidently not intended for our good." He noted that a number of Union transports were observed moving up the river above Vicksburg, some accompanied by ironclad gunboats, and

---

[26] Ibid., 48–49.
[27] Smith, *A Smith in Service*, 44. He perhaps meant "laughable" more in terms of the boys having a good time rather than implying any sort of humor inherent in their execution of commands.
[28] Stamper, "Travels of the 43rd Tennessee," 47.
[29] Smith, *A Smith in Service*, 44.
[30] Ibid.

seemed to be probing conditions up the Yazoo. It was also possible, Wash stated, that some of the boys in blue were being moved back into Louisiana.[31] Rumors had also crept through the camps for several weeks the inactivity of the enemy must have meant they were pulling out to reinforce an anticipated major spring campaign in Middle Tennessee. Though their project to dig the canal had not been successful, scouts had reported that the enemy had work parties mending roads and rebuilding bridges on the Louisiana side as far south as New Carthage. This activity led Pemberton to conclude that Grant planned to move much of his army down river along the Louisiana shore very soon. "Our generals had a sharp eye on it all," Wash wrote in his journal, "and orders were issued that we must be ready to go at a moment's warning."[32]

As a partial response to gauge any enemy movement, Earnest of the 60th Tennessee indicated that his Washington County company was sent in the evening to the trenches at Chickasaw Bayou "in the midst of a heavy rain." He described their march from and return to camp in such unpleasant conditions: "the road [was] as bad as one usually finds [here] being over hills almost perpendicular, perfectly slick with mud and beset on every side with little stumps and brush, to say nothing about wading the creeks and mud shoe-mouth deep in the ravines."[33]

Down the lines at Warrenton, Stamper of the 43rd Tennessee indicated matters were all quiet there, and that another general inspection and review for the brigade was conducted at 11 a.m., which he termed "a magnificent display." His day was spent sitting up until midnight with a soldier identified only as "Bruce" and with the brain-injured John Barnett. After being relieved of the duty, Stamper returned to the 43rd Tennessee's camps amid a deluge. The next morning, he reported that the regiment came in off picket through the mud and beneath a cloudy sky. "Our chaplain had a 'meeting' at four o'clock." That evening, the command performed dress parade, having missed the reviews of the rest of the brigade, and Stamper felt that the 43rd Tennessee "made a nice appearance and the occasion was a good one."[34]

While assembled in regimental formation, the adjutant announced some political news: Captain Anderson. J Cawood of Company B had just been designated senior captain of the regiment, instead of Captain Sterling T. Turner, contrary to what had been decided by a draw at Charleston, Tennessee,

---

[31] Wash, *Camp, Field and Prison Life*, 24.
[32] Ibid.
[33] Northen, *All Right, Let Them Come*, 71–72, 79.
[34] Stamper, "Travels of the 43rd Tennessee," 49.

during initial elections. The 43rd Tennessee also received its rations on this date, Stamper wrote, and "it fell to our company to take a piece of beef which was so bad our men refused to eat it." So, as a matter of principle, the company made do with only bread. "There was no little complaining," Stamper recorded, "though it did no good as it brought no meat." Even in trying times fraught with poor rations, the clever and energetic managed to persevere. Stamper noted that bright and early on 13 April his brother "Bill struck out on a search through the regiment, and came across Zeak Eldridge who had just got some meat from home [in Charleston, Bradley County]." W. D. Stamper managed to talk Ezekiel into dividing the ham, and he brought back two and a half pounds of bacon to his messmates, where, according to Isaac Stamper, "we greased our throats once more."[35]

Good Samaritans Among the Mississippians. On the morning of 14 April, Benjamin C. Giddens of the 3rd Tennessee concluded twenty days on sick leave at the home of the Sextons in the country near Vicksburg. He doubtlessly astounded his wife, Malinda, in a letter with the news that after he had completed his recovery from the ague and "yellow janders," he sought honorably to settle his bill prior to returning to his regiment. "What do you suppose she charged me?" he asked Malinda: "she did not charge me any thing." Giddens probably was in pretty strong disagreement with fellow soldiers who proclaimed that all the citizens of Vicksburg plagued the defenders with inflated prices, ill treatment, and contempt. Giddens then added more good news: Mrs. Sexton "made me promise to come back if I got sick I told her that I would." With the random treatment the sick and wounded received, such a pledge was nearly as good as a discharge. Giddens indicated that he begged Mrs. Sexton to let him pay her for her kindness since he had managed to come up with some money, but she continued to decline, saying that she liked to take care of the sick soldiers "if they behave themselves."[36]

"I was as moral as a preacher of the gospel the whole time," Giddens proclaimed, stating that he always went with the family to their prayers in the mornings and the evenings. Giddens told Mrs. Sexton that he was "a thousand times obliged," and she responded that he was "a thousand times welcome." He wrote with some wry humor that "Brother James had to pay two dollars a day" for his care during his sickness. "I licked it to Jim this load of poles," Giddens boasted, "old dark skinned Ben has good luck some times." He believed that

---

[35] Ibid., 49–50.

[36] Benjamin C. Giddens to Melinda ("Linda") Giddens, 14 April 1863, Giddens Letters.

brother "Jim is still improving" and Giddens himself was "as stout as I was before I got sick and if I get sick I am going back to Mrs. Sexton she has plenty to eat and that is good."[37]

Preparing for the Yankees in Reyonlds's Corps. Rations were at that time fairly good in camp, Giddens told Melinda, and he, like others, hoped that the invaders had "pretty near all left Vicksburg." With that said, however, he indicated that fifty miles to the north there had been skirmishing. "I think there will be a dreadful fight above Vicksburg—the gun boats and transports are all gone up the river," he reported, "[since] the yanks are trying to make a flank movement to get to our rear they want to get to the railroad between us and Jackson and cut off our supplies."[38] Giddens's assessment of the enemy's strategy would prove all too correct, even if he was mistaken about the direction from which Grant would ultimately make his strike. Indeed, Grant had begun to put in motion his grand maneuver to distract Pemberton from his primary plan of landing his men across the river at Grand Gulf. Sherman had again commenced saber rattling along the Yazoo River to create a diversion, which caused Pemberton to expand his limited number of defenders in order to meet the threats from above and below Vicksburg. Regardless of what maneuvering the enemy attempted, Giddens's confidence in his comrades and Confederate fortifications sounded all too familiar by this point in the campaign. "They will be met promptly by our soldiers," he told his wife decisively. "The 52nd Georgia and our brigade [Reynolds's] have gone to where the fight was expected. There were artillerist here enough to defend the City." Prophetically, Giddens declared: "You will hear stirring news in a few days."[39]

As for war matters in Tennessee, Giddens stated that he had heard about fighting near his home at Charleston, and in Middle Tennessee, where "Rosancrans is advancing on Bragg." In response to some of his wife's questions, Giddens wrote, "you asked me if I prayed I do sometimes you want to know if I ever thought of dying yes I have thought of it many times." He encouraged her to "hold on till you get to the good world," despite all the trials and troubles she had suffered, and if "you live religious, I think you can weather the storms of this life." In closing, Giddens told his wife that he had received her letter on 10 April, and "I was truly glad to read it over 4 or 5 times."[40]

---

[37] Ibid.

[38] Ibid.

[39] Ibid. This perhaps explains why the 3rd and the 43rd Tennessee Regiments were sent the month before up to Vicksburg for a time.

[40] Ibid.

Meanwhile, in the nearby camp of the 43rd Tennessee, Stamper indicated that the weather was a bit blustery. His Company F took its turn at picket, though he and others were not called due to some non-combatant duties. He recorded he, brother William , Corporal Peter H. Slagle, and J. W. Fleming, regimental drummer, "went out two miles from our camp and with help from others, made one hundred and forty feet of drum cord for our drums." Private Nelson C. Redman of his company went home on 13 April, carrying a precious discharge in the vent pocket of his shell jacket.[41]

The regiment was out "on review," Private Jimmy Caldwell of the 59th Tennessee noted in a 14 April letter to his cousin Carrie, though he was not required to be present for some reason, resulting in a quiet and restful two hours. Earlier that morning, the 59th Tennessee had a small dress rehearsal for a brigade review later in the day. "We have a tolerably larger brigade [than the others in the division]," he wrote, "and when the boys all 'dress up' and form a line with colors flying and music sounding at their head they make quite a grand appearance indeed." Caldwell remarked that it was no wonder "Gen'l" Reynolds was proud of his "brave mountain boys," as he referred to his brigade. As for the regiment itself, much news was going on within its leadership, he continued, beginning with the fact the command would no longer be called "Cooke's regiment."[42]

"Colonel [James Burch] Cooke has resigned on account of his health," Caldwell reported, "which had been declining for the last six months." Caldwell and the rest of the regiment were saddened by the departure of their old commander, "who has been with us so long, and treated us so well." Cooke had "stuck to us through long marches and never faltered where danger was." Caldwell stated that the colonel was always riding to the front of the regiment when his health allowed, wherever "she was called to go." As for the new regimental commander, Caldwell supposed correctly that Colonel William Eakin would be called to step up. "He is a good officer," Caldwell indicated, "and I know of no one not willing for him to be promoted."[43]

Unlike many other commands camped around Vicksburg, the Monroe County native reported that the health of the 59th Tennessee continued "very good" even with the "change of climate, water, diet, &c." Caldwell recorded,

---

[41] Stamper, "Travels of the 43rd Tennessee," 50.

[42] Jimmy Caldwell to Carrie Stakely, 14 April 1863, Hall-Stakely Papers.

[43] Ibid. Col. Cooke is buried in the Confederate Cemetery adjacent to the campus of the University of Tennessee at Chattanooga. Eakin would earn the promotion and would prove himself to be an able though unspectacular regimental commander. He apparently provided as best he could for his men's health and well-being.

"we have had only a few deaths by disease since we came to Vicksburg." The food situation was "tolerable" for anyone willing to pay fifty cents per pound for "flower." He reported that the regiment had received an ample supply from a Monroe County speculator by the name of C. F. White, who, Caldwell was led to believed, had brought the flour down with him on the railroad free of charge by representing it as property of the government. If the flour had been shipped for free, Caldwell noted, then White was gleaning a profit of "32 cents per pound" for every portion he sold.[44]

"Cousin Jemmy" remarked that he was sitting about camp in the midst of a "dull, dry evening," and though he did not really feel like writing a letter, he did so in hopes that Carrie would be compelled to write him back. Caldwell surmised that the "nonsense" he sent her would provide her plenty of opportunity to "correct" his grammar since he could not really do any better "under the circumstances." He indicated that he felt much like "Flossie" did in regard to her "dear Mr. Reed away over in Kentucky and longing for the time to come when he'll come back again!" The time in camp weighed heavy on the boys when not on picket, and Caldwell indicated that rather than reading the daily newspapers, he spent his spare moments reading Sir Walter Scott's "Lady of the Lake." The poem had left Caldwell feeling "curious, or anxious or filled with pleasure, or something else. I don't hardly know which." Nonetheless, he believed, "it is pleasant to us soldiers to read anything in camps, [and] the much more a splendid poem."[45]

Caldwell reported that "Sam" had come back to the regiment, and Captain Bob Rowan of Company D, 62nd Tennessee, had returned a day or two before with another letter. Caldwell noted that "Nachy," the company comic, declared that his pocket watch "runs right when it lies down," but when in his pocket, it "runs long or rather it don't run atall." Nachy, Caldwell wrote, was cooking supper at that very moment. "He says to tell you all 'howdy,' and also he is cooking a piece of nice beef." This fare supplemented the rest of the menu and also included "liver, boiled beef, biscuit and coffee." Nashoua, Caldwell laughed, "wishes you were here to see if he cooks it well." In closing, he invited Carrie and all who read the letter to write to him. In a postscript, he wondered about "the French class" he and Carrie were once a part of in better times, since she had not reported on it for a time. He also passed on the admonition, "a

---

[44] Ibid.
[45] Ibid.

young gentleman of this Regt. says tell Hessie she mustn't marry while he is in Miss."[46]

Yankee Mischief Afoot up at Snyder's Bluff. Around the middle of April, General Bragg was preparing the Army of Tennessee for the onset of active spring campaigning. A number of his brigades had been dispatched during the winter to meet threats in other departments, particularly to Joseph Johnston's Department of Mississippi and East Louisiana. Now, he wanted the troops returned. On the 15 April, Pemberton issued orders for General John C. Vaughn's Brigade to report to Bragg at Tullahoma. By the next day, however, Pemberton became alarmed by Grant's increased activity and feared that he would soon need every man who could shoulder a musket. He countermanded the directive, deciding to "defer the movement of Vaughn's Brigade until further orders." A train reserved for its transportation at Jackson was also put on hold pending events.[47] The preparations for such a move, however, caused considerable activity in John Vaughn's camps in the upper end of the defenses. The men had no idea where they were to go.

Captain Wash of the 60th Tennessee wrote that, around 2 a.m. on 15 April, the boys of the brigade were "roused from their slumber" and ordered immediately to prepare rations that would last four days, a strong indication of a march toward the enemy was imminent. "At daylight," Wash recorded, "everything was ready—our little trunks packed up to go withersoever ordered."[48] Lieutenant Earnest indicated that he too was awakened. "Got up and found we were ordered to cook five-days' rations and be ready for leaving by nine o'clock," he recalled: "by the time specified, all were ready but we were kept waiting for several hours, when the order came for us to hold ourselves in readiness to move at any moment."[49] Pemberton was compelled to hasten some of his troops north of Vicksburg in the direction of Haynes Bluff and Steele's Bayou to intercept a perceived Federal attack there. This impending feint by Sherman's XV Corps was part of Grant's design to confuse Pemberton as to

---

[46] Ibid.

[47] Gen. John C. Pemberton to Gen. Carter L. Stevenson, 15 April 1863, *Official Records*, ser. 1, vol. 24, pt. 3, p. 744; Gen. John C. Pemberton to Gen. Carter L. Stevenson, 16 April 1863, *Official Records*, ser. 1, vol. 24, pt. 3, p.747; H. C. Tupper to Major L. Mims, 16 April 1863, *Official Records*, ser. 1, vol. 24, pt. 3, p. 749. Had the transfer been consummated, it is interesting to imagine what service Vaughn's East Tennesseans might have provided in the bloody campaigns that lay ahead for the Army of Tennessee.

[48] Wash, *Camp, Field and Prison Life*, 24.

[49] Northen, *All Right, Let Them Come*, 80.

where the threat against Vicksburg was to be directed. But the day passed with no further orders, keeping the boys at the ready and waiting in an awful suspense. Into the next morning they sat nervously along the road leading toward Yazoo City, when another order arrived directing the brigade to keep two days of rations cooked and on hand, and, as armies for time immemorial had been instructed, "to await further orders."[50]

All routines in the East Tennessee brigades of John Vaughn and Alexander W. Reynolds began to take on a new level of seriousness beginning the last half of April. The realization had set in that spring had arrived in earnest and that the Yankees were at last going to exchange bluster and make-work schemes for an unrelenting determination that would not end until their aims were realized, or the Confederates compelled them to leave. The calm staring down of one belligerent against the other across the great river was nearly at an end: After months of playing at soldier, threatening hostile intent should the enemy show themselves, the picket duty guarding against an attack that within their hearts the boys probably believed would never come. Even the random shelling was usually about as threatening as an extravagant fireworks display; all this was nearly all over. But even with a myriad of preparations for the grand maneuver, there still seemed to be some moments left that had little to do with the terrible clash of arms just days away. These pauses in history did much to demonstrate the good nature and humanity of the East Tennessee Confederates so far away from their homes, yet so close to one another.

On 15 April, for example, Isaac Stamper of the 43rd Tennessee recorded that Captain James P. Burem, 31st Tennessee out of Bulls Gap, Hawkins County, and Miss Nettie Green of Warren County, Mississippi, were married around dusk. "The boys gave them a serenade," Stamper reported.[51] Another account described the genesis of the romance as one in which "Captain J. P. Burem, with his command at Vicksburg, and on an early morning in March while returning to camp from picket duty, with another officer he called at the house on the way, where a young lady was playing 'Annie Laurie.' He fell in love with the beautiful player on sight, and they were married on this date [15 April]. The wedding was a sensation, and in response to a serenade, he made a thrilling speech."[52]

---

[50] Wash, *Camp, Field and Prison Life,* 24.

[51] Stamper, "Travels of the 43rd Tennessee," 50.

[52] "Capt. J. P. Burem, Thirty-First Tenn.," *The Confederate Veteran* 3/7: 203; "Capture of the *Indianola,*" *The Confederate Veteran* 32/8:381–82. After the surrender, it was widely reported that Grant loaned Burem and his new bride his personal carriage to get to Enterprise, where they would board the train to Hawkins County. The following

Porter's Navy Makes Its Run Down River. Alas, the time for thrilling speeches, military weddings, and serenades passed forever on 16 April, for on this day Grant set the great machinery of his dreaded forces into motion. The attack began with the violent passage of Admiral Porter's gunboats lashed together in pairs, moving close to the Vicksburg shore where the river batteries had problems depressing their siege pieces low enough to inflict any serious damage. The troop and supply transports rode parallel along the city front, twelve vessels in all.

Sergeant Robert Bachman of the 60th Tennessee, along the upper lines where the first barrages were thrown at the Union gunboats by Battery Tennessee, probably expressed the matter best with his simple eloquence: "For three or four months, we quietly passed the time in camp, drilling a few hours a day. Along the river front for several miles we had heavy cannon." Then, on this dark night in April, he indicated, "the gunboats of the enemy ran our batteries."[53]

"Our gunners were greatly aided in their aim by the light which came from some burning cotton barns on the opposite side," Bachman noted, referring to fires lit by brave Confederate scouts on the enemy's side of the river in the destroyed town of DeSoto. But "while some of the gunboats were disabled, most of them ran the fiery gauntlet without injury." None of the ironclads were seriously damaged, and only one of the transports, the *Henry Clay*, was destroyed. Bachman thought that the terrific cannonading "could probably be heard fifty miles up and down the river."[54]

Captain Wash, in another company of the 60th Tennessee positioned nearby, described the situation this way: "Just at 12 midnight, the booming of the signal gun on the river told us the gunboats were coming." He indicated that the 60th Tennessee rapidly responded to the "long roll" and was formed into line of march. It then moved through the darkness, with a heavy trod, rattling canteen and bayonet, "away to the scene." The 60th's march was a response to the perpetual fear that the Yankees were going try to land their men in front of the upper works on the old Chickasaw Bayou battlefield "under the

---

summer, Burem, like Lt. Calvin Smith, was killed in action at the Battle of Piedmont, VA. His body was never recovered, but his father back in East Tennessee erected a stone in his honor on the family farm, bearing his son's likeness in uniform. For an interesting account of this story, see Fred Brown, "A Monument adorns the Captain's old Home-place," *News-Sentinel* (Knoxville TN), 28 November 1993, Living Section, East Tennessee Chronicles, E1, E7.

[53] Bachman, "Reminiscences of Childhood," 18.

[54] Ibid.

cover of the gunboats." The Confederates moved along the old familiar roads and trails at the double quick, in a darkness occasionally brightened with the discharge of a legion of heavy cannon (mostly from the batteries) and pre-arranged fires lit across the river and at various points along the waterfront at Vicksburg. Wash wrote that the boys finally reached the scene of the action where, one mile off, "the incessant peals from forty or fifty siege guns [from] our water batteries shook the earth, and made the air reverberate for miles around."[55]

With errors in almost every declaration, Wash wrote that eleven boats (actually twelve) started to run the gauntlet, and two of them were believed have been sunk in front of Vicksburg. Some had been holed several times, and there was much confusion on the river attendant to their impudent dash past the batteries, but only the transport *Henry Clay* was actually destroyed. Despite Wash's impression that "many of their crews [had gone] under" aboard sunken men of war, none were actually killed, though some of the Federals were wounded. Wash reported erroneously another enemy warship was disabled and floated to safety beyond the range of the roaring Confederate batteries. "They hurled broadsides of shot and shell into the City as they passed," Wash reported, "doing no damage except killing six mules." In what would prove to be ironic understatement, Wash noted, "this was the most successful of several attempts General Grant made to pass our fortress."[56]

Down on the Warrenton end of the line of defenses, activity was also picking up. In an almost surreal prelude to the events that would transpire in the campaign in the next few days, Stamper of the 43rd Tennessee recorded in his diary on 16 April that his regiment was involved in its usual routine prior to the midnight attacks: company drill at 8 a.m., followed by battalion drill at three that afternoon. His only inkling that something was out of the ordinary prior to the evening hours was his note, "a continual cannonading was kept up about Vicksburg." And it was headed with all its fury down the river. About 1 or 2 a.m., he wrote, "a fleet of eight or nine boats attempted to pass town and did affect their object, with the loss of one boat burned by an exploding shell," a reference to the fate of the transport *Henry Clay*.[57]

[55] Wash, *Camp, Field and Prison Life*, 25.
[56] Ibid.
[57] Stamper, "Travels of the 43rd Tennessee," 50. Quite often, one end of the line was not aware of dangerous situations transpiring on the other end, and would continue typical routine unaware of any crises.

Stamper supposed that their object was Port Hudson. The bulk of Porter's fleet passed the defenses of both Warrenton and Grand Gulf, arriving off New Carthage, Louisiana, to begin preparations for loading General McClernand's XIII Corps and General McPherson XVII Corps for the landing on the Mississippi shore. Sherman's corps remained at Milliken's Bend with some of Porter's gunboats. It would soon be on the move overland along the Louisiana side down the river. Wishful thinking about the Federal designs on Port Hudson aside, Stamper recorded that Reynolds's Brigade fell into line of march about 8 a.m. on 16 April, "to go to Warrenton to prevent a landing in case the enemy decided to do so." Again, the East Tennesseans of Reynolds's command were hurried to the works near Warrenton, "where we expected to engage the enemy," but found once more the Yankees were making no effort at a troop landing there. Port Hudson, Louisiana, according to Stamper's hopeful reckoning, still seemed to be the destination and object of this mysterious Federal activity.[58]

In another regiment belonging to the brigade of Alex W. Reynolds, Lieutenant Calvin Smith, of Persia, Hawkins County, and the 31st Tennessee, recorded that his regiment, under Colonel William M. Bradford, was ordered to sentinel duty as its normal routine, with some of the companies assigned to the standard picket posts sites along the levee's bluff. Companies F and C manned the Fort; Companies A, E, D, and H settled back at their rest area in ready reserve. Then, around midnight, Smith indicated that a heavy cannonade began at Vicksburg. Around one thirty, he was up from his sleep and "saw the reflection of light in the fort." It was then that he heard the call to assembly from the alarm cannon. The boys formed up in columns of four soon thereafter and filed into line of march. "Look out!" Smith wrote, as though acknowledging this reaction was something serious this time. "Soon we were in line—give the road—there goes the bearer of dispatches!" One of these dispatches ordered the reserve to the Fort, under the command of Captain James W. Chambers, senior captain of the regiment and commander of the Company A boys out of Sevier and Knox Counties.[59]

Continuing in a delightful stream of consciousness style, Smith detailed the next moments. "What fire is that yonder in the river—boat burning—forward, march!—close up!—what are you doing back there? Halt!—Look out, shells flying!—Silence, onward, march!" He stated that the remainder of the 31st Tennessee was soon inside Fort Warrenton, and they

---

[58] Ibid.
[59] Smith, *A Smith in Service*, 45.

observed that the boats below in the big bend of the river were now out of the range of their short-range arsenal. "Hush!" Smith recorded. "Somebody in distress—perhaps got hurt by a shot as our 4 small cannon fired 80 times—solid shot." A dispatch from "General" Reynolds stated that eight vessels had passed. With the approach of dawn, the boys were able to see a transport, later identified as the *Queen of the Forest*, anchored off the Yankees' camp. Smith assumed that she had put in was due to some damage it had incurred. Other ships suffered in the run past the city. The transport *Henry Clay*, which Smith identified as the *Silver Wave*, was set ablaze and sunk. The gunboat *Lafayette* was not sunk outright; though it lost the coal barge cabled to it, the *Lafayette* was not seriously damaged.[60]

Smith wrote that a yawl was sent across to the Louisiana side to retrieve five men and a lady shipwrecked on the bank, waving the white flag. The lady informed them that there had been fifteen Union ships that had originally started on the dash, but eight turned around to return to where they came from, "owing to the work being too hot to make the trip." Amidst all this bedlam, Smith noted, a lone Yankee battery was popping at them from somewhere on the Louisiana shore; its fire did little damage to Fort Warrenton.[61]

Despite all that was unfolding, the next few days would find things settling back to normal within the realm of Confederate Vicksburg. Military courts still functioned in the camps. On 17 April, a court-martial was concluded against Private M. D. Mayes of Cocke County and the 61st Tennessee. He was found guilty of desertion and was sentenced to die by firing squad. The specifications were given as follows: "Said Mayes did attempt to reach the enemy by crossing the river in a small boat with another man, and when observed by our picket boats and chased, did jump from his boat to the Louisiana shore, on or about 11 March 1863." The case was referred to Secretary of War James Seddon in Richmond, where it was decided to suspend sentence for thirty days pending review by President Jefferson Davis. The fact that such high ranking governmental officials would be involved indicated even the president of the Confederacy could often be petitioned by the lowliest private. Fortunately (or unfortunately) for Private Mayes, the case was forgotten with the beginning of Grant's offensive, and he soon found himself back on duty. He would taken prisoner at the Battle of the Big Black River on 17 May, forwarded first to the

---

[60] Ibid.
[61] Ibid.

dreaded prison camp at Fort Delaware, and then dying later of small pox at Point Lookout.[62]

Down river, Stamper indicated that the 43rd Tennessee was brought back to its camps from Warrenton on 17 April "to await another scare," which would occur with greater frequency in the days to come. Precious little concern for what was about to transpire had filtered to the lower ranks, for "at two o'clock, the 3rd Tennessee Regiment called on our band to play at the burial of Lieutenant Alexander M. Douglass [of Company B and Monroe County] of their regiment." Stamper indicated that the burial site was three miles away, "we rendered the honors due him." In Stamper's own regiment, Private George Dotson of Rhea County died on this date of fever at an undisclosed location in or near the camps. On Saturday the eighteenth, young Private Dotson was buried with full military honors.[63]

The right wing of the 43rd Tennessee had been called back to picket duty. Stamper indicated that he and Bill Fleming were again out looking for drum cord and made a visit to "the Jets" for them. The Yanks had been shelling Vicksburg nearly all day, though the damage was reported as slight. Adding to the aggravation, Stamper reported that the day was troubled by "one of the heavy spring rains" with which the East Tennesseans had become acutely familiar.[64]

Sherman Leaves Milliken Bend and Marches South. Two unidentified soldiers of the 31st Tennessee who had died recently of fever were buried on 18 April. And, with some foreshadowing of coming events, Stamper wrote that some of the brigade's engineers under the command of Lieutenant Calvin J. Ewing were ordered down to Grand Gulf to assist with work on its fortifications. Stamper stated prophetically that "a fight is expected at that place."[65] Pemberton knew that Grant was marching a large body of men from Milliken's Bend south, and it was becoming apparent that the Union general was not interested in coming ashore at Warrenton. Though all the attention given to the little fort there prompted Stevenson and Reynolds to conclude that enemy troops were to be landed in the vicinity, it had not happened. McClernand's and McPherson's corps had proceeded down river in transports while Sherman's corps maintained a presence in the old camps at Milliken's Bend. He would follow later. Leaving the XV Corps behind served to keep Pemberton guessing.

---

[62] 61st Tennessee, *Compiled Service Records.*
[63] Stamper, "Travels of the 43rd Tennessee," 50.
[64] Ibid.
[65] Ibid., 50–51.

Ultimately, Sherman would set out on the long march down the Louisiana side of the channel first toward New Carthage and then cross to the Mississippi side. For the time being, both Pemberton and Grant, unbeknownst to the other, assumed that the landing would be made under the imposing fortifications and heavy guns implanted at Grand Gulf, above a cove into which the Big Black emptied into the Mississippi. It was Grant who would later change his mind. These decisive occurrences, however, were several days away.

Enough of a routine was reestablished by 19 April for Lieutenant Smith of the 31st Tennessee to record on that date that several of his sick men were under orders to report themselves for convalescent recovery. Privates Jesse W. Webster and John Fite were sent to Lauderdale Springs to recuperate, and Private George Ball was ordered to the 1st Louisiana Hospital at Brookhaven.[66]

Stamper of the 43rd Tennessee indicated in his journal on 19 April that the shelling of Vicksburg continued, and between midnight and daylight the day before, "the boat lying opposite our camp supposed to be damaged, fired up and steamed passed Warrenton." The small caliber guns at Fort Warrenton opened up on her, but apparently did her no further injury.[67] Lieutenant C. M. Smith of the 31st Tennessee correctly identified this vessel, but named her wrongly, calling her the *Queen of the Forest* rather than her true name *Forest Queen*. His observation was that around 4 a.m. on the 20 April, the *Forest Queen* was repaired, floated down river in the darkness, where "she nearly passed before being seen." A couple of shots were taken at her, Smith reported, but "she whistled steam up and was soon out of danger."[68]

The right wing of the 43rd Tennessee returned from picket duty along the Warrenton levee, and Stamper recorded the news that shelling was still being directed at Vicksburg. "In the evening," he stated nonplussed, "I put out a trotline."[69]

Back above Vicksburg in the camps of John Vaughn's Brigade, again belying the impending desperate force of arms, Captain Wash of the 60th Tennessee wrote "one of my sergeants who had been to the country to get some clothes washed brought me a beautiful bouquet, which he said was handed him by an unknown lady." Attached to the arrangement was a gilt-edged note that said "Compliments of Miss C. to Capt. W." Indicating he had only seen her

---

[66] Smith, *A Smith in Service*, 45.
[67] Stamper, "Travels of the 43rd Tennessee," 51.
[68] Smith, *A Smith in Service*, 45.
[69] Stamper, "Travels of the 43rd Tennessee," 51.

once, Wash mused: "'Twas a freak of woman's nature."[70] Earnest of the 60th Tennessee indicated not all was not frivolous within their sphere of influence, however, stating that General Vaughn under orders of General M. L. Smith had his command rush from camp out to their defensive positions in the trenches so it could be determined how long it would take the men to be in place and ready should the Yankees try to land again from the Yazoo River.[71] The boys probably did not appreciate the exercise.

Going to Meet the Yankees at Grand Gulf. "Cloudy and some rain," Smith of the 31st Tennessee suggested in describing weather conditions on 21 April. It was a busy day for Reynolds's Brigade as it made active preparation to meet the boys in blue should they attempt their long anticipated landing down toward Grand Gulf. Colonel Bradford's regiment, along with the rest of the brigade, was ordered to break camp and march to a point two miles east of Warrenton, where they would pick up the road that led toward the Big Black River, Grand Gulf, and points southwest. "We slung our knapsacks and accoutrements and fell into line," Smith wrote. The rain had begun again, so the boys marched through it to their new, temporary campsite. The three regimental supply wagons lumbered on after their line of march carrying "3 pieces of cooking vessels, and 2 tents" allowed for Smith's company. "We faired pretty well," he indicated, "though it rained and thundered all night." Administratively, orders required that one company move at a time in order that the regimental baggage, which had to be considerable in these pre-siege days, might be taken on ahead.[72]

The 43rd Tennessee was also on the move, according to Stamper in his daily entry, but suddenly in a different direction. "In a few minutes, the entire regiment was ordered to move," according to Stamper, with the understanding the camp equipment would be brought on the day after. "At about 2 o'clock orders came from the brigade to move in the direction of Grand Gulf."[73] Some urgency drove each step as the East Tennessee Rebels splashed through the standing water in the road, eyes beneath drooping soggy slouch hat brims darting about toward comrades in the line as they leaned into the driving rain with Enfields slung barrel-downward. Propelled by anxious immediacy, sergeants yelled hoarsely to close up the ranks as the men set off on what they must have felt to be the great adventure of their lives to discover and waylay the infernal Yankees wherever they came ashore.

---

[70] Wash, *Camp, Field and Prison Life*, 25.
[71] Northen, *All Right, Let Them Come*, 83.
[72] Smith, *A Smith in Service*, 45.
[73] Stamper, "Travels of the 43rd Tennessee," 51.

"The drums beat the long roll," Stamper wrote, "and the boys started off with the rain pouring upon them in torrents." Left behind once more in the camp, Stamper was on detail with the regimental musicians who were to follow later. As had all too often been the case, he indicated that by sundown, countermanded orders were issued and there would be "no movement for them for the time being." Stamper reported that he and the others left behind in the tents of the old camp were "pleased." During the night, he noted, the rain came down in earnest, "and it seemed it would drown all the boys who were out in it without tents." Certainly, Smith and the 31st Tennessee, in the shelter-less fields of their new digs, had to agree. Stamper indicated that during their idleness, his brother Joe "found a swarm of bees." Seeming always to have time on his hands, Stamper wrote that they constructed a hive and, near dark, put the colony in it. "We expected to have some honey in case we did not have to leave this section,"[74] he stated

Lieutenant Earnest with the 60th Tennessee in the upper defenses recorded matters pretty much as usual on the Mint Springs Bayou. Incredibly, the regiment was again involved in inspections and drill with General Smith's inspector general. "Made an awful start—Colonel C[rawford] making a complete mess of it," Earnest admitted. Quickly, however, Colonel Gregg and the inspector general took over "and the boys performed well."[75]

"We arose early [on 22 April] and cooked our breakfast which consisted of a piece of meat sop and cornbread," Smith of the 31st Tennessee wrote. Soon, a dispatch came informing those in their new bivouac needed to send back to their old camps for rations, "as we may stay here for a few days." He recorded that he was writing around 2 p.m. and had just recently eaten. From where he was sitting, Smith stated he could hear the heavy cannonade of big guns down at Grand Gulf, and it was now almost a foregone conclusion that the Federals intended to make their landing there.[76] Or, perhaps they would choose to come across somewhere between South Fort and Warrenton. Many also believed that Federals still had large numbers of troops at their main camps at Milliken's Bend to threaten Vicksburg. To attempt to meet the threat from whichever point it came, Pemberton had moved one division under General Forney to the vicinity of the Haynes' and Snyder's Bluffs fortifications. The river batteries and General Martin Luther Smith's division (including John Vaughn's Brigade) were charged with the defense of the Vicksburg should Grant attempt to land at

---

[74] Ibid., 52.
[75] Northen, *All Right, Let Them Come*, 84.
[76] Smith, *A Smith in Service*, 45.

the city's wharves, and the four brigades in Stevenson's Division (Tracy's, Taylor's, Barton's and Reynolds's) were to watch the river from South Fort to Warrenton. All this posturing prompted Smith to observe adequate numbers of Confederate soldiers had been placed all "along the way to watch the enemy."[77] Meanwhile at Grand Gulf, General John Bowen's division, 4,200 strong, waited for Grant to come.

The weather had cleared off for the time being, Smith reported, and had become pleasant. He sat rather serenely beneath the shade of a horn beam poplar as he wrote his observations, and felt led to comment on the variety of trees he had encountered while in this section of Mississippi: "magnolias, live oaks, dog wood, mulberry and many others [except for pine]." He stated that he had found cane in the hollows, "growing 30 feet high or more." Toward evening, Smith recorded the news that Reynolds's men were to be relieved by General Edward Tracy's Alabama Brigade later that night. "Drums beat, wagons were loaded, and we fell into line," Smith wrote. "Generals Tracy and Reynolds sat on their horses while we passed in review, and soon after came Gen. Tracy's Brigade: the 23rd Alabama, 31st Alabama, 40th [46th] Alabama the 20th Alabama and 31st Alabama. Smith called them all "a fine set of soldiers." Lieutenant Smith and most of Reynolds's Brigade went back to their original camp east of Warrenton, "after an absence of 36 hours." Once there, Smith said the boys ate supper and retired wearily to their bedrolls sooner than usual, where they "were soon asleep, and soundly slept up to 12 midnight."[78]

Supply Transports Try to Slip by Fort Warrenton. Stamper of the 43rd Tennessee, ever optimistic, reported in his entry for 23 April that during the night, five or six more transports ran by the batteries at Vicksburg in the secure company of a shepherding gunboat.[79] Earnest of the 60th Tennessee noted that Vaughn's Brigade went at the double-quick to their works around 11 p.m. "When we got there the whole line of batteries along the river were ablaze," he reported, and soon after taking their positions, a house on the [Desoto] peninsula was set afire lighting up the whole river.[80] Although the Yankees had been getting more self-confident of their ability to run the gauntlet, this particular attempt proved less successful. Of the six steamers and twelve barges loaded with provisions, the *Tigress* was shot to pieces, ran aground, and broke up along the shore of the Johnson plantation three miles down river from

---

[77] Ibid., 45–46.
[78] Ibid.
[79] Stamper, "Travels of the 43rd Tennessee," 52.
[80] Northen, *All Right, Let Them Come*, 84.

Vicksburg. The *Empire City* was totally disabled and drifted down to Johnson's Plantation, where she was stopped and lashed to the *Cheeseman* for the run past Fort Warrenton. The *Anglo-Saxon*, the *Moderator*, and the *Horizon* received less damage and made it safely past both hazards at Vicksburg and Warrenton. One of the survivors of the dash reported that the six vessels and the troop barges received "500 shots fired at us, and discharges of musketry was kept up along the bank of the river to pick off the men on the transports, especially the pilots, some of whom had their pilot houses taken down and stood exposed."[81]

In Reynolds's camps in the vicinity of Warrenton, Smith of the 31st Tennessee, whose overview of the entire affair was not nearly as enlightened as the Federal volunteers manning the transports, noted that these vessels did not fire a shot as they passed either Vicksburg or Warrenton. He did have some knowledge, however, of the extremely effective marksmanship poured into the transports' steerage deck, which "killed 5 pilots." These additional vessels increased the fleet below to about twenty boats, he remarked, and still the belief was that the Federals were targeting the troublesome Confederate garrison at Port Hudson. Most of the defenders believed that it would have to be eliminated by the Yankees before they could concentrate their full attention on Vicksburg. Smith declared that the batteries at Fort Warrenton kept up a hot fire on the Federal vessels as they went by, "but so far as we could see, with but little effect."[82] His regiment during the day was relieved from picket duty.

Wash of the 60th Tennessee reported on the passage from his vantage point, indicating that, just before daylight, six additional vessels of the Union fleet made their dash through the "rubicon." There were five transports protected by cotton and hay bales, he tallied, and one ironclad. He indicated that the "searching and galling" fire of the Confederate batteries sank the gunboat *Henry Clay* [the *Tigress*], "and the rest were so riddled they had to lay up several days at a landing below the city."[83]

Colonel Andrew Jackson, Jr., commanding the 1st Tennessee Heavy Artillery Regiment at Battery Tennessee, the first to open up on the enemy vessels, described the action taken by his batteries [including the East Tennessee one under the command of John Lynch] during the night of 22 April:

---

[81] Report of Lorenzo Thomas, 25 April 1863, *Official Records*, ser. 1, vol. 24, pt. 1, p. 564–65.

[82] Smith, *A Smith in Service*, 45.

[83] Wash, *Camp, Field and Prison Life*, 26.

The alarm was given at 11:30 p.m., and soon thereafter, a boat appeared rounding the point above, and was followed by five others at short intervals. The two cone side-wheel, the other stern-wheel transports, all small, light-draught boats, well protected at the sides by barges loaded with coal bales of hay or cotton. Their boilers and machinery were protected by cotton bales. Fire was opened upon each in succession as she came in view, and continued with spirit and accuracy until they were out of range [down river]. All the transports were riddled, and the escape of any seemed miraculous, considering the number of large projectiles sent crushing through them. One of them ran into the Louisiana shore opposite Wyman's Hill battery, and was abandoned by her men, and floated down the river apparently in a disabled condition; another was also badly damaged, and floated down with the current.

"The atmosphere was hazy and close," Jackson reported, "and the smoke settled down over the river, often completely concealing and obscuring the boats, and rendering it almost impossible to fire with accuracy. This was, however, in a measure obviated while houses across the river were burning." Jackson continued, "A 10-inch Columbiad, commanded by Captain Lynch," "jumped the pintle at the twelfth discharge, but was remounted in a short time, and is now ready for action."[84]

These transports were heavily loaded with supplies for the Union army advancing toward the village named appropriately enough, Hard Times, Louisiana, from which Grant, within a week, would launch his crossing over the Mississippi. There was now no further supposition required of the troops around Vicksburg concerning the plans of Ulysses S. Grant, according to Wash of the 60th Tennessee. "From the heights around Vicksburg, we [had seen] the wagon trains moving down the river on the Louisiana side," he stated, adding ominously: "the camps of the foe, so long in our view, were disappearing."[85]

The passage of the six vessels in the darkness had interrupted the sleep of the exhausted soldiers of A. W Reynolds's Brigade. "I was awakened by the cannonade and roar of artillery," Smith of the 31st Tennessee recorded in his

---

[84] Report of Col. Andrew Jackson, Jr., 24 April 1863, *Official Records*, ser. 1, vol. 24, pt. 1, p. 570.

[85] Wash, *Camp, Field and Prison Life*, 26. The forces so long opposite on the Louisiana shore were being marched down to the landings opposite Bruinsburg, where Grant's landing of troops would finally occur.

daily entry. "It came from Vicksburg." He reported a "terrible affair of shooting upon our side" even though some of the siege guns had been taken down and relocated up toward the Yazoo River, where Sherman's men appeared active again. Some other pieces, Smith had been led to believe, had been positioned around Vicksburg to take their place. "They have been belching forth in earnest from midnight to 2 a.m.," he observed, "and with but a few minutes intermission, I could hear our troops' hurrahing and cheering as if some great accident had happened to the Yankees." Just before daylight, he wrote, the firing had moved down toward Warrenton as the addled Federal boats drifted and lurched by the guns at South Fort and Fort Warrenton. Smith indicated he and Captain George Hynds of his regiment went up on Flag Hill [South Fort] where "we could see the fire of our cannon and hear the reports which were terrible."[86] It was a thrilling exhibition that was without a doubt impressive for these infantry spectators.

Last Arrivals at Vicksburg. Stamper of the 43rd Tennessee shared somewhat more cheerful news for 23 April when he stated that, at the time he was writing, "all had become very quiet." The boys, he commented, were appropriately referring to it as "the calm before the storm." Other good news on this evening concerned a shipment of provisions from home that arrived by train in Vicksburg for the boys in the 43rd Tennessee. "Several boxes of bacon and flour were received by the boys of Company F," he wrote. "You know this pleased the boys."[87] This was probably some of the last deliveries the boys would receive from their homes. The East Tennesseans had no way of knowing it yet, but all too soon parcels and letter delivery would be permanently eliminated when Grant's stranglehold closed all forms of communication from the outside world to this celebrated corner of Warren County, Mississippi.

In a bit of circumstantial bad luck, John C. M. Bogle of Maryville, Blount County, found himself on 23 April aboard one of those final trains making it into Vicksburg before Grant's landing. Crossing out the word "Maryville" on his letter as his return address, he informed his wife that he had finally arrived in the camps of the 62nd Tennessee at the Mint Springs Bayou. His military status was somewhat unclear, though it seemed that he was initially some kind of agent or perhaps civilian clerk assigned to Rowan's regiment. Bogle arrived at Vicksburg the previous day around noon, and had experienced no real mishaps

---

[86] Smith, *A Smith in Service*, 52.
[87] Stamper, "Travels of the 43rd Tennessee," 52.

on the trip other than being "considerably delayed" due to the conditions of the Southern Railroad from Meridian to Vicksburg.[88]

"Since I left Mobile, Ala.," Bogle reflected, "I think I must have seen by the lowest calculations about 20 or 25 places on the R. R. at which there had been a run off." He noted that near "Big Chunky Creek [the Chunky River]," the bridge had fallen through some time before and sent the whole train—locomotive and all—crashing into the swollen currents below, where nearly forty soldiers were drowned. "We had the good fortune," he indicated, "of coming through without anything of the kind occurring." He informed his wife that the weather was quite warm and spring had almost turned into summer here. Bogle reported that the peaches in Mississippi were already as big as quail eggs, and what little wheat that grew there was "headed out fully" and probably had been so for two weeks. "The whole land abounds in magnificent collections of flowers & *rare* shrubbery," he told her, "in the zenith of their glory." He wished that he were part genii who could wish such marvels back to East Tenn. for her enjoyment. In Mobile, he saw plenty of nice strawberries and had he had his wife with him, they would have shared a couple of plates of them in cream. But since she was not along, he did not avail himself of any.[89]

Bogle was pleased to find her letter awaiting him when he arrived in Vicksburg. He indicated that he had written her often on the way mailing letters back to Maryville from West Point, Georgia, Mobile, Alabama, and Jackson, Mississippi, and pretended to be miffed that she had scolded him in her correspondence for not writing. He forgave her, however, since he realized that his missives haven't had time to get to her yet. In reference to his journey and current situation, Bogle continued his description: "When I got here I had a good wash & change of clothes & expected a good sleep last night." But between 11 and midnight, he stated that the pickets began to discharge their Enfields, and soon after some of the batteries along the river startled him with the deafening roar of their discharges. (For one unaccustomed to the terrific explosions from the big guns, it must have been a terrifying way to have been awakened.) Their target was a gunboat, which "came plunging around the point & then came the heavy hoarse growl of our batteries each for a short time paying *marked* attention...."[90] The remainder of this letter, unfortunately, has not survived.

---

[88] John C. M. Bogle to "Bessie" Bogle, 23 April 1863, Saffell Family Papers, University of Tennessee Archives, Knoxville TN.

[89] Ibid.

[90] Ibid.

On 23 April, Sergeant James Madison Martin, belonging to Benjamin Giddens's Company G, 3rd Tennessee out of McMinn County, wrote a letter to his sister in Athens. He was happy to receive letters from her and his father, but he had almost despaired of ever receiving any more news from home. He declared that he had written his brother, threatening that he would not write home again until he had received at least five or six letters from there. He did not, however, follow through on his threat. Martin indicated that his sister had received a great many letters from him, and that one had arrived almost every Saturday. He noted his surprise at learning from an acquaintance that his sister had gone to work in a factory, but he was even more surprised to hear that H. Leonard was "hiding out" from the conscript officers. Martin wondered if this was true, or if his father was simply writing to shame Leonard into doing his duty. Martin wanted to know whether his father was joking or not. "From what I can learn, they are going to have hard times in Tennessee," he wrote. "Besides a great deal of stealing and robbing, tell Father to keep my rifle and pistol well-loaded and kill anybody that trys to interrupt him." He besought his sister to tell Ben and Harry to "do the best they can," and "tell them to write to me and tell how much [of a crop] they are tending this year."[91]

"I had much rather they [have] me hear than to go back to Tennessee," Martin declared, "for they are fighting rather to hard for me to want to be there." This was probably a reference to the heavy campaigning the Army of Tennessee had endured the fall and winter before in Kentucky and Tennessee. Martin reported there had been no fighting at Vicksburg yet for the 3rd Tennessee, and he was quite confident that there would not be a fight, "nor will we be attacked," reflecting others' confidence the fortifications and natural defensive strength of the Vicksburg works were just too impregnable. "Six gunboats passed our batteries the other night," he wrote, "and one gunboat was sunk and one steamboat intended to pass but was sunk also." Martin referred to a battle at Coldwater, Mississippi, in the north central portion of the state, where the Confederates were reported to have captured 4,000 prisoners plus many commissary stores.[92] Whether the report was true or not, he could not say. Though there was a lot of cavalry activity in that vicinity during this period, there were no casualties figures reported to the extent to which Martin alluded.

"Me and Bud Rogers went to town yesterday," Martin mused, "and bought two old friends of sure-enough coffee. The boys would ask me where I got it

---

[91] James Madison Martin to his sister May McClain, 23 April 1863, Harr-Morton Letters.
[92] Ibid.

and I told them that that was up to me." Generally, he reported, the boys had plenty to eat, and "they bought as much as they drew." He told his sister that he had plenty of clothes as well, but wished that she would make him a new shirt and send it. He closed his letter with the usual imploring of family and friends to write, and stated that he would write his father in a day or two. "I have declined the idea of marrying," he concluded with an interesting bit of news. "I never will marry."[93]

An East Tennessean Serving with the Alabamians. Samuel A. R. Swan was from Cleveland, Bradley County. He had originally volunteered for service with John Vaughn's old 3rd Tennessee, though he was now serving as a commissary officer in Stephen D. Lee's Alabama Brigade, which, like Reynolds's Brigade, was also in Stevenson's Division. In the opening entry in his diary kept during the Vicksburg campaign begun on 23 April, he described matters as follows: "We [Lee's Brigade] were ordered to move down to 'Warrentown.' The passage of several gunboats by the batteries of Vicksburg a short time previously indicated the intention of the enemy to make a movement of a serious nature below Vicksburg." And indeed such was the case. Swan wrote that a couple of nights after his brigade arrived at Warrenton, "several transports succeeded in passing the batteries that confirmed the impression the enemy desired to cross the river [there]." Suspecting a ruse, Swan indicated that while all this was transpiring, Grant continued to exercise a feint on the Yazoo, "to conceal their design."[94] Though this was certainly the case, even Pemberton at the time did not know the intentions of any of Grant's strategy. Sergeant Robert Bachman of Kingsport, Sullivan County, and the 60th Tennessee, evaluated the Yankees' plan beginning on 16 April as a triumph that allowed "General Grant to transfer his army from the west to the east side of the river a few miles below Grand Gulf."[95]

Officers were still required to spend time in matters unrelated to military preparedness. Captain Wash of the 60th Tennessee indicated that he was appointed to a board of survey on the 24 April by General John Vaughn to examine army clothing to be issued to the troops in the brigade. "Most of the pants were of goods manufactured in Lexington, Ky.," he reported, "and was

---

[93] Ibid.

[94] Samuel A. R. Swan, "A Tennessean at the Siege of Vicksburg: The Diary of Samuel Alexander Ramsey Swan, May 18–July 1863," *Tennessee Historical Quarterly* 14/4 (December 1955): 354.

[95] Bachman, *Recollections of Childhood*, 18.

brought out by General Edmund Kirby-Smith [following Bragg's ill-fated Kentucky invasion] in the fall of 1862."[96]

Despite the seeming lack of immediate reaction on the upper lines to the impending crisis, the entries of Calvin M. Smith of the 31st Tennessee for 24 April dealt more with the serious military situation at hand and focused on the activity of the Union vessels on the river. "I learned today," he reported, "that one of their transports was so disabled that she commenced sinking." Smith indicated that the *Tigress* had finally sunk and had washed aground on a point of a small island near the Jonston plantation. He stated that some of the enemy who had abandoned the *Tigress* and perhaps some of the other transports had survived in their life preservers and surrendered to the pickets once they swam to shore. There they were welcomed by their new hosts to the hospitality of close quarters in Vicksburg. Smith's wing of the 31st Tennessee (Companies A, F, D, I, and C) was assigned to the picket lines on this date near Warrenton, where he learned from his friend Captain Chambers that the lethal Confederate batteries struck repeatedly a second vessel, which went under just above Warrenton, and a third which passed through in sinking condition.[97]

"Thus, out of 6 boats," Smith remarked, "we are sure of 3, and one gunboat and 2 transports got through." But not without plenty of damage and numerous casualties, Smith predicted. He added "I have just heard that the lower boat sunk and was set on fire this morning by the Yankies, [where it] burnt right to the water-line." This reference was not substantiated by fact. Misconceptions that the sudden and increasing activity was a plan to reduce both Grand Gulf and Port Hudson led Smith to conclude that Grant would thereafter make his long expected attack on Vicksburg itself.[98]

Stamper of the 43rd Tennessee noted that all remained relatively quiet, with the weather "very warm and sultry."[99] "Sultry" translated as "humid."

Grierson's Raiders Burn the Mail. While Grant amassed his army around Hard Times and the transports and troop barges were being prepared for hauling his men across the river for a landing at some point he had not yet really decided on, a daring Yankee cavalry raid in conjunction with Grant's overall strategy had been ongoing in Mississippi for eight days. Led by

---

[96] Wash, *Camp, Field and Prison Life*, 27. At that time the East Tennessee soldiers were probably not wearing family-made jean clothes other than a few items that may have been forwarded from home. Some evidence exists, however, that, during the siege, many soldiers wore clothing made from non-dyed off-white jean cloth.

[97] Smith, *A Smith in Service*, 46.

[98] Ibid.

[99] Stamper, "Travels of the 43rd Tennessee," 52.

Brigadier General Benjamin Grierson, the command was composed of three cavalry regiments and a battery of horse artillery, 1,700 strong. The raiders left from Grand Junction, Tennessee, on 16 April and, by 24 April, were straddling the Mississippi Central Railroad at Newton's Station, some fifty miles east of Jackson and twenty miles west of Meridian. There they captured and burned two heavily-loaded trains, one of which had been heading east and the other had been traveling toward Vicksburg. Destroyed on the Vicksburg train were munitions and commissary supplies. Even more devastating for Pemberton's army at Vicksburg, however, was that the train was carrying what would prove to be perhaps the final delivery of mail from East Tennessee, Alabama and Georgia to soldiers from those states.

Colonel Key Reports on His Observations. Mosquitoes, Lieutenant Colonel David M. Key of the 43rd Tennessee wrote in a letter home on 25 April, had become the Confederate soldier's constant companion at Vicksburg. They were, he insisted, the one Mississippi crop "which never failed." Attempts at humor aside, Key indicated that malicious Federal intent was for the moment in remission. Though his letter carried little news about the war, it contained interesting information concerning military life in the field. Key informed his wife, "Lizzie," that her box of supplies containing, among other things, fruit and bacon had been safely received. She had also shipped him a barrel of flour, which, next to bacon, was always gratefully appreciated by the East Tennessee boys. "I have seen no ham in Mississippi which can claim comparison with the ones you send me," Key noted, adding, "long may you live and always have such to eat." In an interesting aside fraught with subtlety, Key noted that two "ladies" had been in camp recently. One was "a blooming young lady of seventeen" who was a refugee at Vicksburg, and the other was a widow he described as "fat and forty." He did not speak to them, "leaving those honors to Colonel Gillespie and the Adjutant." Key noted that such "welcomes" were not very comfortable either for him or "The Major [Lawson Guthrie]," since "gallantry dodges the question." In his only actual war news, Key indicated that the papers had by now informed Lizzie the Yankees had again passed "a batch of their boats" by Vicksburg down river. Addressing Pemberton's necessary over-extension of his forces from Haynes Bluff to Grand Gulf, Key reported, "before the boats went down, ours [Reynolds's] was the only brigade below the city lines." This event led the generals to hasten other commands to Reynolds's support to "resist any attempt of the enemy at landing below [Warrenton]."[100]

---

[100] David M. Key to "Lizzie" Key, 25 April 1863, David M. Key Papers, Bicentennial Library, Chattanooga TN.

Key believed that the men of the 43rd Tennessee were in good health. They were eating quite well just then, and he firmly believed that the residents of the Vicksburg and Warren County were having a harder time dealing with the changing situation than were the soldiers. He noted that other parts of the South assumed that Mississippians lived better lives than others. "They have been so accustomed to raising cotton nearly exclusively," he suggested, "and purchasing provisions from the north and west, getting these shipped in by the river." As matters were now, such an enterprise was impossible since the river in both directions was closed to them.[101]

An educated native of Greene County, Key was an attorney, judge, and politician who settled near Chattanooga after the war. He espoused some controversial views, including some liberal attitudes toward rights that should be afforded freed slaves. Like General James Longstreet, he became a Republican after the war and was selected Postmaster General by President Rutherford B. Hays (1877–1880). Key and others from that section of Tennessee often provided in their writings remarkable observations on the milieu of the country, as well as sociological, historical, and agricultural assessments of the new and unfamiliar environment in which they found themselves.

Mississippians "have never raised hogs," Key noted, "since they could buy their bacon with the proceeds of their cotton." Wheat, he declared, would not grow very well this far south, and whereas corn would, it did not mature as fully as it did in East Tennessee because the weevils "cut it up." Before the war during this time of year, the cotton waited in sheds to be shipped out. Its proceeds would be used to bring back all the luxuries and provisions the people in the area would ever require, Key noted, including all sorts of fruits year round. "The farmers [here] are planting very little cotton now," he observed, with corn and sweet potatoes their chief crop. This early in the spring, Key said, corn was already nearly two feet high and the sweet potatoes the farmers raised were "much better than those we grow in Tennessee." It was at this point in his letter Key meant to address the issue of the "mosquito," but he found himself forced to close hurriedly since the mail was about to be taken to the train. He concluded his letter to Lizzie by asking the Lord to "bless you and the children."[102]

"Slept some last night [but] the muesquetoes was very troublesome," Smith of the 31st Tennessee wrote. "They will get under the blanket of which I

---

[101] Ibid.
[102] Ibid.

was covered up head & foot & sing 'cozen, cozen' in my ears." He added that nothing could be done to dissuade the little fellows. The boys "wanted not their friendship," so they had "declared war on them." Another annoying and more dangerous inhabitant with which the boys coexisted were snakes, "of which there are hundreds here of all kinds and sizes." Some of his comrades were pursuing a favorite past time during the day, Smith wrote, trying to catch fish, but to no avail. The river was apace in its late spring settling, and Smith indicated that their brother brigade of Georgians in the division under General Seth Barton had marched from Vicksburg and passed in general review. "[Barton's men] formed lines, wheeled into columns by company, and passed the General [Reynolds] and his staff, while a brass band played [in their honor, as they] marched back to their camps." The boys enjoyed this spectacle of their fellow brigade, alongside which they would serve for nearly the next two months in joint operations both defensively and offensively during the siege. The large bottoms above Warrenton would soon be dry, Smith stated, and "a good place for [such] reviews." However, developing military emergencies would soon eliminate such needless pageantry. Work continued on the Fort at Warrenton in preparation for anticipated enemy attacks, and Smith reported that he heard occasional cannon discharge at Grand Gulf.[103]

Stamper of the 43rd Tennessee wrote that things were all quiet at Vicksburg, though the boys were pretty angry over the news of Grierson's cavalry raid at Newton's Station on 24 April. What irked the East Tennessee boys the most was that the raid had destroyed the mail aboard the train, and the wrecked track there further hindered future later deliveries.[104] In fact, mail in and out of Vicksburg for Confederate soldiers after 18 May would be completely stopped. Many would have to settle for entering their thoughts in what were known as pocket diaries in hopes of being able to share them with their families later. Still, the anxiety of not knowing what was happening at home coupled with all the other miseries inflicted by the siege would prove nearly unbearable. The burning of the train reminded the soldiers of some of "our tricks by General J. H. Morgan," Stamper observed whimsically.[105] Earnest of the 60th Tennessee was also philosophical about the raid, stating, "I think a letter or two in the lot they got was for 'myself'—but no harm they will not likely enjoy the contents."[106]

---

[103] Smith, *A Smith in Service*, 46.
[104] Stamper, "Travels of the 43rd Tennessee," 52–53.
[105] Ibid., 53.
[106] Northen, *All Right, Let Them Come*, 85.

With all this activity, uncertainty, and disorder, death from the old miseries still called in the camps. Private Llewallyn Henry of the 62nd Tennessee and Cocke County died on 25 April of dysentery while serving at Vicksburg. His family supposed that his illness was brought on by the soldier's improper diet consisting of roots and green corn. Hart's family did not learn of his death until some of his comrades returned to Newport after their surrender and parole in late summer 1863. Family legend says that he was buried at Vicksburg (probably as one of the many unknowns).[107]

The few remaining days of relative inactivity fooled the boys into believing that they could settle back into ordinary routine, and though they were to practice vigilance, it was done with little urgency. Grant was continuing to marshal his massive force across the river for its inevitable crossing at Bruinsburg. Other relatively mundane administrative procedures continued in Vaughn's camps around the Mint Springs Bayou, despite preparations on the lower lines to receive Grant's impending landing. Lieutenant Alexander M. Wood of Morristown and the 61st Tennessee service records noted on 26 April that he received a certificate of disability as a result of "stepping on a knife and severing a tendon in his foot."[108] Since he had no parole document in his service record, he probably made his way home by train before the boys were trapped in the works.

Matters on 26 April did not reflect the impending crisis on the lower lines, either. Smith of the 31st Tennessee reported that Barton's Georgia Brigade was again to drill in the bottoms near Warrenton. Captain George Hynds' company was brought into the works on picket duty around the village to relieve Smith's. The Hawkins County boys returned to their camps around 4 p.m. The weather was very warm. The river had stopped falling, and Smith reported it was now "12 inches lower." Smith, supporting Stamper's report, stated that he had heard that the Yankees had made a raid above Jackson "burning some Depoes." He wrote that some "rascals" tried to burn the Fourteen-mile [Creek] bridge, but they were run off by its guards, whom Smith heard "killed 6" of the would-be arsonists.[109]

Meanwhile, activity in the camps seemed to be returning to normal on 26 April. Stamper stated the 43rd Tennessee stood regimental inspection at 9 a.m.,

---

[107] Walker, "Death and Depredation," *Tales of the Civil War*, 109.

[108] 61st Tennessee, *Compiled Service Records*.

[109] Smith, *A Smith in Service*, 46. This action, of course, transpired during Gen. Benjamin Grierson's infamous cavalry raid designed to disrupt Pemberton's communications and supplies. The raid commenced at Grand Junction, Tennessee, and concluded at Baton Rouge, Louisiana.

a Sunday morning routine, followed an hour later by preaching. At around 5 in the afternoon, there was a dress parade. Around that time, the verdict came in regarding a court martial against Captain Calvin L. Hensley of Company G, 43rd Tennessee and Mossy Creek, Jefferson County: he was cashiered from office and his name was sent home to the enrolling officer in his district to conscript him into service again as a private soldier. Captain James Giddens and Captain William C. Morelock, both of the 3rd Tennessee, were punished for not reporting mutinous activity in their companies. Their sentences were the loss of one-half their wages for the muster period and the suspension from office for three months. Private Andrew Pettit, one of the mutinous soldiers, was sentenced to perform police duty around the regimental camps, to lose three months' pay ($33), and to march at the "mark time" on the barrel head three hours each day for the period of his sentence. Stamper indicated that Sergeant Major Graves acted as "agent."[110]

Once again, Smith of the 31st Tennessee found himself awakened before daylight on the 27 April by the roar of cannon around Vicksburg. The official records did not address what this commotion was about, but Smith thought that some more boats were passing, noting that he heard them puffing their way down the river out from Warrenton, snapped at by "the little Bull Dogs in the fort who showed those for miles around that they were not asleep."[111]

On this date around the Somerset Plantation, fifteen miles down and across the Mississippi River from Warrenton, McClernand's XIII Corps and McPherson XVII Corps were preparing for the landing and attack at Grand Gulf. Porter had seven of his ironclads being fitted to pound the fortifications there prior to the landing, with the date for the onslaught set for the morning of 29 April. Ever the master strategist, Grant came up with a new plan for a diversion. Prior to leading his XV Corps now at Milliken's Bend down river to join in the attack, Sherman was asked to make a demonstration in force against Snyder's Bluff, some twelve miles northeast of Vicksburg. This action would require Pemberton to spread even more thinly his defenders in various directions as he tried to anticipate from which quarter the main attack would be launched.

Because the men in the Confederate camps had even less knowledge than their generals of what mischief was being plotted against them by the Yankees, they contented themselves to rumor mongering. Otherwise, they occupied themselves with routine matters. For example, Stamper of the 43rd Tennessee

---

[110] Stamper, "Travels of the 43rd Tennessee," 53.
[111] Smith, *A Smith in Service*, 46.

recorded, "Captain Hensley started home bright and early—disgraced forever." His transgression was not named. "Great mud puddles were created in camp," Stamper continued, and the rain poured all day making most oppressive the humidity. When evening fell, elections were held in camp for the Company G vacancy necessitated by the cashiering of Hensley. The aspirants, according to Stamper, were Francis M. Pennington, James W. Crookshanks, and Houston C. Witt. The primary vote getters were Crookshanks and Pennington, with the former officer elected to the office. Pennington protested the results, and some of the Jefferson County boys were dissatisfied. "It was left to the General [Reynolds] to decide," Stamper reported, "and he decided in favor of Crookshanks."[112]

Colonel Pitts Conducts a Funeral. Meanwhile, out in the county near the community of Oak Ridge, Dr. Thomas Markham and his wife suffered the death of their small son, Willie. The sexton of Vicksburg's Presbyterian Church was asked to conduct the funeral service in his church, but was told the building and the city itself were unsafe due to the damage inflicted by frequent Federal shelling. Therefore, the young boy was buried in the Vicksburg city cemetery, Cedar Hill, where so many of the dead soldiers from East Tennessee were interred. The Presbyterian minister was out of town when the service was scheduled, so Colonel [Rev.] Fountain E. Pitts, commander of the 61st Tennessee and a former Methodist minister, officiated at the "brief, appropriate and touching ceremony." Willie's body, it was recorded, was sealed in the old city vault at the cemetery "during a drenching rain."[113] Thus, Colonel Pitts, who by now was allowing James G. Rose to direct the daily affairs of the regiment, conducted one of his final duties for the people of Vicksburg before his resignation. Pitts left Vicksburg for home sometime around the first week of May, just before the beginning of the active campaign.

Sounds of War Down at Grand Gulf. The discharge of big guns from the vicinity of Grand Gulf was heard on 28 April, reported Lieutenant C. M. Smith of the 31st Tennessee. The exchange was occasioned by three of Porter's gunboats and their "feeling out" of the batteries there. Smith lamented the fact that, even worse for the East Tennesseans, no one had received any "mail since the Yankie raid."[114] The boys were increasingly more affected by the loss of their only contact with their homes, and it would only get worse.

---

[112] Stamper, "Travels of the 43rd Tennessee," 53.

[113] Gordon A. Cotton, *Vicksburg: Southern Stories of the Siege* (Vicksburg MS: self-published, 1987) 39.

[114] Smith, *A Smith in Service*, 47.

The right wing of his regiment had been called to picket duty, Stamper of the 43rd Tennessee recorded. He heard the heavy fire down river and claimed that it came from the vicinity of New Carthage. From the heights at Grand Gulf, General Bowen could see the Hard Times levee, four miles beyond the point where the river hooked. The levee was lined thickly with barges and transports loading men and equipment. On guard in the river offshore lay Porter's squat gunboats looking like gigantic black flatirons, with their tall stacks belching thick dirty smoke, scattered about like a lioness pride keeping watch over their cubs. Meanwhile, in a surreal image belying the danger one day away, Stamper noted that, while the boys were on picket, they "settled a swarm of bees." Private Andy Turner, who was designated "superintendent" of the find, received several stings that caused him to break out in large welts, making him "scratch like nettles." "He had the boys rubbing him with flour," Stamper wrote, "which caused a great many remarks."[115]

Private Joe Smith Reports on Matters in the 59th Tennessee. Private Joe A. Smith of the 59th Tennessee wrote his cousin Carrie Stakely on 28 April from the camp near Warrenton. Quite possibly she never received it until after the surrender. He was anxious to hear from her, he confessed, realizing that he could not expect to unless he was the first to employ "Dear Ink & Paper." He stated that much time had elapsed since he had last heard from her, causing him to fear that his "once friend and playmate" had forgotten him in far-off Vicksburg, Mississippi. Smith lamented the fact that he had been gone so long from Madisonville, and scarcely a day had passed that he had "not been carried back in my imagination to the same old place to me so familiar with scenes, faces, &c." He was uncertain as to whether she was receiving any mail from the boys of her acquaintance who served with the 59th Tennessee, and if not, he intended to inform her of the regiment's activities since leaving "good ole East Tennessee." They were still in camp four miles south of Vicksburg, he reported, and about that distance north of Warrenton on the banks of the "great Mississippi." Warrenton, he concluded, "is a very small place but now deserted town where our brigade pickets one day out of every seven." This was pretty much the only duty they were called on to do right now, Smith noted.[116]

---

[115] Stamper, "Travels of the 43rd Tennessee," 53–54.

[116] Joe A. Smith to Carrie Stakely, 28 April 1863, Hall-Stakely Papers. Today, Warrenton is unincorporated and straddles the famous US Highway 61. It contains several shopping centers, a coffin manufacturing plant, and the Vicksburg City airport. The roads leading west toward the river from the highway pass a few homes, but the one-time location of Fort Warrenton is not marked.

"Having pretty fair water yet and rations some of the worst," Smith wrote, "but little or no exposure our regiment is perhaps in as good condition and it may be better than it would have been at this time if it had remained in E. Tenn." The regiment had not experienced much sickness so far, Smith reported, "and indeed, I haven't heard of a half dozen deaths in the 59th Tennessee since we have been here." He confessed, however, that most of the boys had little or no desire to remain in Mississippi once summer arrived in a few short weeks. The boys knew that, along with the intolerable weather, they would find most of their sources of water had evaporated, leaving them with only what they bring in from the Mississippi River itself. And this water would have to be hauled by wagons "over the very roughest kind of road" over a mile and a half to the camp. "This I hope and trust before that time shall have arrived, our officers will move us from this locality if not entirely out of the state," he confessed. The boys were anxious to be gone, and they said nearly to a man, according to Smith: "*Lord*, any [duty] rather than Mississippi!"[117]

Smith concluded his letter by indicating that he would now "bring this very dry, dull and uninspired letter to a close." If, however, Carrie deemed it worth her while to respond, he promised that his next effort at letter writing would "improve." In a post-script, he reported to "Miss Stakely" that cousin Jimmy Caldwell is "looking well and apparently enjoying life as well as any person in camp." Indeed, Joe Smith wrote young Jimmy, one of Carrie's many correspondents at Vicksburg, had not been sick since they had been in camps, and most of her other acquaintances in the 59th Tennessee were also "generally well."[118]

Worries about Home. As an indication of the disdain many of the Mississippians held for the East Tennesseans' service in the Cotton State, a letter dated 28 April appeared in the Knoxville *Register* from an unidentified East Tennessee Confederate soldier serving at Vicksburg. This soldier bitterly protested that the boys felt unappreciated and wasted in Mississippi, while their interests and their homes were threatened by an imminent Federal invasion through the Cumberland Gap:

> Our own generals and commanders of regiments know the mountains and passes, they know the people, and they should have been in command in East Tennessee all the time and today we would have a better state of affairs around our homes. But the authorities in

---

[117] Ibid.
[118] Ibid.

Richmond thought otherwise and some great failures have been committed. Commanders placed over East Tennessee soldiers looked upon them as nobody and viewed them all with a suspicious eye. I am willing to make a contact with the government that Burnside and his 30,000 men cannot invade our homes if we are sent there to defend them.[119]

Grant Initiates His Grand Plan. On 29 April, the first stage of Grant's "Grand Maneuver" commenced. Porter's seven ironclad gunboats raised steam and headed across the river toward the high bluffs and the fortifications at Grand Gulf. General John Bowen, from Missouri, had sixteen siege guns and field pieces waiting. The Big Black River emptied into the Mississippi near the upper approach, across from the point of the river basin. Mounted here were four large caliber cannon and a howitzer, and on the bluffs below Grand Gulf were three other large siege pieces and four howitzers. Three other field pieces had been placed in the center among rifle pits manned by Bowen's infantrymen. The Union gunboats began their bombardment of the upper fort (Fort Cobun) at 8 a.m., firing some 2,500 rounds during the next five hours into the bluff earthworks forty feet above the river. Their bombardment failed to silence any of the Confederate cannon. The tremendous cannonade in these lower sections was heard up in the area where Vaughn's Brigade was camped, according to Captain Wash of the 60th Tennessee. "At broken intervals all day we could hear it in the direction of Grand Gulf thirty miles down the river." After dark, he reported, three more gunboats tried to pass the "frowning batteries" and one of them was "badly used up."[120]

Private Joseph Smith of the 59th Tennessee forwarded additional war rumors to his cousin Carrie. He claimed that the Yankees had brought ashore 45,000 troops approximately fifteen to twenty miles to the south at the mouth of the Big Black River. "If this report is true," Smith concluded, "we will have to change our locality sure enough—and that *immediately*." He was relatively certain that there would be no opportunity for the boys to fight them near

---

[119] Unidentified Confederate soldier to the Knoxville *Register*, 28 April 1863, McClung Historical Archives, Knoxville Public Libraries, Knoxville TN. It is no small irony that when the Federal government was scrambling to forward reinforcements from every department to Grant at Vicksburg, John Parke's division was ordered there from Ambrose Burnside's command in Kentucky on 14 June 1863. The loss of these 8,700 men postponed the highly anticipated invasion of East Tennessee for another two and a half months.

[120] Wash, *Camp, Field and Prison Life*, 27.

Warrenton from the rifle pits since the men all knew that "their objective is doubtless to get our roads cut off" and thereby choke off the supplies and trap Pemberton's scattered army. Grant was determined, Smith believed, to "shame us into surrender or into an instant evacuation of the place." He did not believe that the Feds would be successful. "We [and] the enemy will certainly find us prepared to meet them," he boasted, "attack us where they may or where they will." Until something toward that end transpired, Smith stated, "I forbear saying anything further in regard to it."[121]

Another Smith in Reynolds's command, Captain Calvin M. Smith of the 31st Tennessee, reported on 29 April that he would muster the boys for their monthly pay the next day. Some newspapers out of Memphis arrived today, Smith wrote, namely, the *Appeal* and the *City Whig*.[122] He professed no personal knowledge of anything untoward occurring at Grand Gulf. Not so with Stamper of the 43rd Tennessee, who wrote of heavy cannonading near Carthage, and of word that some of the enemy had landed there. Continually, "a fight was generally expected." He reported that, just before dark, the 59th Tennessee was ordered to Warrenton and had left the brigade's camps. "We all expected to go that night," Stamper stated, "but were not called out."[123]

Captain Reuben Clark of the 59th Tennessee wrote in his diary that Grant had landed a division on 29 April near Port Gibson, only thirty miles from where Reynolds' Brigade was located. "I was on picket at Warrenton," he stated, "when orders came to report with my men to Colonel Reynolds without delay." The 59th Tennessee was then hastened on the road by forced march toward Port Gibson, "without time to prepare rations." The regiment, tired and hungry, arrived there around 10 p.m.[124]

Sherman's Ruse on the Yazoo. The great movement of the armies toward one another was underway at other points as well, namely, the upper defenses of Vicksburg. Sherman's men were menacing the city from their old landing on the Yazoo River. Prior to daybreak on the morning of 30 April, Grant had finally managed to land on the eastern bank of the Mississippi 20,000 men of the XIII Corps under General McClernand, along with some of John Logan's Division belonging to the XVII Corps. A Union scout gained valuable information from a slave that their best landing place would be near the abandoned village of Bruinsburg, some 10 miles south of Grand Gulf. Grant

---

[121] Joseph Smith to Carrie Stakely, 28 April 1863, Hall-Stakely Papers.
[122] Smith, *A Smith in Service*, 47.
[123] Stamper, "Travels of the 43rd Tennessee," 54–55.
[124] Clark, *Valleys of the Shadow*, 19–20.

wanted every musket he could gather for the landing, but feared that if he
brought Sherman's corps too quickly, Pemberton would shift his entire force
down to Grand Gulf. So Grant left the XV Corps on the Yazoo for a time to
vex Pemberton's imagination.

Confronting the boys in blue on the upper end of the line, Wash of the
60th Tennessee stated that after delivering a severe shelling on the Confederate
defenses at Snyder's Bluff, Sherman's troops, supported by a half dozen
ironclads and some twenty transports loaded with infantry, went up the Yazoo
River and rushed ashore some of these soldiers. The Confederates there
"suspected it was merely a ruse, to draw our troops from other quarters."[125]
Earnest, also of the 60th Tennessee, agreed that such a demonstration was "not
apt to fool anyone as [it] is undoubtedly a feint." He believed, however, that the
"ball will open tomorrow in earnest—and if not tomorrow, perhaps the next
day."[126] This prediction proved correct, for as night fell, the troops who had
been previously set ashore suddenly returned to their vessels, and the transport
flotilla withdrew to its landing up the river at Young's Point. From there, after
unloading from their transports, they struck out by land, headed southward
toward Hard Times, Louisiana. The part of McClernand's corps that had not
already landed was just ahead moving at the quick march. Wash said that the
gunboats stayed behind and continued shelling the upper Confederate defenses
at Snyder's Bluff. By now the opposing forces were shifting toward Port
Gibson; elements of the Southern army to check the Federals already ashore
and additional reinforcements to meet those Yankees who would soon follow.[127]

Samuel Swan of Cleveland, Bradley County, serving with Stephen D.
Lee's Brigade, wrote on 29 April that the gunboats had been engaging the
batteries at Grand Gulf all day with neither antagonist rendering the other any
real damage. The Union fleet, however, suffered the loss of eighteen sailors
killed and fifty-six wounded in the exchange. By evening, Lee's Brigade was
ordered to march to Grand Gulf and did so after dark. They reached the Big
Black River with their baggage train while the night still lingered on. Swan, as a
commissary sergeant, accompanied his brigade's wagons and reported that they
experienced great difficulty in getting their heavily encumbered conveyances
through the slimy bottoms. The train took the entire day to get through. Lee's
Alabamians, according to Swan, crossed the Big Black by steamboat, and after a
little sleep, were marching early the next morning 30 April. He reported that

[125]Wash, *Camp, Field and Prison Life*, 28.
[126] Northen, *All Right, Let Them Come*, 88.
[127] Wash, *Camp, Field and Prison Life*, 28.

Baldwin's Mississippians had also come up and crossed during the day. They passed Lee's men and continued on with their supply trains. "All day we heard the very heavy firing at Snyder's Bluff," Swan wrote, which led him to surmise that Grant wanted to mount a feint in order to prevent the shift of large numbers of Confederate reinforcements down to Grand Gulf. Grant masterfully kept Pemberton guessing as to where he was concentrating his real efforts: Grand Gulf, or up above Vicksburg around Snyder's Bluff. Swan indicated that at dark Lee's Brigade had moved forward toward Grand Gulf.[128]

Robert Spradling of the 43rd Tennessee reported succinctly, "the Yankees crossed the Mississippi River and landed at Port Gibson on the 30th of April, 1863."[129] The 43rd Tennessee was apparently not called to any action on that morning, and indeed, routine continued be the order of the day. "The regiment had mustered for pay," Stamper of the 43rd Tennessee reported, though the boys had to be distracted by the heavy cannonade kept up by the Yankees at Snyder's Bluff. Incredulously, Stamper recorded that the news "all was quiet about Grand Gulf." The left wing of the 43rd Tennessee was sent on picket to Warrenton in relief of the right wing of the regiment. The routine seemed incredulous, given the activity all around. Company F caught a number of fine fish while on picket, Stamper noted, stating one of them weighed sixty-five pounds.[130] Meanwhile, north of Vicksburg, after the invaders pulled their troops off the old Chickasaw Bayou battlefield for the march down to join Grant, Earnest of the 60th Tennessee indicated that his regiment stood inspection in "a desperately hot sun." He proudly proclaimed: "We bore it like heroes and stood our ground."[131]

Captain Jacob Hays of the 59th Tennessee was also involved in usual routine. He drew from Stevenson's divisional quartermaster clothing and camp equipment for his company, perhaps only hours before the regiment was called to make the long march down to Grand Gulf. His allotment included eight hats, ten jackets, nineteen pair of pants, five cotton shirts, ten pair of brogans,

---

[128] Swan, "A Tennessean at the Siege of Vicksburg," 354.

[129] William Raleigh Clack, "Personal Diary of the Siege and Surrender of Vicksburg, Mississippi, July 4, 1863" (unpublished manuscript), Vicksburg National Military Park Archives, Vicksburg MS) 1.

[130] Stamper, "Travels of the 43rd Tennessee," 54.

[131] Northen, *All Right, Let Them Come*, 87.

seven pair of drawers, one wall tent and fly, five camp kettles, one boiler and lid, one iron pot and skillet, and four mess pans (tin plates).[132]

Calvin Smith of the 31st Tennessee also reported on 30 April that the previous morning, a cannonade at Grand Gulf continued without intermission. He had just made out the muster rolls for the company, when around 10 o'clock he observed a heavy cannonade begun on Vicksburg resulting in "fires I can't count." He added to his report specific details regarding Grierson's raid on the Jackson railroad that destroyed five miles of track, burned twenty boxcars, and "injured" two steam engines. Then the Yankee raiders then rode off. General W. W. Loring offered them a fight, Smith stated, "but they skedaddled." Grierson was riding to join General Nathaniel Banks at the Red River, according to reports Smith had heard. Grierson, of course, would have been ordered to avoid engaging Confederate infantry with his horse soldiers, and to continue his raid right on to Baton Rouge. At midnight, there was rapid firing above Vicksburg at Snyder's Bluff. "Waggoner" Rice told Smith that he had heard that General Vaughn had argued with his superiors to rush the entire army to Grand Gulf and give battle to the Yankees as they were coming ashore, but to no avail, probably because, as Smith predicted: "There will be—no doubt—a heavy fight above Vicksburg." Pemberton and others still were not convinced that Grant would not make his actual assault over the Walnut Hills. Smith reported that the Memphis *City Whig* carried the story about the Yankies attack at "Grand Gulf with 6 gun boats and 3 transports from above [river]." The story indicated that one boat was disabled and floated helplessly past the batteries. "The other steamed up the river after throwing 3000 shells," Smith quoted from the article, "killing our army's Colonel of Artillery [William Wade]" in the works at Grand Gulf.[133] Quite often throughout the campaign, the boys only learned of conditions and incidents around Vicksburg through the newspapers.

Hard Marching Toward Port Gibson. Meanwhile, in their haste to reach Grand Gulf, the boys in the 59th Tennessee were doing some hard marching, an unaccustomed activity after months of routine camp life. The crackle of grasshoppers lofted from the weeds alongside their route across roads that were uneven and rutted, and often slowed their progress when they dropped off into miry ditches containing blackened water with undeterminable bottoms. Grant had McClernand's men moving quickly in the extreme heat and dusty conditions from their point of landing toward Port Gibson seven or eight miles

---

[132] 59th Tennessee, *Compiled Service Records.*
[133] Smith, *A Smith in Service*, 47.

distant. Indeed, all the digging, marching, and work the Yankees had occupied themselves with over the winter would find them in much better physical condition then their Southern counterparts once active campaigning commenced.

After some time, the 59th Tennessee, according to Captain Reuben Clark, "laid down within hearing of the enemy," and found itself much worn out with fatigue, the heat and hunger. They had marched nearly fifteen miles since leaving camp that morning, and, were now a few miles south of the Big Black River. Around daylight on 1 May, they were finally told to stack arms and sleep on the road or along the banks lining it. Their slumber proved short-lived, however, when they were awakened at 2 a.m. and ordered to march in the opposite direction from Grand Gulf. The Yankees had neutralized the defenses there and were speedily deploying along the roads and fanning out to the northeast, straight for either the regiment or the crossing it would use to get back to Vicksburg. Stevenson's Division, which had been rushing toward the landing area as fast as it could go, was now ordered back toward the Vicksburg to avoid being cut off by Grant's forces racing toward the Big Black River crossings, the supposition being that McClernand's goal was to flank them and cut off their retreat. Tramping wearily back in the direction from which they had come, Clark indicated that once the 59th Tennessee made it across the Big Black at Hankinson's Ferry, they were ordered to camp in a large grove of magnolia trees and remain there on guard until further orders.[134] Grant's men, despite making a feint toward the crossing to cut off the Southerners below it, had no intention of moving in the direction of Vicksburg just yet. His men were headed east. The assignment of the Confederate resisters was to keep Grant's hordes on the southeastern side of the Big Black River, which, for the time being, was his intention.

Incredibly, with all the hostile action brewing to the south of the Vicksburg, John Vaughn's men carried on as normal. Captain William A. Wash of the 60th Tennessee noted that on 30 April, that his brigade commander sensed the danger and had issued orders that no soldier or officer was to leave camps without Vaughn's written authority. Such restrictions always seemed to be ignored by the young Kentuckian serving with the Cocke County company, and he managed to slip off with one of his friends to visit a young lady in the

---

[134] Clark, *Valleys of the Shadow*, 20.

country where "Lieutenants Billy R. and Jim B." would be present, playing the violin for her pleasure.[135]

"We studied and calculated between the good to be done obeying the order," Wash wrote, "and the pleasure to be derived from going." The fiddle "out balanced," he admitted, and as soon as darkness descended, off he and his officer friend strolled. They soon arrived at the home of the young lady's father, "Mr. C." Following along immediately behind them were the two lieutenant musicians, but they arrived with no violin. They sent word back to camp for the forgotten fiddle, saying that it was needed for a concert in another part of the camp. "In the meantime," Wash reported, "Miss Mollie and Miss Henrietta happen in." Their parents were dutifully convinced that music with dancing was "no account," but, with a little coaxing, the old folks gave in. After some prancing about on the arbor in front of the house, the young officers decided that it was time for them to be back at their camps. When the sun broke over the horizon to the east on the morning of 1 May, Wash wrote, "no one suspected we had been absent, nor did the secret ever leak out." He was left to conclude, "a soldier may sometimes if he will have as fine times as anybody."[136] The martial activities of the next two weeks would rob him of most of his chances at socializing for a long time.

The bi-monthly musters for March and April were completed during this turning point in the campaign. Six companies serving with Vaughn and Reynolds reported the following status of their men:

> Company C, 59th Tennessee: fifty-four men present for duty during the period, including two men returned from desertion, and three conscripts. The status of four other men was not stated.[137]

> Company I, 59th Tennessee: eighty-two men present for duty during the period, the status of six others not stated. Four men were absent on detached service (including Captain [William] Smith, who was back in East Tennessee recruiting); Four men were absent sick in Vicksburg area hospitals. One soldier was absent without leave back in

---

[135] Wash, *Camp, Field and Prison Life*, 27. According to Lt. Earnest, 2nd Lt. William ("Billy R.") Gammon of his regiment was an accomplished fiddler. Northen, *All Right, Let Them Come*, 69.

[136] Wash, *Camp, Field and Prison Life*, 27–28.

[137] 59th Tennessee, *Compiled Service Records*.

East Tennessee serving with Thomas" Legion. One man received a medical discharge. Three men died of disease during the period.[138]

Company H, 60th Tennessee: Fifty-one men present for duty during the period, including one man returned from desertion; the status of seventeen men was not stated; seven men were sick in Vicksburg area hospitals; two men died of disease, during the period; five men were killed by a tornado; one man was absent on detached service; two men received medical discharges.[139]

Company I, 60th Tennessee: seventy-seven men were present for duty during the period, including four men who were returned from desertion, and one man returned for duty from the hospital; one man was sick in camps; the status of eighteen men was not stated; six men were absent sick in Vicksburg area hospitals; one man was medically discharged; two men were carried on the rolls as deserters.[140]

Company G, 61st Tennessee: sixty-two men were present for duty during the period, including one man who had transferred from the 31st Tennessee, and one man present sick in camps; six men were absent sick in Vicksburg area hospitals; one man transferred to the 31st Tennessee; one man discharged; three men were carried on the rolls as being absent without leave.[141]

Company I, 62nd Tennessee: seventy-four men were present for duty during the period, including one man transferred in from the 5th Tennessee Cavalry; six men were absent sick in Vicksburg area hospitals; one man discharged for an undisclosed reason; five men died of disease during the period; one officer resigned his commission.[142]

---

[138] Ibid.
[139] 60th Tennessee, *Compiled Service Records.*
[140] Ibid.
[141] 61st Tennessee, *Compiled Service Records.*
[142] 62nd Tennessee, ibid.

The last day of April would bring a close to the often comfortable routine of camp life, for on following day, Grant's "grand maneuver" would proceed like some irresistible force long expected and even anticipated. Papering the walls and tables of his headquarters, the topographic maps of his vast defensive responsibility rose in their awesomeness before John Pemberton.

CHAPTER 6

"Fixing Up Our Contraptions for a Yankee Hunt" 1-15 May ("The Grand Maneuver")

Grant Moves Inland—The Battle of Port Gibson. The XIII Corps, some 17,000 strong, under the command of Grant's old nemesis John McClernand, had by daybreak of 1 May found itself ferried across the Mississippi from Louisiana to the abandoned and mostly wrecked hamlet of Bruinsburg. From there, the corps had made its way inland toward the Confederate defensive lines at Port Gibson, some five miles due east. These determined Yankees had been marching most of the night. McClernand feared that the Confederates under the steady hand of General John S. Bowen of Missouri would burn the bridges north of Port Gibson, bottling the Yankee forces below the Bayou Pierre and its tributary, the Little Bayou Pierre, and allowing Pemberton time to rush troops southward to check the Yankee advance. Back at Bruinsburg, John Logan's Division in Major General James McPherson's XVII Corps was also crossing the river to land on the Mississippi side, increasing the strength of the landing party to nearly 25,000 muskets. Bowen realized that if the Yankees captured Port Gibson, the flank of Grand Gulf would be exposed, necessitating its abandonment. The terrain in the Port Gibson vicinity approximated most of the landscape in the Vicksburg area: steep knobs and ridges with eroded ravines snarled with thick weeds, cane and tangled undergrowth.

Around 8 a.m. on the morning of 1 May, the Battle of Port Gibson opened with McClernand overwhelming Bowen's 2,500 Rebels. By dark, Bowen had withdrawn from the field in good order after a desperate and bloody struggle resulting in casualties to nearly 25 percent of his men. His stubborn efforts, however, bought Pemberton time.

Samuel Swan of Edward Tracy's Alabama Brigade, and a native of Cleveland, Bradley County, indicated in his journal entry that, at about 10 a.m. on 30 April, his brigade, like Reynolds's, also in Carter L. Stevenson's Division, was on the move toward the crisis at Grand Gulf and reached "a fork of the road three miles from Grand Gulf and five from Port Gibson." "A fierce battle was then raging on the Bayou Rim," Swan wrote, "some three miles below Port Gibson." The Federals had marched "a large force" by land on the opposite side of the Mississippi. General Bowen's command, Sterling "Pap" Price's old division, had been merged with two brigades of Missourians. Swan indicated that Tracy's Alabama Brigade came on the field about 1 a.m. on 1 May and went immediately into action. Baldwin's Mississippians and Louisianans arrived at about 8 a.m. "General [Edward D.] Tracy was killed about 8 a.m.," Swan wrote, noting that Tracy "was a very brave man and exposed himself greatly, and he was shot by a sharp-shooter."[1]

According to Swan, the boys involved in the action "behaved well and held their position until late in the evening, when the enemy massed his forces on the right flank of our line" turning the Confederate position and compelling them to withdraw northward across the Bayous Pierre. This was done in good order, Swan asserted, though it caused the Southerners to leave their dead, their severely wounded, and nearly 400 of their comrades in the hands of the Yankees. "Our troops fought obstinately all day against overwhelming odds," he reported, and "they suffered severely, several officers, a number of men and many horses being killed and two of their cannon dismounted."[2]

Thus, on the first day of May began a series of battles that concluded on 17 May with the disaster at the Big Black River, and the subsequent beginning of the siege of Vicksburg. General John S. Bowen's forces met Grant as he crossed the Mississippi River below Port Gibson at Bruinsburg. Bowen repulsed the advancing enemy at first, Captain William A. Wash asserted, but his force was small and Grant soon had the whole Union army across and coming against him. After a spirited defense, Bowen thought it prudent to fall back and ordered his men to spike the large unmanageable siege guns that could not be readily withdrawn. This was done on 2 May. Wash wrote that there were considerable losses on both sides: 875 Federal and 787 Confederate.[3]

---

[1] Swan, "A Tennessean at the Siege of Vicksburg," 354.

[2] Ibid. One East Tennessean captured during this action was Pvt. James W. Netherland, 1st Tennessee Cavalry. His company C and other cavalry units were operating as scouts between Grant's advance and Bowen's men checking the Yankees near Port Gibson. During this time Netherland was captured. Interestingly, he was exchanged through the lines on 12 June, perhaps because he had contracted small pox. The Federals probably thought that Netherland could cause more harm among Pemberton's forces within the siege lines. 1st Tennessee Cavalry *Compiled Service Records*.

[3] Wash, *Camp, Field and Prison Life*, 28.

"We lost General [Edward D.] Tracy of Alabama [in the fray]," Wash noted, "and also General Bowen's chief of artillery [Colonel William Wade]." In the delaying action, Wash indicated that Anderson's [Boutetort] Virginia Battery, which had eight field pieces "and the best equipped I ever saw," lost fifty-six horses, six guns, and thirty-seven men. Its two remaining guns would be lost two weeks later at Baker's Creek, and only five men of the battery returned to the Vicksburg trenches.[4]

"My company was detailed on the night of May 1st to go on outpost guard," Wash continued, "in the entrenchments at the bend of the river above Vicksburg." Like Reynolds's Brigade and its levee picket duty at Warrenton, this assignment was the on-going routine for the 60th Tennessee and Vaughn's other regiments: to man the ditches on what had been the left flank of the old Chickasaw Bluff's battlefield. Ever since the Federal fleet first made its appearance above Vicksburg the latter part of January, Wash reported: "Rain or shine, hot or cold, some of us had to lie in the ditches every night so it had become commonplace." He indicated that the night was warm and pleasant, and things were passing off quite agreeable in the camps along the Mint Springs Bayou two miles northeast of Vicksburg. "We placed our guns in proper place in case of alarm," Wash stated, "[and] listened to and chatted a while about the booming cannon down at Port Gibson. Then we spread our blankets and laid on them for a good night's sleep."[5]

Sometime earlier in the day, E. D. Parker, also of Wash's 60th Tennessee, "dropped a few lines" to his wife "to inform you of my health." It was good, he wrote, and he hoped that his wife and his son were also in good health. Though Parker prefaced his letter with the admission that he "had no news," he indicated that matters seemed strange now since "there has bin some fighting 78 miles below and 42 miles above, the result of which is not known yet." The men were expecting an attack "hear day and knight." They had orders to march toward Tennessee, "but I don't think we will leave tel we either whip, run or scare the Yankeys away from this place." Sickness ran rampant through the regiment, he reported, "but almost all of them is improving with a few exceptions."[6]

"We burn, sink or capture a bote occasionally when they attempt to pass our batterys," he indicated, referring to the enemy. "Tel your father I would like to see him & tel him some of my yarns," Parker teased, adding the sad news

---

[4] Ibid., 28–29.
[5] Ibid., 29–30.
[6] E. D. Parker to his wife Susan, 1 May 1863, Parker Letters.

that "Cosen Eligia Brown [of his Company E] is ded he died the 29 of April." He reported that his wife's brother Samuel was well, "though he has a complaint of the bowel." There had been plenty of cornbread and bacon for the past ten days, "but they brought us old poor beef this morning." Moreover, the boys had to pay high prices for anything "to nurish us when our stors is out of order." Some of the prices he quoted were as follows: "Eggs is bringing $2.50; Butter $2; flour 60 cts. per lb.; chickens $3 to $3.50 a piece." Not realizing that the mail would soon be cut off from the outside altogether, he admonished her to "write often" and "give me all the news in the neighborhood."[7]

Colonel Pitts Resigns. Lieutenant Colonel James G. Rose had been managing the affairs of the 61st Tennessee for some time. He indicated that Colonel Fountain E. Pitts, "who was advanced in years and a minister of the Gospel," resigned command of the regiment on 1 May. After this date, Rose stated, Pitts was no longer in camp with the regiment.[8]

Their War Begins in Earnest. On 1 May Captain Robert Hynds of the 31st Tennessee wrote a letter to his mother in Jefferson County "the Yankees made an attack on Grand Gulf the day before yesterday, but [it] was not successful." The shelling there was the heaviest cannonade he had ever heard. "It lasted over 3 hours and there was about 3,000 of the enemy," he noted, "our loss was small, one colonel and three men killed, and only 13 wounded." He reported that the numbers lost by the enemy was unknown, though one of their gunboats was badly crippled and damaged. Hynds asked his mother to tell his little brother Alex that, every time he had been on picket, he caught "plenty of fish."[9]

Sam Dick, a mutual acquaintance, was seeking a sick furlough to come home, and rather than wait for it, he left on his own accord. "General Pemberton ordered him to the hospital," Hynds wrote, "but he went on. He did very wrong for the doctor wanted to see him once more before they would grant him a furlough." He cautioned his mother not to say anything to Sam's parents, but he "is awful sick of the war" and that's "about all that matters with him at this time." While affairs in camps beginning the day for both East Tennessee brigades were mostly routine, the conditions at Port Gibson were spreading northward and would soon attract the attention of most of Reynolds's brigade.[10]

---

[7] Ibid.

[8] Rose, "The Sixty-First Tennessee," in Lindsley, *The Military Annals of Tennessee (Confederate)*, 1: 574.

[9] Robert J. Hynds to Mary Hynds, 1 May 1863, in *Civil War Records*, vol. 78.

[10] Ibid.

"The battle of Port Gibson was fought on Friday, the 1st day of May," Robert Spradling of the 43rd Tennessee wrote in his diary: "our brigade [Reynolds'] started to Port Gibson Friday night and arrived there Saturday evening about sundown."[11] Stamper, also of the 43rd Tennessee, reflected on the strange contrast the day brought, when it dawned clear and beautiful and three companies of the regiment were paid. Before dark, however, many of Reynolds's men were being rousted from their camps and hustled into a line of march, their faces turned toward Port Gibson. "Our forces engaged the enemy for five hours at there," Stamper reported, though "we were repulsed due to superior numbers." Reynolds's men could not reach the field in time and were not actively involved in the battle. The Federals were in possession of the town and its fortifications by 5 p. m. Two hours later, the 43rd Tennessee and the other three regiments in Reynolds' Brigade left camps to reinforce General Bowen's overwhelmed command falling back from Port Gibson. Buttressing Bowen's defense was no longer the objective; the East Tennesseans, along with other elements of Stevenson's Division, were now being charged to protect the upper banks of the Bayous Pierre. The Tennesseans would later be charged with protecting the crossings along the Big Black River itself. The boys endured a forced march, which had begun at sundown, Stamper reported, with the 43rd Tennessee making fifteen miles by 2 a.m., resting "for the night" in the vicinity of Hankinson's Ferry, which traversed the Big Black River.[12] This would be the main escape route for Bowen's (and later W. W. Loring's) defeated forces retreating from Port Gibson.

Orderly Sergeant William H. Long of Morristown, who served with the 59th Tennessee, wrote that Reynolds' Brigade was "sent to Grand Gulf about 52 miles below Vicksburg" to contest Grant's landing. Despite "marching all night & day, some 50 miles in twenty-four hours," the brigage arrived too late to engage the Yankees as they came ashore.[13]

Defending the Western Bank of the Big Black. Orderly Sergeant Murray Brown of Elizabethton, Carter County, and Company C, 59th Tennessee, noted that, on 1 May, his regiment "left Camp Reynolds 3 miles below Vicksburg, Mississippi, and marched in the direction of Port Gibson. The company halted and remained at Hawkins [Hankinson's] Ferry on the Big Black River with four other companies of the regiment until the army fell back across

---

[11] Spradling, "Diary," 1.
[12] Stamper, "Travels of the 43rd Tennessee," 54.
[13] Long, "Autobiography," 1: 58.

the [Big Black] river."[14] This half of the 59th Tennessee was expected to defend this closest northward crossing on the river, the first route the Yankees were expected to try to seize leading as it did directly to Vicksburg. However, Grant continued to be a master of deception, and despite sending sizeable detachments or cavalry in the direction of several crossings over the Big Black, he persistently drove the bulk of his exhausted and water-starved legions on a long, forced march northeast toward Jackson and its railway supply link connection with Vicksburg.

Wash of the 60th Tennessee wrote concerning his watch north of Vicksburg, "at about the hour of midnight leading into Saturday the 2nd of May, we were aroused from our slumbers by the heavy tread of troops crossing the bridge not far from us." He stated that these Confederates marched directly by his regiment, probably heading south toward Port Gibson. "These boys were in high spirits," he noted, "having heard the rattle of musketry before." This was General John C. Moore's Brigade of Mississippians, Alabamians, and Texans, just arriving "from the Yazoo and Deer Creek country," where they had been defending Fort Pemberton.[15] The commanding general for whom the fortification was named continued consolidating all his forces below Vicksburg. The number of men positioned in the upper works was dwindling as more were drawn away to the emergency around Port Gibson, soon leaving only Vaughn's Brigade to maintain the lonely watch for enemy activity on that flank. So far removed, his men were oblivious to the desperate situation to the south that would soon engulf them all. For the present, much of their routine continued as usual.

Serving with the Medical Department, Lemuel Cline, a hospital steward from Dandridge serving with Rose's 61st Tennessee, stated in a letter to Lizzie that he was embarrassed to be writing since Grierson's raiders had torn up the railroad "at some point above Jackson," and as a result, he had received no letters for some time. "The great fight has now commenced on the Mississippi," he wrote, informing about her a the battles south of Vicksburg the past two days near Grand Gulf. He said that word from there indicated that the Southern army "has got the best of it," necessitating reinforcements being rushed there by both sides.[16]

---

[14] 59th Tennessee, *Compiled Service Records.*

[15] Wash, *Camp, Field and Prison Life,* 30. Moore's Brigade had been north of the defenses confronting Sherman's feint against the upper works while most of the Yankees came battled their way by Port Gibson and Grand Gulf.

[16] Lemuel Cline to "Lizzie," 2 May 1863, Lemuel Cline Letter, National Park Archives, Vicksburg MS.

"I think if we prove victorious at that point," Cline predicted, "it will put a stop to fighting in this valley." With the landing down the river, he believed that the Yankees had left their end of the line north of Vicksburg altogether, and "I'm glad of it." He wanted his regiment to "get into a little fight," provided that he came through safely. Cline reported that the enemy was busy on the river, apparently preparing for its fleet's involvement in this new phase of the campaign. He could see their boats from his post near the Mint Springs Bayou. Word had come to him that Lizzie's father had been captured in Kentucky and that one of her brothers had been killed there. Cline hoped that neither report was true. He was sending his letters out by Billy Bowman, "who is starting for home this morning," since the standard Confederate mail service was unreliable now that Grierson's raiders were operating in the area. "I have been anxiously awaiting a letter from you for some time," he noted, "and as yet have not received one for several weeks." He thought that she had stopped writing him, and he had almost stopped since he had gotten so few replies from any of his acquaintances.[17]

"The weather is very warm here," Cline wrote, and the boys believed that they would not get away from Vicksburg before next month, "if then." They knew, however, that they would not be leaving before the Yankees do. "I have been enjoying myself finely for some time here among the sand-lappers of Mississippi," he mused, "and have found a nice lady down here and am afraid I will have to take a *rib* in this part of the Confederacy." Contrary to this affinity for the Magnolia State, Cline suggested that though "the boys are generally well and in fine spirits," they were almost to a man ready to return to serve in East Tennessee. The medical assistant from Jefferson County included with his letter a printed map of Mississippi so that Lizzie could see "what a fine place it is." He indicated that his brigade was two miles to the "left" of town by the map. Once he returned home, Cline promised to show her the principal points on the engraving if she will "preserve it." The hour grew late, Cline conceded, and he would have to close for the time. His fellow steward Thomas Rader of Greene County was, after all, "pestering me so much I can hardly write."[18] Such light-hearted banter for these boys was drawing to an end.

Cline wanted to hear from Lizzie, and he wished that she would inform him about General John Scott's recent cavalry raids in Kentucky, in which a number of East Tennessee Confederate cavalrymen of his acquaintance had participated. Cline particularly wanted information about which of his friends

---

[17] Ibid.
[18] Ibid.

and neighbors had been killed or taken prisoner. In closing, he noted that it was a Saturday evening, and that he had spent the day in town while much of the army was rushing to the invasion site some fifty miles down river. He stated that he would go to preaching on the next day, as he did every Sunday. He only wished that he would be home for the summer. "But Alas!" he exclaimed, "I fear I will be doomed to disappointment."[19]

Calvin Smith of the 31st Tennessee reported in his diary "two hours before sunset yesterday evening [1 May], we and the whole brigade left camp and marched past Warrenton—night overtook [us]—still we traveled on past some pickets and fine farms." The moon was shining brightly and the brigade continued on until midnight, when it halted and lay down to take its rest, "being tired and sore, and not used to marching." Many of the boys were bare-footed. The brigade slept soundly until an hour before daylight, Smith wrote, when "we arose from our rest and fell into line—soon marching." After a brief time, they reached the [Big Black] river, and made their crossing over a pontoon bridge he called "boats lashed together." Here they were halted again and allowed to rest.[20]

Spradling of the 43rd Tennessee stated in his writings, "we started on the retreat at 10 o'clock on the evening of May 2, and got back across the Big Black River Sunday evening [3 May]."[21] Isaac Stamper, also of the 43rd Tennessee, indicated with a bit more precision that his regiment finally reached the Grand Gulf vicinity around sunset after crossing the Big Black River at Hankinson's Ferry early on Saturday morning, 2 May. Hours later, with their supper completed, he indicated that the boys lay down and slept until around 2 a.m. [3 May], when they were awakened. With some urgency, they then marched back to the crossroads at Willow Springs where the enemy was attempting to cut them off before they could cross the river to the elevated upper bank of the Big Black.[22]

The army deployed all along the Bayou Rim along the Big Black. Samuel Swan of Tracy's Brigade, now under the command of Colonel Isham Garrott after Tracy's death at Port Gibson, noted, "sometimes skirmishing with the enemy, who, however, made no serious attempt to cross."[23] Grant's advance had made a feint against Reynolds's placements, as though threatening a direct push

[19] Ibid.
[20] Smith, *A Smith in Service*, 47.
[21] Spradling, "Diary," 2.
[22] Stamper, "Travels of the 43rd Tennessee," 54.
[23] Swan, "A Tennessean in the Siege of Vicksburg," 355.

toward the works at Vicksburg. The Yankees, however, soon resumed their movement northeast toward their primary objective at this stage of the campaign, the state capital, Jackson. Three fine bridges in the area along the Bayous Pierre had been burned the night before to hamper Grant's supposed advance north toward Vicksburg. "That evening [2 May]," Swan recorded, "Reynolds' Brigade arrived, wearied with the long march." Then around dark, Generals W. W. Loring, who would assume field command and supervise the withdrawal toward Vicksburg, and Lloyd Tilghman's Brigade also arrived. At dark, the generals decided to evacuate Grand Gulf due to its indefensible status and fell back northward over the Big Black River toward Vicksburg.[24] Pemberton's intention was to form his defensive line all along the north bank of the Big Black up as far as the Big Black Bridge. The ridge formed by the flow of the river through the centuries had produced a most formidable bluff for defensive placement on the west bank, coupled with the natural obstacle of the Big Black itself then wild and fierce, swollen with collected spring rains.

Standing Guard at the Chickasaw Bayou. With the assaults in the vicinity of Grand Gulf and Port Gibson, and the uncertain intent of Grant's simultaneous designs on the lines above Vicksburg, Wash of the 60th Tennessee wrote on 2 May, "we had to go on picket duty in front of the Chickasaw Bayou." Though there were now no Federals visible in that direction, the northern flank had to be protected against "any emergency." Because the guard line was over a mile long, a nervous Wash noted, "it was not fun posting and instructing sentinels."[25]

"The days were getting hot enough to kill a fat man," Wash recollected, "and at night the mosquitoes were far more terrible than the anticipated Yankee shells and bullets." John Vaughn's men, positioned often as pickets in the vicinity Snyder's Bluff, were ordered back toward Vicksburg that evening. At dusk, Wash and his Cocke County men watched the bulk of the troops north of Vicksburg as they advanced past their picket posts. For three long hours they filed by, he noted, three brigades and several smaller detachments headed to defensive positions to check the enemy thought to be advancing from to the south. "The artillery which can move faster than the infantry, struck camp the day before," he reported, "and away they went, lumbering down the valley." Among this contingent was Captain Ferdinand Claiborne's 3rd Maryland Battery, the only Confederate force at Vicksburg from that state. It was a command that would later serve within the fortifications with A. W. Reynolds's East Tennessee Brigade during the siege. Wash stated that such frenzied

24 Ibid.
25 Wash, *Camp, Field and Prison Life*, 30.

activity, with hundreds of troops being moved in the direction of Grant's landing at Grand Gulf and Bruinsburg, left the small assembly of defenders around Vicksburg feeling "kinder ticklish." Indeed, with the current emergency, Wash indicated that, as far as he knew, no other brigades except John C. Vaughn's East Tennesseans were defending Vicksburg.[26]

"We felt honored by being trusted with so important a duty," Wash declared proudly. All was now on a war footing, and along Vaughn's picket line that night there was another fierce war going on, Wash mused, "between the boys and the mosquitoes." He stated that the soldiers were unable to sleep that night, so they alternated their swearing at the buzzing critters and the Yankee nation.[27] The fields before them, which had been covered for months by the high stage of the Mississippi River overflow, was now a swampy mire where portions of the Chickasaw battlefield had been hatching great swarming squadrons of the pests. After a night of worrying with the "biters," as Wash termed them, he found himself the next morning checking on his picket posts as "the beams of ole Sol were getting nigh perpendicular." Once satisfied that all was secure and his men were poised and alert to any alarm, Wash, as he often seemed to do, found the time and gall to slip off from duty to visit with the ladies in the country with whom he had made previous acquaintance.[28] This was another example of Colonel Crawford's, or Colonel Gregg's, laxity in military discipline, which allowed his junior officers to do whatever they wished, even during emergencies.

"I sauntered leisurely away," Wash reported, "though contrary to a strict line of duty with no one noticing my course." He stated that he got up a half a mile on higher ground, where it was cooler, and felt inclined to "go on further." Along a rugged terrain tangled with the new undergrowth of late spring vegetation. His path led up inclines until he arrived at a "nice little cottage" more than a mile from his post. "Knowing that there was a charming somebody there," he wrote, "and that I might get a good dinner, I accidentally happened in to blow a few minutes." After a couple of hours into his visit, the cook announced to Wash and his hostess that their dinner was ready, which he ate, then concluded his stopover, hastening "back to my post many not knowing I had been absent."[29]

---

[26] Ibid.
[27] Ibid., 31.
[28] Ibid., 32.
[29] Ibid.

Lieutenant Earnest, also of Wash's regiment, noted that the evening heat was "almost insufferable." He had spent the day trying to read a book, but at he had to stop because the mosquitoes began their assault, spreading out over the lines from their swarms that hovered like thick black clouds over damp marsh and depressions.[30]

Orders awaited Wash's company when they came in off picket which almost always indicated preparation for active campaigning: "cook four days' rations and await further orders." In a few hours this task was completed, and "we were now ready for the fray," Wash stated. Scarcely had the regiment lain down for rest when the booming of cannon indicated that something was amiss over on the river. The long roll was sounded and the brigade hurriedly fell in, "though we had been constantly on duty for three days and nights," according to Wash. The East Tennesseans hustled in the darkness toward the river at the double-quick, and as they staggered along at a half run, that heard out on the river the escape of steam making a loud blow, signifying some mortally wounded Union vessel.[31]

"When we gained the top of [Fort] Hill overlooking the scene of the action," Wash noted, "the object was in range of the heaviest and hottest [Confederate] batteries." Allen Wash's friend James Earnest, also of the 60th Tennessee, wrote the that vessel soon turned by "the right oblique" and headed for the Louisiana shore.[32] In a matter of minutes, smoke and flame burst forth from a Yankee, the *George Sturgess*, and the gunners ceased their lethal work. The tugboat, just out in the river from Vicksburg, burned to the water line with twenty-three out of a crew of twenty-five captured, some badly scalded. The boat's contents were medical stores, and it was thought to have been protected on either side by cotton-clad barges carrying, Wash learned later, 50,000 rations for hungry Federal soldiers down river.[33] Wash concluded in his entry for 2 May, "that was our last experience with the night visitors on the water," adding, "they smelt 'a mice' and came no more."[34] Despite this modest victory, the real damage was already done down the river and had left open the route to Grand Gulf on the Mississippi shore.

Another Mississippi Family of Good Samaritans. Lieutenant David Hynds, a native of Mossy Creek, Jefferson County, was a member of the 3rd Tennessee

---

[30] Northen, *All Right, Let Them Come*, 89.
[31] Wash, *Camp, Field and Prison Life*, 33.
[32] Northen, *All Right, Let Them Come*, 89.
[33] Ibid.
[34] Wash, *Camp, Field and Prison Life*, 33.

and not involved in Reynolds's forced march toward Grand Gulf. Hynds wrote a letter to his mother on 3 May from the residence of Mr. Kline, where he almost recovered from a long spell of typhoid fever. His recovery was so sound that he would "be able to return to duty in a short time." Mr. Kline's plantation was called "China Grove," and its owner was a wealthy planter, "clever and a gentleman in every respect." Hynds also described Kline's wife as "clever," and reported, "she has been almost a mother to me since I have been here." Hynds, a handsome lad, was also blessed with the attention of their four daughters, "who seem to take as much interest in my welfare as if I had been a brother." Other boarders in the house included Mrs. Arnold, a widow, her three sons, and a daughter, who Hynds found to be an interesting little girl of eleven.[35]

"I have had every attention paid to me that I could possibly have had if I had been at home," Hynds wrote, "and I must acknowledge that I have been just as well satisfied." He informed his mother that he had been confined to his bed for thirty-eight days, "and much of that time my skin was parched with a burning fever." With all that, however, he marveled that he never once "lost his reason for a single moment." The fever had always been worse from 8 a.m. until around 4 p.m., and he believed that he never became "deranged" because "Mr. Kline's youngest daughter Nannie was constantly by my bed, bathing my head, face and hands in cool water." The experience, he asserted, was anything but disagreeable; the daughters "are both interesting little girls & will long be remembered by me."[36]

Dr. A. C. Blevins, the regimental surgeon, also attended Hynds during the worse days of his illness and "handled my case well according to Sam [David's brother]," which led Hynds to conclude that Blevins was "a splendid surgeon." Disagreements seemed only to have arisen when Hynds was forced to take the "bad taste" of the medicine. Sam also had been with him continuously, and was "here yet," Hynds wrote this letter. "He will go back to camp to make out the company pay roll."[37]

Hynds also wrote about the impending and on-going Yankee activity, noting, "we had a fight with them last Friday at or near Grand Gulf some 30 miles below Vicksburg." He referred to the loss of General Tracy "of our division," and that "our brigade has been sent down there." He had heard that

---

[35] David Hynds to Mary Hynds, 1 May 1863, in *Civil War Records*, 1: 72.
[36] Ibid.
[37] Ibid.

30,000 Confederates were confronting 40,000 Yankees, "but we still send more troops on down."[38]

"Mr. Kline and his son speak of going down [to Grand Gulf] tomorrow," Hynds noted, but he was not sure whether they would go or not. Their inclination seemed to be to "take their guns and go into the fight with the rest of the poor soldiers." Undoubtedly as a matter of pride, the wealthy planter and his son, whose ages were not indicated, felt obligated to defend not only their state but also their own property.[39]

He reported that Joe Shadden (a kinsman or neighbor out of Dandridge, Jefferson County who served with the 31st Tennessee) was also sick in a private house about five miles away. "I will go see him in a day or two," he promised, "for you must know that when I wish to ride, I have a choice of carriage, single buggy or horseback, and some one of the young ladies generally goes with me."[40]

Calvin Smith of Persia, Hawkins County, and the 31st Tennessee, wrote in his journal that the regiment and brigade were fourteen miles south of their Warrenton camps. Referring to the brigade's frantic movements of 1 and 2 May, he acknowledged that General Tracy had been killed in the "hard fight with the Yankies near Port Hudson," and his loss would be severely felt. Colonel Isham W. Garrott of the 23rd Alabama "was seen to fall from his horse [in the fight] and was taken prisoner, but made his escape which gave glorious news." The Federals captured a battery in the fight, but it was reclaimed. "For nine hours, 600 men without any reinforcements kept several thousand in check, reinforced by brigades at a time." Smith stated that the 31st Tennessee was held in support of Waddell's Alabama Battery, composed of seven "fine guns" and toting several loads of ammunition. The East Tennessee boys, Smith remarked, after months of garrison and picket duty, were "ancious to meet the enemy." A large steamboat, he noted, was anchored near their present position, and they were always aware of distant artillery down on the river.[41]

Defending Hankinson's Ferry. At 10 p.m. on 1 May Smith wrote, the brigade was formed into columns of four and marched southward, "passing some large farms of cotton and corn." They arrived at a point on the Mt. Vernon-Willow

---

[38] Ibid.

[39] Ibid.

[40] Ibid.

[41] Smith, *A Smith in Service*, 47. The steamer in question would have been one of four supply transports (the *Charm*, the *Bufort*, the *Paul Jones*, or the *Dot*) trapped in the Big Black River once Grant's men came ashore and cut off their escape via Grand Gulf to the Mississippi.

Spring Road, reportedly only two miles from the Yankees, so close they could hear their drums. The brigade was ordered to fall out and take some sleep, which they were allowed to enjoy for only two hours. The boys were then roused up and ordered to double-quick it back to where they had crossed the Big Black at Hankinson's, at a pace they had to keep up for about nine miles. The feeling in all their minds continued to be that not only was a large body of enemy infantry at their heels, but it could suddenly attack them out of the darkness either from the flank or perhaps face to face. "The cavalry met us there [across Hankinson's Ferry along the north side of the Big Black]," he recorded, "and told us the enemy is near us in heavy forse, aiming to surround us."[42] Though such a strike was never initiated, Spradling of the 43rd Tennessee indicated in a letter written in 1904 that the boys were involved in "heavy skirmishing all day long,"[43] continually halting and forming across the road a line of battle, and facing one way or another seemingly at the whim of their nervous officers in anticipation of a sudden attack from all directions by untold numbers of omnipresent belligerents.

Finally arriving at the Willow Springs crossroads after attempting to distance themselves from Grant's advancing hordes, the regiment and brigade were allowed to rest a few minutes around 7 a.m., taking a quick breakfast from their haversacks before being thrown again into line of battle facing south as rear-guard. "Here, we had hot skirmishing for three or four hours," Stamper wrote, "until the remainder of our army had passed that point, and we were allowed to fall back to safety over on the other [northwest] side of the Big Black River." Reynolds's men had been relieved by Bowen's Missouri brigade, assuming from the East Tennesseans the task of covering the Confederate retreat across the Big Black at that vicinity. Once Reynolds's men had crossed the river, Stamper reported, "we marched about four miles [toward Mt. Vernon] and took up [made camp and slept] until morning [of 3 May]."[44]

"By one o'clock on 3 May, the head of the column was crossing the Black on a bridge of flat boats placed end to end," wrote Swan of Tracy's Brigade, and a native of Cleveland, Tennessee. Reinforcements from General Stevenson's Division (Reynolds' East Tennesseans) were there to meet them at Hankinson's Ferry. Before darkness descended, Swan noted that all the Confederates, totaling some 17,000 men, engaged south of the Bayou Pierre at Grand Gulf and Port Gibson were by this time safely across the river. From the lower bank

---

[42] Ibid.
[43] Spradling, "Diary," 2.
[44] Stamper, "Travels of the 43rd Tennessee," 55.

of the Big Black, the Yankees were "throwing a few shots" in Garrott's direction.[45]

In the early morning of 4 May, Smith of the 31st Tennessee noted Confederate forces on the retreat toward the works at Vicksburg now included the brigades of Generals Bowen, Green, Tilman (Tilghman), Stevens (Stevenson), and Reynolds's. Smith indicated that Reynolds's men, unused to all the marching, were "nearly all asleep" on their feet.[46] These troops were being rushed to the various ferries, bridges, and crossings on the Big Black as far as the Southern Railroad in anticipation of the Federals marshalling their forces to cross further up. Were they to succeed, it would become a foot race to the works at Vicksburg. Reynolds's Brigade was marched toward China Grove plantation, where they and other commands were assigned to keep a watchful eye for an attempted enemy crossing of the Big Black at either Hall's Ferry or Baldwin's Ferry. Half the command was left at the plantation, while W. W. Loring, in charge of the rear guard defense, rushed Bowen's, Cockrell's, Green's, and Taylor's Brigades toward the Big Black River Bridge. The cavalry scouts shadowed Grant's various lines of advance and continued to report that the Yankees were in force close by. Reynolds's Brigade, which had been protecting the crossing over the Big Black at Hankinson's Ferry, was called to again cross the river and meet the Federal advance in that direction.

Battling Grant's Advance. Breathless and sweaty cavalrymen reported that the Federals were now only a few miles south of their position. "[We] fell into line and marched down toward them," Smith reported, where Reynolds formed the brigade as follows: "Our [the 31st Tennessee] was left across the road, the 3rd Tennessee and 59th Tennessee took post further to the left, and the 43rd Tennessee was sent to the front to protect the skirmishers." This line entered the woods, he stated, "and the fighting soon commenced."[47]

"We thought we were now going into it in earnest," Smith recorded. The Yankees had planted a battery and fired a few rounds at the skirmishers and the 43rd Tennessee, which fell back until they reached Reynolds's main line of battle. Another enemy battery was placed on a flank to gain better advantage on Reynolds's artillery support. Waddell's Battery responded by firing many times and, gaining its rhythm, soon commenced a rapid fire. The accuracy of the Alabama gunners caused the enemy to pull their field pieces a mile off, but the Southern "shells continued to be fired [after them] with great effect." The

---

[45] Swan, "A Tennessean in the Siege of Vicksburg," 355.
[46] Smith, *A Smith in Service,* 47.
[47] Ibid.

damage at that distance, however, could not be determined, admitted Smith, who based the effectiveness of the Confederate field pieces on the rapidity with which the Northern guns had had to be moved. Even with the good shooting, the Yankee battery was about a half mile off, causing Smith to declare that their shells came in too quickly to dodge, but were aimed too high to be of any real threat. With their delaying action accomplishing all it could, the 43rd Tennessee, and soon the entire brigade, was ordered to fall back to Hankinson's Ferry. Once again, concerns of a flanking movement by the superior Federal numbers cutting the East Tennesseans off from the Big Black predicated the withdrawal. The scramble toward the river was hastened, and Reynolds's Brigade passed several other brigades and regiments as well as long trains of wagons headed in that direction. Once back across the Big Black, the brigade was ordered camp for the night.[48]

Smith wrote, "we had a fine night rest, having slept less than 5 hours in 2 days & nights, and having traveled 60 or 70 miles." Safely north of the river, he admitted that he was not aware of the numbers of Confederates assembled there, but declared, "we are ready to fight now in earnest." By late the afternoon of the day before (3 May), all the boys had gotten across, and the Confederate pioneers had nearly destroyed the bridge. The Yankee cavalry dashed up and tried to harass their work, but to no avail. No word had been received, according to Smith, that anybody was hurt in the defense.[49]

In the previous afternoon action on the skirmish line, Smith stated that John Kite, Jr., serving as a skirmisher, was shot at, the ball passing "through his clothes above his knees," but not hitting flesh. "All [the skirmishers] escaped" unharmed. If the boys in blue were going to cross the Big Black at Hankinson's, Smith maintained, they had now have to pause first to construct their own pontoon bridges. But he, his comrades, and Pemberton himself had no way of knowing what Grant's ultimate strategy was. Pemberton's intentions were to bring back to the works as many of his soldiers as he could to defend Vicksburg. Regardless, every Confederate command, in anticipation of an impending major battle at or just above the Big Black, was ordered to send back to camps for its walking invalids who could carry a musket in order to swell the defensive ranks. "Lieutenant James Miles [of Strawberry Plains, Jefferson County] was detailed back to [the 31st Tennessee's] camp," Smith reported, "to bring out the able men that might be there." He indicated that the regiment was ordered on the march at around ten that night, and after progressing some six miles toward

---

[48] Ibid., 47–48.
[49] Ibid., 48.

Warrenton and their camps, were halted and told to rest. After a brief period, they were again assembled and marched five more miles near the familiar plantation of Captain Barnes, who was also in the army, where they camped for the night.[50] Barnes's plantation was just off the Warrenton road a few miles from Reynolds's camps, and some five miles southwest of China Grove, where the 43rd Tennessee was bivouacked.

"The Barnes' family was hospitable and patriotic," Smith suggested. They had been very good to the sick East Tennessee Confederates, and, indeed, at that very moment, Lieutenant Robert Long and Private E. H. Long were quartered there under the care of Privates Hugh Harper and I. B. Dykes of Smith's company. The next morning, 4 May, Reynolds's Brigade was marched down to Antioch Church near the Big Black, where the brigade camped on the farm of Mrs. Sexton, another kind lady who had taken in various numbers of sick East Tennesseans. There, Smith observed, half the regiment was kept out on picket toward the river to watch for the Yankees crossing there, but "there were no enemy around this side of the Black River." He reported that he had heard some firing down near the Red Horse Church four to five miles distant, which he supposed to be the enemy's pickets probing ahead of their main advance. He reckoned that the Yankees were preparing their pontoon bridges down there in advance of their crossing of the Big Black to advance toward Vicksburg. Smith supposed that when they came, "we will have a hard fight here, perhaps. Or we're willing to try our luck in Vicksburg itself."[51] Sustenance had been accumulated now inside the lines at Vicksburg, so he knew that Pemberton was anticipating a long siege. Even with that realization, he and the boys were hungry for a fight.

Stamper of Bradley County and the 43rd Tennessee stated, "we marched ten miles [on the retreat from Grand Gulf] and were ordered into line of battle four miles out of Warrenton."[52] Spradling of the same regiment indicated the 43rd Tennessee was at [Hankinson's Ferry near] the Antioch Church [where the defensive stand was to be made], but "the Yankees moved away [after the weak demonstration described] in the direction of Jackson."[53]

Swan reported that the Alabama Brigade had now, after the death of General Edward Tracy, been placed under the capable command of Brigadier General Stephen D. Lee. The Bradley County soldier noted that at midnight

---

[50] Ibid.
[51] Ibid.
[52] Stamper, "Travels of the 43rd Tennessee," 55.
[53] Spradling, "Diary," 2.

the trains of the army were put into motion, "and the troops [from the different commands] are positioned to defend the different ferry roads leading toward Vicksburg across the Big Black River northward." Lee's Brigade was camped four miles east of Warrenton, with the general's "headquarters being located near Gib Gibson's."[54]

"We remained in this position awaiting the enemy to develop his plans," Swan wrote. As an official of the brigade commissary, he noted that the men with that department all through the army were busy "driving in all the cattle and collecting all the corn on the Big Black and hauling it into our lines."[55] It was a precaution taken should unfortunate events allow Grant to force the Confederates inside siege lines at Vicksburg. Though contingencies, maneuvers, and defensive posturing were in play because of affairs around the Big Black, matters back in Vicksburg, where John C. Vaughn's Brigade awaited orders, seemed deceptively routine and ordinary. No movement was anticipated, according to Wash of the 60th Tennessee, so he, Captain Francis S. Blair of Jonesborough, Washington County, and Captain Samuel R. Gammon of Rogersville, Hawkins County, made arrangements with an old black woman there to prepare them a good dinner.[56]

"We got the semi-approbation of Colonel [John C.] Crawford," Wash noted, "not forgetting to prepare for a notification if the regiment should move." It became more apparent that Crawford's junior officers were telling him what they were going to do rather than the officers seeking his permission beforehand. Wash stated, "the old Auntie" fixed up the best dinner they had ever eaten during their sojourn in Mississippi, "with every variety of vegetables, meats and other things, and a splendid dessert." The Washington Hotel in downtown Vicksburg, reputed to be the best in the city, charged $2 for a dinner "not much better than we get in camp." Wash stated that this luxurious meal "only cost us $3." Passing back northward toward their camp, the three captains made their way through the city's cemetery, where all had officiated at the burial of some of their men who had died of disease the four months they had been there. Here, they tarried a moment, Wash recollected, to admire the "many nice marble tombs and beautiful shaded walks." One section in the cemetery was assigned to the Confederate dead, which caused him to remember

---

[54] Swan, "A Tennessean at the Siege of Vicksburg," 355.

[55] Ibid.

[56] Wash, *Camp, Field and Prison Life*, 33.

the "six noble youth of my company entombed there. I wrote all the consoling and encouraging words I could to the parents of each."[57]

Lieutenant Earnest of the 60th Tennessee, attending to his duties, saw to the manning of his picket posts in the familiar trenches at the base of the Chickasaw Bluffs on 5 May. Then, he did a little fishing in the sloughs and bayous nearby. He stated that he watched the massive alligator gars as they prepared to spawn, in their gambol all about him in the shallow waters. Some of these monsters, "were five or six feet long and probably weighed 200 pounds." His luck proved poor, however, so he only caught one small "perch."[58]

War matters to the south of Vicksburg during the morning found scattered Confederate cavalry scouts poking about on the east side of the Big Black River, where they encountered various bodies of enemy cavalry apparently headed directly toward Fisher's Ferry, some five miles up river as the crow flies from Hall's Ferry. The assumption was an infantry force was just behind with intentions of crossing at Fisher's Ferry. General Loring was directing the majority of his forces toward the Big Black River Bridge, where he assumed the main crossing would be forced by the bulk of Grant's horde. There was little concern with defending any ford along the river where smaller detachments might be popping up. To the Confederates, Grant seemed to be probing for a point to cross the Big Black. The Rebels, with the constant marching and counter-marching for the past four days, were exhausted. The veterans of the Port Gibson battle had their energies further drained by that bitter fight. Their opponents, hardened by endless and strenuous work details during the previous months (while their Confederate counterparts watched from picket posts), seemed better conditioned and better able to handle the long, hot, dusty marches.

Stamper of the 43rd Tennessee reported that his regiment was still camped in the fields around the Barnes plantation. Incredibly, it seemed that the crisis had suddenly lost its immediacy. That evening, General Stevenson called among his regiments for musicians to entertain the ladies at the mansion, and Stamper, a regimental drummer, indicated, "we responded with the best we had for one-half hour."[59]

One mile from the Barnes's plantation, General Carter L. Stevenson's men were positioned at Antioch Church, on 6 and 7 May, in the vicinity of Warrenton, to protect that end of the line should Grant force a crossing.

---

[57] Ibid.

[58] Northen, *All Right, Let Them Come*, 90.

[59] Stamper, "Travels of the 43rd Tennessee," 55.

Stamper wrote in his daily journal entry that his regiment was relocated their on 7 May. Detailed as the brigade pickets, the "left wing" of the 43rd Tennessee was called to outpost around the camp below Antioch Church, where it maintained the vigil against possible surprises, according to Stamper.[60] The enemy's plans remained unfathomable.

Captain Wash of the 60th Tennessee recorded that, around 1 May, he had sent one of his men who had suffered a long period of fever into the country for convalescence, "where he could get more tender treatment than in camp or the hospital." Colonel Crawford gave Wash permission a week later, around 8 May, to take the horse of his friend Lieutenant Earnest to Captain Edwards's "mansion," where the sick soldier was. "[Edwards] was the best old farmer in all the country about," Wash noted, and "some four or five other convalescents from our regiment were there."[61]

"Mrs. Edwards cared for them as kindly as if they were her own," Wash indicated, "and the boys loved her for it. She told me there had been no less than thirty-seven sick men in her house since the troops had been stationed there." The unnamed soldier Wash checked on was much better, and would be able to return to camp in a few days. Mrs. Edwards invited Wash to stay for supper, which of course he did. Afterwards, he saddled his horse and set out for to camp. Wash, who always had people to visit regardless of which direction he went on his little trips to the country, stopped off on the way back at the residence of Dr. Cook, "with whose family I was intimately acquainted." Convinced an active and major campaign was imminent, Wash availed himself of this opportunity to stop at the Cooks to tell them farewell for the time being. "I'm not sure that I would ever have known the Doctor but from the fact he had three accomplished and interesting daughters," Wash recollected in his memoirs. Since he had not been there for about a month, the girls, were glad to see him. First, he greeted the girls' mother. "Then, there came tripping in the ones I most desired to see," he remarked, "fresh as morning roses and full of life." The eldest daughter, "Miss Lucy," was thoroughly educated, quite good looking, brilliant, witty, and sarcastic—"she was," he scoffed, "the very kind of 'sawyer' I sometimes like to strike against."[62]

The other daughters, Portia and Mary Vic, while not as brilliant, "were amiable and interesting, and the hours glided by till, the first thing I knew, the sun was gliding by the treetops." Miss Lucy played the piano, and Miss Portia

---

[60] Ibid.
[61] Wash, *Camp, Field and Prison Life*, 35.
[62] Ibid., 36–37.

sung a "vocal melody." Wash was given several bouquets for some of his friends in camp, and the then Don Juan of the 60th Tennessee finally took his "adieu." Perhaps feeling a bit guilty because of all the tarrying, Wash struck out at a lope for camp, the dusk settling before him from across the river toward the west, where he saw the distant roofs of Vicksburg rising behind the earthen battlements, sharply outlined in black against a blood-red stripe caused by the dying sun. Once back in camp, Wash delivered all the mementoes and messages with which he was charged. He found his company had already left on picket down to the river, so he had to hurry along to catch up. "That's the last piano I've heard [at the Cook's]," he wrote from Johnson's Island prison some time later, "and the last parlor I've entered and the last refined society I have been in up to date."[63]

John Allen of the 61st Tennessee, a common soldier who undoubtedly spent precious little time in gentile parlors during his Vicksburg duty, noted in a letter on 8 May to his wife back in Morristown, "since I wrote to you last, the Yankees landed about 60,000 soldiers at Port Gibson below Vicksburg." He stated that the day before, 7 May, found the boys confronting the enemy twenty-five miles below Vicksburg at Grand Gulf, where a severe fight took place. Though he reported that his regiment and Vaughn's Brigade had not yet been engaged, Allen expected that "the main fight will come off Friday." He predicted that the coming week would settle the fate of Vicksburg, adding, "we have been trying to get the Yankees to follow us into our breastworks ever since we have been here, and I think we will make the trip this time." (Allen would learn to be careful about what he asked for in the weeks ahead.) "Don't pay any attention to anything you see in the papers or hear," he suggested, "but look on the bright side and we'll end up well, we feel sure."[64]

Private John Barnett died on 8 May of the head wound he had suffered in a camp fight at the hands of his Private Elisha Scott, Stamper of the 43rd Tennessee recorded. Captain Day paid the right wing of the regiment off after it came in off picket.[65]

Grant Heads Toward Jackson. On 9 May, it seemed to the East Tennessee Confederate soldiers both armies were taking their ease. Little did they know that some of Sherman's XV Corps had begun to arrive across from Bruinsburg after their long march from Milliken's Bend. They would soon be crossing the river into Mississippi to augment McClernand's and McPherson's corps. The

---

[63] Ibid.

[64] John Allen to his wife, 8 May 1863, in *Civil War Records*, 1: 11.

[65] Stamper, "Travels of the 43rd Tennessee," 55.

heat was now constant, intense and oppressive, causing the Yankees to spend considerable effort and time trying to find ample sources of water for their parched army as it pressed relentlessly toward Jackson. They had by this date passed through towns and villages south of the Big Black River as far east as Auburn, less than twenty miles due south of the Southern Railroad depot at Edwards.

Another East Tennessean Arrives as Grant's Men Advance. John C. M. Bogle, now serving with the 62nd Tennessee, wrote his wife, Elizabeth ("Bessie") Cox Saffell Bogle, around dark on 9 May, informing her that he had received her letter and one from his father, "which afforded me much gratification." He was relieved to hear that their two small boys were getting over the "O-ing" (whooping) cough, and he was sorry for not being home to help with their care and to "keep you company in your vigils." He directed his sons to be good little boys and obey mama. "That long looked for fight has not yet taken place," he wrote, "tho' as usual, looks to be not far distant." He informed her that the Midwesterners were fortifying Grand Gulf and Port Gibson, while the Southern army, he believed correctly, was in "position [along] the Big Black River."[66]

"The gunboats are now in the bend [of the Mississippi], and are looked for to come down tonight," Bogle declared. He told Bessie that he had sent her $100 by Private A. O. Howard from Loudon and serving with the 62nd Tennessee, who had been sent home. Bogle promised to try to send more as conditions allowed. He asked his wife to take care of the boys until he got home, though he could not say with certainty that he ever would return, since he could not predict what might happen to him. "But, I am yet in hopes we will whip them here & if we don't, I shall try very hard to make good my way *to hum.*" Bogle delicately advised his wife that if he was killed, she must use her best judgment and listen to the advice of her brother "Dick [Saffell] & Father & Hugh." He implored her to be cheerful and hopeful, and to fight despondency "by conjuring up things to be more than they really are." When she was most fretful, he suggested, she must seek the comfort of the Lord, "whose ability & goodness is never wanting."[67]

Bogle reported the news that fellow Maryvillian Sam Toole, who served with the 3rd Tennessee in Reynolds's Brigade, had been taken prisoner in the action after Grand Gulf, though Bogle did not believe it. He had asked people in Vicksburg about Toole's status, but none could give any definite

---

[66] John C. M. Bogle to "Bessie" Bogle, 9 May 1863, Saffell Family Papers.
[67] Ibid.

confirmation. Though the 62nd Tennessee was still in the same section, the distance between Vaughn's and Reynolds' Brigades was now over seven miles, and Reynolds's men had been moving constantly since 1 May. Ready and accurate news, therefore, about one or the other East Tennessee brigades was always sketchy. "Don't tell Mrs. Toole or *any one else* for I think it would be making her miserable all for nothing," Bogle implored. The mail was long in going out and coming in, he stated, and the wait for a letter was uncertain. He would know more about Sam Toole's situation in a few days and would then write Bessie with an update. Until such time, she was to keep *mum* about it.[68]

Bogle did have some big news about an occurrence in Vicksburg, Bogle reported. The Vicksburg *Whig* newspaper office had burned down that morning. The loss of the newspaper was devastating, for had provided most of the news the boys received. "We are living better than when I used to write you," he indicated with some cheerfulness. "We get some flour some bacon and better beef, &c." Their water, however, was another matter. It was a little brackish and warm, Bogle noted, and contained other disagreeable characteristics as well. "It is alive with wiggle tails & various tribes of smaller 'animalaculae,'" he declared, "which gambol about under your nose quite lively whilst you take a drink." Teasing his wife, Bogle wrote that she would probably "starve" for a drink of water for three or four days before she would take a drink. He preferred water from the Mississippi River "for taste," though it was getting a bit too warm for his preference. "I think there will surely be some decisive move in a few days," he declared, "though I have been saying that for 2 weeks. We have been ordered to cook 2, 3 or 4 days' rations several times & ready for a march at a moment's warning. But we have never yet made the move."[69]

Bogle deemed that the position they held was vital for the protection of Vicksburg, and he supposed that the 62nd Tennessee was not called to Grand Gulf because they were left to defend it from surprise attack from other quarters. Bogle stated that Lieutenant Frank Hannum, who had delivered mail for him on occasion while home on recruiting trips, "was not well—had been on the sick list for several days [and] is a little better now." Though Hannum was able to "walk around," he was still carried on the sick lists and excused from duty. Bogle declared that all the boys were "anxious for Tenn. as well as for V. B. [Vicksburg]," due to the threat posed by Union General Ambrose Burnside's forces in Kentucky posed to invade East Tennessee through the Cumberland

---

[68] Ibid.
[69] Ibid.

Gap. Bogle noted that most of the boys' concerns were not helped by the slowness of mail service, and none of them had any idea what was going on back in their home section. He told Bessie that her brothers, Sam and Dick Saffell, had not been writing him, and he wondered why. Sam was on duty with the 63rd Tennessee back in East Tennessee, and Dick was with the 26th Tennessee in the Army of Tennessee somewhere between Murfreesboro and Chattanooga. Bogle was always concerned about the well being of his brothers-in-law. He also indicated that he had not received a letter from Dick Bowman, then at New Market, Jefferson County and carried on the rolls of the 60th Tennessee.[70] Bowman was possibly on detached service there. In closing, Bogle indicated that he must go to bed and promised, should anything occur over night, he would add it to the letter in the morning.

"The troops were paid off yesterday [8 May] which caused much satisfaction," Calvin Smith of the 31st Tennessee reported in his daily entry. The brigade was still within close marching distance of the Big Black and the works below Warrenton, but calm still reigned in the camps. The Lieutenant from Hawkins County noted that the day's weather was agreeable, with an absence of rain and cooled by a nice steady breeze. The nights were mild and good for sleeping. The brigade still was camped at the Sexton farm, where it enjoyed good cistern water, though Smith believed the rations to be "short," consisting of seven pounds of bacon and a pint of meal per mess per day. In one short month, this would seem like a feast. Rice and molasses continued to supplement their meager rations. In anticipation of a "big fight" occurring soon along the Big Black River, Smith reported, "the farmers are moving their stock and grain up country." Always observant of things about him, he reported that the land abounded in corn, cotton, sweet potatoes and vegetables of all kinds. The plantations and homes roundabout were adorned with "ornamental shrubbery," and Mr. Gibson had the "prettiest yard [I] ever saw." All the woods and yard trees were "loaded with full grown leaves," which prompted Smith to exclaim: "I believe the seasons are two months earlier here than in East Tennessee."[71]

"All along the line matters are quiet just now," Stamper of the 43rd Tennessee noted. It was known the Yankees were active on the lower side of the Big Black River, and the 3rd Tennessee, which had been placed on advance picket, kept an attentive eye toward their every move. The following day, 10 May, enemy gunboats continued to steam boldly up the river from Grand Gulf

---

[70] Ibid.
[71] Smith, *A Smith in Service*, 48.

in order to shell Warrenton. Other than that, Stamper recorded, all was quiet at their current post near Antioch Church. The regimental parson, Archibald P. Brooks, came among the boys during the day and preached a good sermon.[72] Smith of the 31st Tennessee, also in attendance at the service, indicated that the sermon was on "Daniel and the Lyon's den" and was heard by a large and attentive assembly. During the service the congregation heard the shelling toward Warrenton, mentioned by Stamper. Smith believed that the brigade would be breaking camp in a few days, headed in what direction he could not say.[73]

As for Federal activity on 10 May, elements of Grant's army, screened by a large cavalry force, were spotted in strength at Auburn, and advance Yankee scouts were observed at a farm only twelve miles from Raymond on the Utica road. Even with Grant's vanguard way to the east at Auburn, Pemberton still assumed that the enemy would at some point turn north and strike at Edwards' Depot, twenty miles away, before heading west along the Southern Railroad to the Big Black River Bridge. Should Grant instead head in the opposite direction toward Jackson, additional Confederate forces were arriving there daily to augment General Johnston's small army. Finally, Pemberton always had to be on the alert that the Yankees might still try to cross at Hall's Ferry or Baldwin's Ferry and then attack any defenders of the Big Black Bridge from the rear. Once on the west side of the Big Black River, of course, the invaders could choose to ignore any Confederates at the bridge and simply move on Vicksburg itself. Pemberton thought that Grant now had four options, any of which severely taxed his stretched and limited resources.

Regular military routine was again in order, with Vaughn's Brigade commissary on 11 May receiving a supply of sugar and flour, according to Captain Wash of the 60th Tennessee. He noted that he procured the supply allotted to his mess consisting of himself, his three lieutenants, and the cook. Wash drew eighty pounds of sugar at 12¢ a pound and sixty pounds of flour at 20¢ a pound. In addition to the small reserves they had on hand, Wash believed that they were fixed for food for a while. "But, the sequel was," he found, "that we lost it all."[74]

During the evening of 11 May, Lieutenant J. T. Earnest and Captain Wash, borrowed a metal skiff to take a little boat ride out on the "Great Father of Waters." They believed that the Mississippi off Vicksburg was rather placid

---

[72] Stamper, "Travels of the 43rd Tennessee," 55.

[73] Smith, *A Smith in Service*, 48.

[74] Wash, *Camp, Field and Prison Life*, 37.

now since most of the Federals had gone down river. Wash and Earnest wanted to do a little sightseeing over along the Louisiana shore where the Northern camps had once been on the DeSoto Peninsula. The two young officers of the 60th Tennessee, however, received friendly advice from the picket boats of Captain Lynch's "Mosquito Fleet" that their stirring around in that quarter enhanced the probability they would draw fire from the Confederate river batteries. With the nervousness rampant in the army at that time, Wash and Earnest concluded that the time was not good for prowling about the enemy's old camps.[75]

"We thought it discretion to desist," Wash reasoned, so, around dusk, he was back in camp, where he received a message from Mrs. Hinson, a good, poor woman who lived near the camps at Mint Springs Bayou. Mrs. Hinson's husband was in the service, and she sent for Wash and one of his lieutenants, who often checked on her, to ask if the two officers would be so kind as to "sit up with the corpse of one of her children." They could not refuse to go, and Wash along with his unnamed friend were "glad to give rest and comfort to a distressed mother."[76]

In a long letter to his wife dated 11 May, John C. M. Bogle from Maryville, Blount County, serving with the 62nd Tennessee, wrote that he would be forwarding the letter to her by Lieutenant Frank Hannum, who had received a sick furlough home "since he is quite weakly." Bogle was pleased with his young friend's fortune, but he wished that it were he who was going home. "There are a good many in the brigade who are sick," Bogle reported, indicating that two men had died in the 61st Tennessee the day before. One of them had been sick for two days, and the other "was well an hour before he died." The surgeons warned the men that their comrades had probably died of yellow fever. Bogle sought to allay his wife's fears by indicating that his health continued to be "pretty good."[77]

Concerning another issue he addressed in his last letter, Bogle noted that Captain Sam Toole of the 3rd Tennessee had not been captured as previously reported. Bogle promised to send Bessie $100 by Lieutenant Hannum "if I get change." He reported that he was in better spirits today, having heard things that made him confident of Confederate success in defeating Grant, though, he admitted "all is yet in the dark" concerning Pemberton's operational plans. The Federals were busy fortifying near Port Gibson and at Grand Gulf, Bogle

---

[75] Ibid.
[76] Ibid.
[77] John C. M. Bogle to "Bessie" Bogle, 11 May 1863, Saffell Family Papers.

declared, and were present across the river in force: "perhaps 75 or 80 thousand men."[78]

"We have great excitement here occasionally," Bogle reported, "as the Yanks attempt to run their boats by us." These vessels, he wrote, did not return fire, "but jog along as if nothing was happening." Still he believed that the Union ships "get more than half of [the shells directed at them] before they get by." Though his company was raised just across the Blount County line in nearby Mt. Vernon, Monroe County, Bogle wrote that he had not had an opportunity to visit the camps of the Maryville boys assigned to Reynolds's Brigade:_Normally, Captain Toole's company from Blount County in the 3rd Tennessee, and one in William Bradford's 31st Tennessee. "We occasionally meet some of them in Vicksburg," Bogle reported. He continued to be concerned about having not heard from Richard Saffell, his wife's brother who was an officer in the 26th Tennessee serving with the Tennessee army. Bogle was vexed that Saffell did not write. Saffell's brother Sam was also lax in his correspondence, Bogle complained.[79] Sam was an officer with the 63rd Tennessee, (which Bogle called "Fain's regiment," so-named for its organizing officer, Richard Fain), another East Tennessee infantry regiment that served for the time in its home section, protecting the railroad and its bridges, as well serving as garrison troops in and around the Cumberland Gap.

"I hear that Fain's whole regiment are under arrest," Bogle joked, "for want of appreciation of Gen. [Archibald] Gracie's [their New York-born brigade commander] *worth*." This comment seems to be another example of a lack of basic trust or respect for "yankee-born" officers in their ranks, and one most Vicksburg soldiers seemed to share for Pennsylvania native General Pemberton. Bogle directed his wife to tell "Dick Boman" that if Ambrose Burnside succeeded in getting into East Tennessee, Bowman was to keep the Yankees from "getting" Wash, June, and Phil, probably the family slaves. Bogle suggested that his wife keep in close communication with Bowman, and "the times will dictate to you what the course is best to be pursued." Reflecting the feeling of most of his East Tennessee comrades who served around Vicksburg, Bogle noted that he "wished it was so that I could be with you if our valley is invaded." But he did not believe such a catastrophe would ever occur because he did not "think they would be permitted to gain possession of [East Tennessee] for then it cuts off direct communication between the Capital [Richmond] &

---

[78] Ibid.
[79] Ibid.

this country [the western Confederacy]."[80] His confidence in his government's ability to prevent the invasion would not be rewarded in the days ahead.

The defeat of Hooker in Virginia, Bogle predicted, would allow General Lee to free up forces to be sent down to East Tennessee to capture Burnside "if he comes in." Such a circumstance, however, would spell disaster for the home section because it would bleed East Tennessee dry of provisions and forage even if only one army were to occupy it for an extended period of time. "Therefore," he suggested to her with a bit of tongue in cheek, "you had better pack your carpet bag & be ready for any emergency." Bogle begged his wife to continue to write him, even if her letters did not make it through: "if I get them, they will do me much more good & if not, they will do neither you or me any harm."[81]

"I expect we would have removed hence some time since," Bogle continued, "but we still occupy the same position & probably may for some time."[82] Little did Bogle realize that in a matter of hours, his regiment would be on the move eastward, and would forever abandon its camp north of the defensive lines of Vicksburg. His life thereafter during the siege would find him in the trenches on the ridge above their old camps.

In this lengthy letter, Bogle expressed his gratitude for some dried flowers included in an earlier letter from his little son Hugh, and he longed for the day he could return to his family. He believed that he and his wife could nothing more important than give their children "a good education. Any correspondence from home meant much to him, Bogle wrote, indicating, "your letter does much to calm my perturbed spirits." As for the military situation around camp, he reported, "if the post gets much more sickly than it is now, I think I will *vacate* and come home." The Conscript Law was being strictly enforced then, he acknowledged, "so I do not think it would be much better there than here."[83]

"I do not assume my exemption papers would save me," Bogle confessed, admitting that if he could get some sort of office job near home, "it would be much more pleasant."[84] He noted that, with some luck, he "may come home at anytime." Bogle wrote that Major Smith was writing the quartermaster general

---

[80] Ibid.

[81] Ibid.

[82] Ibid.

[83] Ibid.

[84] Bogle's implication was that he was a civilian attached to the army's service, and as such, the law prevented him being "loaned" across the river to the Trans-Mississippi Department.

concerning his case and seemed as intent on keeping the Maryville staff officer there as Bogle was intent on going home. Whatever might happen, Bogle told his wife, she was to contract Sam Wear for corn, wheat, pork, and hay, and he wished that she would continue to keep him informed about matters at home. He told her if the invaders got into Blount County, she was to tell "Sade" to claim all their property, which hopefully would prevent their possessions from being confiscated.[85] Sade's family was perhaps sympathetic to the Union and would be left alone should the Yankees come.

"If *her* sweetheart is [by now] in the Southern army," Bogle teased, "*she* must *discard* him for the present at least." He noted "General" McCampbell had arrived in camps over the past few days.[86] Bogle also reported that he had heard the Reverend James H. Alexander preach to the boys the day before. An acquaintance, John Murrell, had been asking about "Miss Sallie," he reported, and W. C. McCray of the 62nd Tennessee had left for home. Bogle wished that "Will" would write him and complained no one in Maryville other than Bessie was corresponding with him. Concerning money matters, Bogle advised his father to hold onto his cotton for the time being, and suggested that he "pay off your debts and send your money south." "I send you a map of the Vicksburg country which will be a nice thing to refer to," he wrote, "though at present the main point is below V'burg & this shows only the bases of operations above." The boys were ready for the fight so long anticipated, and the sooner it happened, the better. "We get reinforcements," he noted in closing, "and the yanks are making great preparations by getting up mortar fleets & a raft with 60 [pounder] Parrott guns on [them]."[87] Bogle promised to write more in the morning if something transpired during the night.

Smith of the 31st Tennessee noted in his journal entry that, as the evening of 11 May, John Reynolds was "very unwell." Also, W. H. Chesnutt had gone back to the main camp at Warrenton quite ill and had been so for some time. Another of Smith's privates, Henderson Kite, had been vaccinated against small pox, which required him to stay back at Warrenton. General William E. Baldwin's Mississippi and Louisiana brigade was camped close by and shared picket duties with Reynolds' men. Colonel Lillard's 3rd Tennessee was still at Hall's Ferry, according to Smith, guarding a collection of grain until the

---

[85] Ibid.

[86] Apparently, McCampell was a man Bogle little respected, or one about whom he liked to tease his wife. There were several artillerymen by that name serving with Lynch's Battery near their camps, so this individual was perhaps a conscript with that command.

[87] Ibid.

quartermasters and commissary could move it inside the fortifications at Vicksburg.[88]

The Battle of Raymond. "We are accumulating large stores of provisions and forage at Vicksburg," Smith noted, "with the intention of holding the place at all hazards." The principal location and strategy of the Union army was becoming more evident by 12 May.[89] The enemy had advanced as far north as the Fourteen-mile Creek at crossings seven miles south of Edwards' Depot, and equidistant near Raymond to the east. With Joseph Johnston accumulating additional forces around Jackson, Pemberton decided to engage Grant's men in the vicinity of Edwards' Depot. He still believed that any movement the Yankees were making toward Raymond and Jackson was one of Grant's ploys. Consequently, Pemberton ordered General John Gregg's Tennessee and Texas Brigade at Raymond to stall the Union advance. Gregg found himself drawn into a battle with two divisions of McPherson's XVII Corps. After a hot and dusty fight lasting from noon until 2:30 p.m., Gregg's Brigade was forced back by sheer numbers and retreated without pursuit through Raymond to Johnston's army in Jackson. Gregg, an aggressive and capable brigadier, as well as his battle-tested and reliable Tennessee and Texas brigade, was thereby lost to Pemberton because the advance of Grant's forces cut it off. The route for the Yankees to Jackson was now unhindered

J. C. M. Bogle, attached to the 61st Tennessee, added to his lengthy letter of the day before that there was "nothing new this morning." Then he augmented it with additional paragraphs. Bogle referred again to the map he was attaching and wished that he had more time to annotate it for her. He hoped to be home soon to add commentary to it by "demonstration" rather than by "chirography." Even with the lack of notation, he believed that the map would aid her understanding of events then transpiring more than the newspaper accounts she read. He wanted her to show it to Dick Saffell, Bill McCampbell, and Andy McClain for their "especial satisfaction." Bogle stated that he was sending home his tobacco bag by Lieutenant Hannum, since he had not learned to smoke it, lamenting, "I tried it & made a failure of it." He, therefore, had to forgo the "benefits" of such a habit in "keeping off diseases or tooth ackes." Finally, he enclosed for her and Hugh some flowers, of which "we have quite a variety of verbenae and heartease, with no two being alike." Bogle's

---

[88] Smith, *A Smith in Service*, 48.
[89] Ibid.

comments were made prior to the call to arms for Vaughn's Brigade. On this date, the usual routine for the Vicksburg defenders changed forever.[90]

Vaughn's Men Called Forward to the Big Black Bridge. "The morning of May 12th was the last one that ever dawned upon us in our camp [at the Mint Springs Bayou] that had become so like home to us," Wash of the 60th Tennessee recalled. Indeed, matters had been so quiet on this flank of the defenses, the boys "had ceased to be in suspense."[91] With the absence of alarm, they had resorted again to the routine of customary camp life for a few hours. Then at around 2 p.m., events began to unfold which would lead Pemberton's army through the upcoming week from one disaster to the next. For many of Wash's comrades, the misfortunes terminated with them subjected to a long relentless siege. For William A. Wash and many others, they would wind up confined in wretched prisoner of war camps for the next year and a half, almost until the end of the war.

"General Vaughn sent down orders for us to cook three-days' rations," Wash wrote in his memoirs. "We had similar orders before, so it startled us not." The boys of the 60th, 61st, and 62nd Tennessee set about their preparations in a leisurely fashion, and having heard the cry "wolf" so often, few worried about any sort of movement anytime soon. Then at 4 p.m., another order came down, commanding the brigade to be prepared to move out by 6 p.m., "and we were to take nothing but what we had on our backs, one blanket rolled and worn over the left shoulder, war equipments and a single cooking utensil to the mess."[92] Suddenly, the war began to sound all too real to troops who had had become accustomed to the routine of camp life. Anxiety grew that active campaigning was about to begin in earnest, and where it would lead, no man could say. "Everything was now in haste," Wash pointed out, "the hurrying up of the cooking of the beef and cakes; the fixing up of duds to leave in care of the sick, of whom, for our regiment, there was almost a hundred." And as 6 p.m. approached, the haste of preparation accelerated. "At half past five," Wash noted, "the long roll beat for all to arms, and though many of the men had not finished cooking, there was no longer time to tarry." It was the duty of the junior officers to check on those who were not able to go, and to leave instructions for the sick. Probably the ill and the able pitied one another. Wash stated that he had to leave fifteen of his men in camp who were not suited for

[90] John C. M. Bogle to "Bessie" Bogle, 12 May 1863, Saffell Family Papers.
[91] Wash, *Camp, Field and Prison Life*, 37.
[92] Ibid., 37–38.

active duty, "and once we marched away, I never laid eyes on them again."[93] Ironically, if these sick did not die of their ailments, or they were not compelled out to their regiments before the Battle of the Big Black River, they remained under arms for the Confederacy, at least until the 4th of July.

When 6 p.m. arrived, everyone able was in formation, trying to situate their 13–pound Enfield musket comfortably on their right collarbone. The staggered order "forward—march!" echoed down the column of fours, repeated by the sergeants, and the men stepped forward amid the clank and rattle of canteen and bayonet, with the measured trod of hundreds of government brogans or leathery bare feet kicking up a thick cloud of the powdery dirt from off the roadway. Coughs, throat-clearings, and spitting, along with other noises men made at such a times as these were there, but as for talking or wise-cracking, little was to be heard, since, as Wash indicated, most of the boys were "keeping their expressions and feelings to themselves."[94]

"Little did we realize, with our adieus to those left behind," Wash reminisced, "that we were forever leaving our romantic home in the hollow forever." Out on the road, "we were met by the other regiments of our brigade, the 61st Tennessee commanded by Colonel Pitts [actually Lieutenant Colonel Rose], and the 62nd Tennessee, commanded by Colonel Rowan." Being the senior regiment of the brigade, Wash moved his regiment, the 60th Tennessee, to the head of the column, with those following subject to their "stifling dust." He noted that the boys in the ranks had no idea where they were headed. Four hours later, he noted, they turned off the road near Mt. Albion Church around ten miles due east of their Vicksburg camp, and headed into a wood, where they struck camp for the night. "We built huge log fires, and chatted around them for awhile," Wash commented, "then wrapped up in our blanket and laid down to sleep and rest our weary limbs." The boys slept in their humble surroundings for only a few hours. At 3 a.m., the long roll awakened them.[95] Earnest of the 60th Tennessee wrote that they were headed in the general direction of Jackson. By the time they bedded down, he noted that they had progressed only six miles due to delays and "a slow pace."[96]

Already in the field, Swan of Lee's Brigade reported that, on "the evening of the 12th, we moved towards Bovina [Station, two miles west on the railroad

---

[93] Ibid., 38.
[94] Ibid., 38–39.
[95] Ibid., 39.
[96] Northen, *All Right, Let Them Come*, 93.

line from the Big Black River Bridge], arriving there the next day."[97] Wash and the boys were headed in the same direction, scrambling to move out in the early morning of 13 May because at 2 a.m., Pemberton, at Bovina Station, sent orders by courier to General Vaughn, directing him to move his East Tennessee brigade "at once" to the Big Black River Bridge and "occupy the trenches there." It took only fifteen minutes for the boys to get up and pull their accoutrements off the rifle stacks, roll up their bedrolls and loop them over their shoulders, and take their pieces and fall in, ready to march again.[98] From their haversacks some pulled the coarse beef strips they had "tanned" the day before and plied them with perhaps a cake of cornbread, washing them down with water drawn from wherever they could get it.

"Streaks of light were just beginning from the east," Wash noted, as they got on the main road to Jackson near the residence of Dr. Newman. Familiar roads, houses, and other comfortable landmarks took on a far different aspect as the boys prepared their minds for the martial work ahead. They soon entered the intersection of the main road and the Jackson and Vicksburg rail-line, and turned onto the parallel turnpike running alongside the tracks. Soon the brigade was on its way to the Big Black River Bridge, the principal span between Vicksburg and Jackson on the rail line. Their march was to be ten miles. Around 8 a.m., the brigade stopped for awhile to eat breakfast. Then, plodding on, the brigade reached the bridge around noon. Passing over it to that east side, Vaughn's Brigade was ordered several hundred yards forward to the entrenchments just vacated by some troops "called forward" toward Jackson.[99]

"There was a general movement toward the front," Wash wrote, "and two brigades were leaving." He noted that toward evening, General Stevenson's Division passed, including Reynolds' East Tennesseans. Dense clouds of a thunderstorm brewing behind them were already approaching the Confederates, Wash stated, "and all realized that the clash of arms might soon be heard and seen." Reports received indicated that advanced pickets from both armies were already exchanging unpleasantries to their front, and the Yankees "had been making a reconnaissance to within ten miles" of the position Vaughn's boys now occupied. As the East Tennesseans settled into their rough works, important commanders began to arrive at the bridge. "This was the first time I ever saw General Pemberton," Wash recorded, "who was accompanied

[97] Swan, "A Tennessean in the Siege of Vicksburg," 355.
[98] Wash, *Camp, Field and Prison Life*, 39.
[99] Ibid., 39–40.

by his staff and General Tom Taylor of Kentucky. They were headed to the front."[100]

The 62nd Tennessee is Honored. Lost in all the martial fervor, General Pemberton's headquarters on 13 May issued General Orders Number 72, which stated: "In honor to the troops engaged in the fight near Vicksburg, on the 29th day of December, 1862, and in commemoration of their gallant and meritorious conduct on that occasion, the following commands will inscribe on their standards "Vicksburg—viz.: '80th (62nd) Regt. Tenn. Vols.'"[101] This was the early numerical designation for John Rowan's 62nd Tennessee. Its standard would be the only one of Vaughn's three regiments not to be lost in four days at the Battle of the Big Black River bridge. The inscription artist would have fifty-two days to add the battle honor to Rowan's regimental standard.

Pemberton Seeks to Check Grant "in the Field." Spradling of the 43rd Tennessee stated that the regiment and brigade left Antioch Church for Bovina Station on 13 May.[102] Swan's boys with Stephen D. Lee's Brigade were among the troops Wash observed moving toward Jackson. Swan stated, "we were to seek the Yankees and attack him regardless of [his] numbers."[103] As the day faded away toward midnight, Pemberton, at his headquarters at Bovina, received word from his cavalry scouts that the Federal troops that had been lining the lower banks of the Fourteen-mile Creek at Whittaker's Ford and Montgomery Bridge to threaten Edwards' Depot had vanished, presumably to join the divisions gathering around Clinton.

The Evacuation of Jackson. Matters in Jackson on 14 May were dismal. Joseph E. Johnston realized Sherman had his four divisions at Clinton, a mere ten miles west of the Mississippi capital. Considering his forces to be too weak and the defenses too feeble to protect the city, Johnston ordered an evacuation of Jackson around 3 a.m. Leaving behind a small rearguard, Old Joe withdrew his little army twenty miles northeast to Canton. Unrealistic hopes were that Pemberton would march his army there, connect with Johnston's forces, and thereafter bring the fight to Grant.

General John C. Pemberton, in a communiqué to Johnston from what would become his command post at Bovina Station, reported that he was moving his entire force of nearly 16, 000 men from Edwards' Depot toward

---

[100] Ibid., 40.

[101] Special Order of Gen. Martin L. Smith, 27 April 1863, *Official Records*, ser. 1, vol. 17, pt. 1, p. 675.

[102] Spradling, "Diary," 2.

[103] Swan, "A Tennessean in the Siege of Vicksburg," 355.

Johnston's command at Canton, leaving behind Vaughn's Brigade, about 1,500 effectives, at the Big Black Bridge should they have to fall back to Vicksburg. "The men have been marching several days," Pemberton warned Johnston, "are much fatigued, and, I fear, will straggle very much."[104]

Vaughn Charged to Hold the Big Black Bridge. General Pemberton sent two rather nervous dispatches to General John C. Vaughn at his post just to east the Big Black River Bridge at different times the same day. The first directive informed Vaughn that the army was on the march to Clinton. General Lloyd Tilghman's Brigade would join the march, leaving its present position on the Baldwin's Ferry Road that would cause the ferry to be unprotected. If the Big Black Brigade is viewed as the bottom angle of an equilateral triangle formed by the ferry, the bridge defenses at the Big Black, and Vicksburg itself, an enemy force could flank the position at the bridge just by gaining the west bank of the river, and dash toward Vicksburg before the defenders at the bridge could react in time to beat them there in a foot-race. The distance would have been only around ten miles.

Pemberton ordered the Monroe County general to continue to occupy the trenches in front of the railroad bridge, "but keep a sharp lookout for your rear." In the event the East Tennessee Brigade encountered a vastly superior force and was "compelled to fall back," Vaughn was to retreat twelve miles northwest toward Milldale in the vicinity of Snyder's and Haynes' Bluffs to keep from getting cut off. Pemberton indicated that he was sending an officer and twenty cavalrymen as scouts to act as buffers against an approach by the enemy.[105] Shortly thereafter, Vaughn received a second directive from the commanding general that again cautioned him to "be on the alert." Major General Andrew J. Smith's (Federal) Division was still reinforcing Baldwin's Ferry. Pemberton's information came from a captured Union officer.[106]

Matters on the East Bank of The Big Black River. Captain Wash of the 60th Tennessee commented on the "unfortunate position" at which John Vaughn's Brigade now found itself on the east bank of the Big Black. Wash observed, "the country all around is low and level, with a line of entrenchments something over a mile in length [and] had been cut in a zigzag circular shape, crossing the railroad and terminating at the river above and below." Though the typography

---

[104] David M. Smith, ed., *Compelled to Appear in Print: The Vicksburg Manuscript of General John C. Pemberton* (Cincinnati OH: Ironclad Publishers, 1999) 104.

[105] Gen. John C. Pemberton to Gen. John C. Vaughn, 13 May 1863, *Official Records*, ser. 1, vol. 24, pt. 3, p. 874.

[106] Ibid., ser. 1, vol. 24, pt. 3, p. 880–81.

provided no elevations, he indicated that the earthworks were certainly an advantage for the defenders. "The bottom was one vast cornfield, containing perhaps 300 acres," he wrote, with "several gin houses and sheds partially filled with cotton bales, several hundred of which had been used in constructing batteries and defenses for ammunition and anticipated wounded." The planted corn, which had been about a foot high, was trampled flat by the soldiers during their recent construction of the works. Word came back to Vaughn on 14 May, according to Wash, that the Yankees had occupied Jackson with little or no resistance.[107]

Again, even with the probability of imminent hostile action, young Captain Wash, as he was often wont to do, set out on a "foraging expedition." After "a right smart walk," he found a lady who sold him two pounds of butter for $2, and who gave him a gallon of milk for free. While he sat on her portico resting and admiring her flower garden, it rained for about an hour. Once there was a let-up in the deluge, Wash started back for the works, but he still got soaked to the skin. With his company at their place in the line, he wrote, "I found the boys standing around, wrapped in their blankets, and taking the pelting rain like wet turkeys." They took care of their Enfields by keeping them slung over their shoulders, barrels pointed toward the ground.[108]

Conditions deteriorated in the Big Black fortifications as a result of the storm. Wash and the men found the ditches constructed for them filled to the brim by the rain, and "had the yanks come then, it would have been face to face." When the rain stopped, the defenders baled and drained out the standing water, and that night, the wet, cold ground was their mattress and pillow.[109]

While his friend Allen Wash had been cavorting around the countryside, Lieutenant Earnest of the 60th Tennessee indicated that the rest of Vaughn's Brigade "remained in the trenches all day [14 May] without the slightest shelter from rain or sun." The morning's heat was "oppressive," but by evening, the very heavy summer-thunderstorm moved through and gave them all a refreshing drenching.[110]

Reynolds' Brigade was on the road toward the east as part of Pemberton's advance. On 14 May, Spradling of the 43rd Tennessee reported, "we advanced to Edwards' Depot."[111] Edwards was some eighteen miles west of Clinton,

---

[107] Wash, *Camp, Field and Prison Life*, 40.
[108] Ibid.
[109] Ibid.
[110] Northen, *All Right, Let Them Come*, 93.
[111] Spradling, "Diary," 2.

where the Confederates assumed Grant was marshalling his forces. Stamper said that the regiment "arose early, and after breakfast we marched to Edwards' Depot on the railroad." He also noted that the rain came "very hard," and the boys got very "wet and muddy." Reynolds' Brigade was "taken in their camp for the night," and soon, with the assistance of their campfires, set about drying themselves and their "tricks." "We got a good night's sleep on our cotton beds," Spradling recorded, "for there was plenty of cotton going to waste around the Station."[112] Sergeant William H. Long of the 59th Tennessee noted that his regiment "fell back to a place on the railroad between Jackson and Vicksburg: Edwards Depot."[113] Pemberton was obviously massing his forces at this point before they moved northwest toward Canton in hopes of uniting with Johnston's men.

The so-called Battle of Jackson was waged on this 14 May, hampered by the torrential rainstorm, but only Gregg and some scattered forces were left to face Sherman's and McPherson's Corps, advancing on the Raymond and Clinton Roads. The opponents traded artillery for a time. Once the withdrawal was complete from the capital, Gregg withdrew to Canton to join Johnston.

Early on 15 May, General Vaughn received orders from Pemberton indicating "the troops [his army] were about to move from this [Edwards'] depot," and the Monroe County general was directed to "send up one regiment to act as an advance guard [there]." Vaughn was also directed to alert General William E. Baldwin to remain behind at Edwards until the East Tennessee regiment got there to provide a warning link between the advance and the defenders at the Big Black.[114] Baldwin would then join the advance. Captain Wash's 60th Tennessee was not the regiment called forward and remained as part of the bridge guard at the Big Black. Wash wrote they had heard some desultory firing some distance off in "the direction of the enemy," leading many to conclude the battle had begun. The firing, however, was merely General Abraham Buford's Cavalry Brigade "firing off their wet guns." Wash noted that Vaughn's men spent the afternoon in the works, "cleaning up and fixing up our contraptions for the Yankee hunt."[115]

The Night before the Battle of Baker's Creek. "We are quietly basking in the sunshine about our entrenchments," Wash noted, expecting to fight behind

---

[112] Stamper, *Travels of the 43rd Tennessee*, 56.

[113] Long, "Autobiography," 1: 54.

[114] Gen. John C. Pemberton to Gen. John C. Vaughn, 15 May 1863, *Official Records*, ser. 1, vol. 24, pt. 3, p. 883.

[115] Wash, *Camp, Field and Prison Life*, 42.

them if the Federals came. At 3 p.m., however, new orders arrived for the brigade to be ready to move in ten minutes. All rushed to their stacked arms, "for someone whispered the foe [was] not far in the distance." Immediately, Vaughn's men were on the march east to Edwards' Depot, where sizeable collections of Confederate units were being assembled. Arriving there at sunset, Wash indicated, "we camped in an old field hard by." They observed Pemberton's huge supply train shunting slowly eastward toward Clinton and Jackson. The whole army was being assembled there. It would be only a few hours until they marched out to meet the Yankees. During the night of 15 May, Wash's company and Captain Joseph L. Hale's company of Boon's Creek, Washington County, in compliance with orders, posted forward sentinels a half mile out on the main Raymond road. A cavalry picket was in position two miles further down. They were to bring the alarm should the Yankee cavalry come dashing in on them, Wash noted, "but they came not."[116]

Colonel Alexander W. Reynolds stated in his official report of this part of the campaign that he "left Edwards' Depot on the Southern or Jackson Railroad at 12 o'clock on the night of 15 May," serving as the rear guard of the army [which] was then marching toward Raymond.[117] Calvin Smith of the 31st Tennessee noted that his regiment "was at Edwards Depo 18 miles from Vicksburg, [and had] been marching hard." He added that it "rained hard, very muddy[;] the Yankies [were] 12 miles west of Jackson." Pemberton and his staff were there, Smith reported, along with Generals "[Thomas] Taylor, [Abraham] Burford and many other notable leaders." Word had it that Joseph Johnston had returned to the ashes of Jackson once Grant set it afire and left. John Vaughn was at the Big Black River Bridge, twelve miles behind them on the Jackson Railroad. On the march through, Smith met up with his brother Sevier, Lieutenant S. Spears, Thomas Lee, I. I. Lee, and many other Hawkins County acquaintances at the bridge serving with Vaughn's Brigade. W. H. Chestnut caught up with the 31st Tennessee down the road by hustling at the double-quick, and David Booker, who had become sick on the march, stayed back with Vaughn's boys in the fortifications at the Big Black. His friend Deustus Petty attended him there. Smith reported that Doc Toal was with them from camp and brought news that Jay I. Reynolds and Henderson Kite were improving, though Lieutenant Robert Long was "rather worse." Smith indicated that Hugh Harper was waiting on Long at the residence of Captain Barnes some 10 miles

---

[116] Ibid.

[117] Report of Gen. A. W. Reynolds, 27 July 1863, *Official Records*, ser. 1, vol. 24, pt. 2, p. 107.

southwest of Vicksburg. "This makes 6 men left behind," Smith reported, "four at Brook-Haven and 2 at Lauderdale Springs."[118]

There was indication that some fighting had occurred during the day "on this side of Jackson," Smith wrote. He admitted that the boys had been "down in the mouth" the day before due to the hard marching, but now, "we are in much better spirits all considered." He stated that a "grand maneuver" was expected soon, and that there would be "hard work" for them all resulting from it. "Our Regt. numbered last evening 408 privates and 35 commissioned officers," he noted, "and some came back from camp last night making 450 fighting men. Our Regt. [brigade] will average 500 men, making 2000 fightening men." Smith could not even guess the number of men he had seen marching toward Grant's forces, but "suffice it to say, there is enough to do the job." Continuing his census, Smith figured that the long trains of artillery and supply wagons, escorted by Colonel Wirt Adams and his 300 cavalrymen, were indicative of what Grant would face. Smith frequently asked where the marching troops were headed, but he never received answers. Indeed, perhaps the only one who knew, he surmised, was Pemberton himself. With the 20,000 who had passed since Reynolds's men occupied their present location, Smith noted, "it appears we won't lack men to fight or compete with the enemy that might oppose us."[119]

With all the activity and movement toward Grant's forces near Jackson, Smith believed, "we will no doubt move out with our brigade about dark." He watched "many cattle being driven by to feed the soldiers on." As though he had counted them all, Smith noted that fifty-one regiments had moved by their position during the day, and all told, there were now more than seventy regiments from the states of Tennessee, Mississippi, Arkansas, Louisiana, Georgia, Alabama, Missouri, and "perhaps troops from other states."[120]

"These are effective fighting men," Smith boasted, "men who are fightening for the property of their families and rights." He noted that thousands of them had been driven from their homes by the invaders, and such men could not be subjugated. They were unconquerable, Smith declared, "with too much hatred to even wish for peace." All of them were joyful and "full of glee" even as they marched "perhaps right into the jaws of death." Would the God of Battles, Smith wondered "give this splendid army to Lincolns hordes who have robbed the defenseless women and children of the staff of life, taking

[118] Smith, *A Smith in Service*, 48.
[119] Ibid., 48–49.
[120] Ibid., 49.

their possessions, then setting fire to their homes leaving them to shift for themselves?" He declared that the God of Battles would give them victory "in answer to the thousands of prayers that [went] up every day and night in and out of the army."[121]

Stamper of the 43rd Tennessee wrote on 15 May, "we were moved forward some two miles, where we halted until Lowering's [W. W. Loring] Division passed us." At 2 a.m., the brigade of A. W. Reynolds started forward again, and the boys found out later that "our Division [Stevenson's] has been assigned to the duty of guarding Pemberton's immense wagon train [during the pending action]."[122] Spradling, also of the 43rd Tennessee, indicated succinctly, "we moved out on Friday evening to attack the enemy,"[123] and along the march frequently changed their rifles from one bruised shoulder to the other. First Sergeant Murray Brown, of Elizabethton, Carter County, and 59th Tennessee, stated "we moved toward the Big Black River Bridge, which we reached and passed over to Edwards' Depot guarding Ridley's [Mississippi] Battery until the day before the Battle of Baker's Creek. We were relieved and rejoined our regiment."[124]

Swan of S. D. Lee's Brigade reported that the day was spent "cooking rations." Also, some of the men of the brigade were assigned on detail to "build a bridge across Baker's Creek on the Raymond Road." Cavalry scouts reported that the enemy had taken possession of the road to Clinton, and later confirmation came that Joseph Johnston had abandoned Jackson, retiring toward Canton. He left the capital of Mississippi to the mercy of the Yankees, who set it to the torch.[125] Grant never had intentions of staying there long.

[121] Ibid.
[122] Stamper, "Travels of the 43rd Tennessee," 56.
[123] Spradling, "Diary," 1.
[124] 59th Tennessee, *Compiled Service Records*.
[125] Swan, "A Tennessean in the Siege of Vicksburg," 356.

CHAPTER 7

"The Battle Rages with Much Violence on Both Sides" 16 May

The March Toward Baker's Creek. "On the morning of the 16th of May," Captain Reuben G. Clark of the 59th Tennessee declared, "the battle for the possession of the Mississippi valley occurred."[1] General Carter L. Stevenson, commanding the division to which Reynolds' Brigade was assigned, noted that he was summoned at sunrise to appear at headquarters at Bovina Station, where Pemberton informed him that Johnston had ordered them to join up with him at Canton as soon as possible. Pemberton decided to move at once via Brownsville on the north side of the railroad.[2]

Lieutenant Calvin M. Smith of the 31st Tennessee reported, "Saturday morning found us several miles west of Raymond having commenced our march at about midnight." Reynolds's Brigade had been charged with guarding Pemberton's large supply train of wagons, "loaded with the munitions of war."[3] The rumors were rampant that Jackson was now in the hands of Grant's legions.

After only a few hours of sleep and before the 59th Tennessee fell into formation just prior daylight on 16 May, Colonel William L. Eakin handed Clark a form circular from General Pemberton to be read to the troops. Clark dutifully communicated it to his men from Morristown, then composing the largest company in the entire brigade. "This was a dark and gloomy morning," he remembered, "and as I ordered my men in line under the trees to read them the address, the expression on their faces so impressed me that I can never forget the events of that morning." After marching eastward late into the night and into the early hours of the morning of 16 May, the 59th Tennessee, along

---

[1] Clark, *Vallleys of the Shadow*, 21.
[2] Report of Gen. Carter L. Stevenson, 29 July 1863, *Official Records*, ser. 1, vol. 24, pt. 2, p. 93–94.
[3] Smith, *A Smith in Service*, 49.

with the rest of Reynolds's Brigade, was out on the road again east of the Big
Black River, headed toward Joseph Johnston's army near Canton. All knew that
a major engagement with Grant's army was imminent. Clark was resigned to
the fact that Pemberton's army was inadequate to meet the seemingly endless
blue columns they had heard about and seen, nor was its "lieutenant-general
commanding" up to the task of leading any sort of major offensive.
"Incompetent" was the term Clark used to describe Pemberton. "We knew our
chances for victory were hopeless," he confessed, "and that a fruitless sacrifice
of life was to be made this day."[4]

Clark's and Smith's brigade commander, Colonel A. W. Reynolds, had his
men on the march again long before the eastern skies reflected any morning
light, and "the rear of the train and my command reached the junction of the
Clinton and Raymond Roads about daylight." Here, his ponderous collection of
wagons and troops halted to await further orders. They were quick in coming.
The cavalry scouts hurried to inform Reynolds that the train had gotten too
close to the enemy. "At 6 a.m., I was directed to form my brigade in line of
battle on the Clinton road, fronting the road leading in direction of Raymond,"
Reynolds reported, an order which he promptly obeyed. A line of skirmishers
were ordered some 500 to 600 yards to the front, he noted, which "had been
posted but a short time when they engaged the skirmishers of the enemy
moving up the Raymond Road."[5]

The 31st Tennessee was dropped back at the double-quick to the bridge
over Baker's Creek to keep it open should calamity strike, while Reynolds
deployed his other regiments to skirmish with the Yankees on the Jackson
Road, some two miles ahead. While on guard at the structure referred to as "the
little Black bridge," Lieutenant Calvin Smith and the boys of the 31st
Tennessee observed "Cloubourne [Claiborne's] of Latrobe's old battery with six
or seven pieces" rolling by at an impressive gallop toward where the Federal
pickets had been earlier in the morning.[6] Their Maryland friends would be
relied upon to break up any advancing enemy threat.

Guard for Pemberton's Supply Train. "Halten! Enemy in front! Turn back,
31st!" Smith's regiment was warned as the 31st Tennessee took to the post at
the bridge. The Confederates quickly realized that the enemy was seeking to
reclaim this crossing they had previous taken to Clinton, and which they still

---

[4] Clark, *Valleys of the Shadow,* 21.
[5] Report of Gen. Alexander W. Reynolds, 27 July 1863, *Official Records,* ser. 1, vol.
24, pt. 2, p. 108.
[6] Smith, *A Smith in Service,* 49.

considered key to Grant's offensive plans.[7] "Such was the condition of affairs when I was relieved [at this point] by General Stephen D. Lee's brigade at about 8 a.m.," Colonel Reynolds indicated. Pemberton had more pressing duties for the East Tennessee brigade. Couriers delivered orders from General Pemberton placing Reynolds's men in charge of and guard over the army's wagon train, composed of nearly 400 conveyances. He was directed to move immediately the wagons north of the Southern Railroad line to a point on the Brownsville road two and a half miles from the junction of that road and the road that led to Edwards' Depot.[8] Pemberton had intelligence informing him that the Yankees were in the vicinity, seemingly spilling out on every road leading westward by the thousands, and the long cumbersome supply train would appear to be defenseless and an easy target.

General Stevenson reported that Pemberton "directed me to move the trains as rapidly as possible to a point at least three miles beyond the Jackson road [northward toward the Brownsville road], and then halt there." The wagoneers were then to pull their cumbersome charges off to the left and right of the road to provide an ample corridor for the uninterrupted passage of the infantry and artillery. "I immediately caused the trains to be turned, and in charge of my fourth brigade of Col. Reynolds to be moved rapidly to the rear in accordance with the instructions I had received."[9]

"We had just finished breakfast when the enemy came up," Swan of S. D. Lee's Brigade wrote in this day's entry. The Alabamians were still responsible for the safety of Pemberton's supply train, at least for the next few hours. Considerable tumult resulted as the threat of a Union attack required the 400 wagons to be turned in the opposite direction. "The wagon train was reversed and drawn back towards Edwards' Depot, [across the Southern Railroad, and] then driven three miles up the Brownsville Road."[10] Swan noted that Reynolds's Brigade, guarding the depot, formed the entrance left of Lee's lines allowing the wagons to pass through as they were hurried to the rear, and dropped into line of battle as their new protectors.

By 9 a.m., General Stephen D. Lee's Brigade had relieved Reynolds's men at the Raymond-Clinton crossroads, and "in a very short time, [Lee's] skirmishers were engaged by those of the enemy." So, rather than taking over

---

[7] Ibid.

[8] Report of Gen. Alexander W. Reynolds, 27 July 1863, *Official Records*, ser. 1, vol. 24, pt. 2, p. 108.

[9] Report of Gen. Carter L. Stevenson, 29 July 1863, *Official Records*, ser. 1, vol. 24, pt. 2, p. 94.

[10] Swan, "A Tennessean in the Siege of Vicksburg," 356.

the guard of the train as planned, Lee found himself fronting and fighting a large Federal force. "Instead of following up the movement already in part executed by the trains and Reynolds' Brigade," Lee noted in his report, "it became necessary to check this purpose of the enemy," which he felt was to "turn our left flank, and get between our army and Edwards' Depot." If such a maneuver was accomplished, Pemberton's army would be cut off from the most direct route back to Vicksburg. By 10 a.m., Lee stated, "several divisions of [enemy] troops [were] visible in front of our left."[11] The relay of the train's protection down the ranks from one of Stevenson's brigades to the next was now impossible. The long queue of supply wagons were now the sole responsibility of Colonel Reynolds and his men, and their commanding officer was ordered to get these valuable encumbrances headed away from the approaching enemy.

Turning The Train Around. Reynolds's Brigade, according to Isaac Stamper of the 43rd Tennessee, took its place at the rear of the wagon train because the Yankees were reported to be near and were approaching quickly along several different routes.[12] The supply train had first been headed toward the state capital on the Jackson Road before matters toward Clinton necessitated its cumbersome reversal of direction. At once the gargantuan task of turning the many heavy-laden wagons and struggling teams around on the narrow road commenced, sometimes through ditches and over high banks. Great were the applications of whips and oaths administered by the sweating red-faced wagon-masters. Stalled wagons and field artillery pieces blocked the muddy, narrow road. The army wagon train stacked up along the roadside, while the 43rd Tennessee [and the other three regiments of A. W. Reynolds] observed the mess from the woods.[13] Reynolds's men, befuddled by their orders, stood by the side of the road for what seemed an eternity watching the train pass through their position so that they might take their place at its rear to protect it from swooping cavalry raiders known to be in the area.

"I received further directions to so arrange my command as to give the train proper protection, as I would alone be held responsible for its safety," Reynolds declared. He rode to the rear of his column, halted, and turned the brigade around, after having marched his men at the double-quick to overtake

---

[11] Report of Gen. Stephen D. Lee, 25 July 1863, *Official Records*, ser. 1, vol. 24, pt. 2, p. 101.

[12] Stamper, "Travels of the 43rd Tennessee," 56.

[13] David Abshire, *The South Rejects a Prophet* (New York: Frederick A. Praeger, 1967) 45.

the train. The quick march was becoming the only cadence his men would know on this day. Reynolds disposed his troops as follows, according to orders: a detachment in front, one regiment on the right flank to guard against cavalry, and the remainder of the infantry and the battery in the rear to protect the train against the Federals moving on them from behind, from the direction where the Battle of Baker's Creek was commencing.[14] Then off they lumbered, moving with agonizing slowness westward toward the railroad at Edwards' Depot over the tracks and onto the parallel Brownsville Road just north.

According to Pemberton, in compliance with the orders to protect the wagons, "Reynolds' Brigade moved on with the trains, and was thus cut off from participation in the battle almost immediately begun."[15] "We halted again five miles above Edwards' Depot," Stamper wrote in his journal, "since by this time the battle was raging at a point from which we were moving."[16]

"The artillery and musketry have turned loose in earnest," Smith of the 31st Tennessee observed, the men choking back the dust from what the immense train in front of them kicked up. The enemy was feared to be approaching, heading in their direction west along the Brownsville Road as well as another column coming up the road from either Edwards' or Bolton Depots. Reynolds ordered the 31st Tennessee out as skirmishers on the flanks, and it moved forward cautiously toward Baker's Creek to provide warning at the first signs of the Yankees' approach. The 31st soon had an opportunity to do so. Private E. Banton [James Banston?] of Bradford's regiment was killed in action in the skirmish line at the "little bridge" over Baker's Creek just north of Bolton's Depot. The regiment fell back at the "double quick," while the cannons roared and small arms crackled from where the Battle of Baker's Creek raged, the enemy reputedly coming after the wagon train also at the "double quick."[17]

The boys left alongside the wagons listened with some consternation to the heavy cannonading occurring to the east and south. Behind them, they believed that their East Tennessee comrades in Vaughn's Brigade were entrenched on the east side of the Big Black River where the Jackson road crossed as sole protectors of the army's route back to Vicksburg should disaster befall the Confederates. Many accompanying the wagons believed that they

---

[14] Report of Gen. Alexander W. Reynolds, 27 July 1863, *Official Records*, ser. 1, vol. 24, pt. 2, p. 108.

[15] Smith, *Compelled to Appear in Print*, 117.

[16] Stamper, "Travels of the 43rd Tennessee," 56.

[17] Smith, *A Smith in Service*, 49.

should get to the Big Black River Bridge to reinforce their fellow East Tennesseans left their by themselves. The safety of the supply train, however, was the paramount consideration in Reynolds's mind. "General" Reynolds was with his staff riding behind the line of march of his brigade as the wagons rattled along slowly in front of them, all the while aware that the enemy was at their rear. Every cavalry scout who rode up reported that the Federals were just behind and gaining ground. With intentions of checking the impending arrival of the pursuing enemy, Reynolds sent orders for the brigade to halt and form in line of battle to protect the rear of the trains.[18] "I reached the point designated [by Pemberton] at 11 a.m.," Reynolds noted in his report, "when I parked the train and formed my line of battle, facing toward the enemy and in front of the train. My battery was placed in position to protect my front and flanks.[19]

Gillespie's Problems with Reynolds. Smith recalled that, during the chaos, Colonel James W. Gillespie, ranking colonel in the brigade (not including Reynolds, of course), countermanded Reynolds's orders and instead ordered his men toward the Big Black Bridge to reinforce General Vaughn's command. "General Reynolds comes forward then," according to Smith, and ordered Col. Gillespie arrested for disobeying the brigade commander's orders, which would have left the train stopped and in danger of imminent capture. Reynolds, greatly agitated and reportedly a bit inebriated as well, offered upon reflection to restore the popular commanding officer of the 43rd Tennessee to his Regt.[20] Something happened during this day's maneuvers between Reynolds and Gillespie, but what actually led to their falling out is unclear.

Reynolds's incompatibility with the East Tennessee fraternity continued, and its officer cadre's resentment of his placement over them resulted from several issues. Not only was he not an East Tennessean; he was not even from Tennessee. Moreover, he had not been promoted to brigadier, though his name had been brought before at least once before the Confederate congress, which, apparently, had tabled its approval. Finally, in minds of many of his East Tennessee regimental commanders, Reynolds was a drunk, who was often inebriated at times when he needed a clear head.[21] Just as Colonel Cooke of the 59th Tennessee had resented his treatment by General Stevenson, Colonel Gillespie, as a point of honor, for a brief period turned over command of the

---

[18] Ibid.

[19] Report of Gen. Alexander W. Reynolds, 27 July 1863, *Official Records*, ser. 1, vol. 24, pt. 2, p. 108.

[20] Smith, *A Smith in Service*, 49.

[21] Allen, *Rhea and Meigs Counties in the Confederate War*, 57.

43rd Tennessee to his most able lieutenant colonel, David M. Key. Gillespie was content to accompany the command "under arrest."

Another account of this incident was presented by V.C. Allen of the 3rd Tennessee, which he presented as an illustration of "the metal of which Colonel Gillespie was made."[22] Though the point is the same, Allen's particulars were not as accurate. His account was written years after the war and was littered with considerable embellishment.

"The Battle of Baker's Creek had been fought and lost by General Pemberton, and Stevenson's Division had lost heavily in the fracas," Allen recorded. Stevenson's Fourth Brigade, under the command of Colonel Alexander W. Reynolds and composed of four East Tennessee regiments, was, according to Allen "covering the retreat and holding the enemy in check until General Pemberton could get his command across the Big Black River." Reynolds ordered his command to "move in a direction that no *sober man* would have thought about going," according to Allen, and that was back in the direction of the Yankee army. "Colonel Gillespie in ringing tones ordered a halt," Allen recollected, "being the senior colonel, and after a short consultation with the other regimental commanders, took command of the brigade and saved it to the Confederate army."[23]

During the long, hot day, slowly making their way, Reynolds's men and the trains were continuously subjected to warnings and alarms that constantly required the brigade to form lines of battle across the road and fields where they awaited an imminent attack. The brigade was never, according to Stamper of the 43rd Tennessee, seriously tested. In the evening the supply train was ordered toward Bovina and then to the inside of the fortifications at Vicksburg. At dusk, the train and brigade had been once ordered to Edwards' Depot, "but after starting we found that the enemy was there, and we would have to go back about a half mile and take another road [toward Brownsville]."[24]

Battle of Baker's Creek from the Big Black Bridge. On 16 May, Vicksburg's destiny would ultimately be decided. Vaughn's Brigade awaited in the level fields a half mile east of the Big Black River Bridge. Captain Wash of the 60th Tennessee reported, "we could plainly hear the opening contest at Champion's Hill [Baker's Creek]." The skirmish firing, sometimes increasing to volley musketry, introduced the commencement of the Battle of Baker's Creek to the Vaughn's East Tennesseans entrenched there. Joined in short order, he added,

---

[22] Ibid., 57–58; 43rd Tennessee, *Compiled Service Records.*
[23] Allen, *Rhea and Meigs Counties in the Confederate War*, 58.
[24] Stamper, "Travels of the 43rd Tennessee," 56–57.

by a few cannon booming away. As the sun rose toward its zenith, Wash indicated the noise of the battle raged faster and hotter, filtering its way back to the boys at the Big Black Bridge.[25]

Vaughn's boys trembled with anxiety anticipating what the sounds of the battle meant—the hearing but not knowing—the mysteries of struggle a dozen miles to the east near Baker's Creek in which they played no part. The more nervous among them strained to hear, leaning on hands cupped over the muzzles of their Enfields and the butt ends resting in the soft damp earth of their works. Those who could tried to lighten the situation with jokes. Others crouched on their heels or sat silent on the drier spots within their rough defensive works in front of the Big Black Bridge; the introspective among them kept personal and private turmoil locked in fertile imaginations. All sensed, however, the great struggle on the field of battle long anticipated was finally almost upon them.

"For perhaps the first hour of the battle, the artillery roars like thunder, deafening everything else," Wash observed, "and now it measurably ceases; with the din of musketry paramount, sometimes as thick as hail pattering on a tin roof, and other times popping in rapid succession" like a string of firecrackers. "Sometimes successive volleys ring forth, and then again we hear the random, desultory fire," as though surprised pockets of unseen combatants suddenly happened upon one another. Then, Wash noted, the cannon opened again with sparse or concentrated deep rumblings from new points of advantage.[26]

For a while, the deadly sounds of combat intensified, then faded almost into total silence, with only an occasional shot squeezed off at scattered localities. Then, Wash imagined, like a smoldering fire, "the battle sounds burst forth at a new point in all its former fury." Talking amongst themselves, Vaughn's boys hoped that the Yankees were being driven from the field. As Wash described it, "the sound seems to get more distant," which led him and his non-engaged comrades to suppose that the fighting had not stopped, but had only moved into some hollow or to the backside of distant hills, which masked the intensity. Up until noon, the armies were feeling one another out, strategies were implemented, and the opposing forces ran their maneuvers to gain advantage. Wash indicated that the battle lines changed almost perpendicular to their original positions. Then, he wrote, "the work commenced in earnest." In fact, Wash later found out, "there was a mighty slaughter on both sides," with the critical point for near victory lost when the

---

[25] Wash, *Camp, Field and Prison Life*, 44.
[26] Ibid., 43.

Southern army occupied the edge of a wood fronting a cornfield, but could not hold it.[27] "News" that General John Bowen had captured two Union regiments came, Smith of the 31st Tennessee indicated, "and the battle raged with much violence on both sides."[28]

"Twice did the enemy attempt to charge them," Wash was informed, "but each time with a sad result to the attacking party." Grant finally funneled in an endless stream of reinforcements, the story went among the boys, and hit Pemberton "in front and on the flank," which caused his men to be "routed and driven back with heavy loss."[29] It was Barton's and Cumming's Georgia Brigades on Pemberton's left flank that broke and precipitated the route.[30]

March of the Stragglers. Around 2 p.m., the first gaggle of wounded and straggling Confederates began shuffling by Wash's post, headed for the rear. Those who had no wounds, as per orders, were detained by the guard at the Big Black River Bridge and required to stay with the troops there guarding what now had become the route of retreat. These dispirited soldiers proved no boon to the nervous defenders the following day when subjected to another Yankee onslaught. "Within an hour, several hundred men wounded in every

---

[27] Ibid.., 43–44.

[28] Smith, *A Smith in Service*, 50.

[29] Wash, *Camp, Field and Prison Life*, 44.

[30] Reports of Gen. Seth Barton and Gen. Alfred Cumming, *Official Records*, ser. 1, vol. 24, pt. 2, p. 100, 106. Similar to the accusations leveled at Vaughn's Brigade after the Big Black fiasco, Major Raleigh Camp of the 40th Georgia confessed that men from his home state in the Cummings and Barton brigades had their manhood questioned after Baker's Creek: "We have been charged by the citizens and soldiers from other states with cowardice. It has been frequently said, I hear, that the Georgians run." Raleigh S. Camp, "What I Know, I Know, and I Dare Express It: Major Raleigh S. Camp's History of the 40th Georgia in the Vicksburg Campaign," *Journal of the American Civil War* 5/1 (1996): 64. Mary Webster Loughborough shared her disappointment with other troops entering Vicksburg after the disasters in the field on 16 and 17 May: "We are disappointed in you!" cried some of the ladies. "Who shall we look to now for protection?" "Oh!" one of the demoralized soldiers replied. "It's the first time we have run. We are Georgians, and we never ran before; but we saw them all breaking and running, and we could not bear up alone. Mary W. Loughborough, *My Cave Life at Vicksburg* (New York NY: D. Appleton & Co., 1864) 44. See also, Smith, *A Smith in Service*, 49–50. R. S. Bevier, after the stampede at Baker's Creek and the Big Black River, declared that "an uneasy and ominous feeling of distrust imbued the minds of both men and officers, combining a fear of those troops who fled so readily at Baker's Creek (Barton's and Cummings' Georgians) and the Big Black River (Vaughn's East Tennesseans), and a suspicion of the motives and patriotism of Gen. Pemberton." R. S. Bevier, *History of the First and Second Missouri Confederate Brigades, 1861–1865* (St. Louis MO: Bryan, Brand & Co., 1879) 199–200.

conceivable manner passed by," Wash reported, "and about half of them had been shot in the hands and arms, as was usually the case in battle."[31]

Earnest's Washington County company of the 60th Tennessee was ordered to straddle the railroad line to hinder the pace of the shirkers, "but they came on so fast we had quite a time of it." He noted that Reynolds's men came in with the wagon train that had arrived "in a perfect rush." Pemberton's flustered staff officers ordered the 60th Tennessee back to the Big Black Bridge, Earnest continued, "where we were posted for the same purpose as the evening before." Before long, he observed, the vanguard of the enemy came menacingly into view." The 60th Tennessee remained on duty all night.[32]

Meanwhile, alongside the wagons where they were provided a few minutes blow while awaiting further instructions, Smith of the 31st Tennessee remarked on what he and the other wagon guards of Reynolds's Brigade were doing somewhere along the Bridgeport Road. "I hear cannon again," Smith reports, "yet we sit here as if unconcerned." The slow-moving train of the army had been sent on ahead, he noted, adding, "we have been marching 36 hours with but little rest."[33]

Colonel Reynolds received new orders around this time from Pemberton's command post at Bovina Station. The boys were instructed to cook and eat immediately what rations they had in their haversacks because they were to march again soon and to overtake the lumbering wagon train. But then, just as quickly, contrary orders arrived, Smith wrote, with the alert that Barton's Georgians were being hard pressed back in Reynolds's direction after being overwhelmed in the battle, and "we are sent to reinforce him."[34] Two regiments would remain to escort the train. The boys were once again called to form columns of four before stepping out lively eastward toward the battle. But before Reynolds's men could make much progress to reach them, Barton's Brigade, which had broken beneath the crushing assault on their position along General Pemberton's left flank, were stampeding westward on the Jackson to Edwards' Depot road, straight toward the Fourth Brigade.[35]

Saving Pemberton's Wagons. "The position taken by me [guarding the retreat route through Bridgeport] was held until about 3 o'clock," Reynolds noted, when he received a message by courier from Brigadier General Barton

[31] Wash, *Camp, Field and Prison Life*, 44.

[32] Northen, *All Right, Let Them Come*, 94.

[33] Smith, *A Smith in Service*, 50.

[34] Ibid.

[35] Report of Gen. Alexander W. Reynolds, 27 July 1863, *Official Records*, ser. 1, vol. 24, pt. 2, p. 108.

confirming that his line had been broken. This meant that the bluecoats might now close on the army's trains with little impediment since Barton warned Reynolds that his battered and dispirited Georgians would be little help in preventing an attack.[36] Consequently, "Barton directed me to dispatch the train to the rear across the Big Black," Reynolds noted. Not only was Barton going to be unable to help protect the precious supply wagons; he was going to endanger their safety by bleeding off some of Reynolds's boys, since he implored the commander of the Fourth Brigade "to re-enforce him with all available forces as early as practicable."[37] Barton was fearful that his demoralized command would be caught, overwhelmed, and compelled to surrender by the pressing Federals. In his opinion, his brigade's importance to the army far outweighed that of the wagon train.

"I immediately put the train in motion," Reynolds noted, "leaving two regiments and a section of artillery to protect it," and rapidly moving the remainder of the force to the support of General Barton. On arriving at a point near the Baker's Creek Bridge, Reynolds received word that the troops of General Barton's command were moving quickly back toward Edwards' Depot.[38]

Confusion in the Orders. All of Stevenson's brigades that had been battered about on the field at Baker's Creek were suddenly in need of Reynolds's help. As Reynolds rushed toward Barton, orders arrived for the East Tennesseans to support another brigade in their division, Stephen D. Lee's Alabamians. After they had progressed only a short distance toward Barton, Reynolds wrote, "we were ordered to support Lee's men at the Baker Creek's bridge on the Raymond Road."[39]

On this hot and dust-enshrouded afternoon, the frustration and confusion over orders and counter-orders grated on the nerves of officers and privates alike. Reynolds's men must have wondered if anyone in command above regimental level knew what they are doing. "We about-faced and started to [Lee's] support," Stamper of Gillespie's 43rd Tennessee recorded, but they were not able to reach the Alabamians. The fast-pursuing Yankees, flushed with their victory at Baker's Creek, were storming in heavy force along all the roadways leading toward the Big Black River bridge, and had come between Reynolds's and Lee's men. It was then after 4 p.m., and by this time, the enemy

---

[36] Ibid.
[37] Ibid.
[38] Ibid.
[39] Ibid.

had discovered Reynolds's advance and opened on his vanguard with artillery fire, moving with thick concentrations of infantry to cut it off from Edwards' Depot.[40]

"I directed my artillery to rejoin the section left on the Brownsville road as quickly as possible," Reynolds reported, "and I moved with the infantry toward the junction of the [Clinton/Jackson and Raymond] roads." Nearly a division of Federals, according to Reynolds, had already crossed the Baker's Creek bridge and gained a point nearer the depot ahead of the East Tennesseans.[41]

Rushing the Wagons to Bridgeport. Pemberton then issued orders that could not have been clearer: Reynolds was to save the army's train at all costs. Reynolds's men and the wagons would now be unable make it to the Big Black bridge ahead of the Yankees, and were forced to take the parallel road north of the rail-line to Bridgeport. Time was crucial, but with some considerable luck, Reynolds and his exhausted wagon escorts would be able to cross the Big Black River there.[42] These new orders rendered to Reynolds, Smith of the 31st Tennessee indicated, demanded that the brigade "continue our retreat to Vicksburg."[43] The East Tennessee boys in their sweat-soaked woolen uniforms, caked with layers of accumulated dust and dried mud, tried to drag weary legs one before the other. They followed along behind their rickety, cumbersome charges, choking on the dirt-cloud raised by the creaking wheels. After all the brigade had bested to this point through the long steamy day, perhaps the greatest challenge for Reynolds's exhausted men still lay ahead.

"My safety now depended on out-maneuvering [the enemy]," Reynolds declared, stating that his boys marched in parallel lines with the Northerners for at least "half of a mile." Taking advantage of a dense wood that masked the direction his men and the wagons were taking, Reynolds changed his route to the right and quickly joined the other troops of his brigade, who had been rushed back from the Brownsville road. A mile and a half above the Big Black River Bridge lay Bridgeport, where a pontoon bridge had been constructed as an emergency route toward Vicksburg. The bulk of Pemberton's army had crossed where the railroad ran east to west across the Big Black Bridge, but Reynolds's only hope was the parallel route just north to reach the fortifications

---

[40] Stamper, "Travels of the 43rd Tennessee," 57.
[41] Report of Gen. Alexander W. Reynolds, 27 July 1863, *Official Records*, ser. 1, vol. 24, pt. 2, p. 108.
[42] Ibid.
[43] Smith, *A Smith in Service*, 50.

at Vicksburg safely.[44] The wagons were turned to the left and arrived at the ferry on the Big Black River five miles off, with the East Tennesseans "nearly [at the] double quick all the way." Though it took between three and four hours, Smith indicated that the train finally moved across the pontoon safely, except for one caisson "sunk with the boat." Lieutenant Miller of Company B, 31st Tennessee, who commanded the brigade wagons, was "wounded but made his escape."[45] Describing the situation at Bridgeport in some greater detail, Reynolds found there a light pontoon bridge over which he passed two of his regiments and one piece of artillery. But when the boys "attempted to throw over a caisson, the bridge gave way, and carried it down with it."[46]

"I extricated myself from this dilemma by cutting out one of the boats forming the bridge," Reynolds reported, "and by it I crossed my entire command by 3 a.m. on the morning of the 17th." The danger to his command and the wagon train was far from over, however, since Reynolds's men still had nearly twenty miles to cover to reach Vicksburg. After his attempts to assist other brigades in his division, the Fourth Brigade's commanding officer became convinced that his men were on their own and would receive no support or reinforcements. With most of Pemberton's artillery left abandoned on the field to the enemy, it was Reynolds's East Tennessee infantrymen who had to find a way to comply with their commander's admonition to "lose all, or hold the enemy in check."[47]

Hardy Jones and Tobe Fuller of Stamper's Company F, 43rd Tennessee, were among those taken prisoner during the march with the train toward Bridgeport. Corporal Andrew M. Taylor of Elizabethton, Carter County, and the 59th Tennessee, a recent convalescent in camps who had just rejoined the command, was also picked up by the Yankees, exhausted, on the march.[48] Many other weary stragglers met the same fate. "After crossing the river and marching a mile," the boys laid down this night of the 16th and had a good, if brief, sleep.[49]

"We laid down to sleep about 3 o'clock," Smith of the 31st Tennessee declared, and thereafter, they arose and proceeded the north side of the Big

---

[44] Report of Gen. Alexander W. Reynolds, 27 July 1863, *Official Records*, ser. 1, vol. 24, pt. 2, p. 108.

[45] Smith, *A Smith in Service*, 50.

[46] Report of Gen. Alexander W. Reynolds, 27 July 1863, *Official Records*, ser. 1, vol. 24, pt. 2, p. 108–109.

[47] Ibid., 109.

[48] 59th Tennessee, *Complied Service Records*.

[49] Stamper, "Travels of the 43rd Tennessee," 57.

Black leading to Vicksburg. "I have since seen at the forks of the road a sign board, '14 miles to Vicksburg,' and 'five miles back to the bridge passed the place [Bridgeport] where we crossed last night."[50] The Battle for the Big Black Bridge was then in play, its sounds for Reynolds's men had much the same effect Vaughn's men had had the day before listening to the affair at Baker's Creek. "I remained at Bridgeport until near daylight," Reynolds wrote in his official report, "when I destroyed the boats there and at a point one mile above, and moved toward Bovina, sending an officer forward to inform the Lieutenant-General of my whereabouts. I received instructions from the lieutenant-general to proceed to Vicksburg by the nearest route and there await orders."[51]

The Yankee cavalry was galloping into every straggling, disorganized group of Confederates it could find, whether the body of soldiers was large or small. A massed troop of Yankees came after Reynolds's train with reckless abandon just before it made its escape across the Big Black. After what the Union army had done the day before to Pemberton's divided forces, the horsemen undoubtedly believed that the train was easy pickings. "In the swirling, confusing battle, Reynolds' steady infantry and the cavalry detachment from Wirt Adams' [which had just joined them], beat off attack after attack," according to the historian Warren Grabau.[52] The terrain, densely wooded and crisscrossed with eroded gullies, served the East Tennesseans well, and the cavalry could not get their horses at them. They had to settle for the harassment they had already done and be content with that. Soon the train was safely on the other side of the Big Black's muddy waters and on its plodding way to the works at Vicksburg, leaving the destroyed pontoon bridge behind. Also tarrying behind was a spunky annoyance for the cavalry following.

Lieutenant Ewing's Rear Guard Stalls the Yankee Advance. Reynolds left behind a handful of brave volunteers from Gillespie's 43rd Tennessee, a gaggle of Chattanooga boys under the command of Lieutenant Calvin Ewing charged with holding in check for as long as possible an undeterminable number of Yankee troops led by a cavalry advance which continued to press in the direction of the crossing at Bridgeport. The 6th Missouri Cavalry, under

---

[50] Smith, *A Smith in Service*, 50.

[51] Report of Gen. Alexander W. Reynolds, 27 July 1863, *Official Records*, ser. 1, vol. 24, pt. 2, p. 109.

[52] Warren E. Grabau, *Ninety-Eight Days: A Geographer's View of the Vicksburg Campaign* (Knoxville TN: University of Tennessee Press, 2000) 318.

Colonel C. Wright, arrived first in the Federal vanguard.[53] Unlike Pemberton down the river a mile and a half at the Big Black Bridge, Colonel Reynolds had had the wisdom to place this tiny rear guard on the *western* bank of the river. Wright's Yankee horsemen galloped up to find fragments of the pontoon bridge in the water, and in short order received fire from the detachment of East Tennessee Confederates on the opposite shore, whose audacity was not to be believed and whose number was unknown. The troopers returned fire with their Sharps' carbines and Colts revolvers, and were soon supplemented by the arrival of the first elements of Andrew Jackson Smith's Yankee infantry division, which exchanged fire with the handful of boys from the 43rd Tennessee. "A half an hour banging away produced no noticeable diminution in the Rebel's reply," Wright confessed, so General Smith ordered forward a couple of 12–pounder howitzers from the 1st Illinois Light Artillery. The spot in the river was only forty yards across, and after several lethal charges of canister were sent crashing through their cover at pointblank range, Colonel Gillespie's East Tennessee "rear-guard" concluded that this phase of the war for them was over.[54]

Lieutenant Calvin J. Ewing of Hamilton County and the 43rd Tennessee was the young engineering officer left in charge of this small party of miners and sappers, according to Captain J. N. Aiken, his commanding officer from Chattanooga. "And in the face of a terrific fire from the advanced guard of the enemy," Aiken continued, "[Ewing's men] cut up and destroyed the pontoon bridge."[55] The Yankees discovered the little squad of East Tennessee "rear guards" who fell into their hands, despite their bravery, were "universally despondent, and think there is but little doubt of our capturing Vicksburg."[56] Ewing and perhaps others in the party made their escape and later rejoined their comrades back in the works.

Saving the Camp Equipment. Sergeant George W. Crosby of Morristown and the 59th Tennessee noted that Lieutenant Ewing "and ten or twelve of his men of the brigade gave fight and saved all the train." With the Yankees now running helter-skelter in all directions leading toward Vicksburg, the camps outside the fortifications of Vicksburg proper were in considerable danger.

---

[53] Report of Col. Francis P. Blair, 24 May 1863, *Official Records*, ser. 1, vol. 24, pt. 2, p. 256; Report of Giles A. Smith, 26 May 1863, *Official Records*, ser. 1, vol. 24, pt. 2, p. 263.

[54] Ibid.

[55] J. N. Aiken, "The Forty-Third Tennessee," in Lindsley, *Military Annals*, 1: 523.

[56] Report of Col. Francis P. Blair, 24 May 1863, *Official Records*, ser. 1, vol. 24, pt. 2, p. 256.

Crosby indicated that around this time he had been detached from the regiment back to the Big Bayou, "to move all the sick and camp equipment as could be saved back to the ditches." "I had charge of the wagons and also of the sick," Crosby noted, "though the sick that could walk were held back for later transport." The men who needed to be taken to the hospitals were hauled away in the first wagons. Soon into the relief effort, however, "some lieutenant" assumed command and ordered Crosby and his fellow soldiers to leave as quickly as they could. "You stay here until the first wagons come back for the second load," Crosby told the unidentified officer, who was greatly agitated and in an excited state. 'You damned fool!' the officer responded: 'We can't stay here! Look yonder at the Yankees crossing the river!'" At that moment, they saw a wagon and team lumbering toward them at a rush, with its driver yelling, "Bring up the artillery! Be quick!" The boys loaded the wagons back at the Big Bayou camps, and then made another trip to continue loading more until they were able to get most everything inside the fortifications. Crosby's colonel, William L. Eakin, recalled that the regiment was unable to save its tents before entering the siege lines, but other regiments in Reynolds's Brigade seemed to have been more successful in retrieving theirs.[57]

In the early evening the whole army was in full retreat, according to Wash, who was back at the Big Black Bridge with his 60th Tennessee. "Several brigades [were] tarrying on the battlefield to hold the enemy in check," he reported. While fighting with the army's rear guard, Wash indicated that his fellow Kentuckian, General Lloyd Tilghman, "lost his life late in the evening while keeping the enemy back at a bridge on the left."[58] Swan of Stephen D. Lee's brigade suggested that while he had no intelligence on the order of the battle just fought, "the battle went against us, and our lines fell back and could not be restored."[59] Captain Clark of the 59th Tennessee summed up the day's sad events by declaring, "Grant's lines were being thrown in our rear since his lines were so much longer than ours."[60]

The only field artillery left in Stevenson's entire division, Swan noted, belonged to Colonel Reynolds. The Cleveland, Tennessee, soldier had also received word that "our loss [today] was quite heavy in men." All of Pemberton's men made it over the Big Black at the two crossings, the Big Black Bridge and Bridgeport, except for most of the division of W. W. Loring, which

---

[57] Hodges, *The Crosby Collection*, 413.
[58] Wash, *Camp, Field and Prison Life*, 45.
[59] Swan, "A Tennessean in the Siege of Vicksburg," 356.
[60] Clark, *Valleys of the Shadow*, 21.

had been cut off on the retreat and forced to head toward Hazlehurst. Loring also suffered "the loss of all his cannon." The only bright spots in the miserable day for Stevenson's Division, Swan reported, was "the brilliant work done by Lee's brigade in the battle" and the efforts of Alexander Reynolds and his men, who finally got the supply train to safety inside the fortifications at Vicksburg.[61]

"Why General Pemberton left the high commanding points on the Vicksburg side of the river," Captain Clark of the 59th Tennessee wondered, "and crossed to the low flat to meet Grant, leaving him in the heights and the Mississippi River behind, has always been a mystery to me."[62] Clark's orderly sergeant, William H. Long of Morristown and the 59th Tennessee, seemingly little concerned with such tactical considerations, shared the bit of trivia that the battle fought on 16 May known in history by three different names: Baker's Creek, Champion Hill, and Edwards' Depot. "Our regiment lost 72 men," Long indicated, "& we were cut off from the main army & had to run around the Federal army a distance of 8 miles." He recorded that this amazing feat, which Captain R. G. Clark timed on his watch, was accomplished in fifty-five minutes.[63] For all the complaints the East Tennesseans had about Colonel Reynolds, he retained the regard of his superior officers and perhaps even the grudging respect of his "mountain boys."

"We were on the field of the Battle of Baker's Creek," Orderly Sergeant Murray S. Brown of Elizabethton, Carter County, and the 59th Tennessee, posted in the company's record of events, "but were not closely engaged with the enemy." He noted, with some considerable understatement, that "we retreated to Vicksburg, at which place we arrived on 16 [17] May 1863; the men being greatly exhausted."[64] His company lost six stragglers who were captured by the Yankees on the long retreat. Sergeant William H. Long of Morristown and Company I, 59th Tennessee, noted that three men in his command were also captured during the same activity.[65] The service records of Company C, 1st

---

[61] Swan, "A Tennessean in the Siege of Vicksburg," 356.

[62] Clark, *Valleys of the Shadow*, 21.

[63] Long, "Autobiography," 2: 54.

[64] 59th Tennessee, *Compiled Service Records*.

[65] Ibid. A soldier in a Mississippi regiment described the grueling march as follows: "some of the troops passed our camps worn down and exhausted from repeated forces marches. The enemy had been pursuing them, hanging upon their rear, capturing those that were unwell or too much exhausted to march and causing our men to push forward with all their might. There they go—covered with dust—with a swinging gait, hungry, thirsty, tired, sleepy and discouraged. I heard one remark that he had not slept any for two nights." Kenneth Urquhart, *Vicksburg: Southern City Under Siege: William Lovelace*

Tennessee Cavalry indicated that that command lost three troopers, whose exact status was unknown, on the retreat, and that 2nd Lieutenant Thomas Miller was killed in action during the unit's scouting activities on the fringes of the battle.[66]

"[The Battle of Baker's Creek] resulted into a hot contest," Stamper of the 43rd Tennessee, Reynolds' Brigade, noted, "so much so that our forces had to fall back with considerable loss [the next day] to Vaughn's Brigade." He reported that when the Yankees cut off their route into Vicksburg, Reynolds's men and the wagon train "had no alternative but to take the nearest road [Brownsville] to Vicksburg and get inside our fortifications." This amazing journey, Stamper wrote, concluded "an hour by the sun, Sunday evening [17 May]."[67] But that happy event would not occur until the following day. Even as the Big Black River battle was in progress on 17 May, as Reynolds's East Tennesseans followed the rumbling creaking wagons rattling along, the news passed among the boys that Vaughn and his men had abandoned the bridge. All were withdrawing back toward Vicksburg where everyone was headed now, some as commands, some as individuals, some with more order than others.

Reports of the just concluded battle at Baker's Creek continued to take more form and detail. The boys on the march learned that the left of the army had at first driven the enemy back, but their numbers were such that they recovered and smashed General Barton's center, severely cutting up his brigade, according to Calvin M. Smith of the 31st Tennessee. The rushing Yankees overran Waddell's battery, and all the others Pemberton took to the field with him, as it turned out. Smith noted the Waddell battery "lost every man killed or taken prisoner, but one, who had his arm shot off."[68] Describing the day's events as concisely as possible, George Hynds of the 31st Tennessee wrote six words in his journal summarizing the past twenty-four hours: "Battle of Edwards' Depot, Confederates defeated."[69]

The aftermath of the battle was also disheartening for those not witnessing it, whether among the citizens in Vicksburg or the boys who stood on the guard at the Big Black Bridge. Demoralized and straggling men, replete with stories of

---

Foster's Letter Describing the Defense and Surrender of the Confederate Fortress on the Mississippi (New Orleans LA: Historic New Orleans Collection, 1980) 1.

[66] 1st Tennessee Cavalry, *Compiled Service Records.*

[67] Stamper, "Travels of the 43rd Tennessee," 57.

[68] Smith, *A Smith in Service,* 50.

[69] George H. Hynds, "Original Handwritten Notes of the Siege of Vicksburg from May 16th to July 4th, 1863" (unpublished manuscript), National Park Archives, Vicksburg MS, 1.

defeat and disaster, complained that the Yankees were too many in number. The stream of the battle weary intensified as men headed past Crawford's regiment rearward, and Captain Wash of the 60th Tennessee admitted that the results were now painfully clear. By 4 p.m., he noted, the road was clogged with exhausted stragglers from fragmented regiments and crushed batteries,[70] the latter without most of their fine horses and equipment, their caissons or their field pieces.

"Half an hour later, General Pemberton came up to my post and asked why my company was not to the front," Wash stated. "I told him we were on picket, and he acknowledged it was all right." Wash, though only a junior officer, had the impudence ask his commanding general about the result of the day's battle, to which Pemberton replied: "We are whipped, but the enemy outnumbered us three to one." Wash noted that the Lieutenant General commanding was calm in conduct, but "greatly agitated in mind." A courier arrived soon thereafter with a dispatch for General Pemberton from General Joseph Johnston. Wash watched Pemberton read it, study it a moment, then, gritting his teeth, remark to his staff: "Had General Johnston sent me this dispatch yesterday, this battle would not have been fought!" His adjutant was handed the correspondence, with orders to "preserve it," because Pemberton believed that it might be "of value to me someday." I later found out that the dispatch was an order to avoid a collision with the enemy," Wash remembered, "and [Pemberton] was ordered to unite his force with Johnston's in the vicinity of Clinton."[71]

---

[70] Wash, *Camp, Field and Prison Life*, 45; Loughborough, *My Cave Life at Vicksburg*, 41–45. One Confederate described as follows the experience of a straggling friend on the retreat from Baker's Creek who wound up as one of the unfortunate pick-ups:

> Near the middle of the afternoon [of 16 May] they saw a troop of cavalry galloping towards them and they were not long in discovering that they were Federals. Hugh could have escaped to the woods, but he would not leave his lieutenant.
>
> "Hello, Johnnies! Which way?" was the greeting given by the officers in the front.
>
> "We are attempting to overtake our command," replied the Confederates.
>
> "You have fallen in with the wrong command, haven't you?"
>
> "From your garb, we think we have," the boy said, dryly.
>
> "We'll take good care of you," said the Yankee officer. Joe Wright Crump, "A Boy Soldier's Fidelity," *The Confederate Veteran* 4/4 (April 1896): 119.

[71] Wash, *Camp, Field and Prison Life*, 45.

Wash continued describing post-battle scenario. He indicated that Pemberton's army was now in full retreat, though it appeared a rear guard action was offered at Edwards' Depot by the few Confederate commands which fell back from the battle and rallied to brunt Grant's advance.[72] Few there were of these heroes who could be stopped to face the relentless approaching foe.

While the events that surrounded the Battle of Baker's Creek drawing to an end, Robert Bachman of the 60th Tennessee noted that Vaughn's men were to take part in the battle along Baker's Creek, but they were instead ordered back to the Big Black River to protect the bridge over which Pemberton's forces were to escape. "The retreat was at night and in great confusion," Bachman confessed. "In the darkness, a great many soldiers became detached from their companies and regiments." But when "strayed men" reached the river, they were corralled, with each one ordered to call out his regiment: "59th Tennessee," called out one, "25th Georgia," another, and "15th Alabama," yelled a third. "And so it went," Bachman continued, "until all the lost soldiers are back with their proper regiments." As darkness neared, the army continued its way westward toward and over the Big Black.[73]

At Edwards' Depot, the Confederates left train carloads of provisions, ammunition ,and medical stores, not to mention all the cotton storage houses there. All were set on fire to deprive the Yankees of their spoils. The rear guard fell back a stone's throw ahead of the enemy's vanguard, Wash indicated, and the enemy artillery sent grape and canister to hurry the Southern soldiers along, "but pursued no farther." Around 10 p.m., he recalled, another part of the army reached the Big Black and passed across the planked-over railroad bridge and the steamer *Dot*, which had been jammed on one side of the riverbank and its stern wedged on the other. These defeated soldiers made with all haste left in their weary bodies for the safety of Vicksburg. General Bowen's division of Missourians and Arkansans arrived and were placed on the left and right flanks of Vaughn's men.[74] Bowen, who was becoming one of the generals in whom all the troops at Vicksburg had great confidence, without a doubt proved a calming influence on the men left behind to defend the bridge. Due to rank, he was in field command of the defensive line in front of the Big Black River bridge when the Yankees finally arrived to test it.

Preparing for the Onslaught of the Victorious Yankees. Long into the night, preparations continued for the anticipated battle just east of the Big Black

[72] Ibid.
[73] Bachman, "Reminiscences of Childhood," 18–19.
[74] Wash, *Camp, Field and Prison Life,* 45.

bridge the next morning. The 60th Tennessee, Wash noted, was ordered out to the extreme right of the defensive line, "beyond the real line of defense." The anxiety attendant to the perceived imminent arrival of Grant's victorious forces played on the men's minds as Crawford's regiment "took its position behind the levee." The East Tennessee boys wondered about the malevolent forces swarming out there in the darkness toward the east as they occupied themselves applying spades to their defenses, or dragging logs and other brush in an effort to construct what Wash termed "rough earthworks" some distance removed from the actual defenses. "That night while entrenching," he remembered, "I said to our Colonel [Nathan Gregg] and several others that we would surely go up right there, for there were no means of retreat, the river being directly in our rear and no crossing save near the bridge, and that was frail and inadequate."[75]

Reflecting on the situation several years later, Wash stated that it would have taken at least four times the number of Confederates already there to hold against the Yankee hordes coming against them at daylight. He believed that it was "preposterous" to think the force at hand could have held out for more than a few hours. "However," he added with resignation, "nothing daunted, and we made the best preparation we could to receive them." Some 4,000 men, along with twenty pieces of artillery, were in place to defend the bridge, with the belief the boys in blue would be upon them with first light. "After midnight," Wash reported, "and after the excitement of the day and our night march, we wrapped our martial cloaks about us and slept till day."[76]

"In the evening of 16 May, while the Battle of Baker's Creek was in progress," Colonel James G. Rose of the 61st Tennessee recorded, "General

---

[75] Ibid., 45–46.

[76] Ibid., 46. One of the units purloined at the defenses was the 4th Mississippi of W. E. Baldwin's Brigade, Martin L. Smith's Division. Although marginally involved in the battle of Baker's Creek, the 4th Mississippi was placed within Vaughn's Brigade to augment his numbers and "add to their morale," according to Baldwin's report. As an indication of the limited number of rifles the 4th Mississippi brought to bear, there were fewer than 300 men on its rolls at its reorganization in October 1862. Although Bearss indicated it was on the extreme right flank of Vaughn's Brigade, a number of East Tennessee participants stated the 60th Tennessee's right flank rested against the mound of the railroad. Baldwin in his report indicated that though he desired to recall the regiment to his brigade, "it would not be brought off [since] General Vaughn [at the time] was warmly engaged with the enemy." Baldwin then declared that the 4th Mississippi "gallantly held its position on the other side [of the line] until left alone by the other commands adjoining," presumably Vaughn's north of the railroad and Cockrell's to the south. Report of Gen. W. E. Baldwin, 10 July 1863, *Official Records*, ser. 1, vol. 24, pt. 2, p. 400–401.

Vaughn's Brigade was placed in position to protect the railroad bridge at the Big Black River some six miles in rear of the Confederate line of battle." Shortly after dark, his regiment watched the defeated Confederate troops engaged in the day's fight slowly make their way toward them and across the bridge. "The crossing continued through the night and until daylight," Rose indicated, "when all had crossed except for a few stragglers." General Vaughn's position at once became critical, according to Rose. It occupied a line of unfinished earthworks, with "the Big Black River deep and sluggish in its rear," and the East Tennesseans were the only organized force standing between Grant's advance, "flush with the preceding day's victory," and Vicksburg. "The peril of the situation was realized by every private," Rose noted, "and orders for the withdrawal of the brigade across the river were momentarily expected." The position was, according to Rose, untenable, and indeed, the bridge itself was no longer of use to the Confederates, since the army was well on its way toward the fortifications of Vicksburg.[77]

Basic military tactics suggest that a force should never take up a defensive position with a body of water at its rear, so it seemed that Pemberton set these men up for disaster by placing his works on the east side of the Big Black rather than on the western bluffs, which would have proved to be at least as formidable to attack as had been his defenses at the Chickasaw Bluffs back in December 1862. More formidable indeed, the swollen river would have been to the Confederate front. Pemberton feared, with justification, that even had the Confederates placed all their troops, instead of just the remainder of Lee and Baldwin's Brigades, on the western bluffs where the railroad bridge ran across, Grant would have merely by-passed the crossing there and placed his pontoons up and down the river, flanking the position. Grant would later fortify those bluffs by digging trenches on the west bank of the Big Black as a defense against the much-anticipated attempt by Joseph Johnston to raise the siege.

In his defense of strategy at Vicksburg, Pemberton initially stated that the earthworks had been placed on the eastern side of the Big Black long before so that the troops who manned them could launch a counterattack against any assault made on it. Pemberton believed the position to be so strong that even with the dire circumstances his army found itself in after Baker's Creek, the right troops, and under his most trusted lieutenant, John Bowen, could stop Grant's march toward Vicksburg dead in its tracks. Pemberton also gave as an excuse for leaving Bowen's and Vaughn's men in the advanced positions long

---

[77] Rose, "Sixty-First Tennessee," in Lindsley, *The Military Annals of Tennessee (Confederate)*, 2: 575.

past the time they were needed: so that Loring's Division, which had been separated from the main force and was unaccounted for, might still be looking for a way get over the Big Black to rejoin the forces withdrawing into the Vicksburg fortifications.[78] "Onward came Grant's victorious columns," Colonel Rose concluded, skeptical of Pemberton's grandiose plans, "but the order for the withdrawal of the brigade came not."[79]

---

[78] Report of Gen. John C. Pemberton, 25 August 1863, *Official Records*, ser. 1, vol. 24, pt. 1, p. 266.

[79] Rose, "Sixty-First Tennessee," in Lindsley, *The Military Annals of Tennessee (Confederate)*, 2: 575.

CHAPTER 8

"Who Can Appreciate a Moment of Such
Extreme Solitude?"
17 May
("The Battle of the Big Black River")

Description of the Big Black Battlefield. Colonel James G. Rose of the 61st
Tennessee provided in his reminiscence a topographical description of the
works east of the Big Black River Bridge. They were shaped like a letter "V," he
noted, with both flanks resting on the river above and below the bridge, "and
the apex at the railroad, nearly a mile east of the river." His regiment was
positioned on the left of the brigade, which defended originally a line extending
from near the railroad north to the river. The 62nd Tennessee manned the
center of the line assigned to Vaughn, and the 60th Tennessee was on the right
somewhat forward, with its farthest company resting its flank against the
elevated bed of the railroad. "Earthworks had been hastily thrown up on each
end of the line," Rose continued, "leaving a space of about two hundred yards
near the center without defensive works." This space would be critically
important during the battle. Rose believed that no effort had been made to dig
trenches there because the plot of ground "was probably covered with water
when the works were being constructed" due to the spring rains. Now, with the
approach of Grant's hordes, the swampy expanse had evaporated, and the
ground was now firm enough, allowing, Rose predicted with some trepidation,
for "the movement of troops."[1]

General John C. Pemberton, in his official report, provided a similar
image of the battlefield at the Big Black River:

> The river, where it is crossed by the railroad bridge, makes a bend
> somewhat in the shape of a horseshoe. Across this horseshoe, at its
> narrowest part, a line of rifle pits had been constructed, making

---

[1] Ibid.

excellent cover for infantry, and at proper intervals dispositions were made for field artillery. The line of pits ran nearly north and south, and was about one mile in length. North of and for a considerable distance south of the railroad and of the dirt road to Edwards' Depot, nearly ran parallel to it, extended a bayou, which in itself opposed a serious obstacle to an assault upon the rifle pits. This line abutted north on the river and south upon a cypress brake, which spread itself nearly to the bank of the river. In addition to the railroad bridge, which I had caused to be floored for the passage even of artillery and wagons, the steamer *Dot*, from which the machinery had been taken, was converted into a bridge, by placing her fore and aft across the river.

Between the works and the bridge, about three quarters of a mile, the country was open, being either old or cultivated fields, *affording no cover should the troops be driven from the trenches* [italics added]. East and south of the railroad the topographical features of the country over which the enemy must necessarily pass were similar to those above described; but north of the railroad and about 300 yards in front of the rifle pits a copse of woods extended from the road to the river.[2]

Pemberton's confidence in the men charged to hold their ground placed in this position was unflinching, given the seeming impregnability of the breastworks, especially with the arrival and placement of Bowen's Division (composed of Cockrell's and Green's Brigades) on the flanks. Bowen's men had been tested and found reliable the day before at Baker's Creek and at Port Gibson two weeks previously. The right of the line below the south side of the railroad was manned by General Francis Cockrell's Missouri brigade, and on the left flank, judged equally steady were General Martin Green's Brigade of Missourians and Arkansans. John Vaughn's boys manned the center of the works between Green's right flank and the railroad line. The East Tennesseans would be entrusted with the critical obligation to hold the center. Their dependability was the great unknown. In Pemberton's opinion, these East Tennesseans had yet to really prove themselves despite their success at the Chickasaw Bluffs. "General Vaughn's Brigade had not been engaged at Baker's Creek," Pemberton noted, "and his men were fresh, and I believed were not demoralized."[3] One of those fresh troops was Sergeant Robert Bachman of the

---

[2] Report of Gen. John C. Pemberton, 25 August 1863, *Official Records*, ser. 1, vol. 24, pt. 1, p. 266.
[3] Ibid.

60th Tennessee, who, in describing the events that led to the disaster at the Big
Black River, indicated ominously: "the enemy followed our retreating army, and
by daylight [of 17 May] were ready for another battle."[4]

Isaac Stamper of the 43rd Tennessee, along with the rest of Reynolds's
Brigade marching behind the wagon train toward Vicksburg just north and now
west of the river, stated that at 8 a.m. on the morning of 17 May, after another
sleepless night, the boys heard the heavy firing coming from the vicinity of the
Big Black River Bridge.[5] "It is with no little anxiety that I can sit here when our
retreat may be cut off or we might render Gen. Vaughn great assistance," wrote
Calvin Smith of the 31st Tennessee during a respite in their march as escort of
the trains. He felt that the brigade should have been "pressing forward and
engaging the enemy, so as to assist our friends and acquaintances." Those
orders were not forthcoming, however. As he pondered these and other
matters, Smith and the boys watched "companies of cavalry passing along the
road."[6] And though he did not indicate where the riders were heading, it was
probably back in the direction of Bovina Station and then toward the Big Black
Bridge, to keep an eye on the Yankees' forward progress.

The Battle Commences. The first indication the Federals were ready to press
their advantage on the Big Black defenders was when "the enemy opened his
artillery at long range," Pemberton wrote in his official report. "Very soon, he
pressed forward with infantry into a copse of wood north of the railroad."[7]
Colonel James G. Rose of the 61st Tennessee indicated that, once the morning
got light enough to see movement in the black woodline before them, his
regiment observed "the Federal sharp-shooters … appearing on our front."[8]
From there, they began plying their lethal trade against any movement detected
in the Confederate works while their columns moved into place for the assault.

Captain Wash of the 60th Tennessee reported that the battle commenced
around 7 a.m. when "our pickets began a brisk fire with their cavalry advance."
Less than an hour later, he noted, the Yankee artillery and infantry came up,
and soon, the opposing batteries began to duel for a half hour. The
Northerners discontinued their shelling after that time and limbered up their
guns to haul them to points of closer proximity in an effort to disillusion the

---

[4] Bachman, "Reminiscences of Childhood," 19.

[5] Stamper, "Travels of the 43rd Tennessee," 57.

[6] Smith, *A Smith in Service*, 50.

[7] Report of Gen. John C. Pemberton, 25 August 1863, *Official Records*, ser. 1, vol. 24,
pt. 1, p. 267.

[8] Rose, "Sixty-First Tennessee," in Lindsley, *The Military Annals of Tennessee
(Confederate)*, 2: 575.

Confederates in their works. Their trajectories were too high, however, and Wash believed that the enemy guns did no serious damage. "The whistling rifled cannon balls that split open trees in our rear made some of the boys open their eyes," he observed, "but most of them were perfectly calm."[9] Despite Wash's optimistic evaluation of the morale of the men, Major Samuel Lockett, Pemberton's chief engineer, noted in his report that the troops in the defenses seemed to him to be "unsteady."[10] Predictably, the Yankees' nearly point-blank barrage must have had that chilling effect. James E. Payne of the 6th Missouri, Francis Cockrell's Brigade, indicated, "men of many battles told me they had never before been exposed to so deadly a fire as Grant's gunners turned loose on Bowen and Vaughn that morning."[11]

Certainly one soldier whose eyes were opened a bit wider than most had to be General John C. Vaughn himself, who, while riding behind his lines during this bombardment, had the reins of his horse cut by fragments from a near miss. "I got off my horse to re-tie them," Bob Houston, one of General Vaughn's staff recorded. "I saw General Vaughn under the most terrible fire. He was cool and collected" and "seemed unconscious of fear."[12] Meanwhile, six brigades of McClernand's XIII Corps continued their deployment across the field in the woods facing the Confederate left flank. The greater concentration of their forces was massed before the defender's center and left on the oblique in anticipation of the impending attack. Rushing up with six full brigades composed of twenty-eight regiments, the Union troops, soon joined by General Grant himself, had every right to expect that this day would, as had the day before, belong to them.[13]

"I found on reaching the field just east of the Big Black River," Colonel Albert Lee, commanding a brigade in General Peter Osterhaus' Federal division, noted. "Lawler's brigade of [our] division deployed in line before the enemy's works." Two of Lawler's regiments were on the left and rear, Lee wrote, with a section of a battery on the right, banging away almost point-blank

---

[9] Wash, *Camp, Field and Prison Life*, 46–47.

[10] Report of Samuel Lockett, 23 July 1863, *Official Records*, ser. 1, vol. 24, pt. 2, p. 73.

[11] James E. Payne, "Missouri Troops in the Vicksburg Campaign," in *The Confederate Veteran* 36/7 (July 1928): 302–303.

[12] Bob Houston, "A History of Vaughn's Brigade," in *A Soldier's Story of the Siege of Vicksburg, from the Diary of Osborne H. Oldroyd*, ed. Osborn Oldroyd (Springfield IL: H. W. Rokker, 1885) 154.

[13] Charles E. Hooker, *Mississippi*, vol. 12 of *Confederate Military History: A Library of Confederate States History*, ed. Gen. Clement Evans (Secaucus, NJ: The Blue & Grey Press, 1899) reprint, 148–49.

into the Confederate works. To the right of his formations were Lawler's two
other regiments supporting General Eugene A. Carr's division. "In front of us
was a long line of earthworks filled with guns," Lee reported, "and a quarter of
a mile distant from our deployed line." Lee took special notice of the bayou that
ran in front of the length of the Confederate works, causing him to realize that
the men who would make the attack at this point would have to wade through
water and muck "12 or 15 feet across and difficult of passage." This observation
led Lee to conclude that any advance over this treacherous ground, which was
also well covered by no less than five Confederate batteries in the center, would
be "impracticable."[14]

Perhaps an hour was occupied by the Yankees moving their considerable
infantry formations in position for the assault during and after the time their
artillery did its work. The Northern lines encompassed the entire defensive
line, Wash asserted with some nervousness, and in the breaks in the trees dense
columns of the boys in blue could be seen advancing methodically into place.[15]
The psychological effect on the defenders having to watch and wait for such
vast numbers of their foe, as they coolly prepared for their concentrated sweep
on the Confederate works a mile in front of the Big Black River, can not be
overstated. The Battle of the Big Black River would be a victory of intimidation
as opposed to a victory of brute force.

"On our left a thick forest was within a half mile of our line," Wash
recollected, "and there it was that the enemy made their first demonstration."[16]
The Yankee skirmishers spread out and advanced toward the Confederate
defenders on the left flank commanded by General Martin E. Green. Wash
affirmed that the enemy's strategy, with heavy skirmishing against the center of
the defenses, was somewhat unnerving. "This brisk fight at long range," he
noted, "continued for perhaps an hour."[17] Rose of the 61st Tennessee recorded
that this "heavy line of Federal sharp-shooters kept up a continuous and deadly
fusillade from the woods in front of the regiment," which caused him to feel
uneasy about the attention given his position. He expected that all those
Yankees would fall upon his men. Rose's adjutant, James D. Thomas, was sent
off to remind General Vaughn of the problem of the marshy gap at their
position between his left flank and the right flank of Greens' Brigade, which

---

[14] Report of Col. Albert Lee, 22 May 1863, *Official Records*, ser. 1, vol. 24, pt. 2, p.
132.
[15] Wash, *Camp, Field and Prison Life*, 47.
[16] Ibid.
[17] Ibid.

had the potential of allowing the Yankees to dash into it, and from which advantage they could get in their rear and render an "enfilading fire which would force us from our position."[18]

Meanwhile, Rose reported, Captain Thomas's mission to procure any reinforcements from General Vaughn failed, "though frequent application was made for more troops to mass on the left."[19] Captain Houston of Vaughn's staff reported that Vaughn was not the one who had refused to supply reinforcements. The matter was laid at the doorstep of the commanding general, Houston, who "was as helpless and undecided as a child." Houston indicated that the sparseness of numbers required defenders to be spaced one every four feet in the works before the Big Black River Bridge, and there was no additional support to be spared.[20] Rose noted that the regimental adjutant's effort "was nonetheless gallant, because the enemy's sharp-shooters swept the whole field with their murderous fire, and Thomas went and returned at the imminent risk of his life."[21]

The boys in Vaughn's command, with their pulses thumping dully at the double-quick in their ears, had spent the morning, when daylight finally permitted, watching the Yankees as they massed their forces for an assault through the fields and woods described by Captain Wash. Hidden by trees was Mike Lawler's Brigade, which had moved into a sizable swale along the river bank to their left front. From that vantage point, Lawler's infantry prepared, in relative safety for their impending attack, his advanced regiment only a stone's throw away from the Confederate works.

"Finally the regiments that were to lead the charge formed with bayonets fixed," General Michael Lawler declared. In the edge of the woods along the riverbank, he wrote in his report, they coiled to strike. "All things being in readiness, the command 'forward!' was given, and the noble regiments sprang forward toward the works."[22] Lawler, in his shirtsleeves, was among the troops, waving them on.

---

[18] Rose, "The Sixty-First Tennessee," in Lindsley, *The Military Annals of Tennessee (Confederate)*, 2: 575.

[19] Ibid.

[20] Houston, "A History of Vaughn's Brigade," in *A Soldier's Story of the Siege of Vicksburg*, 154.

[21] Rose, "The Sixty-First Tennessee," in Lindsley, *The Military Annals of Tennessee (Confederate)*, 2: 575.

[22] Report of Gen. Michael Lawler, 26 May 1863, *Official Records*, ser. 1, vol. 24, pt. 2, p. 137.

"Pretty heavy skirmishing was kept up for awhile along our whole line," General Pemberton observed, "but presently the enemy, who had massed a large force in the woods immediately north of the railroad, advanced at a run with loud cheers."[23] Wash of the 60th Tennessee noted with some admiration that "several brigades of [enemy] infantry, like brave Spartans, came out into the open ground." They attacked at the oblique, only to be met initially by the intense fire of the Missouri and Arkansas boys of General Green, who soon "made them hustle back to the cover of the timber."[24]

Colonel Elijah Gates, commanding the 1st Missouri Cavalry Regiment (dismounted) in Green's Brigade on Vaughn's left, described what he observed: "The enemy formed their men on the river in the timber, where we could not see them. They brought their men out by the right flank in column of fours, about 140 yards in front of my regiment, at the double-quick." Gates's men opened up a "terrific fire" on the advancing bluecoats until they passed out of sight into a grove of timber to his right.[25] Lawler, who had commanded the attackers against Gates's men, reported that his men had endured "a galling fire from the sharp-shooters [Gates' men] on the right."[26]

"After they passed me," Colonel Gates recorded, "we listened for our men to open a heavy volley on my right and drive the Yankees back."[27] He contended that such punishment, surprisingly, was not forthcoming from the Enfields of Vaughn's Brigade. "Three rounds of 'buck and ball' [one .577 rifle ball with three buckshot on top of it] had been issued to us," Sergeant Robert Bachman of the 60th Tennessee noted. "This ammunition was especially used in resisting the enemy's charge, which we were expecting."[28] Close work had been anticipated in front and inside the trenches, and the nearest ammunition the rifleman had to canister was their "buck and ball." With these rounds, the Confederates expect to rebuff the Yankees in close quarters' fighting, despite the enemy's superior numbers and its confidence earned the day before along Baker's Creek. Colonel Gregg's 60th Tennessee was on the extreme right of Vaughn's position, with its right flank buttressed by the elevation of the railroad

---

[23] Report of Gen. John C. Pemberton, 25 August 1863, *Official Records*, ser. 1, vol. 24, pt. 1, p. 267.

[24] Wash, *Camp, Field and Prison Life*, 47.

[25] Report of Col. E. Gates, 1 August 1863, *Official Records*, ser. 1, vol. 24, pt. 2, p. 119.

[26] Report of Gen. Michael Lawler, 26 May 1863, *Official Records*, ser. 1, vol. 24, pt. 2, p. 137.

[27] Report of Col. E. Gates, 1 August 1863, *Official Records*, ser. 1, vol. 24, pt. 2, p. 119.

[28] Bachman, "Reminiscences of Childhood," 19.

bed, Bachman reported, where "we could see the enemy deploying in front of us."[29]

The Unsteady Defenders. There remained, then, the gap that had caused Colonel Rose some considerable alarm and had precipitated his alert to General Vaughn. No sooner had Adjutant Thomas returned with the bad news that no men were to be sent to plug the hole than the "anticipated assault broke upon the regiment in all its fury." In his description of the situation, Rose stated: "the assaulting columns proved to be from General Osterhaus' division, which had been massing in a depression hidden by timber near the bank of the river." These audacious Midwesterners were formed into five lines of battle, which easily overlapped the entire defensive line assigned to the 61st Tennessee, and were "moved from its cover into an open field in our front in magnificent array, with banners flying and their burnished arms reflecting back the rays of the morning sun."[30] From within this "magnificent array," Colonel T. E. Buehler, commanding the 67th Indiana, sent one of his companies ahead as skirmisher before making his advance "by the right oblique through brush and bayous, over fences and hedges, advancing at a rapid rate."[31] Colonel Rose of the 61st Tennessee, rarely given to exaggeration, recalled that his East Tennesseans had been able to count seventeen regimental flags advancing against their position.[32] This mass of attackers caused more than one rifleman in the Confederate works to look over his shoulder toward the bridge and calculate the time it might take to flee there.

Then, "despite a weariness caused by the oppressive heat of the previous day," Buehler's Hoosiers, in sight of the breastworks at the Big Black, "and with a shout unequaled," dashed forward at the double-quick over the plowed field and across the bayou.[33] Also on the attack was Lee's Brigade. "I deployed two companies of the Second Brigade as skirmishers," Colonel Albert Lee wrote, regarding the deployment of his men, and "directed their advance through a point of wood some distance to our left, to reconnoiter the left flank of the works opposed to us." Here awaited Vaughn's East Tennesseans and General

---

[29] Ibid.

[30] Rose, "The Sixty-First Tennessee," in Lindsley, *The Military Annals of Tennessee (Confederate)*, 2: 575.

[31] Report of Col. T. E. Buehler, 25 May 1863, *Official Records*, ser. 1, vol. 24, pt. 2, p. 596.

[32] Rose, "The Sixty-First Tennessee," in Lindsley, *The Military Annals of Tennessee (Confederate)*, 2: 575.

[33] Report of Col. T. E. Buehler, 25 May 1863, *Official Records*, ser. 1, vol. 24, pt. 1, p. 596.

Green's right flank. Two regiments of Lee's brigade advanced behind the cover of this skirmish line, before the whole struck the left flank occupied by Rose's 61st Tennessee.[34]

Sergeant Bachman of the 60th Tennessee indicated that from his vantage point the Yankees advanced toward the works manned by his brigade, across a level field of four or five hundred yards, "alternately advancing and faltering under our galling fire of buckshot and ball." All the regiments on the left and center were issuing volleys except for the rather isolated 60th Tennessee near the railroad embankment.[35] This observation was supported by General Lawler, who indicated that, as his infantry continued toward the center of the Confederate line, the men of 61st and 62nd Tennessee rose up from their works with Enfields leveled and cut loose with "a terrible fire of musketry."[36]

"Soon a column was seen filing to the right of our line, and we were fully expecting a brush there," Captain Wash of the 60th Tennessee, recorded. Then, around eleven o'clock a.m., the Yankees, alerted by a deserter, took advantage of a flaw in the works, namely, "an unguarded space in about the center of our left wing."[37] It was Rose's undefended gap. "[The attacking Yankees] dashed bravely on," Lawler continued, "[through a] perfect hailstorm of bullets poured into them with destructive effect ...[three regiments] pressed onward, nearer and nearer to the rebel works, over an open field of 500 yards, under a wasting fire, and up to the edge of the bayou." At this point, Lawler's Iowa and Wisconsin troops halted "only long enough to pour into the enemy a deadly volley."[38]

This concentrated fire, from which hundreds of minie balls zinged into the position held by the 61st and 62nd Tennessee, sent chunks flying out of the snarled limbs and logs, kicked up puffs of dirt, and smacked with violent thuds into the cotton and hay bales the East Tennesseans were using as cover. Some of the Union lead found other marks. Private John B. Browne of Company B, 62nd Tennessee, out of Rogersville, Hawkins County, and Privates William Crump, Joseph McCrary, William Miller, and Nathan Shipley, all of Company

---

[34] Report of Col. Albert Lee, 22 May 1863, *Official Records*, ser. 1, vol. 24, pt. 2, p. 132.

[35] Bachman, "Reminiscences of Childhood," 19.

[36] Report of Gen. Michael Lawler, 26 May 1863, *Official Records*, ser. 1, vol. 24, pt. 2, p. 137.

[37] Wash, *Camp, Field and Prison Life*, 47.

[38] Report of Gen. Michael Lawler, 26 May 1863, *Official Records*, ser. 1, vol. 24, pt. 2, p. 137.

E, 61st Tennessee, out of Blountville, Sullivan County, were killed.[39] At least one soldier in Rose's command, in receipt of this volley, would carry with him a horrible reminder of this morning's experience the remainder of his life. Private George Washington Smith of a company from Morristown with the 61st Tennessee indicated in his application for membership in his local Confederate Veterans' association: "I was wounded at the Big Black River, where I had my left eye shot out."[40]

The Dash for the Bridge. The volleys sent their way from the distance of a football field end-zone to end-zone provided the sudden impetus for the East Tennesseans to reconsider their options. General Michael Lawler noted in his report that the 23rd Iowa in his brigade "broke the enemy's line from a swamp at the edge of the timber, and poured an enfilading fire into the ditches." This, he observed, was what "routed the rebels in confusion."[41] Captain Houston of Vaughn's staff described the scene as he saw it: "Grant's victorious forces, ten times our numbers, moved rapidly forward, and while they were checked two or three times, they soon found our unprotected left, and with one grand bound it seemed to me, carried our whole line."[42] Vaughn's men received the brunt of the attack, but, according to Pemberton, "did not remain to receive [the Yankees], but broke and fled precipitately."[43]

"We had [gotten to] within 100 yards of the works, [with] a bayou to cross, [which was] filled by a heavy abatis," wrote Colonel James Keigwin of the 49th Indiana, General T. T. Garrard's Brigade, "[when] the enemy commenced putting cotton [lint from the bales used as breastworks] on their ramrods, and showed a willingness to surrender."[44]

"The two companies of skirmishers deployed on my left had meanwhile advanced," Lee noted, "and as our line moved forward, charged at the double-

---

[39] Rose, "The Sixty-First Tennessee," in Lindsley, *The Military Annals of Tennessee (Confederate)*, 2: 582; 61st and 62nd Tennessee, *Compiled Service Records*.

[40] Membership Applications, (William B. Tate Camp 725, United Confederate Veterans, Morristown TN) 105

[41] Report of Gen. Michael Lawler, 26 May 1863, *Official Records*, ser. 1, vol. 24, pt. 2, p. 137.

[42] Houston, "A History of Vaughn's Brigade," in *A Soldier's Story of the Siege of Vicksburg*, 154.

[43] Report of Gen. John C. Pemberton, 25 August 1863, *Official Records*, ser. 1, vol. 24, pt. 1, p. 267.

[44] Report of Col. James Keigwin, 18 May 1863, *Official Records*, ser. 1, vol. 24, pt. 2, p. 23.

quick,"[45] lest the cotton lint wavers be inclined to change their minds. Lawler's men "dashed forward through the bayou filled with water, fallen timber and brush, on to the rebel works with the shout of victors, driving the enemy in confusion from their breastworks and rifle pits."[46] Keigwin of the 49th Indiana declared that his regiment was the second one inside the Confederate works, "although they had farther to charge and deeper water to wade through than three others that started in advance of us."[47] Lawler's Brigade hit the gap between the 60th Tennessee and the 62nd Tennessee, and was quickly into the works, "just as the enemy was leaving them."[48] An overwhelming number of Yankees, according to Wash, rushed through this uncovered gap, suddenly finding themselves in the Confederate flank and rear.[49] Lack of confidence over Vaughn's assigned position had added to the East Tennessean's "unsteadiness," and despite the efforts of officers to calm their men to do the work at hand, some of the boys started scrambling over the rear of their ditch and heading for the bridge blockhouses from which the generals and even some of their own field officers were apparently observing the sorry spectacle. In the twinkling of an eye, dozens of Confederates, then hundreds, began the panicky stampede for the Big Black Bridge.

"Before we fired a gun," Bachman of the 60th Tennessee indicated, the line gave way on the left of the brigade, forcing the center and right to fall back and cross the Big Black River, nearly 500 yards to the rear.[50] Vaughn's men were not the only ones to run. As soon as the defenders were aware of the massive penetration of their line, the "skedaddle" began. All the Confederates on both sides of the railroad abutment were now compelled to run for their lives and liberty. "The boys now had no earthly show of resistance," Wash noted, "they must run, or surrender, or be shot down." He indicated that

---

[45] Report of Col. Albert Lee, 22 May 1863, *Official Records*, ser. 1, vol. 24, pt. 2, p. 132. Lee indicated that, with this maneuver, his brigade "cut off an entire regiment of the enemy [the 60th Tennessee], who laid down their arms and surrendered." In a bit of mild complaint, he added: "As the surrender was being made, some mounted staff officer from [A. J.] Smith's division rode through our line and received it from the rebel colonel [Nathan J. Gregg]." Lee, however, emphasized that his men had made the unhappy plight of the 60th Tennessee a reality.

[46] Report of Gen. Michael Lawler, 26 May 1863, *Official Records*, ser. 1, vol. 24, pt. 2, p. 137.

[47] Report of Col. Keigwin, 18 May 1863, *Official Records*, ser. 1, vol. 24, pt. 2, p. 23.

[48] Ibid.

[49] Wash, *Camp, Field and Prison Life*, 48.

[50] Bachman, "Reminiscences of Childhood," 19. Other combatants estimated the distance to have been between three-quarters of a mile to a mile.

General Vaughn, comprehending the situation, ordered the boys to evacuate as quickly as they could. It did not take long for everyone to determine that most of the Yankees pouring through their line could reach the Big Black Bridge ahead of most of the defenders.[51]

Vaughn sent his young aide Lieutenant John Toland of the 3rd Tennessee, and Talbott, Jefferson County, to order the withdrawal of the troops, which was mostly a formality by this time. Toland "rode up boldly to the lines and gave the orders," according to Adjutant Houston. In the course of carrying out his assignment, Toland was once thrown from his panic-stricken horse in the excitement of the action and, like many others, had to flee on foot to the river, where he made his escape by swimming across to the safety of the west bank.[52]

Colonel Rose at once ordered his 61st Tennessee to get out of the works and make for the bridge and river as fast as they could. This quick reaction on his part allowed him save "a portion of the 61st Tennessee."[53] Yankee officers also focused their attention to matters at hand. "I sent the 11th Wisconsin to occupy the ground between the enemy and the bridge," General Lawler reported, "and thus cut off their retreat." With considerable understatement, he added, "the movement was successful."[54]

With the center of line held by Vaughn's Brigade now dissolved, resistance on the wings also crumbled. Cockrell's men south of the railroad, "after a lively skirmish fire had been kept up for some time along our whole front," saw the East Tennesseans "beginning to give way and then running in disorder."[55] Cockrell, crouching atop the railroad abutment, quickly realized that the

---

[51] Wash, *Camp, Field and Prison Life*, 48. James E. Payne of the 6th Missouri noted that after the bombardment of the works at the Big Black, "There followed a strong infantry assault, during which Vaughn's command gave way and escaped. Bowen's men, seeing they would be cut off from the bridges, then abandoned their place and sought safety beyond the river." Payne, "Missouri Troops in the Vicksburg Campaign," 36/7 (7 July 1928): 302.

[52] Houston, "A History of Vaughn's Brigade," in *A Soldier's Story of the Siege of Vicksburg*, 154. Toland was an Irish immigrant adopted as a boy by Congressman Albert Watkins of Jefferson County, and raised with Watkins's children. At the start of the war, Toland was a student at Mossy Creek Baptist College nearby and enlisted with his brother Isaac Watkins in Vaughn's 3rd Tennessee on 6 May 1861, the day Tennessee formed a military alliance with the Southern Confederacy.

[53] Rose, "The Sixty-First Tennessee," in Lindsley, *The Military Annals of Tennessee (Confederate)*, 2: 575.

[54] Report of Gen. Michael Lawler, 26 May 1863, *Official Records*, ser. 1, vol. 24, pt. 2, p. 137.

[55] Report of Col. Francis Cockrell, 4 August 1863, *Official Records*, ser. 1, vol. 24, pt. 2, p. 113.

Yankees were getting between his brigade and the bridge, so he also ordered his men to make their escape to the rear as hard as they could go. Wash noted that the 60th Tennessee, being on the extreme right just below Cockrell's vantage point on the railroad elevation, was unaware of the catastrophe unfolding for some minutes, and once they were alerted, a necessarily brief consultation among the regimental officers was held. Lieutenant Colonel Gregg ordered all who could to dash to the rear toward the river. This they did.[56]

Gregg, who was in field command of the 60th Tennessee, ordered his men to follow him along the railroad to the river where the steamer *Dot* was wedged from one bank to the other, and there they would cross. As feared, the Yankees were ahead of them and cut off their escape, resulting in Gregg's immediate surrender of a large number of his regiment unable to escape.[57]

Other accounts of the ignoble capitulation of the 60th Tennessee its final time under arms at relatively full strength may render Wash's version the romantic ideal. "Our company, being on the left of the Regiment, went up the river to the railroad bridge upon which we expected to cross," Bachman of the 60th Tennessee recorded. All the while the Yankees were closing in and firing on them. He indicated that the boys resisted as best as they could while running for the bridge, but as they neared it, the East Tennesseans discovered the Major Samuel Lockett and his over-zealous engineers had already fled and burnt the bridge behind them.[58] Pemberton had left instructions, should it become necessary, to burn the span to prevent the enemy from gaining an easy crossing. Unfortunately, Lockett could not wait for all the panic-stricken Confederates to cross, so the bridge's destruction trapped many of the Confederates on the east side of the river.[59]

Bob Houston, Vaughn's adjutant, helped destroy the bridge. He asserted: "I had turned over the barrels of turpentine, and under orders, set fire to the

---

[56] Wash, *Camp, Field and Prison Life*, 48.

[57] Ibid. The reason for the absence of the regimental commander, Col. John C. Crawford, is unknown. He was an older man and may have been in ill during most of the Vicksburg campaign. Based on the writings of his younger officers, Crawford was considered an obliging father to them. Capt. John Bachman would assume command of the remnants of the 60th Tennessee after its return to the trenches. Crawford's activities and whereabouts during the 47–day siege were not noted in available sources. He would return for a time to command what remained of his regiment after it was exchanged. Vaughn lost nearly a third of his 1,500 men at the Big Black, the majority of which were with the 60th and 61st Tennessee.

[58] Bachman, "Reminiscences of Childhood," 19.

[59] Report of Samuel Lockett, 23 July 1863, *Official Records*, ser. 1, vol. 24, pt. 2, p. 73.

boats out of which we had made a pontoon."[60] Grant later affirmed that the time he lost having to construct a pontoon bridge for his army to cross was the principal reason he was unable to move rapidly on Vicksburg and quickly affect its capture.[61]

Down the river a short piece below the bridge, Bachman and some of his fellow soldiers were unwilling to submit quite as easily as their colonel had. They observed the bridge made from steamship *Dot*, and the Sullivan County native declared, "I was among the last to cross upon it." A number of others determined to swim across the river jumped in and braved the fire of the Union soldiers from the elevation behind them. "One of them [was] my brother," Bachman indicated.[62] As the senior captain and ranking officer of the 60th Tennessee who had escaped capture at the Big Black, John W. Bachman would command what remained of the regiment throughout the siege.

Pemberton reported that, during the aftermath of the action at Big Black, little military discipline was observed because everyone was caught up in reaching the bridge to gain the security of the river's western bank. "Many were unable to do so, but affected their escape by swimming the river," he stated. Others, not being able to swim, were drowned in the high waters and swift currents. "There were a considerable number," he admitted, "who were unable to swim, and others too timid to expose themselves to the fire of the enemy in an effort to escape."[63] These men remained subdued in the trenches or wandered aimlessly around the field behind them and were made prisoners.

Prisoners of War. Captain Wash of the 60th Tennessee described what had happened to those who surrendered. Like Bachman's company, Wash and some of his men sought to get to the bridge or the steamer in order to cross the Big Black. "But we had only gone a little way," he noted, "when we saw ourselves hemmed in, and the bluecoats swarming from the brush a half mile to our front." Colonel John Crawford had made his escape before the action began, Wash indicated, and the fate of most of Wash's men was in the hands of

[60] Houston, "A History of Vaughn's Brigade," in *A Soldier's Story of the Siege of Vicksburg*, 154.

[61] Samuel H. Lockett, "The Defense of Vicksburg," in *Battles and Leaders of the Civil War*, ed. Robert Underwood Johnson and Clarence Clough Buel (New York: Thomas Yoseloff, 1956; repr., Secaucus, NJ: Castle Publishing, 1989) 3: 515.

[62] Bachman, "Reminiscences of Childhood," 19.

[63] Report of Gen. John C. Pemberton, 25 August 1863, *Official Records*, ser. 1, vol. 24, pt. 1, p. 268.

Lieutenant Colonel Nathan Gregg. He consulted with his officers, and the consensus was the only thing they could logically do was surrender.[64]

General Stephen Burbridge described in his report what happened next: "A white handkerchief was displayed on their intrenchments," he recorded, "upon which Lieutenant Conover, my acting assistant adjutant general, and Captain Keigwin, acting aide, who were in advance of the skirmishers, rode forward and received the surrender of the forces and colors of the 60th Tennessee Regiment under command of Lieutenant Colonel Nathan Gregg, and reported them to me."[65] Gregg was probably escorted back to the place of surrender.

The 60th Tennessee's flag was not the only banner from Vaughn's Brigade to suffer the degradation of falling into the enemy's hands. "Lieut. Rawlings of Company F, 23rd Iowa," Colonel Lawler recorded, "captured the colors of [Colonel Rose's] 61st Tennessee, wresting them from the rebel color bearer." He added that another lieutenant with the 23rd Iowa snatched the colors of the 21st Arkansas of Green's Brigade.[66]

"We formed as a regiment [for the final time in the war in these numbers]," Wash wrote, and "threw down our arms and accoutrements. Colonel Gregg rode out to meet the enemy, who were rushing on with wild huzzas."[67] After the surrender, one of Albert Lee's staff rode through the line and received the sword of Colonel Gregg.[68]

Many Yankee regiments claimed the honor of capturing Crawford's regiment. "We received the surrender of the 60th Tennessee Regiment," Buehler of the 67th Indiana claimed.[69] And yet another Union regiment, based

---

[64] Wash, *Camp, Field and Prison Life*, 48.

[65] Report of Gen. Stephen Burbridge, 24 May 1863, *Official Records*, ser. 1, vol. 24, pt. 2, p. 32. One of the 60th or 61st Tennessee's flags remains a "prisoner of war" over 140 years later. Despite efforts of Tennessee state officials through the years to have the banner returned, the "battle trophy" is still in the possession of the Iowa Deparment of Archives and History in Des Moines. The colors are of a large first national pattern with thirteen seven-pointed stars arranged in a circle on the blue field. One white "bar" of these "stars and bars" was painted with the words "In God We Trust." Howard Michael Madaus and Robert D. Needham, *The Battle Flags of the Confederate Army of Tennessee* (Milwaukee WI: Milwaukee Public Museum, 1976) 46.

[66] Report of Gen. Michael Lawler, 26 May 1863, *Officials Records*, ser. 1, vol. 24, pt. 2, p. 137.

[67] Wash, *Camp, Field and Prison Life*, 48.

[68] Report of Col. Albert Lee, 22 May 1863, *Official Records*, ser. 1, vol. 24, pt. 2, p. 132.

[69] Report of Col. T. E. Buehler, 25 May 1863, *Official Records*, ser. 1, vol. 24, pt. 1, p. 596.

on the report of its commander Colonel F. W. Moore of the 83rd Ohio, sought the glory attributed to being the regiment that captured of the bulk of the hapless 60th Tennessee. Moore wrote that his men "advanced on the morning of the 17th at the best speed of which they were capable, passing through Edwards' Depot, and reaching Black River in season to charge the left of the enemy's intrenchments at the time they were being most heavily driven in on the right, and participated in the capture of the Sixteenth [60th] Tennessee Regiment, and some 100 stragglers besides, who fell into the hands of the First Brigade." He added, "with renewed satisfaction, I am able to say this success was bloodless, not costing us a man."[70] This was most likely because the battle was over by the time Moore's brave Buckeyes made their "charge." They had to content themselves in the "mopping up" and with making boasts.

Particularly aggravating to the men of Lawler's Brigade were the actions of General Stephen Burbridge's staff officers. Though Lawler's men were mostly responsible for the results of the battle north of the railroad, Burbridge's aides-de-camp rushed in on horseback to claim the spoils of the hard work done by Lawler's Brigade. Burbridge, who had commanded a brigade on the southern side of the railroad line fronting Francis Cockrell's Missouri Brigade, found itself involved in the sweep toward the Big Black Bridge collecting prisoners. When the day's reports were filed, commanders had difficulty spreading the credit among the Yankees.

The Confederate troops who did escape joined the remainder of Pemberton's army headed west toward the lines at Vicksburg. From the bluffs on the west side of the river, Baldwin's and Lee's Brigades kept the enemy from crossing until adequate time was allowed for the shaken bridge defenders to get a good head start. The fact that the bridge was destroyed bought time for the rear guard as well. Covering the twelve miles to Vicksburg on foot as best they could, Sergeant Robert Bachman of the 60th Tennessee noted that he and numerous other Big Black defenders who were able to escape finally made it during the evening of 17 May, into the chaos ruling the streets leading into the city.[71] Lieutenant Earnest of the 60th Tennessee termed the dash to Vicksburg

---

[70] Report of Col. Frederick W. Moore, 25 May 1863, *Official Records*, ser. 1, vol. 24, pt. 2, p. 37.

[71] Bachman, "Reminiscences of Childhood," 19. Mary Loughborough described the chaos in Vicksburg: "The stir of horsemen and wheels began, and wagons came rattling down the street—going rapidly one way, and then returning, seemingly, without aim or purpose; now and then a worn and dusty soldier would be seen passing with his blanket and canteen; soon, straggler after straggler came by, then groups of soldiers worn and dusty with the long march. 'What can be the matter?' we all cried, as the streets and

"a foot race," and upon arriving there, all the men were "completely broken down and strangling for water." After about a three-hour rest, he and the other survivors of the past two days were ordered to a place below town, "marching nearly all night before we could find out where [Vaughn's] Brigade was."[72] The soldiers from the broken commands hammered at Baker's Creek and the Big Black milled about the streets, certain that it was only a matter of hours before Grant's men entered the fortifications and made them all prisoners. Some of the officers were already busying themselves with putting on their best dress uniforms to look nice for their passage "north of the Ohio."

The Spoils of War. Before pressing their advantage with any seriousness, however, the Yankees at the Big Black occupied themselves with tallying their spoils. General Lawler, whose men inflicted this disaster, noted that, based on initial battlefield estimates, the haul for the Yankees was considerable and included eighteen field pieces, large quantities of ammunition, thousands of small arms, and 3,000 prisoners. Later, with more specificity, he amended the trophies of war to be 1,460 small arms, several hundred accoutrements, 1,120 prisoners, and four stands of colors, two of which came two from Vaughn's Brigade.[73]

Colonel Albert Lee noted that the Confederates at the bridgehead "abandoned eighteen pieces of light artillery with caissons, their ammunition, &c., and retreated rapidly over the Big Black River, burning the fort [blockhouses] and railroad bridge."[74] Colonel J. J. Guppey of the 23rd Wisconsin, which had also been involved in the horserace toward the bridge, stated in his report: "when the 60th Tennessee Regiment surrendered to this brigade, three hundred and sixty stand of [their] arms [were] captured, the destruction of which was assigned to [the 23rd Wisconsin], and they were

---

pavements became full of these worn and tired looking men. We set down to ask, and the reply was: 'We are whipped; and the federals are after us.'" Mary Loughborough, *My Cave Life at Vicksburg*, 42.

[72] Northen, *All Right, Let Them Come*, 94. Earnest reported that most of his company and Company G from Sullivan County made their escape.

[73] Report of Gen. Michael Lawler, 26 May 1863, *Official Records*, ser. 1, vol. 24, pt. 2, p. 137–38.

[74] Report of Col. Albert Lee, 22 May 1863, *Official Records*, ser. 1, vol. 24, pt. 2, p. 132. All the artillery was lost because Pemberton, for unknown reasons, ordered the caissons and teams removed to the western side of the river before the action began. His supposed confidence in the outcome of the action led him to sacrifice the bulk of his field pieces when a victory was not realized.

accordingly destroyed under my supervision."[75] General Lawler was the first to admit that the battle was not completely without cost to the boys in blue. "This brilliant success was not accomplished without considerable loss," he lamented, stating that his command lost fourteen men killed and 185 men wounded "in the space of three minutes, [which was] the time occupied in reaching the enemy's works." "[This result] attested [to] the severity of the fire to which my men were subjected," he concluded.[76] Some of these casualties could be attributed to Green's Arkansans and Missourians, and the volleys of John Vaughn's East Tennesseans.

Aftermath of the Big Black River Battle. Regardless of the excuses the followed the disaster, this engagement, unlike the one at Chickasaw Bluffs in December, did *not* find Vaughn's East Tennesseans "holding their position with great steadiness and nerve." In response to the well-deserved criticism Vaughn's men received for their lack of resolve during the Battle of the Big Black, several feeble attempts to explain away the conduct of the East Tennessee brigade were offered by some of the participants and their comrades in Reynolds's Brigade. For example, Colonel James Rose of the 61st Tennessee pointed out, "the assault fell with all its fierceness almost exclusively on the 61st Tennessee, which was well-nigh annihilated." Rose indicated that he brought nearly 400 men into the works the day before, and only 112 were able to make it back inside the lines at Vicksburg the evening after the battle. "Nearly 300 men were killed, wounded or captured,"[77] according to his figures, though the vast majority of these casualties were made prisoners of war during the debacle at the Big Black River.

Captain Wash of the 60th Tennessee indicated that he and his men "shed tears for a few moments [after their officers surrendered them]," but then they "summoned up their manhood" when he directed his company not to be dejected or cowed, "but [be] as valorous as ever, for we had tried to do our whole duty and were guiltless." As though to justify the course of action taken as the only rational one, Wash added, "had the engagement lasted a half hour longer, a whole division of troops and twelve rifled cannon would have come against our single regiment."[78] Already the rationalizers were forming excuses

---

[75] Report of Col. J. J. Guppey, 25 May 1863, *Official Records*, ser. 1, vol. 24, pt. 2, p. 39.

[76] Report of Gen. Michael Lawler, 26 May 1863, *Official Records*, ser. 1, vol. 24, pt. 2, p. 138.

[77] Rose, "The Sixty-First Tennessee," in Lindsley, *The Military Annals of Tennessee (Confederate)*, 2: 575.

[78] Wash, *Camp, Field and Prison Life*, 48.

regarding what happened at the Big Black River. These prisoners, for the most part, would have over a year and a half in wretched Yankee prison camps to remember the events of the morning of 17 May as they crafted their story, that is, those who were able to survived their ordeal up north.

Wash, as though to summon some of his "manhood," stated incredulously: "we were going to try them a whack," though he believed that, regardless of what they had done to resist, the defenders at the Big Black would have been overpowered quickly. In that assessment, he was most likely correct. "Our boys' nerves were all braced for the unexpected contest," Wash declared, "and the boys would have battled valiantly."[79] Thus, someone had let them down, and it was probably their officers who had lost the will to "try the Yankees a whack."

The other East Tennesseans under the command of A. W. Reynolds also had ample opportunity to come to the defense of their sister brigade. Calvin Smith of the 31st Tennessee had a personal interest in Vaughn's men and their welfare, since he had a brother and neighbors serving in the brigade. Smith and his brigade had been a few miles north of the railroad during the battle, attempting after many long hours on the march to get the trains safely into the works at Vicksburg. Once there, Smith was provided with some initial information that was not entirely accurate, and some of which was fanciful. "All fighting seem[s] to have ceased [at the bridge]," he opined, "and we get word that General Vaughn has fallen back as well. Colonel Crawford's Regt. [the 60th Tennessee] attempted to cross the river on a drift."[80]

"I see the curling smoke at the bridge," Smith stated, "and a large steam boat [the *Dot*] that is lying there."[81] The smoke was visible from where the brigade was on the road with the wagons.

The reports began to make there way to Reynolds's men, possibly by stragglers finally getting into Vicksburg, that the entire 60th Tennessee had been made prisoners of war, except for two companies. Captain Samuel R. Gammon's company, which had been recruited in Rogersville, Hawkins County, was reportedly among those captured, Calvin Smith noted with distress. His brother Sevier and close friends Thomas and Jesse Lee had been captured, along with "many others of my acquaintance were thrown in the hands of the enemy."[82]

---

[79] Ibid.

[80] Smith, *A Smith in Service*, 50.

[81] Ibid.

[82] Ibid. Capt. Johnny Bachman of the 60th Tennessee, suddenly thrust into regimental command due to the capture of all the field officers after the Big Black, submitted the following regimental return: "We had 1 Lieut. Colonel, 1 Captain, 3 1st

"They were opposed by an overwhelming force [with] no less than 13 Yankee flags [representing 13 regiments] in the charge," he reported, facing Vaughn's men and supporting artillery, loaded with "double loads of canister [discharged] at full 50 yards distance." As a result, Smith's imagination envisioned hundreds of Federals being swept down "like wheat to the scythe in the hands of a skilful mower." Such suppositions were fed by further rumors coming in from the battle at the Big Black that stressed that the Northerners suffered many more casualties than did the Southerners. The boys took some comfort in the "news" that, according to witnesses, the Yankees were "lying in piles for a mile in front as they approach the ditches before the Big Black Bridge."[83]

"Colonel Pitts' boys [the 61st Tennessee] laid them awfully before he was forced to leave," Smith had heard, "but [in turn] lost many men in the retreat." The facts of the day's events would not such bravado. Lieutenant Sam Spears of Hawkins County and the 60th Tennessee; Sergeant James O. Senter of Jefferson County and the 31st Tennessee; J. Lawson of an unspecified unit; Jake Miller of Hawkins County and the 60th Tennessee; John Owens of 61st or the 62nd Tennessee; "and one or two others that were on detail service, were saved [from capture at the Big Black]," Smith was pleased to report.[84]

Why the Debacle at the Big Black? How could that disaster at the Big Black have occurred? According to General Vaughn's chief of staff, Bob E. Houston, the works at the Big Black River bridge on the day before the battle were manned only by his brigade.[85] As Pemberton stated, the line of works was a mile long from north to south and was initially manned by Vaughn's 1,500 East Tennesseans. On the evening after the Battle of Baker's Creek, 16 May, the flanks were ultimately filled in by Green's and Cockrell's brigades, which had performed bravely in the day's struggle, leaving the center, a distance of some 500 yards, covered by Vaughn's three regiments. If Vaughn had 1,500 to 1,800

Lieuts., 7 2nd Lieuts., and 6 Brevet 2nd Lieuts. Captured at the Big Black. Enlisted men captured numbered 239, belonging to Companies A, B, C, D, E, F, H, and I." 60th Tennessee, *Compiled Service Records.* There were at least three captains of the regiment captured at the bridge: Capt. James Hodges of Company H, Capt. William A. Wash of Company I, and Capt. Samuel Gammon of Company B. Eleven men from Company C, 62nd Tennessee, were captured at the Big Black, and one man was wounded. Company D, 62nd Tennessee, had one man killed, three wounded, and four captured at the Big Black River. 62nd Tennessee, *Compiled Service Records.*

[83] Smith, *A Smith in Service*, 50.

[84] Ibid.

[85] Bob Houston, "History of Vaughn's Brigade," in Lindsley, *The Military Annals*, 1: 140.

men in the works, would negate the argument made by Houston that "in no instance was this part of the front line protected by more than one soldier to every four feet." He used this excuse to justify the "necessarily feeble" resistance offered in the battle by Vaughn's East Tennesseans.[86]

In some places, Grant's legions came in solid lines two regiments deep, and though they were superior in numbers, Houston indicated, "our forces received their attack with firmness." He was referring, one can suppose, to the efforts made by General Green's men on the left, but not to a measured and consistent resistance of most of the East Tennesseans. Houston further asserted that, unknown to Confederate officers, the receded river bottom on the left flank was capable of supporting heavy infantry numbers and "gave ready opportunity to the enemy for flanking." Of course, this tactic was not required due to the unexpected success of the attack on the center. "With one grand bound," Houston suggested, "they swept our lines creating confusion and producing panic." The result was that "of the 3,800 men [the total number of defenders on the east bank of the Big Black River] who went out a week before to the front, only 2,000 were able to return to the trenches."[87]

"During this battle, the men and officers displayed the worthy qualities of the soldier," Houston noted as though he believed it, "and only abandoned their positions when further peril would have been manifest folly." Houston closed this portion of his analysis by stressing, "the gallantry of General Vaughn was the pride of his soldiery."[88]

General Vaughn found little to highlight in either the actions of himself or his men, leaving Pemberton to note in his official report, "I have received no report from Brigadier-General Vaughn of the operations of his brigade on this occasion."[89] Such a report would have been rather painful and embarrassing to write, and Vaughn, certainly a man of independent mind, apparently never tried to put his brigades' activities in an official record. So, without an explanation, Pemberton was left to arrive at his own conclusions.

"The troops occupying the center did not do their duty," Pemberton was left to conclude. He noted that though the Yankees had to attack across an almost impassable bayou, Vaughn's men "shamefully abandoned their positions almost without resistance."[90] Indeed, many fled before the enemy was still two

---

[86] Ibid.

[87] Ibid.

[88] Ibid.

[89] Report of Gen. John C. Pemberton, 25 August 1863, *Official Records*, ser. 1, vol. 24, pt. 1, p. 267.

[90] Ibid.

hundred yards to their front, if enemy reports are to be believed, struggling toward the East Tennessean's position through the muck and mire of the bayou bottoms in the open fields to their front. Even worse are the reports that Colonel Gregg had determined to surrender before the attack was even really underway. Pemberton's chief engineer, Samuel Lockett, that architect of the fortifications at the Big Black Bridge, indicated, "about 9 o'clock [a.m.], our troops on the left [center] broke from their breastworks and ran pell-mell toward the bridge."[91]

"After the stampede at the bridge," Lockett, who often exaggerated his reports, suggested that "4,000 troops deserted in a solid body to the enemy."[92] That number of "deserters," of course, would have probably exceeded the total number of men Pemberton had in the Big Black works. Probably the most accurate conclusion that could be drawn about the behavior of the East Tennesseans on that May morning was expressed by one historian who postulated that they "simply lacked the will to fight this day."[93] As for the impression made on the Federals, Colonel James Keigwin of the 49th Indiana, whose men helped precipitate the route, noted that the defense at the Big Black was "the poorest fight I ever saw the rebels make."[94]

Any small confidence the commanding general had in Vaughn and his men based on the Chickasaw Bluffs battle back in December was now frittered away. The murmuring about the mettle and loyalty of the East Tennessee Confederates would now undoubtedly resurface. It was no accident Vaughn's Brigade would be placed on the extreme left flank of the Vicksburg defenses, where the height and works of Fort Hill would make its assigned position impregnable. The other commands, such as Cumming's and Barton's Georgians, that "sinned" at Baker's Creek, according to the historian Ed Bearss,[95] would also rank equally low in Pemberton's estimation and would find themselves assigned to the extreme right flank on either side of Reynolds's Brigade. Frequently serving together during the siege in mixed commands on

---

[91] Report of Samuel Lockett, 23 July 1863, *Official Records*, ser. 1, vol. 24, pt. 2, p. 73.

[92] Ibid.

[93] Todd Groce, *Mountain Rebels: East Tennessee Confederates and the Civil War, 1861–1870.* (Knoxville TN: University of Tennessee Press, 1999) 101. Most of the men captured on this morning were held as prisoners and were not exchanged until two months before Lee's surrender at Appomattox.

[94] Report of Col. James Keigwin, 18 May 1863, *Official Records*, ser. 1, vol. 24, pt. 2, p. 23.

[95] Edwin Bearss, *The Campaign for Vicksburg*, 3 vols. (Dayton OH: Morningside Press, 1986) 3: 737.

tactical sorties outside the ditches, elements of these three brigades in
Stevenson's Division would prove themselves over and over.

In the final analysis, there was considerable blame to go around for what
happened at the Big Black on 17 May. Pemberton has to be singled out for
allowing his despondent troops to have been involved in a meaningless
engagement one day after his army had been so badly whipped by Grant. He
was also responsible for the placement of the defensive works on the east side of
the bridge, trapping three brigades of his soldiers with their backs to a swollen
river with only one narrow bridge as a viable escape route. Given those factors,
however, the lion's share of the blame falls on the excuseless retreat precipitated
by the East Tennesseans, who apparently felt they had as much entitlement to
be demoralized and to run as anyone else in Pemberton's army. After all, they
had seen hundreds do it with little apology the afternoon and night just after
the whipping at Baker's Creek.

Colonel Rose evaluated Pemberton's suspect tactics by stating that
Pemberton "decided to meet Gen. Grant in the open field, and the battles of
Grand Gulf, Raymond, Baker's Creek (or Edwards' Depot), and the Big Black
River followed in rapid succession, resulting in a series of defeats for the
Confederates."[96]

Undoubtedly, Grant's forces relished the thought of chasing Pemberton's
army back into the works at Vicksburg. Their confidence in the capture of
Vicksburg must now be concluded in short order, based on the haphazard
resistance offered by Pemberton's men on 16–17 May. While he had no desire
to criticize Pemberton or the disposition of his forces, Rose nevertheless
asserted that preceding the surrounding of Vicksburg, mistakes were made in
the piece-meal and confused handling of the army, which played right into
Grant's hands. "This was the misfortune which the 61st Tennessee suffered in
common with the rest of our ill-fated army. The regiment, out in the field, was
not engaged in any of the battles … but that of the Big Black some ten miles
east of Vicksburg on the Jackson Road, and resulted most disastrously to the
[command]."[97] Tellingly, Pemberton admitted in his official report of the
operations: "it had become painfully apparent to me that the *morale* [italics
added] of my army was not such as to justify an attempt to hold the line of the
Big Black River. Not only was it greatly weakened by the absence of General

---

[96] Rose, "The Sixty-First Tennessee," in Lindsley, *The Military Annals of Tennessee
(Confederate)*, 2: 575.
[97] Ibid.

Loring's Division, but also by the large number of stragglers, who, having abandoned their commands, were already making their way into Vicksburg."[98]

But perhaps it was Colonel James G. Rose of the 61st Tennessee who had the best explanation by any participant given for what had happened that day at the Big Black River. He suggested few could appreciate a moment of such extreme solitude, who have never witnessed such a hostile display by such numbers bent on overwhelming a position in which its defenders had so little faith.[99] And to be fair, it must be assumed that even had the East Tennessee troops at the bridgehead done their whole duty, pouring out buck and ball until their Enfields became too hot to load, and doing their part at turning back three attacks "with great slaughter," Grant would have continued to pour wave after wave of his Midwestern cannon fodder in on them until the end result, like the final result of the siege itself, would have still been the same. Muster reports for April and May for selected companies engaged at the Big Black River indicated the following representative losses in Vaughn's regiments:

> Company H, 60th Tennessee, lost 55 percent of its present strength as prisoners of war at the Battle of the Big Black River (twenty-nine men out of fifty-three engaged, including its captain, James C. Hodges).[100]
> Company I, 60th Tennessee, lost 60 percent of its present strength as prisoners of war at the Battle of the Big Black River (fifty-one men out of eighty-five engaged, including its captain, William A. Wash).[101]
> Company G, 61st Tennessee, lost 64 percent of its present strength as prisoners of war at the Battle of the Big Black River (forty-four men out of sixty-four engaged).[102]
> Company I, 62nd Tennessee, lost only 6 percent of its present strength as prisoners of war at the Battle of the Big Black River (five men out of seventy-seven engaged).[103]

---

[98] Report of Gen. John C. Pemberton, 25 August 1863, *Official Records*, ser. 1, vol. 24, pt. 1, p. 268.

[99] Rose, "The Sixty-First Tennessee," in Lindsley, *The Military Annals of Tennessee (Confederate)*, 2: 575.

[100] 60th Tennessee, *Compiled Service Records*.

[101] Ibid.

[102] 61st Tennessee, *Compiled Service Records*.

[103] 62nd Tennessee, *Compiled Service Records*.

The 62nd Tennessee, of Vaughn's entire brigade, escaped the fiasco with the greatest number of men. In the works, it was the left-most regiment, with the 60th Tennessee on the far right and the 61st Tennessee in the center. Once the line was breached, the majority of Colonel Rowan's regiment escaped, perhaps due to the concentration of the Yankees on the center of the works. It seems that Rowan's regiment, perhaps the better disciplined one in the brigade, kept its head under direction of their capable commander and slipped to the rear with the men of Green's Brigade on their left flank. The 62nd Tennessee, incidentally, was the only command in Vaughn's Brigade to escape with their regimental colors.

What of the East Tennessee soldiers who did not make it to safety? W. A. Wash of the 60th Tennessee related some of their experiences as prisoners of war. He noted, "now comes a new era in our existence as soldiers." The boys were no longer armed and willing to rush into the fray against the hated enemy, under the direction of officers they respected and followed without question, he wrote. Though they still possessed their physical qualities and loyal hearts, they were powerless to make any difference in the campaign. As prisoners of war, Wash declared, "we are subject to the will and mandates of those into whose hands we have fallen."[104]

The prisoners were in the hands of the exalting Yankees as the "battle" made its way to the rear toward the Big Black Bridge. Within minutes, Wash stated the Confederate prisoners were formed into two lines and marched along the line of their poorly defended, and now deserted entrenchments toward a shady woodland a half mile off. As they were herded away, Wash indicated, the prisoners looked back over their shoulders toward the Big Black Bridge. They had been called on to defend it at all costs, and it was now in flames, "and a sharp cannonade was going on between our men over the river and the Yankees who were trying to cross."[105] It was Lee's Alabamians and Baldwin's Mississippians and Louisianans using the heights there to their advantage to

---

[104] Wash, *Camp, Field and Prison Life*, 51.

[105] Ibid. Wash at different times called the bridge "frail and inadequate," but then as it burned, "a splendid structure." The supports and pilings of the old bridge are still standing or lying about the base of the newer bridge. It is said that at low water, the "ribcage" of the steamer *Dot*, over which Bachman made his escape, can still be seen. Mark Morgan, "Preservation Report," *Journal of the American Civil War* 2/1 (1st Quarter 1992): 73. Although the river at low levels looks about like a good-sized creek, local fishermen told the author that when the spring showers are falling, the river can rise up some fifteen to twenty feet along the bluffs. They maintain at any time of year, the strong currents keep their lines continually fouled.

stall the foe and to provide a covering fire for the final few Confederate defenders who were attempting to swim across the river and those who were scrambling up the bluff to get out of the line of fire. It was at this position where Vaughn's and Bowen's men should have been deployed in the first place.

S. A. R. Swan of Stephen D. Lee's Brigade, providing his impression of the sorry day's work, wrote in his daily journal that Bowen's Division of "perhaps 3000 men" were charged with defending the rear of the army as it made its way over the Big Black Bridge on retreat toward Vicksburg, "but the trenches were stormed and carried, and all the cannon lost and about half the command captured."[106]

"Thus disaster follows disaster," Swan lamented, as the defeated army of John Pemberton made its way back to the trenches around Vicksburg, "wearied and depressed." Few people, whether they were soldiers, civilians, or Yankees, believed that these defeated men could hold back the relentless foe "flushed with victory," until General Johnston can do "something."[107]

Lee and Baldwin's men, after fighting a brief rearguard at the Big Black River, withdrew to the works with the rest of Pemberton's shaken forces, and all were ultimately assigned their respective defensive positions within the lines at Vicksburg, with "what encouragement could be given, urging them to hold out to the last," according to Swan. "That evening," he reported, "our lines were inverted on the left from the river around to some distance below the railroad, and the attack commenced by the enemy with their incessant musketry and artillery fire."[108]

Reynolds's Brigade and its massive wagon train had since also arrived at Vicksburg safely after their grueling march. "I reached Vicksburg at 5 p.m. on the 17th," Colonel A. W. Reynolds wrote in his report, "and encamped in rear of the intrenchments near the Jackson road. The trains which were placed under my charge arrived in safety, with the exception of one ordnance wagon which broke down crossing the Big Black swamp."[109]

In his report on the Vicksburg campaign, Pemberton heaped considerable praise on the work done by Colonel Alexander Reynolds in saving the entire train of the army. "Under the judicious management of Reynolds commanding a Tennessee Brigade of Stevenson's Division, [the train] was crossed without

---

[106] Swan, "A Tennessean in the Siege of Vicksburg," 357.

[107] Ibid.

[108] Ibid.

[109] Report of Col. Alexander W. Reynolds, 27 July 1863, *Official Records*, ser. 1, vol. 24, pt. 1, p. 109.

loss, though the movements of the enemy compelled the brigade to cross the Big Black above the railroad bridge."[110] The contribution of Colonel Gillespie on the march was not stated. Little wonder, however, due to his coolness in times of crisis, he and his 43rd Tennessee were to be one of the two often-utilized reserve units for Stevenson's entire division in the forty-seven days ahead. In essence, they were the shock troops called to stand in the gap whenever there was a threat the lines would be breached. They were called on numerous time to do this, and never did they fail

Abandoned forever were the old camps for Reynolds's and Vaughn's men, which had been their homes for the past five or six months on the Mint Springs and Big Bayous. Captain William A. Wash of the 60th Tennessee, now a prisoner of war, later addressed the loss he suffered: "My journal account books, clothing, many highly prized letters and tokens from friends, all are perhaps now moldering in the ruins and waste about Vicksburg. That was the third time I had lost all my clothing, and the second my journal, precious at least to me, by the vicissitudes of war."[111]

With simple eloquence, Sergeant William H. Long of Morristown and the 59th Tennessee, noted, "on the 17th of May, we fell back into the trench around Vicksburg."[112] At Vicksburg, Swan of Lee's Brigade and Cleveland, Tennessee, recorded in his diary, "our men lie very close in the trenches and reserve their fire."[113] This statement would become for the besieged of Vicksburg an accurate summation of their new routine for the next forty-seven days.

---

[110] Report of Gen. John C. Pemberton, 25 August 1863, *Official Records*, ser. 1, vol. 24, pt. 1, p. 266.
[111] Wash, *Camp, Field and Prison Life*, 18.
[112] Long, "Autobiography," 1:54.
[113] Swan, "A Tennessean in the Siege of Vicksburg," 357.

CHAPTER 9

"The Hardships and Privations of the Men Were Beyond Description" 18-31 May ("The Investment")

Affairs within the Beaten Army. On 18 May, amid confusion and panic created by the failed adventures of Pemberton's confrontations with Grant, the exhausted and universally despondent Confederate army continued pouring into the works around Vicksburg, the long cloud of dust from their feet drifting above the trees along the Jackson Road toward the Big Black. One observer noted that he "saw our army in retreat, and in utter confusion; a long line of stragglers. There would be a squad of infantry, a horseman, a gun, a few more infantry, and so on; with no more order than travelers on a highway, seeking Vicksburg as shelter. This stream of stragglers continued nearly all day."[1]

These demoralized men were sent to various regrouping areas to rest, and subsequently issued assignments in the entrenchments around Vicksburg. Most now believed that, once pontoon bridges were completed to bring his army across the Big Black, Grant would soon come to complete his task. Vaughn's East Tennesseans were positioned on the extreme left flank of the works along the high ridge that included Fort Hill. Reynolds's men were placed on the far right of the works one brigade up from the trenches occupied by Seth Barton's Georgians. "During the forty and four days of the Vicksburg siege," B. E. Houston of Vaughn's staff recorded, "this brigade covered and protected the upper river batteries under Fort Hill and opposite the Edwards house to 'Razor Hill.' During these memorable days, the batteries of Gen. Vaughn were frequently disabled, but his lines were never broken. Now and then the ranks were thinned by the enemy's shot and shell, but in every instance their perilous places were at once voluntarily supplied."[2]

---

[1] Bachman, "Reminiscences of Childhood," 22–23.

[2] Houston, "History of Vaughn's Brigade," in Lindsley, *The Military Annals*, 1: 140. According to the distances between the National Park markers at Vicksburg, the front

Colonel Eakin of the 59th Tennessee noted in a letter to the Vicksburg Park Service many years after the war:

I reached Vicksburg the evening after the Battle of Baker's Creek. We were ordered to occupy from one point to another, of what was called trench. The line of defense had doubtless been fixed by engineers with the apprehension of a siege at some future period. A trench not more than perhaps a foot deep had been thrown up, when it was not filled up by the washing of the sandy soil. I was ordered to occupy this trench with all my regiment continuously. We did not have any tents (they were left behind when we went to Baker's Creek). We soon had a trench deep enough for the men to stand, or walk erect without exposure to musketry and sleep diagonally across with a parapet in front to fire from, protected by a head log in front. The five companies of the 3rd Tennessee, Colonel Lillard's regiment, Reynolds' Brigade, occupied a trench on the right of Capt. Claiborne's battery and a little in advance on the line on their right and left. The ground they occupied was some higher than that upon either side and the sharp-shooters got nearer to them sooner when they advanced upon parts of the line. I had cross trenches in my rear and no filth accumulated in the trench; vermin accumulated in the absence of soap and water.[3]

After some busy hours of positioning themselves in the trenches and squaring away his men, Smith, whose 31st Tennessee was just to the left of Eakin's, stated that he had already conversed with General Vaughn and with several others who were there for the "awful course of the 2 days fighting." Smith was led to believe that there "were many prisoners taken on both sides but no doubt the enemy lost the most killed & wounded."[4] This assumption was one for which he would find "correction" during his later investigations.

---

manned by Vaughn's three regiments (not including the Mississippi State troops assigned to him) was approximately 600 yards long.

[3] Eakin to Rigby, 12 March 1904. In this letter Eakin noted that during the siege he was allowed to send only two men from each of his companies each day to do laundry for the balance, and that Reynolds "would not permit me to leave my trench except on some duty." One year later at the Battle of Piedmont, VA, Eakin was captured and spent the rest of the war at Johnson's Island, Ohio. He indicated that his two brothers were in the federal service during the war, and that afterwards, he practiced law in Chattanooga with a partner who had been a Union officer.

[4] Smith, *A Smith in Service*, 50.

Some of Vaughn's soldiers captured at the Big Black the day before were, on the morning of 18 May, a living testimony to conditions on the other side of the lines. As a new prisoner of war, Captain Wash of the 60th Tennessee recorded as the contest at the Big Black River was "waging hot," [though it was pretty much over by then], "the shade to which we were escorted [by their Yankee captors] was quite pleasant."[5] Stragglers had been gathered up in all directions, and soon "our captive band amounted to 1,000, the whole number captured." Wash's numbers are conservative and incomplete. A guard line was established around the prisoners allowing the captives several acres in which to roam.[6]

"The Yankee boys soon mixed all among us," Wash remarked, "and are very anxious to know why we rebels were fighting so ardently against 'the best government the world ever saw.'" General debates erupted, and all sides were heard. As usually seemed the case, Wash had adapted quite nicely to his change in circumstance and was soon making the best of it. His remorse at being made a captive did not trouble him for long. After the prisoners were secured, various Yankee officers came into the compound, and once they had located their kindred number in the gray ranks, they "talked with our 'big officers' about things in general."[7]

Dealing with the Big Black Prisoners. In addition to their jubilation over the bumbling at Baker's Creek and the Big Black River fiasco, the captors were thrilled because word had been received that "Richmond had fallen," prompting the boys in blue to declare that "they were going to take Vicksburg the every next day like a flash." Noting his opinion that neither catastrophe had nor would occur on the enemy's prescribed timetable, Wash continued to illustrate the scene around him. He called the intermingling of gray jackets and bluecoats "a fit subject for the graphite pencil of an artist." As the day passed, Wash stated that the rear of the Union army (wagon trains, cavalry escorts, general plunderers, and pillagers, as well as the swelling number of contrabands) was "constantly arriving."[8]

---

[5] Wash, *Camp, Field and Prison Life*, 52.

[6] Ibid. The surrender of most of the 60th Tennessee would not be the first during the campaign. The day before at the Baker's Creek battle, the 46th Alabama of S. D. Lee's Brigade, while pressing ahead a supposed advantage, found itself surrounded in a ravine ahead of the line of battle and was surrendered by its colonel, Michael L. Woods. The Alabamians were left unsupported by the panicky skedaddle of Barton's and Cumming's Georgia Brigades.

[7] Ibid.

[8] Ibid.

"They [the yanks] had the best equipped wagon train I ever saw," he noted, "with nearly all covered wagons drawn by six-horse teams of splendid stock, and all in seemingly excellent condition." He admitted that the sight of the Union army's prowess was awe-inspiring, and it amazed him and his fellow prisoners of war to see the three heavy siege guns go through, drawn with slow deliberateness by teams of twelve oxen each. "These guns were fifteen feet long," Wash wrote, "and otherwise in proportion."[9] The prisoners wondered how the Northerners had dragged such ponderous behemoths all the way upland from Port Gibson on the sorry roads gashed far too often with deep erosions.

The woodlands where the boys were biding their time was one that was "thick with Yankees, Confeds, stock, wagons, and colored folk." The "loyal troops," as Wash sarcastically called his enemy, were busy wolfing down hearty snacks. Wash was disappointed, however, since he and the other prisoners who had not eaten anything in a day and a half received nothing from their guards. A large house nearby within the· guard line had been abandoned when the battle engulfed it was now being "sacked by the northern soldiery" of everything of value, including its splendid furnishings and choice library, "right under the eyes of several generals who had made their headquarters there."[10]

Throughout the scorching afternoon, Wash reported the Yankees were busily engaged in tearing down several barns to make pontoon bridges over the Big Black River. Just before nightfall, "the bulk of their army passed over and on to take Vicksburg 'the next day.'" As darkness descended, the boys were invited by their hosts to sleep where they were standing, and with the coming day, they were promised to at last draw rations.[11]

Assuming Defensive Positions within the Vicksburg Trenches. Robert Bachman, part of the 60th Tennessee not made prisoner at the Big Black, noted on this first day of siege, "the enemy captured our regimental camp [on the Mint Springs Bayou] which was beyond our line of trenches." Consequently, "we lost everything: knapsacks, extra blankets, books and photographs." He lamented the boys did not have a stitch of clothes other than what they wore on their backs. His recalled that during the siege, the quartermasters did not issue any change in clothing because he supposed they did not have them. "I did not have

---

[9] Ibid.
[10] Ibid., 53.
[11] Ibid., 54.

a bath in that time," he confessed, meticulous about his personal hygiene, "nor water enough to thoroughly wash my hands and face."[12]

"Our trenches were semi-circular," Bachman explained, "running from the river north of the city down to Warrenton, some ten miles down the river." Within the fortifications were nearly thirty thousand men and batteries affixed at strategic points in the line. "Soon after entering the city," Bachman pointed out, "Grant ordered a charge to be made on the center of our line, hoping to break it and capture the city at once. This effort wholly failed."[13]

Convinced later that such tactics were futile, Grant entrenched his vast army around Pemberton's and settled down for a regular siege. "The 61st Tennessee constituted a part of the garrison at Vicksburg till its capitulation to Gen. Grant, July 4, 1863," wrote Colonel James G. Rose, who had also succeeded in getting away from the Big Black. The regiment's position in garrison was above the city, on the bluffs overlooking the Mississippi River, and its daily duties early in the siege consisted of picketing, always observing the activities of William T. Sherman's men on the ridge opposite. Rose indicated that as Grant collected his large army, "the 61st Tennessee literally slept on its arms within a hundred yards of the works assigned it to defend." He stated that each company was opposite its position in line, and that each soldier in his regiment knew his exact spot in the works. Upon signal, whether day or night, the works held by the 61st Tennessee were instantly manned.[14]

"On the morning of May 18," Colonel A. W. Reynolds, commanding the East Tennesseans in the lower works, wrote in his official report, "my brigade was assigned its positions on the line of intrenchments, on the left of General Barton, whose brigade occupied the extreme right, my left resting on the Halls' Ferry Road, and on the right of General Cumming's."[15] The troops assigned to the "ditches," as Reynolds and most of his men called them, were the 31st Tennessee, the 59th Tennessee, and five companies of the 3rd Tennessee. The reserves behind the lines were the 43rd Tennessee and the other five companies of the 3rd Tennessee. His artillery redoubts were occupied by "five light pieces under Captain F. O. Claiborne [commanding the 3rd Maryland Battery] in the

---

[12] Bachman, "Reminiscences of Childhood," 23.

[13] Ibid., 20.

[14] Rose, "The Sixty-First Tennessee," in Lindsley, *The Military Annals of Tennessee (Confederate)*, 2: 575.

[15] Report of Gen. Alexander W. Reynolds, 27 July 1863, *Official Records*, ser. 1, vol. 24, pt. 2, p. 355.

center and right center of the line."[16] Claiborne's battery was unique because it was the only Confederate unit in the Vicksburg siege from that state and the only field battery involved in the previous days' battles not losing its guns.

Reynolds reported that upon taking up his positions, the "works were so weak and easily enfiladed that it was necessary to fill up some of the trenches and dig others." Then, he noted, new redoubts for his field guns were also constructed. On the night of the eighteenth, Reynolds threw out a line of pickets about a half mile in front of the works. They often exchanged fire with enemy's pickets across the way positioned in front of their defenses being thrown up with all due haste.[17] "Each officer and soldier was assigned his place in the rifle-pits," Reynolds recalled, "and my reserves in proper position. The precaution of throwing out pickets at some distance in front had the effect of keeping the sharp-shooters of the enemy at a distance, and prevented my line being annoyed." He stated that Cumming's Georgians on his left did not do so and suffered because of it, right "from the beginning."[18]

Keeping the Feds at a distance, Reynolds observed, was only one element of his precautions, but it gave his men a chance to strengthen his works unmolested. "Notwithstanding my line for the time being little harassed by the enemy in my front," the commander of the 4th Brigade indicated, "it was greatly annoyed by the shells from the gunboats and mortars established on the peninsula and the river, which opened [up] daily on our rear."[19] Calvin Smith of the 31st Tennessee wrote, "we arrived at Vicksburg and took over our position in the ditches." Word had come to the lines that one of his friends and fellow officers, Lieutenant Robert Long of Smith's Company D, "was dying the morning of the 18th, but [we] can't go see him due to the enemy, in line of battle beyond." He reiterated, as though providing some comfort, that Private Hugh Harper was with him.[20]

---

[16] Ibid. R. S. Bevier indicated that units designated as "reserves" during the siege were those "that [were] the steadiest and most reliable troops in the army ... and to them was entrusted the safety of every weak point in the defenses. Whenever the danger was most imminent, the charge of the enemy the most determined, or the fighting waxed the warmest, there the reserves were rushed at the double-quick, to fill the breach and restore the alignment." Bevier, *History of the First and Second Missouri Brigades*, 200. Often called upon in times of desperate need by Gen. Stevenson, the 43rd Tennessee, during the long (and for it, bloody) siege, never faltered in its duty.
[17] Ibid.
[18] Ibid., 355–56.
[19] Ibid., 356.
[20] Smith, *A Smith in Service*, 50.

The enemy, Smith noted, had "destroyed Warrenton, landed on the big levee and marched into our old camps out of town, before heading to Vicksburg, Miss." Except for some of their tents and other camp equipment evacuated on 16 and 17 May, Reynolds's Brigade had left all they had in there at the Big Bayou. The Yankees were now free to pilfer through their stuff as they wished. Smith noted that Lieutenant Long had "died at Capt. Barnes' 5 miles south east from Vicksburg, and will be interred at Antiock Church 4 miles east of Warrenton on Monday, 18th." None of his friends would be able to attend the funeral. "This is the second Lieut. our Co. has lost to disease," Smith wrote, the first being "2nd Lieut. Isham Reynolds and [now] 3rd Lieut. Robert Long. We mourn the loss[es] [as] they were valuable officers both gallant and brave and always ready to do their duty."[21]

Isaac Stamper of the 43rd Tennessee noted in his diary that the day for Reynolds's Brigade "was devoted to the arranging of our troops in the trenches." His regiment, being held in reserve in trenches overlooking the river, "did not get in our position until nearly dark." He noted that the 31st Tennessee, the 59th Tennessee and a portion of the 3rd Tennessee were placed in the ditches, and he indicated the rest of the 3rd Tennessee and 43rd Tennessee were held as reserves, some few hundred yards on the bluff of the river to their rear.[22] William H. Long of Morristown and the 59th Tennessee, remarked "on the 18th of May, I was sent to the hospital with intermittent fever."[23] There he remained for many days before rejoining his command in the trenches, coming to the conclusion the hospital was doing him more harm than good.

S. A. R. Swan of S. D. Lee's Brigade noted, "the line of investment was drawn around the town, and firing commenced immediately to the left." The Confederates at Snyder's Bluff to the north had been quickly drawn inside of the works around Vicksburg, "sending the boats and destroying everything else." He contended that the day was a "gloomy one for our troops."[24]

"The boldness of the enemy in carrying the slight earthworks at the Big Black Bridge had discouraged our men greatly," he admitted, "and the feeling was general that they would overrun our entrenchments at the first outset." Everyone Swan encountered displayed "gloomy forebodings" in their countenances. He noted most of the officers were seen putting on their best

---

[21] Ibid.
[22] Stamper, "Travels of the 43rd Tennessee," 57.
[23] Long, "Autobiography," 1: 54.
[24] Swan, "A Tennessean in the Siege of Vicksburg," 357.

uniforms, and all seemed to be readying themselves for the dreaded voyage up to Camp Chase. The quartermasters and commissaries had parked their wagons in preparation for the torch, and the mules were set loose inside the works where they roamed about, "trying to pick up a scanty supper."[25]

The Big Black Prisoners Wonder about Supper. Wash explained that he and his fellow prisoners were brought into columns on the morning of 18 May, where they counted "by twos" several times. After a final counting, the officer prisoners of war were invited to give up their pistols and swords. Many, however, had thrown theirs away while the Yankees were not looking rather than let their captors have them. At 2 p.m., the officer in charge promised the prisoners that after they were marched back to Edwards' Depot, they would receive food. "Our escort[s] were the 3rd Iowa and the 54th Indiana," Wash wrote. After pulling along "in the ankle-deep dust" of the road for a time, the prisoners of war, upon their arrival at the depot, found the men of General Alvin P. Hovey's Division loitering about the place, the Yankee soldiers occupying farm houses "made desolate" by their presence. Most of the citizens had fled.[26] Incredibly, many of these unfortunate people had fled into Vicksburg to the "protection" of Pemberton's army rather than face the uncertainty they had encountered among the invaders. They would share the trying days ahead with Pemberton's men.

From the depot, the Big Black prisoners were marched a half mile more to an old field that was blessed with a water source nearby, where they were instructed by their captors to pitch their camp again. "It is now sundown," Wash indicated, "and from long fasting our appetites were whittled down to a keen point." The commander of the guard was once more ready with promises and indicated that the poor Southern soldiers should have rations before they slept. It had now been two days since most of the boys had had a bite to eat, Wash declared, and only now and then did one of their captors feel compelled to share a morsel of his rations with the prisoners. Finally, at 10 p.m., subsistence came in the form of sugar and meal, but there was neither salt for

---

[25] Ibid.

[26] Wash, *Camp, Field and Prison Life*, 54. Wash added the following anecdote: "My revolver had been taken by an insolent puppy of a staff officer. Without orders, and with a haughty air, he ordered me to give it to him. I told him I had been thus ordered several times, but had refused; and did not intend on giving it up unless ordered by a competent authority. A Major General was standing nearby. I approached him and asked if I must deliver it. He said, 'yes,' and I did so. The pompous, contemptible manner of being with shoulder straps on who demanded it deeply aroused my indignation, and I had a burning desire to tell the chap what I thought of him."

flavoring, nor any utensils for cooking. So, once again the Big Black River captives wrapped themselves up in "the arms of Morpheus," as the captain from the 60th Tennessee phrased it, "and dreamed of good things to eat—just out of our reach."[27]

After being awakened early on Tuesday morning, 19 May, Wash, his comrades of the 60th Tennessee, and others detained against their will at the Big Black were marched on "the back track" toward the Big Black again. At dusk, they crossed over the river on the pontoon bridge thrown together by the Federal pioneers in the general areas where all their troubles had begun. They were settled in a cornfield on the river bluff for the night, during which Colonel Elijah Gates and his adjutant, Frank Clewell of the 1st Missouri Cavalry (dismounted), absented themselves from the rest and found their way back to their command within the ditches surrounding Vicksburg.[28]

Toward those ditches manned by the supposedly demoralized Confederates, Grant hurriedly brought up his three infantry corps under McClernand, McPherson, and Sherman. What they saw as they were marching up the Jackson Road toward these fortifications for the first time was described by one of Grant's staff officers: "A long line of high, rugged, irregular bluffs, clearly cut against the sky, crowned with cannon which peered ominously from embrasures to the right and left as far as the eye could see. Lines of heavy rifle-pits, surmounted with head longs, ran along the bluffs, connecting fort with fort and filled with veteran infantry."[29]

The 19 May Assault. Undaunted, the determined Grant decided to press his fleeting advantage and order an immediate attack on 19 May. He believed that the shaken morale of Pemberton's army would bring about a speedy conclusion to this affair. Unfortunately for him, as Pemberton's chief engineer, Lockett, pointed out, not all the men in Pemberton's command had been involved in or demoralized by the battle, and these men were still itching for a fight.[30]

William Sherman, Grant's most trusted lieutenant, launched a major assault on 19 May against the left center of Pemberton's works at the Stockade Redan. The brigades of Louis Hebert and Francis Shoup manned these defenses, and Bowen's battle-tested brigades under Cockrell and Green were brought up as primary support. The Yankee brigades of Hugh Ewing, T. K.

---

[27] Ibid., 54–55.

[28] Ibid., 55–56.

[29] Alan Hankinson, *Vicksburg: 1863: Grant Clears the Mississippi* (Oxford: Osprey Publishing Ltd., 1993) 62.

[30] Lockett, "The Defense of Vicksburg," 3: 488.

Smith, G. A. Smith, and John Thayer spearheaded the main thrust of the attack. Initially, the abatis and other obstacles hindered their approach toward the elevated casemate, and upon nearing its base they were cut down by the concentrated fire of the Confederate defenders. Sherman's attack was to have been replicated and supported by assaults launched to his left and right by elements of McPherson's and McClernand's corps, but coordination was disjointed and their efforts were timid and ineffective. The usually sure-footed Grant, free-wheeling and able to marshal his concentrated forces wherever he had wished, was guilty of hasty preparation and coordination. He also underestimated the resolve of his enemy, now secure in their impenetrable works. Grant's failure on 19 May provided encouragement to Confederate defenders from one end of the line to the other, canceling the good work the Yankees had previously done to destroy their will to fight. Grant suffered nearly 1,000 dead and wounded in the debacle, while the defenders' losses were only around 200. Suddenly the nagging questions returned on the Federal side concerning the invincibility of Fortress Vicksburg. Obviously, the news of the attacks on the Stockade Redan occupied the writings on 19 May of the East Tennessee chroniclers.

"Cannonade commenced yesterday evening above the railroad," Smith of the 31st Tennessee wrote in his journal, with one battery being engaged. Suddenly four or five batteries joined the chorus, he noted, and the "fight assumes a threatening aspect." He heard the small arms fire of musketry, "as if the Yankies are making charges," but since the Confederates were at their posts in the ditches protected by earthworks and head logs, with slots or notches in the timber to fire through or to fire over, he felt that his old comrades were "well situated" to defend themselves and their positions. Smith indicated that for a "third time our troops surrounded and took the whole lot of them." Back in Reynolds's works, Smith recorded some of the things on his mind that day. "Companies A, F, D, and I, numbering 135 muskets, and the other 6 companies are [at the ready] in the other ditches," he wrote. Concerning his own men, Smith wondered in particular about Private W. H. Chestnut, who had not been heard from since they had left Edwards' Depot in flames, where "I saw the fire and heard the reports of shells as the fire reached them."[31]

By 9 p.m., the cannonade was now heavy all around Fortress Vicksburg, and Smith acknowledged that Confederates "are completely hemmed in," with the Yankee navy back up river firing from all their available boats. Down at

[31] Smith, *A Smith in Service*, 51.

their Big Bayou camps now occupied by the enemy, the Federal infantry was rattling away with musketry.[32]

George Hynds, in another company of the 31st Tennessee, wrote on 19 May, "the attack is renewed on our left and center, and continued all day." The enemy had made several desperate charges upon the Confederate lines, but was repulsed with heavy losses. Hynds reported Confederate casualties to be thirty to forty and Yankee casualties to be 1,000 killed and wounded.[33] The boys felt that there was some leveling of the score on this date, balancing the casualties at Baker's Creek and the Big Black, with the Union dead piled literally knee deep against the steep Confederate embankments of the upper works. Stamper of the 43rd Tennessee noted with simplicity in his journal, "the enemy attacked us in our fortifications on the left; we repulsed them."[34]

"General Grant invested Vicksburg on the 18th of May," Captain Reuben Clark of the 59th Tennessee observed in a matter-of-fact manner as well, "and stormed our fortifications on the 19th. This effort to carry our position by storm was disastrous to the Federals." He recounted the attacks as "battle lines, one after the other, emerging from the woods, coming across the old field in our front three lines deep, when all but the front line gave way under our deadly fire." The attack was unsupported, Clark indicated, "and moved right up under the galling fire of shot and shell from our fortifications," adding, "much to their credit." The Yankees made it as far as the front of the works, where, finding no support, "they had no alternative but to surrender."[35]

Their numerous men killed in the charge were left in front of the works until long after decomposition had set in, leaving the air most foul and offensive.[36] Suspicions were that Grant purposely left his dead to decay in the heat at the foot of the Confederate embankments as another of his ploys to wear down the resolve of the suddenly obstinate Southern defenders.

"The firing opened by day break," Swan of S. D. Lee's Brigade recorded, "with small arms and as the day advanced, battery after battery of the enemy would belch forth their hissing balls and shells as they would get into position." The Confederate defenders fired but little, conserving their precious reserves. They were only to shoot when the shot was sure, and, Swan reported, it was around 2 p.m. when the firing on the left of the line became "terrific." The

---

[32] Ibid.
[33] Hynds, "Original Handwritten Notes," 1.
[34] Stamper, "Travels of the 43rd Tennessee," 57–58.
[35] Clark, *Valleys of the Shadow*, 23.
[36] Ibid.

continuous roar of heavy guns and small arms "showed that an assault of a most desperate character was being made on our lines." In three quarters of an hour, Swan noted, the firing slackened and a heavy cheer rose from the Confederate works. This roar of voices was carried soon up and down the line from the left of Lee's Brigade. "We had repulsed a furious assault with immense slaughter," Swan indicated, this time with no exaggeration. He pointed out that the Yankees, in agreement with Smith's account, charged right up to the trenches, and those who found a brief respite from the hail of musket balls, canister, and grape met with the bayonet and were compelled to "either surrender or be killed." Though the assault was general, it was most fierce on the left center of the line. Unfortunately for Yankees, Swan stressed, "our huge guns commanded a good part of that ground, and the firing [and its effect] were terrific."[37]

Meanwhile, the Confederates back in control of the burned-out Jackson (now referred to as "The City of Chimneys") welcomed the arrival of General States Rights Gist and his division of 5,500 men. Johnston's little army was now about 13,000, and would increase the next day when the 5,000 man division of W. W. Loring (lost on the retreat from Baker's Creek but thereby saved from the siege) joined "Uncle Jo" in the ashes of the newly reclaimed Mississippi capital.[38]

The Big Black Prisoners March toward the River and Their Trip North. Among the Big Black prisoners, William Wash of the 60th Tennessee noted that the morning of 20 May found the boys finally eating a meal of beef and meal. Wandering nonchalantly through the guard line, he went on a little foraging expedition, and the enterprising captain from Kentucky managed to "borrow" some coffee and bacon from the Yankee camps. He also happened upon a little coffee pot that he later carried off to the officer's prison at Johnson's Island, Ohio. Unfortunately, he had little time to spare for preparing his newfound rations since orders came to have the Big Black River prisoners move out.[39]

"By eight o'clock, we were traveling toward Vicksburg," Wash reported, and while en route, the boys passed many beautiful mansions, "and everywhere the ladies came out to give us a look of profound sympathy." Perhaps mirroring the expressions of the vanquished as they marched by, the ladies appeared to have had their "hopes and fortitude … almost sunk; [they] shed tears." But, Wash maintained, other women, "with stronger and braver hearts," waved their handkerchiefs, expressed their blessings on the boys, and called out for them to

---

[37] Swan, "A Tennessean at the Siege of Vicksburg," 357–58.

[38] Smith, *Compelled to Appear in Print*, 199.

[39] Wash, *Camp, Field and Prison Life*, 56.

return soon to continue the battle for Southern rights. "We gave them cheers," Wash remembered, and "told them all would yet be well," though some of the prisoners whose feelings were more tender "could not restrain the teardrops that flowed in sympathy for those noble women of the South." Around dinner time, the column stopped for water and rest directly at the rear of Vicksburg, only "a few hundred yards behind the enemy's line of investment."[40]

Wash noted a brisk cannonade in the lines was then going great guns, rounds and shells being traded from both sides. Within sight of where the boys rested in the road, Wash saw the proud residence of Dr. Cook, where he had wiled away many hours in days past. The good doctor, Wash discovered, had decided to take his family into the lines at Vicksburg, and was now in his city residence among the besieged. Cook's fine country house, where the vanquished now lingered to catch their breath and escape for a moment the exhausting heat, was serving as a hospital. The yard, fields, and orchard were crowded with parked ambulances and other supply wagons. "After an hour's rest, we march on," Wash proclaimed, "going close by our old camp ground, and moving in the direction of Snyder's Bluff." Their stroll carried them three miles further before the column was turned sharply to the left and descended the sharp and rugged hills that overlooked the memorable spot where many of Vaughn's Brigade first "saw the elephant": the battle ground of Chickasaw Bayou. This bloody ground where four hundred had been captured and at least a thousand killed and wounded, only covered around four acres.[41]

Many of the prisoners, Wash stated, began boasting of their contributions to the Yankee disaster in those final days of 1862. Indeed, some of the prisoner escort, the 54th Indiana, also had reason to remember the field across which they now trod, having left 200 casualties from their regiment there. "It was there that we commenced meeting wagons laden with army stores for the troops besieging Vicksburg," Wash reported. "They came over a corduroy road from Lake's Landing on the Yazoo, where still other boats were then landing even more Yankee soldiers." Snyder's Bluff, which had "withstood many a pelt from the yankee ironclads," was now vacated, and several Federal gunboats were going pell-mell up the river toward Yazoo City in hopes of snagging the two Confederate ironclads known to be under construction there. Before Porter's men of war could get to them, however, these vessels suffered the fate

---

[40] Ibid., 56–57.
[41] Ibid.

of so many Confederate warships in the war: they had been torched to prevent capture.[42]

On his current line of march, Wash reported, "we were passed by a train of over a hundred wagons," as well as a brigade of infantry headed toward Vicksburg. With some cat-calling back and forth, he noted that the boys yelled at the Yanks that though Vicksburg may be where they were headed, "admittance will come dear." Around dark, the column of now non-combatants with their blue-clad guards reached the Yazoo River wharves, after having marched over twenty miles since 8 a.m., "most of the time through a stifling dust cloud" raised by the feet of their own comrades up ahead.[43]

"We found a dozen transports and a host of soldiers, citizens and boatmen" at the wharves, Wash reported, "all full of joy, for they thought one half of Pemberton's army was defenseless before them." Within the hour, "we got splendid rations, but again, no way of cooking them," which was just as well because the boys were then so weary that all they could think about was lying down and going to sleep. All night long, they tossed and turned to the gentle melody of the mortar boats, which flung, with deep-throated "whumps," their huge iron balls toward the beleaguered and defiant city of Vicksburg, Mississippi.[44]

While at the prisoners' compound, one East Tennessee Rebel took the advantage of all the mingling and pressing of humanity about the large group of prisoners to make his escape. "Pikey John" Allen of Cocke County and the 62nd Tennessee declared that he had been imprisoned on the second floor a building at the Yazoo and Mississippi Rivers confluence. While looking out the window,

---

[42] Ibid., 58–59; H. T. Reid to U. S. Grant, 12 May 1863, *Official Records*, ser. 1, vol. 24, pt. 3, p. 303–304. There were actually three vessels being constructed as or converted into ironclad rams at the yard in Yazoo City (in addition to a number of other vessels in the assembly area): the *Mobile*, "a small boat, … being converted into an ironclad gunboat," was complete except for her armor; the *Republic*, "a large boat," was a side-wheel ram, which had railroad iron attached as armor; and a third unnamed vessel was to be a large ironclad ram, but "the water has been around her, so they have not been able to work on her for the last three months." Moreover, Reid reported that the ground under her had "caved in," causing her to "careen over to one side." She was a large vessel, some 310 feet long with the "frames of the hull not all up," but the Confederate builders "have a great deal of timber ready to go into her as soon as the water falls," Reid noted. However, all were burned to prevent capture with the abandonment of Yazoo City. See also Fletcher Pratt, *Civil War on Western Waters* (New York NY: Henry Holt, 1956) 133, 230.

[43] Pratt, *Civil War on Western Waters*, 230.

[44] Ibid.

he felt homesick and hungry, and decided to escape. The building was close enough to the Yazoo River, so he jumped from the window into the river. From there, he swam to the opposite shore where it was not so crowded. The fall injured him, and though wracked with pain and weariness, Allen pulled himself up on the bank, where he rested in some cover as quietly as he could. When his strength returned, he set off as fast as he could go, not toward the works at Vicksburg but toward his home in East Tennessee.[45]

According to his family's oral tradition, "Uncle Pikey traveled by night and slept by day, living on raw potatoes, and some corn thrown in when he could find it." Along his long route home, Allen found "shattered homes" that often proved good places to scavenger for food. He stated that, daring to move only in the dark of night, he took over two months to "scout" his way home to Cosby Creek, deep in the Smoky Mountains. Pikey John's family welcomed him home after such a long a time away, all superfluous flesh wasted away, his clothes ragged and filthy.[46]

The heavy firing continued until dark on 20 May, according to Smith. The musketry and battery fire began at daylight and continued all day. One shot, he reported, shattered the pole above the parapet on which the 31st Tennessee's flag flew defiantly over their position, bringing it down. The boys scrambled to repair the staff, and their ensign was soon run back up again.[47] How often this ritual was repeated by all the commands in the ditches during the siege can be easily imagined.

"Our siege guns, I think, will keep the yankees out of Vicksburg," Smith predicted. After days of disappointment and a seeming inability to defeat the foe, there suddenly returned a confidence evident earlier in the Confederate arms at Vicksburg. Smith reflected such confidence with these words: "Our men fought like veterans—yielding not an inch of ground though heavily charged and repedly."[48]

Rumors were running rampant at Vicksburg, and Smith repeated them: General Nathan Bedford Forrest had arrived in the Vicksburg area by the Yazoo route. Another tale indicated that General Joseph Johnston was "fighting the enemy in the rear." As the siege crawled along in the weary days ahead, daily rumors had Johnston intervening to end the siege. Another yarn spun on this on 20 May was that John Vaughn's Brigade, on the opposite end of the line,

[45] Walker, "Close Calls and Narrow Escapes," *Tales of the Civil War*, 61–62.
[46] Ibid.
[47] Ibid.
[48] Ibid.

had been influential in the repulsing of Sherman's attack on the nineteenth, holding "the enemy back, slaying thousands."[49] Great was the distance between the two flanks in physical as well as factual terms.

"Our men would cheer and holler in derision," Smith recorded, regarding the Yankees' disastrous attacks of the previous day. He was proud that these assaults, no matter where they were made on the line, had all been repulsed. Thus, for the time being, the enemy had initiated their routine of cannon fire from daylight until dark, with sharpshooting commencing at first light. Their gunboats moved up from the lower river and fired their guns, which were seen as white puffs gently floating sideways, then melting. Then, they floated back out of range of the still dangerous river batteries. Smith declared Reynolds's Brigade was in the center of the right wing of the army, "and we have not yet fired a gun, but will not remain idle long from present indications."[50] George Hynds of the 31st Tennessee wrote, the "battle still continues, but our men seldom fire." There were no charges made by the Yankees today on 20 May, he indicated, though the gunboats and mortar boats shelled Vicksburg all day and all night.[51]

"At daylight the fire commenced," Stamper of the 43rd Tennessee noted in his diary, "and at eight it ceases." At 4 p.m., the regiment, in its capacity as reserve, was suddenly called up to support the left wing of the division (Stephen D. Lee's Brigade) where the Federals were believed to be preparing for a charge. "We marched under the fire of the enemy to our post with the bullets singing all around us," Stamper reported. In the volleys, Private Jessie Addison of Company A took a ball in the leg, and Lieutenant Hopkins was stuck "slightly" in the breast. Another casualty was Lieutenant Colonel David M. Key, who was reportedly stung in the thigh by a spent ball that did not penetrate the flesh.[52] The seriousness of the wound was more significant, and while recuperating in a Vicksburg hospital, Key contracted a much more debilitating condition, malarial fever, or "the ague" as the physicians of the day called it.[53]

---

[49] Ibid.

[50] Ibid.

[51] Hynds, "Original Handwritten Notes," 1.

[52] Stamper, *Travels of the 43rd Tennessee*, 58.

[53] Ibid. The date given for Col. Key's injury was 22 May. For a dramatic rendering of the action, see Abshire's *The South Rejects a Prophet*, 47–48. Although Stamper indicated that the ball did not penetrate the flesh, Key's wound was apparently more severe. Capt. J. N. Aiken of Chattanooga and the 43rd Tennessee wrote: "Our able land efficient lieutenant colonel D. M. Key, was also wounded [on 20 May], and before he recovered

In Stephen D. Lee's Brigade on the left of Stevenson's Divisional trenches, S.A.R. Swan observed that the firing was getting hotter, and that the minie balls were now reaching every exposed spot in the Confederate works. "A good many struggling mules and horses were killed and a number of men wounded in passing to and fro in the trenches," he wrote. Confederate losses, however, were relatively small because the boys made every attempt during the hail of musketry to "keep under cover as much as possible."[54]

"During the afternoon of the 21st," Captain Wash of the 60th Tennessee recalled, the prisoners from the Big Black "managed to get our appetites satisfied and our bodies well saturated, for a beating rain poured on us for an hour." In addition to the shower, he noted that the boys were allowed to take a "refreshing bath in a bayou nearby." All day long the heavy cannonade aimed at Vicksburg continued, both from the gunboats and mortars, interspaced by the Union infantry with their small arms fire. Such firepower led even the captive Southerners to conclude that, with the fury of so much of Grant's seemingly infinite force, "Vicksburg must succumb in a few days." Late in the evening, some of the transports were called to take the prisoners over to Young's Point on the Louisiana side of the river opposite the mouth of the Yazoo. Apparently they had to pass the hat to pay for their own fare because since the boys in the 60th Tennessee contracted with the steamer *Chancellor* for their passage. As the faint colorless light that follows the glow of sunset settled in, the vessels bearing the East Tennesseans moved off the Yazoo and into the broad Mississippi, where at 8 p.m., it "rounded to at Young's Point, and remained there overnight."[55]

"We could plainly see the mortar boats shelling Vicksburg" in full view of their position, Wash noted. He stated that they could only distinguish the light of the fuse bombs "which would go up and up for several thousand feet, then down, down, down into the devoted City, but not more than half of them exploded." These mortars, which one Confederate described as looking like a potash kettle, could throw shells a distance of two and a half miles. Wash

from his wound was stricken down with malarial fever, from the serious and debilitating effects of which he did not recover until long after the war was over. This was an irreparable loss. He had drilled and disciplined the regiment, and made it one of the best commands in the whole Southern army. Had his health permitted him to remain in the active service, he would unquestionably have greatly distinguished himself." J. N. Aiken, "The Forty-Third Tennessee," in Lindsley, *The Military Annals*, 1: 524.

[54] Swan, "A Tennessean in the Siege of Vicksburg," 358.

[55] Wash, *Camp, Field and Prison Life*, 59–60.

recalled that it "was a beautiful sight to behold those seeming streaks of light traverse the midnight darkness in pleasing curves."[56]

George Hynds of the 31st Tennessee, defending those works in "the devoted City" that Wash watched from the other side of the river, wrote that the "sharp-shooters commenced firing at daylight and kept it up all day." The boats continued their shelling. A battery played on Reynolds's line, as well as a line of sharpshooters "farther to the right."[57] Most of the fire Reynolds's men received from this quarter was particularly troublesome because it was delivered enfilade into their right flank. The curve in the line from Barton's to Reynolds's position allowed the boys in blue down toward Warrenton to fire straight across and through the East Tennesseans' trenches.

"Vicksburg is surrounded by hostile foes," Lieutenant Smith of the 31st Tennessee recorded. "We are now in a state closely beset on all sides by cannon which are playing from all quarters by day and night." The Yankees had charged the fortifications time after time, he noted, "leaving on the ground their dead and wounded, while our men suffer but little." He postulated that "we will be able to hold out as long as the enemy is willing to keep us here." Though the Yankees had shelled the town the day and night of 20 May, little damage was done. "I don't hear of many killed on our side," he reported. Three gunboats approached Vicksburg from down river in the evening and shelled the fortifications, doing little damage. "Our batteries don't open fire often," according to Smith, at the end of his daily entry.[58]

"At daylight [on 21 May] the fire opened again," Isaac Stamper of the 43rd Tennessee recorded, "and one minie ball struck P. H. Slagle, cutting his clothes and bruising his skin." Otherwise, he was unhurt, though shaken. Hot firing was kept up all day, and the regiment in its reserve status was able to "take shelter behind a hill."[59] They were not alone in seeking refuge on opposite sides of the many hills that were prolific in the Vicksburg landscape. "The non-combatants hunt for safer places," Swan of S. D. Lee's Brigade wrote, "when intervening lulls afforded some defense against the flying balls." On this date he recorded that the fierce bombardment continued on their works "from all sides." The Yankee gunboats came up the river and made an attack on the water batteries, "throwing shot all over the lower parts of our lines."[60]

---

[56] Ibid., 60.
[57] Hynds, "Original Handwritten Notes," 2.
[58] Smith, *A Smith in Service*, 51.
[59] Stamper, "Travels of the 43rd Tennessee," 58.
[60] Swan, "A Tennessean in the Siege of Vicksburg," 358.

The 22 May Assault. At daylight on 22 May, a ferocious artillery barrage was unleashed on the works at Vicksburg from the enemy on land and on the river. At 10 a.m., Grant ordered another assault on the fortifications, this time from all his corps in concert. Sherman again attacked the Stockade Redan area of the line and was thrown back. McPherson's corps advanced again in columns down the Jackson Road against the so-called "Great Redoubt," where, after heavy fighting, it too was repulsed by the Confederate defenders. McClernand's corps proved the more successful at the terrible work, attacking the area between the 2nd Texas Lunette, the Railroad Redoubt, and the Square Fort. Mike Lawler's heroes of the Big Black forced a temporary abandonment of the Railroad Redoubt, but with counterattacks from the Lee's men and the reserves, including the 43rd Tennessee, previous conditions were restored. At a crucial juncture in the attack, Lawler's corps commander, John McClernand, made a plea for reinforcements, but there were none to be had. Yankee casualties for the day numbered an astonishing 3,200 men, with Pemberton's defenders suffering fewer than 500. The Northern newspapers began to embellish Grant's growing reputation as a butcher of his own men.

Descriptions of the 22 May attack were again encouraging. Though the action was "furious and obstinate," Swan indicated from the riverside, the ironclads proved no match for the accuracy and effectiveness of the Confederate land batteries, which usually caused the men of war to be "hauled off much damaged." While the opposing gunners on land and on the river banged away at one another, the Yankee infantry had again tested the lines ringing Vicksburg. Referring to the day's fierce attacks, Swan indicated that the Yankees had waged a particularly vigorous assault on the center where the Southern railroad entered Vicksburg.[61]

"An Iowa regiment [as part of McClernand's vanguard] charged up and succeeded in planting their standards on one of our redoubts," Swan reported. Despite this momentary success, the Hawkeyes were soon overwhelmed by a Confederate counter-attack which drove them into the ditch dug in front of the embankment. There, they were compelled to lay in the trench at the base of the works, afraid to run for it or surrender. Lee's men lit fuses on artillery shells and threw or rolled them down the slope to where the enemy soldiers crouched, killing many and causing fourteen men and a lieutenant colonel "to ask for terms." Swan recorded that the slaughter was "terrific," and the Yankee casualties "scattered over the ground in front of our lines[;] their dead and wounded for days a sickening sight indeed." Some Alabamians were killed as

---

[61] Ibid.

well. Swan focused special attention on Colonel Edmund W. Pettus of the 20th Alabama, who "behaved gallantly leading a charge made by a portion of Waul's Texas Legion [as reserves] against the redoubt in possession of the enemy." Pettus tore down a Union regimental flag, trampled it under foot, and then led the charge that drove the enemy back.[62] The 43rd Tennessee was also brought up to shore up the defenses. "The Yanks charged our breastworks several times, and were repulsed with great slaughter," James Henry Darr of the 43rd Tennessee reported, losing three of their regimental flags taken by Stevenson's men. As for his own regimental losses, Darr noted, "Captain Sterling Turner was killed (shot through the head) as well as 'the tall man' [Private Heard] in Captain McKamy's company."[63] Enemy losses were considered heavy and the Confederate loss, "very small."

A frustrated Grant decided after the fruitless hot work on 22 May to settle into a proper siege, convinced as he was that the Confederates in those formidable works before him "could not last always." The War Department in Richmond also continued to reinforce Joseph Johnston's command in Jackson. On this date General Nathan G. "Shanks" Evans arrived with his brigade of 2,000 men, and was assigned to General Loring's Division.[64]

The mortar boats from the river threw shells at night, which "burst in every direction over the beleaguered City, adding to the hideous concert going on around us." With instant death a distinct possibility, Swan reported that the nervous defenders could only catch a little sleep during this night. Provisions were prepared behind the lines and carried to the boys in the ditches after dark, according to Swan, "and the dead animals hauled off [and dumped in the river]" where the "water [is drawn] and brought to the boys in barrels."[65]

Writing also on 22 May, Private James Darr, of Charleston, Bradley County, and the 43rd Tennessee, noted in his journal the men were already watching anxiously for relief from either Joseph Johnston or General Franklin Gardner, commander of the garrison at Port Hudson, Louisiana. Both of these generals, however, had troubles of their own. Darr indicated that it was the fourth day of the "fight" (siege), and that none in his Company I had been wounded yet. However, later he reported that Private Richard Bradshaw was wounded in both thighs the day before, though no bones were broken. The

---

[62] Ibid.

[63] James Henry Darr, "Diary" (unpublished manuscript), Ron Evans Private Collection, 1. A copy of this document is available in Vicksburg National Military Park Archives, Vicksburg MS.

[64] Smith, *Compelled to Appear in Print*, 200.

[65] Swan, "A Tennessean in the Siege of Vicksburg," 358.

morning brought nothing new, only the continual "popping away" of the sharpshooters. Then around 10 a.m., Darr indicated that the Yankees had brought up five gunboats that rapidly shelled Vicksburg. Their bombardment continued into the morning, he noted, "the shells bursting and flying in all directions." Later that evening, Darr indicated that the firing on the lines had ceased, after "there had been most awful fighting since 2 o'clock."[66]

"From our camps around Vicksburg, we had seen the Federal fleet anchored at Young's Point since Christmas Day, 1862," Wash of the 60th Tennessee wrote from the camps he now shared with his fellow prisoners of war, "but had never dreamed of being there in this capacity; though the boys often joked each other about going to 'Camp Chase' and other northern prisons." The area where the captives were detained around Young's Point was "a low, flat and often swampy country behind a levee," both filthy and splotchy with algae and scum, and dotted with stumps awash in standing pools of stinking stagnant black water where the nameless vermin dwelled. Wash noted that the Confederates had often heard that they were not the only ones who suffered horrendous fatalities as a result of disease and the unhealthy environment.[67] Indeed, it had always been believed there had to be great mortality within the invader's ranks.

"All along the levee were thick groups of graves," Wash noted, "with some poor, deluded fellow, who thought he was fighting for the preservation of the government in its purity, instead of for the subjugation of the rights and institutions of the Southern people." On 22 May, Wash stated that the Big Black River Bridge captives, officers and privates, were separated in preparation for their big voyage up the Mississippi to prison camps where most would spend the remainder of the war. "North of the Ohio River," as the Federal authorities wrote in their records, these men would be the guests of the world's greatest government, at Fort Delaware, Johnson's Island, and, finally, Point Lookout, where they would be sent before being exchanged.[68]

The officers were quarantined a quarter mile away from their men, and Wash indicated that it was only with the greatest of difficulty that they received permission to return to check on their sick. The prisoners found that they had to walk a half mile to the river to get water and firewood with which to cook, and even then, the guards would allow only three men to go at once, "always under the escort of a chap wearing a blue coat and sporting a musket and a 'six

---

[66] Darr, "Diary," 1–2.

[67] Wash, *Camp, Field and Prison Life*, 60.

[68] Ibid., 61.

shooter.'" Wash reported that the total number of prisoners collected on this side of the river from various quarters had grown to 3,500, of which 170 or so were fellow officers. The air was heavy and undulating, and quickly bathed in sweat those moving about. "The sun was almost unbearably hot," Wash concluded in his daily entry, "and we made shades with brush, and with our blankets stretched on poles."[69]

Meanwhile, back within the works of the Confederate defenders, George Hynds of the 31st Tennessee recorded that the 22 May assaults had led to "one hundred and twenty prisoners [being] taken." With contempt, he added: "all of whom were drunk." Alcohol was perhaps the only way the prisoners' officers could compel them to make such a desperate charge. The battle continued to rage, Hynds reported, and the boys "still, for the most part, hold their fire." He remarked on the continual shelling from the boats all night, but little damage had been done to their targets.[70]

The day's action commenced about 9 a.m. when the Yankees opened fire from several of their gunboats, which was instantaneously joined by the batteries from their works. "[Their fire] was promptly replied to by our guns," Hynds noted. "Under this fire, the enemy made three desperate charges upon our left, and after gaining the entrenchments, was repulsed in handsome style." During this futile assault the 120 inebriated warriors were captured by their Confederate foes. This assault was another example, it seemed, of Grant's ends-justifying-means through which perfectly sane men lost their reason to alcohol and undertook this suicidal charge. Down on Reynolds's end of the line, the boys in blue had further extended their lines to the right, leaving the Fourth Brigade's picket posts untenable. Consequently the brigade was called back into the safety of the works. "Our batteries threw shells into the timber to our front," Hynds stated, "to drive the sharp-shooters out." Around 11 o'clock, the gun and mortar boats ceased their shelling, abandoning their mission at least for the day. Apparently so had Grant in his disastrous efforts to storm Vicksburg with major all-out assaults. He probably concluded that the people in the city were no longer "demoralized," and that any further Yankee attacks would be much more modest.[71]

Calvin Smith of Hawkins County and the 31st Tennessee noted in his daily entry that the Yankees had posted three or four "mortar rafts" off Vicksburg, and that three gunboats came up the evening before. They

---

[69] Ibid.

[70] Hynds, "Original Handwritten Notes," 2–3.

[71] Ibid., 3.

commenced shelling Vicksburg and Reynolds's lines in the morning, "wounding but two men."[72]

"A Yankee battery east of the City is playing upon our trenches," Smith wrote, "and our nearest battery is firing at [it]." He believed that it would have to move or be taken by assault "or otherwise." The enemy shells flying east from Porter's gun and mortar boats and west from Grant's batteries were "passing each other with terrible explosions." The cannonade was unceasing, and the sharpshooters plied their trade as soon as it was light enough in the morning to see, lasting until that moment at the edge of darkness when human objects could be discerned no longer from other shadows. "I could see the mortars throwing shells last night and could see the course of the shells, marked out by the fire tail bomb ejecting a star-like tail and whistling noise passing high in the heavens, seemingly among the starry orbs of the heavenly firmament," Smith noted. Smith reported that the distance the boys were from the river made the sound of the mortars' actual firing unheard, but when the huge rounds struck, "explosions [were] much nearer and terrible, scattering missiles and fragments everywhere to the certain destruction of any living animation."[73]

In a skirmish after dark between the pickets outside the lines, Smith stated that the 59th Tennessee, whose turn it was at that dangerous post, lost a couple of men killed, though "several of the enemy" had also been killed. The 43rd Tennessee supported the line and was assaulted by three Yankee regiments, he added, "repulsing them with great slauter." Though the Union batteries shelled the works and inflicted some damage, the Confederate pioneers continued to keep up repairs during the night and always had them viable again the next morning. All the while, Smith concluded, "the enemy is suffering greatly." He noted that their gunboats had thrown shells "fast and thick" within Reynolds's lines, but the boys were all secure in their ditches. "Fragments would fall close to us," he recorded, "[and] the boys jump out and pick them up as they were glad to see them."[74] These fragment would be souvenirs for the folks back home, if ever the mail could run through again, or if these Confederates could ever make it back home. There would be days ahead when they could pick up all the scrap metal they wished without leaving their position in line, though with the enemy sharpshooters daily improving their aim, none dared raise their heads above the parapet.

---

[72] Smith, *A Smith in Service*, 51.
[73] Ibid.
[74] Ibid.

Describing the 43rd Tennessee's role in repulsing the 22 May Yankee attacks, Spradling of that regiment wrote, "we reinforced the 20th and 23rd Alabama Regts. in the heavy charge." It proved to be a tragic day for Company F; its Captain, Sterling Turner, was killed in the action, as well as Private John Shamblin and several other unnamed men in Gillespie's regiment. The Federals, Spradling reported, were thrown back with severe losses.[75] Fleshing out Spradling's report some, Isaac Stamper indicated that Captain Turner was shot through the head, "when the enemy reached our trenche," where they were repulsed, leaving forty prisoners and one regimental flag behind. Samper recorded that the regiment had been ordered at noon to reinforce Stephen D. Lee's Alabamians, necessitating the 43rd Tennessee "to march under some of the hottest fire for a half mile."[76]

"Ed Cox was wounded in the leg, and William McCarrel slightly in the face," Stamper wrote, Harrison Eaton in Company D was wounded in the hand, and Private Simon Heard in the same company was killed in the ditches, like Turner, shot in the head. A great many Northerners were killed, in addition to the prisoners taken during the repeated and concentrated attacks, which availed them nothing.[77] After the desperation of fighting the day before, 23 May "was a dull monotonous day," according to Wash of the 60th Tennessee, "except when relieved by the artillery duels going on around the City." At 2 p.m., he noticed that the gunboats in the river seemed bent on silencing the stubborn river batteries once and for all, though word had come to the prisoners that one ironclad was sent to the bottom. Rumor or not, Wash indicated, "men came from that direction dripping wet and the firing had died away."[78]

Hynds of the 31st Tennessee in the ditches below Vicksburg down river from where Wash watched at Young's Point noted that everything the night before was mostly still. Not a gun was heard, Hynds reported, until about 3 a.m. when the river batteries let loose their heavy cannon on the gunboats. As darkness gave way to dawn, the fight again commenced on the left, and continued all day at long range. The enemy made no charge, though the gunboats and mortar boats were still firing away, some of their shells bursting near the 31st Tennessee's entrenchments. Hynds recorded the death of Captain Turner ("the old hero," as Stamper had called him) in the 43rd Tennessee the day before, as well as a private soldier unnamed serving with the 59th

---

[75] Spradling, "Diary," 2
[76] Stamper, "Travels of the 43rd Tennessee," 58.
[77] Ibid.
[78] Wash, *Camp, Field and Prison Life*, 61.

Tennessee.[79] Turner was 52 years old. Smith of the 31st Tennessee indicated that two men with the 59th Tennessee who were killed in this action, along with "several of the enemy." The Persia native reported that the 43rd Tennessee, in front of the trenches, was charged by three regiments of Yankees and turned them away with "great slaughter." During the cannonade of the day before, Smith wrote that the embankments of their trenches were damaged, but repaired by the tireless pioneers during the dark of night. He repeated his feeling the enemy had to be suffering greatly.[80]

"Three gunboats threw shells fast and thick yesterday evening," Smith reported, though the men felt safe and secure in their ditches. He noted all was quiet during the night until around midnight when the "morter" boats commenced their frightful work on Vicksburg, undoubtedly doing much damage, he supposed, but they "couldn't or haven't burnt the City yet." "Our position is strong," Smith asserted, "and will be hard to take."[81]

Three men with the 43rd Tennessee recorded brief observations regarding the day's activities: W. R. Clack noted the Yankees made a charge on their breastworks the day before, but were driven back with "great slaughter." The annoying sharpshooting and cannonading continued all day.[82] Spradling wrote that Nathan Colbaugh of his company was killed by a sharpshooter, and that Francis "Nute" Million, I. H. Fisher, and R. G. McAdon of the regiment were killed on this date by a single shell burst from the Union batteries.[83] Jacob E. Sliger of McMinn County and the 43rd Tennessee reported that he was wounded then, and "wasn't able to do much [else] since I was at the fort … and a bomb shell came through near Nute Milam [Million] and myself killed him and wounded me I was knocked down and parcel covered with dirt was taken out and sent to hospitle."[84]

Finally, Stamper recorded that at 1 a.m. on 22 May, the 43rd Tennessee hustled to the support of General Cumming's Georgians at their place in line to Reynolds's left, and the boys took their position to Cumming's rear "under a

---

[79] Hynds, "Original Handwritten Notes," 3. Pvt. John A. Richie of Company E, 59th Tennessee of Madisonville, Monroe County, was killed on 22 May and was buried at Soldier's Rest, Cedar Hill Cemetery, Vicksburg.

[80] Smith, *A Smith in Service*, 52.

[81] Ibid.

[82] William Raleigh Clack, "Personal Diary," 1. Million's tombstone in Cedar Hill Cemetery states only that he was killed in 1863, but records indicate the date of his death was 23 May.

[83] Spradling, "Diary," 1.

[84] *Civil War Veteran Questionnaires*, eds. Dyer and Moore, 5: 1973.

high hill which protected us from the fire of the enemy."[85] Private Darr, also of the 43rd Tennessee, wearied of the fighting that continued along their lines the whole morning and had killed and wounded so many of his comrades. He observed that the Yankees continued to shell Vicksburg "at a heavy rate" from the river. Though there was the usual sharpshooter activity, he noted that the skirmishing seemed to have played itself out. Detailed as a clerk for the regiment, it was his duty on this date to order the making of coffins for both Captain Turner and the "tall" man (Heard) referenced the day before, as well as draw up clothing requisitions for some of the men.[86]

Preparations were made, according to S. A. R. Swan serving with Lee's Brigade, to assemble all of Pemberton's wagons (the very ones defended to the extreme by Reynolds's Brigade after the Baker's Creek fight) in one large area used for commissary stores, medical and ambulance services, and other duties, in the event they had to be destroyed. The corn used for feed held by the quartermaster department was turned over to the commissary to be used for bread. Forage for the animals was stopped, and, Swan reported, "the poor mules are turned loose to pick what little grass they could." Rations to the boys were reduced somewhat. "Thus," Swan recorded, "the siege of Vicksburg commenced, which is destined to exert an immense influence on the result of the war, however it may end." The defenders had now been in the trenches for six days and nights and had endured "almost unremitting fire of shot, shell, and a pitiless storm of minie balls from a strong line of sharp-shooters."[87]

From the river, the mortar boats flung huge projectiles over Vicksburg, and in no part of the Southern lines, according to Swan, was there to be found a place "where some missile does not penetrate." Every "hiddy hole," as the East Tennessee portion of the defense called them, was occupied during the shelling by somebody, either a citizen, a servant, or a soldier. And the topography of the area was "very favorable in this respect," Swan reported, "being formed into numerous ravines and little hills that afford much protection." Despite these rather favorable conditions for humans, however, the mules went about grazing as best they could, though they were "constantly shot." The boys called it "going up" when referring to the killing of their animals. The men passed about as their duties required and "ran great risks from shells and minie balls constantly dropping over our lines."[88]

---

[85] Stamper, "Travels of the 43rd Tennessee," 58.
[86] Darr, "Diary," 2.
[87] Swan, "A Tennessean at the Siege of Vicksburg," 358.
[88] Ibid.

As for the citizens of Vicksburg, Swan pointed out that they were generally safe from most alarm, retreating to bunkers or caves in times of danger. He marveled at the shells crisscrossing one another coming from the river to the west and from the land batteries to the east until it was too dark to take aim. Commissary details were assigned to cook and carry rations to the men in the trenches, as well as the unpleasant task of loading on wagons the dead mules and driving them down to the river, "where they were discarded." Thus, with each passing day in this first week of siege, Swan indicated that the boys were "getting a little more used to the situation."[89]

With the opening of another Sabbath day on 24 May, Wash of the 60th Tennessee, among the Big Black prisoners on Young's Point, Louisiana, stated, "everybody but us put on [their best] clothes, and sauntered about to see what they could find." Some of the Yankee officers who had yet to view a real live Rebel up close came to the prisoner yard, loitering on the fringes, according to Wash, while they studied the "general physiognomy of the boys and old men that were fighting against 'the best government the sun ever shown on.'" The Confederate captives talked freely with these heroes in blue, and though agreement and concessions on some points were made, no one on either side seemed to be convinced or converted.[90]

Around noon, Wash observed a "stately column" approaching their position from the interior of Louisiana, "and we perceived it to be composed of nearly three hundred contrabands, with their cubs and bundle of rags, hunting freedom." He noted that all about them were already hundreds of black folks, "squatted about in squalid hovels and tents, with no means of subsistence, save the scraps they could pick up around the soldiers' camps."[91]

"Twill be a dear bought freedom to them," Wash predicted, "for the Northerners don't really love them, and won't take them into brotherhood." He believed that the enemy sought "only to destroy the institution [of slavery]" without any concern of what would become of these "unfortunate wretches."[92] In the midst of these fleeing black people in numbers few of them had ever seen before, many of the East Tennessee captives probably agreed with Wash's assessment of matters.

In the works across the way, other East Tennessee Confederates still under arms watched the routine that had become so familiar to them. The mortars on

---

[89] Ibid.
[90] Wash, *Camp, Field and Prison Life*, 62.
[91] Ibid.
[92] Ibid., 62–63.

the river shelled their lines during the night "at regular intervals," and at daylight, the Yankees provided their usual wake up call of musketry and battery work into the Confederate positions. George Hynds of the 31st Tennessee indicated that his side replied only with artillery when "heavy volleys of musketry are heard on the extreme left [in the vicinity of Vaughn's lines]." Across the way from Reynolds' lines, Hynds noted the Federals had been busy placing a battery, though it had not opened fire during day. "On the 22nd when the enemy charged the works defended by Lee's Brigade," he reported in his journal, "they drove our men back and had possession of the battery for a while, but [our] reinforcements were soon brought up and drove the yankees out."[93]

Calvin Smith, also with William "Reshy" Bradford's regiment, wrote that the cannon commenced their awful work early, and that the enemy was busy at night all along the lines, digging closer "ditches," from which they "would sharp shoot our men from light to dark as regular as clock work." As a man of obvious learning, Smith noted that he had spent this Sunday reading his New Testament and Tacitus, just as he would be doing were he back home in Hawkins County on a Sunday. It got him to thinking of "those enjoyments that I once had at home with my wife & children."[94]

"What a contrast and a change," Smith wrote, "here in the ditches some 800 miles from those I love better than my own self, here surrounded by hostile foes throwing shells and shot exploding all around me … after having to dodge the balls as they pass me but alas this is the fortunes of war." And though surrounded by a malevolent host of unknown proportions, Smith declared that the boys felt safe because "our army is in the rear of the enemy under General Joseph E. Johnston and Gen. [Bedford] Forrest who will deliver from this 'bag,' as the Yankies call it."[95] Like so many of the besieged chroniclers, Smith found himself becoming fully comforted in the arms of wishful thinking.

Robert Spradling of the 43rd Tennessee, in his succinct manner, indicated that the sharpshooters and cannonading resumed as usual and continued all day.[96] His compatriot Isaac Stamper of the same regiment believed that this fire was not as heavy as it had been, though he noted that two men in adjoining brigades had been killed as a result of it. He noted that the night was mostly quiet, and the boys all "got a fine sleep."[97]

---

[93] Hynds, "Original Handwritten Notes," 3–4.
[94] Smith, *A Smith in Service*, 52.
[95] Ibid.
[96] Spradling, "Diary," 2.
[97] Stamper, "Travels of the 43rd Tennessee," 59.

James Darr of the 43rd Tennessee wrote on this Sunday morning that the Yankees had shelled Vicksburg throughout the night at a heavy rate of fire and were continuing through the morning and into the afternoon. The sharpshooters continued to "peg" away. He reported that a man in Captain McKamy's company had been killed the day before as had another out of Company D. While the enemy fire continued to slam into their lines, Darr noted, the remainder of the army's mules were driven out of the works to the mercy of the Yankees. At 3 p.m the fighting was confined to mostly artillery fire, though the sharpshooters expended rounds occasionally. Pursuant to orders, Darr requisitioned three more coffins to be made.[98]

The Burial Truce Ruse. Sunday brought to mind for S. A. R. Swan, serving in Stephen D. Lee's Brigade, "a difference from the quiet peaceful Sabbath I have spent at my home in [Cleveland], Tennessee." No church bells rang in the besieged Vicksburg, calling the people to the houses of worship and to the praise of the God of peace and love, he lamented, "only the angry roar of cannon and the rattle of musketry."[99] The misery in the lines was compounded by the choking stench of the festering and reeking Yankee dead in front of their works, killed in Grant's futile assaults. Some had been lying under the hot sun since the previous Tuesday.

Around the time Wash was observing the approach of the ex-slaves, Swan indicated that Grant had sent forth a delegation under flag of truce near the center of the Confederate works. Others sources indicated that the contact was originated by Pemberton. When the flag was carried, "a large number of the enemy who had been lying in a ravine under the range of our guns where they had taken shelter in the assault made on Thursday evening ran back towards their lines." Grant's tricks continued unabated, though Swan wrote, "our boys fired into them when the flag returned."[100]

As darkness returned, Swan noted, the mortar boats had resumed their work "with vigor." Though they fired throughout the day, the heaviest shelling seemed always to occur after dark, when precise aiming was impossible and the general terror from randomly placed explosions served only to demoralize. Even with all the blasting and explosions, however, rarely were there any casualties from this method of harassment, though Swan admitted that accurate statistics at his level in the chain of command were difficult to come-by.[101]

---

[98] Darr, "Diary," 2.
[99] Swan, "A Tennessean in the Siege of Vicksburg," 358.
[100] Ibid., 358–59.
[101] Ibid., 359.

The Big Black Prisoners Finally Head North. "On the morning of the 23rd [25th], we were notified that steam boats were coming to transport us up the river," Wash of the 60th Tennessee reported. The Yankees provided each of the prisoners with three days' rations, which were to last them until they reached occupied Memphis. They were then ordered to prepare for their long journey. At 2 p.m., the Big Black River prisoners collected their scanty possessions and their bedding, and were marched to the landing, under the watchful eye of their blue-clad guards from the 23rd Wisconsin and 8th Ohio. There, they observed the transport steamers awaiting their Confederate cargo: the *Crescent City*, the *Ohio Belle*, the *Omaha*, the *Gladiator*, and the *General Robert Allen*. Off from the landing was a gunboat assigned to accompany them because Confederate guerillas infested the river at all points and plagued shipping anyway they could. The gunboat mounted ten heavy guns, and half of its crew were "gallant boys all the way from Africa."[102]

"I was on board the *Omaha*," Wash wrote, "which contained some 800 men." Meanwhile, the faith of the prisoners "in the invincibility of Vicksburg was growing stronger," he noted, with the repeated news that Federal frontal assault after assault had been repulsed with great slaughter. Wash, on his way to Johnson's Island officers' prison near Sandusky, Ohio, indicated that around 4 p.m., the flotilla, with its captives aboard, steamed off. Most of prisoners would spend the next year and a half at Johnson's Island, Fort Delaware, and Point Lookout before being exchanged for Union captives in Confederate prisons, their active service against the "greatest government on the face of the earth" virtually at an end. The vast majority of them would be exchanged late in February 1865 and awarded a minimum of a month's paroled prisoner's furlough. They would be home in East Tennessee at the time of Lee's surrender. "We took one last lingering look at the gallant City, as she fade[d] off in the distance," Wash sighed, "and leaving our blessings and best wishes with her noble defenders," though, he added, "we were glad to get away from the hearing of the contest in which we felt so deep an interest, but could not lend a helping hand."[103]

Bonafide Burial Truce. As the smoke from the stacks of the transports traced the prisoners' departure, a burial truce was now in effect between the belligerents. Vaughn's assistant adjutant, Lieutenant John Toland, forwarded on 25 May orders from General Martin Luther Smith that "a flag of truce regarding the burial of the enemy's dead has been sent by General Pemberton,

---

[102] Wash, *Camp, Field and Prison Life*, 63–64.
[103] Ibid., 64.

who directs that should they cease firing along their lines, there will be no firing along ours." General Vaughn attached to his directive the following command: "the officers in command of troops in this brigade will conform strictly with the accompanying order."[104]

Some hours before the truce, the battle for Vicksburg "was opened this morning at daylight by the sharp-shooters and artillery." A Yankee battery to the front of Reynolds's lines threw some rounds toward the Confederates without effect. Then, at 2 p.m., Captain George Hynds of the 31st Tennessee reported, the firing ceased in order to give the enemy a chance to bury their dead, estimated to be 2,500 to 3,000. Some of the bodies had been lying where they had fallen for seven days. Reports among the men set Southern losses since entering the defenses at 600.[105]

Before the truce went into effect, "a Yankie piece was let off at us from the south [a distance of] one mile," Calvin Smith of the 31st Tennessee noted at the beginning of his journal entry for 25 may. He noted that the round was a solid rifled cannon bolt "which came whistling across us," doubtlessly generating some considerable attention. But the Confederate batteries gave back as good as they got, he wrote, so the enemy took care "not to show themselves." A flag of truce was brought over by the Feds several days ago "requesting to bury their dead," but Smith stated it was refused since the Yankees would not let the Confederate dead be buried at Port Gibson. Today another flag of truce was accepted in the Confederate lines, and this time Pemberton acquiesced, since the stench was making life almost unbearable for his troops. Hostilities were to be discontinued at least until dark.[106]

"Our soldiers and the Yankies got together and joked about shooting at one another," Lieutenant Smith remarked. The boys in blue told the East Tennesseans that Grant had lost around 6,000 men killed and twice that number wounded since the siege began on 18 May, which led Smith to conclude, "we have not lost 100 men killed and wounded" in the same period of time. Interestingly, Smith recorded that he, Captains Neil and Mason, and unnamed officer, "not hearing of this transaction" until an hour before sundown, set out on a little walk along the lines across the way as far as the Southern railroad line, strolling along two full miles of the enemy's ditches, which they observed were "full all the way around of armed men, many

---

[104] Melancthon Smith to John C. Vaughn, 25 May 1863, in *A Soldier's Story of the Siege of Vicksburg*, 200.
[105] Hynds, "Original Handwritten Notes," 5.
[106] Smith, *A Smith in Service*, 52.

batteries on the way someplace, and enemy batteries not over two hundred yards from us."[107]

They noticed eight graves of their dead on the hill tops 150 yards from the 31st Tennessee's lines, and watched discretely as their burial parties began hunting their comrades who had been wounded and whose only recourse had been to crawl into brush piles out of the line of fire to die. "Some have been lying 10 days," Smith stated, "and I could smell them of a mile or more." Those retrieved were pitched unceremoniously into rough holes and covered over quickly by their own men because of their advanced state of decay.[108]

"We set out to return to [our] ditches," Smith reported, "so we took down the railroad to the depot near the river." He made an informal reconnaissance of the subsistence holdings of his own army, and observed "a house full of flour, large quantities of salt, corn meal, 5 engines and 50 to 75 cars, 2 steam mills grinding, perhaps 6,000 beeves, nearly 2,000 mules and horses." A member of his regiment, whom he identified only as "Harris," returned to their trenches one hour *after* the truce had expired.[109]

After the truce was concluded, Smith noted that the Yankees made another limited assault against Stephen D. Lee's entrenchments, but only got into his forward picket positions at the base of the works. "Lee yelled down to them if they didn't surrender, he would be compelled to kill them there, but they did not seem to be afraid," according to Smith. "So, Lee's men again lighted and applied fuses to their battery shells and toss them over into the ditches." In the darkness, the Yankees could not see the danger they were in, and the shells went off and killed around 100 of them. The twenty who survived surrendered without further negotiation.[110]

On the far right flank of the army next to Reynolds's men was a brigade of Georgians under the command of General Seth Barton. During the night of 25 May, he sent out a party of men with axes to cut down trees that enemy pickets had been using for cover. Their musket fire, however, kept the Georgians from their work. The excursion, however, was not a totally wasted effort, and "our men surrounded and took 97 prisoners and marched them into Vicksburg." From this little sortie, the Georgians and their East Tennessee support "got crackers, clothing, hats and many other tricks." Meanwhile, the grapevine telegraph spread incorrect intelligence that in front of John Vaughn's lines

---

[107] Ibid., 52–53.
[108] Ibid., 53.
[109] Ibid.
[110] Ibid.

nearly 3,000 yanks had been killed during the assaults. The Yankees killed on the upper lines were victims of Shoup's, Hebert's, and Bowen's men, not Vaughn's. With good rumors following great ones, Smith reported that another had General Johnston hard at work, "whipping the Yankees back in this direction." Indeed, the rumor that Johnston was active was rampant in Grant's camps. He had detached some 12,000 of his men under General Francis Blair up the "Mechanicsburg Corridor" toward Satartia to investigate the possible advance by Johnston's so-called Army of the Relief. Otherwise, all these fanciful tales were excellent for the garrison's morale, which was reflected in Smith's next comment: "I feel confident that we can hold our ground until the Yankees will be glad to cross the river."[111]

With the sun and renewed firing signaling a new day, 25 May, Isaac Stamper of the 43rd Tennessee and his comrades were again rushed to the support of General Lee's men and were lined up behind Colonel Franklin K. Beck's 23rd Alabama. During the brief skirmish, the 43rd Tennessee's surgeon, W. B. Johnson, received what would later be a fatal wound from the Yankee sharpshooters. Correcting a previous report, Stamper wrote that, during the previous evening, Pemberton had been the one to send a flag of truce so that the Federals could bury the men killed in the 19 and 22 May assaults. "The stench was becoming unbearable," Stamper affirmed. In agreement with Smith's report, the deadline was set at 8:30 p.m., Stamper wrote, "and some of our boys went over and had a great deal of chat with the Yanks during the truce." There was a general swapping of knives, canteens, and other items, and all agreed it was a glorious thing to "hear the big guns hushed for even a short time, for they had been roaring for more than a week."[112]

Clack of the 43rd Tennessee recorded the events of 25 May with the same opening used by most on these days of siege: "dueling commenced early this morning." However, around 3 p.m., he reported that the flag of truce was received with the Yankees asking to bury their dead. This request was granted. "All is now quiet on our line," he stated, enjoying the few hours of tranquility as the bluecoats went about their grim tasks in front of the ditches.[113] Reuben Clark of the 59th Tennessee also indicated that the truce was initiated by the Confederates, as if Grant had to be taught the Christian thing to do. If Grant had no intention of burying his soldiers killed in the assaults, Clark wrote, we asked him "to suspend hostilities until we could bury them ourselves." A detail

---

[111] Ibid.

[112] Stamper, "Travels of the 43rd Tennessee," 59.

[113] Clack, "Personal Diary," 1.

of Yankee soldiers, once the truce was in place, came from their lines, and "holes were dug and the dead were shoveled into them without removing cartridge boxes or any of their equipment." Clark suspected that Grant intended "to leave his dead near our line to make it so disagreeable that we could not endure the stench."[114] The Confederates were nearly at that point.

"Hostilities have entirely ceased," Darr of the 43rd Tennessee observed, causing him wonder what was going on. The day had opened with firing between the sharpshooters on both sides, though the artillery had ceased for the time. The Yankee navy had shot shells into Vicksburg again most of the previous night. "This is the seventh day since the Yanks commenced to storm this place," he wrote, "and I do not see they have accomplished anything."[115] After the usual firing that commenced at daylight concluded at 3 p.m., word of a truce was received so that the enemy could bury their dead. "Men on each side now met each other in friendly conversation," he remarked, "and there was quite a mingling of the two armies in front of our lines for a short time." When each side returned to its respective lines, the battle resumed as before. "The short cessation in the firing was a great relief to we tired men," Darr indicated, "and the spirits of all went up." The boys of the garrison eagerly inquired about activities outside the lines, and after some talk with the Yanks, Swan wrote, "all came to the conclusion our case was not quite as desperate as had been thought." Porter's mortar fleet was given the night off, and "the boys all got a good night's rest."[116]

Swan noted that several hundred weapons were gleaned from the field between the lines during the dark hours the past few nights, and all the boys in the trenches were amazed to discover that the Yankees were using Enfield muskets, the same weapon employed by the Confederates. According to Swan, before this discovery, the Confederates had believed that the enemy had access to "better arms" than they had themselves. An enemy rifled cannon had been throwing shells constantly while the Confederate batteries were silent, and in some instances, the earthworks had been damaged and a few Confederate field pieces were dismounted, temporarily placing them out of commission. The Federals had by now dug rifle pits for their skirmishers almost to the edge of Lee's breastworks and thereby kept up a repetitious fire from about 4 a.m. until eight in the evening. "Whenever one of our men raised his head above the earthworks," Swan indicated, "he instantly became the mark for fifty rifles."

---

[114] Clark, *Valleys of the Shadow*, 23.
[115] Darr, "Diary," 2.
[116] Swan, "A Tennessean at the Siege of Vicksburg," 359.

When particularly bored, the boys often put a hat on a ramrod, held it above the head log, and watched as it instantly drew dozens of minie balls from the Union lines. This kind of event was the usual course at any moment in Lee's trenches. On Lee's right, he indicated, were the Georgians of General Cumming's Brigade. Still farther down, was Reynolds'S Brigade of East Tennesseans, containing his old regiment, the 3rd Tennessee. Beyond them going in a hook back toward the river was Seth Barton's Georgia Brigade constituting the extreme right of the Confederate Army at Vicksburg. The day saw little small arms fire, though a "battery opened on Reynolds' Brigade west of the Hall's Ferry Road, throwing an occasional shot" into his lines.[117]

"A line of the enemy's skirmishers took positions in a cane brake in front of the old 3rd Tennessee," Swan wrote, "but two companies charged through and dislodged them." It was on this evening that Seth Barton sent out a large detachment that cut off and captured four companies of Federals on the Warrenton road. Barton reported that the Confederates did their best counterattacks during the night. They had learned from Grant's foolhardy attacks that daylight offensive action had "played out." The gunboats still came up the river and threw shells from the rear into Lee's and Reynolds's line. As a buttress, the 43rd Tennessee marched over to support Lee's men as reserve during the assault on Thursday, "and suffered some," Swan concluded.[118]

Though the night entering 26 May seemed to be a restful one, Calvin Smith of the 31st Tennessee wrote, "early this morning commences the day with sharp shooting, cannonade and shelling in every direction." Reports reached the boys through the grapevine that the Big Black River prisoners were being sent across the river today, though they had been there for several days. This report led Smith to think of his brother Sevier Smith, in Company B, 60th Tennessee, and of Jesse Lee, of the same command, who was also recruited in Rogersville, Hawkins County. Smith hoped that Sevier, Lee, and the rest of his acquaintances captured at the Big Black were alive and safe, and "will hold out until exchanged." An exchange had to come soon, Smith asserted, since "we are collecting quite a fine lot [of prisoners] in Vicksburg." He noted that the "whether" was extremely hot, dry, and dusty, "but we have very good water."[119] The weather would prove consistent in this regard, but water would not.

Smith remarked that during the previous night the men had been disturbed by the rattle of musketry and the usual discharge of cannon, which

---

[117] Ibid., 359–60.
[118] Ibid., 360.
[119] Smith, *A Smith in Service*, 53.

seemed aimed in all directions. He believed that the enemy was "trying to change their luck" by concentrating their attention on another part of the line, since the middle had proved so difficult for them to uproot. "For some cause or other [Confederate] troops are collecting heavily on our right," he noted, "probably expecting an attack from the direction of Warrenton which is now held by the enemy." Spies had been captured sneaking up the river bank, Smith reported, and the pioneers were busy in the construction of new ditches to confront the enemy's lines along the lower flank.[120] It looked like Barton's boys, as well as Reynolds's and perhaps Cumming's reserves as well, would be called on to be ready for any emergency.

George Hynds of Jefferson County and the 31st Tennessee wrote in his journal that the night before, "eighty-seven prisoners were taken on our extreme right without much resistance." The fight commenced at daybreak and continued all day long "at long range." It looked like the mortar boats were targeting one of the hospitals in Vicksburg. Hynds stated that the boys continued to look for Johnston to hit Grant's rear so the garrison might be relieved.[121]

The 43rd Tennessee, which seemed to be most active at night these days, was awakened and formed at around 3 a.m. on 26 May, and ordered from their position in the rear of Reynolds's lines to support General Seth Barton's Georgians down on the extreme right flank "on the Warrenton road." They were in place by sunup, Stamper noted, and "Companies A, F, D, and C were put in the ditches on the extreme left of a large gun [at the South Fort] overlooking the Mississippi River." Companies B and G were placed on the right, in Barton's trenches. With no attack forthcoming, the rest of the 43rd Tennessee was held back in reserve. Stamper reported that all was quiet on the right after this false alarm, "except an occasional sharp-shooter or a shell from our guns."[122]

"The enemy opened fire at daylight this morning [26 May]," Clack of the 43rd Tennessee stated in the opening of his daily entry. Gillespie's regiment was on the move early and relocated "just before daylight to the river below town," taking their places in the trenches. Around 9 a.m., enemy land batteries commenced their ritual of shelling Vicksburg, and a number of the Union gunboats moved into position to assist, Clack recorded, weary with the

---

[120] Ibid.
[121] Hynds, "Original Handwritten Notes," 5–6.
[122] Stamper, *Valleys of the Shadow,* 59.

predictability of it. "Oh! May God in Heaven aid and deliver us from this unhappy state!" he prayed.[123]

"Our men keep close under cover of their breastworks and suffer but little," Swan announced. The Yankee artillery struck close and was very annoying, he reported. "Shells are bursting in almost every portion of the ground inside our lines and a caisson filled with shells was blown up today in one of our redoubts, injuring eight men of the 20th Alabama." The endurance of the men in the ditches was stretched to the maximum, he wrote, "having to lie motionless all day under a burning sun." Some of the boys rigged tent flies or blankets to lie under, and they provided the only shade for the boys. "Unless God Himself in His mercy, favors us and brings us deliverance," Swan lamented, "we will have to succumb at last." Hopes persisted that Johnston would be the Lord's instrument of rescue, for many believed that Johnston continued to collect an army equal to this considerable task. The Yankees, Swan realized, possessed the area around Snyder's Bluff to the north of the city and "have uninterrupted communication by the Yazoo with their forces in the rear of Vicksburg." Prophetically, Swan predicted, "it looks much like the fate of the war is to be decided here."[124]

General Thomas H. Taylor, Pemberton's assistant inspector general, issued a report submitted on 26 May detailing the conditions of the brigades defending Vicksburg. Taylor noted that General Vaughn's Brigade had 1,156 effectives in the ditches sharing 917 rifles. They had 70,920 rounds in their cartridge boxes, and the brigade ordnance officers had on hand another 35,000 rounds. On this particular day, Vaughn's men had fired their rifles 120 times. The condition of their ammunition was categorized as "doubtful." Taylor reported that Vaughn's men had suffered one man killed and three men wounded on 26 May. Conditions around Vaughn's camps were described as "generally good." Taylor indicated that Reynolds's Brigade had 1,759 effectives, and each man had his own weapon. Reynolds's men had 73,360 cartridges in their boxes, with their ordnance officers in possession of 53,000 more. The men had fired only twenty times on 26 May. One man was reported missing from the Fourth Brigade, and Reynolds's camps were described as "tolerable." Regarding the evening's sortie on 25 May with the men of Barton's Brigade, the Georgians were given credit for the capture of 114 combatants: two captains, three

---

[123] Clack, "Personal Diary," 1.

[124] Swan, "A Tennessean in the Siege of Vicksburg," 360.

lieutenants, and 109 infantrymen. No mention was made of the assistance rendered by Reynolds' men.[125]

The Sinking of the "Cincinnati." Rare indeed at this point of the siege were occurrences that gave the garrison succor and comfort with any frequency from the tedium it daily endured. But 27 May would be just such a day when an incident transpired not of fiction or imagination to be passed along from boredom or ignorance, but an actual victory observed or heard about by most everyone in the trenches. It would inspire the Vicksburg garrison for days to come.

"The Yankies thought they would try another trick to day," Lieutenant Calvin Smith of the 31st Tennessee continued in his daily entry. Three gunboats came steaming along down river at the same time as two others cruised up from the lower river, "all firing at our batteries together with the mortar fleet which was under the far banks of the peninsular out of sight."[126] As the war dogs crept around the bend across from Fort Hill, the upper battery (Lynch's battery) of the 1st Tennessee Heavy Artillery bade them the usual welcome. Known collectively as "Battery Tennessee," the guns here were under the overall command of Colonel Andrew Jackson, Jr., the stepson of the seventh president of the United States. Suddenly, all the batteries joined in, pounding the ironclad *Cincinnati*. "Captain [John P.] Lynch's battery," Smith wrote, "sent a few well-directed shots [that so] battered her hull and iron sides, she sank very soon, and the other paddle wheeler skedaddled." He noted that the other vessels coming from the south "fell" with the current back down river, "proud that they had escaped so well." Even in their defeat, Smith admitted, "they threw a few shells, and several came over near our ditch." These missiles sunk mostly in the dirt, but one did explode, "and killed 4 soldiers near one of our batteries."

One of the boys in the regiment, A. H. Owens, who had been in Vicksburg on 27 May, returned with news that for all their bluff and hardware flinging through the skies, the Yankees "had not done as much damage as expected" to the city.[127] "From the time and number of shells one would think that this 'Gibraltar of the West' would have been destroyed [in] 7 or 8 days and nights," Smith scoffed. He reported three mortar boats had been shelling the Warren County seat with "thousands of shells" in a vain attempt to "fire the town,"

---

[125] Gen. Thomas H. Taylor to Gen. John C. Pemberton, 26 May 1863, *Official Records*, ser. 1, vol. 24, pt. 3, p. 923–24.

[126] Smith, *A Smith in Service*, 53.

[127] Ibid., 53–54.

continuing as they had done for five months with the result thus far that "perhaps 20 men have been killed or wounded during that time."

On 27 May, Smith concluded the section of his diary relating to his activities in the Vicksburg campaign. He stated, "of course 'everything' is not correct as it is very difficult to get the truth of transactions as they transpire." Should he "get killed or loose this book," he implored anyone who found his journal to his wife, Nancy, back at the Persia Post Office, Hawkins County, Tennessee. "My wife and children, Mother and companion, would confer a lasting thanks and friendship to their enemies should this book fall into their hands," Smith promised. His desire was that his wife and children "William Sylvester, Cornelia Frances, Marcus Lafayett, Laura Manurva, George Ridley and Tabitha Jane" might "learn to hear what I was doing while absent from them for so long." Concerning dear little ones, he remarked, "how I would like to see them, how I left them in good health last October." "No doubt they often think and talk of me as lost from their sight forever on this earth," he wrote, "but I have always felt that providence would always deliver me safe in their presence again." His prayers, he indicated, were to see the day he could return home.[128] Smith's journal and a subsequent one that he kept during the siege happily made their way safely home.

"Along about 11 o'clock [a.m.]," George Hynds of the same regiment recorded in his daily journal, "a gunboat [the Cincinnati] attempted to run down by our batteries, and was sunk by Lynch's Battery." With understandable pride in his fellow Jefferson Countians caught in Grant's "jug" at Vicksburg, Lieutenant Hynds boasted, "Lynch has done more effective work with his battery than has been done with any other on the river."[129] Clerk Darr of the 43rd Tennessee recorded that the Yankee gunboats attacked Battery Tennessee at the bend in the river, fired some twenty shots, and tried to run back up the Mississippi once her hull had been pierced. She sank to the bottom, according to Darr. "A prisoner we took says only a fourth of the crew of 120 made their escape," he declared, adding, "the boat was riddled to pieces."[130]

The Yankees kept up their heavy fire on the left of Stevenson's division, according to Isaac Stamper of the 43rd Tennessee, and attempted a charge there in the evening with the usual unsuccessful results. "Five gunboats, two above and three below town, made an attack on the City and our fortifications," he noted, referring to the sinking of the ill-fated *Cincinnati*. The lower boats did

---

[128] Ibid.
[129] Hynds, "Original Handwritten Notes," 6.
[130] Darr, "Diary," 3.

no harm, with the exception of killing one man, and did not "stay very long within reach of our river guns." And except for this sinking of "one boat carrying fifteen guns sunk by our batteries above town," Stamper reported that all was quiet on the right flank where he and his East Tennessee comrades were operating.[131] "Three gunboats came up opposite our line," Clack of the 43rd Tennessee noted from the reserves' vantage point on a bluff of the river behind Reynolds' works, "but none of our regt. was hurt." He recorded, however, that a soldier off to the right of the 43rd Tennessee's position had "had his head shot off," and two of his companions were wounded. Another gunboat, the *Cincinnati*, from the upper end of the river attempted to pass the batteries, he declared, and was sunk. Sharpshooting and cannonading continued as usual along the back lines, "and a general engagement is expected daily." The rumor circulated again that Johnston had attacked the Federals at the rear along the Black River. Clack indicated that in front of their ditches "the Yankee pickets have come into sight" of the defenders.[132]

Writing for the *Confederate Veteran* many years after Vicksburg had fallen, F. W. Merrin, an eyewitness of the sinking of the *Cincinnati*, presented the following narrative concerning the day's big excitement:

> A few days after the fruitless efforts of Gen. Grant to carry the Confederate lines by heavy and successive charges, one beautiful morning about eight o'clock a considerable commotion was noticed from the position occupied by the writer on the old Spanish Fort Hill, the extreme northern point in the Confederate lines. It was on a high bluff. There was commotion, too, in the river at Milligan's [Milliken's] Bend, above the city, the headquarters of Commodore Farragut, commanding at that point. In a very little while, we plainly saw one of the largest gunboats of the fleet moving out and down the great river. Majestically and slowly she moved, keeping on the north side of the great Vicksburg Bend, and partially hidden by the intervening banks. While passing exposed places some shots from the river batteries were fired at her, including a few shots from the noted gun, 'Whistling Dick,' but on came the war dog. With ports closed and a good head of steam on, she majestically swept around the big bend and into the main channel leading by our river line of batteries and the city of Vicksburg. After making the curve, and until she had passed the besieging line of

---

[131] Stamper, "Travels of the 43rd Tennessee," 59–60.
[132] Clack, "Personal Diary," 1.

the federals, our river batteries had but little chance to fire, and the high bluff field batteries none at all. For the next twenty or thirty minutes, thousands of spectators from the two out-stretched battle lines and thousands of citizens crept from their hiding places to witness it.

On came the *Cincinnati*. 'Whistling Dick' managed to get a shot or two at long range and at a sharp angle up the river. The river batteries could only await their time, and were on the alert. Just as the huge ironclad was passing the first battery, the open port of the vessel was shown, and no sooner did the great beam sweep out of the way than a solid shot from one of the guns of the battery entered the opening, and as the sequel proved, cut its way clear through the vessel, passing out below the water line on the opposite side. Those of us who witnessed this terrific scene from the higher bluff could see at once that great harm had been done the vessel. The port was closed at once; not a gun was fired from the vessel. We saw the water spout out for some distance beyond the boat. Her wheels were stopped, and the great warship seemed to drift with the current; but in a very little while, her engines started up again, and her propelling power seemed to be as good as ever. She made a gentle curve from our batteries, and turned back up the river. Our batteries improved this time, and the ironclad was doubtless hit a number of times, but we could discern no other damage to her. When the *Cincinnati* had passed above the federal lines, we were soon convinced of the terrible effect of the first shot. The monster ironclad was headed for the shore; her seamen and soldiers were seen taking to the water from all sides, with such drifting facilities as they could get hold of, and finally, when about the length of the vessel from shore, she quietly settled to the bottom of the Mississippi River. Such a shout went up from the Confederate lines as was never heard before.

The 'Yah! Yah!' which came back from the other side was ludicrous.[133]

S. A. R. Swan of S. D. Lee's Brigade gave his version of the story in his daily entry. "At about ten o'clock this morning, three of the enemy's gunboats made their appearance below and commenced throwing shot and shell," he reported. At the same time, the *Cincinnati*, mounting thirteen guns, came down from the upper fleet and attacked the batteries at short range. Giving a picture

---

[133] F. W. Merrin, "Sinking of the *Cincinnati* at the Siege of Vicksburg," *The Confederate Veteran* 5/5 (May 1897): 201.

of the effectiveness of the river batteries at Vicksburg and indicating why Grant feared them so, Swan noted that the "battle" was of short duration, and the Yankee ironclad was pierced at the water's edge and began to sink. "She signaled for help," the Bradley County native indicated, "and several tugs made their appearance but dared not to come to her relief." Like some huge dying prehistoric beast, the *Cincinnati* turned and made her way slowly around the point, finally jamming her prow into bank. Her crew hastened through the shallow water to land, and in a short time, her stern settled down into the water, leaving only her prow visible still stuck into the bank. "It was cheering indeed to see her go under," Swan recorded, adding, "the [other] boats immediately hauled off, and moved down stream."[134]

"You heard of *our* sinking the gunboat," Sergeant Jacob Alexander of Lynch's Battery wrote his friend John T. Moffitt in regard to the fate of the *Cincinnati*. "It is generally allowed that we did it." Alexander knew who did it because, he stated, "I stood by and saw the battery which did the work. It was a shot from the banded [reinforced] 62–pounder on the hill below the Water Batteries." The scene was "intensely exciting, especially as we saw her careening."[135]

"Shout after shout went up from one end of the line to the other," Alexander reported, "which was well understood by the yankees to mean their defeat. Prisoners told us that it made the enemy furious, astonished as they were at the fate of their most powerful vessel." The struggle for Vicksburg continued to put a heavy toll on the enemy fleet was attempting to subjugate the city. "You have seen it stated that there were 4 boats," he wrote, but "there were only two in range of our guns. Two others came down a ways, merely as spectators." When the mighty *Cincinnati* was lost, however, they lost their stomach for the dash, he noted. "Our success has done the boys much good." Corporal James Barnes of Sullivan County, commanding the rifle on the hill, fired the fatal rounds into the warship. "Since the fight, they have given us a 10–inch Columbiad," Alexander reported, as though it was a reward earned.[136] Though many of the observers argued over to whom the credit for the sinking of the monster ironclad should belong, one artilleryman serving with the next battery down the river indicated he felt "safe in saying that Capt. Lynch is

---

[134] Swan, "A Tennessean at the Siege of Vicksburg," 360.
[135] Jacob Alexander to John T. Moffitt, 30 March [May] 1863, Moffitt Papers.
[136] Ibid.

entitled to the honor of sinking the *Cincinnati*. [Lynch's] was a splendid company."[137]

The mortar batteries from down river were doing yeoman's work prior to the Yankees' disaster, "but they too soon ceased." Swan of Lee's Brigade noted, as many others had, that it was amazing that with all the "immense masses of iron" the Yankees hurtled at the works and Vicksburg, the results were so miniscule. "It is a grand and terrible sight," according to Swan, "to see them rushing madly through the air at night and bursting high above the City, scattering whizzing fragments over the heads of men, women and children." Only by the grace of God, he concluded, were the missiles "turned aside and suffers not the helpless inhabitants of this beleaguered City to be mangled by them."[138]

The sinking of the *Cincinnati*, following within a week of the disastrous attacks on the works by Grant on 19 and 22 May, seemed to bring new life into the East Tennesseans and all the garrison's defenders. George Hynds of the 31st Tennessee noted on 28 May, the "gunboat sunk yesterday was a new one, and was considered to be the best on the river." Her battery, according to the Dandridge native, was composed of "13 nine-inch rifle guns," and the grapevine telegraph indicated incorrectly that none other than David Porter himself had commanded her. This imprecise news service, Hynds seemed to admit, did not provide information on whether the vice admiral had made his getaway or not. (Porter was not aboard, as his flagship was the "timberclad" *Black Hawk*.) The siege continued at long range, and Hynds forwarded the accurate appraisal that the Yankees had lost their stomach for direct assaults on the impregnable Confederate trenches.[139] As a consequence, on this date, U. S. Grant made another request to Washington for heavy reinforcements. His wishes were always granted by Abraham Lincoln.

The sharpshooters pecked away as soon as there was enough light for them to draw a bead, according to Clack of the 43rd Tennessee, and the boys saw "a few can be seen in sight of our line again this morning." The gunboats that shelled them the previous morning lay at anchor, deceptively still and silent two miles down the river.[140] Isaac Stamper of the same regiment stated that firing was resumed at daylight and continued until dark: the continuous, nerve-wracking, and wearisome mantra repeated day after day. The enemy gunners at

[137] W. L. Kidd to W. T. Rigby, 27 June 1903, W. T. Rigby Correspondence.
[138] Swan, "A Tennessean in the Siege of Vicksburg," 360.
[139] Hynds, "Original Handwritten Notes," 6–7.
[140] Clack, "Personal Diary," 1.

a gin house down near Reynolds's old camps in the direction of Warrenton threw a few shells into the works, which caused Seth Barton to send some of his Georgians out after them. The Federals quickly removed the battery, thereby saving it for another day. Stamper wrote that the enemy drew unexpected attention from the Georgians, which caused the blue-clad artillerymen "get up and dust." And finally, the "official" news came down to the boys in the lines that "assistance was coming to us," he reported. Morale peaked considerably the last few days among the defenders, and they were all glad at last, for "the enemy would be defeated after so much time and expense in trying to take Vicksburg."[141] James Darr of the 43rd Tennessee noted that by 10 a.m. on 28 May, there had been little fighting, except for the usual sharpshooting and occasional cannon fire. He recorded that Dr. W. B. Johnson, still suffering from his 25 May leg wound, seemed to be doing some better that morning.[142]

The weather was moderate and pleasant, Swan noted in his journal entry 28 May. He believed that the Northerner's fire was "rather spiritless," particularly from the mortar batteries. Echoing the optimism ranging through the Confederate works, Swan supposed that the Yankees' lack of effort was due to their discouragement over the repeated failure of their gunboat attacks. This conclusion caused him to predict, if "we only had enough heavy guns to sink every boat that tried to pass, we would not be beleaguered now on the land side." He believed that the Confederate government had provided too many heavy guns for the defense of Charleston harbor, and that Jefferson Davis and Pierre G. T. Beauregard, commanding the defenses there, would have to answer to history should Vicksburg fall because of a lack of sufficient siege pieces.[143]

Another boost to Confederate morale occurred when a visitor made his way into the lines on 28 May, Swan noted, "which all day long animated the troops." The visitor was the famous partisan scout Lamar Fontaine sent from Joseph Johnston. He brought the cheering news that General Robert E. Lee had defeated Joseph Hooker at the Battle of Chancellorsville and had driven the Yankees back across the Potomac, leaving Lee's forces "in possession of Arlington Heights [overlooking Washington, DC]." Fontaine also declared that Johnston was quickly assembling his Army of the Relief. All this information was presented to the boys in the trenches where it was "received with cheering." Swan reported that the famous scout, a veteran of numerous of "hair-raising

---

[141] Stamper, "Travels of the 43rd Tennessee," 60.
[142] Darr, "Diary," 3.
[143] Swan, "A Tennessean in the Siege of Vicksburg," 360–61.

adventures" and a "recipient of many wounds," had made his way down the Yazoo River "disguised as a fisherman, and was picked up by our men who were searching for the crew of the gunboat sunk that morning." These survivors from the *Cincinnati*, Swan noted, "were supposed to be wandering about lost in the Yazoo swamps." The scout Fontaine also brought with him a large quantity of percussion caps for the garrison's Enfield muskets, Swan noted "of which the supply is scarce." Others described Fontaine's sneaking through the lines in far more dramatic terms.[144]

Colonel Alexander W. Reynolds wrote in his report "on or around 29 May," the "enemy by a superior force drove in my picket line. After night fall, I attacked them in turn and reestablished [it]."[145] About 6 a.m., George Hynds of the 31st Tennessee noted that a fierce artillery duel had begun, which lasted for a full half hour. Hynds stated that it was the heaviest firing he had yet heard during the siege. At 6 p.m. that evening, the cannonade commenced again with volleys exchanged from both lines. The men were put on alert in their trenches expecting another massive general assault, but Grant had been taught his lesson. None was forthcoming.[146]

The day opened with gunfire and shells, and by 8 a.m., there was a general heavy bombardment going on along the back lines of Reynolds's positions where Gillespie's reserves were often camped. According to Clack, this barrage lasted for an hour or two. Around 3 p.m., everything was then quiet along the back lines. A dozen transports accompanied by a couple of gunboats steamed down river and anchored out "in line of battle" above Vicksburg. Another gunboat, he wrote, approached from the lower river, and shelled the lower end of the lines for a while, doing no damage. Swarms of heavy clouds appeared as dusk approached, Clack recorded, accompanied by thunder and the appearance of rain. The gunboats threw a few shells in their direction once it got dark.[147]

The rifled cannon that had caused considerable annoyance to the boys was dismounted on 29 May by one of the large Confederate siege guns on the left of

---

[144] Ibid., 361. Capt. John S. Bell of the 12th Battalion, Arkansas Sharp-shooters, described this phenomenal incident as follows: "We were getting short of gun caps when one night some daring fellow drifted down the river through the yankee fleet between two logs covered with brush to bring us quantities of percussion caps 'done up' in oil cloth to prevent them from getting damp." John S. Bell, "Arkansas Sharp-shooters at Vicksburg," *Confederate Veteran*, 12/9 (September 1904): 446.

[145] Report of Col. Alexander W. Reynolds, undated, *Official Records*, ser. 1, vol. 24, pt. 2, p. 356.

[146] Hynds, "Original Handwritten Notes," 7.

[147] Clack, "Personal Diary," 1.

General Stevenson's line, according to Isaac Stamper of the 43rd Tennessee. A spirited cannonade ensued, as though the boys in blue had been insulted, and the Southern guns traded them round for round for nearly two hours. He confirmed the gunboats were at work on the back lines along the river, but no harm resulted. "We were all snug on our couches when the gunboats attacked us again," Stamper noted, citing the time as about 9 p.m. "We all hustled to our ditches and had our night's rest spoiled." Just as quickly as it had begun, however, the warship stopped its firing and moved away. During the day Private Jessie Addison of Company C died of his wounds suffered in action on 20 May. Other news that Stamper shared was that Pemberton had ordered all the stock that could be spared be driven out of the lines "because we had nothing on which to feed them." It was an ominous development for the boys, Stamper acknowledged, for "it made known to us the scarcity of supplies."[148]

Private Darr of the 43rd Tennessee remarked that the cannonading took on a personal reality on the morning of 29 May when a ball passed through his tent erected on the back lines near the river. Fortunately for him there was no one in it at the time. The evening brought with it an increase, as usual, in the Yankee artillery. "I wish Jef Davis and all the men who had a hand in bringing this war was in heavy loss," he maintained, "and then we would have peace."[149] It was one of the few times any of the Confederates blamed their own president for the war rather than the other side.

A most terrific cannonading from the enemy's lines marked the rising of the sun on 29 May, S. A. R. Swan wrote in his daily entry. "The shells were whistling through the air and bursting almost without intermission for nearly two hours." Other than that, little transpired during the day worthy of being written down until about 5 p.m., "when the enemy amused themselves by another furious bombardment." Their rifled guns sprayed shot and shell "all over the ground" inside the Confederate lines. The men got to their ditches, where they knew they were as safe as could be expected, and the non-combatants, Swan noted, "gathered in little squads around where the commissary and quartermaster men congregate," where they cooked the pitiful victuals for the soldiers, or assembled for ambulance duty near the hospital camps if required. "The boys sought the protection of a hillside and trees with an alacrity that was quite commendable to see," he noted. It was almost as if the citizens realized that the troops always knew where the safest places were. As a commissary officer, Swan recollected that on this date Pemberton sent around

---

[148] Stamper, "Travels of the 43rd Tennessee," 60–61.
[149] Darr, "Diary," 3.

his famous directive that required the name of every man for whom rations were to be drawn. "It is now becoming a question of bread with us," Swan admitted. The directive from the commanding general stressed, "we can hold Vicksburg as long as we have a ration or a cartridge," so the decision was made that rations should be "economized with the utmost care possible." The large quantities of field peas and rice were to be used to spread out the limited amount of corn, and what meat remained was to be carefully conserved.[150]

"If we have to remain cooped up here for two months eating mush made of cornmeal, peas and rice mixed together," Swan indicated, "[while] lying in the trenches under a hot sun by day and heavy dews by night, with shells from land and water dropping around and amongst us all the time, shall we have not earned a little rest?" His suggested that his government "encourage the men with the hope of furlough, to see their homes and families as soon as the siege has passed."[151]

The enemy's sharpshooting ritual, General John C. Vaughn wrote in a daily report, began as usual on 30 May. Around 5 p.m., the enemy cut loose for at least an hour with their batteries across the Mint Spring Bayou for all they were worth. Their attention drew no casualties among his brigade high atop the ridge or the batteries and Mississippi State home guards attached to his command. "The men are at work every night," he noted, strengthening their fortifications along his lines.[152]

Hynds of the 31st Tennessee shared old news on this date's entry when he got around to reporting the arrival of the courier Fontaine, but added that Fontaine had brought a dispatch from Johnston and "20,000 [percussion] caps, an article we are likely to run short of." In matters concerning their commanding officers, complaints often came from various quarters the generals were seldom seen outside their headquarters, but Hynds noted on this date, both Stevenson and Pemberton reviewed the boys "in the trenches."[153]

With the dawning of 30 May, "the sun arose in its undimmed splendor this morning," Clack of the 43rd Tennessee wrote, "and all is quiet and still around old Vicksburg." Not even a gun being fired could be heard along the lines. Anchored out in the river were the gunboats, but no hostile intent was evident from their dark foreboding presence. By seven that evening, some mortar fire

---

[150] Swan, "A Tennessean in the Siege of Vicksburg," 361.
[151] Ibid.
[152] Report of Gen. John C. Vaughn, 30 May 1863, *Official Records*, ser. 1, vol. 24, pt. 2, p. 690.
[153] Hynds, "Original Handwritten Notes," 7.

from the rafts out in the river had begun, with an occasional round from a gunboat in the lower channel.[154] Stamper of the 43rd Tennessee also commented on the clear and calm day, adding, "not a gun to be heard." As the day progressed, however, the Yankee fire increased as heavy and steady as ever. By nightfall, the enemy had opened up with their mortars on the position occupied by the Gillespie's reserves, shelling his men until 9 p.m. The massive rounds resulted in little damage, Stamper observed, though a Louisiana artilleryman nearby suffered a mortal wound. "It gives us great trouble seeing one hundred pound balls falling all around us," he asserted, "sometimes bursting over our heads with the fragments flying in every direction." In a fatality not attributed to hostile action, Stamper indicated that Sergeant William J. Lawson of Rogersville, Hawkins County, and Company "E died in the hospital of fever.[155]

"How I would like to hear from home," wrote James Henry Darr of the 43rd Tennessee, a thought that must have been in the mind of every man in the ditches. It was the source of considerable "uneasying" for him. The usual sharpshooting and cannonading continued, he wrote, adding to the typical random mortar fire from the river during the night hours. "We look for General Johnston next week," he sighed. "We hope to be able to hold out till he arrives. We have 15 thousand men against 100 thousand."[156] Though overestimating his enemy's and underestimating his own army's numbers, the heavy enemy fire directed toward their positions must have made the disparities seem plausible.

Good weather and a cool breeze refreshed Yankee and Rebel alike, Swan of Stephen D. Lee's Brigade reported, and the "cumulus clouds afford shade to the boys in the trenches." Swan's rations for the day consisted of field peas, corn, and rice ground up together, making a substitute for bread. "It is impossible to make it palatable by baking in the ordinary way," he wrote, and the "men are required to boil it thoroughly into mush, then fry it, [though] lard issues come in small quantities for that purpose." When the mortar boats throw shells, Swan observed, the river batteries on their end of the line tended to reply, if only in a modest manner. These gun and mortar boats had been lengthening their range as of late, and smacked Vicksburg indiscriminately.

---

[154] Clack, "Personal Diary," 2.
[155] Stamper, "Travels of the 43rd Tennessee," 61.
[156] Darr, "Diary," 3.

Swan was amazed that "though a number of houses are struck, no great damage is being done."[157]

General Vaughn, commanding his brigade on the far left flank and northern edge of Vicksburg, noted in his daily report for 31 May that his lines had received "heavy" artillery fire the preceding day, but his men had not return it.[158] Occasionally, the sharpshooters from the foe's fortifications across the draw from him fire sometimes, and his men in return let off "an occasional shot" when the enemy presented himself. "About an hour before daylight this morning the enemy opened fire upon our trenches," George Hynds of the 31st Tennessee reported, "and we supposed again they were going to make a general attack." At daylight the firing died off, however, and all the routine returned to its usual volume. Around 11 o'clock (probably p.m.), the mortars commenced their shelling into Reynolds's lines, and "they fell a good deal too close to be comfortable." Hynds wrote that the shells continued to fall really close to him, but none had exploded. (Few, seemingly, ever did, since the fuse system of the day was extremely crude and inefficient. Oftentimes the flaming fuse was actually extinguished by the act of being fired or soon into its flight.) "The day was very hot and sultry," Hynds concluded in his daily entry,[159] indicating that a suffocating humidity intensified in the bottoms of the ditches where they crouched.

Concerning the "fierce bombardment," Lieutenant Calvin M. Smith of the 31st Tennessee pointed out "the whole line seemed to be in a blaze, doing our trenches some damage." The men had been ordered to have plenty of ammunition and await any emergency. Smith also noted that the "yank pots" continued throwing mortar rounds their way, but as Reynolds's lines (with the exception of the 43rd Tennessee in reserve) were out of their view, they were not shelled as much. "Some shells," he asserted, "fell to the ground before bursting, then exploded, tearing up the earth and dust, resembling a coal pit."[160] Their regimental chaplain, Napoleon Bonaparte Goforth, had conducted a prayer meeting the evening before and intended to have another that day after dark. The sharpshooters in both lines continued to be active, according to Smith, with Reynolds's marksmen believed to have killed several careless Yankees. Smith recorded that, by using a spyglass through an observation port,

---

[157] Swan, "A Tennessean in the Siege of Vicksburg," 362.

[158] Report of Gen. John C. Vaughn, 30 May 1863, *Official Records*, ser. 1, vol. 24, pt. 2, p. 690.

[159] Hynds, "Original Handwritten Notes," 61.

[160] Smith, *A Smith in Service*, 55.

he had watched Federal sharpshooters as they loaded and fired. Up and down the river the enemy continued to move transports filled with troops and munitions of war. "The yankies have placed a gun battery to our right and are firing it at our [Claiborne's] battery," Smith wrote, "which sometimes passes over our heads making a hideous noise as they drive through the tree limbs over us."[161] The boys in the back trenches on the bluff over the river took note of the racket to and from Reynolds's main line, Stamper of the 43rd Tennessee noted. "There was a constant flashing and roaring of artillery, so much so we thought a general engagement had commenced."[162]

"We put on our tricks," Stamper wrote, "and held ourselves in readiness for an attack on our part of the line, but no demonstration was made." Indeed, as it was later discovered, the fire was merely a cannonade and not a general attack. Down on the lines observable to Stamper, the day was quiet, with only an occasional shell from the mortars across the river.[163] These did no damage to men or to the breastwork.

William Clack of the 43rd Tennessee stated, however, at 3 a.m. on 31 May, the heavy cannonading resumed all along the lines. Then an hour later, the gunboats added to the barrage. Through all this, Clack noted that only one man in the 3rd Maryland Battery was wounded. At 6 a.m., the shelling slacked off, and only an occasional cannon shot disturbed the peace the remainder of this Lord's Day.[164]

James Darr of the 43rd Tennessee took a walk up town on this Sunday, 31 May, though he found little to do in Vicksburg. Once back in the works, he found nothing happening and became convinced that the Yankees had decided to starve them out since they could not whip them in their works. As for the best place to avoid fragments or sharpshooter injury, Darr suggested, "the ditches are the safest plan."[165]

The Federals initiated "a furious cannonade from their land batteries" at daylight, Swan wrote in his journal, though it let up a half hour later. These shells landed all about the city streets, and there seemed to be "no place within our lines...beyond their reach." He did report, however, that the little knolls around town tended to provide shelter from the Union guns. "Every little dell is filled up with wagon mules and the corps of commissaries and quartermasters

---

[161] Ibid.
[162] Stamper, "Travels of the 43rd Tennessee," 61.
[163] Ibid.
[164] Clack, "Personal Diary," 2.
[165] Darr, "Diary," 4.

and their assistants engaged in cooking, and the like," Swan noted, being one of their number. The water for the boys in the trenches was brought in at night from the river.[166] The Father of Waters off Vicksburg also served as a dump for dead animals, refuse, and other filth contributed to both by the Confederate garrison and the Yankees besieging from the upper ditches they occupied.

"The barrels [in which the water comes in] is covered in bundles and blankets [which] makes very good drinking," Swan recorded. He asserted that the boys had been confined in the trenches for fourteen days as the month of May 1863 expired, and there was among them a growing anxiety to hear "the distant booming of Johnston's cannon." Down on the right flank of the army, the Feds were beginning to concentrate some forces, which, Swan observed, had caused the pickets of Stevenson's Division (as Reynolds reported earlier) to be brought in.[167]

---

[166] Swan, "A Tennessean in the Siege of Vicksburg," 362.
[167] Ibid.

CHAPTER 10

"There Is No Romance to the Actors"

1-15 June

The Tedious Routine Continues. The last day of May and the first few days of June found the heat pouring down like a fiery wave striking point blank on the dirt ditches and what sparse scorched grass remained around the soldiers at Vicksburg. Gun barrels left in the sun raised blisters when touched. Trees within the works not killed by the constant barrage drooped motionless as the life was sucked from them by the heat and lack of moisture. The blinding haze of the Mississippi summer seemed to make objects in the distance shimmer and quiver. After two weeks, the air was thick around the boys, with the smells of baked filth that plagued confined men, and the stench of death and rot from the slaughter yards where the last of the cattle (and later the mules) were prepared for their consumption. These young men aged beyond their years with the permanent sun squints were filthy and were dressed in crusty uniforms stained with the accumulation of their daily sweat. These men moved no more than required because they respected their enemy's inerrant sharpshooters, and because they were becoming too feeble and weak for wasted motion.

By 1 June more Southern reinforcements had arrived in Mississippi, few of whom would ever be called to lift a finger in relief of their Vicksburg brethren. The Confederate infantry division of W. H. T. Walker containing some 7,500 men detrained at Yazoo City joining other commands there. Additionally on this date, General John C. Breckenridge's division of 5,500 men dispatched from Bragg's Army of Tennessee arrived in what remained of the burned out capital of Jackson. Joe Johnston was nearby in Canton with a portion of his Army of the Relief, whose total numbers, augmented by Breckenridge and Walker, were now some 22,000 men.[1] Pemberton's numbers, of course, remained static at around 29,500 in the defenses of Vicksburg, though many

---

[1] Smith, Appendix C: Opposing Forces, Vicksburg Campaign, *Compelled to Appear in Print*, 200–201.

were unfit for duty. Grant had accumulated 51,000 men in the vicinity, with reinforcements on the way.

General Vaughn stated in his 1 June daily report to his divisional commander Martin Luther Smith that at 3:30 the night before, the Yankees began a heavy artillery barrage on the lines occupied by his brigade and attached units of home guards. The sleep of his men was interrupted for about one hour. Each of these nightly "wake ups" brought the whole brigade at a rush to their position in the works (a routine all were accustomed by this time), though by now they had doubtlessly stopped worrying about any enemy assaults up Fort Hill. Later at about 8 a.m., Vaughn reported that the enemy had focused their artillery on his 32–pounders' position on the extreme right. The gun returned fire for a time, but "due to some deficiency in the carriage," it discharged only a few rounds. Thereafter, he noted, "everything was unusually quiet the remainder of the day."[2]

The Mississippi State Troops. At around 10 p.m., on 1 June, Vaughn indicated that he sought to strengthen his line on that quarter by moving Major J. R. Stevens's Mississippi State troops to the extreme right at a point, he lamented, that "is not yet strong enough."[3] These state troops had been assigned to Vaughn to shore up the numbers of his depleted brigade, which was smaller than average even before losing so many men at the Big Black Bridge. Subject to considerable ridicule from the veterans in the army, these Mississippi home guard forces were placed initially between the 60th Tennessee as Vaughn's left flank and the artillery atop Fort Hill covering a half-mile of the line. Vaughn's own men by this point of the campaign were no strangers to the snide asides of others, so doubtlessly they had their fun with these Mississippians who were either too old or too young to serve as regulars, but were compelled to do their duty during the present emergency. Bob Houston, serving as General Vaughn's chief of staff, commented as an impartial observer in regard to their trench construction peculiarities: "As to how deep [their] ditches would have been dug by the time the siege was over, this deponent saith not. These state troops were worse than groundhogs, for they soon had their ditches so deep that they could not reach the top of them with the muzzles of their guns, and orders had to be made to fill them up."[4]

---

[2] Report of Gen. John C. Vaughn, 1 June 1863, *Official Records*, ser. 1, vol. 24, pt. 2, p. 691.

[3] Ibid.

[4] Houston, "A History of Vaughn's Brigade," 200.

Another Confederate chronicler with a Louisiana regiment noted that near their camps prior to the siege "was an encampment of the Mississippi militia, composed of men of good intentions, but most woefully ignorant of tactics and discipline." He noted that their attempts at drill gave rise to some "rich, racy and laughable scenes." These home guards, he wrote, "afforded the never-ending source of amusement to the disciplined veterans of the regiment, and an opportunity for indulging their propensity for fun."[5] He recollected:

> the drill of the militia was always the occasion for outbursts such as the following: "Now, men, mind you stand up straight, and form a line like a ram's horn." "Now mind, I'm going to fling you into fours." "Into fours—git!" "Into twos—git!" "Now I'll swing you like a gate." "Swing like a gate—git!" This new style of issuing orders was always received with uproarious mirth, and so confused the amateur soldiers as to completely incapacitate them for performing any evolutions.[6]

There is little doubt that Vaughn's men, after their shameful performance at the Big Black River, enjoyed having such irregulars around to absorb some of the contempt that had previously fallen on them from the other brigades in Martin Luther Smith's Division. Despite being made sport of by all "regular" Confederate soldiers, these old men and boys in the days ahead were killed or wounded by the sharpshooters and artillery shells in numbers proportionate to the other commands on the upper lines. Vaughn reported that his 60th Tennessee suffered one wounded, and that the Mississippi State Troops, also under his command, had another man wounded during the bombardment on the town.[7]

Pea Bread, Sugar and Molasses. Robert Bachman of the 60th Tennessee addressed the degenerating food and water rations by observing that their poor quality and low quantity caused the men in the ditches to lose strength and weight rapidly. Some of the men became so weak and sick that "they had to be sent to the field hospitals, such as we had." Those remaining did what they could to bolster spirits. "The boys in the trenches nearest me," Bachman wrote, "often talked of the good food we used to have in our far away Tennessee homes, and of how we would feast if we ever got back to them." Bread and

---

[5] Tunnard, *A Southern Record*, 204.

[6] Ibid.

[7] Report of Gen. John C. Vaughn, 1 June 1863, *Official Records*, ser. 1, vol. 24, pt. 2, p. 691.

butter, all the milk they could drink, cheese and ham and chicken, he indicated, "never looked so good to us, before or after." Remembrance of his hungry days in the trenches, he wrote years later, "will always move me to feed any hungry man who comes my way, however much of a tramp he may be."[8]

The Yankees Move in More Field Pieces to Reynolds's Front. Alexander W. Reynolds as a part of his official report related to his brigade's activities during the Vicksburg campaign indicated that the Yankees were also troubling his position. They placed "a battery about 800 yards to my front and opened fire on me," he reported. This annoyance was short-lived, however, since Ferd Claiborne's 3rd Maryland Battery, as partial artillery support for the brigade, skillfully employed its own rifle pieces and soon rendered the Northern guns silent.[9] Otherwise, matters in Reynolds's trenches, Stamper of the 43rd Tennessee indicated in his journal, were pretty quiet in front of the ditches. There had been, however, some firing all day all along the line. That evening he reported that rations were brought out "composed of beef, molasses and bread made of 1/3 meal, 1/3 rice, and 1/3 field peas."[10] Though some of the boys did not like this, others of a patriotic bent declared, "if Vicksburg can be held by eating such food, they would willingly live on it for a long time yet." Regardless, Stamper opined with a bit of resignation, "it was mighty tough."[11]

"Heavy cannonading was heard this morning [1 June] just at daybreak on our left," Clack of the 43rd Tennessee stated in his diary on this date. The boys made ready to shoulder their weapons, with all believing that there had to be an assault on the lines somewhere. By 7 a.m., he wrote, all became relatively quiet again. An hour later, the cannonading slackened off from that experienced at daylight, though it continued "in a mild manner all day long against the front lines."[12] James Darr of the 43rd Tennessee agreed in his journal entry, though there was some shelling from the river, it was basically calm along the lines.[13]

Captain George Hynds of the 31st Tennessee reported the day's weather to be quite warm, "and the Yankees have made it warmer still with their shells." There had been no unusual small arms activity, except between the various picket posts. "The army is now living on poor beef and coarse meal made of

---

[8] Bachman, "Reminiscences of Childhood," 22.

[9] Report of Gen. Alexander W. Reynolds, undated, *Official Records*, ser. 1, vol. 24, pt. 2, p. 356.

[10] Stamper, *Travels of the 43rd Tennessee*, 61–62.

[11] Ibid., 62.

[12] Clack, "Personal Diary," 2.

[13] Darr, "Diary," 4.

corn and stock [field] peas," he wrote, "but the men are in good spirits and ready for the enemy to make an attack on us."[14]

"These 15 days we have held the ditches and still we feel as able to defend as at the first," Calvin Smith of Persia, Hawkins County, and the 31st Tennessee stated, echoing Hynds's sentiment. He added: "Nay, more willing than ever, as the enemy is so certain of victory and no doubt they would let us march out with the army and all our arms and munitions of war just to gain possession of this devoted city." Such would not happen, however, until Joseph Johnston himself ordered it, Smith declared. "General Pemberton came around and thinks we can hold this place until our stock of provisions becomes exhausted," Smith reported. Their rations were now one-third corn, one-third field peas, and a third rice, ground together. He noted that this was despite the fact that the army had a large number of beef cattle being fed on cane and grass. The horses and mules had for a time been allowed no corn as feed, and still seemed to be doing well. The water supply continued "pretty good," according to Smith.[15]

"Our pickets are and have been popping off at the enemy pretty close for some time," Smith stated. "Company G had one private, Nathan Ball, son of Thomas Ball [of Bulls Gap, Hawkins County], shot in the hips this morning, but [it was] not considered mortal." Several Yankees, according to Smith, were seen to fall in exchanges between the pickets. The Northern navy out on the river continued to throw an occasional shell toward their ditches. Describing other conditions around the lines, Smith noted that the Feds had placed a battery to their front the night before, "but it had done no harm yet." Other infringements to which the besieged were becoming acclimated were not being able to "stray off [get up, move around]." The cooking was done in the hollows and cane breaks; the water within the lines was brought up and divided by sergeants designated for such duty. "Our men are in good spirits," Smith believed, "and there is very little sickness ... considering the numbers, climate and everything." The boys were ready to fight in the ditches if attacked, even though many suffered from bowel complaints that weakened them. Smith noted that it would be hard for many of them to make a march of any distance, should they be called upon to "cut" their way out.[16]

Captain Clark of the 59th Tennessee noted on 1 June that the "hardships and privations of the men were beyond description." One source of supplies had

---

[14] Hynds, "Original Handwritten Notes," 8–9.
[15] Smith, *A Smith in Service*, 55.
[16] Ibid.

been cut off before the siege commenced, he wrote in his journal, and "we had been living for months on beef from cattle that were so poor, they could not get back up off the ground when down."[17] Two brigades over to the left of Reynolds's men, Samuel Swan, who seemed to have as much free time and abundantly more writing paper than any one, wrote in his diary on this date that "at 3 o'clock this morning the enemy opened a vigorous fire of artillery, throwing their projectiles at random over almost every part of the ground inside the entrenchments." He reported that such had been the Yankees' practice for the past couple of mornings, but little damage resulted from it other than "the extreme annoyance of the missiles flying in every direction." Swan indicated that their firing usually lasted a half hour in duration and reoccurred at intervals all day. The Federals began to press Barton's Georgians on Reynolds's right, he reported, with close skirmishing. "Our troops are planting some new batteries of siege guns at different places along inside our works," Swan noted, "which are intended to cover any attempt to advance their lines." These pieces, as of 1 June, were not yet operational.[18]

The wind commenced that night as a stiff breeze, Swan reported, and coupled with the shells falling thick and fast, "the night was a night of terrors." The Union gunners' indiscriminate shelling was said to have set fire to the south side of Washington Street, where many Vicksburg businesses were, and burned down a "whole square" of commercial buildings. Within some of the warehouses there, Swan wrote, "several hogsheads of sugar belonging to private parties were destroyed." It was later claimed, however, that these storage facilities belonging to speculators were not burned by the enemy shelling at all, but had fallen victim to the righteous indignation of some of the soldiers in the garrison. If the troops were not going to be allowed to partake of the foodstuffs contained inside, neither would anyone else. As a commissary officer, Swan noted that there was a concerted effort by the quartermasters to drive most of the governmental mules and horses out of the Confederate lines because these animals competed with the cattle for the limited patches of grazing area that remained. The quartermasters also had the unpleasant duty of having to haul off dead animals after dark and throw them in the river, along with generally policing Vicksburg and lines of trash and debris. As for the horses and mules, for which there was now no need within the army, Swan wrote, "hundreds" of

---

[17] Clark, *Valleys of the Shadow*, 24.
[18] Swan, "A Tennessean in the Siege of Vicksburg," 362.

them had been chased out toward the bluecoat lines, though large numbers of them were still within the confines "running at large and often getting shot."[19]

Vaughn's Annoying 32–Pounder. On 2 June, General Vaughn reported in his daily summary that the Yankee artillery was still determined to destroy the 32–pounder of Lynch's Battery on the right of his line. The enemy's preoccupation with that gun could only be supposed, but perhaps it had been doing effective work either on the river or on Sherman's lines on the other side of Mint Springs Bayou. The gun was mounted high and visible on the ridge east of Fort Hill, and had become a major irritant to the enemy soldiers across the draw. Vaughn stated that its crew tried to answer the enemy's fire "for the purpose of finding the range," but the embrasure that protected it would not allow the piece to be depressed enough to hit anything down in the Mint Springs hollow. During an exchange with opposing batteries, Vaughn reported, "one man was killed and three wounded" among its gun crew, along with one man wounded in the 3rd Battalion of the Mississippi State Troops. Even with all that artillery activity, Vaughn reported that the day was otherwise "unusually" quiet except for a little sharpshooting.[20]

The Grapevine Telegraph. The boys in Reynolds's Brigade, according to Captain Hynds of the 31st Tennessee, "were twice aroused and ordered into the trenches believing the Yankees were going to make an attack on our batteries," but after some spirited musketry from the Confederate trenches, the Federals' desires soon waxed cold. Hynds addressed the burning of the city block in Vicksburg, while noting that the two Union cannon mounted in front of Reynolds's works the previous night were now firing at them. "The shells whistled and exploded too close to our entrenchments to be comfortable," he contended. Other batteries were being implanted close to the lines, "and it is believed that they will make a general attack soon."[21]

"I was officer of the guard last night [2 June]," Calvin Smith of the 31st Tennessee noted in his daily journal entry. He made rounds of the brigade's ditches around 11 p.m., and then turned in. Sometime later, Sergeant Ball awakened him and warned that the enemy pickets were advancing. Lieutenant Smith went back to the ditches and found the boys all alert with Enfields pointed in the direction the enemy was thought to be approaching. Again, it

---

[19] Ibid.

[20] Report of Gen. John C. Vaughn, 2 June 1863, *Official Records*, ser. 1, vol. 24, pt. 2, p. 691.

[21] Hynds, "Original Handwritten Notes," 9–10.

proved a false alarm.[22] Generally, heavy rifle fire could be heard occasionally, he wrote, along with a few cannon discharges.

Dispatches had come through the lines that indicated that General Edmund Kirby-Smith's army was at "Natches," and that General Sterling Price had his forces "at the mouth of the White River above." If both reports proved true, Smith maintained, the Federals would be in as bad a fix as they thought they had the garrison. He reported that the enemy battery to their front was now set up, but had not thrown any rounds their way yet.[23] He added the interesting news that the city's Negroes had been turned out of the lines and told to make for Jackson, which led him to conclude "not many of them got there, I reckon."[24] Perhaps he thought that they had either become "contrabands" and subject to the pleasure of their Yankee liberators just across the way, or had been killed in the attempt.

Though occasional cannon discharges could be heard, Clack of the 43rd Tennessee wrote in his journal, "all appears tolerably quiet." He was writing in his journal at 11 p.m., and stated that the moon was shining brightly while the Northerners continued the shelling of Vicksburg. Sounding incredibly commonplace and routine, Clack reported that Lieutenant James C. Hopkins had "started home tonight."[25] It was mind-boggling to consider the extreme daring it would have taken to get through the lines at this point in the siege.

Stamper wrote that it was unusually quiet on 2 June, which "satisfied us that the enemy was tired of trying our works." They had become content apparently to wait until the Confederates' rations ran out. The garrison, however, still had hoped that Johnston's Army of the Relief would "cut them out." Rations for the day were pea bread, Stamper recorded, "which by this time proved not to be good food."[26]

Cannonading and the proportionate number of casualties continued, according to Swan with Lee's Brigade. The grapevine telegraph was busy, he recorded, with all sorts of sensational nonsense. The fact that the boys knew that a courier had recently gotten through the lines from General Joseph

---

[22] Concerning the fire in Vicksburg, Smith reported that it was set "supposedly by the hand of the incendiary, [and] consumed several large store houses and their contents. Very little was saved …though the soldiers managed to carry out some tobacco." (Smith, *A Smith in Service*, 55). "One square of the city burned up last night," Darr of the 43rd Tennessee wrote.

[23] Ibid.

[24] Darr, "Diary," 4.

[25] Clack, "Personal Diary," 2.

[26] Stamper, "Travels of the 43rd Tennessee," 62.

Johnston gave "plausibility to every tale that is started." Swan believed that many of the rumors actually originated within the Federal lines since in many places the pickets from both sides coexisted in such close proximity before their trenches that some had become quite friendly. "They meet and trade coffee for tobacco," he stated, and by this fraternization, the gossip of each camp was exchanged. Though all this sort of "news" was suspect, Swan indicated, each morsel had "an effect on the morale of the soldiers." One of the rumors that circulated on this date was that the distant firing heard to the east was supposed to be around the Big Black, and the boys "thought it to be Gen. Johnston's cavalry advance."[27] Should this be true, of course, the hope-starved garrison knew that it was the beginning at last of the initial probe coming towards them from the so-called Army of the Relief. With this, Swan still believed that the men around him by this point of the siege were generally more concerned with getting "out of the jug" alive and safe than they had been during the first days when they had determined to fight to the last ration and the last cartridge.

"No one who has never been in the same condition," the Bradley County native wrote, "can appreciate the feeling that pervades a beleaguered [besieged] army, cut off from communication with friends, surrounded by forces they know not how numerous, [and] uncertain when the attack will be made." Compounding this instability, he acknowledged, was the awareness that the Confederate lines were so vast and distant that "one side may be carried and the other side may be ignorant of it until too late to remedy it." These factors all worked against the defenders, he lamented. Swan closed his daily entry with the poignant desire that "I hope never to be besieged again."[28]

By 3 June, Johnston's numbers at Canton had swelled with the arrival of the cavalry division of William H. Jackson, numbering some 3,000 troopers. Around the same date, Grant received General Nathan Kimball's division from Stephen Hurlbut in Memphis composed of twelve regiments of infantry.[29] This allotment allowed Grant to complete his encirclement of all the Vicksburg fortifications, since he now had enough men to close off the Confederate far right flank from the vicinity of the Warrenton road to the river. The brigades of General Seth Barton and Alexander Reynolds now had facing them for the first time during the siege significant numbers of Union infantry. The rifle pits and ditches below them seemed now to seethe with bluecoats. Obviously,

---

[27] Swan, "A Tennessean at the Siege of Vicksburg," 362.

[28] Ibid., 363.

[29] Smith, Appendix C: Opposing Forces, Vicksburg Campaign, *Compelled to Appear in Print*, 201.

Pemberton's numbers remained constant in the aggregate, though ever dwindling in effectives due to sickness, wounds, and deaths.

General John Vaughn in his daily report indicated that though the men under his command suffered no casualties the day before, the Yankees again opened "heavy artillery fire" on his brigade about 1 a.m., 3 June. After the firing ceased, all was quiet, he reported, until 9 a.m. the next morning. Then, it was again a battery from the enemy's works that threw shells at the 32–pounder on the right of his line high atop the ridge. This fire was ignored. The enemy kept up their fire for nearly a half hour, and then, "with the exception of an occasional shot from a sharp-shooter," quiet prevailed until nearly 6:30 p.m. when they suddenly began shelling Vaughn's lines with six pieces of artillery until dark.[30]

Watch was kept in earnest during the night just passed, Calvin Smith of the 31st Tennessee reported, but all remained quiet and the enemy attempted no mischief. There was news that the Federals were seriously fortifying along the western bank of the Big Black River in the vicinity of the 17 May battlefield in anticipation of an advance by Johnston's army. A major engagement was predicted there soon. "A great battle may be fought here in this quarter, or again a retreat," Smith suggested, adding, "this would be equal to a heavy defeat to the army that attempts to escape without a fight." He indicated that the day's weather was good, warm, and humid, though the breezes from the river helped. Sleeping was comfortable with just one blanket, as the night air cooled the trenches some. "I am preparing to send a letter by the first mail through," Smith reported, "though we are surrounded, and it takes a cunning man to get through the lines at night." The "present emergency," as the besieged termed their plight, was not expected to last since General Pemberton, according to Smith, had ordered full rations for the men. Smith noted his personal commissary bill for the month of April had been $30.50, while his bill for May had only been $6. He indicated that the reason for the lower bill was that the boys were constantly on the march during May, with little time for drawing rations or cooking.[31]

"The boys have holes in the ground to get in when the Yanks throw shells," James Darr of the 43rd Tennessee wrote in his journal. "All look like hogs [and] are a heap more dirty." Though it was relatively quiet around the lines in the morning, according to Darr, the Yankee gunboats flung rounds

[30] Report of Gen. John C. Vaughn, 3 June 1863, *Official Records*, ser. 1, vol. 24, pt. 2, p. 691.

[31] Smith, *A Smith in Service*, 55–56.

their way occasionally. At around 5 p.m. a shell from a gunboat wounded Private Charley Graves, whose leg would probably have to be amputated. After dark, Darr, for the first time found himself out on picket between the lines. From there, he heard heavy fire on the left, which added to his nervousness even with an Enfield in his hands.[32]

Stamper of the 43rd Tennessee noted that the pickets engaged in some exchange of musket fire today, during which Lieutenant John H. Cody of Monroe County and the 3rd Tennessee was killed. There was also some shelling directed toward their works from the vessels on the river, according to Stamper. Repeating Darr's news, Stamper noted that Private Charley Graves of Company I caught a fragment from one of these exploding shells, shattering the bone between his ankle and knee, and necessitating the amputation of his leg. The 43rd Tennessee, as part of the reserve for Stevenson's Division, was called up just as darkness closed in to support General Cumming's Georgians on their left. They moved to the rear of Cumming's right flank, where we "lay down and slept till daylight." Stamper also indicated that there was a considerable degree of shelling that night coming in from the river.[33]

Clack recorded in his diary that the morning was calm and quiet, though beginning about 3 p.m., the gunboats began shelling. Though the boys wrote continuously that the shelling did not worry them much, it still had an unsettling effect when a "lucky" shot fell in their midst, for it brought all too clearly to their attention that serious wounds or even death could occur randomly to themselves or fellow soldiers with whom they had been conversing with just moments before. At 4 p.m., there was heavy cannonading on the back lines and some musketry along the main line. The grapevine telegraph spread the word that Johnston's attack on Grant's rear was set for Friday, 5 June. Clack also indicated that the 43rd Tennessee left their trenches at 8 p.m. and moved up the line to the left to support a weak point there where the Halls' Ferry Road entered the works. This point was known by the boys as "The Georgia Salient," due to Cumming's Brigade being positioned there, and always proved to be a hot spot right between the left flank of Colonel Reynolds's position and the right flank of the Georgians. Clack stated that cannon fire was currently targeted for that vicinity. An hour later the gunboats had "come up" and were

---

[32] Darr, "Diary," 4.
[33] Stamper, "Travels of the 43rd Tennessee," 62.

rapidly shelling the bottoms in the direction of town. After an hour or so, the shelling ceased and "we got to sleep a little."[34]

George Hynds of the 31st Tennessee reported in his daily entry that the mortars were busy on the river. In front of their works, Reynolds's pickets were shooting at the bluecoats, who "never fail to fire in return." In the exchange Lieutenant Cody of the 3rd Tennessee "was killed in front of our trenches by a ball from the Yankee pickets." To the left, Hynds reported, other fighting was heard.[35]

Despite all this activity just down the works, Swan, with Lee's Brigade, thanked kind Providence for the unusual quiet that prevailed up the line in front of his position and "for protecting us day by day." He reported that sickness minimal and that the weather was "favorable." "Oh, that men would see the goodness of the Lord," he proclaimed, "and our nation would humble itself before Him and acknowledge Him in all our ways." He liked to believe that the "good people throughout the Confederacy" were lifting up their hearts in supplication to the Lord, for the "safety of their country in this its trying hour." A Northern victory here, Swan asserted, would undoubtedly encourage them not only to open up the Mississippi for their malicious ends, but also to prolong the war. About sundown, Swan reported, "a furious artillery duel commenced" because some Confederate batteries that had been established at the beginning of the siege were being fired to "find the range." This annoyed the Yankees, and soon the exchange "became general." A gunboat came up river and threw a considerable number of large caliber shells whose "whizzing fragments landed in the City, thus giving an idea of their tremendous power." He believed that even with that the ordnances' terrible potential, evidence of damage was not considerable. "One loaded shell from a Parrott gun struck a tree at the root of which a number of us were sitting," he wrote, "and dropped, half burying itself in the ground a few feet from us and scattering splinters

---

[34] Clack, "Personal Diary," 2. Sometimes the constant bombardment had the opposite effect. One of the besieged soldiers described one particularly violent evening: "The hill trembled as if shaken be an earthquake. The effect on the men was as a rocking cradle to a sleepy babe, and when a messenger reported to our colonel that the line up in the trenches was in danger of breaking and needed support, in calling the regiment into line he found all but half a dozen or so soundly sleeping. But a few of us were awake, and we were soon rushing toward the firing line." Payne, "Missouri Troops in the Vicksburg Campaign," 36/7 (July 1928): 377.

[35] Hynds, "Original Handwritten Notes," 10.

around at our feet."[36] Swan's strong belief in a merciful God was strengthened even more as a result of their miraculous escape from injury.

In a rather rare display of Confederate artillery prowess, at 8:30 a.m. on 4 June, Vaughn ordered his 32-pounder naval gun to open up on the enemy lines "for range." This piece was soon augmented by the firing of one of his 24-pounder siege cannon and a 3–inch rifle. The Union forces returned "a desultory fire during the day," Vaughn reported. His intent was to draw away the increasingly effective barrage on his second 32-pounder, where "the night's work [might go on] undisturbed." During the night Vaughn had his 24-pounder siege pieces continue to fire, hoping that they would discourage the Yankees from trying to plant a cannon at the Edwards's house. Although the Yankees had previously tried to do this, he stated that there was no sign "of it being in position yet." He reported that their sharpshooters had now advanced along the Mint Springs Bayou as far as "the mound near Colonel Pitts' former headquarters." Three men in his brigade, Vaughn noted, were wounded the previous day: one man in the 60th Tennessee and two in the 62nd Tennessee.[37]

On the lower end of the line, Colonel Alexander W. Reynolds stated that during the nights of 3 and 4 June the Yankees had positioned four heavy caliber guns "which opened up on the 5th at daylight." This time the 3rd Maryland Battery could not deter them from their work because of their distance deep within the federal lines just beyond range of the lighter caliber Confederate field pieces. Reynolds indicated in his official report that these guns "continued to play upon my works incessantly throughout the siege, except at night and a few hours during the heat of the day."[38]

Picket Duty between the Ditches. On 4 June, Lieutenant Calvin M. Smith of the 31st Tennessee provided details of what it was like to go on picket during the siege. "I was detailed to take charge of the guard this morning," he wrote, and just before daylight he took twenty men and two sergeants into the hellish uncertainty between the lines. Once there, he set up two posts composed of four men each, taking the rest of the detail back to the ditches set up for the picket reserve. From this point, the posts were relieved at 1 p.m., 8 p.m., and 1 a.m. The Confederate posts were within 400 yards of the Federal's ditches and 600 yards away from their batteries. "During these 24 hours, thousands of

---

[36] Swan, "A Tennessean in the Siege of Vicksburg," 363.

[37] Report of Gen. John C. Vaughn, 4 June 1863, *Official Records*, ser. 1, vol. 24, pt. 2, p. 691.

[38] Report of Col. Alexander W. Reynolds, undated, *Official Records*, ser. 1, vol. 24, pt. 2, p. 356.

musket shots were fired at us," Smith indicated, "some shell and canister clipping close to our heads, making a noise overhead like an over-grown [wasp] drone." Understandably, the men on picket were constantly ducking their heads involuntarily, in a routine he viewed as both terrifying and comic.[39]

"After dark," Smith continued, "the Yankie ditches, batteries and gunboats cut loose like volcanoes. Missiles were flying in every direction as if an eruption was in operation." The Yankees had made several charges that evening, leaving the ground covered with their dead and wounded. With the all the activity, Smith had grave concerns that his little outpost would be cut off from their lines. He cautioned his boys to be ever vigilant. They did not need to be reminded. Smith himself stood sentry with one of his men for a time, until giving in to exhaustion and returning to the reserve area where he fell asleep. The pickets stayed awake all night and watched the enemy. Smith wrote that Claiborne's 3rd Maryland Battery was directed to shell a strip of timber near where his pickets were positioned after those of Cumming's Brigade had "shamefully" run off when the Yankees began firing at them. Smith indicated that a major and perhaps half of the 3rd Tennessee (one half of the regiment was in the trenches, and the other half was held in reserve with the 43rd Tennessee) ventured forth to find where the enemy pickets were. For their trouble they found themselves fired on by other nervous pickets with the Georgians' outposts. Within moments, Smith indicated, Lillard's men returned fire.[40] If the boys in blue knew what was happening, they must have found it amusing to see sets of pickets from neighboring Confederate brigades firing away at one another. Fortunately, due to darkness and perhaps to panicky marksmanship, no harm was done to either command.

After being relieved from picket duty, Smith reported immediately to Colonel A. W. Reynolds, his brigade commander, suggested that a ditch be cut to form an embankment to provide protection for the pickets. Reynolds sent out a bold squad of volunteers to perform the task, immediately drawing the attention and fire of the enemy batteries, which sent the volunteers scurrying back to the main trenches. Apparently, Lieutenant John M. Carson, who had been involved in the *Webb* naval battle, had drawn the dangerous assignment, and he and Smith reported the situation to Reynolds. Will T. Dykes and John McClain of Smith's company were with the party, and upon their return were pronounced "brave men" by their comrades. After they left their attempt at the entrenching work, Dykes and another man returned to the scene with

---

[39] Smith, *A Smith in Service*, 56.
[40] Ibid.

considerable caution to see what the situation looked like. They found an Enfield musket left on the ground, abandoned by one of their men who had gone to a nearby spring for water, only to draw the fire of the Yankees. Unable to get back to his piece, he left it. Why the fortunate private in this dangerous arena did not take his rifle with him was unexplainable.[41]

James Darr of the 43rd Tennessee reported hearing heavier fighting the night before on the center and left, accompanied by heavy cannonading all night and into the morning. "This is horrible to be penned up in as small a place of two square miles to be butchered like so many hogs," he lamented, adding whimsically, "Am it not?" By 5 p.m., the cannonading had continued sparsely all day, and the men were getting tired of eating only pea bread only once a day. Their grumbling had intensified because they believed that more rations were available. "They think that there is 700 barrels of flour on hand," Darr suggested with considerable logic; "eat that first and if not relieved, then eat peas as bread."[42] But the generals rarely listened to the lowly soldier.

Clack of the 43rd Tennessee wrote on 4 June that the regiment found itself positioned "in Col. Bradford's [31st Tennessee] rear on the Hall's Ferry Road." As was routine now, he indicated that the sharpshooters began their specialty at daylight to the brigade's front. That day, an attack was expected. "The minies and shells are now whistling over our heads," he reported, causing him to add, "may God speed the happy hour when we shall be delivered from this unhappy state." Clack noted that at 5 p.m. word had come through the lines that some of the Louisianans had gone across the river the previous night and spiked the mortars that were opposite the town. A young black boy who lived in a house near the breastworks was decapitated by one of the liberators' cannon balls, he stated, and two others in the household were wounded. The residence was close to Reynolds's positions in the trenches, and the horrible occurrence was "in sight of us," Clack indicated. At dark, the firing had almost ceased with only an occasional "sharp and jarring report [of a musket] from the pickets."[43]

Taking and Defending the Picket Posts. "At daylight [on 4 June] the enemy opened fire with two batteries and a long line of sharp-shooters on our brigade and a Georgia regiment," George Hynds of the 31st Tennessee entered in his journal. Though the brigades on either side of Reynolds were both from Georgia, it was probably Alfred Cumming's men to the left of Reynolds's position. Just after sunset, the Yankees made a charge on the pickets' ditches in

---

[41] Ibid.
[42] Darr, "Diary," 4.
[43] Clack, "Personal Diary," 2.

front of the parapet, Hynds wrote, "and drove them back into the [main] lines." Hynds stated the night before two gunboats bombarded the Confederate hospital in Vicksburg for about an hour, "throwing 64-pound shells at it."[44]

"The sharp-shooters began their work at daylight," Stamper of the 43rd Tennessee recorded in his diary on 4 June, "and this they kept up till darkness enveloped us." That night at 2 a.m., he reported, the regiment was ordered to take a position on the right Reynolds's Brigade to await the enemy's pleasure after they had again driven in the pickets. In short order, the counterattack was launched, driving the Federals from the positions they had taken. After that, Stamper recorded, "we went back to our old position, getting there by daylight."[45]

On 4 June, Sergeant William H. Long of the 59th Tennessee returned to his command after being confined since the first day of the siege to a city hospital. Soon after he rejoined the regiment in the ditches, he "had a lock of whiskers shot from under my right ear without drawing a drop of blood."[46] No doubt Long was instantly impressed with the aim of the enemy's sharpshooters.

In regard to the mission leading to the destruction of the Union mortars, Swan wrote that since so few shells came from across the river, "it occasioned a report spread among the troops that a regiment of our men had gone over and captured and spiked them." Despite that good work, however, he stated that a number of men in Lee's Brigade had been wounded that day due to the bursting of another mortar round. Swan observed that another line of batteries mounting heavy guns were being positioned behind Lee's defenders, and had been placed "so as to fire once or twice within so that if our first line were stormed, the Yankees could hardly be able to hold their gain." The men continued to look anxiously for Johnston to move his forces up and raise the siege. "Continual duty in the trenches during the very hot weather and the poor food is telling on [the besieged] slowly," Swan observed. He stated that most believed the lines would be held until subsistence finally ran out, and many predicted that their rations could last for only another month.[47]

Vaughn's daily report on 5 June indicated that there was the usual annoying sharpshooting against his line, "interspersed with artillery fire." Major Stevens's Mississippi home guards, in their advanced position on the high embankment where the Mint Springs Bayou ran into the river and kept up a

---

[44] Hynds, "Original Handwritten Notes," 10.
[45] Stamper, "Travels of the 43rd Tennessee," 62.
[46] Long, "Autobiography," 1: 54.
[47] Swan, "A Tennessean in the Siege of Vicksburg," 363.

constant fire on the mound across the hollow, preventing Grant's men from throwing up any new fortifications there. The effects seemed rewarding since "no new works can be discovered at that point." Vaughn indicated that three men were was wounded during the day.[48] In Reynolds's Brigade, according to Stamper of the 43rd Tennessee, there had been "no change in affairs," though provisions were getting sparse. Though the grapevine telegraph had reported that today was the day that Johnston's Army of the Relief would initiate the attack to relieve the Vicksburg garrison, it never occurred. Ever optimistic despite enduring the whole siege up to that point, Stamper now questioned not *when* Johnston would strike, but *if*. The firing of the occasional enemy cannon led him to conclude that its purpose was to signal others rather than to harass or cause harm.[49]

In comparison to previous days' hostile activity, Clack of the 43rd Tennessee reported, "things are tolerable quiet this morning." The usual firing, now so routine, continued along the lines. In their reserve status, the boys of his regiment were still in their own ditches fronting the river. At seven that evening, all remained relatively quiet, and Clark prayed, "Oh! Lord, watch over us while we sleep tonight."[50]

James Darr of the 43rd Tennessee reported that a man named "Shamblin" was wounded accidentally through the arm on 5 June. Though the sharpshooters "popped" away all day, there had been little fighting. "Oh that I could see home and enjoy its pleasures once more," Darr lamented. "Oh that I was out of this place!"[51]

"It is now more dangerous for a man to expose himself anywhere along our line on account of the sharp-shooters," George Hynds of the 31st Tennessee confirmed. He indicated that the day was a hot one beneath a pitiless sun, during which several shells and minie balls had passed "within a few feet of my fly."[52] The boys had early on erected shelters composed of branches or tent-flies stretched over poles, usually behind their main trenches.

Though the firing continued, Swan of Lee's Brigade and Cleveland, Tennessee recorded that there were few casualties. The quartermaster boys had been busy the past few days, he noted, "paying off the soldiers, providing clothing, balancing the books, &c." Homesick and heart sick, Swan lamented

---

[48] Report of Gen. John C. Vaughn, 5 June 1863, *Official Records*, ser. 1, vol. 24, pt. 2, p. 691–92.

[49] Stamper, "Travels of the 43rd Tennessee," 62.

[50] Clack, "Personal Diary," 3.

[51] Darr, "Diary," 4.

[52] Hynds, "Original Handwritten Notes," 10–11.

the fact that so many of the boys were anxious with "inexpressiveness in regard to the loved ones back home." He believed that the brave men who surrounded him sighed and expressed their heart break "in the twilight hour," when they talked with one another about the anxiety of friends and family back home ignorant of their Vicksburg acquaintances' welfare. The soldiers referred to their state of affairs as "being in a sack." But with stubborn spirits, he said with stiffened resolve, "they refuse to bow to the invader and are ready to hold their ground to the last man against Lincoln's missions [minions]." After concluding that "war is a horrid business," Swan longed for the time when the "kingdoms of this earth become the kingdoms of Christ the King of Peace." He yearned for a time when the war alarms were no more, and he prayed that the Confederate nation "would humble itself by its rulers and people before the Lord God of Hosts." "[We should] supplicate His mercy that He suffer [us] not to fall into the hands of [our] enemies," Swan suggested. He concluded that it would indeed be a cruel fate now "if God were to permit our enemies to obtain the dominion over us."[53]

"Everything was unusually quiet on my line," Vaughn reported in his daily submission on 6 June. He stated that there was only a little sharpshooting and artillery fire until the evening hours, after which "the enemy shelled my line for a short time." Casualties for the day included the death of one man in Major Stevens's Mississippi State troops and one man wounded in the 62nd Tennessee.[54]

"This is the 22nd day of the great battle for the capture of Vicksburg," George Hynds of the 31st Tennessee declared, "and the enemy has made but slow progress towards the taking of the place." He indicated that though batteries and rifle pits nearly surrounded the vast lines of defenses, what the final result would be, no one knew. There was sparse firing on the previous night, he noted. "The weather is very warm and dry," he remarked, "equal to August in Tennessee."[55]

Agreeing with most commentators on 6 June, Calvin Smith of the 31st Tennessee commented that the firing was less than usual. A farcical story reached the lines stating that Joseph Johnston had fought the Yankees seven hours and had taken around 10,000 prisoners. Other information traveling along the grapevine telegraph indicated that the "Old Jo" was also on the march

---

[53] Swan, "A Tennessean in the Siege of Vicksburg," 363–64.

[54] Report of Gen. John C. Vaughn, 6 June 1863, *Official Records*, ser. 1, vol. 24, pt. 2, p. 692.

[55] Hynds, "Original Handwritten Notes," 11.

toward Grant's rear. Whatever maneuvers were being undertaken on their behalf, Smith had to admit that the Federal army continued to extend its lines around the garrison both to the right and up on the left. Their supply of troops must have seemed limitless. With these rumors, another one just as fantastic arose, Smith said. This tale proclaimed that Rosecrans's Army of the Cumberland was moving behind Joseph Johnston's Army of the Relief, and that Braxton Bragg and the Army of Tennessee was following Rosecrans. (It must have sounded like all the armies in Mississippi, Louisiana, and Tennessee were congregating around Vicksburg for one final apocalyptic Armageddon.) Smith wisely noted that he did not consider any of this information too reliable. The night had passed quietly because the river had been falling, backing the mortar rafts out of range. But after forty-eight hours, the rafts were back as methodical as ever, supplementing the resumption of renewed enemy sharpshooting.[56]

"Our regiment was permitted to sleep all night," James Darr of the 43rd Tennessee recorded in his daily diary entry, which was unusual for the garrison. At noon the situation continued to be relatively quiet, though he reported some heavy firing from the gunboats. Darr believed all the men were getting sick.[57]

Some sharpshooting occurred at daylight, Clack of the 43rd Tennessee reported from the lower end of the line, "but in a milder manner than common," though it lasted all day. Clack was content that night had come again with skies speckled with stars, "while we again lay us down to sleep upon the rough ground of Vicksburg." His only supplication was: "I pray heaven's blessings to rest upon us."[58]

Others in Reynolds's command, however, did not rest during this lull. The compiled service records of the 59th Tennessee indicated that Privates Dillon Blevins, John Blevins, Jr., Azariah Grace, James F. Jones, Isaac Nideffer, John Spires, and Emanuel White deserted their company through the lines.[59] All from Carter County, these boys had had enough.

Swan of Stephen D. Lee's Brigade wrote about a good deal of firing around the line at all points, but few were hurt. With the worsening rations, dysentery was beginning to spread among the men, though they continued "to keep up wonderfully." Swan observed that as time moved slowly along, the men became more hopeful of receiving Johnston's salvation. They anticipated it daily, he reported with the belief that soon his "Army of Relief's" artillery must

---

[56] Smith, *A Smith in Service*, 56.
[57] Darr, "Diary," 4–5.
[58] Clack, "Personal Diary," 3.
[59] 59th Tennessee, *Compiled Service Records*.

be heard in the distance pounding the Yankee rear. In matters closer to his personal observation, Swan recorded that a shell had dropped over Lee's breastworks that day wounding two lieutenants in the 31st Alabama. "I saw their wounds dressed," he recorded. "It was a horrid sight."[60]

Vaughn reported that his men were greatly annoyed by the sharpshooters to the left of his line in his 7 June summary to division headquarters. At times the artillery fire was heavy, but it was inconsistent. One man was wounded in Major Stevens's Mississippi Battalion.[61]

"Each army had its sharp-shooters, those who were good marksmen," Bachman of the 60th Tennessee stated, "and who especially picked off men who exposed themselves to view." He indicated that while confined in the trenches, he used his shell jacket for a pillow. One morning, Bachman rose and laid the coat, just as it was folded, on the backside of his place in the trench. As must have happened hundreds of times a day during the siege, he forgot about the sharpshooters and stood erect for a moment or two to stretch his cramped limbs. "One of the yankee sharp-shooters apparently saw me and took aim," he recollected, "for just as I stooped for a moment for some purpose, a rifle ball zipped over me and struck my coat, cutting four holes through it." Had he stood for only an instant longer, "I would have been killed."[62]

Kirby-Smith Attacks Milliken's Bend, Young's Point. On the sweltering morning of 7 June, some troops from the Department of the Trans-Mississippi (that is, Texas, Arkansas, Missouri and portions of Louisiana west of the Mississippi) attempted to draw away Grant's total concentration from Pemberton's confined forces at Vicksburg. General Henry McCullough's Texas Brigade of 1,500 men attacked the Union garrison and depots just up river on the Louisiana side at Milliken's Bend. The fortifications there were manned by 1,000 troops belonging to the 23rd Iowa (veterans of the Big Black River battle)

---

[60] Swan, "A Tennessean in the Siege of Vicksburg," 364.

[61] Report of Gen. John C. Vaughn, *Official Records*, ser. 1, vol. 24, pt. 2, p. 692–93.

[62] Bachman, "Reminiscences of Childhood," 23. A Mississippi soldier described the daily experiences of soldiers in the trenches: "How long shall the endurance of our men be tested? Whoever heard of men lying in ditches day & night exposed to the burning sun & drenching rains for a period of thirty days & that too under continual fire & on quarter rations—their limbs stiff—their strength frittered away—their flesh leaves their limbs & muscles relax & their eyes become hollow & their cheeks sunken. One cannot rise to adjust his blankets or relieve his cramped limbs without great risk. Their clothes are covered with dirt & 0 horrible their bodies are occupied by filthy vermin, the detestable bodyguards [lice]. Nor could this be avoided, for the ditches were alive with these crawling pests & to escape was impossible." Urquhart, *Vicksburg: Southern City Under Siege*, 47.

and three new Louisiana regiments of black soldiers recruited from the local plantations. As they made their advance across the cleared ground, the Texans sensed little resistance. Shouting "No Quarter!" they pressed their assaults. The defenders were overwhelmed by superior numbers and lost 652 men killed, wounded, and captured. Before the base could be captured and destroyed, however, Porter's most formidable ironclad gunboat, the *Choctaw*, sent several well-placed salvos into the Confederate flanks from her 100 Parrott and 9-inch Dahlgren rifles. Compounding the Texans' problems was the intense heat (approximated at 95 degrees with correspondingly high humidity) sapping the assailing force physically and necessitating their withdrawal with their prisoners. At the same time, a coordinated attack had also taken place against the defenses at nearby Young's Point by General James Hawes' Brigade, composed of the 12th, 18th, and 22nd Texas. This strike was also thwarted by strong infantry reinforcements and gunboat support. Hawes' Texans also suffered severely from the heat and humidity, with nearly half of the force taken down with heat exhaustion. Hawes and McCullough had no recourse except to return to their base at Richmond, Louisiana.[63] These were two rare instances during the war when it was just too hot to fight. Though their efforts were unsuccessful, the sound of the heavy guns and steady musketry up the river aroused the curiosity and hopes of the Vicksburg defenders.

"Early this morning [we] heard the very distant firing of large caliber guns up the river," Calvin Smith of the 31st Tennessee wrote. He believed correctly that "somebody" (one of the Trans-Mississippi forces) had perhaps turned up there. The boys were now living off short rations, and all believed that soon all beef, bacon, rice, field peas, meal, sugar, and molasses would be used up. Of these staples to their menu, the men had most days drawn small portions in varying variety. The weather, Smith reported, was quite warm, though tempered at times by breezes from the river, particularly on the high ground. The temperatures in the ditches where all air movement died was excruciating. The men had been confined to the trenches for their fourth Sunday, and Smith indicated that their health, overall, was excellent considering their duty and environment. He thought that, if necessary, they could stick it out perhaps for four more weeks before their provisions would be expended.[64]

---

[63] Report of Henry E. McCulloch, 8 June 1863, *Official Records*, ser. 1, vol. 24, pt. 2, p. 467–70; Report of J. M. Hawes, 9 June 1863, *Official Records*, ser. 1, vol. 24, pt. 2, p. 471–72.

[64] Smith, *A Smith in Service*, 56.

Smith predicted that the Confederate sharpshooters were killing as many Yankees as the enemy was them. The musket in the hands of a skilled marksman, he had heard, could kill a man a half mile away. Though the weather had been stifling, Smith reported that a shower of rain had moved in during the morning and delivered its contents in torrents, providing a brief respite. He had spent the day reading "principally the Testament," which he declared he had read all the way through. "Very little firing is done on our part," he recorded. "The greatest danger is that we may become too scarce to hold out until succor reaches us." Smith believed that the garrison still had the ability, the strength, and the munitions to defend Vicksburg, and he declared all were getting along well so far.[65]

Captain Hynds of the 31st Tennessee wrote in his daily entry that heavy artillery fire continued for several hours during the morning, sounding as though it was about ten miles off at Milliken's Bend and Young's Point. "Several rumors [were] afloat as to the cause," he stated, hoping that it was Johnston at last being aggressive on the garrison's behalf.[66]

"No relief brought us," Stamper of the 43rd Tennessee said, expressing with simplicity the disappointment the defenders dealt with during this period. He stated that everything continued about as usual, though there was nothing usual in the mortal wound suffered by Private William J. Adams of Company K and Ooltewah, Hamilton County, when he was struck by a minie ball.[67] Clack of the 43rd Tennessee indicated that at 9 a.m., Adams was wounded "just now" from a sharpshooter's "spent [deflected] ball, thought mortal." Clack stated that the cannonading on Vicksburg had resumed after a hiatus of two days.[68]

"I am dirty as a hog," James Darr of the 43rd Tennessee reported honestly. He pleaded for word from home and the ability to communicate with his family. The boys were all worn out lying continuously in the ditches, as they had been doing for twenty-two days. He prayed that they all would be spared to return to their homes. As though interrupted in mid-thought, Darr stated he could hear some heavy cannonading in the distance, though he could not tell from what point. The shelling on Vicksburg was "very dangerous," Darr noted, and the misery was intensified by the "most awful" heat. He wondered if any

---

[65] Ibid., 56–57.
[66] Hynds, "Original Handwritten Notes," 11–12.
[67] Stamper, "Travels of the 43rd Tennessee," 63.
[68] Clack, "Personal Diary," 3.

soldier could endure more under their present circumstances. "If any man in the world deserved merit it is the soldier at Vicksburg," he declared.[69]

Swan of S. D. Lee's Brigade reported that three weeks had passed since "we have been shut up in this beleaguered city." And though he was bemused by the idea that some people not among them might have found such a circumstance fascinating, the Bradley County Rebel declared, "there is no romance to the actors." "Any moment is liable to bring a deadly missile from the rifle ball to the 13–inch shell," he realized, and he had often seen little groups during the siege talking together when the dull boom of the mortar announced that a shell was in flight. "All give a moment's attention to the unwelcome guest," he declared, lending an ear to ascertain its direction. If it sounded to their trained hearing as though the shell would pass over, the conversation continued. "But when the [balls] from rifles pass," he added, "there is no time to speculate if they are falling near and all rapidly begin to look out for safer quarters."[70]

Swan addressed the sad plight of the mules and artillery horses, noting they had "cropped the grass bare all about and the hills are naked and desolate." He believed that all of the livestock were starving by degrees, and that in a few days, the animals would all be dead. "There was a cane field south of the city to which they were all driven," he related, "but that is now consumed." Matters were dire for man and beast. All this led Swan to conclude, "the prospect is gloomy in the extreme."[71]

"How many anxious thoughts this day are turned towards our homes," Swan wondered, "where we used to go up in peace to the House of God in company of friends and neighbors?" The Yankees believed in their awful engines of war and their terrible ships of iron, but he asked his God to intervene on the South's behalf at Vicksburg. "Oh God, we have sinned and Thou has punished us sorely and brought us to this extremity," he confessed. "Let thy compassion now return, and save us. Put Thy fear upon our people, and our rulers, and may we become a nation whose God is the Lord!"[72]

More Yankees Oppose Reynolds's and Barton's Lines. And still the enemy's reinforcements poured in. General Francis J. Herron's Division, composed of 5,100 men in eight regiments and three batteries, was dispatched to Grant from Major General John Schofield's Department of Missouri and arrived down river

---

[69] Darr, "Diary," 5.
[70] Swan, "A Tennessean at the Siege of Vicksburg," 364–65.
[71] Ibid.
[72] Ibid., 364–65.

on 8 June, further swelling Federal army.[73] The arrival of Herron's Division would have an immediate impact on the East Tennesseans of Alexander Reynolds and the Georgians to their right under Seth Barton. Herron's men would augment General Jacob Lauman's Division fronting these two Confederate brigades posted from the Hall's Ferry Road around to the South Fort on the river. Fronting Reynolds's men were Lauman's Division composed of the Illinois Brigade of Col. Cyrus Hall and a brigade of infantry from Illinois, Indiana and Wisconsin under Colonel C. E. Bryant. Enemy artillery support facing Barton, Reynolds, and some of Cumming's lines were ten guns of two companies belonging to the 2nd Illinois Light Artillery, six guns each served by the 5th Battery and the 7th Battery of the Ohio Light Artillery, and two field pieces manned by elements of the 15th Battery, Ohio Light Artillery. When Reynolds's men were called to support General Barton's men below them in the line, it was usually against William Orme's Brigade, Herron's Division, made up of the 94th Illinois, the 19th Iowa, the 20th Wisconsin, and four guns of Company B, 1st Missouri Light Artillery. These hearty Midwesterners would spend the remainder of the siege testing the right flank of the Southern defenses.

General Vaughn reported no casualties for 8 June "and less sharp-shooting than usual." Only a few rounds from Union gunners disturbed the peace of the night, he stated, when artillery fire was kept up on his right.[74]

More of the Grapevine Telegraph. The mind-numbing routine of the Confederates was often jolted by acts of sudden violence in and in front of Reynolds's ditches. Clack of the 43rd Tennessee stated that one man in Company D was wounded in the morning. At 7 p.m. that night, firing appeared to him to be rapidly delivered. Word had filtered down to the common infantryman, he asserted, through Johnston's couriers and the usual grapevine telegraph sources that an English fleet had come to the South's aid and was now in possession of New Orleans. An equally incredible story stated that "General Lee" had taken possession of Helena, up the Mississippi River, and finally, in "news" closer to their proximity, General W. W. Loring had retaken Snyder's Bluff, up on the Yazoo.[75] All were favorable reports that by this point in the siege meant they were all false.

---

[73] Smith, Appendix C: Opposing Forces, Vicksburg Campaign, *Compelled to Appear in Print*, 201.

[74] Report of Gen. John C. Vaughn, 8 June 1863, *Official Records*, ser. 1, vol. 24, pt. 2, p. 693.

[75] Clack, "Personal Diary," 3.

At around 2 a.m., George Hynds of the 31st Tennessee recorded, the Union sharpshooters fired several volleys "to annoy us." But the boys were so accustomed to the shells and sharpshooter noise by then that they "paid but little attention to them." He reiterated that the Southern artillery rarely responded to the incessant fire of the foe's batteries.[76]

Heavy musketry was evident on the lines the previous night, James Darr of the 43rd Tennessee wrote. He reported that one man was wounded in the 43rd Tennessee's Company D during the morning, after heavy cannonading had been going on all night. "When shall we get help?" he wondered.[77] Spradling of the 43rd Tennessee indicated in a letter to the Vicksburg National Park years after the war that his friend Corporal Thomas Houts was the man wounded on this date by the Yankee sharpshooter.[78] Stamper of the 43rd Tennessee affirmed this incident, spelling his name "House," and reported that he was "wounded in the legs." Stamper noted that the pickets continued to exchange fire with one another all through the night. Still, the monotonous pace of the siege continued with little variance, he lamented, and all the boys continued to look longingly for the arrival of Joseph Johnston's legions to cut them out. Great was the idle talk about rations, he reported, specifically about what was on hand, how long it would last, and so forth. "All are beginning to suffer with hunger," he wrote.[79]

After all the miserable days and evenings they had spent freezing in the dampness of winter and early spring, as well as suffering under the pelting of heavy showers, Swan of S. D. Lee's Brigade wrote in his daily entry that "scarcely a sprinkle of rain has fallen since the siege commenced." He reported that the boys had been under constant fire and completely invested now for twenty-one straight days. All the soldiers were hungry not only for rations but also for news, causing Swan to assert: "rumors of the most unreasonable character are started and handed around." The hottest rumor of the day in his trench was that General John Bankhead Magruder and his troops aboard a cotton-clad fleet (along with other gunboats from Mobile) had recaptured New Orleans. In addition, the story circulated that General Sterling Price had retaken Helena, Arkansas, and with it, eighty heavy guns. Such news, had it been true, would really have posed a serious threat against Grant's communications and supplies by the river.[80] Variations on these reports spread

---

[76] Hynds, "Original Handwritten Notes," 12.
[77] Darr, "Diary," 5.
[78] Spradling, "Diary," 1.
[79] Stamper, "Travels of the 43rd Tennessee," 63.
[80] Swan, "A Tennessean at the Siege of Vicksburg," 364.

within Reynolds's lines. Such reports were pitiful inventions to assuage desperate hearts.

Swan wrote that he had the opportunity of reading a dispatch from General Stephen D. Lee to General Carter L. Stevenson which reported that a lieutenant in Waul's Texas Legion, while out between the lines on picket duty, had met and talked "in a friendly" way with a Union sergeant. This enemy picket provided news pertaining to General Robert E. Lee's victory over Hooker in Virginia, at the Battle of Chancellorsville, the burning of the "long bridge" over the Potomac, and the fears reigning through the North about the imminent danger to Washington itself. Other news provided by the Yankee sergeant pertained to the threat against Helena by General John S. Marmaduke's forces, and finally, the best news of all, related to the activities of General Edmund Kirby-Smith and his Army of the Trans-Mississippi. Kirby-Smith, the dispatch said, "was reportedly advancing on the opposite [Louisiana] side of the river requiring two divisions to be sent from Grant's forces across to meet him, and that the heavy firing in the distance yesterday morning was the gunboats shelling the woods about Milliken's Bend where some of Price's or Kirby-Smith's men had made their appearance."[81]

The dispatch also included information that General Johnston's forces had been skirmishing with Grant's outposts on the banks of the Big Black for two days, causing the Federals to become increasingly uneasy about Confederate intentions. Most of this information, according to Swan, seemed to confirm much of the grapevine dispatches, and it helped inflate the spirits of the troops in the trenches. He indicated that when the men were in high spirits, they did not get sick as often. At that time, nearly 1,000 soldiers were on the sick and wounded rolls from Stevenson's Division, which included Swan's brigade commanded by Stephen D. Lee, Alexander W. Reynolds' East Tennessee brigade, and the two Georgia brigades of Cumming and Barton. As for his duties, Swan remarked that all procedures within the brigade commissary were now reduced to a system. The cooking of rations was carefully attended to, and the portions issued were closely measured so that nothing was hoarded or wasted. He stated that the men "do not suffer," though their rations' portions were greatly reduced.[82]

A remaining stock of supplies by this time, according to Swan, was a small amount each of corn meal, rice, peas, beef or bacon, lard, sugar and molasses. About 1/2 lb. of corn meal, 1/2 lb. of beef, or 1/2 lb. of bacon formed the usual

[81] Ibid.
[82] Ibid.

ration, he wrote, augmented by a small quantity of the other articles for the daily allowance. "Each day brings us nearer to the crisis," Swan indicated. He felt that if the army was not relieved by the time the present supply was exhausted, the garrison must capitulate or cut its way out. Swan predicted that the garrison could hold out for a month yet, "if sickness does not break out." He concluded in his daily entry: "the summer heats are terrible, though the nights have thus far been cool enough to sleep pleasantly—but the mosquitoes are very troublesome." Finally, he reported, the shelling of the mortar boats from the river continued all night.[83] Despite all this, Swan marveled at the endurance of the besieged.

Vaughn stated in his 9 June daily report that five men had deserted from the 61st Tennessee. Enemy activity began briskly enough, but the sharpshooting tapered off around noon. The Yankee cannon were active in the morning and at noon, he reported. Later in the evening, "a heavy fire was kept up on my right during the night." The mortar boats opened fire about noon on the right of his line as well, but it resulted in no casualties.[84]

Colonel Reynolds indicated in his official report on this date that the Federals mounted several 20–pounder Parrotts within 400 yards of his line, which necessitated a gradual withdrawal of his pickets back into the trenches. This unfortunate circumstance allowed the enemy to cut a zigzag approach to within seventy-five yards of his brigade's position, where they had "thrown up works much stronger than those occupied by our troops." Their parallel lines ran the entire length of the East Tennesseans' fortifications, Reynolds reported. In these ditches were positioned dozens of sharpshooters who kept up such a continuous fire on Reynolds's line that "to show any part of the body above the parapet was almost certain to be struck." Reynolds stated that he sent frequent sorties out at night whose mission was to drive the pests from the ditches and then to work at filling them up with dirt. Unfortunately, he explained, his men could not hold these positions because of the superior numbers of Yankees firing relentlessly on them from their back lines. As the days progressed, Reynolds stated the enemy continued to mount other large caliber siege guns and steadily increase their number of sharpshooters.[85]

---

[83] Ibid., 364–65.

[84] Report of Gen. John C. Vaughn, 9 June 1863, *Official Records*, ser. 1, vol. 24, pt. 2, p. 693.

[85] Report of Col. Alexander W. Reynolds, undated, *Official Records*, ser. 1, vol. 24, pt. 2, p. 356.

Captain George Hynds of the 31st Tennessee wrote in his journal on 9 June that there had been "a gentle breeze" that blew throughout the night and into the morning hours. He wondered how the grapevine telegraph could work overtime providing the most absurd tales when no real news could get through the lines. Still, he confessed, "there are plenty of believers."[86]

Private W. J. Routh of Company K, 43rd Tennessee, according to Stamper of that regiment, died in the hospital of "continued sickness." Otherwise, there was "no change of affairs."[87]

Some sporadic shooting at supposed phantoms continued through the night, Clack of the 43rd Tennessee wrote in his journal, with serious firing resuming its usual routine at first light. As darkness approached, the Northerners commenced shelling Vicksburg from across the river on the DeSoto Peninsula.[88] James Darr of the 43rd Tennessee noted simply that the fighting continued all day.[89]

S. A. R. Swan of Cleveland, Tennessee and serving with the commissary in General Stephen D. Lee's Brigade, agreed with Hynds's observations that the only news circulating was what had been invented in the trenches. During lulls in the shooting, the boys were subjected to the taunts of the enemy pickets who often boasted: "they [were] our jailors" and were merely engaged in guarding prisoners. "They did a right smart job of keeping an eye on us," Swan confessed. He maintained that it was a miserable time for all who were shut up in the place, as well as for those friends and relations at home who remained ignorant of the defenders' situation. Swan declared that if the garrison was ultimately fortunate enough to "get off safe and hold our ground," they owed their success entirely to a merciful Providence, since the Federals "[were] straining every nerve to accomplish our capture." Brought to bear on the Vicksburg garrison was "every appliance of military science," he wrote, "the most approved engines of destruction by land and water, and limitless uninterrupted communications for supplies and reinforcements—all belonged to the Yankees."[90]

Like almost all his comrades, Swan was starved for a single good night's sleep. The unrelenting sharpshooters and the constant bursting of shells over their heads sapped their strength. Shut up in the hot dirty place where they

---

[86] Hynds, "Original Handwritten Notes," 12.
[87] Stamper, "Travels of the 43rd Tennessee," 63.
[88] Clack, "Personal Diary," 3.
[89] Darr, "Diary," 5.
[90] Swan, "A Tennessean at the Siege of Vicksburg," 366.

were made to lie prone and still in filthy ditches littered with weeks of the worst discards of their comrades, infested with vermin and disease, and breathing the moldering odors of decay and the leavings in the sinks behind their trenches, these East Tennesseans and their Confederate comrades were dead in spirit and starved for a drink of cool fresh water or a decent bite to eat. Swan confessed: "sometimes I almost despair for relief and am driven to leave all in the hands of God."[91]

After several days of concentrating on his right, the invaders shifted all their heavy artillery fire against the water batteries and the left of his line, General Vaughn recorded in his 10 June report.[92] "This morning we had a very hard shower of rain which cooled the atmosphere and made it quiet pleasant for awhile," reported George Hynds of the 31st Tennessee. The humidity was so thick in the ditches during this time of year that a man could see the hole his finger poked through it. The humidity would have been relieved only for a brief time by a rain, since the shower's after effects served only to intensify what the boys called the atmosphere's "sultriness." The tease of cool air always quickly gave way to an increase in the heat and heavy humidity. Hynds stated that the thunder accompanying the summer storm "surpassed in sublimity all the artillery on earth," including the guns Grant had ringing them in from all sides of the trenches and out on the Father of Waters. The sharpshooters "were again at their trade," Hynds wrote, rarely abandoning their craft for any reason. Captain Joseph A. McDermott of Madisonville, Monroe County, and the 59th Tennessee, died on this date in a freak accident when his own pistol accidentally discharged. Private Henderson Shield of Company A in Hynds's regiment and a native of Sevierville was mortally wounded by enemy fire.[93]

Clack of the 43rd Tennessee confirmed Hynds's report about the blessing of a fine rain around 4 p.m. The night approached with a heavy wind picking up, with dark clouds rolling in, and the lightning playing across the heavens, punctuated by "an awful thunder that seems to shake the whole earth." This terribly sublime scene inspired Clack to pray to Jehovah, "who rides upon every tempest, protect me tonight!" Within an hour of the storm's passing, the Federals resumed with their batteries, firing constantly.[94]

---

[91] Ibid.

[92] Report of Gen. John C. Vaughn, 10 June 1863, *Official Records*, ser. 1, vol. 24, pt. 2, p. 693.

[93] Hynds, "Original Handwritten Notes," 12–13.

[94] Clack, "Personal Diary," 3–4.

James Darr, serving in the 43rd Tennessee, noted that the fighting continued all day. Though he had been sick, Darr reported that he felt better today.[95] Stamper, also of the 43rd Tennessee, reported, "we had copious showers today and tonight."[96] War matters were consistent in their unrelenting routine.

Swan noted in his diary that though the enemy's fire continued to be annoying, it had not been destructive for several days. What he read into that he did not indicate, for he had administrative matters to occupy his attention. Much confusion arose today, Swan declared, in the new procedures laid out for issuing rations. Many men failed to draw rations because they were left off the commissary census as ordered by the commanding general, which caused a "great dissatisfaction." The intent of Pemberton's edict was to ensure that the exact number of men on the rolls received the one ration to which they were entitled, so as to stretch the food reserves as far as was possible. There were obviously some problems yet to be worked out with the system, Swan stated. Though he was concerned about the morale of the army under the circumstances they were in, few desertions had occurred as of this date. He believed that it was not because of the efforts of the officers, but because of the constancy of the private Confederate soldier "who was cheerfully undergoing such hardships for the love of his country." If success was attained in defending Fortress Vicksburg, Swan believed that the private soldier, who exhibited unfathomable fidelity and endurance, would be the reason, though likely he would remain unknown and unremembered. Swan noted that the feeling now was that there would be no "great battle," since it was obvious that the Yankees intended on starving the garrison out rather than risking any more bloody and futile direct assaults.[97]

Some of the newspapers that had made it into Confederate lines indicated that the Yankees had finally admitted to heavy losses at the Big Black River, in addition to many more casualties suffered during their disastrous attacks on the fortifications in the first days following the investment. According to Swan, the Confederates in the lines thought, if only the Federals would resume their bloody attacks on the fortifications, they would discontinue their efforts, abandon the field, and adjudge their campaign to have been a failure. He commented on the heavy showers that had succeeded in making the ditches muddy. The showers brought behind them a heavy wind, which added to the

---

[95] Darr, "Diary," 5.
[96] Stamper, *Travels of the 43rd Tennessee*," 53.
[97] Swan, "A Tennessean at the Siege of Vicksburg," 366.

misery, he noted, since "the men, wet to the skin, stood or crouched in the muddy trenches shivering all night." The scene, he observed, was one of "terrible grandness," with the roaring of the cannon often muffled out by the roar of the "heavenly artillery," and the incessant flashes of lightning exceeded any muzzle flashes the enemy's artillery could produce.[98]

Henry Ginder, a resident of Vicksburg, wrote concerning the evening of 10 June, "I pitied our poor soldiers the night of the rainstorm, lying in it all night and unable to do anything else the next morning for fear of the Yankee sharp-shooters, who expend more ammunition in one day than we have on hand. If they don't get this place, it will have been a most unprofitable and costly job for them; if they do get it, it will be a very cheap bargain."[99]

As this summer storm blew through, Grant received another division of infantry on this date under the command of W. "Sooy" Smith. The command, nearly 7,500 men, had been previously employed in West Tennessee and Northern Mississippi. Grant now had over 75,000 men around Vicksburg. Lincoln and his war department continued to take the capture of Vicksburg seriously. The influx of invaders would not cease there. Three days later, 8,700 more Union soldiers arrived at Young's Point.[100] The swelling numbers filling the ditches across the way were becoming painfully obvious and demoralizing to the Confederate defenders.

Vaughn reported on 11 June that a happy consequence of the storm the night before was that little sharpshooting and no cannonading had occurred. He stated that his trenches were still full of water, and as a result, could not be occupied. He repeated the news that five men from the 61st Tennessee had deserted on Tuesday, 9 June, "but were not reported until after the report was forwarded yesterday."[101] The reason for Colonel Rose's tardy submission was not indicated.

There were no changes in affairs in Stamper's sphere of interest, and he stated that the same firing transpired on this date as it had on all previous days. The weather cleared off, he was glad to report, and the day continued unusually cool and pleasant.[102] Clack of the 43rd Tennessee remarked that the day was

---

[98] Ibid.

[99] L. Moody Simms, ed., "A Louisiana Engineer at the Siege of Vicksburg: Letters of Henry Ginder," *Louisiana History* 8 (1967): 148.

[100] Smith, Appendix C: Opposing Forces, Vicksburg Campaign, *Compelled to Appear in Print*, 201.

[101] Report of Gen. John C. Vaughn, 11 June 1863, *Official Records*, ser. 1, vol. 24, pt. 2, p. 693–94.

[102] Stamper, "Travels of the 43rd Tennessee," 63.

cloudy and damp in the morning. "It rained very hard last night," he wrote, "and our things are nearly all wet." The sharpshooting had resumed, and he worried, "we are liable to be stuck with a ball any minute" since "we are in a position where they fall around us and in our midst." The blessings of the Lord were on Private J. L. Miller of his company, Clack reported, who was "struck with one [minie ball] today." Since the ball was "well spent," it did not break skin,[103] but probably left a terrible bruise.

Clack said that the word traveling through the grapevine was that Grant had asked Lincoln for 100,000 more men to reinforce him. The old rumor of "Old Pap" Price recapturing Helena continued to make its rounds, and, as a result, the men believed that Grant's supplies had been cut off. As for the number of Confederates defending Vicksburg, Clack estimated that there were 31,380 men with thirty to forty days' rations.[104]

"Everything [was] quiet this morning except the mortars shelling the City," according to James Darr of the 43rd Tennessee. He reported that Benjamin Herman of Company C, 31st Tennessee, was wounded slightly, and he predicted that Dr. W. B. Johnson, who had been wounded on 25 May, would not live.[105]

"The hospitals begin to be filled up," Swan reported in his journal entry for the day, "showing how much exposure, fatigue, hot weather and short rations and wounds are diminishing our effective force." Such complaints were of what Swan termed a "slight character," and he thought that if the boys could just get out and move about a bit from the narrow limits within which they were confined, such indispositions would be alleviated. The hospital records indicated that one third of the forces within Vicksburg's defenses were under the charge of the surgeons, a total of nearly 10,000 men. "After a few days of rest [outside the confines of the ditches]," Swan reported, they improved and were able to go back on duty in the trenches."[106]

Vaughn indicated in his daily report on 12 June that he had finally allowed his infantrymen to fire their muskets, though not necessarily at the irritating Yankee sharpshooters. The firing had been only "for the purpose of discharging guns that were exposed to the rain during the previous day." The Northern artillery continued to fire some, succeeding in disabling one of Vaughn's 24-pounder siege guns. One of his men in the 62nd Tennessee was killed in the

[103] Clack, "Personal Diary," 4.
[104] Ibid.
[105] Darr, "Diary," 6.
[106] Swan, "A Tennessean at the Siege of Vicksburg," 366–67.

exchange, and another man belonging to the Mississippi State troops wounded.[107] Otherwise, the tedium around the still muddy ditches continued.

As an example, Robert Bachman of the 60th Tennessee wrote, "Every few days, I would take off my shirt and pick body lice from it. As I looked up and down the trenches, I saw other soldiers doing the same thing. In merriment, some fellow would call out, 'Boys, here's a big one—branded C.S.A.!'"[108]

Major Joseph A. Boyd, 3rd Tennessee," according to Stamper of the 43rd Tennessee, "a brave and patriotic soldier, shown by his early enlistment and life in the cause of the South, died this date of sickness." Stamper also noted, "several in our regiment were sent to the hospital," and it was "alarming to think we would be compelled to stay so far south through the hot season of the year." Sergeant Harvey Walker of Company A was wounded in the hand slightly by enemy fire.[109]

"Quiet today with the exception of the artillery," James Darr of the 43rd Tennessee recorded. He noted, however, that a "Maj. Bage," probably Major Wyatt T. Baylis of the 7th Mississippi Infantry Battalion, had died the night before of "flux." Darr had been detailed to the hospital to care for Dr. W. B. Johnson of the 43rd Tennessee. From what he observed there, Darr believed that half the army must now be sick, and that "all would be sick if they do not quit pea bread." He wrote that he too was not feeling well, probably a result of the heavy rain a few nights before. He wished that every man responsible for this war they were fighting was "somewhere else" since the boys were all worn out and sick. "Stop it!" Darr demanded, "Stop it, I say!"[110] George Hynds of the 31st Tennessee wrote the Federals were also continuing to annoy his regiment with their shells and sharpshooters. They seemed to have been firing more on the left than usual, he noted.[111]

The mortars continued to pound Vicksburg "without doing any very great damage," Swan of S. D. Lee's Brigade declared. He found it incredible that with all the shells the Yankees threw at them, the casualties remained smaller than expected. The latest word around camp indicated that a courier from Johnston had made it through the lines into Vicksburg. And while contents of his dispatches were not known, he brought with him several Jackson newspapers that were turned over to the army printers in town who were making extra

[107] Report of Gen. John C. Vaughn, 12 June 1863, *Official Records*, ser. 1, vol. 24, pt. 2, p. 694.
[108] Bachman, "Reminiscences of Childhood," 23–24.
[109] Stamper, "Travels of the 43rd Tennessee," 63.
[110] Darr, "Diary," 6.
[111] Hynds, "Original Handwritten Notes," 13.

copies for the boys. Each little bit of hope encouraged the army, Swan felt, and gave them "strong faith in relief if we can hold out long enough."[112]

Though Reynolds reported that circumstances had required him to bring in his picket line some days before, the duty had apparently resumed some time before 12 June. Sergeant James Henderson Everhart of Hawkins County and the 31st Tennessee on that date accidentally shot himself in the wrist with his own Enfield while on the dangerous assignment between the lines. On 24 June, due to "inflammation," surgeons amputated Everhart's arm below the elbow.[113] The boys often leaned with wrists crossed on the muzzles of their muskets while the butts rested on the ground. Sometimes they jarred and went off. It was the next morning before Everhart had his wound dressed by a surgeon. Smith escorted him to the Fourth Brigade Hospital, where his company commander took pains to find him "a good tent" with comrades J. Grigsby and J. Dykes, who were there sick. He endured much pain for nearly two weeks. Smith diagnosed all three men's conditions to be "poorly."[114]

"I saw many men at the hospital that were bad off," Smith wrote in his daily journal, "but the majority of these are fast recovering from diseases and wounds." Even with this optimistic prognosis, Smith was obliged to admit that "many will never get well." To round out his duties for the day, Smith noted that he also made a stop at brigade headquarters. "I carried the adjutant's report [there] late in the evening," he reported. "[It] gave our total of men [in the 31st Tennessee] for duty 399, of which 20 are cooks, 4 pioneers." While there, he heard considerable talk, joking, boasting, and "bragadation generally." He found the visit most interesting.[115]

Vaughn wrote in his daily report for 13 June that the sharpshooting continued, with some cannonading in the evening. There was no movement of the Union troops to his front the day of the report. He indicated that one man in the 3rd Battalion of the Mississippi State Troops was wounded, and one in Ward's Artillery Battalion was also wounded.[116]

"Many a time at night I have watched the great mortar shells with the lighted fuse rise toward the zenith," Sergeant Robert Bachman of the 60th Tennessee recollected, "and then gracefully curve down to the City; sometimes exploding in the air, sometimes in the town, sometimes in the ground." He

[112] Swan, "A Tennessean at the Siege of Vicksburg," 367.
[113] 31st Tennessee, *Compiled Service Records*.
[114] Smith, *A Smith in Service*, 57.
[115] Ibid.
[116] Report of Gen. John C. Vaughn, 13 June 1863, *Official Records*, ser. 1, vol. 24, pt. 2, p. 694.

pointed out that they looked like huge lightning bugs circling in the dark skies, and when they came earthward and struck the ground, "they make an excavation in which an elephant might be buried."[117]

The enemy's cannonade continued heavy all night and into the morning, Darr of the 43rd Tennessee wrote. He noted that a courier had come from General Johnston's headquarters, bringing with him news that the Army of Relief would be making its move soon. Darr also reported that his patient, W. B. Johnson, spent a restless night.[118]

"This is the fifth Sunday since we came into the ditches," recounted Lieutenant Smith of the 31st Tennessee. Incredibly, he felt that the time was passing quickly. He noted that the men spent much of their time lying around, some sleeping, some reading, and others talking with their comrades about the war and particularly about their homes, family, and children. "Dear children," he sighed. "We think more than we express to each other, but many of us will never live to see those that are near and dear to us." He was thankful that his health and strength were still excellent, and he believed that if he were to see the folks at home, though they would be changed, he would still know them, and they him. "What a time we would have!" Smith exclaimed. "Ah! Little can you imagine what a joyous time it would be to me. But this is the life that suits me except it is rather too confining, though I find enough to do."[119]

"While I am writing, the roaring of cannon and whistling of bullets are continually flying," Smith remarked, "and I am as liable to be shot as anyone." The Northerners, with their rifled cannon, he noted, had the ability to kill them from a distance of eleven miles. But on to better things: meals. He wrote he had bought 8 1/2 lbs. of sugar for $5.00, and that he and Sergeant Owens had just cooked some rice and corn, had bread, and made coffee. Smith indicated that he still had not heard from his brother-in-law and company commander Captain

---

[117] Bachman, "Reminiscences of Childhood," 21. Another Confederate soldier enduring the siege described the cannonading's effect on the boys in the trenches: "At night, the firing increases. They burst above the valley and send their howling fragments into the vale below.... The shells come rushing overhead—everyone appearing as if they would fall right upon your head. We could not sleep at night—were always in dread. No sooner had sweet refreshing sleep closed our eyelids, but some thundering shell would explode above our heads and drive slumber far from our weary eyes. The well and sound could not sleep with unbroken slumber—but would be awakened out of a sound sleep a dozen times during the night by these unwelcomed messengers. None who lie down at night had any assurance but that before the day should dawn his body would be torn in pieces by a fragment of shell." Urquhart, *Vicksburg: Southern City Under Siege*, 37.

[118] Darr, "Diary," 6.

[119] Smith, *A Smith in Service*, 57.

James D. Spears, who had been caught outside the lines when the investment was initiated on 18 May. Two of the 31st Tennessee's field and staff, Major Bob McFarland and Adjutant William H. Hawkins, however, had had the misfortune of arriving in Vicksburg on the last train in before the siege commenced. McFarland indicated that Spears and some of his men had been left off their train on the way back due to lack of room. "I would like to have him here," Smith wrote of Spears, "but I'm glad he is not for if he is living, he can send word home of how affairs are down west." His news source reported that perhaps these men had been captured, paroled, and sent home, or forwarded to some other place for exchange.[120]

Stamper recorded the roar of cannon and "the crackling of musketry between our men in the trenches and the enemy" as usual awakened the boys. He indicated that picket duty in front of the works had resumed, and Company H of the 43rd Tennessee had taken positions before Colonel Bradford's regiment, the 31st Tennessee.[121] Firing at broken intervals continued all night, Sergeant Clack of the 43rd Tennessee stated, and the sharpshooters seemed to be beginning earlier and in a "little warmer manner than usual."[122]

Reliable information, according to Swan, was making the rounds that General Johnston was still busy organizing an army to come to the relief of the Vicksburg garrison. "This gives great encouragement to our poor wearied men," he indicated. Another courier made it though the lines the night before, Swan wrote, and brought with him two hundred thousand percussion caps.[123]

Opposite the brigades of Barton and Reynolds, General Francis J. Herron's Division was now entrenched astraddle the Warrenton Road in the vicinity of the Big Bayou. His eight regiments from Illinois, Iowa, Wisconsin, and Indiana had finally completed Grant's total encirclement of Fortress Vicksburg, on the north, south and east by land, and on the west by water. The aggravation these Midwesterners rendered in the enfilade with their sharpshooters and artillery upon Reynolds's Brigade in particular would remain unabated until the surrender.

The usual sharpshooting came from the Union works, according to Vaughn in his 14 June report, with some cannonading during the day. He stated that his command suffered one man each wounded in the 60th Tennessee, the 62nd Tennessee, and in the few men from Loring's Division serving under him

[120] Ibid.
[121] Stamper, "Travels of the 43rd Tennessee," 63.
[122] Clack, "Personal Diary," 4.
[123] Swan, "A Tennessean at the Siege of Vicksburg," 367.

not cut off with the majority of that command after the Battle of Baker's Creek.[124]

Hynds of the 31st Tennessee recorded that another Sabbath day had dawned on the weary army in its trenches. "Instead of church bells ringing to call the people to the house of God to worship as in days gone by," he lamented, "the air is loaded with the sound of artillery and musketry." How long must this continue, Hynds wondered, ever aware that no one could tell. "There has been more firing today than there has been for several days," he wrote, "but not so much immediately over my fly."[125]

"Our army is nearly half sick," speculated James Darr of the 43rd Tennessee, serving still on detached duty attending W. B. Johnson at the hospital. He repeated that everyone had expected Joseph Johnston to free them long before this time. Though it was a Sabbath day, Darr declared that the Federals never observed it. There was heavy fighting all day, and a report stated that the enemy on the other end of the line had made a charge to no effect.[126]

Stamper of the 43rd Tennessee declared that the Confederates had been in the fortifications for one month, but there nothing had changed. He indicated that the army still had some rations, but there was no real sign of relief. Stamper observed, "Vigilantly, we have watched and patiently we have waited for the hope of relief and deliverance from Vicksburg." Private William Adams of Company K died on 14 June of his wounds suffered seven days earlier. Companies A and E went on picket to relieve Company H.[127]

All around the lines it was quieter than usual during the night of 13 June, Clack of the 43rd Tennessee recorded, "but we were awakened from our sleep early this morning by the sharp-shooters." Around noon, extremely heavy cannonading erupted on the left of Reynolds's lines toward Lee's Brigade, and many Confederates supposed that the bluecoats were preparing to make an attack there. By 7 p.m., however, there had been no news of any such assault. Had it come, Clack and his comrades would likely have been rushed into the line there to help meet the threat. "Another Sabbath has passed and we are still confined to this same unhappy place," Clack deplored, with no real hope of being delivered. "Oh Lord!" he prayed, "how long shall we remain in this state? Deliver us at once!"[128]

---

[124] Report of Gen. John C. Vaughn, 14 June 1863, *Official Records*, ser. 1, vol. 24, pt. 2, p. 694.
[125] Hynds, "Original Handwritten Notes," 13–14.
[126] Darr, "Diary," 7.
[127] Stamper, "Travels of the 43rd Tennessee," 63–64.
[128] Clack, "Personal Diary," 4.

Swan, in Lee's Brigade off to the left, echoed Clack's sentiments: "Oh, when shall we cease to hear the noise of battle breaking in on the quiet of our Sabbath?" Adding to the danger was the fact the picket lines of both armies "were thrown forward [toward each other] at night." In such close proximity, Swan indicated that they did not always fight, however, and opposing pickets were known to converse occasionally. The night before, for example, the pickets in front of Lee's Brigade were within ten steps of their enemy, Swan recounted, "and remained the balance of the night talking about the state of affairs." Even with their unlimited access to the news of the day, Union camps were infested with rumors nearly as bad as those within the Confederate fortifications. Obvious conclusions were drawn that the Federal army was now massive and able not only to close all the potential escape gaps in the lines but also to fortify the east along the banks of the Big Black River to discourage any assistance Johnston might seek to render. "A great battle is looked for very shortly," Swan said, closing his entry for the day.[129]

In his 15 June report Vaughn noted that sharpshooting was sparce the previous day. In addition, the enemy's land batteries had been "unusually quiet" until evening, when they opened fire on his left. From artillery over on the peninsula, he noted that a few shells fell on the left of his line, but "the proximity of their own line [to his left flank] prevented them from shelling it to any extent." The night of 14 June, the Union gunners had opened fire from their land batteries "on what was supposed to be some boats going in the direction of the [wreck of the] gunboat *Cincinnati*," for what purpose his men had no idea.[130] Obviously, these Yankees were trying to salvage the gunboat's battery.

The day of 15 June was cool and pleasant, Hynds of the 31st Tennessee reported, and the enemy commenced firing at daylight, as was their routine.[131] After some picket firing, Calvin Smith of the 31st Tennessee noted that an artillery duel began from both sides, which made "the earth and heavens fairly shake." The soldiers went about with their mouths open to relieve the strain on their ears. He indicated that the Confederate pieces were extremely effective. "I think I could see our shells burst with a seeming hatred amongst the Yankies," Smith declared, "we lost none—can't tell as to the enemy." He reported awakening with the morning, fresh from a dream about someone returning

---

[129] Swan, "A Tennessean at the Siege of Vicksburg," 367.
[130] Report of Gen. John C. Vaughn, 15 June 1863, *Official Records*, ser. 1, vol. 24, pt. 2, p. 694.
[131] Hynds, "Original Handwritten Notes," 14.

from Hawkins County with the news all was well with his family. Conditions, however, soon brought him to the realization the siege raged on.[132]

Word began to filter back that a fierce Federal charge on the left had occurred, gaining some ditches, but the Yankees had again been thrown back with severe losses. As Smith spent his time writing, he noted that a heavy cannonade was going on. He noted also that he had read in a small Vicksburg newspaper that during the siege thus far, the Yankees were said to have suffered 15,000 killed and 45,000 wounded, lost, and missing, for a total of 50,000–60,000 casualties. The little paper wondered how long Grant could keep up the siege at that rate. Still, the federals bragged that soon the garrison would be totally annihilated.[133]

"I went for water a while ago," Smith reported, "and several balls struck close to me. A musket ball passed through my tent today; one came inside yesterday. Got use to them, but when they come whizzing close, I can't help dodging a little." Smith confessed that he wrote so "indifferently" about such occurrences because he fully expected to return home to his family, though he admitted that he "was as liable to be killed as anyone." He endured this danger for his country because of the disastrous war foisted on it, which he believed sought as its primary aim the destruction of the South. The Confederacy was defending itself against invasion, plunder, subjugation, and extermination. The South had "not … fought or marched over one foot of their soil as I know of," Smith believed. "We are therefore justified to cherish those rights that are mine and yours."[134]

The day broke with the appearance of rain, Clack of the 43rd Tennessee wrote in his daily journal entry, with the usual degree of sharpshooting. As though something major was anticipated by the generals, he wrote that the brigade surgeon had ordered all convalescents "who were able" to return to their commands. This order led Clack to speculate that a major attack was anticipated. The grapevine telegraph was full of the "news" that Grant continued to be heavily reinforced. At 7 p.m., Clack stated that the day had passed relatively quiet. "We wait impatiently for the hour of our deliverance," he noted, imploring Providence: "May God speed the hour!"[135]

---

[132] Smith, *A Smith in Service*, 57.

[133] Ibid., 57–58.

[134] Ibid., 58. On this evening of 15 June, while Smith was making his journal entry, the vanguard of Gen. Robert E. Lee's Army of Northern Virginia—Maj. Gen. Robert Rode's division—crossed the Potomac River into Williamsport, Maryland, to commence the invasion that would culminate in the Battle of Gettysburg.

[135] Clack, "Personal Diary," 4.

Though there had been some little picket fighting, James Darr of the 43rd Tennessee reported the morning to be somewhat quiet. He believed that the Yanks had tried to burn Vicksburg using cotton and turpentine, but failed. Darr was still an attendant at the Fourth Brigade hospital, caring for Dr. W. B. Johnson, who he noted was resting some easier. Darr was weary with the trials. "No relief yet—how long—how long!" he wailed. "Oh! that I could hear from home!"[136] Stamper of the same regiment indicated there was continual firing the whole day. He also reported that all the hospitalized who could walk were sent back to their regiments. "Some who could hardly stand alone," he noted, "were forced to come." As a consequence, he acknowledged, some of their good boys soon "relapsed and died" and were buried beneath the sod of the Mississippi Valley.[137]

"The day passed," Swan of Lee's Brigade wrote in his daily entry, "with nothing of interest to vary the monotony of the siege."[138] Sometimes, however, Pemberton sought to help the men pass the time pleasantly by providing libations for those so inclined. "In view of our exposure in the trenches," wrote Sergeant Robert Bachman of the 60th Tennessee, "liquor was issued as a ration a few times. I never drank my portion. Doubtless it went to some other fellow, and probably he was the worse for it. At any rate, I endured the hardship of trench life just as well, if not better, than the men who drank their liquor rations."[139]

---

[136] Darr, "Diary," 7.
[137] Stamper, "Travels of the 43rd Tennessee," 64.
[138] Swan, "A Tennessean at the Siege of Vicksburg," 367.
[139] Bachman, "Reminiscences of Childhood," 22–23.

CHAPTER 11

"The Siege Drags Its Weary Length Along"

16-30 June

General John Vaughn reported on 16 June the usual sharpshooting, with cannon fire directed "altogether" on the right of his assigned position on the far left flank. He believed that the Federals opposite him were constructing new works around the Edwards's house to his front. One man with the 61st Tennessee was reported killed.[1]

Fraternization. In another of Vaughn's regiments, Robert Bachman of the 60th Tennessee noted: "we had to stand picket in front of the breastworks, down in the hollow." Just as in front of Reynolds's lines, the picket posts of both armies here were also close to each other, "and sometimes we would agree not to fire on one another, and then have a friendly conversation."[2] George Hynds of the 31st Tennessee described the day as refreshingly cool, cloudy, and a little rainy. He continued the discussion about the "social chats" between the Rebel and the Yankee pickets transpiring frequently during this time of the siege. "Neither side gives the other any information that would be of benefit to their commanders," Hynds noted. He suspected that the enemy had spies within the fortifications "because whenever we get up any 'grapevine news,' they are certain to ask our men about it in less than 24 hours." As a favorable consequence of such fraternizations, he reported that the Yankee sharpshooters sometimes yelled for the boys to "get in their holes" when they got ready to shoot.[3]

Morale Among the Besieged. Smith of the 31st Tennessee earmarked 16 June as their thirtieth in the trenches. He believed that his regiment was fortunate for not having been heavily assaulted yet, though they did have to contend daily

---

[1] Report of Gen. John C. Vaughn, 16 June 1863, *Official Records*, ser. 1, vol. 24, pt. 2, p. 695.

[2] Bachman, "Reminiscences of Childhood," 24.

[3] Hynds, "Original Handwritten Notes," 14–15.

with the enemy's sharpshooters and batteries. He was proud to proclaim that no man in his company had yet been hit by enemy fire. He attributed such good fortune to the purposes of God Almighty himself. Smith's company also had fewer deaths because of disease than any other company in the regiment. He attributed this good fortune to the industry of his men. Realizing that Smith was an older man and a Mexican War veteran, the boys looked to him as their authority and listened to him when he told them to "take exercise" and keep themselves as clean as they could. He felt that the government was lax in its distribution of soap, and he and the boys often had to wash without it. When they could find some, they often paid one to three dollars a pound for it. As others had stated, the men also had the option of hiring black women to wash their clothing for twenty-five cents an article, though Smith indicated that such a service quickly consumed the men's wages. Food from citizens was also becoming hard to come by, and Smith related that he saw that day a small "rice pie" bought for $2.50.[4]

As for war news, Smith passed on the latest rumors. One was that most of the Union troops were being drawn away to defend their back lines against Joseph Johnston, who was thought to be pressing them from Jackson. Smith had also heard that General John Breckenridge and even the popular, hard-drinking Tennessee General Frank Cheatham (who was still with the Army of Tennessee near Chattanooga) were now in the fray, "moving their lines steady and sure of certain victory." Smith believed that the garrison had to hold for only ten days or two weeks more before Johnston finally had "his host in hostile array" against Grant's rear. The garrison, then, would not be surprised to awaken one morning soon to find the Federal army fleeing from the "scene of strife," according to Lieutenant Smith.[5]

"We are closely watched and invested on every side," Smith wrote, "but seem to be cheerful reading Testaments, tracts, singing, talking, laughing and enjoying merriment generally." (Such laughter had to be the sort of raspy humorless laughter generated by the repetition of tattered old jokes, the monotony of which was matched only by the boredom of confinement.) Smith stated that he had turned forty-one years old on 10 June, and had since determined to read the New Testament all the way through. He indicated that the rations were now less than a pint of corn meal per day, sometimes mixed with rice and peas, a spoonful of lard, a quarter-ounce of tobacco, a small portion of salt, and sometimes sugar or molasses. "We understand we get only a

---

[4] Smith, *A Smith in Service*, 58.
[5] Ibid.

few of these articles at a drawing," he stated, "and are perhaps better off than if we got plenty."[6]

The main regret of most of the men was that they were denied news from home. Of all of Grant's cruel and effective weapons, this denial was perhaps his most powerful against the morale of the Confederates. Thus, instead of writing letters, many of the boys like Lieutenant Smith spent their time filling up their so-called pocket notebooks. He closed his daily entry indicating that it had rained some that evening, cooling the atmosphere and making the weather comfortable for a time. He had had a wrenching toothache the night before, Smith disclosed, which caused his jaw to swell considerably. He would have the tooth pulled if it afflicted him again. "The Yankies fire heavily," he concluded, "[their missiles] whizzing through the cane and timber overhead close to us."[7]

Stamper of the 43rd Tennessee wrote in his daily entry there was "no change" in circumstances, though there had been a "fierce" cannonading from the Northern batteries. "Several shells burst over our company," he stated, "scattering fragments through the air." He indicated that one piece struck near his head covering those around him with dirt, but doing no real harm. At sunset, Stamper reported Companies F and D relieved Companies I and C. Private John Brank of Company A died due to continued sickness.[8] Otherwise, the day was pretty much as usual, with no change in matters as far as Clack of the 43rd Tennessee knew. He wrote in his journal at 7 p.m. after duty ended, "a warm firing has been kept up all day." His prayer, as he lay down beneath "the ethereal blue for covering," was that the "Lord [will] watch over me while I sleep."[9]

James Henry Darr of Charleston, Bradley County, and the 43rd Tennessee was pleased to note that the boys were getting better rations than they had gotten for weeks. They received rye bread now instead of cowpeas. There was "considerable stir" around the lines during the morning hours from both artillery and musketry. The firing continued the whole day and was heavy after dark, he wrote. "Oh could my wife know that I am not wounded," he implored to no one in particular: "I should be better but so it is."[10]

Nearness of the Picket Lines. "For a short time, our picket lines were kept in front of the entrenchments," Captain Reuben G. Clark of the 59th Tennessee

---

[6] Ibid., 58–59.

[7] Ibid., 59.

[8] Stamper, "Travels of the 43rd Tennessee," 64.

[9] Clack, "Personal Diary," 4.

[10] Darr, "Diary," 7.

stated, "but they were finally driven back into the breastworks." He described in his entry the "roads" the Yankees had dug up right against the base of the Confederate works. And once there, they then cut parallel trenches deeply enough to "run four-horse teams at close range in perfect safety."[11]

"In fact," Clark wrote, the Yankees "have worked themselves up so close, that it was worth one's life to put his head above the breastworks for any length of time." He described the ground that stretched between the two lines as being covered "with thickets of bushes, briars, &c." At night the pickets were placed in front of the lines to avoid surprise attacks. On one occasion, he was the Field Officer of the Day, a terribly dangerous duty in which he had to work his way carefully from picket post to picket post. The next morning, the duty officer was required to report the night's activities to headquarters. "I had passed my men and was coming very near the Yankee posts," Clark stated, "which would have cost me my life within a moment's time had I not heard a gentle whistle of warning" from some of his own pickets nearby. He verified the report of others that at this point of the siege the posts were so close together that none dared to make any noise when out there in the darkness.[12]

The Shelling and Sharp-shooting Continues. Swan of Stephen D. Lee's Brigade indicated the day was rather uneventful, though the "rumors rife." The extra run of the newspaper repeating the news in the courier-delivered Jackson editions was made available to the boys in the lines today.[13]

The usual sharpshooting and some cannonading, General Vaughn reported, echoing the usual scenario in his lines. The only new wrinkle on 17 June was the establishment of a new enemy position in front of Vaughn's left near "the Edwards' negro quarters." One of Vaughn's men with the 62nd Tennessee was killed during this reporting period.[14]

Captain Hynds of the 31st Tennessee wrote that a hero of the Grand Gulf battle, Colonel Isham W. Garrott of the 20th Alabama, Lee's Brigade, was killed during the morning. The Yankees were attempting to move another battery in front of their works, he added, "but Captain [Ferdinand O.] Claiborne [of the 3rd Maryland Battery placed within Reynolds's lines] threw a few shells into their parapet which made them leave."[15]

---

[11] Clark, *Valleys of the Shadow*, 24.

[12] Ibid., 24–25.

[13] Swan, "A Tennessean at the Siege of Vicksburg," 367.

[14] Report of Gen. John C. Vaughn, 17 June 1863, *Official Records*, ser. 1, vol. 24, pt. 2, p. 695.

[15] Hynds, "Original Handwritten Notes," 15.

"There was a right smart of shooting during last night," Clack of the 43rd Tennessee reported. At 6 p.m. Companies B and G started out on picket in front of the trenches. Clack was with them and stated that by 7 p.m. they had settled into their picket posts. "The bullets cut pretty close to us out here," he noted with profound understatement. He asked the Lord to speed the hour of their deliverance from that place.[16] Stamper of the 43rd Tennessee also noted the death of Colonel Garrott, indicating that "he was shot dead through a port hole in our fortifications by a yankee sharp-shooter." "One Yankee came into our lines and surrendered while we were on picket," Stamper noted.[17]

"Firing was just as heavy as yesterday," Darr of the 43rd Tennessee recorded. "The sergeant major of the 3rd Tennessee was seriously wounded." As of 17 June, according to Darr, one month had passed since the garrison had been hemmed inside its narrow confines. Darr contended, "there has not been one day but what we have been fighting." The boys knew nothing of what was going on in the world outside, particularly matters back home. What was going on around their lines was quite enough: heavy fighting on the left all evening with small arms representing some sort of desperate fracas. Darr was still attending to Dr. Johnson, who was "sinking very fast." He empathized with the plight of the surgeon, dying in such a place among strangers while cannon roared all around and small arms rattled. "Oh God!" he begged, "Save me from it—save me from such a death!"[18]

While not significant in the great scheme of things, especially when compared with the death of a notable like Colonel Garrott, company reports indicated that Private James L. Smith of Carter County and the 59th Tennessee shared Garrott's fate, having been shot in the head by a Federal sharpshooter while at his humble post in the fortifications.[19]

The enemy, Swan of Lee's Brigade wrote, had been firing shells into town from a Parrott gun battery across the river somewhere on the peninsula. To its disadvantage, however, the gun had been placed within effective range of the Confederate river batteries and drew their ire. "I think the enemy is making steady advances and if we are not relieved," Swan contended, "we must inevitably yield before a great many days longer." The Confederate garrison, he

---

[16] Clack, *Diary*, 4.
[17] Stamper, "Travels of the 43rd Tennessee," 64.
[18] Darr, "Diary," 8.
[19] 59th Tennessee, *Compiled Service Records*. Smith is buried at Soldier's Rest under one of the many "unknown' Confederate stones.

reported, had now been cooped up so long that "we can't do much beside hold our lines and wait patiently for Gen. Johnston."[20]

Another man in the 62nd Tennessee was killed 18 June, Vaughn reported, though the action of the day was pretty routine: the usual sharpshooting at his men, a bit more cannonading than usual during the early part of the day, and then matters then settling down into a quiet night.[21]

Robert Bachman of the 60th Tennessee wrote in his memoir that life in the trenches was excruciatingly monotonous because the soldiers had to remain in them day and night in all sorts of weather. They suffered indescribably for adequate food and decent water. "Under the darkness of night," he reported, "water was hauled in barrels from the river and placed in the trenches. The summer sun soon made it tepid and unpalatable. Yet it was so precious it was only used for drinking purposes. Our dirty hands and faces were strangers to water for many days." In agreement with others, he recorded that at the beginning of the siege the food supply for Pemberton's army was limited and had to be measured carefully. As the days dragged along, the rations became smaller until meat and corn bread soon disappeared from the menu. All around Vicksburg, he wrote, mule meat hung in the markets. Starved cattle had all been killed and consumed. "Wharf rats," he purported, "were considered a delicacy by many of the soldiers."[22]

As the siege drew toward an end, the daily ration consisted of about one half a pint of pea soup and a finger length of pea or rice bread. "The peas," Bachman explained, "were those usually fed to cattle. They were ground into meal, mixed with water and salt, and cooked in a dutch oven." He indicated that even "as hungry as we were, about all we could get of such bread was the crust, as the inner portion was practically raw." The cooking was handled, as Samuel Swan had described, by a detail of soldiers who worked their business in the "hollows back of the trenches," where they were out of the attention of the enemy's sharpshooters.[23] Captain Bob Houston, General Vaughn's Inspector General, described the rations as "peas mixed with corn and wheat, which were to be ground." Mule meat was introduced to the brigade by a detail of a Texas regiment, who "jerked" it for the men. "The mule meat was good," Houston admitted, "and in a few days very few were heard to grumble; but the grinding

[20] Swan, "A Tennessean at the Siege of Vicksburg," 367.

[21] Report of Gen. John C. Vaughn, 18 June 1863, *Official Records*, ser. 1, vol. 24, pt. 2, p. 695.

[22] Bachman, "Reminiscences of Childhood," 21.

[23] Ibid., 21–22.

of the peas seemed to have poisoned [us]. While you could fry them they tasted good enough, though the stomach could not retain them very long."[24]

Meanwhile, another fire had broken out in Vicksburg during the night, Captain Hynds of the 31st Tennessee reported, though word to the extent of damage had not reached Reynolds's men in the lower fortifications yet. Hynds indicated, "Sergeant Robert Hill of Knoxville and Company A was shot through the body this morning "and lived but a few minutes."[25] Hill had been lying in his ditch, Smith added, when a ball came through and struck him in the breast, killing him instantly. "It's a sad sight to see a stout man killed so suddenly," Smith of the 31st Tennessee reported. "If the abolition leaders could see with their own eyes the horrors of the battlefield, they would certainly be willing to let us alone. The blood of thousands of brave men is more upon their heads but still they cry for more."[26]

The day before, the Federals had made three charges on the left of the line, according to Smith, where they were repulsed "with great slaughter." He knew that the losses were "considerable," and Waul's "Texicans" met them face-to-face during one attack at 100 yards. Other losses the day before included the sharpshooter killing of Colonel Garrott of the 23rd (20th)Alabama, whom Smith called "a brave and energetic officer." Seeking a remedy to the constant sharpshooting led the men of the 31st Tennessee to place banks of dirt atop the parapet to shelter Bradford's regiment from their antagonists straight ahead, as well as enfilading fire directed at them from Herron's works astraddle the Warrenton Road to their south. "Kelly Allen was sitting in my tent yesterday," Smith remarked, "when a ball struck him on the hip and bounced off. His wound is not considered dangerous, though it left him considerably bruised."[27]

It was also an eventful day for Isaac J. Stamper of the 43rd Tennessee who was elected (by vote of 47 to 15) 3rd lieutenant of his company over W. T. Lenoirs, due to the death of Captain Sterling T. Turner, killed in action on 22 May. J. J. Cox was elected 5th sergeant, and R. D. Rady was elected 4th corporal. Stamper indicated, "we had some fun in our electioneering." Around 10 p.m., the day's fun ended. Stamper reported that the Yankees attacked Cumming's and Reynolds's picket posts around the Hall's Ferry Road.

---

[24] Houston, "A History of Vaughn's Brigade," 155.

[25] Hynds, "Original Handwritten Notes," 15–16.

[26] Smith, *A Smith in Service*, 59. Smith indicated that Hill was a private and could have been from Sevierville.

[27] Ibid.

Company K was in the reserve and called into the engagement. The fight continued for about two hours, with the 43rd Tennessee boys "holding their position." Private Harry Marbury of Company K suffered a wound to the jaw and shoulder, though it was not thought to be mortal. Some others "were merely marked."[28]

The rest of the regiment was hurried into Cumming's ditches to support Colonel Barkuloo's 57th Georgia, anticipating a new threat from Lauman's infantry supported by Herron's Brigade along the Hall's Ferry Road, as Clack had reported. No charge, however, was forthcoming. After sunup, Stamper stated, "we returned to our respective places in reserve."[29] Clack's rendition of the night's events reflected the evening before had "passed off tolerably quiet, though the sharp-shooters opened up early this morning." One of the Georgia boys sharing the 43rd Tennessee's picket post had been killed during the morning. Clack stated that they were relieved at 6 p.m. by Company K. Then the boys returned, ate supper, and then lay down for the night. Clack had just drifted off to sleep when he was awakened by the rattle of musketry. The Midwesterners were again trying to drive in Reynolds's pickets and gain possession of their posts. The 43rd Tennessee, sleepy and unsettled by the sudden danger, was ordered forward, taking its position in the trenches with Colonel Barkuloo's 57th Georgia.[30] One Confederate involved in the counterattack had been wounded, but the firing soon ceased when the Feds returned to their ditches, leaving matters to remain as they had before their incursion. "Everything is quiet this morning," Darr of the 43rd Tennessee wrote in his diary. "Not a gun to be heard on our line."[31] It would not last. By evening, he reported, the intense firing had resumed.

Swan of Lee's Brigade observed, "the weather is very pleasant, the nights cool and the atmosphere seems to be pure and healthful." Care had been taken to remove all the dead animals, which were thrown into the river. The water was regularly hauled from the river during the night and taken to the men in the trenches. "Not much sickness in the army," Swan stated, though some other journalists had reported otherwise. The small reserve of corn meal had been used up, and rations were supplanted with field peas, flour, and rice meal, which made an awful unpalatable mess that even starving men found impossible to keep down. Across the river, the bluecoats were firing on the city with a couple

---

[28] Stamper, "Travels of the 43rd Tennessee," 64–65.
[29] Ibid., 65.
[30] Clack, "Personal Diary," 5.
[31] Darr, "Diary," 8.

of field pieces planted in the woods on the peninsula, Swan wrote. These guns were effective because they were light and easily moved around once the bigger caliber river batteries targeted their location. These two 12–pounders vexed the water haulers, who seemed to be the central focus of their harassment, and inflicted some damage to buildings on the lower streets of Vicksburg near the wharves.[32]

"Indications Point to a Speedy Surrender." On 19 June, Charles A. Dana, a Correspondent, issued to his newspaper in Washington the following report of what he believed was happening in the Confederate trenches across the way:

> All indications point to a speedy surrender of this place. Deserters who came out yesterday say that the Tennessee and Georgia regiments have determined to stack their arms within three days and refuse to continue the defense on the ground that it is useless, and that it is impossible to fight on the rations they receive. All the deserters are worn out and hungry, and say the whole garrison are in the same condition, besides, the defense has for several days been conducted with extraordinary feebleness, which must be due either to the deficiency of ammunition, or exhaustion and depression in the garrison, or to their retirement to an inner line of defense. The first and third of these causes no doubt operate to some extent, but the second we suppose to be the most influential.[33]

Despite Dana's optimism over an impending Confederate collapse, General John C. Vaughn in his 19 June report stated that it seemed to him that Grant's men were the one who were continuing their harassment with "extraordinary feebleness," since the hostilities *against* the Confederate lines were "unusually quiet." Around 10 p.m., the enemy's artillery opened fire along the river at some skiffs being prepared by details of Pemberton's men for a possible escape across the river to the now largely unoccupied peninsula.

These boat-builders were dismantling a number of structures to use their lumber to construct several watercraft, should desperate measures be required, to float the garrison across. Such a passage would have been frightening, for it would mean rowing thousands of defenseless men in 2,000 skiffs over open water for nearly a mile while subject to the guns of the enemy fleet. Unrealistic

---

[32] Swan, "A Tennessean at the Siege of Vicksburg," 367.

[33] Charles A. Dana to Edward M. Stanton, 19 June 1863, *Official Records*, ser. 1, vol. 24, pt. 1, p. 98.

as it sounded, it was one desperate option Pemberton was considering. In unrelated matters, Vaughn reported that one man was killed and one man wounded in the 60th Tennessee since he had last reported.[34]

On 19 June on the other end of the line, Captain George Hynds of the 31st Tennessee indicated that a "sharp skirmish took place in front of our right between our pickets and a force of Yankees sent to drive them in."[35] "The enemy has kept up a regular fire upon our line for about 25 days," he wrote. "They have shot thousands of shells and bushels of bullets without inflicting any serious loss upon our army." Despite all that, Hynds admitted, Vicksburg was the last city he wanted to be in when facing an enemy as well prepared for the business as the bluecoats were.[36] Smith of the 31st Tennessee described the melee referred to by Hynds involving men from his company as follows: "After dark, the Yankies charged our pickets [from Smith's company] under Lieut. Davis," Smith recorded. The sentinels who had been sent in advance of the others fell back, with the exception of seven men "who were most exposed." It was feared they all had been captured. Davis's men were sent right back to retake their posts, supported by a company from the 43rd Tennessee also out of Rogersville. These two companies of Hawkins County men poured a concentrated fire into the Federals, keeping them at bay and suffering one man wounded. Meanwhile, in the pitch darkness streaked by the flashes of random musket fire, interested observer Smith and his "ditch sentinels" kept a nervous eye on what was transpiring should they be ordered forward in the event of a pitched battle. "The men lay in the ditches," Smith wrote, "and I acted as officer of the ditch sentinels; Captain James P. Burem was officer of the day. The cannon and musketry played incessantly on us for two hours." He noted that one Northern shell passed dangerously close to them and completely tore up the tent of "Pony" Chestnut, which was back behind the fortifications. Smith feared the extreme darkness, for the Yankees might be able to creep right up over the lip of the trench and gain entry before the defenders were even aware they were there.[37]

Clack of the 43rd Tennessee stated that his regiment left the trenches among Cumming's men at daylight and came back to their reserve position in the hollow near the river. Though he noted that a little sharpshooting occurred,

---

[34] Report of Gen. John C. Vaughn, 19 June 1863, *Official Records*, ser. 1, vol. 24, pt. 2, p. 695; Gen. U. S. Grant to Admiral David D. Porter, 21 June 1863, *Official Records*. ser. 1, vol. 24, pt. 3, p. 423–24.

[35] Hynds, "Original Handwritten Notes," 16.

[36] Ibid., 16–17.

[37] Smith, *A Smith in Service*, 59.

he indicated that the morning passed off tolerably quiet.[38] Flour was issued to the boys on 19 June.

"Dr. W. B. Johnson died this morning at 2 a.m.," James H. Darr of the 43rd Tennessee stated matter-of-factly. Darr's duty at the hospital was now finished. He recorded that Private Harry Marbury in the 43rd Tennessee's Company K had been wounded the night before, and there was some sharpshooting going during the morning. The drudgery continued unabated with no hopes of relief in sight. Few Confederates expected any external aid to the garrison now, according to Darr. "They have gone out to bury Dr. Johnson," Darr noted, "and I am nearly worn out sitting up and waiting on him."[39] Stamper also recorded that the 43rd Tennessee lost its surgeon, Dr. Johnson, to the wounds he had received from the enemy shelling. "He was greatly mourned by our regiment," Stamper wrote, "for we looked to him for medical aid. He was a distinguished physician." One soldier each in the 59th Tennessee and the 31st Tennessee were killed in action on 19 June, and Stamper confirmed Clack's report that "we drew flour bread for our rations."[40]

S. A. R. Swan, in his lines with Stephen D. Lee's Brigade, believed that casualties were increasing in the ditches due to the weakened condition of the soldiers who were becoming too confused from hunger to demonstrate the carefulness they needed to avoid being shot by sharpshooters. Though it seemed that Grant no longer had any stomach to launch a concentrated attack in the vain hope of carrying the garrison's defenses, according to Swan, his cruel strategy to starve the garrison out apparently was working. "Their zigzag trenches and planting of batteries nearer to our lines for the purpose of battering down our defenses," Swan marveled, was proving to be a highly effective strategy. He noted that the boy in blue had gotten within two hundred yards of Lee's lines with their rifle pits. "With that," he wrote, "the pickets stand at night in some places no more than fifteen paces apart, but by agreement, do not fire on each other."[41]

On 20 June, Vaughn reported that the routine was a bit different this evening. His 3–inch rifle had been shooting infrequently from Fort Hill as its crew tried to get the range of the Union lines across the hollow in an effort to dissuade them from their various enterprises attempted during the hours of darkness. With this small rifle's occasional targeting, the left of Vaughn's line

---

[38] Clack, "Personal Diary," 5.
[39] Darr, "Diary," 8.
[40] Stamper, "Travels of the 43rd Tennessee," 65.
[41] Swan, "A Tennessean at the Siege of Vicksburg," 367–68.

soon drew some heavy artillery fire in return. Like a boiling nest of fire ants, the Federals continued their work on the hill above the Edwards's house. Vaughn indicated that they were also constructing some new positions toward the river near the Indian mound at Mint Springs Bayou. At daylight, a furious barrage was commenced, which continued along the upper lines for four hours. The Madisonville general reported that the enemy had now added four more field pieces directed at his trenches.[42]

One man in Company C was badly wounded in the face by the explosion of a shell, Hynds of the 31st Tennessee stated. All the wounds suffered by the men of Colonel "Reshy" Bradford's command up to this point had been life-threatening.[43] Isaac J. Stamper of the 43rd Tennessee agreed with Hynds concerning the cannonade they faced at daylight, calling it horrific. "There was scarcely a minute that the roar of cannon did not fill the valley," he stated. Rather than cause despair, however, the intensity of the adversary's fury was judged by Stamper to be a result of Joseph E. Johnston's pressing Grant's rear. They hoped that relief was now at hand, Stamper wrote, "and we wait patiently for his cannon to announce his arrival." Companies I and D of his regiment relieved Companies H and G from picket duty. Lieutenant Elijah Vincent of Company D was slightly wounded in the side during this picket, and Private John Dennis of Company H died in the hospital of sickness.[44]

"Heavy cannonading commenced at daylight this morning," Clack of the 43rd Tennessee recorded on 20 June, "and continued until 11 o'clock." He indicated that the bombs exploded, casting about their pieces "which fell all around us and among us," but hurt no one. The evening passed off tolerably quiet, and Clack thanked "high heaven" for its protection.[45] Darr of the 43rd Tennessee described the bombardment on 20 June as "the heaviest cannonading that has ever been yet on the line." J. L. Christian of Company G, 31st Tennessee and Bulls Gap, Hawkins County, had been shot through the head the night before.[46] Christian was probably the individual Hynds had mentioned.

Smith of the 31st Tennessee noted that he went up town during the day to try to draw some shoes and boots for the company. All were either too large or too small, so he drew none. He observed several shells falling inside Vicksburg

---

[42] Report of Gen. John C. Vaughn, 20 June 1863, *Official Records*, ser. 1, vol. 24, pt. 2, p. 695.

[43] Hynds, "Original Handwritten Notes," 16.

[44] Stamper, "Travels of the 43rd Tennessee," 65–66.

[45] Clack, "Personal Diary," 5.

[46] Darr, "Diary," 9.

while he was there, found a couple of newspapers, and headed back down to his brigade trenches. Once there, he read the papers to "the nervous set" and to those who were illiterate. He rarely saw any newspapers, and he had learned that the printers in the city were now taking their paper from ceilings and walls, and striking printed matter on the un-patterned side. The garrison still had no real news from the outside, although everyone believed that their imminent relief was only a matter of days. "I will stop," he wrote in conclusion for the day, "as our artillery—the baby-waker—has let off something."[47]

Lieutenant Calvin Smith had felt certain the pitch darkness of the early morning hours of 20 June would certainly encourage some sort of Yankee sally. Though they obviously could not see what they were firing at, he indicated that the enemy was pouring free fire (both musketry and artillery) into the Confederate works nearly as fast as they could load and bust a cap. Smith indicated that as he sat writing by candlelight, their artillery's discharges shook his tent. Amid the darkness, the 59th Tennessee had had a man shot through the head (probably James L. Smith of Carter County) killing him instantly. "I don't think the Yankies kill one of our men to a bushel of bullets," Calvin Smith wrote, "but it is a perpetual whizzing and chattering over our heads." He described his idea of a defensive mound mentioned the day before by indicating that he had had his men construct a pile of dirt at the head of the company's positions to stop the enemy's fire from the flanks.[48]

The placement on 13 June of the division of General Herron near the old camps of Colonel Reynolds just west of the South Fort and Warrenton had allowed Grant to augment General Lauman's Division in the vicinity of the Hall's Ferry Road. The Federals had thereafter been able to place field pieces and rifle pits whose lines of fire enfiladed the trenches in the left flank of the Georgians and right flank of the East Tennesseans. As if that were not bad enough, Barton's and Reynolds's reserve regiments would now find themselves having to scurry to defend against attacks at this new point almost as frequently as they had had to in support of the positions held to their left by Cumming and Lee. The full occupation of these positions would be the first time these two brigades of Georgians and the East Tennesseans had numbers of the enemy opposing them nearly equal to those of other commands up and down the trenches. Two assaults occurred on consecutive nights. One commenced at dark on 19 June, and the next began on 20 June. In the darkness of both nights, Barton and Reynolds concluded that the nearness of these sharpshooters' rifle

---

[47] Smith, *A Smith in Service*, 59.
[48] Ibid.

pits so close to their works had to be addressed. Seemingly, there would be no end to the terrible events during these two nights.

In a rare double entry dated 20 June, Calvin Smith of the 31st Tennessee wrote that the pickets for his regiment had been increased and reinforced by those from the 43rd Tennessee and subject to a heavy cannonade during the daylight hours, finally ceasing at dark. Smith indicated that, as officers of the guard, he and Captain James W. Chambers of Knoxville and the 31st Tennessee carefully inspected the regiment's sphere of responsibility. He learned sometime later that Private Isaac Christian of Captain Burem's Company G had been shot through the head. Smith repeated the news that both the 3rd Tennessee and the 59th Tennessee had also had men killed the past few days in a similar manner.[49]

When daylight broke on 20 June, the Confederates discovered that the Northerners had planted two batteries opposite Reynolds's and Barton's lines, and soon there erupted a furious artillery duel. To compound their advantage, the Yankees brought up on the river opposite the Confederate rear the gunboats *Benton* and *Mound City* to join in the fray. Soon, all batteries and sharpshooters in the line were involved "full blast." Smith indicated that the Confederate batteries joined the battle, occasionally throwing their shells with considerable accuracy. The casualties in the 31st Tennessee at the conclusion of this bedlam were that a man in Company C had been shot "through the jaws," and another soldier from Company B had been wounded. Smith chose a pathetic incident to close out this entry: "A wounded mule came to our ditch today and seemed to have no sensation of fear," he wrote. "The Yankies fired 50 or 60 rounds at him. Finally, he staggered and fell into our ditch and died, though we tried to drive him off." Smith indicated that the boys had to work some to get him out of the ditch after darkness fell.[50]

Finally, Swan of S. D. Lee's Brigade also spoke of the "tremendous" cannonade that, according to him, ran from daylight to 8 a.m. "For three hours a perfect storm of shot and shell was hurled upon us from nearly their whole line," he noted, with the shells bursting and scattering fragments about "like rain," though few were hurt. "It is believed that Johnston's army was making an attack on them from outside," Swan added with some considerable degree of wishful thinking.[51]

---

[49] Smith, *A Smith in Service*, 60.
[50] Ibid.
[51] Swan, "A Tennessean at the Siege of Vicksburg," 368.

The Yankees, at around 4 a.m. on the morning of 21 June, opened up "a heavy fire of artillery and sharp-shooters" along his entire line, General Vaughn noted in his daily report, "which [was] kept up until around 9 a.m., when it gradually ceased." Some of his line was also subjected to the attention of the two annoying field pieces being moved with regularity about on the peninsula to avoid a fix on their position by Confederate gunners. He reported that one man in Ward's Artillery Battalion was wounded, and three men with the 61st Tennessee also hurt as result of enemy artillery fire.[52]

Hynds of the 31st Tennessee indicated that the night passed with extreme silence, leaving the boys to believe that the Northerners were "fixing for a general assault," though none was made. Grant had learned the futility of "charging entrenchments defended by brave men supported by cannon double-shotted with grape and canister," Hynds supposed.[53]

"This is the sixth Sunday since we came into the ditches that surround the Hill City of the Mississippi," Lieutenant Smith of the 31st Tennessee wrote in his daily entry, the second time in two days that he made two entries for the day in his journal. Finding a tattered silver lining in an immense and deep thunderhead, he indicated that the Confederates had little territory to protect, while the Federals must concern themselves with some thirty to forty miles to their front and rear. Any day Smith expected to hear the deafening roar of Johnston's cannon, driving Grant's minions pell-mell before the Confederate advance all the way to the banks of the great Mississippi itself.[54]

"The Yankies have kept up a heavy picket fire today," Smith noted, "sometimes with whole volleys poured in at a time. A man in Company B died last night from a wound received yesterday on picket. Company C had one shot in the jaw today—not serious." Smith reported that the balls flew thick around them wherever they were, and it might seem unusual to the outsider that they walked about seemingly oblivious to all danger. And even in their dire straits, the boys found time to talk. "Some talked of going up to Camp Chaice [Chase]," he indicated. "Some talked of good things they used to eat at home." With that, Smith believed that the men stood it "first rate." He noted that it was "difficult" for any man to be surrounded and shot at by numerous foes, living on one-third rations, shut off from all communication with their homes and the outside world. Many of the boys found it hard not to rail against their

---

[52] Report of Gen. John C. Vaughn, 21 June 1863, *Official Records*, ser. 1, vol. 24, pt. 2, p. 695.

[53] Hynds, "Original Handwritten Notes," 17–18.

[54] Smith, *A Smith in Service*, 60.

superior officers, Smith believed, but for all that, the last people the men would want to see captured, killed, or wounded would be their generals.[55]

The First Violent Sortie, 21 June. Perhaps Smith felt obligated to make another entry on 21 June because of all the hostile action that took place outside their lines on the night of 21 June. He wrote that at midnight, two companies of the 43rd Tennessee and one company of the 57th Georgia, under direct command of Colonel William Barkuloo, attempted to storm only a few yards over some of the Federal forward rifle pits probably occupied by one or more of Cyrus Hall's Illinois regiments. Because of their proximity, these pits had become a source of considerable annoyance. Though initially the tactical strike was a surprise and successful, the Georgians and East Tennesseans were forced back due to the withering fire from several well-placed rifle pits on their flanks, resulting in the loss of Lieutenant James Crookshanks killed and four or five men wounded. The Yankees' casualties were unknown. Some of the young lieutenant's men braving brisk musketry carried Crookshanks's body back to their works. "This ditch will be a source of much annoyance to us as long as they continue to occupy it," Smith predicted. "They kept up a nice fire and showered balls all over us."[56]

Soon after, some of the enemy batteries in the vicinity were roused and sent several projectiles whistling into the Confederate battlements. Smith believed that some of the shells traveled nearly three miles before striking their works. "A shell came like a stray messenger and struck the ground 40 yards from my tent [failing to explode on impact]," he declared. "1st Sgt. W. T. Dyer and Pvt. Hugh Harper got it and attempted to unload it." The terrible projectile exploded, and Smith believed it to be a miracle that neither of the men was killed. In fact, only Harper sustained a slight injury from the experience. Smith marveled at their foolishness and believed that these men "would not trifle with any more [unexploded ordnance] soon." He noted that some of the shells contained numerous musket balls in a tin box full of powder, and "made an especially loud report when they exploded, scattering deadly minies in all directions."[57]

Providing additional details regarding the deadly sortie, Sergeant Stamper of the 43rd Tennessee noted that at sunset, Companies A and F relieved Companies D and I in the forward picket line. At 11 p.m. a "battalion" of Georgia troops, which Stamper indicated belonged to Barton's rather than

---

[55] Ibid.
[56] Ibid.
[57] Ibid.

Cumming's Brigade, was sent along with Companies B and G of the 43rd Tennessee to charge and occupy the near ditches bristling with enemy sharpshooters. These rifle pits had been constructed recently and were a short distance in front of Reynolds's lines. "We succeeded in running them out of the works," Stamper recorded, "but it did us very little good as the yanks came back the next day and recaptured the ditches." Their success could not be allowed to stand. Since Stamper's regiment was involved, he was able to provide more complete information on the casualties. Lieutenant James W. Crookshanks of Stamper's company was killed. Captain Andrew J. Cawood of Company B was wounded in the leg, Sergeant A. Russell Denton of Company G was mortally wounded, and "Gib Murray [Company G] was shot in the nose." Companies F and A held steady at their positions during the engagement to the left of where it was fought.[58]

Out in this advanced position in front of the trenches, Private Darr of the 43rd Tennessee later recorded on this night of mayhem that he was "out on picket outside of our lines [though probably not when the attack was initiated]." His description indicated that "the Yankees are shooting over us all the time—have to stay here till night—considerable firing of small arms—we are between the fire of our men and the Yanks."[59]

Clack of the 43rd Tennessee, who was personally involved in the attack, wrote: "it was with great reluctance that I went into it, but I said nothing." He noted that even if the Confederates had captured these pits, they would never have been able to hold them. Some of the boys in his regiment (Companies B and G) and a company from the 57th Georgia rushed the entrenchments before their lines in order to drive the bluecoats out of the ditches they had constructed close to one of Colonel Reynolds's picket posts. "We succeeded in driving them from their first ditch," Clack wrote, but overwhelming numbers in the darkness opened fire on the attackers, causing the East Tennesseans and Georgians to fall back in good order. He noted that the way the enemy rifle pits were constructed with their protective parapets facing the Confederate works. Hence, "they afforded no protection from the enemy's lines."[60] Additionally, Stamper added, the 57th Georgia suffered one man killed and two wounded.[61]

Captain Hynds of the 31st Tennessee indicated that two companies of the 43rd Tennessee and two from "a Georgia regiment" launched the attack. They

---

[58] Stamper, "Travels of the 43rd Tennessee," 75.

[59] Darr, "Diary," 9.

[60] Clack, "Personal Diary," 5.

[61] Stamper, "Travels of the 43rd Tennessee," 75.

assaulted the rifle pits of the enemy's sharp-shooters to the front of Reynolds' and Cumming's lines. "They charged and took the first ditch," Hynds noted, "but were unable to hold it." Falling back with the loss of ten brave men wounded and one "brave and gallant young officer," Lieutenant James Crookshanks, killed. "Crookshanks never spoke a word after the ball struck him," Hynds wrote, "but fell from his feet a corpse." He confirmed that Captain Cawood and Sergeant Russell Denton were also among those wounded.[62]

Clack of the 43rd Tennessee reported that another Sabbath (21 June) had rolled around after the chaos of the night before, and it found the Confederate soldiers of East Tennessee and their comrades from other states still "confined to the neighboring hill of Vicksburg without any better prospects of our deliverance." Reports that Johnston had finally attacked Grant's rear circulated, but Clack was skeptical. The sharpshooters "are pecking away this morning as usual," he stated, and the firing was maintained the whole day.[63]

"We have now been shut up for thirty-six days and under fire for thirty-five since the 18th of May," Swan of Bradley County serving in S. D. Lee's Brigade noted in his entry on 21 June. "The experience of such strife is not to be forgotten in a life time." He indicated that if the good Lord spared him, he would dedicate the remainder of his life to his service "with more of zeal and thoughtfulness than before." Swan had witnessed an acquaintance of his "torn to fragments" by an exploding shell nearby, which also wounded several others. The minie balls from the sharpshooters the day before struck quite close for three hours, and spent balls dropped "in about every direction." Yet, he wrote, "I feel more anxiously the danger to my country than to myself if the enemy should wrest this stronghold from us." He prayed to God that it would not be allowed to happen. "How pleasant it would be to sit today," Swan yearned, "quietly in church at Cleveland, surrounded by friends as of times gone by, and join in the solemn hymns of praise and thanksgiving." He noted that every Sabbath day since 1 May had been disturbed by the sound of hostile cannon "nearby," and it was on the first Sabbath in May that "we retreated from Grand Gulf pursued by the enemy." On the second Sabbath, his brigade was within the sound of the skirmishing at the Big Black River, and on the third, "we were retreating to Vicksburg from the unfortunate field of Baker's Creek." Since that time, the Sundays had been profaned by the "continuous conflict around Vicksburg." Swan noted that today he was unwell and had been for several days,

---

[62] Hynds, "Original Handwritten Notes," 18.
[63] Clack, "Personal Diary," 5.

believing that "the usual disease of summer [possibly diarrhea] is prevailing to a very considerable extent."[64]

The Folks at Home Worry. The siege was also extremely trying on the families back home in East Tennessee, mainly because they had no way of knowing anything specific about their loved ones confined at Vicksburg, and the general news they read in papers describing the terrible events could do nothing but fuel their anxiety. "Your note of [June] 18th containing the painful intelligence of my brother's being wounded is too hard," wrote the sister of Lieutenant Colonel David M. Key of the 43rd Tennessee, identified only as "E.K.B." She had addressed the letter to Key's wife, Elizabeth, and added, "I need not tell you that it distresses us very much for he is so fleshy and the weather so warm, that if he is seriously wounded, it will doubtless go very hard for him." Key's sister ventured naively the suggestion that if "Lizzie," as Key's wife was nicknamed, "could go to him, it would be a great blessing," but she realized "it is not likely you could get through the Yankee lines."[65]

"We have felt much concern for our folks this long while," E. K. B. told her sister-in-law, "and still the siege continues. We cannot know their fate." She hoped that something could be done soon to relieve Vicksburg, and she believed that all the other troops in the region "are said to be coming to the rescue." Her hoped and prayed that these forces could "relieve our brave and suffering friends," and she encouraged Lizzie to be as hopeful as she could be. "When all is known," Key's sister feared, despite her cheering words, "there will be trouble at every hearthstone." She shared the news that Mr. Johnson in Madisonville had received a telegram from Tate Hain at Jackson, Mississippi, which indicated that their son, Jimmie Johnson of the 62nd Tennessee, had been reported missing since the Battle of the Big Black River. The family was, as Key's sister reported, "much afflicted on account of it." "Mrs. Johnson is so nervous she can hardly bare anything," E.K.B. wrote, "this will about kill her unless she can hear something to relieve her mind."[66]

As much as the poor boys sent to the vile Federal prison camps would suffer, there were usually mothers at home who fretted away the time with them. Key's sister also informed Lizzie about the evil events occurring in East Tennessee during this period. "No doubt a great deal of mischief is being done," E. K. B. reported, adding, "there are not enough troops in this part of the country to hinder the vandals from accomplishing all they wish." There had

---

[64] Swan, "A Tennessean at the Siege of Vicksburg," 368.

[65] E. K. B. to "Lizzie" Key, 21 June 1863, Key Papers.

[66] Ibid.

been a rumor that bushwhackers had burned a factory of some sort at Lenoirs, but that had proved false, though "it created a painful excitement throughout the section." Still, she assumed the report of fighting going on in Knoxville might be true; she anticipated news on it that day. But her thoughts were never far from David Key and his comrades in far away Mississippi. "Let the fate of Vicksburg be what it may," she suggested, "but I do hope our dear ones may be spared." She begged Lizzie to write soon if she heard anything at all about her brother, "whether good or bad. Mother is very anxious."[67]

General John Vaughn reported on 22 June that a few shots had been exchanged between his guns and an enemy battery on the lower line during the evening, though sharpshooting mercifully had been rather slight. "The enemy are making a line of intrenchments from the battery recently established," he noted, "from near the river to the valley road, perhaps as a rifle pit, or more likely as a protection to get in and out of the battery." His brigade lost during the reporting period one man in the 62nd Tennessee killed.[68]

The Second Sortie, 22 June—Getting It Right. Though the attack the night before on the Yankee rifle pits outside their lines had been ultimately unsuccessful, another attempt by portions of Reynolds's and Cumming's reserves would be attempted the next night. This time they would utilize the sufficient numbers required to force the invaders out permanently. Stamper of the 43rd Tennessee indicated that the action transpired on the night of 22 June, and it is possible that Clack may have confused the dates and circumstances since they happened two nights in a row. He started off his entry calmly enough by acknowledging that at dark the Confederate pickets withdrew "a little." Clack surmised insufficient numbers had led to the Confederates' failure to hold what they had captured the night before, the 22 June sortie had fully half of the 57th Georgia (Cumming's reserve regiment) and three-fifths of Gillespie's 43rd Tennessee attacking the enemy's rifle pits again around midnight. The attack drove out all the Yankees (except for those captured) back to their main line. The boys then set to filling in the works with available dirt that had been used to brace the pits. The desperate affair, often involving hand-to-hand grappling, Clack noted, was attended with casualties on both sides, during which the Confederates captured a lieutenant colonel and nine or ten men, but the Southerners had two men killed and twenty wounded on the

---

[67] Ibid.

[68] Report of Gen. John C. Vaughn, 22 June 1863, *Official Records*, ser. 1, vol. 24, pt. 2, p. 696.

Southern side. The enemy numbers killed and wounded were not indicated, but were likely much greater.[69]

Specifically, the casualties in Company B, according to Stamper, were Private George Loy, killed in action, and Private A. J. Houghton, mortally wounded and dying the next day. Private William Boles was wounded in the leg. Wounded in Company D was Private Jack Waller, who suffered a gunshot to the leg. Casualties in Company G were Private Albert Jarnigan, mortally wounded; Private Huston Witt, wounded in the arm; Captain William H. Wiseman, wounded in the arm, and Private Thomas J. Newman, in the jaw. Sam Dennison suffered a mortal wound. Losses in Company I were Captain William H. McKamy, who received a severe wound in the shoulder that later required the removal of three inches of bone. Private James Henry Darr suffered a slight wound. Wounds incurred in Company H were Private Tom Farmer, wounded in the shoulder, and C. M. Riggins, a slight wound in the ankle. Losses in Company E were Sandy Henry, killed in action, Peter Southerland, wounded in the arm, and Bill Fryerson, a slight wound in the hip. Stamper indicated that several others were wounded slightly by minie balls and bayonets, and some were "burned a little" due to circumstances not indicated.[70]

Calvin Smith of the 31st Tennessee issued his version of the melee, indicating that sometime after 10 p.m., Colonel Barkuloo again led the Georgians and East Tennesseans on the second sortie, taking the ditches occupied by the Federals just to their front. The firing from small arms was heavy for nearly half an hour. Losses were not yet available.[71] Hynds of the 31st Tennessee reported on the second attack in as many nights by elements of the 43rd Tennessee, adding that they were supplemented not only by their usual friends the Georgians, but also by some of the Missouri reserves as well. The result was a success. Hynds supposed, however, the casualties to be high for the 31st Tennessee's sister regiment: one killed, three mortally wounded, and seventeen severely wounded. Captain William H. Wiseman, he noted, was among the wounded. The Yankee loss in killed and wounded was not known, though the attack netted a lieutenant colonel and nine riflemen prisoners. From these prisoners, the Confederates learned that the Federal army was busy digging a tunnel toward the upper works in order to "lay a mine and blow up one of our batteries." "They beat all creation to work," Hynds marveled.[72]

---

[69] Clack, "Personal Diary," 5.
[70] Stamper, "Travels of the 43rd Tennessee," 66–67.
[71] Smith, *A Smith in Service*, 60.
[72] Hynds, "Original Handwritten Notes," 19.

Though Stamper of the 43rd Tennessee stated on this date that there was "no change along the line," matters in his own regiment had changed.[73] Spradling of the same regiment wrote that the 43rd Tennessee had "done considerable picket duty outside our ditches." He added that on the night of 22 June the old 43rd Tennessee charged the enemy that had succeeded in entrenching themselves close to and parallel with the Confederate ditches. "We routed them completely," Spradling noted proudly, but, he acknowledged, "we lost 23 killed and wounded in less time almost than it takes to write about it." Among those wounded was one of Spradling's friends, Andrew Jackson "Jack" Waller.[74]

Clack, also of Gillespie's regiment, wrote in his journal, "another attempt was made last night [22 June] to charge the enemy trenches" by six companies of the 43rd Tennessee and a "squad" of Georgians, "which was successful." Though the attack drove the Yankees back and allowed the boys to fill up the ditches, Clack agreed with all the others who reported on the attack that the 43rd Tennessee suffered severely: "21 killed and wounded." Private George Loy of Company B was killed, and Andy Hughes and William Boles were wounded. Despite all the sacrifice and bravery, Clack admitted, "the Yankees occupy the same ground again today that they did yesterday." He stated that Andy Hughes died the next day, 22 June, of his wounds, and that Loy had not been killed instantly, but had died later that morning.[75]

"Last night [21/22 June] was a terrible and long-to-be remembered night," James Darr of the 43rd Tennessee wrote in reference to the fierce skirmish fought outside the ditches the night before. He indicated that his regiment was ordered out at midnight to run their adversaries from outside the entrenchments they had captured, which, Darr felt, "had been cowardly abandoned by [Cumming's] Georgians." His description of the action was extremely detailed and explained the reason for the 43rd Tennessee's excessive casualties. "We went out and found them ready for us," Darr noted, "and the first thing we knew, they were shooting at us from all directions. Yet, we run them off after having one man shot dead and 21 others wounded." Among these twenty-one were Captain William H. McKamy, Captain Wiseman, Albert Jarnigan, and Houston Witt. He also listed himself as one of the wounded.

---

[73] Stamper, "Travels of the 43rd Tennessee," 67.

[74] Spradling, "Diary," 1.

[75] Clack, "Personal Diary," 5.

Jarnigan's wound proved fatal, as did two others, according to Darr: "Captain McKamy had all the bones taken out of his shoulder."[76]

The heavy concentration of casualties as a result of this sortie can probably be best explained by the words of the great Russian novelist Lev Tolstoy, describing the instinctive reaction to sudden ambush: "When you are out on a raid, and when they begin firing, don't get into a crowd where there are many men. When you fellows get frightened you always try to get close together with a lot of others. You think it is merrier to be with others, but that's where it is the worse of all! They always aim at a crowd."[77]

This "little occurrence was spread through the camps afterwards," according to William Tunnard of the 3rd Louisiana. Among the overwhelmed Midwesterners occupying the ditches, Lieutenant Colonel Camm of the 14th Illinois, seeing that he was either to be captured or forced to run the gauntlet to get back to his main lines, "decided to lie down among the dead in the ditch, expecting to remain 'perdue' until our forces retired, and then his escape could be secured." Once the Georgians and East Tennesseans began to fill in the ditch as graves to the dead there, the Yankee officer came back to life, "and the dead, to all appearance, rose up and walked, declaring he was not ready to be buried alive."[78] In short order Camm became the reluctant guest of the Vicksburg garrison.

The boost to the garrison's morale resulting from this little engagement was reflected in the diary of a Louisiana soldier in the upper works who wrote: "Two regiments on the right—Texans we believe—charged upon the enemy outside the lines, capturing a colonel, lieutenant-colonel, a captain, and eight privates; one hundred and fifty stands of arms, spades, shovels, &c.; killed and wounded forty, losing only eight men. This little episode of the siege caused much excitement and enthusiasm along the whole line."[79] Another inaccurate report as to the composition of the attacking force indicated: "a couple of Georgia regiments charged a federal breastwork about 50 yards to their front which had been thrown up [on the night of 21 June]." A regiment of bluecoats in the trenches soon found themselves dislodged at the point of bayonet, and

---

[76] Darr, "Diary," 9.

[77] Lev Tolstoy, *The Cossacks*, trans. Louise and Aylmer Maude (New York NY: Alfred A. Knopf, 1994) 174.

[78] Tunnard, *A Southern Record*, 225.

[79] Bearss, *The Campaign for Vicksburg*, 3: 887; Report of Gen. Carter L. Stevenson, 29 July 1863, *Official Records*, ser. 1, vol. 24, pt. 2, p. 345.

the works were "taken with very slight loss." These ditches were refilled using the entrenching tools the Federals had used.[80]

Smith of the 31st Tennessee indicated that the day of 22 June had dawned peacefully and a calm fine one, cool and spring-like similar to a many mornings he had experienced back in "old Hawkins County." Roasting ears of corn and blackberries had been ripe for nearly two weeks, and he fondly recollected picking the berries back home, stewing them in sugar. Though there were numerous bushes between the opposing works, the boys could not get to them for the Yankees' shooting. Smith looked forward to being on picket at night when the boys could pick and eat all they wanted with less danger. That night, however, would be no time for picking blackberries.[81]

"Parson Goforth told us last night that J. H. Everhart's arm would be cut off today at 10 a. m.," Smith noted, adding, "I think I will be there if my presence is not needed here." He indicated that he had made a porthole in the trench parapet so he could observe the enemy without being seen or shot at. "The cannon shot last night presented a lively scene," he recollected. "Four or five batteries were firing through the darkness of the night by guess. The shells would often pass each other while others at right angles followed by a streak of fire emitted by the fuse by which the powder in the shell is exploded." He noted that the projectiles often came straight towards them, striking the ground or passing overhead. Either way the boys never failed to dodge. "John Reynolds was on picket yesterday," Smith wrote, "and could not scarcely move without being shot at." Porter's gunboats were booming out on the river as Smith wrote, "though they keep a respectful distance from our batteries in the City."[82]He longed for the day when the garrison would hear "the bulldogs in the rear, baying at the Yankies like frightful demons." Cheers would ring the knobs and valleys around Vicksburg, he proclaimed, and if it could only happen on the Fourth of July, "what a jubilee!" He knew that the men had suffered many hardships and privations, but "I think too much of my country to say ought against the Confederacy or our peerless liberty."[83]

"Equal rights is the go with many of us," Smith reported, "while others live in constant fear of being subjugated." He indicated that his health

[80] A A. Hoehling, *Vicksburg: 47 Days of Siege* (New York NY: Fairfax Press, 1969) 212.
[81] Smith, *A Smith in Service*, 60.
[82] Ibid.
[83] Ibid.

continued "good," which he attributed strangely enough to the boys' "light diet." He believed that the wounded and sick were mending quickly and rejoining their comrades in the ditches. Smith noted that J. R. Dykes and Jesse Grigsby had both returned to the 31st Tennessee's fold some days ago. J. A. Tucker was still in the hospital, however, and Smith feared such would be the case for some time. "I think bad management has been given J. H. Everhart," Smith suggested, "or his hand would not have had to be cut off." The usual care given such wounds, he indicated, was continuous coldwater application to the injury.[84]

When he would have the time to sort out the facts, Smith wanted to give a "true" statement of the fight outside the works the night before. From what he had gathered by the time of this entry, the second picket charge from the Fourth Brigade found the 43rd Tennessee engaged both times, losing a few men killed and wounded. Some of these wounded had since died. The attack allowed the men to fill up the enemy's ditches, and they captured one lieutenant colonel and nine of his men, in addition to 500–600 ditching tools. "Nothing can resist the impetuous charge of our pent up boys," Smith declared. He noted there were five companies involved in the attack: two from East Tennessee, two from Georgia, and one from the Missouri reserves.[85]

Swan of S. D. Lee's Brigade wrote that the firing throughout the night and day was continuous. "When we lie down at night, the chances increase that we will be struck any moment by a ball or shell fragment," he perceived. A massive 65-pounder siege gun planted on their right and continuously slamming mammoth shells into their lines was particularly worrisome to Lee's men,. "This morning, one burst and tore up the ground in our fireplace, and scattered pieces about our little nook in every direction," he noted. Whenever his acquaintances became casualties, they reminded him that "death [is] very near to us." As if to illustrate his point, Swan wrote that Ben Murphy had been wounded that day and had probably died. Skirmishing was fierce at night all up and down the line, he indicated, and the "greatest battle of the war" was anticipated daily. "May God in mercy prosper our arms and drive back the invaders discomfited in their own land, and give us peace," he prayed.[86]

Vaughn's report indicated nearly the same routine on 23 June as the day before, and for some days before that: some sharp-shooting, with an occasional shell from their cannon here and there, until about 8 p.m., when a heavy

---

[84] Ibid.

[85] Ibid., 60–61.

[86] Swan, "A Tennessean at the Siege of Vicksburg," 368–69.

concentrated explosion of artillery broke out all along the line north and south lasting for almost two full hours. The East Tennessee general stated that the Yankees were still busy with their entrenchment work in the valley at the base the Confederate abatis. His men suffered no casualties this daily report period.[87]

Flag of Lynch's Battery. Lynch's Battery overlooking the bend in the river above Vicksburg was always threatened during the siege by gunboats and land batteries fixed on its position, or subject to a quick raid by Sherman's infantry that could have separated it and the other guns of Battery Tennessee from infantry support on the high prominence behind them. Lynch's guns' close proximity to Sherman's batteries on the garrison's extreme left (and northern) flank resulted in most of the East Tennesseans' siege pieces being at times disabled. One of Vaughn's aides, General Jackson "Crozier" Ramsey, son of the influential Dr. J. G. M. Ramsey of Knoxville, placed atop the parapet of one of Captain Lynch's guns a "beautifully finished [first national] flag, made and presented to the brigade by his deceased sister." Young Ramsey, like Lieutenant John Toland, another of Vaughn's aides, was a scion of a prominent pro-Confederate family in East Tennessee, and had likely been assigned to duty on the general's staff, where it was thought he would be relatively safe from danger. His flag, however, "at once became a target for the enemy's artillery," Ramsey's father remembered, and on more than one occasion, the Federals were said to have made attempts to take it. After the surrender, Crozier secreted the tattered and torn flag in his trunk and took the flag safely home.[88]

Johnston Begins to Annoy Grant's Back Lines. Word was again making the rounds that Johnston and his forces were pressing the federal rear from the east side of the Big Black based on the sounds of cannonading heard from that direction the day before, according to Swan of Bradley County. "Each day brings us nearer to the decisive moment," he wrote, "and the long agony must close before many more days." The anxiety over Johnston and whether he could be successful added to the boys' distress because they realized that should he be defeated in battle with Grant, "our fate will be sealed." All that was propping up the garrison now was the forlorn hope that imminent relief was soon forthcoming. Once that hope vanished, Swan admitted, "we will have to succumb." Though subsistence might last another twenty-five to thirty days should tragedy befall Johnston and his long awaited rescue attempt, Swan

---

[87] Report of Gen. John C. Vaughn, 23 June 1863, *Official Records*, ser. 1, vol. 24, pt. 2, p. 696.

[88] William B. Hasseltine, *Dr. J. G. M. Ramsey: Autobiography and Letters* (Nashville TN: Tennessee Historical Commission, 1954) 124.

indicated, "the spirits of the men would be gone and demoralization would become general." His trust in God remained since he had "sustained us during two years of fierce war."[89]

The Enemy's Fire Intensifies. During the day, Swan wrote that he had heard about the activities of the 43rd Tennessee and the 57th Georgia the night before, and of the desperate fight that transpired in front of the ditches to Reynolds's and Cumming's front. "A number of men and officers on our side were killed outright," he noted, "and a number wounded." The Confederates were said to have held their ground until daylight, when they "filled up the ditches, burying the Yankee dead in the trenches they themselves had dug."[90]

The usual sharpshooting was reported on Wednesday, the twenty-fourth, Vaughn wrote, but little cannonading. None of his men were casualties during the day.[91] Hynds of the 31st Tennessee wrote that though another long day had passed, "it has not been long enough to tire the Yankees." He believed that more firing than usual was kept up along Reynolds's lines, and the Confederate river batteries and Porter's gunboats traded insults all day long. Whether incredibly prophetic or whether written after the war provided him with some new material, he stated: "if Johnston don't come in ten days from this time, we will have to go up the spout for want of provisions." For days the Federals had been firing directly at the positions of the 31st Tennessee, he wrote, with a seven-inch rifle playing on their works, throwing "a shell faster than any I have ever heard." Another siege piece to the right had been also firing on their lines all day.[92]

The regiment was charged with the night's placement of pickets, according to Smith of the 31st Tennessee, consisting of thirty men under the command of his friend Lieutenant James A Webster. The Yankees charged Barton's works with a sizable force, necessitating the withdrawal by Webster and his pickets who were exposed to heavy fire. They occupied another position a bit less exposed and remained there until daylight, when they were ordered back into the main works. Smith indicated that he checked on J. H. Everhart the day before and found out that he would have to have his arm taken off that day. The operation occurred some hours later, and Smith noted that Everhart "bore

---

[89] Swan, "A Tennessean at the Siege of Vicksburg," 369.

[90] Ibid.

[91] Report of Gen. John C. Vaughn, 24 June 1864, *Official Records*, ser. 1, vol. 24, pt. 2, p. 696.

[92] Hynds, "Original Handwritten Notes," 20.

it fine." The wound could not have been cured without the operation, according to the Persia native.[93]

"There is heavy firing on both sides today," Smith wrote. "More than usual." He was quick to note, "our boys are plugging away, too" even though the Yankee infantry were in their ditches 600 yards away. Regardless, he boasted, "they dodge back very quick when they hear our shots." Smith suggested that though he had first doubted such reports, he had seen too many instances through his "port hole" of times when some of the Confederate marksmen hit the boys in blue across the way at a range of what Smith guessed to be nearly 800 yards. "The mules and horses often graze between us, and the Yankies kill every one they see," he recorded. "Perhaps a 1000 head of cattle and horses have been killed since the siege commenced." Grants men shot slow moving milk cows routinely whenever they appeared between the lines to prevent them from reentering the Confederate works to provide aid, comfort, and nourishment to the Southern cause. Smith indicated that this slaughter required the men to dig holes after dark in order to cover up the poor beasts.[94]

The Death of Captain Claiborne, 3rd Maryland Battery.

"There were a great many casualties during the siege," Captain Reuben G. Clark of the 59th Tennessee remembered, also in the vicinity. "I cannot tell you how many men I saw killed in various ways: some torn to pieces by accidental shells, others shot in the head by sharp-shooters, &c." He stated his was one of two companies that supported the 3rd Maryland Battery under the command of Captain Claiborne, "who was shot almost to pieces in an artillery duel three weeks after the siege began." Clark reported that he was standing by afterward stunned and transfixed by the frightful spectacle, unmindful then of his own personal danger. The shells were still coming in and the Yankees had the range. "Get out of the way, Clark! You'll be killed!" someone yelled at him, making him aware of his exposure. The greatest mortality to the Vicksburg army, however, during the siege and the campaign in general, according to Clark, was sickness.[95]

The 43rd Tennessee Is Called Forward Again. Clack of the 43rd Tennessee, in reporting the assault the previous night, noted that the next regiment on their left charged the Yankee ditches just to the front of their works "and drove them back," but the enemy was back in their old positions that next day. He also

[93] Smith, *A Smith in Service*, 61.
[94] Ibid.
[95] Clark, *Valleys of the Shadow*, 25.

observed that a mortar battery on the rafts out on the river was shelling the town, and that the sharpshooting was pretty much as usual.[96]

"Companies D and I relieved Companies K and E at picket," Stamper noted. Companies A, F, G, and B were sent to the ditches with Colonel Barkuloo's regiment, the 57th Georgia as support, where "his men dug a ditch in front of his cannon to prevent the enemy from undermining our works." The men of 43rd Tennessee and the 57th Georgia, having shared so much together in the front of their works the past few days, were finding themselves by now perhaps on first-name bases. While involved in this fortification assignment, Stamper reported, the boys were charged by the enemy "and driven back into our ditches." At midnight, he recorded, at the conclusion of one long day, "we were ordered to General Barton's right, fronting the river." We went into the ditches at daylight, he noted.[97] Whose "ditches" he did not specify, though Barton's would be the ones. The regiment, from its reserve lines on the river, carefully made the short traverse from their positions to those across the hollow with several stops and starts.

Meanwhile, up the line in the Fourth Brigade Hospital, James H. Darr of the 43rd Tennessee continued to mend from his "slight," though unspecified, wound suffered in the previous evening's assault. He resided in the same tent quartering the severely injured Captain McKamy and Charley Graves, who had earlier had his leg amputated as a result of a shell fragment received on 3 June.[98]

Swan, writing from the left of Stevenson's lines, stated that the Yankee mortars were busy nearly all day, and that some of the land batteries of heavy Parrott guns on the peninsula fixed on the river batteries and continued a lively fire as well, doing no damage.[99]

Grant Sets Off a Mine. Though 25 June would dawn routinely enough, it would be a day of considerable excitement when Grant's sappers set off a massive mine composed of 2,200 pounds of black powder under the center of the Confederate works. Vaughn noted in his report for the period, however, that the day for his men had been typical and composed of a little sharpshooting from his front, accompanied by an occasional shot in return from his own men. Little shelling transpired, and most things were quiet along his line, especially during the night. "No casualties," he indicated.[100]

---

[96] Clack, "Personal Diary," 6.

[97] Stamper, "Travels of the 43rd Tennessee," 67.

[98] Darr, "Diary," 10.

[99] Swan, "A Tennessean at the Siege of Vicksburg," 369.

[100] Report of Gen. John C. Vaughn, 25 June 1863, *Official Records*, ser. 1, vol. 24, pt. 2, p. 697.

Officer Controversy in the 62nd Tennessee. Military matters and internal squabbles among Vaughn's officers were not entirely laid aside with the crisis confronting the army. On 25 June, General Pemberton received the following letter from Captain Nathaniel Atkinson of the 62nd Tennessee:

Sir: I would respectfully request to you that there is a contest between myself and Capt. William R. Smith of Company I, as to who is entitled to the promotion of major which place has recently been made vacant by the resignation of Major [Simeon D.] Reynolds. The facts from which you will be entitled to decide who is entitled to the promotion are these: the companies composing the Regt. were very humbly gotten up and organized, it was not known who of the officers elected were entitled to seniority in consequence of priority of organization. So it was proposed by the Col. (nearly all the Capts. being present), that we decide both letter and rule of the draw. This proposition was agreed to by all present and the drawing was supervised by Col. Rowan and Maj. Reynolds with the result of assigning to me the position of ranking captain of the regiment and A Company of the regiment. And so far as I have heard both officers and men are satisfied. On this capacity I have been acting since the organization of the Regt. Captain Smith has been giving his tacit consent to this draw for nearly eight months, and therefore waived his right to the promotion, if he ever had any. Besides, his Co. did not draw rations nor perform any kind of military service for several days. No one heard him complain when there was reason as he thought for promotion, while I have been discharging the duties of Ranking Capt. of the Regt. all that while. I would further state that if Capt. Smith's claim were recognized it would have the effect of producing great dissatisfaction in the Regt. And involve the necessity within the Regt. of being a source of great confusion thereafter as to rank. I was authorized by Maj. Gen. John P. McCown, commanding the Dept. of East Tenn. on the 3rd day of Sept., 1862, to raise a Co. of infty. for the war and appointed recruiting officer for the same, but my Co. was not organized until the 20th of the month. Yet I might have had from Jan. 3rd as the Co. was received by the War Dept., & authority given by Genl. McCown recognized by the Same. As the only field officer we have present is sick, I earnestly request that you decide the matter as soon as possible. I have the honor to be very respectfully, your obedient servant, Nat'l Atkinson, Capt., comdg. Co. (A), 62nd Regt. Tenn. Vols.[101]

When matters were settled, Captain Smith of Cocke County was promoted to "major."[102]

The Boys Are Called to Be Ever Vigilant. "The enemy was quite still today," George Hynds of the 31st Tennessee reported, "until about 4 o'clock when they opened a heavy fire upon our line with artillery and small arms, lasting about one hour." The enemy's motive was unknown to those inside the fortifications. Hynds noted that if the Yanks thought they would scare us, "they were very much mistaken."[103]

The distance from the explosion of the mine would keep the initial news of its ignition from the East Tennessee defenders, though the sound of its discharge would have had to impress them as something more than just a few siege pieces being discharged. Though there was no demonstration on the right, Stamper of the 43rd Tennessee wrote that the enemy engaged in considerable cannonading and sharpshooting in front of General Seth Barton's line, Barton's Georgians constituted the extreme right flank of the Confederate works at Vicksburg. Stamper stated that Major Lawson Guthrie received a slight flesh wound in the thigh during the shooting, and C. W. Cruse of Company K died of "sickness" during the day[104]

"Four companies of the 43rd Tennessee were ordered out last night," Clack reported, to reinforce Colonel Bradford's 31st Tennessee, where a heavy attack was expected. The 43rd Tennessee remained in close quarters in those ditches with their fellow East Tennesseans "until 11 or 12 o'clock" when the regiment was relieved, having received orders to move back toward the old position on the river. With the dawning of a new morning on 25 June, an attack was still considered likely any moment. The sharpshooters, according to Clack, were hard at work, and Grant seemed to be testing the lines. Clack also noted the wounding of Major Lawson Guthrie by a sharpshooter. "We had heavy cannonading here on the lower end of our lines this evening," he wrote. As was the custom, Clack noted, one third of the men in the works were held on watch while the other two thirds attempted to sleep. His prayer was that "Heaven's

---

[101] 62nd Tennessee, *Compiled Service Records.*
[102] Ibid.
[103] Hynds, "Original Handwritten Notes," 21.
[104] Stamper, "Travels of the 43rd Tennessee," 67.

blessings rest on us, and that the all seeing eye of Jehovah may watch over us and protect us from all danger and harm."[105]

Firing occurred along the line as usual on 25 June, according to James H. Darr of the 43rd Tennessee, and from his hospital vantage point he perhaps saw a fellow East Tennessean, Bill Harman, brought in with an undesignated wound. Darr reported that Captain McKamy was doing as well as could be expected, with most of his shoulder bones having been removed. Along around five in the afternoon, Darr reported that Major Guthrie of the 43rd Tennessee was brought in with a gunshot wound in his thigh. At that time of day, Darr heard heavy cannonading going on all around the lines. Something was certainly up, he suspected.[106]

The 4 p.m. bombardment, which Swan termed "the hottest yet," suggested that a major Union assault was imminent, but enemy "made only a partial one on the Jackson Road." Using some of his men who had been coalminers in Pennsylvania, Grant had a couple of shafts dug from his works to points underneath the Confederate lines. At their terminus were planted massive charges of powder, through which Grant hoped to set off explosions to cave in strategic points in Pemberton's line. After the gunpowder was detonated, massive assaults would be launched when it was believed the defenders would either be crippled and killed, or be thrown into dazed confusion. On 25 June, the Yankees blew up one of the bastions on the middle line beneath the 3rd Louisiana Redan. Their attack there, according to Swan, was a formidable one, but, like every major Union thrust against the fortifications, a failure. Sensing something was afoot, the Louisianans manning the position were pulled back to a secondary defense, reducing the effects of the explosion. A small number of Mississippians seeking to initiate a counter-explosion beneath the redan were killed in the blast, though casualties were much fewer than Grant had hoped for. Swan indicated that the closeness of the left flank of Lee's Brigade's to the explosion resulted in eight or ten Alabamians killed or wounded.[107]

Among the casualties during the day was Swan himself, though not by the force of the immense blast. He recalled that the balls fell fast and thick in the little nook in which he and his comrades were measuring out the scanty three days of rations for the boys in the 20th Mississippi. After they moved their operations a bit further back from the brewing hostilities, Swan stated that he was making the measurements and calculations when a descending minie ball

---

[105] Clack, "Personal Diary," 6.
[106] Darr, "Diary," 10.
[107] Swan, "A Tennessean at the Siege of Vicksburg," 369.

passed through the fleshy part of his left forearm, just missing the bone. Had it struck the bone, he knew that he would undoubtedly have lost his arm. He believed that a bit of a shift in his weight to the wrong side would have sped the ball right through to his heart.[108] Like Bachman's experience with sharpshooters, however, he survived.

Even prior to his wound, Swan's "general health" was "not good." He indicated that his bowels had been out of sorts for some days; however, he believed that "God spares me from day to day by His tender mercies." Swan's wounded arm seemed to "bid fair to do well." His friends and comrades, he wrote, cared for him in his time of need.[109]

On Friday, 26 June, the Yankees kept up their sharpshooting until about 5 p.m., Vaughn reported, at which time the enemy opened fire with heavy artillery and started sharpshooting in earnest all along his entire line. With the coming of night, he stated, things quieted down. One man was killed in the detachment belonging to Loring's Division, and one was killed and three were wounded among the Mississippi State Troops.[110]

The unrelenting assault of the "soldiers that bore no arms," however, did their most annoying work after the night air "chilled" the atmosphere. "When on picket I dreaded the mosquitoes more than the Yankees," Robert Bachman of the 60th Tennessee wrote. He stated that once dark descended, he was always forced to press his old hat tightly over his face, and then wrap his blanket around his head. He then sought to protect his hands by concealing them under his armpits within his semblance of a shell jacket. Even with these precautions, Bachman indicated, "the mosquitoes would so bite me as to make me look in the morning as if I had the chicken pox."[111]

George Hynds of the 31st Tennessee wrote that all was more quiet than usual "on the Potomac" today, though the day before the Yankees blew up a mine they had dug under one of the parapets on the left, which killed and wounded several men. The resulting Federal charge into the crater found the Bluecoats contained and trapped. After a limited initial success, the Yankees were driven out or captured after a couple hours of desperate hand-to-hand struggle. The impressive engineering attempt resulted in forty Confederate dead and wounded, with their enemy suffering a loss of nearly 200.[112] Again, the

---

[108] Ibid.
[109] Ibid.
[110] Report of Gen. John C. Vaughn, 26 June 1863, *Official Records*, ser. 1, vol. 24, pt. 2, p. 697.
[111] Bachman, "Reminiscences of Childhood," 24.
[112] Hynds, "Original Handwritten Notes," 21.

Southern defenders proved up to the task, and Grant's attempt to force the issue by direct assault through yet another creative scheme failed.

There had been some firing on the right the night before, according to Calvin Smith of the 31st Tennessee. There were also some distant cannon heard to the east along the Big Black River Bridge. The besieged believed that the Yankees, whose firing to the front had slackened a bit, were running all the available troops they had to their defenses in those works to confront Joseph Johnston's advancing Army of Relief.[113]

The Effectiveness of the Sharpshooters. Since a number of Barton's Georgia brigade pickets had been surprised, overwhelmed, and captured some nights before, Reynolds and Barton no longer sent them out during the day, Smith wrote. The Federals had placed a large siege piece some 500 yards directly in front of Reynolds's lines on the opposite ridge, and had also dug more rifle pits in its vicinity. Giving the Yankees a bit of their own medicine, Smith noted that the 31st Tennessee now kept five sharp-eyed men who had proven themselves marksmen detailed as sharpshooters to fire on every bluecoat who showed himself across the way. Now the enemy would have to use caution in moving anywhere around their parapets. Within a distance of 500 to 700 yards, a man had to be more careful than usual, according to Smith. Anytime a man raised his head near the parapet, he could count on drawing a half dozen minie balls. Smith indicated that, with some trial and error, the Confederate marksmen had gotten to where they could "hit [a target] the size of a man at 600 to 800 yards." Undoubtedly, the Union sharpshooters were just as skilled. "The enemy shoots bushels of balls at us every day," Smith estimated. "No doubt we send balls through their port holes every day, but we can't tell [to] what effect."[114] He noted that, as far as he knew, None of the Confederates within his sphere of interest had been killed or wounded that day, which was certainly a rare occurrence this late in the siege.

"Sharp-shooters firing away as usual this morning," Clack of the 43rd Tennessee reported. At 4 p.m., the regiment had orders to move back into the trenches to support Colonel Barkuloo's 57th Georgia. By 7 p.m., they were on their way to comply.[115] It was yet another call up for the 43rd Tennessee, where either the action was anticipated or hottest. Such was their lot for the entire siege.

---

[113] Smith, *A Smith in Service*, 62–63.
[114] Ibid., 63.
[115] Clack, "Personal Diary," 6.

The enemy's pressure on the lines continued, according to Stamper of the 43rd Tennessee, and the whereabouts of Joseph Johnston were still unknown. Just after dusk, the 43rd Tennessee was ordered to its old position behind Colonel Bradford's and Colonel Barkuloo's positions. Companies I, J, E, and K were sent into new ditches behind the 57th Georgia in case it was required to fall back from its initial line, which was "very much exposed." The night passed quietly, though Stamper reported that Orderly Sergeant Russell Denton of Company G and New Market, Jefferson County, died of his wounds received on 26 June. Monroe Ballard of Company F died of sickness. In other regimental matters, officers who had been promoted due to election were notified of their new offices to date from the time of the death of Captain Sterling Turner. His election being approved, Stamper indicated that his date of rank was established as 1 June. Joe Kethcort was elected third lieutenant to replace Lieutenant Crookshanks.[116]

Captain Claiborne Is Laid to Rest. At 11 a.m. on 27 June, Ferd Osman Claiborne, the Maryland battery commander in Reynolds's Brigade, was buried in a plain black coffin and accorded the rites of the Lutheran Church, which were administered by a licensed minister, Major Henry D. Giesler of "the 59th Tennessee Rifles." Claiborne died the previous day when, at his post, he believed that he observed some Yankees advancing toward Reynolds's lines. Receiving a field telescope from his cousin William Claiborne, serving as an aide-de-camp to Colonel Reynolds, the staff officer hurried through the ditches with it toward his cousin's position, where he witnessed the horror of seeing his kinsman killed. Captain Claiborne had barely given the order to open fire when he was struck in the face by a shell fragment. He died a few minutes later without gaining consciousness. That night, Captain Claiborne's body, in full uniform, was laid in Colonel Reynolds's tent and attended by an honor guard while mourning comrades filed past. "I wish to have [had] the service read by an Episcopal clergyman, but we failed to find one," noted William Claiborne. He described the service for his cousin as follows:

> He was buried on a little knoll about 100 yards north of Reynolds' quarters at a place selected by Frank and Major Phifer. I was feeling too badly to go out. I regret that there are no trees near the spot to shelter it from the sun and rains, but this was almost unavoidable. I will soon as possible procure a stone with a suitable inscription to mark the spot. His burial was attended by the Colonel and staff, the members of his

---

[116] Stamper, *Travels of the 43rd Tennesee*, 67–68.

company, and a large number of devoted friends. All were more affected than I remember to have seen on any former occasion. The general [probably referring to Reynolds] wept like a child.[117]

The Wearing Down of the Garrison Continues. "Still the endless dropping sounds [of spent minie balls] and the heavy roar of cannon salutes us," Swan wrote. The day was without interest to him. "The musketoes are getting to be very annoying at night," he complained.[118] Though James Darr of the 43rd Tennessee indicated things were quiet along Reynolds's front, he reported the massive explosion at the 3rd Louisiana Redan. The Yankees made a charge, but, according to his sources, were "driven back with great slaughter." Captain McKamy suffered through the day with great pain, Darr observed.[119]

Not much sharpshooting occurred along his line, Vaughn reported on 27 June. "Everything unusually quiet."[120] The Yankees made no attacks, but they continued their annoying shellfire, according to Captain George Hynds of the 31st Tennessee. While looking through an observation port in his works, General Thomas Green of Missouri, who had commanded the left wing of the defenses at the Big Black River, was killed on this day by a sharpshooter. Captain B. F. Gaddis of the 3rd Tennessee was also stuck and killed by a sharpshooter. The mortar boats in the river on the far side of the peninsula were at their work again, Hynds wrote, but all their shells fell short.[121]

Clack of the 43rd Tennessee recorded that needed rest was welcomed the night of 27 June, and things were quiet along the lines all during the darksome hours. The quiet ended with the sunrise, however, when the firing resumed. Also at 8 a.m., the mortar boats were dropping shells about the Confederate lines. He marveled that they were flinging the huge projectiles now some five miles. At 7 p.m., the boys were called back to the trenches again, and "a young

---

[117] Hoehling, *Vicksburg: 47 Days of Siege*, 253.

[118] Swan, "A Tennessean at the Siege of Vicksburg," 370.

[119] Darr, "Diary," 10. One Confederate soldier described conditions within army hospitals as follows: "The weather is excessively hot & the flies swarm around the wounded—more numerous where the wound is severest. In a few days the wounds begin to be offensive & horrid! The vile insect finds its way into the wounded part & adds to the pain & terror of the poor sufferers. Nor can this be avoided, unless a nurse were detailed for every wounded man, but there is only one allowed for every eight men. Those that can hold a brush in one hand must use it constantly & those that are helpless must suffer." Urquhart, *Vicksburg: Southern City Under Siege*, 19.

[120] Report of Gen. John C. Vaughn, 27 June 1863, *Official Records*, ser. 1, vol. 24, pt. 2, p. 697.

[121] Hynds, "Original Handwritten Notes," 22.

man named Garghess belonging to the 3rd Tennessee Regt. was killed here in fifty yards of me this evening by a piece of shell." Clack wrote in closing: "Oh Lord! I pray for thy protection!"[122]

Quartermaster John Fleming of Company F died 27 June of sickness, Stamper of the 43rd Tennessee indicated. Otherwise, not much change in circumstances, he indicated, though there was "great talk of surrendering." Captain Benjamin Franklin Gaddis of Company D and Polk County died of wounds.[123] "My wound [is] doing very well," Darr of the 43rd Tennessee wrote in his journal. "Capt. McKamy [is] some better." Darr noted that General Green had been killed that day. Thom Hamilton was also "slain." Their rations for the day consisted of four ounces of flour, two ounces of field peas, and one ounce of rice.[124]

"On such a morning I have walked or ridden by the wheat fields and watched the waving of golden grain as the fitful breeze passed over," Swan of Bradley County waxed poetic in his diary, "and listened to the rustle of the corn and inhaled the fragrance of the new mown hay." How different the situation was now for him now that he was "wounded enough to cause pain, sick in body and sick in heart with hope deferred." He suffered the additional agony of being far away from friends and home and of being "liable at any moment to be swept away."[125]

Grant's Leaflets Speak for the Besieged? The desperation the garrison was feeling was supposedly evident in following letter, attached to the correspondence General John C. Pemberton had collected during his command at Vicksburg:

> In the Trenches, Near Vicksburg, June 28,1863.
> General J. C. Pemberton:
> Sir: In accordance with my own feelings and that of my fellow soldiers with whom I have conferred, I submit to your serious consideration the following note:
> We have as an army as much confidence in you as a commanding general as we perhaps ought to have. We believe you have displayed as much generalship as any other man could have done under similar

[122] Clack, "Personal Diary," 6. Garghess was perhaps "Hargess," of whom there were several in the regiment. Pvt. S. A. Gray of Benton, Polk County, and of the 3rd Tennessee was also killed by this shell.
[123] Stamper, "Travels of the 43rd Tennessee," 68.
[124] Darr, "Diary," 11.
[125] Swan, "A Tennessean at the Siege of Vicksburg," 370.

circumstances. We give you credit for the stern patriotism you have evinced in defense of Vicksburg during a protracted and unparalleled siege.

I also feel proud of the gallant conduct of the soldiers under your command in repulsing the enemy at every assault, and bearing with patient endurance all the privations and hardships incident to a siege of forty odd days' duration.

Everybody admits that we have all covered ourselves in glory, but alas! General, a crisis has arrived in the midst of our siege.

Our rations have been cut down to one biscuit and a small bit of bacon per day, not enough scarcely to keep soul and body together, much less to stand the hardships we are called upon to stand.

We are actually on sufferance, and the consequence is, so far as I can hear, there is complaining and general dissatisfaction throughout the lines.

We are, and have been, kept close in the trenches, day and night, not allowed to forage at all, and, even if permitted, there is nothing to be had among the citizens.

Men don't want to starve, and don't intend to, but they call upon you for justice, if the commissary department can give it; if it can't, you must adopt some means to relieve us very soon. The emergency of the case demands prompt and decided action on your part.

If you can't feed us, you had better surrender us, horrible as the idea is, than suffer this noble army to disgrace themselves by desertion. I tell you plainly, men are not going to lie here and perish, if they do love their country dearly. Self-preservation is the first law of nature, and hunger will compel a man to do almost anything.

You had better heed a warning voice, though it is the voice of a private soldier.

The army is now ripe for mutiny, unless it can be fed.

Just think of one small biscuit and one or two mouthfuls of bacon per day. General, please direct your inquiries in the proper channels, and see if I have not stated stubborn facts, which had better be heeded before we are disgraced.

From—MANY SOLDIERS.[126]

---

[126] "From Many Soldiers" to Gen. John C. Pemberton, 28 June 1863, *Official Records*, ser. 1, vol. 24, pt. 3, p. 982–83.

Though purported to be written and supported by "many" Confederate soldiers, the thousands of copies of this letter were probably dropped from kites lofted over Vicksburg by the Union navy out on the river. The letter was perhaps another of the psychological ploys Grant always seemed to have at his disposal. Whether it had any impact on adding to Confederate morale problems or not is unknown. Matters by then were about as distressing as they could get.[127]

"I Am Yet Counted among the Living." Little sharpshooting and shelling occurred the day before, on 27 June, Vaughn reported, which resulted in only one man wounded serving with the 3rd Battalion, Mississippi State Troops.[128] Hynds of the 31st Tennessee recorded that the Yankees were keeping up their usual amount of firing, which caused him to doubt that they had any respect for the Sabbath, else "they would have rested today." Only one man was slightly hurt during the day in his lines.[129]

"I am yet counted among the living [that] are besieged by the enemy at Vicksburg," Smith of the 31st Tennessee noted. He believed that by taking considerable exercise, he was able to retain good health, though he had to confess that such might not be the case with most of the men around him, suffering as they did with "bowels out of order, slight fevers, heat of the climate, light diet, and their lack of active exercise." He cited one extreme example: "I sent Peter Brown to the hospital this morning, who had [been] reduced to a mere skeleton." Smith had admonished him constantly, but Brown would never do what he was told unless Smith threatened punishment. While accompanying Brown to the hospital, Smith checked on Sergeant Henderson Everhart, who appeared odd "with his arm off." But Everhart was to be discharged and would be sent back home to Hawkins County. Smith did not know how Everhart would get through, but if he did, Smith would send his writings home by him. "I can't tell whether we will be defeated or come out victorious," Smith stated, though the boys were getting used to "hard times with this climate." Half rations any time would be gratefully received, he asserted. At 3 p.m., Smith visited the Fourth Brigade Hospital, where he found Peter Brown, J. A. Tucker, and Henderson Everhart doing better. Smith saw hundreds of wounded and sick, "some of who were mere skeletons [and] cannot recover." He tarried for a time and watched the surgeons cut a minie ball from the jaw of Private William

---

[127] Bearss, *The Campaign for Vicksburg*, 3: 1281.

[128] Report of Gen. John C. Vaughn, 28 June 1863, *Official Records*, ser. 1, vol. 24, pt. 2, p. 697.

[129] Hynds, "Original Handwritten Notes," 22.

Clevenger. Smith was amazed at how flat the soft lead had been mashed, and he remarked that the young Talbott Station, Jefferson County, native suffered little, since he was under the influence of liberal doses of chloroform, scarcely moving at all during the operation. "Lieut. Clepper [also "Klepper"], a fine fellow of Captain Huffmeister's company, was shot [by a sharpshooter] through the head this morning," Smith recollected. "His brains ran out, but he lived until evening, died and was buried."[130]

"Cannonballs crossed my path as I returned [to camp]," Smith wrote, "tossing up dirt and dust." On his walk "home," he observed two gunboats were anchored out in the river beyond the range of the Vicksburg batteries. Smith indicated that the word was going around that mules were being killed "and dying for our consumption." His reaction to this news was a bit different than others who addressed the added menu item: "I'm sure to eat some as soon as I get the chance." As for Fortress Vicksburg itself, Smith pointed out that despite their furious encirclement and six weeks of bombardment, the invaders seemingly were no closer to its capitulation.

"Another Sabbath [28 June] has found me alive and well for which I feel very thankful," recorded Clack of the 43rd Tennessee. He stated that the night before passed quietly, and that he was detailed during that period to help "plant a battery." The sharpshooters commenced their work at first light, he added, noting that, during the morning, their deadly efforts mortally wounded Lieutenant Wilson Clepper of Company E while he was in the trenches.[131] "The Yanks are keeping Sunday," according to James H. Darr of the 43rd Tennessee in his daily entry, "but they will spill it yet." Other interesting news Darr had heard was that the commissaries were "killing mules today and making beef of it."[132] Stamper of the 43rd Tennessee indicated that the sharpshooting directed toward Bradford's 31st Tennessee and Barkuloo's 57th Georgia appeared considerable, possibly because of their battery emplacement work, and he stated that Lieutenant "Culpepper" had been killed. A Georgian also was killed during the period, and a member of either Company A or F was wounded. "All hopes of relief about gone," Darr sighed, noting, "the men are hungry and worn out."[133]

Rations Are Expanded. Sergeant W. H. Long of Morristown and the 59th Tennessee remembered that on 28 June "the Confederacy killed enough mules

[130] Smith, *A Smith in Service*, 62.
[131] Clack, "Personal Diary," 6–7.
[132] Darr, "Diary," 11.
[133] Stamper, "Travels of the 43rd Tennessee," 68.

to give rations for each Confederate soldier one pound." As acting orderly sergeant at the time, Long had to take a detail to the slaughter yard near Vicksburg to procure enough meat for his entire company. "I suppose the yard was so disgusting," he recalled, "[that] I could not eat of it, and gave my meat to a man by the name of Pvt. Calvin Wright." Other men in his company were just as repulsed and gave theirs to Wright also. "He ate six pounds of it," Long mused, "and suffered no inconvenience."[134]

Private Robert "Newt" Fender of the 43rd Tennessee, described happy times during his boyhood back in Sweetwater, Monroe County, when he used to roll biscuits down a hill near his home just to watch the family dogs run after them. During these final days of the Vicksburg siege, he later recalled, he used to dream in fitful sleep of racing the dogs for one of those biscuits.[135]

Samuel Swan, serving with Stephen D. Lee's Brigade, recognized that he was close to giving into his despondency, and that "our days are numbered here and but few until the crisis will be upon us." Subsistence was almost gone, and many men shared his sense of hopelessness. "The enemy has wormed his way up so close to our lines," he wrote, "and has our works so completely covered with cannon and small arms, that our men can scarcely put their hands above the embrasures to look out without being shot." His fears remained that by the Fourth of July, the Federals could, "with proper boldness," storm the works. Swan also had deep concern over the demoralization of the boys, and that "a certain class of men" who, when they reached their limits on physical sufferings, "will forget principle and succumb." Indeed, he reported, many men within the lines had not deserted to the enemy yet because they held on to belief that Joseph Johnston would rescued them in just a few more days. Swan believed that it was too much to ask of the defenders to hold out hope when they were kept by the infernal Yankees from hearing from their loved ones at home. No mail had gotten through since the siege commenced 18 May.[136]

Swan also thought that the "authorities" were experimenting with mule meat on the menu in order "to be prepared in case of emergency." He believed that the boys would consent to eat it for a few days, if doing so would save Vicksburg. His admiration for the soldiers in the Southern army generally, and the Vicksburg garrison in particular, remained strong. "There have been very few desertions," he noted, "and the men submit themselves to the greatest

---

[134] Long, "Autobiography," 1: 54–55.
[135] Donn Patton Brooks, *East Tennessee's Forgotten Soldiers: The Forty-Third Tennessee Infantry Regiment, CSA* (Kyle TX: Westpump Publishers, 1995) 57.
[136] Swan, "A Tennessean at the Siege of Vicksburg," 370.

hardships with cheerfulness if there is a hope held out that by means success can be achieved in the end." Swan's complaint against the leadership were that "Pemberton and Stevenson are both too distant, [and] do not go amongst their men enough to be popular." He indicated, however, that there were "brigadiers in whom the troops have confidence." One of these generals was obviously Swan's own Stephen D. Lee. Reynolds, however, was not one of the popular brigade commanders, nor probably was John Vaughn. "If Pemberton would take the right method and encourage his men by visiting them and showing himself to them and speaking a hopeful word, unpopular as he is," Swan declared, "they would be greatly encouraged, and would do more likely to resist the final assault." He feared that history would be insufficient in rendering complete justice to the Confederate soldiers who served at Vicksburg, "through the antecedent battles and movements, and the siege." Despite his own opinion about where the praise should fall, he suspected that the generals would "claim credit and character if we get out safely."[137]

On Monday, 29 June, Vaughn's men were disturbed by a little cannonading and sharpshooting, he reported in his daily summary. He noted that two men from the 26th Mississippi (Loring's Division) had deserted to the enemy the night before, and that three men were wounded due to enemy fire: one in the 61st Tennessee, and two others in the Mississippi State troops.[138]

Given circumstances where the opposing forces were in such close contact, the men not only had their enemy to worry about; they also had to worry about fatal accidents resulting from friendly fire. Calvin Smith of the 31st Tennessee wrote about one such dreadful accident. "Lieuts. King Stallcup of Company F and Henderson of Company K [were] officers of the picket guard last night," he noted. "They were going about the different posts...[when] Stallcup approached the post where Pvt. J. M. Fitzpatrick was, [and he] halted." The sentinel did not hear the lieutenant respond to the sentry challenge, so he fired and hit Stallcup in the upper breast. Stallcup died within five minutes. "He was brought in a litter to the ditch and is here now, recorded Smith, adding: "He was a fine fellow and generally beliked by all. A man of fine sense and talents ...[who] was courageous in his defense of Southern rights."[139]

Stamper of the 43rd Tennessee indicated that around sunup, Private Jackson Mathis of Company F died of spasms. "He did not live five minutes

---

[137] Ibid.

[138] Report of Gen. John C. Vaughn, 29 June 1863, *Official Records*, ser. 1, vol. 24, pt. 2, p. 697.

[139] Smith, *A Smith in Service*, 62.

after he took sick," Stamper stated. The day was quiet, he noted, and some of his friends bought some small cakes of corn bread for four or five dollars apiece. "[The result of the rations they were receiving] was almost starvation," he remarked, though with some determination he added: "All are willing to hold on as long as there was any hopes of relief rather than submit to Yankee tyranny."[140]

Clack of the same regiment indicated that the determined sharpshooters plied their usual trade. He also noted the death of Private "Mathias" due to cramps. Apparently Mathias's poor system could no longer deal with the lack of and quality of food. He survived only ten minutes after he was struck down. In the 31st Tennessee, Clack recorded, "Private [Lieutenant] King Stalcup was killed last night by some of our own men." The Northerners pressed a limited attack on their right during the evening, but it was, as were all others, turned back.[141] "My wound is doing finely," James Darr of the 43rd Tennessee wrote, adding: "Oh that I was at home." Only cannonading disturbed the quietness of his morning.[142]

"Our prison life is now in the forty-third day," Swan wrote from S. D. Lee's lines. Everyone was expecting "an episode" this week. All eyes were turned toward the approaching Fourth of July holiday, when many believed that "the Yankees will try hard to do something by that time."[143] What better way to celebrate their premier national holiday than to force the garrison into submission?

Request for Passage Through the Lines. One man was wounded in Ward's Artillery Battalion, according to Vaughn's daily submission on 30 June, and he "respectfully reports but little sharp-shooting on my front yesterday; some cannonading in the evening."[144] The day did not pass, however, without event for the Monroe County general. Sometime in the afternoon, he received guests from Vicksburg who sought his council and assistance in getting them through the lines. The young woman who visited his tent offered the following anecdote:

---

[140] Stamper, "Travels of the 43rd Tennessee," 68.
[141] Clack, "Personal Diary," 7.
[142] Darr, "Diary," 12.
[143] Swan, "A Tennessean at the Siege of Vicksburg," 370.
[144] Report of Gen. John C. Vaughn, 30 June 1863, *Official Records*, ser. 1, vol. 24, pt. 2, p. 698.

General V[aughn] offered us seats in his tent. The rifle bullets were whizzing so zip, zip from the sharp-shooters on the federal lines that involuntarily I moved my chair.

He said, "Don't be alarmed; you are out of range. They are firing at our mules yonder."

His horse, tied by the tent door, was quivering all over, the most intense exhibition of fear I've ever seen in an animal. General V[aughn] sent out a flag of truce to the federal headquarters, and while we waited, wrote on a piece of silk paper a few words.

Then he said: "My wife is in Tennessee. If you get through the lines, give her this. They will search you, so I will put it in this toothpick." He crammed the silk paper into a quail toothpick, and handed it to H. It was completely concealed. The Flag-of-Truce officer came back flushed and angry. "General Grant says that no human being shall pass out of Vicksburg; but the lady may feel sure danger will soon be over. Vicksburg will surrender on the 4th."

"Is that so, general?" inquired H. "Are arrangements for surrender made?"

"We know nothing of the kind. Vicksburg will not surrender."

"Those were General Grant's exact words, sir," said the flag officer, "of course it is nothing but their brag."[145]

Waiting to Get "Cut Out." "General Pemberton came around to view the works accompanied by General [Carter L.] Stevenson and others," Calvin Smith of the 31st Tennessee wrote, "[indicating that they] admired our position. We formed our company in the ditches, but were not ordered to salute." Smith accorded the lieutenant general commanding to be a "fine-looking man," but as others concluded, "not calculated to head a large army." There were supposed to be between 20,000 and 25,000 defenders inside the works, but Smith admitted that as of yet, the 31st Tennessee had not been directly engaged. One night, a courier had come through the lines and brought word that Johnston had received reinforcements and was soon to relieve them. The courier also said that Johnston had also brought with him 20,000 musket caps, which, Smith indicated, were "sorely needed."[146]

George Hynds of the 31st Tennessee wrote, "it has been very hot today." Fortunately, the Yankees had been quiet all day long. He stated that only a few

---

[145] Hoehling, *Vicksburg: 47 Days of Siege*, 253.
[146] Smith, *A Smith in Service*, 62.

random shots had been fired from any cannon, and "for the first time, their sharp-shooters seem to be resting."[147] Clack of the 43rd Tennessee related a slightly different story. He wrote that the pickets had been involved in an exchange of gunfire the previous evening, and that sharpshooting had resumed again by daylight. By 10 a.m., heavy cannonading had picked up on the right of the line. The boys, including his 43rd Tennessee, were all now attempting to wrest a few hours of sleep in the trenches in constant readiness for the anticipated major assault. "The sun has now set beneath the western horizon for the last time in June 1863," he reported, "and we are still in possession of Vicksburg."[148] But only for four more days.

Things were now unusually quiet, Stamper of the 43rd Tennessee wrote, "with no assurance of speedy relief." The final destiny of the garrison, he submitted, was fast approaching. The regiment was on the move during the evening, with Companies A and F being relived by Companies H and E. Stamper indicated that his company came out of the ditches and "lay in the rear of J and I as support." News among the boys included that a man named Keaton of Company K died in the hospital, and that William "Bill" Boles of Company B succumbed to the wounds he had received in the assault on 23 June. O. S. Jones of Company E was elected by his company to 3rd lieutenant to fill Wilson Clepper's office.[149] Private James Darr of the 43rd Tennessee indicated that the men would have to eat mule meat in a day or two. The rumor was going strong on this date that Joseph Johnston would be coming "this week" to the garrison's aid. "Oh Life!" Darr exclaimed, "how many strong cares lie thickly strewn in all thy crooked paths!"[150]

Swan in S. D. Lee's Brigade noted that June was almost gone, and that the army was still shut in with no immediate prospects. He reported that the few couriers now who got into the fortifications were often eight days "on the road" between Vicksburg and Johnston. As for Johnston's movements and intentions, nothing was really known. The boys in the trenches had been led to believe that an attempt to cut them out would be initiated by the end of June. All they did now was wait and listen. Rations were scarcer, mules were being butchered, "and the men are trying to prepare themselves to relish mule steaks."[151]

---

[147] Hynds, "Original Handwritten Notes," 22.

[148] Clack, "Personal Diary," 7.

[149] Stamper, "Travels of the 43rd Tennessee," 68–69.

[150] Darr, "Diary," 11.

[151] Swan, "A Tennessean at the Siege of Vicksburg," 370.

"They are testing it [mule meat] around," Swan recorded, "perhaps mainly for buncombe but it is a known fact that we will shortly be reduced to that or starvation." Swan's disposition was undoubtedly affected by the pain of his wound, and he stated that it caused him to be laid "up completely with a high fever and a racking pain in the head." He had found no refuge or shade to lie in until a citizen acquaintance, a Mr. Arthur, "kindly agreed to let me stay at his house, and I had my pallet spread on his porch," where the poor weary soul was finally able to sleep for awhile.[152]

---

[152] Ibid., 370–71.

CHAPTER 12

"We Held a Terrible Foe 48 Days on 12-Days' Rations"

July

Still Watching for Johnston. "Johnston has delayed his expected attack so long that our prospects for going up to Camp Chase seem to be very good," George Hynds of the 31st Tennessee complained as the siege dragged its way into July. Another agonizing month opened, exacerbated by the insufferable heat. Hynds noted that the gunboats had come up river again and gave the Confederate river batteries a good shelling. The Yankees had set off another mine in the lines, he wrote, blowing up one of the works on the left end (actually the middle), killing eight and wounding over a hundred. Grant did not feel, however, that the damage was sufficient to try another follow-up attack in force by his infantry.[1] He always continued to learn.

All was very still, according to Stamper of the 43rd Tennessee, and the talk about cutting their way "out of the sack" was circulating with desperate sincerity. He indicated that such talk created anxiety and howls from the sick and wounded, however, because they knew that they would have to be left behind in the hands of the "merciless foe." And many Confederates would be unable to make any resistance. Stamper stated that J. H. McCoy was elected orderly sergeant of his Company F, Robert N. Fender was unanimously elected sergeant, and P. H. Slagle was elected 4th corporal. Stamper repeated the news that the Yankees had blown up part of the works that day, killing and wounding about sixty men.[2] Hynds put the number at forty.[3] The shelling of Vicksburg continued all night.[4]

---

[1] Hynds, "Original Handwritten Notes," 23.
[2] Stamper, "Travels of the 43rd Tennessee," 69.
[3] Hynds, "Original Handwritten Notes," 23.
[4] Stamper, "Travels of the 43rd Tennessee," 69.

Mule Steaks. "'Here's your mule,' was the tune in every soldier's mouth," James H. Darr of the 43rd Tennessee noted in his daily entry. "But now, the boys were singing: 'Here's your mule *meat*!'" He indicated that the men constantly anticipated the booming of Johnston's guns, but no such sound was forthcoming. Indeed, he wrote, the only sounds were of a little cannonading on the left of the garrison's lines.[5]

All hope for relief has about played out, Swan declared, and the shelling from the Yankee fleet on the river had increased. Despair had settled into the "devoted army," he noted, "but they will exhibit a fixed determination to hold the works to the last." His wound still pained him dreadfully, and he had to keep it continually bathed in the coldest water he could get to keep the inflammation reduced.[6]

General Vaughn in his daily report on 1 July noted that the sharpshooting and cannonading were considerable during the morning and the evening of the previous day. The day following, Vaughn reported that his men had been subjected to the usual degree of sharpshooting, and that around three in the afternoon there was a bit of cannonading. There were no casualties in his command during the day.[7]

Can the Men Cut Their Way Out? Matters were desperate. Pemberton, who was trying to decide on whether to cut the garrison out or seek terms from Grant, sent requests to his brigade and division commanders concerning the morale and physical condition of their men. Alexander W. Reynolds replied with this dispatch:

> July 2, 1863.
> General: In reply to your inquiries as to the condition of my troops and their ability to make the marches and undergo the fatigue necessary to accomplish a successful evacuation, I have the honor to report that the condition of my troops is not good. Owing to the reduced quantity and quality of rations on which my men have subsisted for more than six weeks, to their close confinement in the trenches, constant exposure to the intense heat of the sun and frequent rains, and to impure water they are obligated to drink, they are much reduced in strength, and in many instances entirely prostrated. It would be utterly impossible for most of

[5] Darr, "Diary," 11.
[6] Swan, "A Tennessean at the Siege of Vicksburg," 371.
[7] Report of Gen. John C. Vaughn, 1 July 1863, *Official Records*, ser. 1, vol. 24, pt. 2, p. 698.

them to make a forced march of any distance. Many of my men are in the hospital, and many of those reported for duty in the trenches are extremely weak, and unable to undergo the slighted fatigue. Perhaps, on an average, two hundred men from each of my regiments, animated by patriotic motives and a desire to be free, might be able to make a march of ten or fifteen miles and still be in condition to give battle to the enemy, but hardly more than that number.

The spirits of my men are good, and I believe that almost to a man they would be willing to make vigorous efforts to strike a blow for freedom; but, I regret to say that two-thirds of my men are unable to endure a march of ten miles.[8]

Though individual responses for John Vaughn and other brigade commanders on the left flank did not make it into the records, the division commander, General Martin L. Smith, submitted the following evaluation on the physical condition of his men:

There are about 3,000 men in my division (including the Mississippi home guard) in condition to undertake a march of 8 or 10 miles a day in this weather, if there is an opportunity of resting at intervals. Out of those 3,000 men, only about 2,000 are considered reliable in case we are strongly opposed and much harassed. A secret evacuation I consider almost impossible, on account of the temper of many in my command, who would, of necessity, be left behind, not to mention their natural timidity when left alone, which would induce them to at once get into communication with the enemy for their *own fancied safety*.[9]

---

[8] Report of Col. A. W. Reynolds, 1 July 1863, *Official Records*, ser. 1, vol. 24, pt. 2, p. 348–49.

[9] Report of Gen. Martin L. Smith, 2 July 1863, *Official Records*, ser. 1, vol. 24, pt. 1, p. 282. Emphasis added. Because William Baldwin and Francis Shoup's Mississippians and Louisianans had served well, it can be assumed that Smith's concern was over Vaughn's command. The irony of this assumption, however, is that, after the surrender, most of the 27th Louisiana (Shoup's Brigade) and perhaps other soldiers from the Pelican State were observed deserting across the Mississippi in skiffs. Gen. John C. Pemberton to Gen. U. S. Grant, 8 July 1863, *Official Records*, ser. 1, vol. 24, pt. 3, p. 488. The 17th and 31st Louisiana from Baldwin's command, after passing the Union check-points, "disregarded the commands and expostulations of their officers," and scattered in small groups, setting "their faces homeward." Their officers appealed to the Yankee guards for help in stopping the deserters, but the guards merely laughed at them. William Pitt

Captain John W. Bachman of the 60th Tennessee, as a result of the capture or incapacitation of all his regiment's field officers, found himself as ranking captain in command of the regiment. "When he was called with other officers to a council of war by General Pemberton," Bachman was in the minority of regimental commanders who "voted to cut their way out through the enemy rather than surrender."[10]

George Hynds believed that there had been more firing all along the line on 1 July than any previous day since the siege began. The mortar boats and the guns on the peninsula were giving Vicksburg a terrible shelling. "The heat is now so oppressive," he noted, "that the men could not stand it to fight long at a time now."[11]

"We have listened for Genl. Johnston's artillery for many a night," Lieutenant C. M. Smith of the 31st Tennessee wrote in his journal entry, "[and] to have heard the roar of his artillery would be better than long rations; and this could not be excelled by anything." Even the ever-optimistic Smith, long a rock of hope and determination for his men, found his spirits giving in to the inevitability. With all the garrison had endured, he could not "tell with any degree of certainty how [the siege] would terminate." He felt that a "grand display" must be made to get the garrison out or they would now, due to exhausted provisions, be forced to capitulate. "We have bravely defended this place and many valuable men have sacrificed their lives in the defense of this devoted place," he argued, "and surrender [would only come] on the grounds that provisions were out."[12]

Everything was relatively quiet, Stamper of the 43rd Tennessee wrote in his journal 1 July, except for ongoing cannon discharges from the infernal gunboats. Grant's awesome host was seen in the shimmering heat planting mortars and new batteries. "Our cooks brought out our little rations to us, and told us that the meat had played out," he noted, "and they did not know where the next would come from."[13] The enemy pickets made great sport of yelling that the Confederates now had a new general in the trenches with them: "General Starvation."

Chambers, "My Journal," *Publications of the Mississippi Historical Society*, Centenary Series, 21/6 (June 1913): 281.

[10] "Chattanooga's Most Beloved Citizen," *The Confederate Veteran* 21/6 (1 June 1913): 281.

[11] Hynds, "Original Handwritten Notes," 23.

[12] Smith, *A Smith in Service*, 63.

[13] Stamper, "Travels of the 43rd Tennessee," 69.

Just as the children of Israel had wandered aimlessly through the desert, whining about their difficult circumstances, so too there arose a "great murmuring among the troops," Stamper reported. Vicksburg was "going up the spout," as the boys termed it, and the garrison must either be surrendered, Stamper lamented, or "we would have to cut our way through the enemy lines and make our escape."[14]

Clack of the 43rd Tennessee wrote in his diary that the firing was kept up all night from the mortar batteries on the opposite side of the river. Sharpshooters also did their part when it was light enough to see and the thick dews lay on the ground and wool uniforms like rain water. Even so, Clack reported, the evening was "tolerably quiet."[15]

Darr of the 43rd Tennessee believed that, based on the volume of their artillery barrage, the Yankees were doing all in their power now to silence the Confederate batteries along the river. The South Fort was particularly heavily bombarded from the Mississippi and batteries on the eastern side of the Warrenton Road. Still no Johnston, he lamented.[16]

"Our days are numbered," Swan of S. D. Lee's Brigade predicted. Succumbing somewhat to fatalism, he indicated that the shells were falling dangerously close to him. "I look for a fragment to tear me to pieces," he said with heartfelt despair. He betrayed, however, a faint glimmer of faith and hope when he added: "Providence has protected me so far."[17]

There was little sharpshooting to the front of Vaughn's lines the day before, and some cannonading occurred in the evening. Vaughn recorded in his 3 July report that one of his men in the 62nd Tennessee was accidentally killed, and another man in the 61st Tennessee was wounded.[18] Lieutenant J. Kelsey of Rheatown, Greene County, and the 61st Tennessee died on this date and may have been the man whom Vaughn mentioned.[19]

"The siege dragged its weary length along," Robert Bachman of the 60th Tennessee wrote in his memoirs, "with matters all the while growing worse for us." The food supplies had been depleted, and everyone believed that Joseph

---

[14] Ibid.

[15] Clack, "Personal Diary," 7.

[16] Darr, "Diary," 12.

[17] Swan, "A Tennessean at the Siege of Vicksburg," 371.

[18] Report of Gen. John C. Vaughn, 3 July 1863, *Official Records*, ser. 1, vol. 24, pt. 2, p. 698.

[19] United Daughters of the Confederacy, "Record Book of Confederate Soldiers Buried at Cedar Hill Cemetery, Vicksburg," unpublished manuscript, 1958, Old Court-house Museum, Vicksburg MS. Burial Records, Cedar Hill Cemetery, , Vicksburg MS.

Johnston would not be able to save them. "At length, the afternoon of July 3rd arrived," Bachman noted, "and a flag of truce went up all around the battle line. All firing had ceased. General Pemberton and his staff rode to General Grant's headquarters, some three or four miles northeast of Vicksburg." The result, according to Bachman, was the revolting decision to surrender the garrison the next day.[20]

Signs and Wonders. "Vicksburg—signs and wonders," exclaimed Lieutenant C. M. Smith of the 31st Tennessee in his journal. In a particularly routine and ironic manner, he noted that he awoke to the usual early sharpshooters' musketry, which came from the Union lines, and set out soon thereafter to procure cartridges and musket caps for his men's Enfields. "On returning," he observed incredulously, "I saw the men in the trenches without guns carelessly looking on the enemy's lines and soon saw the Yankies were in the same predicament." Smith was told that the flags of truce had been interchanged, and all firing between the infantry lines had ceased, though he could still hear the gunboats out on the river keeping their steady bombardment on Vicksburg. Indeed, even the Confederate hospitals, he learned, were not immune from these shells, which threw fragments and explosions in the midst of the helpless wounded and sick.[21]

"I in the company of others walked up to the left," Smith wrote, "where hundreds of Yankies were seen walking about there, the two armies were seen gazing upon each other with perfect ease and tranquility as though wishing that we were friends again." The boys were soon into swapping, Smith noted, seeing pen knives and even galluses changing hands. Soon, a loud commanding voice ordered all back to their posts. Smith was surprised to find that the enemy's works were much closer to the garrison's trenches here than imagined; in some places they were only fifty yards apart "by digging crooked [zigzag approaches] lines." The cause of the sudden cessation of hostilities was a mystery to the soldiers, Smith declared, and some ventured to guess that the garrison had been surrendered. Others supposed that Grant was negotiating with Pemberton to have the women and children removed from Vicksburg before the Yankees commenced an even more heinous and intensified bombardment the city. A few thought that the ceasefire was to protest the Federal bombardment of the soldiers' hospitals. As the evening encumbered the men in the still stubbornly-held works, Smith noted that the cannonade continued with more violence than ever. Bacon was now gone, and though others in the garrison and in Reynolds's

---

[20] Bachman, "Reminiscences of Childhood," 24.
[21] Smith, *A Smith in Service*, 63.

Brigade reported eating mule meat long before this, Smith stated that it had not yet made its way to the 31st Tennessee, but some men predicted that it was to be substituted in their rations shortly. "Faces are very long now," he wrote, "but we are prepared to celebrate the 4th of July, perhaps to their detriment. We are willing and anxious to shoot the last ball tomorrow." If a surrender was pending or in progress, he indicated, it would probably occur within the next three days. "I think [there is] some talk [by the generals] of cutting our way out," Smith had heard, "but that would be disastrous to us as it will be to the Yankies if they try to storm Vicksburg without our consent."[22]

Motive was a matter of interest as well to George Hynds, also of Smith's 31st Tennessee, who had never had much confidence in the Northern-born commanding general in the first place. Hynds echoed the feelings of many of his angry fellow soldiers: "I believe we have been sold and Pemberton is now giving a bill of sale for us and receiving his reward." He indicated that it was difficult to be the product sold and "not receive a part of the purchase money." The flags of truce passed most of the day, he stated with obvious disdain, and the soldiers of both armies "came out of their ditches and held friendly communication."[23]

On this most atypical day, Clack began his entry incredulously with the words that "things are rocking along as usual this morning." But by 10 a.m., word was scattering about the lines like an exploded mortar shell that Pemberton had sent out a flag of truce and asked Grant to stop targeting the soldiers' hospitals. Beginning at 1 p.m., and lasting for two hours, heavy cannonading occurred along the river. At 6 p.m., another flag of truce came out, and this time the word had spread through the ranks that Pemberton was seeking terms for the surrender of the garrison. An hour later, Clack with unmistakable resignation declared, "we all go to the trenches. All is very quiet now."[24]

Matters on the land were quiet, Stamper of the 43rd Tennessee stated, but there was fierce cannonading coming from the river. He reported that Generals Forney and Bowen had been sent out under flag of truce at 8 a.m. to make terms with Grant concerning the surrender. "We came out of our trenches and walked about, looking on our enemy who had come out of their works," Stamper noted. "Yanks and Rebels seemed to take pleasure in conversing with

---

[22] Ibid.
[23] Hynds, "Original Handwritten Notes," 23.
[24] Clack, "Personal Diary," 7.

each other." Land matters were quiet and cordial, he remarked, "but the enemy, from the river, [continued to] shell Vicksburg."[25]

"General Johns[t]on must be fighting the Yanks somewhere outside of the lines," James Darr of the 43rd Tennessee wrote, "for it is awfully smoky." The naval guns had a lot to do with that. Matters about Vicksburg, however, were relatively quiet except for the cannonading from the Mississippi. Darr indicated that beef was now going for a dollar a pound, a chicken cost $5, and a turtle dove cost $1.50. The government, he noted, still furnished tobacco. Mule beef (as he called it) was the cheapest meal. Roasting ears cost $1.50 a piece, meal was a dollar a pint, and flour was scarce at any price. "Captain McKamy's case is doubtful," he reported, as the wounded officer fought to recover from his frightful shoulder injury. The last word in Darr's entry for the day was "Armistice."[26]

Despite the flag of truce passing through the lines, Swan of Bradley County contended the shelling from the river from the Parrott batteries and mortars was "terrific." It was as if Grant was reminding Pemberton that his decision to capitulate was the right one. The final artillery duel of the siege and campaign ensued, Swan said, when the often-successful, though often-silent, Confederate river batteries replied one last time.[27] It was as though the days of sitting passively and receiving the Yankee shot and shell had finally been taken long enough, the other cheek had been turned long enough, and now it was time "to give as well as they got" for the brief bit of life this maligned garrison had left to it. The roar of the proud cannon, which had long terrorized anything Grant tried to run by Vicksburg, fairly raged, representing all the 30,000 men who had had no options, and who had been forced to lie still and wait with growling, cramped stomachs and filthy bodies for a chance to fight another day which, for this army, would never come. "At 4 p.m. on the 3rd," Colonel Edward Higgins, commanding all the mighty siege guns facing the Mississippi, declared: "I opened fire all along my lines, and at 5 p.m., the last gun was fired by the river batteries in defense of Vicksburg."[28] It was all sound and fury, signifying nothing.

S. A. R. Swan with Lee's Alabamians, sick, heartbroken, and wounded, indicated that "such events occur but seldom in a lifetime: the deafening roar,

---

[25] Stamper, "Travels of the 43rd Tennessee," 69–70.

[26] Darr, "Diary," 12.

[27] Swan, "A Tennessean at the Siege of Vicksburg," 371.

[28] Report of Col. Edward Higgins, 25 July 1863, *Official Records*, ser. 1, vol. 24, pt. 2, p. 339.

the whistling of shot, the bursting of shell, the dense stifling sulphurous smoke that settles around illuminated by the flashes of the guns, altogether makes a fit representation of Pandemonium." The fragments flew about the house of Mr. Arthur, on whose porch Swan, the Cleveland, Tennessee, soldier reclined on his sick pallet, causing him to note, "the roof was struck once, [and] many fragments dropped in the yard."[29]

The Surrender of the Garrison. The Fourth of July, 1863, the eighty-seventh anniversary of a now divided nation's declaration of independence, dawned with quiet significance. "At about nine o'clock this morning," Robert Bachman of the 60th Tennessee wrote from Vaughn's works, "the soldiers in all our trenches were ordered to step to the rear and stack arms." Then, they were ordered to return to their ditches. The Union soldiers were also ordered to stack their weapons, and then, in "broken ranks," they swarmed over the embankments the garrison had held for so long, "calling to us in a jocose way; extending their hands in friendly greeting." There was a mingling of gray coats and blue coats, "as if there was no difference between us and them, and never had been," Bachman reported.[30]

Bachman found himself conversing with a Hawkeye of the 9th Iowa, and during the conversation, he shared news about the loss of all his meager belongings in the old camp down along the Mint Springs Bayou. In that camp, Bachman had made a pet of a small dog he had named "Bob Hatton" after the Tennessee general in Lee's Army of Northern Virginia killed the spring before during the Seven Days' Battles. The Yankee soldier was amazed and informed Bachman that he might have found the dog when the Iowa regiment was in that vicinity at the beginning of the siege. Iowan had sent it home by steamboat all the way up the Mississippi River. Bachman told the soldier that he was glad that the little dog had found a good home, "as I could not have him."[31]

Around 10 a.m., a triumphant Ulysses S. Grant rode into the city he had been after for nearly eight months, and "the United States flag was run up on the court-house." Soon thereafter, Bachman wrote, the enemy's gunboats and transports began filling Vicksburg's wharfs. Grant, who had been trying to starve all the Confederates to death for a month and a half, turned magnanimous and ordered all the 30,000 prisoners now in his custody receive three full-day's rations. "How good the bread and meat and hard-tack and

---

[29] Swan, "A Tennessean at the Siege of Vicksburg," 371.
[30] Bachman, "Reminiscences of Childhood," 24.
[31] Ibid., 24–25.

coffee and sugar all tasted to us hungry almost starved men," Bachman recalled, "can well be imagined."[32]

Captain George Hynds of the 31st Tennessee was furious over the circumstances surrounding the surrender, writing in his journal, "it is very humiliating to give it up this way." He placed all the blame on John Pemberton, to whom "is due all the honor" for the loss of Vicksburg. Hynds believed that the Southern army had been "sold, if not directly, then indirectly," but he tempered his disgust with the rationalization that "we fought as long as we had rations to eat and could not stand to fight without eating something."[33]

"This doomed city has surrendered," Calvin Smith of the 31st Tennessee stated simply in the opening of his daily entry. He had heard Pemberton had met with his officers in a council of war concerning affairs. Some voted to cut their way out, and others to surrender to "Unconditional Surrender" Grant conditionally; two generals [Lee and Baldwin] wanted to continue the siege at the expense of the mules, jack or horse flesh, and "fight until the last."[34]

"The white flag was hoisted at 9 o'clock," Smith reported, "and we formed in front of our ditch with arms and accoutrements on. General Pemberton and an aide came along the line, took a stand out in the center, and read the orders of surrender, which was to stack arms." Smith noted with some bitterness, "the general made some pathetic remarks, threatening vengeance on the Yankies for lying out to us into starve into submission." Smith indicated that the lowliest private was aware such a strategy was the ultimate aim from the first day of the siege. "We never had more than 18,000 effective men, and a little over 12,000 on the day we surrendered," he wrote, while the Yankees admitted to having nearly 175,000 on their front and their back lines awaiting an attack by Johnston. The Federals, Smith maintained, were surprised to see their prisoners "looking so well," and that there were so few of them—"not more than one soldier for every six feet of line"—whereas Grant's men had been packed in nearly shoulder to shoulder in their broad works surrounding Vicksburg. The boys in blue came among Reynolds's men, Smith indicated, appearing friendly and giving out crackers and coffee, while the trading of personal items continued to take place. In turn, the Rebels visited the Union camps, where they were lavished with "many presents."[35]

---

[32] Ibid., 25.
[33] Hynds, "Original Handwritten Notes," 23.
[34] Smith, *A Smith in Service*, 63–64.
[35] Ibid., 64.

Even with such apparent hospitality and friendliness, insurmountable differences still remained. "Our men would get into strong debate on the war question," Smith reported with some satisfaction. "We show them that in surrender we are not subdued, and both agreed to fight each other again when arrayed against each other another day." Both armies agreed that they deplored the state of affairs bought on by the war, and they both promised to be friends again once it was concluded. Finally, Smith stated that the Union fleet moved up and down the river to the landing at Vicksburg, where he heard reports that six or seven gunboats and forty to seventy-five steam tugs had anchored, along with an assortment of other vessels. The Confederate arms were ordered to be delivered from where they were stacked, according to Smith, and the generals "will be given 30 to 40 waggons to transport out their baggage."[36] This undoubtedly engendered some considerable irritation for the typical, lowly private, who would have to carry out all his "baggage" in his greasy, filthy haversack.

Stamper of the 43rd Tennessee recorded that "at nine o'clock, we hoisted the white flag and stacked our arms, surrendering the place to Grant." Because Grant did not want to get such a large collection of men to the already over-taxed Yankee prisoner of war camps, Stamper seemed relieved to report, "the conditions [are] that all men and officers [are to] be paroled." Additionally, officers were to be allowed to retain their side arms, and all private property "was to be respected." These two stipulations would be ignored by the conquerors at the field level. According to Stamper, 29,000 Confederates surrendered, and army property lost was valued at $200,000. "At 12 noon," he continued in his entry, "the 43rd Tennessee Regiment stacked arms, and 'General' Reynolds gave a short lecture, and sent us back to our respective places above Vicksburg to await the enemy's disposition of us." Though sorry to "bow to our oppressors," Stamper wrote, "we were thankful to be alive."[37]

Also included in the surrender were the regimental flags. The 43rd Tennessee's magnificent first national banner (referred to popularly as the "stars and bars") made from silk presented to Colonel Gillespie and the boys by the ladies of Mt. Sterling, Kentucky, during Bragg and Kirby-Smith's invasion. It showed the effects of defiant display on the parapets and the action taken by the command as reserves. The obituary of Private Walter Thomas Lenoir of the 43rd Tennessee stated, "at the surrender of Vicksburg, less than half of the regiment answered roll call, and their battle-scarred flag, with its 975 bullet

---

[36] Ibid.
[37] Stamper, "Travels of the 43rd Tennessee," 70.

holes, bore mute testimony to the whereabouts of many of the missing."[38] The surrendered battle flag of the 59th Tennessee was also a first national Confederate flag with thirteen white stars arranged in a circle. On its white bar (left side) was painted the legend "Liberty or Death."[39]

"We are proud to know that we had held a terrible foe 48 days on twelve days' rations," Stamper noted, "and [the Yankees] told us we had done very well and deserved credit as gallant soldiers." He indicated that his adversaries "[were] very kind to us" and freely divided up their "crackers" with the conquered. Except for "a little mule meat, which some of us refused to eat," the boys had not eaten any meat for several days, so the crackers were a welcome addition to their diet. "Soon after the City was surrendered," Stamper noted in this entry, "it was full of Yanks plundering stores and loading themselves down with such things as they could find whether they were needed or not."[40] Plundering would be a skill many of these enemy soldiers who would later serve with Sherman would not forget and would utilize again the following year in their triumphant looting of the noncombatants in the state of Georgia.

Clack of the 43rd Tennessee remarked, "all is very quiet around Vicksburg this morning," and "the boys and the Yanks are conversing together." Around 10 a.m., the official surrender ceremony was accomplished "on account of our rations giving out." Even after all they had been through, Clack still felt the necessity of rationalizing the end result: "We marched to 'General' Reynolds' headquarters and stacked our arms," and then returned to the old positions, "where we expect to remain until we are paroled." The evening, he noted, passed quietly.[41]

"There has been an armistice since yesterday," Private James Henry Darr of the 43rd Tennessee recorded in his journal. "I suppose it is for the purpose of surrender, as the mules are getting scarce and poor." The calm now without the roar of cannon, the whistling and explosion of their shells, and the pop and whiz of minie balls was overpowering. Darr noted that the garrison had been surrendered, but he did not know what the terms were. Then, came the word: prisoners were to be paroled, and everyone was allowed to retain their personal

---

[38] W. E. Clark, , "The Last Roll—Walter Thomas Lenoir," *The Confederate Veteran* 38/4 (May 1930): 194.

[39] Carl Jenkins, interview by William D. Taylor. Jenkins is "commander" of the 59th Tennessee reenactment unit and has done a lot of research on the regiment. He is a high school history teacher. All the regimental flags carried by Lynch's Battery and Vaughn's and Reynolds's East Tennessee Brigades were of the first national design.

[40] Stamper, "Travels of the 43rd Tennessee," 71.

[41] Clack, "Personal Diary," 7.

property, as pitiful and scanty as it might be.[42] Many were too sick to stand their parole, so they took their oath in the hospitals and waited to be sent down river through New Orleans to Mobile, Alabama. One such soldier was Private William Casey of Carter County and the 59th Tennessee, who wrote, "I was took sick with chills and fever and was taken to the hospital in Vicksburg where I remained for some time." He indicated that he finally made it home later in the fall.[43]

"General Grant," Clark of the 59th Tennessee recounted, "thinking possibly we were starved out, permitted his men to come among us with well-filled haversacks which they opened at once asking us to help ourselves from them, saying 'we know you must be hungry.'" Apart from being a humanitarian gesture, Clark though that it was good generalship. "The contrast was so great between their well-fed and bountifully supplied army and our starved forces," he noted, "that it disaffected many of our men, especially the lower classes, so that when we were exchanged, it was impossible to get many of them back into the army." Showing a rather bourgeois contempt for a rather considerable number of men making up the Confederate army, Clark went on to say, "this class" had had enough of privations and suffering, "and having but little pride or character, they preferred the disgrace which attached to desertion rather than continue in the service."[44]

Lucy McRae, a Vicksburg citizen, described watching the defeated army milling among the victors: "How sad was the spectacle that met our gaze, arms stacked in the center of the streets, men with tearful eyes and downcast faces walking here and there; men sitting in groups feeling that they would gladly have taken their life-blood on the battlefield rather than hand over the guns and sabers so dear to them!" She continued: "The drummer boy of a Tennessee regiment, rather than give up his drum, gave it to my brother, but it was very soon taken away from him. One poor fellow gave me his horse, which was branded with the letters 'C. S.' and my two brothers hid him in the yard; but it was only a little while before a Federal soldier took him. The instruments of the band of the Tennessee regiment were stacked on the corner in front of our house," McRae continued, "while the guns were stacked in the middle of the

---

[42] Darr, "Diary," 12.
[43] 59th Tennessee, *Compiled Service Records.*
[44] Clark, *Valleys of the Shadow,* 25.

street. Men looked so forlorn, some without shoes, some with tattered garments, yet they would have fought on."[45]

In a consolidated statement of prisoners of war from the surrender of Vicksburg, Mississippi, the following are total numbers for Vaughn's and Reynolds's brigades:

Second [Vaughn's] Brigade, Martin Luther Smith's Division: 3 colonels, 3 lieutenant colonels, 5 majors, 33 captains, 30 first lieutenants, 33 second lieutenants, 19 third lieutenants, 15 non-commissioned staff, 10 first sergeants, 119 sergeants, 91 corporals, 1216 privates, for a total of 1,576 in the aggregate. Whether these numbers include the Mississippi State Troops and the residue of Loring's Division is not indicated, though such is probably the case.

Fourth [Reynolds's] Brigade, Carter L. Stevenson's Division: 4 colonels, 3 lieutenant colonels, 3 majors, 36 captains, 40 first lieutenants, 41 second lieutenants, 33 third lieutenants, 10 non-commissioned staff, 33 first sergeants, 148 sergeants,140 corporals, 1,602 privates, for a aggregate total of 2,093.

Surrender numbers for some of the companies in Vaughn's and Reynolds's commands were as follows:

> Company H, 60th Tennessee, Vaughn's Brigade: twenty-three men in the trenches surrendered; the status of eight others was "not stated," though they were absent sick or wounded.[46]
>
> Company I, 60th Tennessee, Vaughn's Brigade: twenty-four men in the trenches surrendered; the status of eleven others "was not stated."[47]
>
> Company G, 61st Tennessee, Vaughn's Brigade: twenty-four men in the trenches surrendered; six others surrendered in the hospitals were confined sick; four others status was "not stated."[48]
>
> Company I, 62nd Tennessee, Vaughn's Brigade: fifty men in the trenches surrendered; nine others surrendered at the hospitals with the sick and wounded; the status of sixteen others was "not stated."[49]
>
> Company C, 59th Tennessee, Reynolds's Brigade: thirty-seven men surrendered in the trenches; three others surrendered with the sick and wounded in the hospital.[50]

---

[45] Lucy McRae, "Reminiscences of Lucy McRae Bell," *Harpers Weekly* 56/2894 (8 June 1912): 12–13.

[46] 60th Tennessee, *Compiled Service Records.*

[47] Ibid.

[48] 61st Tennessee, *Compiled Service Records.*

[49] 62nd Tennessee, *Compiled Service Records.*

[50] 59th Tennessee, *Compiled Service Records.*

Company I, 59th Tennessee, Reynolds's Brigade: eighty-four men surrendered in the ditches; the status of three others was "not stated."[51]

A survey of the individual records of Company C, 1st Tennessee Cavalry (the only East Tennessee unit of horse soldiers serving at Vicksburg) showed that only one muster report (dated from 28 February through 30 June) was generated during the campaign,. The company had been raised in Athens, McMinn County, and was under the command of Captain R. S. Van Dyke. It was detached from its regiment probably sometime in February and lent eighty troopers to serve as scouts and an escort for General Carter Stevenson and his division. Of the eighty men, fifty-five were paroled on 10 July by Captain W. Pullen of the 20th Illinois Infantry. Another seven were in various Vicksburg military hospitals listed as sick and wounded, and were paroled on 15 July and transported via occupied New Orleans to Mobile. Their paroles were countersigned by Captain John C. Ferry of the 20th Ohio. Five were on detached duty at division headquarters when surrendered, serving as personal escorts for General Stevenson, with one cavalryman designated as a member of the general's personal bodyguard. They were paroled on 6 July with the general's staff, and their paroles were signed by Captain C. Hairston of the 124th Illinois.

Others accounted for were three who were "missing since the Battle of Baker's Creek" and can be assumed to have been made prisoners of war. Four others were outside the lines at a Jackson hospital and therefore not surrendered. Two men died in camp from undisclosed illnesses. One trooper deserted on 15 March, and another with chronic rheumatism was given a medical discharge. Private James Netherland was captured on a scout during the action around Port Gibson on 1 May, and exchanged 12 June after being diagnosed with small pox. Second Lieutenant W. Thomas Miller was killed in action during the Battle of Baker's Creek, 16 May.[52]

"The long agony is over," Swan of S. D. Lee's Brigade announced. "Vicksburg has fallen." As with so many, though they had predicted for weeks this inevitability, he seemed to be in shock and disbelief. The garrison would be paroled and leave the works they had defended for so long. Swan confirmed the final ritual stacking of arms outside the trenches at 10 o'clock. "Some of the enemy's troops marched in, and the United States flag was hoisted up the court

[51] Ibid.
[52] 1st Tennessee Cavalry, *Compiled Service Records*.

house amidst the firing of salutes," he remarked. "All the munitions belonging to the Army of the Mississippi passed into [their] hands."[53]

"The damage to our cause is incalculable," Swan feared, adding, "I refrain from suggesting where the blame should rest."[54] "We are still lying behind our ditches with our arms stacked in front of them," Hynds wrote in his diary on 5 July. The boys watched with contempt as the Yankee sentinels "walked upon our works." The victorious Union troops were strolling in every direction, really enjoying the quiet morning. Hynds's bitterness escaped through the pages of his journal when he maintained, "this lesson ought to teach President Davis that it won't do to place a Yankee general over a Southern army."[55]

Pemberton Attempts to Keep His "Army" Together. Pemberton decided to march his surrendered army, minus the troops from the Trans-Mississippi, east to Demopolis, Alabama, where the Vicksburg parolees would encamp until exchanged. Confederates from across the Mississippi River were no longer subject to Pemberton's orders because most of the Louisiana, Arkansas, Texas, and Mississippi troops had already fled to their homes. The only Trans-Mississippians who had not left were the Missourians who had no homes to which to flee. Theirs were behind the Federal lines.[56] A copy of these orders was the only entry in the 31st Tennessee's Calvin M. Smith's journal. Addressed to Colonel William M. Bradford from "Headquarters, Paroled Prisoners, Vicksburg, Miss., July 5, 1863," the orders read:

No. 1. Immediately after the troops of this army shall have been paroled at the several points designated for the respective organizations, each will be marched back under its commissioned officers to its proper camps. Neither officers nor soldiers will be permitted to leave their camps unless by authority of brigade or division commanders.

No. 2. It is to be distinctly understood that all previous existing rules of organization, discipline and police for the governance of this

[53] Swan, "A Tennessean at the Siege of Vicksburg," 371.
[54] Ibid.
[55] Hynds, "Original Handwritten Notes," 23.
[56] Gen. John C. Pemberton to Jefferson Davis, 17 July 1863, *Official Records*, ser. 1, vol. 24, pt. 3, p. 1010. Pemberton, accompanying the parolees eastward toward Enterprise, complained that he needed to promise the men immediate furloughs in order to ever hope of getting them back into the army. He noted, "nearly all of the Trans-Mississippi troops and those from the State of Mississippi have already deserted," causing him to predict that those from Georgia, Tennessee, and Alabama "will also go when they draw nearer their homes."

army continue in full force. The parole in no manner relieving officers
or soldiers from such duty as do not infringe upon the terms of parole.

No. 3. Soldiers, your defense of Vicksburg has gained for you the
respect and admiration of the enemy against which you have so long
nobly contended, then let them see that notwithstanding your service
you can still maintain the discipline of a well-organized army of the
Southern Confederacy. So soon as I can confer with our government, I
shall endeavor to procure for those of you who desire it the privilege of
visiting your homes, your wives, your children.

John C. Pemberton, Lieut. Gen.[57]

The Yankees up Close and Peaceful. Clack of the 43rd Tennessee, adjusting to
his plight, indicated that "another Sabbath morning has rolled around, and I
(with many others) as a prisoner." The day passed off "calmly," and the
"Yankees visit us today, and we converse in a very free and friendly manner."[58]
The day, according to Stamper of the 43rd Tennessee, "is devoted to preparing
for the paroling of the army." The allowance for his company, he stated, had
been only "peas and sugar." He noted that some of the garrison had already left
for Jackson after receipt of their paroles. Stamper mentioned a couple more
casualties in the regiment: Thomas McAllen of Company F died of sickness,
and Samuel Patillo of Company G succumbed to wounds suffered in the hostile
action on the night of 22 June.[59] Patillo would be one of the final Vicksburg
deaths due to enemy fire suffered by Reynolds's brigade.

Lieutenant John Shields of Morristown and the 59th Tennessee reported
after the war: "after our arms were stacked on the evening of the 5th, General
Grant and his staff rode horse-back around our breastworks." Shields was
amazed that Grant's "dress was like a common soldier," wearing an old dirty felt
hat and a blouse coat, with a black beard that reminded Shields of "a man I
knew well in north Walker County, Georgia," where he was a refugee for a
time after the war.[60]

With each hour, the boys grew more nervous. S. A. R. Swan of Lee's
Brigade wrote, "we are now anxiously awaiting our paroles." Feeling compelled
to explain their plight, Swan noted, "our rations were out, and starvation was
before us." As a commissary agent, he knew there were only peas and sugar and

---

[57] Smith, *A Smith in Service,* 64.
[58] Clack, "Personal Diary," 7.
[59] Stamper, "Travels of the 43rd Tennessee," 71.
[60] John Brabson Shields, "Reminiscences," *East Tennessee Roots* 7/1 (Spring 1992): 6.

mule meat in the larders to last for only a few more days. "Being a prisoner of war," he acknowledged, "we are now supplied by the enemy: two days subsistence consisting of crackers, bacon, pork, coffee, &c. was issued to us yesterday."[61] Though the boys did not find out until later, Grant, far from being magnanimous, probably supplemented their rations from the stores remaining in the Confederate supply depots, that is, from the foodstuffs Pemberton had so jealously parceled out during the siege.[62]

"Captain J. C. Davis was telling 'round that we had only 12 days' rations at Vicksburg when we entered the ditches 16 May," C. M. Smith of the 31st Tennessee noted. "Full rations, I suppose, which was or has been lengthened out to 50 days, 48 days besieged and 2 days after the surrender." Smith confirmed that the boys would "draw Yankie rations today." The men were becoming increasingly anxious to leave. The sight of Vicksburg crawling with their enemies sickened them. Everyone expected to leave "at any hour." Their first destination was as yet undisclosed, but Smith figured that it would be in the direction of Jackson.[63]

Smith was now addressing his entries to his wife, Nancy, and his children, as though to make up for letters not sent for so many months. He indicated that he might actually be able to see them "in the month of August or sooner." At noon he was enjoying a nice dinner of rice and sugar, and plenty of good coffee, "compliments of our Yankie friends." They had also provided the men with plenty of "crackers." In another instance of bearing gifts, Aaron S. Heck had traded away Smith's wooden canteen to a bluecoat for a nice tin one.[64]

"They have a nice sutler's store here where goods can be bought cheap," Smith wrote, "but they won't take our money." In fact, Smith noted, all the Yankees seemed to have plenty of counterfeit Confederate money of their own that they passed off on every occasion when they got the chance. But those enterprising East Tennessean, those "grand speculators on a small scale," had acquired some of the bad money and traded it off as souvenirs to the boys in blue for smaller denominations of "greenbacks." Smith promised that he would

[61] Swan, "A Tennessean at the Siege of Vicksburg," 371.
[62] Gen. U. S. Grant to Gen. John C. Pemberton, 3 July 1863, *Official Records*, ser. 1, vol. 24, pt. 1, p. 284. Grant's specific offer to Pemberton as part of the surrender terms was that "any amount of rations you may deem necessary can be taken from the stores you now have, and also the necessary cooking utensils." It was reported the commissary stores in Vicksburg held enough food to last another week beyond 4 July at the reduced rations rate then in effect.
[63] Smith, *A Smith in Service*, 64.
[64] Ibid.

try to send his little "book" on ahead to Hawkins County if he found someone leaving earlier than he could leave. He told his wife, Nancy, to tell her brother Captain James D. Spears that if he was at home, he should come forward as quickly as possible and assume command since Smith desired to spend time of his own in the bosom of his family in "old Hawkins." He also wrote that his other brother-in-law, Lieutenant Sam Spears, was in or near Jackson, where he had remained since being cut off from the regiment before the siege. Smith had heard that Spears was "lazy and in good health," though due to circumstances he had not seen Spears since entering the ditches.[65]

Addressing Sylvester, his oldest boy, Smith admonished his son to continue working at learning to read and write. "Sylvester, here is men that can't read and write," he noted, referring to men in his company. During their time in the trenches, the pressures of command left Smith free to try to help his men in other ways: "how they hate it; they give me $50.00 to learn them to write, but they are so lazy they won't get paper and ink and I can't afford to buy it for them." But he could afford to buy some clothes. He informed Nancy that he had procured various pieces of clothing, many for their children, and would try to get his men to help him sneak the clothes out. Smith had a coat he paid $8 for which was too small for him and too large for the children, so he decided to give it to Private Dan Kite since he thought it would fit him. "I know when I leave here," he declared, "I will fatten like an old hog or something else." He want to tell Mrs. David Reynolds that her son John was currently in the hospital, "though not sick." The surgeons thought that a march of twenty miles a day would cause heat exhaustion and would prove disastrous. Smith indicated that young Reynolds looked better today than he had for the past four grueling months.[66]

"J. H. Everhart is getting well fast and will be able to start home before long," Smith noted, referring to the soldier who accidentally shot himself in the wrist, necessitating the amputation of his arm below the elbow. Other soldiers belonging to Smith's company still in the hospital included Peter Brown, Jacob Tucker, E. H. Long, and J. R. Dykes. Colonel Bradford had ordered that no man be allowed to leave for home unless he was physically able, and Smith believed that it would be better for them to wait behind until the crowds had thinned. The Yankees were trying to hasten their repairs on the railroad toward Jackson some miles past the Big Black Bridge, so indications were that the repairs were finished, the sick and infirm would not have as far to walk to catch

---

[65] Ibid., 64–65.
[66] Ibid., 65.

other trains east. When Joseph Johnston learned of Pemberton's surrender, he removed his so-called Army of the Relief northwest to avoid having all of Grant's forces immediately turned on him. Without Johnston there, the roads east for the surrendered army would be open. "Our army is by no means cowed," Smith asserted, "though the Yankies tell us that the war will soon be over, that our armies will be defeated, and, of course, we will soon be subjugated." He noted that the men vehemently responded that the struggle had just begun, and though "the North now holds the big river, let them come out into the hills and we will whip [them] to death and [they] will think properly of us."[67]

The Yankees Enroll the Former Slaves. "When I hear them say that it's right to take the Southern Negroes and put them in the [Union] army to fight us," Smith complained, "it makes my blood boil within me." He cited instances at Milliken's Bend and Port Hudson when poorly trained black troops were thrown pell-mell against impregnable Confederate fortifications and slaughtered, their dead littering the ground for acres. "I heard a *smart* Yankie say yesterday he was opposed to having them in the army," Smith noted, "and that the men of the North hated them and that he would not eat the victuals that they would cook." He went on to proclaim that the enemy soldiers he had come in contact with were not fighting the war to free anyone but to subjugate and exterminate "us from the face of the earth."[68]

The day passed still without being paroled, Stamper of the 43rd Tennessee fretted in this day's entry. "[We are] still at our old camp," he added, "or not a camp, but a place where we had been held in reserve for six months." He noted that Vicksburg was crawling with Yankee soldiers now, "enlisting all the Negroes they can."[69] The thick, dry summer dust was "suffocating," according to Swan, "and the time drags slowly until we are paroled and turn our faces toward home." He worried about his mother back in Cleveland, Tennessee, and was anxious to send some word to her and others who missed him and wondered about his present condition. Another matter no doubt related to his weakened state also caused him concern: "I dread the march to our parole camp," he wrote.[70] With no rest for the weary, the garrison would be required to reassemble at various points after a long train ride to wait exchange for Yankee prisoners of war. Reynolds's men had been told that they would

---

[67] Ibid.
[68] Ibid.
[69] Stamper, "Travels of the 43rd Tennessee," 71.
[70] Swan, "A Tennessean at the Siege of Vicksburg," 371.

reassemble at Decatur, Georgia, and Vaughn's men would reorganize at Jonesborough in Washington County. Matters at Vicksburg, however, seemed stalled. The boys still had no word as to when they would get released. Meanwhile, they had to watch in disgust as the Federals enlisted "contrabands" into their army. "I am tired and sick of the Yankees doings," Swan grumbled, "conspiring with the Negroes and even carrying them off by force to form them into regiments."[71]

Even the silencing of the guns conspired against the prisoners, for it did not allow them any better rest after dark. "The sound of musketry and artillery seldom ceased an hour, night or day, during the entire siege," Robert Bachman of the 60th Tennessee recalled. "We became so used to the noise, that it was hard for us to sleep a few nights after the surrender. We missed the cracking rifles and the roaring cannon."[72]

Still nothing happened in Reynolds's Brigade on 7 July related to their parole, Stamper of the 43rd Tennessee reported. The boys tried patiently to await their turn, he indicated, but it was difficult for them as they observed other segments of the army marching east after receiving their paroles.[73] It seemed all were being marched off but them. Long would be line of march heading toward Jackson as Pemberton's army filed out slowly and methodically. During the morning, Swan and the other men of the quartermaster's went to Pemberton's headquarters department, where they received their paroles. He also noted that the time dragged slowly, and that it will be "some days yet before the whole army is paroled."[74]

"All are anxious to be moving towards home," Smith asserted, "and out of sight of the enemy," though superficially at least there was "generally the best kind of feeling between our soldiers and the Federals." Little squads of five or six of the former combatants could be seen in clusters talking over the late occurrences related to the siege, Swan seethed, exhibiting "the greatest good humor." Most of the boys he observed, however, "show an unbroken spirit, and declare to the Yankees their firm intentions to fight them again with more obstinacy than ever" as soon as they were exchanged. In a scene heavy with pathos, Swan outlined the news that only one or two days after the surrender, word reach Vicksburg that Johnston had at long last attacked Grant's rear near

---

[71] Ibid., 371–72.
[72] Bachman, "Reminiscences of Childhood," 23.
[73] Stamper, "Travels of the 43rd Tennessee," 71.
[74] Swan, "A Tennessean at the Siege of Vicksburg," 372.

the Big Black battlefield "and gained a decided advantage."[75] Johnston's success was greatly exaggerated and merely a tentative probe. He was now doing all he could to escape Grant's undivided attention. "As soon as our men heard it, though," Swan wrote, "they let up a cheer which was carried around all the camps of those awaiting paroles." The abolitionists were hard at work, he indicated, "tampering with the Negroes and poisoning their minds as far as possible." Using intimidation, the federal authorities were marching them off in large numbers before "their bayonets to put them into camps of instruction or work gangs." Their Yankee taskmasters, Swan sneered, were much better at getting work out of them than their old supervisors had been.[76]

As the few concessions of the surrender terms favoring the conquered army fell away one by one, Swan noted that the next "privilege" to be revoked by the Federals was the one allowing servants of the officers to accompany them out of enemy jurisdiction. "Passes had been produced for the servants for that purpose," he wrote in his daily entry, "but the abolition element stirred up such a mess that orders were countermanded and passes revoked."[77]

Colonel William Eakin of Monroe County and commander of the 59th Tennessee addressed his experience when he attempted to bring his servant out. "I was unable to get permission to bring him away after the surrender. There were some five or six colored men attached to my regiment. We left some of them shedding tears; they all overtook us before we reached Meridian. [They] said they told the Yankees that the Rebels had impressed them, and they much desired to visit their wives and children, and were given rations and turned loose."[78]

Paroled. Each Confederate soldier had to sign an individual parole witnessed by a Federal officer, which guaranteed the parolee freedom from molestation by the victors as long as he abided by its stipulations. The parole document was worded as follows:

---

[75] Ibid. Unfortunately, much of this was bluster. Few of the East Tennessee Confederates would return to the field even after their exchange. Indeed, many were, as the terminology of the day described it, "used up." The son of the Reverend W. W. Lord, whose father conducted services every day at Christ Episcopal Church during the siege, concluded: "the soldiers, carrying with them little but their clothing, limped off to their homes in Mississippi, Louisiana and other portions of the South and Southwest. Only a few would have the heart and strength to rearm and fight again." W. W. Lord, "A Child at the Siege of Vicksburg," *Harpers Weekly* (December 1908) 44–53.

[76] Swan, "A Tennessean at the Siege of Vicksburg," 372.

[77] Ibid.

[78] Eakin to Rigby, 12 March 1904.

Vicksburg, Mississippi, July _____, 1863,

To All Whom It May Concern, Know Ye That:

I, _____, a _____ of Co. _____, _____ Regt., _____ Vols., CSA, being a prisoner of war, in the hands of the United States Forces, in virtue of the capitulation of the city of Vicksburg and its garrison, by Lieut. Gen. John C. Pemberton, CSA, commanding, on the 4th day of July, 1863, do in pursuance of the terms of said capitulation, give this my solemn parole under oath _____ that I will not take up arms against the United States, nor serve in any military police, or constabulary force in any Fort, Garrison or field work, held by the Confederate States of America, against the United States of America, until duly exchanged by the proper authorities.

Sworn to and subscribed before me at Vicksburg, Miss., this _____ day of July, 1863.

_____

[Parolee's signature or mark]

_____

[Signature and regiment of the paroling officer][79]

"The Yankies came along our company and inquired who it was that wore a red shirt," Smith of the 31st Tennessee recorded in his diary on 8 July. They said that they would give $40 for the man's gun since he had "killed four men at one of their port holes, and scarcely ever missed it." Being no fools, none of his men stepped forward. Smith was sorry that his men rarely had a chance to use their pieces until the siege was almost over, though he felt that this example had proved his men to be good marksmen. Smith reported that a Union officer came around about 10 a.m. where the boys were waiting the Yankees' pleasure and informed Colonel Bradford that his regiment would have to move since he wanted his men to occupy the 31st Tennessee's old positions. A new holding area was prescribed closer in toward Vicksburg, and the regiment finally abandoned their old ditches. At 3 p.m., officials Smith termed "pay-rollers" came among them, passed out their paroles, and had Bradford's men complete them. Smith indicated that the boys were now ready to take the oath of parole,

---

[79] 1st Tennessee Cavalry, 3rd Tennessee, 31st Tennessee, 43rd Tennessee, 59th Tennessee, 60th Tennessee, 61st Tennessee, 62nd Tennessee, and Lynch's Battery, *Compiled Service Records.*

promising not to serve the Confederacy again as soldiers until they were properly exchanged, effective the moment they wrote their names or made their marks on the forms. "[I] was very anxious to get [to Vicksburg]," Smith wrote, "and now as much to get away. Fifty-two days in this prison. How long will we remain here? We have no business here now." Still, as though fully aware of the historical significance of what he and his comrades had been through, Smith indicated that he would not "take the world for the trip."[80]

Private William Hill of Company B, 43rd Tennessee, died on 8 July in the Vicksburg hospital from a "continued illness," according to Stamper.[81] Clack of the 43rd Tennessee noted a "Private William Casey was seriously burnt this evening by foolishly setting powder on fire." Such foolishness indicated that he boys needed something to occupy their time. Paroles for the regiment were expected the following morning, Clack wrote.[82] "Still two brigades [one being Reynolds'] of Stevenson's Brigade [Division] to be paroled," Swan reported, "which will take all day tomorrow."[83]

Interestingly, many in the river batteries, including Lynch's Company, and others in the 1st Tennessee Heavy Artillery and the Alabama and Louisiana Artillery detachments had apparently conspired to refuse to sign their paroles once their appointed time came, though the Yankees would compel them to do so a week and a half later.[84] A random check of the compiled service records of a 40–man sample serving with John Lynch's Light Artillery Company raised in New Market Jefferson County, showed that only half their number received their paroles on their appointed date, 8 July.[85] Rather than attributing patriotic motives to their stubbornness, however, the truth was that those who would not comply were doing so to keep from serving in the army again after exchange. A few of these artillerymen whose positions had been continually pounded throughout the siege, actually returned to the lines after signing their paroles, at which point they were summarily arrested and made prisoners of war. Though

---

[80] Smith, *A Smith in Service*, 66.

[81] Stamper, "Travels of the 43rd Tennessee," 71.

[82] Clack, "Personal Diary," 8.

[83] Swan, "A Tennessean at the Siege of Vicksburg," 372.

[84] Gen. James B. McPherson to Gen. John C. Pemberton, 7 July 1863, *Official Records*, ser. 1, vol. 24, pt. 3, p. 484; Gen. U. S. Grant to Gen. James B. McPherson, 8 July 1863, *Official Records*, ser. 1, vol. 24, pt. 3, p. 488. Of the approximately 1,500 artillerymen initially refusing to sign paroles, nearly half continued in their declination despite the threats paroling officers. These gunners were shipped off to the various Union prisons.

[85] Lynch's Battery, *Compiled Service Records*.

some were sent to prison camps with the Big Black River captives, many others were taken to the Gratiot Street Military Prison in St. Louis, where they were allowed to take the Oath of Allegiance to gain their release.[86] Many in Lynch's Company, records indicated, used their conscript status to convince their conquerors they should be freed from any military obligation since they had been impressed against their wills. Finally, being a conscript had its rewards.

"We have just returned from town with our paroles," Clack of the 43rd Tennessee indicated the next morning, 9 July, with some relief.[87] Stamper of the same regiment confirmed this report, stating that it transpired at around 2 p.m. He finally believed "that we would [now] be free of Yankee insults."[88] Bradley County's Swan noted in his journal that he was still "spending time at Mr. Arthur's for the benefit of shade and water." He generally took his meals in camp, though sometimes, "I get a plate of soup and a dish of tomatoes at Mr. Arthur's which is a great luxury and for which I am very thankful." Swan indicated that a paroled Lee's Brigade would be leaving Vicksburg the next day.[89]

Lieutenant Calvin Morgan Smith of the 31st Tennessee recorded on Friday, 10 July, that his regiment marched into Vicksburg, each man gave his parole of honor, which they signed by name or mark, and had it countersigned by a designated Yankee officer. The men were then marched back to their camping ground, where the different companies had their rolls called, and the men removed their hats and raised their right hand to give their verbal oath to what they had signed. Smith indicated that the men taking the oath in his company were: C. M. Smith; J. A. Webster; J. R. Dykes; N. Chestnutt; L. D. Spears; J. R. Ball; W. T. Dykes; J. M. Tucker; A. G. Wright; A. N. Owens; Kelly Allen; J. G. Brandon; D. Booker; J. M. McClain; W. McClain; T. H. McClain; Henderson Kite; Dan Kite; John Kite, Sr.; John Kite, Jr.; T. Dykes; J. M. Fitzpatrick; I. Gaibia; Hugh Harper; C. Hughes; Aaron S. Heck; J. P. King; S. Kenade; G. Leonard; E. H. Long; D. Petty; John Reynolds; R. Smith; B. Smith, and J. Webster—thirty-four parolees in all. Five other men on the company rolls were sick or recovering from wounds at the Fourth Brigade hospital and were would be paroled there: Sergeant J. H. Everhart; J. R. Dykes; Jess Grigsby; Peter Brown, and Gabriel Tate, serving as a nurse. These men were not well enough to undertake the exhausting march to come over hot

---

[86] Ibid.
[87] Clack, "Personal Diary," 8.
[88] Stamper, "Travels of the 43rd Tennessee," 71.
[89] Swan, "A Tennessean at the Siege of Vicksburg," 372.

dusty roads which would of necessity be crowded with soldiers on their way to the place of transportation, thought to be either Jackson or Meridian. "Many will start from here that cannot keep up," Smith knew, "and I fear having a scarcity of money will be troubled to keep up or to get along." Therefore, Smith dedicated himself to keeping his company together and to assisting those along the way so that all might reach home near the same time. "What joy it would give our friends at home!" Lieutenant Smith exclaimed.[90]

General Vaughn, Colonel Reynolds and their staffs were included in the census of "generals and staff" coordinated through Pemberton's headquarters.[91]

The Boys Head for Home. By 7 July, he throng of soldiers seeking to leave Yankee-occupied Vicksburg was becoming impatient and uneasy, according to Stamper of the 43rd Tennessee. The regiment was still there, he wrote, "waiting for the first part of the army to move out of the way." So far, they had not been able to accomplish getting all the parolees out for the past two days.[92] Stamper's comrade Clack noted that William Hill died the night before, 9 July, and that a friend whose name has not survived Clack's tattered manuscript died during the previous day. With hopes full of anticipation, Clack reported that the 43rd Tennessee expected to be away from their forlorn works by the following morning.[93]

"We had orders to leave at 3 o'clock this morning [10 July]," Calvin Smith of the 31st Tennessee reported, "but something delayed us at headquarters, but no doubt we will start east in less than 24 hours." The orders came to Reynolds's camp before daylight that all the men were to remain in their camps ready to answer to their names when rolls were called. Smith noted that if any man was absent, he would be retained and "sent north," that is, to confinement in one of the Yankee prisons where their friends and neighbors captured at the Big Black were already being quartered. Later, another order came for the boys to be ready to leave at 10 a.m. "So all are anxious and ready to make the start," Smith asserted.[94] The tardy departure was caused by the troops who refused to sign their paroles and whom the Federals were trying to convince that not doing so would result in their imprisonment in prisoner of war camps up north.

The long-awaited moment arrived with the rising sun on 11 July, and Stevenson's Division was finally on the march away from Vicksburg. As a final

[90] Smith, *A Smith in Service*, 66.
[91] Consolidated Statement of Prisoners of War, Vicksburg, Miss., 4 July 1863, *Official Records*, ser. 1, vol. 24, pt. 2, p. 324–25.
[92] Stamper, "Travels of the 43rd Tennessee," 71.
[93] Clack, "Personal Diary," 8.
[94] Smith, *A Smith in Service*, 66.

irritation that must have been almost unbearable, "Reynolds' Brigade was last" in line, according to Stamper of the 43rd Tennessee.[95] The troops in the rear of the column nearly suffocated in the dense dust kicked up by anybody else on the road ahead. Most likely in an army where the pecking order was always considered by date of rank, Reynolds's Fourth Brigade (in a division of four brigades) had little expectation of a better spot, which was compounded by the fact that their commander was a colonel and all the other brigades were commanded by brigadier generals probably resigned them to their lot in line.

Beginning their exodus at around 8 a.m., Isaac Stamper wrote, "we had marched but two miles when we were halted, and inspected by the enemy pickets to ascertain if we were carrying out anything contrary to their wishes." The Yankees were particularly interested in keeping behind body servants. Once the inspections were completed, the brigade moved through the initial security line due east of Vicksburg. After about eight miles, "we took up for the night." The boys had a good rest, Stamper indicated, "and we slept well until disturbed by a light shower of rain, which put everything in good order for the next day."[96] His reference here was positive since the spray on the dry roads settled the dust a bit.

Clack added that the regiment left around 7 a.m. on 11 July, heading toward Jackson and having drawn "six days' rations preparatory for the march." They camped along the railroad "after about 7 1/2 miles," where the night again had "an appearance of rain."[97] Along the line of march, the local citizens were either without much in the way of provisions for the paroled army, or were trading pretty high for what they had sell.

"Oh, save me from my friends the Mississippians!" James Darr of the 43rd Tennessee begged. "The good Mississippians who sold Southern soldiers roasting ears at 2 dollars a dozen are now selling the same to the Yankees at ten cents. Beef to us at $1 a pound now sells at 15 cents—and they all took the oath [of allegiance]!" Perhaps summarizing the feelings of many of his comrades, Darr exclaimed: "Curse ye the Mississippians!" He continued: "Curse ye them bitterly—so say I!"[98]

Fifteen miles were covered the next day, 12 July, Clack of the 43rd Tennessee recalled, and "we marched out this morning at 4 o'clock and struck camp at 6 o'clock p.m." within 8 1/2 miles of Raymond. The sudden exertion

---

[95] Stamper, "Travels of the 43rd Tennessee," 71.
[96] Ibid.
[97] Clack, "Personal Diary," 8.
[98] Darr, "Diary," 12.

over the two days after long weeks of inactivity and poor diet, aggravated some by the shower they encountered, led him to report, "I had a pretty severe chill this evening with fever."[99]

Sergeant William Long of the 59th Tennessee reported that his Morristown company did not receive their paroles until 12 July, though he was probably wrong. "We had to walk 200 miles before we could get on a railroad," he remembered, adding: "We had a rough time."[100]

And on they went, according to Stamper, who wrote, "at daylight on 13 July, we took up a line of march to the Big Black River four miles distant." They shambled on past Bovina Station and arrived at the Big Black River bridge, where the brigade paused to eat its breakfast.[101] There, perhaps some reflected on two months before when their friends and comrades of Vaughn's East Tennessee brigade had been wrecked there. Evidence of the war on the scarred battlefield lay before them yet, the landscape where destroyed and abandoned instruments of war still cluttered the earthworks. Between the bluffs, where the narrow and now much shallower river ran, rose the pylons and remaining crumpled superstructure of the burned bridge, as well as the charred wooden ribcage of the *Dot*, providing breakers for the swift current passing through it. In passing the battlefield Lieutenant Smith of the 31st Tennessee reported seeing many graves, and "many trees are shot down by cannon shot, and limbs are dead caused by shell and shot."[102]

"Breakfast dispatched," Smith continued, "we rolled on slowly, resting often as we were well loaded with rations." The Yankees had provided them with ten days' worth of meat rations and six days of bread.[103] After about twelve miles, Stamper and his comrades stopped for the night. "All along this march," he recollected, "we had roasting ears, for our army was falling back, leaving the country to the mercy of the enemy." As a patriotic duty to deny the Yankees, forage, he indicated that the boys "made free to eat corn," which was a nice supplement to their crackers and meat.[104] Every patch of green corn along the route was covered at once with scarecrow-like parolees, thick as locusts.

"We marched out at 5 a.m. on 14 July," Clack of the 43rd Tennessee indicated in his journal, "and came via Raymond to Cooper's Wells—a distance of 13 1/2 miles." While tarrying a bit in Raymond, he reported that Lieutenant

---

[99] Clack, "Personal Diary," 8.
[100] Long, "Autobiography," 1: 55.
[101] Stamper, "Travels of the 43rd Tennessee," 72.
[102] Smith, *A Smith in Service*, 66.
[103] Ibid.
[104] Stamper, "Travels of the 43rd Tennessee," 72.

J. H. Pyott and Private Thomas Roddy of the regiment were left sick at the hospital there.[105] Then the march resumed again, and they moved along the road without respite in the endless clouds of dust. Stamper of the 43rd Tennessee wrote that the march was resumed at sunup and was directed toward Raymond, "where we expected to pass the [final] outposts of the Yankee army." The route of march was fairly and serenely quiet, though on occasion, while plodding along, the men were forced to the side of the road by several enemy ambulances racing by, removing their sick and wounded to their new base at Vicksburg. "Our scouts had been in Raymond ahead of us this morning," he noted, so the parolee army had ample warning about what to expect "up the road."[106]

After a three-hour rest, Stamper continued, "we struck out and traveled four miles to what is called Cooper's Wells"—once a fashionable health resort where the idle wealthy had whiled away the hot days of the summer. This stop was a great boon for the filthy and louse-ridden brigade, he reported, for "we found plenty of good water to wash with and to drink." Afterwards, the boys spread out again on the shady ground beneath the spreading oaks and "took another good old-fashioned sleep."[107]

Lieutenant Calvin Smith of the 31st Tennessee (who indicated that the events reported today occurred on 13 July; his entries from here are dated one day early) agreed with William Clack that the parolees left at 5 a.m. and arrived at Raymond around noon, where they rested for nearly two and a half hours. "This is a pretty little town," Smith indicated, "but [is] now filled with sick and wounded of both armies." Even then, Smith observed the Yankee wagons arriving under a white flag to carry off their own sick and wounded from the place. In agreement with the other chroniclers, he recorded that the boys left for Cooper Wells, five miles away, which he called "a watering resort for unhealthy people" containing "many large buildings" that had rooms for nearly 500 visitors.[108]

"A great many of the men are barefooted and sore," Smith remarked, indicating that the brigade and four or five wagons had traveled thirty-five miles in three days. All along the choking white dust clogged the air, covering all, and through it moved the ranks of hidden soldiers, the horsemen, and the slow creaking wagons. Smith indicated that he heard the familiar sound of muffled

---

[105] Clack, "Personal Diary," 8.
[106] Stamper, "Travels of the 43rd Tennessee," 72.
[107] Ibid.
[108] Smith, *A Smith in Service*, 66.

cannon towards Jackson and believed that Johnston was fighting in that direction some ten or fifteen miles off to the right of the line of march. No longer directly influenced by the conflict between Johnston and Grant, the parolees' plan for the march was to reach Brandon east of Jackson, some twenty-five miles away, where they would finally board the trains for home. "Just had fried green corn for supper," Smith noted, "having a pine light for the first time in near 6 months." The boys were eating all the watermelon and corn they could hold in their shrunken stomachs. "The people sympathize greatly for us," he observed.[109] The parolees began to realize for the first time that they were considered heroes.

With the morning light on 14 July, the column passed through Byram ("a small town") and made its crossing over the Jackson and New Orleans Bridge spanning high above the Pearl River. Once across, Stamper of the 43rd Tennessee indicated that the boys were able to take another "a pleasant bath" and another good rest. As an added surprise, he wrote, "some of the boys found several barrels of whiskey which had been buried to prevent the Yankees finding it." All were allowed to drink as much as they wanted, and "several got more than they could carry." "We had quite a lively brigade," Stamper mused, and after a month and a half of serious work, "some few took to a little 'wool-pulling' [rough-housing]." Incredibly, the brigade managed after this refreshment to make another five miles that day before stopping for the night.[110]

Lieutenant Smith of the 31st Tennessee indicated the men were on the march early on 15 July, and their next stop was at Byram on the Pearl River. There they saw the Jackson and New Orleans depot ruins, burned the Sunday before along with a number of cars. As in many other towns and communities Reynolds's men passed through now, they found many of the inhabitants fleeing as refugees toward Alabama ahead of the Yankees. Civilians and soldiers alike found themselves intermingled on the journey. The farms and plantations on their route boasted large crops of early corn, field peas, and sweet potatoes. While awaiting stragglers, the brigade took to the water for a refreshing swim, after which, Smith saw hundreds of his comrades lying fast asleep in the shade of trees. "Some of Johnston's cavalry are scouting about here," Smith observed, "and I can still hear the cannon about Jackson."[111] Smith also recorded the whiskey incident, noting some of the men found the barrels buried in the

---

[109] Ibid., 66–67.
[110] Stamper, "Travels of the 43rd Tennessee," 72–73.
[111] Smith, *A Smith in Service*, 67.

ground, smashed them up, and helped themselves to what they wanted. The results were that they "whooped and hollowed like wild fellows." Reynolds's East Tennesseans were camped near a large church where foot-sore stragglers continued to arrive all through the night.[112]

While the 31st Tennessee and 43rd Tennessee seemed to be taking their leisurely time, members of another regiment in Reynolds's Brigade had already begun to arrive home in East Tennessee, particularly some of those in its officer cadre. Captain Reuben Clark of the 59th Tennessee outdistanced much of his brigade to reach the railway where a train waited to take him home. He stated that on 15 July, "I arrived at Knoxville, Tennessee, by railroad and I greatly enjoyed the hospitality of my old friends."[113] Lieutenant John Shields of Morristown and of Clark's company in the 59th Tennessee, described their route, indicating, "we left for home by rail to Selma, Ala., where we took a boat to Montgomery. At Montgomery, we went by rail to Atlanta, from Atlanta to Dalton, from Dalton, Ga., to Knoxville finally to Morristown."[114]

Stamper of the 43rd Tennessee indicated that at daylight on the morning of 16 July, "the tour continued" of this section of Mississippi. As was now the routine, the boys were up early to make as much distance as they could before the suffocating heat of the day sapped all their strength, at which time they rested until sundown, then continued on until dark. Nearer to Brandon they came and what was anticipated to be the end of the march: the first functioning station on the railroad east of Jackson, where they were supposed to board the trains that would ultimately take them home.[115] "But by this time," Stamper wrote with heavy disappointment, "it was found we could not get transportation [here] on account of Johnston having to send so much government property up and down the road from Jackson."[116] Though Johnston came to be much beloved by the Army of Tennessee in the last year and a half of the war, his name at that point probably drew the same ire from these East Tennessee Confederates as would Pemberton's. After countless disappointments, none were in any mood to be thwarted in their weary attempt to finally get home.

The parolees had to go eighty more miles along the powdery roads, swirling with the thick dust clouds. The conquered defenders of Vicksburg moved on, flanked by the flat sun-withered Mississippi countryside they would

---

[112] Ibid.
[113] Clark, *Shadows of the Valley*, 26.
[114] Shields, "Reminiscences," 6–7.
[115] Stamper, "Travels of the 43rd Tennessee," 73.
[116] Ibid.

have to traverse by foot to the Mobile and Ohio Railroad station at Enterprise, Mississippi. Resigned to the fact that they were never going to have an easy time in this state, the men marched another fifteen miles in that direction before "taking up" for the night.[117] At the head of the column the stamping of feet often stopped, and in quiet waves the cessation of all movement spread to the rear ranks. In the confused, furnace-hot mist came moments when utter quietness, a unfathomable submission to endless exhaustion, reigned. The paroled rebels cursed at every unexplained delay and blew their noses through their thumbs and forefingers to bring up the stifling dust. Many tied rags across their mouths and noses to catch the grime.

Adding to the men's misery was the word from Pemberton that the men would no longer be allowed to help themselves to whatever they found to eat along the march. Smith of the 31st Tennessee reported in his journal that orders were issued to cease killing the stock they encountered near their route, since depredations from this point on would be blamed only on the parolees. Such action would be seen as crimes against loyal citizens, many of whom, Smith noticed, continued to head their wagons east away from the direction Johnston's army was taking to the northeast, since only his force remained now to draw the wrath of Grant's legions. Considerable fighting was occurring even now, Smith noted, with Johnston battling the Yankees for the sixth straight day, though "Uncle Jo" was thought to be merely fighting a delaying action as he fell back since he was able to muster only 30,000–35,000 men against at least twice that number of Federals. General John C. Breckenridge was also reported to be active in the vicinity, "killing and capturing nearly a whole brigade" of Yankees in action the previous Monday. "Deeds of heroism are displayed on every hand," Smith indicated. But all the Vicksburg parolees could do was stay out of the way and try to find a train heading east into Alabama. They had become an invisible army. Many of the citizens headed the same way on the road were doing likewise, while doing what little they could to help the soldiers. "The ladies would walk along behind their wagons," Smith wrote, "while they allowed sick soldiers to ride instead," serenaded by the rattle of wheels over the hard deeply rutted roads. It was perhaps unnecessary for Smith to add, "all are loyal through this section."[118]

Clack of the 43rd Tennessee noted on 17 July that he was afflicted with "the chills," as were many of his comrades on the road with him, and he indicated, "I cannot keep my journal any longer." After the long weeks of

[117] Ibid.
[118] Smith, *A Smith in Service*, 67.

confinement on skeleton rations and putrid water, the sudden exertions in the relentless heat and the desire to be home as rapidly as possible struck down a great number of the boys with heat exhaustion, or worse, sunstroke. "We are moving along the best we can," Clack asserted.[119] Great sections of the column began lagging farther behind. Not all could make a more strenuous effort; the heat and exhaustion were becoming unconquerable. Along the road the wide empty space between the head and rear columns steadily lengthened.

Stamper noted that sunup on 17 July found them up and moving again, and soon they plodded through the little town of Cato, "which on account of the war has almost gone to wreck." He noted that the brigade moved another ten miles and after stopping, spread out in the wood and field to sleep.[120]

About this time, Lieutenant John Shields of the 59th Tennessee noted that he and his friend Lieutenant John M. Carson, who had been aboard the gunboat *Webb* back in February, finally arrived at the depot in Morristown (now Hamblen) County. "More than 1000 people had assembled there to meet friends and relatives from the siege of Vicksburg," Shields noted, but these anxious families and friends were doomed to disappointment. There were "but few of us arrived," he continued, "as we got ahead of nearly all our command." Many were sadly disappointed, Shields reported, "as Lieut. Carson and I bore the first reliable news they had had from Vicksburg since the siege began. It was a great trial upon us to report to parents and loved ones the deaths of their sons and friends."[121]

On 17 July, a worried General Pemberton notified President Davis that significant numbers of desertions continued among his men on the road toward Demopolis, Alabama, where his plan was for the Vicksburg army to gather at the parole camp to await exchange. The ex-lieutenant-general commanding feared that as soon as the column reached Demopolis, the Georgians, Alabamians, and Tennesseans would all scatter for their homes, as most of the Trans-Mississippi and Mississippi troops had already done. Ideally, he desired that the paroled prisoners be kept together and put back under arms as soon as a prisoner exchange was completed. As a compromise, Pemberton felt compelled to recommend a furlough for the half-starved and exhausted troops. He feared that without some time at home, many of these men "deserting" on

---

[119] Clack, "Personal Diary," 8.
[120] Stamper, "Travels of the 43rd Tennessee," 73.
[121] Shields, "Reminiscences," 7.

the march would never return to active service.[122] Since many of Pemberton's men on the road to Demopolis had already awarded themselves a "furlough" by getting to Enterprise earlier and getting out on a train, they had not waited around for Davis's approval.

Others were not so fortunate to be further along on the road home; they continued their slow and steady progress on the morning of 18 July. Some of the boys had taken to strolling through the night hours as they hurried eastward to narrow the distance. They also believed that marching in the dark was much more pleasant than marching in the oppressive heat, even when unsure of their direction. An added motivation was that if the energetic ones arrived at Enterprise ahead of most of the others on the march, they would be assured of a place on the train then loading at the depot.

But their comrades who had become used to the routine of their more leisurely daily march were up at daylight as usual and again on their hot, sweaty haul toward the Strong River, a distance of fifteen miles, where the line of their progression temporarily ceased due to nightfall. All the marchers were caked in white dust. It rained occasionally, and continued raining on and off all night. Stamper of the 43rd Tennessee wrote that the boys did not mind it in the least, as it did little to disturb their sleep.[123]

It was about this point in the journey that Reynolds's Brigade began to break up, with the segments that felt more motivated "racing" ahead of some of the weary, the exhausted, and the ill. "The night before," Stamper recorded, "so many of the 59th Tennessee went on ahead, that Colonel Gillespie did not intend to try to march as a regiment but told his boys who had stayed back to be their own commanders and get to Enterprise the best they could."[124] The 59th Tennessee, which had been blessed during the siege with few illnesses when all about them suffered, proved at this point to also be the command with the stamina to outdistance all others in their brigade. With Eakin's men leaving the others of their brigade behind, according to Stamper, parts of three regiments (not including the 59th Tennessee), for so many in Reynolds' other commands

---

[122] Gen. John C. Pemberton to Jefferson Davis, 12 July 1863, *Official Records*, ser. 1, vol. 24, pt. 3, p. 1010.

[123] Stamper, "Travels of the 43rd Tennessee," 73–74.

[124] Ibid., 74. Unlike some of the other paroled commands, the East Tennessee Confederates were probably allowed to leave when every they were able, regardless of whether unit integrity was maintained. Col. Gillespie urged his men to make their own way, and apparently many of the 59th Tennessee's officers were already home by 19 July.

had gone on ahead "to prevent their having to march during the heat of the day."[125]

"The 43rd Tennessee was still together the next morning [19 July]," Stamper wrote, at least enough to still call it a regiment. The 3rd Tennessee and the 31st Tennessee had fragmented, he observed, and gangs and groups of men from each were making their own way southeast toward Enterprise.[126] A number of men now, representing in all the brigades in Stevenson's Division, moved along together, be they officer or private, all equal in the sight of God, excused for the time being to never give nor respond to orders.

"We marched to the Leaf River," Stamper noted, "about twelve miles by one o'clock, where we stopped for dinner consisting of roasting ears." The yankee rations by this point in the great exodus of the Vicksburg parolees had "played out," and their government was in no position to supply them more since Johnston had all supplies diverted to him from Confederate-controlled areas around Jackson. This development led Stamper to conclude, "the condition of that part of the Confederacy, at that time, would not justify a surplus of provisions at any point on our line of march."[127] Such was the unfortunate position in which these famished men found themselves: they were still soldiers of the Southern nation, but they were not serviceable, making them the lowest priority when it came to consideration for either food or transportation. As they had done for long weeks, they would have to look only toward their own initiative and energy to succeed. After they ate their skimpy meal and rested a bit, Stamper and his little unarmed army proceed another six miles before "taking up for the night."[128]

"Some of us had been fortunate enough to get some cornbread and bacon," Stamper stated, source and means not specified, "on which we made a good supper." Afterwards, he went to the home of a doctor in the area and bought two dollars worth of onions and a dollar's worth of tomatoes. Upon his return to the boys, "Lieut. Rep Jones took half of my onions and I kept the remainder for the next day." Stamper and his brother Joe "fell in on my tomatoes" and had quite a feast. "We then went to bed and snoozed sweetly." The next morning, 20 July, Stamper reported, "we struck out pretty brisk," being motivated strongly by the fact that they had to make twenty miles on the march to reach Enterprise by the end of the next day. He indicated that the day

---

[125] Ibid.
[126] Ibid.
[127] Ibid., 74–75.
[128] Ibid., 75.

was "pretty warm," so frequent rests when shade trees were near or along the line of march were always in order. Even with that, they made good time—"about twelve miles against twelve o'clock"—before they halted for dinner and a rest until the relative cool of the day arrived. While lounging around alongside the road, Stamper indicated a sizeable number of "cattle beef" belonging to Johnston's Army were driven by them, headed in the same direction as the parolees. "Those in charge of the cattle told us that Johnston was a few miles south of Brandon," he noted, "and would be falling back toward Meridian." They were obviously thankful that Johnston's so-called "Army of the Relief" would stay north of them. Stamper's little army "rolled out again," as the cool of the evening loomed, and made six miles toward Garlandsville before stopping two miles short. "We remained there all night," he noted, "eighteen miles from Enterprise."[129]

To add to the motivation for the troops, Pemberton on 20 July was authorized by Richmond to grant furloughs of between fifteen to thirty days to the Vicksburg parolees. Reynolds's and Vaughn's men were to receive the maximum allowed because of the great distance they had to travel to get home. After their furloughs were over, Reynolds's men would be ordered to report to the Army of Tennessee near Chattanooga, and Vaughn's men were to report to the parole camp at Jonesborough, Tennessee. Matters transpiring after the Battle of Missionary Ridge on 25 November 1863, however, necessitated that the few men of Reynolds's brigade reporting were forced to make their way instead to Decatur, Georgia, where a parole camp had been established.

The Race for Enterprise. Pressing onward early the next morning of 21 July, Stamper noted that they marched twelve miles toward Enterprise and stopped at noon to eat and rest. Then, with a new urgency in their step, the boys continued on until "rolling into Enterprise at sundown." Once there, they ran into their fellow East Tennessee comrades from John Vaughn's Brigade already "on cars bound for Mobile": the first leg home. Tired and relieved, Stamper wrote that at sundown, a heavy shower commenced that "sprinkled the boys very snugly."[130]

Meanwhile, William Clack of the 43rd Tennessee lifted the postponement of his diary on 21 July, when he noted that he had also arrived today at Enterprise, "the place so long looked for." He may have been traveling with the same group as Stamper. Clack was told that their train would be arriving in the morning at 7 a.m. to take them toward Mobile and out of Mississippi for the

---

[129] Ibid.
[130] Ibid.

last time. "My health is improving," Clack reported, and though it was now pouring rain, "we are under shelter."[131] Their train was not ready at 7 a.m. on the 22 July as promised. Indeed, Vaughn's boys did not get out themselves until after 8 a.m., according to Stamper. Most of the brigade had now made it to Enterprise, he noted, "except for some sick that had to take their time on the march." The East Tennesseans were ordered, finally, aboard the train at 10 p.m., which was to carry them southeast to Mobile. "We got on the train," Stamper wrote, "but we did not leave Enterprise that night."[132]

Stamper of the 43rd Tennessee continued to describe the long trip home. Private George Wilson of Company F was only briefly in the hospital at Enterprise before he died of some undisclosed cause. Then, at 8 a.m., 23 July, with the boys aboard, the train lurched out of the Enterprise station headed south for Mobile, Alabama, via Selma. "Every station was bountifully supplied with fruit and watermelon," he indicated, "all got as many as they wanted." He declared that some of the boys "begged," some "bought," and some "stole," making it "a high day for the Vicksburg prisoners." After starving for so long, Stamper stated that it was "quite a luxury to get apples, peaches, watermelons" and the like.[133]

That night around eight o'clock, the train arrived at the western outskirts of Mobile. The men were led to a large railroad shed where they spread out and slept. The following morning Reynolds's' men were each given two-day's rations of crackers and meat, which was to last them until they got to their homes. At Mobile before they left, Stamper met up with an old friend by the name of Busch, who was serving in the artillery coastal defenses in the forts between Mobile and the Gulf. They had a long talk, and Busch told Stamper that he would see him the next morning before they left, but he did not make it back.[134]

"We left Enterprise yesterday morning at 8 o'clock," Clack of the 43rd Tennessee noted, "and arrived in Mobile at 8 o'clock at night." At 7 a.m. on 24 July, the boys were on "boats" to pass up "the Tom Bigbee."[135] The last time the 43rd Tennessee was on this waterway, it was crossing the bay for the trains to Vicksburg just after Christmas 1862. What an eternity ago that must have seemed as they stared out on the bay, lost in their thoughts.

---

[131] Clack, "Personal Diary," 8.
[132] Stamper, "Travels of the 43rd Tennessee," 75–76.
[133] Ibid., 76.
[134] Ibid.
[135] Clack, "Personal Diary," 8.

Stamper of the same regiment stated that at "six o'clock, we marched down to the wharf." As the boys awaited the boats that would ferry them across the bay, he indicated, "we supplied ourselves with watermelons of the finest quality at reasonable figures." An hour later, they were sailing up the Tensaw River. By 10 a.m., they debarked at the Tensaw Landing. At 4 p.m., they left the nearby depot by train for the state capital at Montgomery, retracing their steps of seven months before. "We traveled slowly all night, and daylight saw us at Pollard, [Alabama], only 50 miles from the river," Stamper wrote in his daily journal entry. "The rest of the brigade did not get off till night." Life was getting better for the Vicksburg veterans from East Tennessee. Stamper indicated that after leaving Pollard, at sunup on 25 July, they "traveled over a good road and made good speed," gorging themselves on fruit and melons at every stop,[136] and visiting with the people coming out to see these now celebrated survivors of the terrible siege of Vicksburg.

"A little before sundown, we arrived at Montgomery and marched through town to the cars on the Atlanta road by way of West Point, Georgia," Stamper noted. There were enough cars there for the whole regiment, and they chambered themselves aboard, believing that the train would soon be pulling out. It did not leave, however, until the next morning at around 7:30, Stamper recorded. When the boys found out that they would not be leaving immediately, they sauntered downtown hoping to do a little trading. With their hats cocked on the sides of their heads, a little money in their pockets, and a bit of a swagger in their step, the heroes of Vicksburg were out to pick up a few bargains before heading on home aboard the train. "But when we got there and saw the high prices," Stamper wrote, "we saw our trading would be slim." Undeterred, some of the fellows bought themselves new hats at $25 a piece, and looked pretty sporting in contrast to their ragged clothes and uniforms. Afterwards, they drew and ate their supper rations, and then lay down around the depot area and slept till morning.[137]

The final entry in Clack's diary read: "I arrived home today [27 July]."[138] Stamper of his regiment, always chattier, detailed the ride home. At 7 a.m., they left for Dalton, Georgia, arriving around 3 p.m., "having made good time" from West Point.[139] Entering their first mountainous country just north of Atlanta after so long an absence must have seemed like home to many.

---

[136] Stamper, "Travels of the 43rd Tennessee," 76.
[137] Ibid., 76–77.
[138] Clack, "Personal Diary," 8.
[139] Stamper, "Travels of the 43rd Tennessee," 77.

Homecomings. At Dalton, as fortune would have it, there was only one train and the 43rd Tennessee was welcomed aboard for the ride back toward Knoxville that night. By 4 p.m., the train pulled out of Dalton and began its last leg of the journey on the East Tennessee & Georgia Railroad. On the state line at Red Clay, Stamper wrote, "a portion of Company K got off the cars, and met their wives, friends, brothers, sisters, fathers and mothers." As the rest of the East Tennesseans watched, the yearning and anticipation in their hearts for pending reunions must have been almost physically painful. "It was a pleasing sight to witness the smiles on the faces of those who had been separated in such perilous times," Stamper reported.[140]

The train then shunted on forward, and as it pulled along, the stops became more frequent, with a few or many of the Vicksburg heroes stepping off at every one. Stamper's stop was close to Dalton since he, like Swan, was from Cleveland. He and a considerable number of others got off the old "iron horse" to receive the welcome of friends and friends. Stamper's own father had much to be overjoyed about because he welcomed the return of all three of his sons safe and sound from their life-changing experience at the siege of Vicksburg.[141]

"This was a time of glad hearts," Stamper noted. "The regiment was losing a great many soldiers who approached their homes to the embrace of anxious hearts." He stated that he, his father, his brother Joe, and his brother Will started for home five miles into the interior of Bradley County, where they soon found welcomed and fond embraces in their family, "which came flying to meet us, with tears and a multitude of questions." Stamper concluded, "We found all well, with a great deal to talk about, so we made bedtime come rather late."[142]

Robert Bachman of the 60th Tennessee indicated that his journey back to Kingsport in Sullivan County on the upper end of East Tennessee concluded somewhat differently. "Together with some of my company," he reported, "I started for East Tennessee. I made a considerable portion of the trip on foot, as some of the railroads were out of commission." After many days, and "varied experiences," Bachman noted, "I reached my old home, dirty, ragged, hungry, yet happy in the assurance of rest, food and shelter for days to come." His homecoming was not as satisfying as Stamper's was since "no one was there to greet me save the negroes and tenants," though they were all glad to see him and gave him a cordial welcome.[143] His prominent Sullivan County family had

---

[140] Ibid.

[141] Ibid., 77–78.

[142] Ibid., 78.

[143] Bachman, "Reminiscences of Childhood," 25–26.

apparently had sought refuge in some other quarter of the Confederacy in anticipation of hard times to come.

Stamper of the 43rd Tennessee, now home on furlough after his long ordeal, stated that remained home from 28 July until 25 August 1863, "enjoying good health and friends." After that time, he reported as ordered to Athens, Tennessee, "for further instructions" from his brigade regarding movement to parole camps. "We received two months' pay here," he wrote, "and the next day returned home to meet again Wednesday, the 2nd of September, for further orders."[144]

Though few of these participants would have believed it, the war would last for another twenty long months after September 1863. Many of the Vicksburg parolees who made it home, as Clark and Swan feared, would never return to the army after its exchange that month. They had had their patriotism sliced right down to the bone at Vicksburg. Many of their comrades, particularly in Vaughn's Brigade captured at the Big Black, would serve out on average eighteen of the war's remaining months in prison hell-holes, quartered in ragged tents often in cold as extreme as the heat they had endured at Vicksburg. A considerable percentage would die of disease and exposure, and even if they survived to be exchanged, it typically occurred only two months before Lee's surrender at Appomattox. They had long forgotten how to be soldiers, and they no longer had the desire to relearn. Others, like Isaac Stamper, Reuben Clark, Calvin Smith, and the Beelers would return and serve until the end.

The Vicksburg Veterans from East Tennessee. The great surprise for the vanquished East Tennessee Confederates from Vicksburg was what they found at stops along the railroad home after leaving Mississippi. Their spirits picked up the further away they got from the city, though they had no idea how they would be received by citizens elsewhere. They had, after all, failed, through no fault of their own, to hold Vicksburg. What they found, however—particularly in Alabama—were citizens who rushed out to provide them with food and fruit, encouraged them along their way, and otherwise extended their appreciation for what these East Tennesseans had suffered for their country during the long siege.

These citizens starved for war news read the papers of their day, which had for months been full of the news of Vicksburg and its ordeals. If half of what they had read about the demanding duty there was true, then these transients and their compatriots were heroes indeed and worthy of awe and admiration.

---

[144] Stamper, "Travels of the 43rd Tennessee," 78.

Old men, always flushed with patriotism, and mothers with little children, wanted to see "the boys" all along their route home. It was as though they had the foreshadowing of a day ahead when all the Confederate soldiers who survived would return home in the end "played out." The mothers and wives who were after the war to be the defenders of the cause and its history, knew that, like those writing letters home and keeping diaries during the Vicksburg campaign, it was a little something they could do to snatch and retain a small bit of their epic for themselves: despite how horrible the recent experiences in Mississippi burned in the hearts of the Vicksburg parolees themselves.

Perhaps one day long after when grown old, the children who witnessed this brief stop-over would tell their own grandchildren of the day they had been too young to appreciate that hot summer afternoon in the middle of July 1863 when the war was lost and the survivors of Vicksburg slowed at their whistle stop long enough to accept melons, water, and scramble to relieve themselves discretely out-of-sight behind the trees just beyond the right of way. They would recall how they had seen all those sallow-faced and gaunt East Tennessee Confederate soldiers in their greasy, tattered uniforms, soldiers who were dirty, smelly, and played out.

Unloved in the days ahead by so many of their own who were disloyal or had become disillusioned, these East Tennessee boys must have relished the adoration of the strangers in those times long ago, at an instant when their train paused for a moment at the depots along the line, allowing those soldiers so inclined to pinch a baby's fat cheek or pat some little tow-head before heading on home.

Appendix A

The Vicksburg Garrison (18 May–4 July 1863)

Stevenson's Division (Maj. Gen. Carter L. Stevenson)

First Brigade (Brig. Gen. Seth M. Barton)

40th Georgia (Lt. Col. R. M. Young)

41st Georgia (Col. W. E. Curtis)

42nd Georgia (Col. R. J. Henderson)

43rd Georgia (Capt. M. M. Grantham)

52nd Georgia (Maj. J. J. Moore)

Henderson's (MS) Battery

Pointe Coupee (LA) Artillery (3 guns section) (Co. A) (Lt. J. Hoist)

Pointe Coupee (LA) Artillery (Co. C) (Capt. A. Chruff)

Second Brigade (Brig. Gen. Alfred Cumming)

34th Georgia (Col. J. W. Johnson)

36th Georgia (Maj. E. C. Broyles)

39th Georgia (Lt. Col. J. F. B. Jackson)

56th Georgia (Lt. Col. J. T. Slaughter)

57th Georgia (William Barkuloo/Col. M. D. V. Corpo)

Cherokee (GA) Artillery (3 guns Capt.)

Third Brigade (Brig. Gen. Stephen D. Lee)

20th Alabama (Col. I. W. Garrott/Lt. Col. E. W. Pettus)

23rd Alabama (Col. F. K. Beck)

30th Alabama (Capt. J. C. Francis)

31st Alabama (Lt. Col. T. M. Arrington)

46th Alabama (Capt. G. E. Brewer)

Waddell's (AL) Battery (6 guns) Capt. J. F. Waddell

Fourth Brigade (Col. Alexander W. Reynolds)

3rd Tennessee (Col. Newton J. Lillard)

31st Tennessee (Col. William M. Bradford)

43rd Tennessee (Col. James W. Gillespie)

59th Tennessee (Col. James B. Cooke/Col. William L. Eakin)

3rd Maryland Battery (7 guns) (Capt. F. O. Claiborne)

Waul's Texas Legion (Col. T. N. Waul)

1st Infantry Battalion (Maj. O. S. Bolling)

2nd Infantry Battalion (Lt. Col. J. Wrigley)

Cavalry Battalion (Lt. T. J. Cleveland)

Zouave Battalion (Capt. J. B. Fleitas)

The Artillery Company (Capt. J. Q. Wall)

Fortney's Division (Maj. Gen. John H. Forney)

Hebert's Brigade (Brig. Gen. Louis Hebert)

3rd Louisiana (Maj. D. Pierson)

21st Louisiana (Lt. Col. J. T. Plattsmier)

36th Mississippi (Col. W. W. Witherspoon)

37th Mississippi (Col. O. S. Holland)

38th Mississippi (Capt. D. B Seal)

43rd Mississippi (Col. R. Harrison)

7th Alabama Battalion (Capt. A. M. Dozier)

2nd Alabama Artillery Battalion (Co. C) (Capt. T. K. Emanuel)

Appeal (AR) Battery (8 guns) (Capt. W. N. Hogg/Lt. Rn. N. Cotton)

Moore's Brigade (Brig. Gen. John C. Moore)

37th Alabama (Col. J. F. Dowdell)

40th Alabama (Col. J. H. Higley)

42nd Alabama (Col. J. W. Portis)

1st Mississippi Light Artillery (Col. W. T. Withers)

35th Mississippi (Lt. Col. C. R. Jordan)

40th Mississippi (Col. W. B. Colbert)

2nd Texas (Col. A. Smith)

Sengtak's (AL) Battery (Capt. H. H. Sengstak)

Pointe Coupee (LA) Artillery (Co. B) (Capt. W. A. Davidson)

Smith's Division (Maj. Gen. Martin Luther Smith)

Baldwin's Brigade (Brig. Gen. William Baldwin)

17th Louisiana (Col. R. Richardson)

31st Louisiana (Lt. Col. S. H. Griffen/ Lt. Col. J. W. Draughon)

4th Mississippi (Capt. T. P. Nelson)

47th Mississippi (Col. C. W. Sears)

Tobin's (TN) Battery (Capt. Thomas F. Tobin)

Vaughn's Brigade (Brig. Gen. John C. Vaughn)

60th (79th) Tennessee (Col. John Crawford/Capt. J. W. Bachman)

61st (81st) Tennessee (Col. Fountain E. Pitts/Lt. Col. James G. Rose)

62nd (80th) Tennessee (Col. John A. Rowan)

Mississippi State Troops (Brig. Gen. John V. Harris)

5th Regiment (Col. H. C. Robinson)

3rd Battalion (Lt. Col. T. A. Burgin)

Detachment, Loring's Division

Shoup's Brigade (Brig. Gen. Francis A. Shoup)

26th Louisiana (Lt. Col. W. C. Crow)

27th Louisiana (Col. L. D. Marks/ Capt. J. T. Hatch)

29th Louisiana (Col. A. Thomas)

McNally's (AR) Battery (2 guns) (Capt. E. McNally)

14th Mississippi Light Artillery Battalion (Maj. M. S. Ward)

Mississippi Partisan Rangers (Capt. J. S. Smyth)

Signal Corps (Capt. M. T. Davidson)

Bowen's Division (Maj. Gen. John S. Bowen)

First (MO) Brigade (Brig. Gen. Francis Cockrell)

1st Missouri (Col. A. C. Riley)

2nd Missouri (Lt. Col. P. Seteny/Maj. T. M. Carter)

3rd Missouri (Maj. J. K. McDowell)

5th Missouri (Col. J. McCown)

6th Missouri (Col. E. Erwin/Maj. S. Cooper)

Guibor's (MO) Battery (4 guns) (Lt. C. Heffernan)

Landis's (MO) Battery (4 guns) (Lt. J. M. Langan)

Wade's (MO) Battery (4 guns) (Lt. R. C. Walsh)

Second Brigade (Col. T. P. Dockery)

15th Arkansas (Capt. C. Davis)

19th Arkansas (Capt. J. K. Norwood)

20th Arkansas (Col. D. W. Jones)

21st Arkansas (Capt. A. Tyler)

1st Arkansas Cavalry Battalion (dismounted) (Capt. J. J. Clark)

20th Arkansas Battalion (sharpshooters) (Lt. J. S. Bell)

1st Missouri Cavalry (dismounted) (Maj. W. S. Parker)

3rd Missouri Cavalry (dismounted) (Capt. F. Lotspeich)

3rd Missouri Battery (1 gun) (Capt. W. E. Dawson)

Lowe's (MO) Battery (4 guns) (Lt. T. B. Catron)

River Batteries

1st Louisiana Artillery (26 guns) (Lt. Col. D. Belzhoover)

8th Louisiana Heavy Artillery Battalion (3 guns) Maj. F. N. Odgen)

22nd Louisiana

1st Tennessee Heavy Artillery Regiment (Col. Andrew Jackson, Jr.)

Caruther's (TN) Battery (Capt. J. B. Caruthers)

Johnston's (TN) Battery (Capt. T. N. Johnston)

Lynch's (TN) Battery (Capt. John P. Lynch)

Valden's (MS) Battery (11 guns) (Capt. S. C. Bains)

Miscellaneous

54th Alabama (detachment) (Lt. J. P. Abney)

1st Tennessee Cavalry (Co. C) (Capt. R. S. Vandyke)

Vicksburg City Guards (Capt. E. B. Martin)

Signal Corps (Capt. C. A. King)

Botetourt Virginia Artillery (Lt. J. P. Wright)

APPENDIX B

IDENTIFIED EAST TENNESSEE CONFEDERATE SOLDIERS WHO DIED IN THE VICINITY OF VICKSBURG DURING THE CAMPAIGN

Adams, William J., Pvt.; Company K, 43rd Tennessee; mortally wounded by a spent ball, 7 June; died 14 June; place of burial unknown; enlisted at Hiwassee Mines (now Ducktown), Polk County.

Addison, Jessie, Pvt.; Company A, 43rd Tennessee; wounded in the leg, 20 May; died 29 May; buried at Soldier's Rest; enlisted at Hiwassee Mines (now Ducktown), Polk County.

Addison, Thomas, Pvt.; Company A, 43rd Tennessee; died 22 March at Hospital #3; buried at Soldier's Rest; enlisted at Hiwassee Mines (now Ducktown), Polk County.

Aiken, Thomas, Pvt.; Company K, 43rd Tennessee; died 11 July; buried at Soldier's Rest; enlisted at Ooltewah, Hamilton County.

Allen, Alexander, Pvt.; Company H, 80th (62nd) Tennessee; died 3 February; place of burial unknown; enlisted at Madisonville, Monroe County.

Allen, Archibald M., Sgt.; Company G, 61st Tennessee; died 20 June; buried at Soldier's Rest; enlisted at Morristown (now Hamblen) County.

Almarand, George, Pvt.; Company E, 61st Tennessee; died 8 April; buried at Soldier's Rest; enlisted at Blountville, Sullivan County.

Armstrong, Alexander, Pvt.; Company E, 62nd Tennessee; died 28 [27] February at Hospital #2; buried at Soldier's Rest; enlisted either in Bradley or Polk County.

Austin, David, Pvt.; Company C, 43rd Tennessee; died 28 February; buried at Soldier's Rest; enlisted at Pikeville, Bledsoe County.

Bacon, Montgomery, Pvt.; Company E, 60th Tennessee; died either 9 or 10 March at Hospital #2; buried at Soldier's Rest; enlisted at Fordtown, Sullivan County.

Bailey, Samuel, Pvt.; Company G, 31st Tennessee; died 12 June; place of burial unknown; enlisted at Rogersville Junction (now Bulls Gap), Hawkins County.

Baker, George, Pvt.; Company E, 62nd Tennessee; died of small pox either 19 or 20 March at the Pest House; buried at Soldier's Rest; enlisted either in Bradley or Polk County.

Ball, Spencer A. Pvt.; Company C, 60th Tennessee; died either 19 or 20 March at Hospital #3; buried at Soldier's Rest; enlisted at Jonesborough, Washington County.

Ballard, J. Henry [also T. H.], Pvt.; Company H, 43rd Tennessee; died 17 June; buried at Soldier's Rest; enlisted at Riceville, McMinn County.

Ballard, J. Monroe, Pvt.; Company F, 43rd Tennessee; died 26 June; buried at Soldier's Rest; enlisted at Loudon (now Loudon) County.

Barham, James, Pvt.; Company A, 61st Tennessee; died 5 July; place of burial unknown; enlisted at Rheatown, Greene County.

Barnett, John N., Pvt.; Company I, 43rd Tennessee; died 29 June of a head wound received in a fight in camp, 8 May; buried at Soldier's Rest; enlisted at Charleston, Bradley County.

Bayless, J. S., Pvt.; Company D, 61st Tennessee; died 24 July; place of burial unknown; enlisted at Henderson Mills, Greene County.

Beaver, Andrews, Pvt.; Company B, 80th (62nd) Tennessee; died 21 February; place of burial unknown; enlisted at Benton, Polk County.

Bell, John, Pvt.; Company E, 43rd Tennessee; date of death unknown; buried at Soldier's Rest; enlisted at Rogersville, Hawkins County.

Bett, John, Pvt.; Company H, 62nd Tennessee; died 27 May; buried at Soldier's Rest; enlisted at Madisonville, Monroe County.

Bible, Jacob [tombstone reads J. Bibb], Sgt.; Company I, 61st Tennessee; died 31 March; body shipped home; enlisted at Warrensburg, Greene County.

Bishop, J. W. [or M.], Pvt.; Company G, 3rd Tennessee; died 25 June; buried at Soldier's Rest; enlisted at Athens, McMinn County.

Black, Joseph, Pvt.; Company A, 62nd Tennessee; died 7 April; place of burial unknown; enlisted at Cleveland, Bradley County.

Black, Martin, Pvt.; Company I, 60th Tennessee; died 2 March at Hospital #2; buried at Soldier's Rest; enlisted at Newport, Cocke County.

Boles, William, Pvt.; Company G, 43rd Tennessee; mortally wounded in the leg at the Georgia Salient, 21 June; died either 28 or 30 June; buried at Soldier's Rest; enlisted at Bulls Gap, Hawkins County.

Booher, John, Pvt.; Company H, 79th (60th) Tennessee; died 18 March; place of burial unknown; enlisted at Morristown (now Hamblen) County.

Booker, William, Pvt.; Company E, [has two markers—one says that he was a member of Company B], 61st Tennessee; died 12 February at the City Hospital; buried at Soldier's Rest; enlisted at Blountville, Sullivan County.

Bowers, G., Pvt.; Company I, 61st Tennessee; died 26 April; body shipped home; enlisted at Warrensburg, Greene County.

Bowman, Alfred, Pvt.; Company F, 79th (60th) Tennessee; died of small pox 29 March; place of burial unknown; enlisted at Jonesborough, Washington County.

Bowman, Archibald, Pvt.; Company G, 60th Tennessee; died 2 July; place of burial unknown; enlisted at Blountville, Sullivan County.

Bowman, D. K., Pvt.; Company D, 60th Tennessee; died 9 May; place of burial unknown; enlisted at Boone's Creek, Washington County.

Boyd, Joseph C., Maj.; Field &Staff, Company K, 3rd Tennessee; died 12 June of sickness; buried at Soldier's Rest; enlisted at Madisonville, Monroe County.

Boyles, Westley W., Pvt.; Company I, 59th Tennessee; died 24 February; buried at Soldier's Rest; enlisted at Morristown (now Hamblen) County.

Branch, L. F., Pvt.; Company D, 60th Tennessee; died 1 June; place of burial unknown; enlisted at Boone's Creek, Washington County.

Brank, John J., Pvt.; Company A, 43rd Tennessee; died 16 June of sickness; buried at Soldier's Rest; enlisted at Hiwassee Mines (now Ducktown), Polk County.

Brooker, G. W., Pvt.; Company E, 82nd (?) Tennessee; died 1 January at the City Hospital; buried at Soldier's Rest.

Brougher, James, Pvt.; Company G, 79th (60th) Tennessee; died 20 March at Hospital #3; buried at Soldier's Rest; enlisted at Blountville, Sullivan County.

Brown, Elijah, Pvt.; Company E, 60th Tennessee; died 29 April; place of burial unknown; enlisted at Fordtown, Sullivan County.

Brown, Felix W., Pvt.; Company C, 81st Tennessee; died 26 January at Hatch's; buried at Soldier's Rest; enlisted at Greeneville, Greene County.

Browne, John B., Pvt.; Company B, 62nd Tennessee; mortally wounded 17 May at the Battle of the Big Black River; place of burial unknown; enlisted at Rogersville, Hawkins County.

Buckner, Jesse F., Pvt.; Company H, 59th Tennessee; died 12 May; place of burial unknown; enlisted at Athens, McMinn County.

Bugart, Joseph, Pvt.; Company F, 62nd Tennessee; died 26 June; buried at Soldier's Rest; enlisted at Loudon (now Loudon) County.

Burgess, Coleman, Pvt.; Company I, 80th (62nd) Tennessee; died 6 January; buried at Soldier's Rest; enlisted at Newport, Cocke County.

Burgess, James W., Pvt.; Lynch's Battery; died 30 March at the hospital in Jackson; place of burial and enlistment unknown.

Burns, Arthur, Pvt.; Company B, [a record also has him with Company H, 59th Tennessee out of Athens, McMinn County] 43rd Tennessee; died 2 July; buried at Soldier's Rest; enlisted with Company B out of Sulphur Springs, Rhea County.

Burwell, R. A., Pvt.; company unknown, 79th Tennessee; died of small pox 7 March at the Pest House; buried at Soldier's Rest; place of enlistment unknown.

Bush, S., Pvt.; Company I, 31st Tennessee; died 19 December 1862 at the City Hospital; buried at Soldier's Rest; enlisted at Talbott Station, Jefferson County.

Byers, William R., Pvt.; Company F, 80th (62nd) Tennessee; died 13 January at the City Hospital; buried at Soldier's Rest; enlisted at Roane County.

Cain, William, Pvt.; Company D, 79th (60th) Tennessee; died 25 February at the City Hospital; place of burial unknown; enlisted at Boone's Creek, Washington County.

Campbell, A. A., Pvt.; Company A, 61st Tennessee; died 26 or 28 June; buried at Soldier's Rest; enlisted at Rheatown, Greene County.

Caneghran, Isaac, Pvt.; Company G, 62nd Tennessee; died 2 July; place of burial unknown; enlisted in Monroe County.

Carden, James L., Pvt.; Company C, 59th Tennessee; died 13 January; place of burial unknown; enlisted at Elizabethton, Carter County.

Carson, T. M., Pvt.; Company K, 59th Tennessee [also the 60th Tennessee]; died 3 July; place of burial unknown; enlisted at Athens, McMinn County.

Casteel, Benjamin L., Pvt.; Company H, 43rd Tennessee; died 15 July; buried at Soldier's Rest; enlisted at Riceville, McMinn County.

Cawood, Andrew J., Capt.; Company B, 43rd Tennessee; mortally wounded 22 June at the Georgia Salient; died 5 August; place of burial unknown; enlisted at Sulphur Springs, Rhea County.

Chase, R. F., Pvt.; Company E, 60th Tennessee; died 30 April at Hospital #2; buried at Soldier's Rest; enlisted at Fordtown, Sullivan County.

Chesnutt, W. W., Pvt.; Company D, 31st Tennessee; died 16 May; place of burial unknown; enlisted at Dodson's Creek, Hawkins County.

Christian, Isaac. L., Pvt.; Company G, 31st Tennessee; killed 21 June by a sharpshooter; buried at Soldier's Rest; enlisted at Bulls Gap, Hawkins County.

Clark, David, Pvt.; Company I, 79th (60th) Tennessee; died 12 May; buried at Soldier's Rest; enlisted at Newport, Cocke County.

Clark, James, Pvt.; Company H, 43rd Tennessee; died 28 June; place of burial unknown; enlisted at Riceville, McMinn County.

Clark, William P., Pvt.; Company I, 59th Tennessee; died 8 April; place of burial unknown; enlisted at Morristown (now Hamblen) County.

Clepper [also Klepper], William [also Wilson], Lt.; Company E, 43rd Tennessee; mortally wounded and died 28 June; buried at Soldier's Rest; enlisted at Rogersville, Hawkins County.

Click, David, Pvt.; Company I, 79th (60th) Tennessee; died 18 February; place of burial unknown; enlisted at Newport, Cocke County.

Click, Isaac, Pvt.; Company I, 79th (60th) Tennessee; died 7 February at the City Hospital; buried at Soldier's Rest; enlisted at Newport, Cocke County.

Cline, D. V. L., Pvt.; Company E, 3rd Tennessee; died 25 May; place of burial unknown; enlisted at Monroe County.

Coats, Callancy [marker reads Calvin], Pvt.; Company E, 31st Tennessee; died 1 June; place of burial unknown; enlisted at Strawberry Plains, Jefferson County.

Coats, Calvin, Pvt.; Company E, 31st Tennessee; died 21 May at City Hospital; buried at Soldier's Rest; enlisted at Strawberry Plains, Jefferson County.

Cody, John H., Lt.; Company H, 3rd Tennessee; killed in action, 3 June; buried at Soldier's Rest; enlisted at Madisonville, Monroe County.

Coffey, John, Pvt.; Company I, 31st Tennessee; died 6 March; place of burial unknown; enlisted at Talbott Station, Jefferson County.

Colbaugh, Nathan, Pvt.; Company D, 43rd Tennessee; died 23 May; buried at Soldier's Rest; enlisted at Decatur, Meigs County.

Cole, J. W., Pvt.; Company I, 43rd Tennessee; died on an unknown date in July; place of burial unknown; enlisted at Charleston, Bradley County.

Collins, Bailey, Pvt.; Company D, 60th Tennessee; died 13 May; place of burial unknown; enlisted at Boone's Creek, Washington County.

Combs, Moses, Pvt.; Company E, 79th (60th) Tennessee; died 14 March; body shipped home; enlisted at Fordtown, Sullivan County.

Conner, John M., Pvt.; Company F, 31st Tennessee; died 28 January; place of burial unknown; enlisted at Mouse Creek (now Niota], McMinn County.

Coyle, William, Pvt.; Company A, 62nd Tennessee; date of death unknown; place of burial unknown; enlisted at Cleveland, Bradley County.

Crookshanks [also Cruikshanks], James W., Lt.; Company G, 43rd Tennessee; killed in action, 21 June; buried at Soldier's Rest; enlisted at Mossy Creek, Jefferson County.

Crump, William, Pvt.; Company E, 61st Tennessee; died 20 May of wounds suffered 17 May at the Battle of the Big Black River; place of burial unknown; enlisted at Blountville, Sullivan County.

Cruse, George W., Pvt.; Company K, 43rd Tennessee; died either 24 or 25 June; buried at Soldier's Rest; enlisted at Ooltewah, Hamilton County.

Crye, Jonathan, Pvt.; Company F, 62nd Tennessee; died 9 April; place of burial unknown; enlisted at Lenoir's Station (now Loudon) County.

Curley, Calvin A., Capt.; Company H, 80th (62nd) Tennessee; killed in action 28 December 1862 at the Battle of Chickasaw Bluffs; place of burial unknown; enlisted at Madisonville, Monroe County.

Daniel, J. W., Pvt.; Company G, 61st Tennessee; died on unknown date in August, after the surrender; place of burial unknown; enlisted at Morristown (now Hamblen) County.

Davis, J., Capt.; company unknown, 79th (60th) Tennessee; mortally wounded at the Battle of Chickasaw Bluffs; died 29 December 1862 at the City Hospital; buried at Soldier's Rest; place of enlistment unknown.

Davis, J. R., Pvt.; Company C, 59th Tennessee; date of death unknown; place of burial unknown; enlisted at Elizabethton, Carter County.

Davis, John, Pvt.; Company H, 43rd Tennessee; date of death unknown; buried at Soldier's Rest; enlisted at Riceville, McMinn County.

Davis, Lewis, Pvt.; Company G, 61st Tennessee; date of death unknown; place of burial unknown; enlisted at Morristown (now Hamblen) County.

Davis, R. B., Sgt.; Company D, 3rd Tennessee; died 4 July; buried at Soldier's Rest; enlisted at Benton, Polk County.

Davis, Robert P., Pvt.; Company I, 59th Tennessee; date of death unknown; place of burial unknown; enlisted at Morristown, now Hamblen County.

Day, Samuel, Pvt.; Company G, 43rd Tennessee; died 23 January at Cox's; buried at Soldier's Rest; enlisted at Mossy Creek, Jefferson County.

Dean, James M., Pvt.; Company C, 31st Tennessee; date of death unknown; place of burial unknown; enlisted at Dandridge, Jefferson County.

Delph, William, Pvt.; Company E, 43rd Tennessee; date of death unknown; buried at Soldier's Rest; enlisted at Rogersville, Hawkins County.

Deniston, Amos, Pvt.; Company I, 31st Tennessee; died 27 or 28 March of small pox at the Pest House; buried at Soldier's Rest; enlisted at Talbott Station, Jefferson County.

Dennis, John, Pvt.; Company H, 43rd Tennessee; died 21 June; place of burial unknown; enlisted at Riceville, McMinn County.

Dennis, Preston, Pvt.; Company D, 43rd Tennessee; died 16 July; place of burial unknown; enlisted at Decatur, Meigs County.

Denson, A. J., Pvt.; Company A, 80th (62nd) Tennessee; died 10 or 11 March at Hospital #3; buried at Soldier's Rest; enlisted at Cleveland, Bradley County.

Denton, A. Russell, Sgt.; Company G, 43rd Tennessee; mortally wounded at the Georgia Salient, 22 June; died 26 June; buried at Soldier's Rest; enlisted at New Market, Jefferson County.

Denton, Abraham, Pvt.; Company C, 1st Tennessee Cavalry; died 11 June; place of burial unknown; enlisted at Athens, McMinn County.

Dockery, William H. Company D, 43rd Tennessee; died 21 February at the City Hospital; buried at Soldier's Rest; enlisted at Decatur, Meigs County.

Dodson, George W., Pvt.; Company B, 43rd Tennessee; died 17 April; initially buried in the Hopewell Baptist Church Cemetery, then moved to Soldier's Rest after the war; enlisted at Sulphur Springs, Rhea County.

Dooley, Aaron, Pvt.; Company H, 60th Tennessee; died 20 February; place of burial unknown; enlisted at Morristown (now Hamblen) County.

Douglas, Alexander M., Lt.; Company B, 3rd Tennessee; died 1 May, buried about three miles from the 43rd Tennessee camp in Warrenton; enlisted at Monroe County.

Douglass, R. G., Sgt.; Company G, 43rd Tennessee; died 7 May at Hospital # 3; buried at Soldier's Rest; enlisted at Mossy Creek, Jefferson County.

Doyle, R. G., Pvt.; Company G, 43rd Tennessee; date of death unknown; buried at Soldier's Rest; enlisted at Mossy Creek, Jefferson County.

Duncan, Isaac N., Pvt.; Company C, 59th Tennessee; date of death unknown; buried at Soldier's Rest; enlisted at Elizabethton, Carter County.

Dunivan, James, Pvt.; Company A, 62nd Tennessee; date of death and burial place unknown; enlisted at Cleveland, Bradley County.

Dunn, John, Pvt.; Company K, 59th Tennessee; died 23 June; place of burial unknown; enlisted at Athens, McMinn County.

Dunsmore, E. H., Pvt.; Company H, 61st Tennessee; died 7 April; place of burial unknown; enlisted at Tazewell, Claiborne County.

Eden[s], Michael, Pvt.; Company D, 60th Tennessee; died 1 July; place of burial unknown; enlisted at Boone's Creek, Washington County.

Edmonds, Garner, Pvt.; Company B, 31st Tennessee; killed in action 24 February by the *Indianola* while aboard the *Queen of the West*; place of burial unknown; enlisted at Maryville, Blount County.

Edwards, Samuel J., Pvt.; Company F, 31st Tennessee; died 3 May; place of burial unknown; enlisted at Strawberry Plains, Jefferson County.

Emmert, Henry, Pvt.; Company B, 61st Tennessee; died 4 July; buried at Soldier's Rest; enlisted at Rogersville, Hawkins County.

Epperson, Levi, Pvt.; Company D, 3rd Tennessee; died 19 January; buried at Soldier's Rest; enlisted at Benton, Polk County.

Erwin, J. R., Pvt.; Company C, 43rd Tennessee [tombstone also states that he was in Company G, 3rd Tennessee out of Athens, McMinn County]; died 6 January buried at Soldier's Rest; enlisted at Pikeville, Bledsoe County.

Everhart, John, Pvt.; Company B, 79th Tennessee; mortally wounded 29 December 1862 at the Battle of Chickasaw Bluffs; died the same day at the City Hospital; buried at Soldier's Rest; enlisted at Rogersville, Hawkins County.

Ferguson, Albert, Pvt.; Company C, 43rd Tennessee; date of death unknown; buried at Soldier's Rest; enlisted at Pikeville, Bledsoe County.

Fisher, I. H., Pvt.; Company D, 43rd Tennessee; killed 23 May by a shell in the trenches; place of burial unknown; enlisted at Decatur, Meigs County.

Fleming, John R., Q. M. Sgt.; Company F, 43rd Tennessee; died 27 June; buried at Soldier's Rest; enlisted at Roane County.

Gaddis, Benjamin F., Capt.; Company D, 3rd Tennessee; mortally wounded 27 June by a shell; buried at Soldier's Rest; enlisted at Benton, Polk County.

Gamm, James, Pvt.; Company K, 3rd Tennessee; died of small pox 11 April at the Pest House; buried in Soldier's Rest; enlisted at Madisonville, Monroe County.

Garghess, _____, Pvt.; Company __, 3rd Tennessee; mortally wounded 27 June by bombshell and died same day; buried at Soldier's Rest; place of enlistment unknown.

Gibboney, John A., Pvt.; Company H, 43rd Tennessee; died 20 July; buried at Soldier's Rest; enlisted at Riceville, McMinn County.

Givens, Alexander, Pvt.; Company A, 43rd Tennessee; died 1 May; initially buried at Hopewell Baptist Church Cemetery, then moved to Soldier's Rest after the war; enlisted at Hiwassee Mines [now Ducktown], Polk County.

Glass, Alexander H., Pvt.; Company E, 59th Tennessee; died 24 June at Hospital #1; buried at Soldier's Rest; enlisted at Madisonville, Monroe County.

Glenn, Jeremiah, Pvt.; Company E,31st Tennessee; died 2 April; place of burial unknown; enlisted at Strawberry Plains, Jefferson County.

Glover, Samuel G., Pvt.; Company C, 59th Tennessee; died 28 June; buried at Soldier's Rest; enlisted at Elizabethton, Carter County.

Good, William, Pvt.; Company K, 60th Tennessee; killed in action 18 June, possibly by artillery fire; enlisted at Leesburg-Longmire, Washington County.

Goodman, John, Pvt.; Company G, 79th Tennessee; killed 29 December 1862 at the Battle of Chickasaw Bayou; buried at Soldier's Rest; enlisted at Blountville, Sullivan County.

Goodman, Thomas J., Pvt.; Company F, 43rd Tennessee; died 21 June; buried at Soldier's Rest; enlisted at Loudon (now Loudon) County.

Goodwin, Thomas J., Pvt.; Company F, 43rd Tennessee; died 20 January; place of burial unknown; enlisted at Mossy Creek, Jefferson County.

Gowan, William D., Pvt.; Company F, 43rd Tennessee; died 17 February at the City Hospital; buried at Soldier's Rest; enlisted at Roane County.

Gray, S. A., Pvt.; Company C, 3rd Tennessee; killed 22 June in the trenches; place of burial unknown; enlisted at Benton, Polk County.

Grubb, Newton, Pvt.; Company D,80th (62nd) Tennessee; died 28 January; place of burial unknown; enlisted at Sweetwater, Monroe County.

Gully, H. J., Pvt.; Company G, 62nd Tennessee; died 28 May; buried at Soldier's Rest; enlisted at Monroe County.

Hale, John, Pvt.; Company G, 79th (60th) Tennessee; died 10 March; place of burial unknown; enlisted at Blountville, Sullivan County.

Haley, John, Pvt.; Company B, 31st Tennessee; killed 24 June on picket duty; buried at Soldier's Rest; enlisted at Maryville, Blount County.

Hall [or Wall], David K., Pvt.; Company G, 60th Tennessee; died 15 June; place of burial unknown; enlisted at Blountville, Sullivan County.

Hamilton, Alexander, Pvt.; Company F, 81st (61st) Tennessee; died 21 December 1862; place of burial unknown; enlisted at Mossy Creek, Jefferson County.

Hamilton, Thomas H., Pvt.; Company G, 3rd Tennessee; killed 27 June by shell fragments; place of burial unknown; enlisted at Athens, McMinn County.

Harlis[s], Rueben, Pvt.; Company G, 31st Tennessee; died 25 February at Hatch's; buried at Soldier's Rest; enlisted at Bulls Gap, Hawkins County.

Harmond, John, Pvt.; Company A, 80th (62nd) Tennessee; died 15 February at the City Hospital; buried at Soldier's Rest; enlisted at Cleveland, Bradley County.

Harrison, William, Pvt.; Company G, 80th Tennessee; killed in action 28 December 1862 at the Battle of Chickasaw Bayou; place of burial unknown; enlisted at Morristown, now Hamblen County.

Hayes, James, Pvt.; Company K, 60th Tennessee; died 1 April; place of burial unknown; enlisted at Leesburg-Longmire, Washington County.

Hayes, John S., Pvt.; Company H, 31st Tennessee; died 29 June; buried at Soldier's Rest; enlisted at Midway, Greene County.

Heard, _____, Pvt.; Company D, 43rd Tennessee; shot in the head and killed by a sharpshooter, 22 May; buried at Soldier's Rest; enlisted at Decatur, Meigs County.

Heart, Simon, Pvt.; Company E, 43rd Tennessee; killed by a sharpshooter, date unknown; buried at Soldier's Rest; enlisted at Rogersville, Hawkins County.

Heaton, Sidney R., Corp.; Company K, 43rd Tennessee; buried at Soldier's Rest; died on an unspecified date in July; enlisted at Ooltewah, Bradley County.

Helm, G. T., Pvt.; Company F, 81st (61st) Tennessee; died 2 January; place of burial unknown; enlisted at Mossy Creek, Jefferson County.

Helton, G. W., Pvt.; Company G, 81st (61st) Tennessee; died 24 February; place of burial unknown; enlisted at Morristown (now Hamblen) County.

Henry, J. S., Pvt.; Company C, 3rd Tennessee; died 14 May at Hospital #3; buried at Soldier's Rest; enlisted at Benton, Polk County.

Henry, Llewallyn, Pvt.; Company I, 62nd Tennessee; died 25 April of dysentery; place of burial unknown; enlisted at Newport, Cocke County.

Henry, Sandy, Pvt.; Company E, 43rd Tennessee; killed in action 21 [22] June at the Georgia Salient; buried at Soldier's Rest; enlisted at Rogersville, Hawkins County.

Hensley [also Kensley], James K., Corp.; Company C, 43rd Tennessee; died 23 February; buried at Soldier's Rest; enlisted at Pikeville, Bledsoe County.

Hibberts, J. M. L., Pvt.; Company G, 3rd Tennessee; died 20 January; place of burial unknown; enlisted at Athens, McMinn County.

Hicks, Eldridge, Pvt.; Company C, 59th Tennessee; died 20 December 1862 in Montgomery on the trip Vicksburg,; place of burial unknown; enlisted at Elizabethton, Carter County.

Hicks, Isaac, Pvt.; Company G, 31st Tennessee; died 25 or 27 February at Hospital #1; buried at Soldier's Rest; enlisted at Bulls Gap, Hawkins County.

Hill, Eli, Pvt.; Company I, 62nd Tennessee; died 11 April; place of burial unknown; enlisted at Newport, Cocke County.

Hill, [S.] R., Pvt.; Company G [?], 31st Tennessee; date of death unknown; buried at Soldier's Rest; enlisted at Bulls Gap, Hawkins County.

Hill, Robert, Sgt.; Company A, 31st Tennessee; killed 18 June by a sharpshooter; place of burial unknown; enlisted at Knoxville, Knox County.

Hill, William, Pvt.; Company B, 43rd Tennessee; died 8 July; buried at Soldier's Rest; enlisted at Sulphur Springs, Rhea County.

Hinson, [J. K.] Polk, Pvt.; company unknown, 43rd Tennessee; died 22 February at Hospital #1; buried at Soldier's Rest; place of enlistment unknown.

Hodge, [E.] C. W. [tombstone reads Hedge], Pvt.; Company E, 81st (61st) Tennessee; died 2 April at Camp Timmons; buried at Soldier's Rest; enlisted at Blountville, Sullivan County.

Holland, W. L., Pvt.; Company D, 43rd Tennessee; date of death unknown; place of burial unknown; enlisted at Decatur, Meigs County.

Holloway, R. G., Pvt.; Company B, 43rd Tennessee; died 17 April; place of burial unknown; enlisted at Sulphur (now Rhea) Springs, Rhea County.

Holly, John, Pvt.; Company B, 31st Tennessee; died 20 June; place of burial unknown; enlisted at Maryville, Blount County.

Houghton, A. J., Pvt.; Company B, 43rd Tennessee; Mortally wounded 21 June at the Georgia Salient; died 22 June; buried at Soldier's Rest. Enrolled at Sulphur (now Rhea) Springs, Rhea County.

Hugh[e]s, Andy J., Pvt.; Company G, 43rd Tennessee; mortally wounded 21 June at the Georgia Salient; died 22 June; buried at Soldier's Rest; enlisted at Mossy Creek, Jefferson County.

Humphreys, John E., Pvt.; Company A, 81st (61st) Tennessee; died 22 March at Hospital #2; buried at Soldier's Rest; enlisted at Rheatown, Greene County.

Hurley, Jeremiah, Pvt.; Company C, 61st Tennessee; died 28 June; buried at Soldier's Rest; enlisted at Greeneville, Greene County.

Ingerham [a.k.a. Ingram], Isaac, Pvt.; Company D, 62nd Tennessee; died 8 April; buried at Soldier's Rest; enlisted at Sweetwater, Monroe County.

Ivy, C. F., Pvt.; Company H, 60th Tennessee; died 4 June; buried at Soldier's Rest; enlisted at Morristown, Hamblen County.

J_____, A. W., Pvt.; company unknown, 43rd Tennessee; date of death unknown; buried at Soldier's Rest; place of enlistment unknown.

Jack, Samuel, Pvt.; Company A, 59th Tennessee; died 27 June; buried at Soldier's Rest; enlisted at Firestones, McMinn County.

Jackson, Elihu H., Pvt.; Company B, 80th (62nd) Tennessee; died 12 March of small pox at the Pest House; buried in Soldier's Rest; enlisted at Benton, Polk County.

Jarnigan, Albert M., Sgt.; Company G, 43rd Tennessee; mortally wounded 2 June at the Georgia Salient; died 23 June; buried at Soldier's Rest; enlisted at Mossy Creek, Jefferson County.

Jay, Alfred, Pvt.; Company I, 31st Tennessee; died 20 March; place of burial unknown; enlisted at Talbott Station, Jefferson County.

Jenkins, Collins, Pvt.; Company B, 81st (61st) Tennessee; died 12 February at the Vicksburg Hospital; buried at Soldier's Rest; enrolled at Rogersville, Hawkins County.

Jenkins, R. F., Pvt.; Company H, 43rd Tennessee; died 22 December 1862 at the City Hospital; buried at Soldier's Rest; enlisted at Midway, Greene County.

Johnson, _____, Pvt.; Company E, 3rd Tennessee; buried at Soldier's Rest; enlisted at Maryville, Blount County.

Johnson, James M., Pvt.; Company F, 31st Tennessee; died 2 February; place of burial unknown. Enrolled at Mouse Creek (now Niota), McMinn County.

Johnson, Joel, Pvt.; Company H, 81st (61st) Tennessee; died 17 March at Hospital #2; buried at Soldier's Rest; enrolled at Tazewell, Claiborne County.

Johnson, Murrell, Pvt.; Company E, 43rd Tennessee; date of death unknown; buried at Soldier's Rest; enlisted at Rogersville, Hawkins County.

Johnson, W. B., Surgeon; Field & Staff, 43rd Tennessee; mortally wounded in leg and side by rifle fire, 25 May; died 19 June; buried at Soldier's Rest; place of enlistment unknown.

Jollorray, Isaac, Pvt.; Company E, 81st (61st) Tennessee; died 8 March at Hospital #3; buried at Soldier's Rest; enlisted at Blountville, Sullivan County.

Jones, Andrew, Pvt.; Company B, 61st Tennessee; died 29 April at Hospital #3; buried at Soldier's Rest; enrolled at Rogersville, Hawkins County.

Jones, Francis M., Pvt.; Company D, 43rd Tennessee; died 10 July; buried at Soldier's Rest; enlisted at Decatur, Meigs County.

Keaton, _____, Pvt.; Company K, 43rd Tennessee; died 30 June; buried at Soldier's Rest; enlisted at Ooltewah, Hamilton County.

Kelly, John, Pvt.; Lynch's Battery; died 8 April at Hospital #1; buried at Soldier's Rest; place of enlistment unknown.

Kelsey, J., Lt.; Company A, 61st Tennessee; died 2 July; buried at Soldier's Rest; enlisted at Rheatown, Greene County.

Ketcherside, T. F., Pvt.; Company A, 43rd Tennessee; died 4 May; initially buried at Hopewell Baptist Church Cemetery, then moved to Soldier's Rest after the war; enlisted at Hiwassee Mines (now Ducktown), Polk County.

Kinkaid, Asa G., Pvt.; Company F, 43rd Tennessee; died 18 January; initially buried at Hopewell Baptist Church Cemetery, then moved to Soldier's Rest after the war; enrolled at Roane County.

Kittrell, John, Pvt.; Company C, 62nd Tennessee; date of death and place of burial unknown; enlisted at Monroe County.

Lampkin, Alvin, Pvt.; Company H, 3rd Tennessee; died 27 June; place of burial unknown; enrolled at Madisonville, Monroe County.

Lauderdale, J. M., Pvt.; Company H, 31st Tennessee; died 21 January; place of burial unknown; enlisted at Midway, Greene County.

Lawson, William J., Sgt.; Company E, 43rd Tennessee; died 30 May; buried at Soldier's Rest; enlisted at Rogersville, Hawkins County.

Leadbetter, John, Pvt.; Company H, 43rd Tennessee; died 23 May; buried at Soldier's Rest; enlisted at Riceville, McMinn County.

Leasbeaugh, D., Pvt.; Company G, 60th Tennessee; died 22 June; buried at Soldier's Rest; enlisted at Blountville, Sullivan County.

Light, J. M., Pvt.; Company I, 79th (60th) Tennessee; died 7 February at a Vicksburg hospital; buried at Soldier's Rest. Enrolled at Newport, Cocke County.

Lindsey, A. B., Pvt.; Company H, 80th (62nd) Tennessee; killed 28 March by a tornado; place of burial unknown; enlisted at Madisonville, Monroe County.

Lindsey, Harvey, Pvt.; Company H,80th (62nd) Tennessee; killed 28 March by a tornado; place of burial unknown; enlisted at Madisonville, Monroe County.

Livingston, A., Pvt.; Company G, 61st Tennessee; died 6 August at Vicksburg after the surrender; place of burial unknown; enlisted at Morristown (now Hamblen) County.

Loaming, M. H., Pvt.; Company A, 79th (60th) Tennessee; died 19 March at the City Hospital; buried at Soldier's Rest; enlisted at Jonesborough, Washington County.

Lockmiller, Harrison, Pvt.; Company D, 43rd Tennessee; died 4 February; buried at Soldier's Rest; enrolled at Decatur, Meigs County.

Long, James F., Sgt.; Company F, 79th (60th) Tennessee; died 3 June at the City Hospital; buried at Soldier's Rest; enlisted at Jonesborough, Washington County.

Long, Lawson H., Pvt.; Company H, 79th (60th) Tennessee; died 27 February; place of burial unknown; enrolled at Morristown (now Hamblen) County.

Long, Levi H., Pvt.; Company H, 79th (60th Tennessee; died 1 March at the City Hospital; body shipped home and buried in the Morelock Cemetery, Morristown; enlisted at Morristown (now Hamblen) County.

Long, Nelson A., Pvt.; Company C, 79th (60th) Tennessee; mortally wounded 17 May at the Battle of the Big Black River; died 18 May at the City Hospital; buried at Soldier's Rest; enlistedat Washington County.

Long, Robert, 3rd Lieut. Company D, 31st Tennessee; died 18 May; place of burial unknown; enrolled at Dodson's Creek, Hawkins County.

Lover, Joseph, Pvt.; Lynch's Battery; died 4 June; buried at Soldier's Rest; place of enlistment unknown.

Lowens, W. H., Pvt.; Company D, 80th (62nd) Tennessee; died 9 February; place of burial unknown; enlisted at Sweetwater, Monroe County.

Loy, George, Pvt.; Company G, 43rd Tennessee; killed in action 21 June at the Georgia Salient; buried at Soldier's Rest; enlisted at Mossy Creek, Jefferson County.

Lynville, John, Pvt.; Company G, 79th (60th) Tennessee; died 12 March; place of burial unknown; enrolled at Blountville, Sullivan County.

Lyon, Jeremiah, Pvt.; Company C, 59th Tennessee; date of death and place of burial unknown; enlisted at Elizabethton, Carter County.

Malone, J. H., Pvt.; Company B, 80th (62nd) Tennessee; died 25 February at the City Hospital; buried at Soldier's Rest; enlisted at Benton, Polk County.

Malone, Samuel, Pvt.; Company I, 81st (61st) Tennessee; died 4 March at the City Hospital; buried at Soldier's Rest; enlisted at Warrensburg, Greene County.

Malone, Thomas, Pvt.; Company H, 80th (62nd) Tennessee; killed 28 March by a tornado; place of burial unknown; enrolled at Madisonville, Monroe County.

Maloy, Valentine S., Pvt.; Company I, 79th (60th) Tennessee; died 6 February at the City Hospital; buried at Soldier's Rest; enlisted at Newport, Cocke County.

Manis, Sterling, Pvt.; Company E, 43rd Tennessee; died 11 May at Hospital #3; buried at Soldier's Rest; enlisted at Strawberry Plains, Jefferson County.

Manners, Sterling, Pvt.; Company E, 43rd Tennessee; died 11 May; place of burial unknown; enlisted at Rogersville, Hawkins County.

Martin, Isaac, Pvt.; Company K, 43rd Tennessee; died either 25 or 26 March; buried at Soldier's Rest; enrolled at Ooltewah, Hamilton County.

Martin, William, Pvt.; Company D, 80th (62nd) Tennessee; died 3 March; place of burial unknown; enrolled at Madisonville, Monroe County.

Mathes, Allen, Pvt.; Company I, 80th (62nd) Tennessee; died 13 January; place of burial unknown; enlisted at Newport, Cocke County.

Mathis, Jackson, Pvt.; Company F, 43rd Tennessee; died 29 June of cramps; place of burial unknown; enrolled at Roane County.

Mattock, J., Pvt.; company unknown, 62nd Tennessee; died 24 June; buried at Soldier's Rest; place of enlistment unknown.

Maxwell, H. L., Pvt.; Company K, 43rd Tennessee; died 1 July; place of burial unknown; enrolled at Ooltewah, Hamilton County.

Maxwell, Jardon, Pvt.; Company H, 59th Tennessee; died 21 June; place of burial unknown; enlisted at Athens, McMinn County.

McAdoo, R. G., Pvt.; Company D, 43rd Tennessee; mortally wounded 23 May by a shell; died 15 July, after the surrender; buried at Soldiers Rest; enlisted at Decatur, Meigs County.

McAllen, Thomas, Pvt.; Company F, 43rd Tennessee; died 5 July, after the surrender; buried at Soldiers Rest; enrolled at Roane County.

McCaw, John, Pvt.; Company K, 43rd Tennessee; died 13 February at the City Hospital; buried at Soldier's Rest; enlisted at Ooltewah, Hamilton County.

McCaw, William, Pvt.; Company K, 43rd Tennessee; died 11 February; buried at Soldier's Rest; enrolled at Ooltewah, Hamilton County.

McCrary, Joseph, Pvt.; Company E, 61st Tennessee; died 17 June of wounds suffered at the Battle of the Big Black River, 17 May; enlisted at Blountville, Sullivan County.

McCraw, William, Pvt.; Company K, 43rd Tennessee; died 2 July; buried at Soldier's Rest; enlisted at Ooltewah, Hamilton County.

McDermott, John A., Capt.; Company E, 59th Tennessee; killed 10 June by accidental discharge of his pistol; buried at Soldier's Rest; enlisted at Madisonville, Monroe County.

McGinty, John, Pvt.; Company D, 59th Tennessee; died 2 or 3 January at the Vicksburg Hospital; buried at Soldier's Rest; enlisted at Knoxville, Knox County.

McGuire, William H., Pvt.; Company F, 31st Tennessee; died 22 February; burial place unknown; enrolled at Mouse Creek (now Niota), McMinn County.

McKinney, J. C., Pvt.; Company C, 31st Tennessee; died 7 April; enrolled at Dandridge, Jefferson County.

McNeese, F. M., Pvt.; Company A, 61st Tennessee; died 14 July, after the surrender; enlisted at Rheatown, Greene County.

Medlin, Thomas, Pvt.; Company H, 60th Tennessee; died 6 or 8 March at the City Hospital; buried at Soldier's Rest; enlisted at Morristown (now Hamblen) County.

Melton, William, Pvt.; Company H, 43rd Tennessee; died 26 February; buried at Soldier's Rest; enlisted at Riceville, McMinn County.

Messer, Elijah, Pvt.; Company E, 31st Tennessee; date of death unknown; buried at Soldier's Rest; enrolled at Strawberry Plains, Jefferson County.

Metlock, R. B., Pvt.; Company B, 79th (60th) Tennessee; died 12 March; place of burial unknown; enlisted at Rogersville, Hawkins County.

Miller, B. F., Pvt.; Company D, 43rd Tennessee; died 5 February; place of burial unknown; enlisted at Decatur, Meigs County.

Miller, George, Pvt.; Company D, 60th Tennessee; died 4 June; place of burial unknown; enlisted at Henderson's Depot, Greene County.

Miller, Jeremiah, Pvt.; Company H, 79th (60th) Tennessee; killed 28 March in camp by a tornado; place of burial unknown; enrolled at Morristown (now Hamblen) County.

Miller, W. Thomas, 2nd Lieut. Company C, 1st Tennessee Cavalry ; killed in action 16 May at the Battle of Baker's Creek; place of burial unknown; enlisted at Athens, McMinn County.

Miller, William, Pvt.; Company E, 61st Tennessee; killed in action 17 May at the Battle of the Big Black River; place of burial unknown; enlisted at Blountville, Sullivan County.

Million, Francis N., Pvt.; Company D, 43rd Tennessee; mortally wounded 23 May by a shell in the trenches; buried at Soldier's Rest; enlisted at Decatur, Meigs County.

Mills, J. W., Pvt.; Company H, 80th (62nd) Tennessee; died 6 January; buried at Soldier's Rest; enlisted at Madisonville, Monroe County.

Milton, William, Pvt.; Company H, 43rd Tennessee; died 28 February at Hospital #2; buried at Soldier's Rest; enlisted at Midway, Greene County.

Morris, Thomas [a.k.a. Samuel Norris], Pvt.; Company I, 80th (62nd) Tennessee; died 4 February at the City Hospital; buried at Soldier's Rest; enrolled at Newport, Cocke County.

Morton, William G., Pvt.; Company G, 60th Tennessee; died 3 July; enlisted at Blountville, Sullivan County.

Mosley, Jonathan, Pvt.; Company H, 61st Tennessee; died on an unknown date in July; buried at Soldier's Rest; enlisted at Tazewell, Claiborne County.

Murray, Ira G. [also J. G.], Pvt.; Company E, 60th Tennessee; died 9 or 10 April; place of burial unknown; enrolled at Fordtown, Sullivan County.

Murry, J. G. [or J. B.], rank unknown; Company E, 79th (60th) Tennessee; died either 6 or 10 April at the City Hospital; buried at Soldier's Rest. Enrolled at Fordtown, Sullivan County.

Myers, L. W., Pvt.; Company H, 81st (61st) Tennessee; died 31 January; place of burial unknown; enlisted at Tazewell, Claiborne County.

Mynatt, Alison W., Pvt.; Company D, 59th Tennessee; died 5 March at Hospital #2; buried at Soldier's Rest; enlisted at Knoxville, Knox County.

Nelson, David M., Pvt.; Company H, 31st Tennessee; date of death unknown; buried at Soldier's Rest; enlisted at Midway, Greene County.

Newman, J. L., Pvt.; Company A, 62nd Tennessee; died on unknown date in June; place of burial unknown; enrolled at Cleveland, Bradley County.

Nichols, William, Pvt.; Company K, 61st Tennessee; died 20 April; enlisted at Zollicoffer (now Bluff City), Sullivan County.

Noblin, C. F., Corp.; Company H, 61st Tennessee; died 17 June; buried at Soldiers Rest; enrolled at Tazewell, Claiborne County.

Nunn, Isaac, Pvt.; Company H, 81st (61st) Tennessee; died 31 January; buried at Soldier's Rest; enlisted at Tazewell, Claiborne County.

O'Dell [tombstone reads Odle], Abraham, Pvt.; Company A, 79th (60th) Tennessee; died either 2 or 10 March at the City Hospital; buried at Soldier's Rest, two men in the box, with O'Dell's headstone to the west; enlisted at Jonesborough, Washington County.

Ogle, John, Pvt.; Company E, 3rd Tennessee; died 15 March at the City Hospital; buried at Soldier's Rest; enlisted at Maryville, Blount County.

Oren, Dennis, Pvt.; Company H, 43rd Tennessee; died 24 March; initially buried at Hopewell Baptist Church Cemetery, then moved to Soldier's Rest after the War; enlisted at Riceville, McMinn County.

Osteen, _____, Pvt.; Company C, 43rd Tennessee; died 27 February from measles; place of burial unknown; enlisted at Pikeville, Bledsoe County.

Owens, John A., Pvt.; Company H, 79th (60th) Tennessee; killed in camp 28 March by a tornado; place of burial unknown; enlisted at Morristown, now Hamblen County.

Padget, Daniel, Pvt.; Company I, 79th (60th) Tennessee; died 6 February at the City Hospital; buried at Soldier's Rest; enlisted at Newport, Cocke County.

Painter, Ira, Pvt.; Company D, 61st Tennessee; died 26 February at Hospital #2; buried northwest of Soldier's Rest in Cedar Hill Cemetery; enrolled at Henderson's Mills, Greene County.

Painter, James, Pvt.; Company D, 81st (61st) Tennessee; died 28 February; body was shipped home; enlisted at Rogersville, Hawkins County.

Painter, Joel, Pvt.; Company D, 61st Tennessee; killed 15 June in the trenches by artillery bombardment; enlisted at Rogersville, Hawkins County.

Painter, Thomas J., Pvt.; Company D, 81st (61st) Tennessee; died 23 January at Hatch's; buried at Soldier's Rest; enrolled at Rogersville, Hawkins County.

Pannel, G. W., Pvt.; Company E, 61st Tennessee; died 16 July, after the surrender; enlisted at Blountville, Sullivan County.

Parmley, Ira, Pvt.; Company D, 61st Tennessee; date of death unknown; buried at Soldier's Rest; enrolled at Henderson Mills, Greene County.

Patterson, N. W., Pvt.; Company I, 43rd Tennessee; died 22 February of small pox at the Pest House; buried at Soldier's Rest; enlisted at Charleston, Bradley County.

Patillo, Samuel, Pvt.; Company G, 43rd Tennessee; mortally wounded 21 June in the shoulder at the Georgia Salient; died 5 July; buried at Soldier's Rest; enrolled at Mossy Creek, Jefferson County.

Phillips, Benjamin, Pvt.; Company E, 61st Tennessee; died 20 May; buried at Soldier's Rest; enlisted at Blountville, Sullivan County.

Phillips, George, Pvt.; Company A, 79th (60th) Tennessee; died on an unknown date in March; place of burial unknown; enrolled at Jonesborough, Washington County.

Phillips, James [a.k.a. Isaac], Pvt.; Company K, 3rd Tennessee; died 25 March of small pox at the Pest House; buried at Soldier's Rest; enlisted at Madisonville, Monroe County.

Pinion, Jackson, Pvt.; Company H, 79th (60th) Tennessee; killed 28 March in camp by tornado; enrolled Morristown (now Hamblen) County.

Presley, Hyram, Pvt.; Company B, 61st Tennessee; died 24 April of small pox at the Pest House; buried at Soldier's Rest; enlisted at Rogersville, Hawkins County.

Pressley, James M., Pvt.; Company B, 61st Tennessee; died 27 April; place of burial unknown; enlisted at Rogersville, Hawkins County.

Price, Thomas H., Pvt.; Company D, 43rd Tennessee; died 4 May; buried at Soldier's Rest; enrolled at Decatur, Meigs County.

Ramsey, E[dmon], Pvt.; Company I, 79th (60th) Tennessee; died 8 March in Hospital #3; buried at Soldier's Rest; enrolled at Newport, Cocke County.

Raper, Larkin W., Pvt.; Company K, 31st Tennessee; died 17 April; place of burial unknown; enlisted at Sweetwater, Monroe County.

Ray, S. F., Pvt.; Company K, 79th (60th) Tennessee; died 2 March; place of burial unknown; enrolled at Leesburg-Longmire, Washington County.

Ray, William, Pvt.; Company K, 60th Tennessee; died 15 June; place of burial unknown; enlisted at Leesburg-Longmire, Washington County.

Rayston, E., Pvt.; Company K, 61st Tennessee; died 9 July, after the surrender; enlisted at Zollicoffer (now Bluff City), Sullivan County.

Reed, S. J., Pvt.; Company A, 31st Tennessee; died 8 June; place of burial unknown; enlisted at Knoxville, Knox County.

Remage, William, Pvt.; Company C, 62nd Tennessee; died on an unknown date in May; place of burial unknown; enlisted at Monroe County.

Rennod, J. W., Pvt.; Company I, 3rd Tennessee; died 4 July; place of burial unknown; enlisted at Decatur, Meigs County.

Rich, Jacob N., Pvt.; Company H, 79th (60th) Tennessee; killed 28 March in camp by a tornado; enrolled at Morristown (now Hamblen) County.

Rich, Thomas J., Pvt.; Company H, 79th (60th) Tennessee; killed 28 March in camp by a tornado; enrolled at Morristown, now Hamblen County.

Richeson, Andrew J., Sgt.; Company E, 59th Tennessee [also Company H, 3rd Tennessee]; buried at Soldier's Rest; killed in action on an unknown date; enrolled at Madisonville, Monroe County.

Richey, J. A., Pvt.; Company E, 59th Tennessee; died 22 May; buried at Soldier's Rest; enrolled at Madisonville, Monroe County.

Riley, W. H., Pvt.; Company F, 81st (61st) Tennessee; died 17 April at Hospital #3; buried at Soldier's Rest; enlisted at Mossy Creek, Jefferson County.

Roaden, Marion D., rank unknown; Company B, 59th Tennessee; accidentally killed 18 February on the Southern Railroad; enlisted at Madisonville, Monroe County.

Robertson, [W.] Garrot, Pvt.; Company H, 79th (60th) Tennessee; died either 6 or 14 March; buried at Soldier's Rest; enlisted at Morristown (now Hamblen) County.

Rogers, W. R., Pvt.; Company H, 3rd Tennessee; died 28 June; place of burial unknown; enlisted at Madisonville, Monroe County.

Roland, L. C., Pvt.;Lynch's Battery; died 30 April; buried at Soldier's Rest; place of enrollment unknown.

Rose, Isaiah, Pvt.; Company A, 79th (60th) Tennessee; died 26 May; buried at Soldiers' Rest; enlisted at Jonesborough, Washington County.

Routh, W. J., Pvt.; Company K, 43rd Tennessee; died either 20 May or 9 June; buried at Soldier's Rest; enrolled at Ooltewah, Hamilton County.

Rutledge, David, Pvt.; Company K, 3rd Tennessee; died 3 April of small pox in the Pest House; buried at Soldier's Rest; enrolled at Madisonville, Monroe County.

Sane, J. H., Pvt.; Company H, 31st Tennessee; died 17 April; place of burial unknown; enlisted at Midway, Greene County.

Saver, Nathan, Pvt.; Company C, 79th (60th) Tennessee; died 4 February at the City Hospital; buried at Soldier's Rest; enlisted at Washington County.

Scalf, James, Pvt.; Company C, 79th (60th) Tennessee; died 29 March; place of burial unknown; enrolled at Washington County.

Scott, Elijah, Pvt.; Company C, 81st (61st) Tennessee; died 22 March at Hospital #3; buried at Soldier's Rest; enrolled at Greeneville, Greene County.

Shamblin, John, Pvt.; Company I, 43rd Tennessee; mortally wounded 22 May during the repulse of Grant's attack on the lines; died 23 May; buried at Soldier's Rest; enlisted at Charleston, Bradley County.

Sheets, Marion, Pvt.; Company D, 62nd Tennessee; date of death unknown; buried at Soldier's Rest; enlisted at Sweetwater, Monroe County.

Shelton, J. J., Pvt.; Company B, 80th (62nd) Tennessee; died 7 January at the City Hospital; buried at Soldier's Rest; enrolled at Benton, Polk County.

Shelton, Riley, Pvt.; Company B, 62nd Tennessee; died 4 June; buried at Soldier's Rest; enrolled at Benton, Polk County.

Shields, W. Henderson, Pvt.; Company A, 31st Tennessee; killed10 June by a sharpshooter; buried at Soldier's Rest; enlisted at Knoxville, Knox County.

Shipley, Nathan, Pvt.; Company E, 61st Tennessee; killed in action 17 May at the Battle of the Big Black River; place of burial unknown; enrolled at Blountville, Sullivan County.

Shropshire, John, Pvt.; Company H, 79th (60th) Tennessee; died 8 April; body shipped home; enlisted at Morristown, now Hamblen County.

Smith, J. M., Pvt.; Company H, 31st Tennessee; killed in action 19 June either by a sharpshooter or artillery; place of burial unknown; enlisted at Midway, Greene County.

Smith, J. Marion, Pvt.; Company D, 81st (61st) Tennessee; died 3 March at Hospital #1; buried at Soldier's Rest; enlisted at Henderson Mills, Greene County.

Smith, James L., Pvt.; Company C, 59th Tennessee; killed 19 June by a sharpshooter; buried as an unknown at Soldier's Rest; enrolled at Elizabethton, Carter County.

Smith, Joseph P., Pvt.; Company K, 59th Tennessee; died on an unknown date in July; buried at Soldier's Rest; enlisted at Athens, McMinn County.

Smith, Lewis, Pvt.; Company D, 80th (62nd) Tennessee; died 27 April at the City Hospital; buried at Soldier's Rest; enlisted at Monroe County.

Smith, Robert, Pvt.; Company D, 80th (62nd) Tennessee; died 28 March at the City Hospital; mortally injured by a tornado; buried at Soldier's Rest; enlisted at Monroe County.

Smith, William J., Pvt.; Company H, 59th Tennessee; died 25 June; place of burial unknown; enrolled at Athens, McMinn County.

Smithpeter, James, Pvt.; Company I, 80th (62nd) Tennessee; died 20 January; place of burial unknown; enlisted at Newport, Cocke County.

Sneed, George, Pvt.; Company I, 62nd Tennessee; died 3 June; buried at Soldier's Rest; enlisted at Newport, Cocke County.

Snoddy, J. L., Lt.; Company F, 81st (61st) Tennessee; died 22 March; body shipped home; enlisted at Mossy Creek, Jefferson County.

Spoon, James, Pvt.; Company G, 61st Tennessee; died 12 May at Hospital #1; buried at Soldier's Rest; enrolled at Morristown, now Hamblen County.

Spriggs, Henry, Pvt.; Company B, 61st Tennessee; died 12 May at the City Hospital; buried at Soldier's Rest; enlisted at Rogersville, Hawkins County.

Stafford, Joseph, Pvt.; Company H, 80th (62nd) Tennessee; killed 28 March by a tornado; enlisted at Madisonville, Monroe County.

Stalcup, Alfred King, Lt.; Company F, 31st Tennessee; killed accidentally 28 June by one of his own men while on picket; buried at Soldier's Rest; enlisted at Mouse Creek (now Niota), McMinn County.

Stall, A. K., Lt.; Company F, 43rd Tennessee; date of death unknown; buried at Soldier's Rest; enrolled at Roane County.

Standifer, J. S., Pvt.; Company A, 62nd Tennessee; date of death unknown; place of burial unknown; enlisted at Cleveland, Bradley County.

Stephen[s], W. K., Pvt.; Company A, 60th Tennessee; died 25 June; place of burial unknown; enlisted at Jonesborough, Washington County.

Stewart [a.k.a. Stuart], William, Pvt.; Company B, 80th (62nd) Tennessee; died either 9 or 10 April at the City Hospital; buried at Soldier's Rest; enlisted at Benton, Polk County.

Strandell, H. F., Pvt.; Company A, 43rd Tennessee; died 14 February at the City Hospital; buried at Soldier's Rest; enrolled at Hiwassee Mines (now Ducktown], Polk County.

Strutten, Hiram L., Pvt.; Company G, 43rd Tennessee; died 14 February; buried at Soldier's Rest; enrolled at Mossy Creek, Jefferson County.

Swaffar, B. L., 1st Sgt.; Company C, 1st Tennessee Cavalry; died on an unknown date in July, after the surrender and being paroled; enrolled at Athens, McMinn County.

Swafford, B. F., Pvt.; Company H, 43rd Tennessee; died 11 July, after the surrender; buried at Soldier's Rest; enlisted at Riceville, McMinn County.

Swafford, John, Pvt.; Company H, 43rd Tennessee; died 25 June; place of burial unknown; enrolled at Riceville, McMinn County.

Swann, Daniel F., Pvt.; Company C, 31st Tennessee; date of death unknown; place of burial unknown; enlisted at Dandridge, Jefferson County.

Taylor, Charles, Pvt.; Company F, 60th Tennessee; died 16 May at Hospital #1; buried at Soldier's Rest; enlisted at Jonesborough, Washington County.

Taylor, James, Pvt.; Company I, 62nd Tennessee; died 10 April at the City Hospital; buried at Soldier's Rest; enlisted at Newport, Cocke County.

Taylor, Joseph, Pvt.; Company H, 80th (62nd) Tennessee; died 28 February; place of burial unknown; enlisted at Madisonville, Monroe County.

Taylor, William, Pvt.; Company E, 80th (62nd) Tennessee; died 10 April of small pox at the Pest House; buried at Soldier's Rest; enlisted at Bradley County.

Teefalaller, W., Pvt.; Company B, 31st Tennessee; date of death unknown; buried at Soldier's Rest; enlisted at Maryville, Blount County.

Thomas, Leander, Pvt.; Company E, 61st Tennessee; died 27 April at the City Hospital; buried at Soldier's Rest; enlisted at Blountville, Sullivan County.

Toney, W., Pvt.; Company B, 79th [60th] Tennessee; mortally wounded 29 December 1862 at the Battle of Chickasaw Bluffs; day 29 December at the City Hospital; buried at Soldier's Rest; enrolled at Rogersville, Hawkins County.

Treadway, John R., Pvt.; Company B, 43rd Tennessee; died 15 July, after the surrender; buried at Soldier's Rest; enrolled at Sulphur (now Rhea) Springs, Rhea County.

Tullock, David, Pvt.; Company A, 61st Tennessee; died 15 April; place of burial unknown; enlisted at Rheatown, Greene County.

Turner, Sterling T., Capt.; Company F, 43rd Tennessee; killed in action 22 May, defending against a general assault on the line; buried at Soldier's Rest; enrolled at Roane County.

Unknown Confederate soldier from East Tennessee; unknown company, 43rd Tennessee; died 5 February of small pox at the Pest House; buried at Soldier's Rest.

Unknown Confederate soldier from East Tennessee; unknown company, 43rd Tennessee; shot for desertion 6 March; buried on NE corner of potters' field marked No. 1.

Unknown Confederate soldier from East Tennessee; regiment and company unknown; shot for desertion 6 March; buried at Soldier's Rest.

Unknown Confederate soldier from East Tennessee; regiment and company unknown; shot for desertion 6 March; buried at Soldier's Rest.

Unknown Confederate soldier from East Tennessee; company unknown, 31st Tennessee; died 19 June; buried at Soldier's Rest.

Unknown Confederate soldier from East Tennessee; regiment and company unknown; died 19 June; buried at Soldier's Rest. [Possibly Pvt. James L. Smith of Company C, 59th Tennessee and of Elizabethton, Carter County; killed this date by a sharpshooter.]

Unknown Confederate Soldier from East Tennessee; company unknown, 3rd Tennessee; killed 27 June by a shell. [Pvt. __ Garghess of this regiment was killed on this date and under similar circumstances.]

Unknown Confederate soldier from East Tennessee; company unknown, 43rd Tennessee; died 8 July, after the surrender; buried at Soldier's Rest.

Vaughan, David L., Pvt.; Company E, 3rd Tennessee; killed either 8 or 9 June by a sharpshooter; buried at Soldier's Rest; enrolled at Maryville, Blount County.

Vaughn, James, Pvt.; Company E, 81st (61st) Tennessee; died 1 April at the City Hospital; buried at Soldier's Rest; enlisted at Blountville, Sullivan County.

Viars, Riley, Pvt.; Company F, 80th (62nd) Tennessee; killed in action 28 December 1862at the Battle of Chickasaw Bluffs; place of burial unknown; enrolled at Loudon, then Roane County.

Wall, David K., Pvt.; Company G, 60th Tennessee; died 15 June; buried at Soldier's Rest; enlisted at Blountville, Sullivan County.

Watterson, Thomas, Pvt.; Company G, 31st Tennessee; died 4 May; enlisted at Rogersville Junction (now Bulls Gap), Hawkins County.

White, James, Pvt.; Company D, 61st Tennessee; died 10 May; place of burial unknown; enlisted at Henderson's Mills, Greene County.

Willet, J. W., Pvt.; Company K, 61st Tennessee; died 1 July; place of burial unknown; enlisted at Zollicoffer (now Bluff City), Sullivan County.

Willet, N. R., Pvt.; Company K, 61st Tennessee; died 5 July; place of burial unknown; enlisted at Zollicoffer (now Bluff City], Sullivan County.

Willis, John W., Sgt.; Company E, 80th (62nd) Tennessee; died 13 January at Walls; buried at Soldier's Rest; enlisted at Polk County.

Wilson, G. W., Pvt.; Company F, 43rd Tennessee; died 18 July at Enterprise, MS, after parolee's march from Vicksburg; place of burial unknown; enlisted at Roane County.

Wilson, J. C., Pvt.; Company G, 61st Tennessee; died 9 June; buried at Soldier's Rest; enrolled at Morristown (now Hamblen) County.

Wilson, James, Pvt.; Company G, 62nd Tennessee; died 20 July; place of burial unknown; enlisted at Monroe County.

Wilson, R. H., Pvt.; Company C, 62nd Tennessee; died 25 June; buried at Soldier's Rest; enlisted at Monroe County.

Winstead, Marion, Pvt.; Company B, 79th (60th) Tennessee; died 17 February; place of burial unknown; enlisted at Rogersville, Hawkins County.

Witt, Houston, Pvt.; Company G, 43rd Tennessee; died 29 August of complications to an arm wound suffered during the 22 June sortie; place of burial unknown; enlisted at Mossy Creek, Jefferson County.

Witt, N. G., Pvt.; Company C, 61st Tennessee; died 20 May; buried at Soldier's Rest; enlisted at Greeneville, Greene County.

Wright, Henry, Pvt.; Company E, 31st Tennessee; date of death unknown; buried at Soldier's Rest; enlisted at Strawberry Plains, Jefferson County.

Wright, J. W., Pvt.; Company B, 31st Tennessee; killed in action 24 February by the *Indianola*, while serving aboard the *Queen of the West*; enrolled at Maryville, Blount County.

Youngblood, J. S., Pvt.; Company B, 62nd Tennessee; killed in action, date of death and circumstances unknown; enlisted at Benton, Polk County.

Appendix C

Identified East Tennessee Confederate Dead during the Vicksburg Campaign

(Breakdown of Casualties by Command)

43rd Tennessee Infantry
Total killed as a result of hostile action: 22
Total identified as dying of disease: 34
Total whose cause of death is unknown or due to other reasons: 39
Total number of deaths: 95

60th (79th) Tennessee Infantry
Total killed as a result of hostile action: 6
Total identified as dying of disease: 32
Total whose cause of death is unknown or due to other reasons: 24
Total number of deaths: 62

61st (81st) Tennessee Infantry
Total killed as a result of hostile action: 5
Total identified as dying of disease: 30
Total whose cause of death is unknown or due to other reasons: 24
Total number of deaths: 59

62nd (80th) Tennessee Infantry
Total killed as a result of hostile action: 5
Total identified as dying of disease: 27
Total whose cause of death is unknown or due to other reasons: 23
Total number of deaths: 55

31st Tennessee Infantry
Total killed as a result of hostile action: 7
Total identified as dying of disease: 13
Total whose cause of death is unknown or due to other reasons: 20
Total number of deaths: 40

3rd Tennessee Infantry
Total killed as a result of hostile action: 7
Total identified as dying of disease: 8
Total whose cause of death is unknown or due to other reasons: 8

Total number of deaths: 23
59th Tennessee Infantry
Total killed as a result of hostile action: 2
Total identified as dying of disease: 7
Total whose cause of death is unknown or due to other reasons: 14
Total number of deaths: 23
Lynch's Light Artillery Company
Total killed as a result of hostile action: 0
Total identified as dying of disease: 3
Total whose cause of death is unknown or due to other reasons: 1
Total number of deaths: 4
Deaths in East Tennessee Commands Not Identified
Total killed as a result of hostile action: 0
Total identified as dying of disease: 0
Total whose cause of death is unknown or due to other reasons: 4
Total number of deaths: 4
Company C, 1st Tennessee Cavalry
Total killed as a result of hostile action: 1
Total identified as dying of disease: 0
Total whose cause of death is unknown or due to other reasons: 2
Total number of deaths: 3

APPENDIX D

372 IDENTIFIED EAST TENNESSEE CONFEDERATE DEAD

Breakdown of Casualties by County during the Vicksburg Campaign
(Many of whom are buried at Soldiers' Rest, Cedar Hill Cemetery,
Vicksburg, Mississippi)

Monroe County 38
Jefferson County 30
Sullivan County 30
Hawkins County 30
McMinn County 29
Washington County 28
Greene County 25
Hamblen County* 24
Polk County 20
County of origin unknown 20
Cocke County 16
Bradley County 12
Meigs County 12
Blount County 8
Roane County 8
Carter County 7
Hamilton County 7
Claiborne County 6
Rhea County 6
Knox County 5
Bledsoe County 5
Loudon County** 3
Bradley or Polk County 3

* County founded after the war; part of Jefferson and Grainger Counties before the war.

** County founded after the war; part of Roane County before the war.

Bibliography

Abshire, David M. *The South Rejects a Prophet*. New York: Frederick A. Praeger, 1967.

Allen, V. C. *Rhea and Meigs Counties in the Confederate War*. Dayton TN: self-published, 1908.

Bachman, J. W. "Chattanooga's Most Beloved Citizen." *The Confederate Veteran* 21/6 (June 1913): 281–82.

Bachman, Robert Luckey. "Reminiscences of Childhood and the Civil War." Unpublished manuscript, Old Courthouse Museum Archives, Vicksburg MS.

Bachman, R. L. "That Perilous Ride at Chickasaw Bayou." *The Confederate Veteran* 10/9 (September 1902) 408–409.

Ballard, Michael B. *Pemberton: A Biography*. Jackson: University Press of Mississippi, 1991.

Barber, Flavel C. *Holding the Line: The Third Tennessee Infantry, 1861–1865*. Edited by Robert H. Ferrell. Kent OH: Kent State University Press, 1994.

Bearss, Edwin. *The Campaign for Vicksburg*. 3 vols. Dayton OH: Morningside Press, 1986.

Beeler, Enoch. Letters. David C. Smith Collection, New Market TN.

Beeler, W. T., Letters, David C. Smith Collection, New Market TN.

Bell, John S. "Arkansas Sharpshooters at Vicksburg." *The Confederate Veteran* 12/9 (September 1904): 446–47.

Bell, Lucy McRae. "Reminiscences of Lucy McRae Bell." *Harpers Weekly* 56/2894 (8 June 1912): 12–13.

Bevier, R. S. *History of the First and Second Missouri Confederate Brigades, 1861–1865*. St. Louis MO: Bryan, Brand & Co., 1879.

Bible, Donahue. *From Persia to Piedmont: Life and Death in Vaughn's Brigade*. Mohawk TN: Dodson Creek Publishers, 1995.

Blair, John J. "Diary of John J. Blair." Unpublished manuscript, Tennessee State Library and Archives, Nashville TN.

Bowman Family Papers. East Tennessee State University Archives, Johnson City TN.

Brooks, Cora Davis. *History of Morristown, 1787–1936*. Nashville TN: Historical Records Survey, 1940.

Brooks, Donn Patton. *East Tennessee's Forgotten Soldiers: The Forty-Third Tennessee Infantry Regiment, CSA*. Kyle TX: Westpump Publishers, 1995.

Camp, Raleigh S. "What I Know, I Know, and I Dare Express It: The History of the 40th Georgia Infantry in the Vicksburg Campaign." *Journal of the American Civil War* 5/1 (1st Quarter 1996): 45–91.

"Capt. J. P. Burem, Thirty-first Tennessee." *The Confederate Veteran* 3/7 (July 1895): 203.

Carson, John M. "Capture of the *Indianola*." *The Confederate Veteran* 32/8 (August 1924): 380–83.

Chambers, William Pitt. "My Journal." *Publications of the Mississippi Historical Society*, Centenary series 5. Jackson MS: Mississippi Historical Society, 1925.

Civil War Records of Tennessee. 3 volumes. Nashville TN: Works Progress Administration, 1939.

Civil War Times Illustrated. Struggle for Vicksburg: The Battles & Siege That Decided the Civil War. Gettysburg PA: Civil War Times Illustrated, 1967.

Clack, William Raleigh. "Personal Diary of the Siege and Surrender of Vicksburg, Mississippi, July 4, 1863." Unpublished manuscript, Vicksburg National Military Park Archives, Vicksburg MS.

Clark, W. E. "That Last Roll—Walter Thomas Lenoir." *The Confederate Veteran* 38/4 (May 1930): 194.

Clark, Willene B., editor. *Valleys of the Shadow: The Memoir of Confederate Captain Reuben G. Clark*. Knoxville TNUniversity of Tennessee Press, 1994.

Cline, Lemuel, to "Lizzie," 2 May 1863. National Park Archives, Vicksburg MS.

Compiled Service Records of Confederate Soldiers Who Served from the State of Tennessee RG 109. National Archives, Washington DC.

Confederate Pension Applications, Soldier's Pensions Applications. Tennessee State Library and Archives, Nashville TN.

Cotton, Gordon A. *Vicksburg: Southern Stories of the Siege*. Vicksburg MS: self-published, 1987.

———, and Jeff Giambrone. *Vicksburg and the War*. Gretna LA: Pelican Publishers, 2004.

Darr, James Henry. "Diary." Unpublished manuscript, Ron Evans Collection.

Crump, Joe Wright. "A Boy Soldier's Fidelity." *The Confederate Veteran* 4/4 (April 1896): 119.

Davis, William C. *Rebels & Yankees: The Fighting Men of the Civil War*. New York NY: Salamander Books, Ltd., 1989.

Foote, Shelby. The Civil War: A Narrative. 3 vols. New York: Random House, 1963.

Fremantle, Arthur J. L., *Three Months in the Southern States, April–June 1863*. Edited by Walter Lord. Boston: Little, Brown and Co., 1954.

Fullenkamp, Leonard et al., editors. *Guide to the Vicksburg Campaign: The US Army War College Guide to Civil War Battles*. Lawrence: University of Kansas Press, 1998.

Giddens, Benjamin C., Letters. Old Courthouse Museum Archives, Vicksburg MS.

Goodson, Gary Ray, Sr., editor. *Georgia Confederate 7,000: Part II, Letters and Diaries*. Shawnee CO: self-published, 1997.

Grabau, Warren E. *Ninety-Eight Days: A Geographer's View of the Vicksburg Campaign*. Knoxville: University of Tennessee Press, 2000.

Groce, Todd. *Mountain Rebels: East Tennessee Confederates and the Civil War, 1861–1870*. Knoxville: University of Tennessee Press, 1999.

Hall-Stakely Papers. McClung Historical Collection, Knoxville Publick Libraries. Knoxville TN.

Hankinson, Alan. *Vicksburg 1863: Grant Clears the Mississippi*. Oxford: Osprey Publishing Ltd, 1993.

Harr, William, and William G. Morton. Letters. Old Courthouse Museum Archives, Vicksburg MS.

Hasseltine, William B. *Dr. J. G. M. Ramsey: Autobiography and Letters*. Nashville: Tennessee Historical Commission, 1954.

Hodges, Shirley C. *The Crosby Collection: "For Love of Family."* Morristown TN: self-published, 1998.

Hoehling, A. A. *Vicksburg: 47 Days of Siege*. New York NY: Fairfax Press, 1969.

Hooker, Charles E. *Mississippi*. Volume 12 of *Confederate Military History: A Library of Confederate States History*. Ed. Gen Clement A. Evans. Atlanta GA: Confederate Publishing Co., 1899.

Hogane, J. T. "Feiminiscences of the Siege of Vicksburg," *Southern Historical Society Papers* 11/1 (January 1883): 291–92.

Houston, Bob. "A History of Vaughn's Brigade." In *A Soldier's Story of the Siege of Vicksburg from the Diary of Osborne H. Oldroyd*, edited by Osborne Oldroyd, 200. Springfield IL: H. W. Rokker, 1885.

Hynds, George H. "Original Handwritten Notes of the Siege of Vicksburg from May 16th to July 4th, 1863." Unpublished manuscript, Vicksburg National Park Archives, Vicksburg MS.

Jenkins, Carl. Interview by William D. Taylor.

Kellogg, Theodore. Letters. Unknown private collection.

Key, David M., Papers. Bicentennial Library, Chattanooga TN.

Lockett, Samuel H. "The Defense of Vicksburg." In volume 3 of *Battles and Leaders of the Civil War*, edited by Robert Underwood Johnson and Clarence Clough Buel, 482–92. New York: Thomas Yoseloff, 1956. Reprint, Secaucus, NJ: Castle Publishing, 1989.

Korn, Jerry, editor. *The Civil War: War on the Mississippi*. Alexandria VA: Time-Life Books, 1985.

Leverett, Rudy H. *The Legend of the Free State of Jones*. Jackson: University Press of Mississippi, 1984.

Lillard, Newton J., Papers. Tennessee State Library and Archives, Nashville TN.

Lindsley, John B., editor. *The Military Annals of Tennessee (Confederate) 1st Series Embracing a Review of Military Operations, with Regimental Histories and Memorial Roles, Compiled from Original and Official Sources*. 3 vols. Nashville TN: J. M. Lindsley & Co., 1886.

Lord, W. W. "A Child at the Siege of Vicksburg," *Harpers Weekly* (1908) 44–53.

Loughborough, Mary W. *My Cave Life at Vicksburg*. New York: D. Appleton and Company, 1864.

Lynch, Rene. *Rebel's Rest Remembers: Sewanee Summers When We Were Very Young*. Sewanee TN: Proctor Hall Press, 1998.

Lynch's Company of Light Artillery. Papers. Vicksburg National Park Archives, Vicksburg MS.

Madaus, Howard Michael, and Robert D. Needham. *The Battle Flags of the Confederate Army of Tennessee*. Milwaukee: Milwaukee Public Museum, 1976.

Martin, James Madison, to his sister May McClain, 23 April 1863. Harr-Morton Letters. Vicksburg National Park Archives, Vicksburg MS.

Membership applications, William B. Tate Camp Number 725, United Confederate Veterans, Morristown TN.

Merrin, F. W. "Sinking of the *Cincinnati* at the Siege of Vicksburg." *The Confederate Veteran* 5/5 (May 1897): 201.

Moffitt, John Thomas. Papers. McClung Historical Collection, Knoxville Public Library, Knoxville TN.

Morgan, Mark. "Preservation Report." *Journal of the American Civil War* 2/1 (1st Quarter 1992): 69–74.

Nelson, T. A. R., Papers, McClung Historical Collection, Knoxville TN.

Northen, Charles Swift. *All Right, Let Them Come: The Civil War Diary of an East Tennessee Confederate*. Knoxville: University of Tennessee Press, 2003.

Official Records of the Union and Confederate Navies in the War of the Rebellion. 31volumes. Washington DC: Government Printing Office, 1895–1929.

Parker, E. D. Letters. In "King History." Typescript, Kingsport TN.

Parks, Joseph H. *General Kirby-Smith, CSA*. Baton Rouge: LSU Press, 1954.

Payne, James E. "Missouri Troops in the Vicksburg Campaign." *The Confederate Veteran* 36/7 and 36/10 (July 1928): 302–303, 377–79.

Pemberton, John C., Papers. National Archives, Washington DC.

Pemberton, John C. *Pemberton: Defender of Vicksburg*. Chapel Hill: University of North Carolina Press, 1942.

Pratt, Fletcher. *Civil War on Western Waters*. New York: Henry Holt, 1956.

Reynolds, Alexander W. Letters. Brian Green Collection, Private Collection, Kernersville NC.

Rigby, William T. Correspondence. Vicksburg National Parks Archives, Vicksburg MS.

Ritter, William L. *Biographical Memoir and Sketch of the Third Maryland Artillery*. Baltimore: John S. Bridges & Co., 1900.

———. "Captain Ritter's Account of Operations of [a] Section of Third Maryland Battery, Spring of 1863." *Southern Historical Society Papers* 7/1 (January–February 1879): 247–49.

———. "Sketch of the Third Battery of Maryland Artillery." *Southern Historical Society Papers* 10/1–2 (January–February 1882): 328–32, 392–402, 464–471.

———. "Maryland Artillery—Sketch of the Third Battery." *Southern Historical Society Papers* 11/1 (January–February 1883): 113–18, 186–93, 433–42, 537–44.

———. "Sketch of the Third Maryland Artillery." *Southern Historical Society Papers* 12/1–2 January–February1884): 170–72.

———. "Tennesseans with a Maryland Battery." *The Confederate Veteran* 378/6 (June 1950): 237.

Saffell Family Papers. University of Tennessee Archives, Knoxville TN.

Sharf, J. Thomas. *A History of the Confederate States Navy: From Its Organization to the Surrender of Its Last Vessel.* 1887; Reprint, New York: The Fairfax Press 1977.

Shea, William L., and Terrence J. Winschel. *Vicksburg Is the Key: The Struggle for the Mississippi River.* Lincoln: University of Nebraska Press, 2003.

Shields, John Brabson. "Reminiscences." *East Tennessee Roots* 7/1 (Spring 1992): 1–10.

Simms, L. Moody, editor. "A Louisiana Engineer at the Siege of Vicksburg: Letters of Henry Ginder." *Louisiana History* 8.

Simpson, John A., editor. *Reminiscences of the 41st Tennessee.* Shippensburg PA: White Mane Books, 2001.

Smith, David M., editor. *Compelled to Appear in Print: The Vicksburg Manuscript of General John C. Pemberton.* Cincinnati OH: Ironclad Publishing, 1999.

Smith, Leland L., editor. *A Smith in Service: Diaries of Calvin Morgan Smith, 1847–1864.* Rogersville TN: Hawkins County Genealogical and Historical Society, 2000.

Smith, Timothy B. *Champion Hill: Decisive Battle for Vicksburg.* El Dorado Hills CA: Savas Beatie Publishers, 2004.

Spradling, Robert. "Diary." Unpublished manuscript, Vicksburg National Park Archives, Vicksburg MS.

Stamper, Isaac J. "Travels of the 43rd Regiment, Tennessee Volunteers: Diary of I. J. Stamper." Unpublished manuscript, Cleveland Library, Cleveland TN.

Swan, Samuel A. R. "A Tennessean at the Siege of Vicksburg: The Diary of Samuel Alexander Ramsey Swan, May 18–July 1863." *Tennessee Historical Quarterly* 14/4 (December 1955): 353–72.

Taylor, F. Jay, editor. *Reluctant Rebel: The Secret Diary of Robert Patrick, 1861–1865.* Baton Rouge: LSU Press, 1987.

Taylor, William D. "Brigadier General John C. Vaughn, CSA: An East Tennessean Leading East Tennesseans in East Tennessee." *Faculty Studies* 7/4 (Fall 1993): 33–41.

_____. *Home-Growed Rebels: Carter County's Company "C," 59th Regiment of Tennessee Infantry, CSA.* Morristown TN: Mossy Creek-Zollicoffer Press, 1992.

Tennessee Civil War Centennial Commission. *Tennesseans in the Civil War: A Military History of Confederate and Union Units with Available Rosters of Personnel.* 2 volumes. Nashville TN: Civil War Centennial Commission, 1964–1965.

Tennessee Civil War Veterans' Questionnaires. Edited by Gustavus Dyer and John Trotwood Moore. 5 volumes. Easley SC: Southern Historical Press, 1985.

Tolstoy, Lev. *The Cossacks.* Translated by Louise and Aylmer Maude. Alfred A. Knopf: New York, 1994.

Tunnard, William H. *A Southern Record: the History of the Third Regiment Louisiana Infantry.* Baton Rouge LA: privately printed, 1866.

United Daughters of the Confederacy. "Record Book of Confederate Soldiers Buried at Cedar Hill Cemetery, Vicksburg." Unpublished manuscript, 1958, Old Courthouse Museum, Vicksburg MS.

Urquhart, Kenneth Trist. *Vicksburg: Southern City Under Siege: William Lovelace Foster's Letter Describing the Defense and Surrender of the Confederate Fortress on the Mississippi.* New Orleans: The Historic New Orleans Collection, 1980.

Vicksburg: War, Terrible War, Had Come to Our Very Hearthstone. Alexandria VA: Time-Life Books, 1997.

Walker, Edward, III, editor. *Tales from the Civil War.* Newport TN: self-published, 1983.

War of the Rebellion: A Compilation of the Official Records of the Union and Confederate Armies. 128 Parts in 70 volumes. Washington DC: Government Printing Office, 1881–1901.

Wash, William A. *Camp, Field and Prison Life: Containing Sketches of Service in the South; and the Experience, Incidents and Observations Connected with Almost Two Years Imprisonment at Johnson's Island, Ohio Where All Confederate Officers were Confined.* St. Louis MO: Southwestern Book and Publishing Co., 1870.

Webster, Gary W. *Confederate Roll of Honor: Confederate Dead Vicksburg Campaign, January 1862–July 1863.* Vicksburg MS: Ole Sow Publications, 1998.

Wenschel, Terrence J. "Chickasaw Bayou: A Battlefield Guide." Tour Guide Brochure. Vicksburg MS: National Park Service, 1989.

Index

186-87; Reynolds troops camp at their farm in early May 1863, 241, 248

"shebangs", 17, 24, 81

Sherman, General William T., battle at Chickasaw Bluffs, 5; ordered to Memphis in December, 1862 in preparation for Vicksburg, 26; departure of troops from Memphis for Vicksburg, 33; arrival by boat north of Vicksburg on December 24, 1862, 36-37; Confederate fortifications and terrain near Vicksburg, 40-42; landing of troops and battles of Chickasaw Bayou and Chickasaw Bluffs, 42-54; withdrawal of troops, 54-55; Federal army lingers at Chickasaw Bluffs area and departs on January 1, 1863, 56; capture of Fort Hindman on Arkansas River, 57; January 2, 1863, end of attempt to capture Vicksburg and withdrawal from Chickasaw Bluffs area, 63; McClernand given command of Army of the Mississippi and becomes his superior, 70; return to Milliken's Bend on Mississippi River in renewed attempt to take Vicksburg, January 20, 1863, 81; DeSoto canal project, 87; April 1863, leaves Milliken's Bend and marches south, 196-98; directed by Grant to attack Snyder's Bluff area as diversionary tactic, 212; attacks Snyder's Bluff area on Yazoo River to draw attention from Grant's forces landing near Port Gibson, then sets out southward by land to meet Grant, 218; forces arrive near Bruinsburg and begin trek to join Grant's forces heading for Jackson, 245-46; May 14, troops positioned at Clinton very near to Jackson, 258; May 19 assault on Vicksburg, 323, 324; May 22 assault on Vicksburg, 333

Shields, Lieutenant John, 468, 482, 484

Shiloh, battle of, 20

Shoup, Francis, brigade at May 19 assault on Vicksburg, 323

60th Tennessee Infantry, renamed from 79th Tennessee, 14; travels from Tennessee to Mobile, November 1862, 17-18; census of Company H at end of December 1862, 57; sinking of federal gunboat Indianola, 130; troop census of

February 1863, 136; casualties from tornado of March 28, 1863, 169; muster for March and April of 1863, 223; picket duty at old Chickasaw Bluffs battleground, 227; position at Big Black River battlefield, 288; 294-95; rout of other two regiments causes 60th to flee for their lives, 298; Gregg orders regiment to dash for river, and cut off by Federals, large portion of 60th surrenders, 300; surrender to Federals, 301-02; losses at Big Black River, 306n-307n, 311; prisoners of war, 312; surrender at Vicksburg and troop count, 465

61st Tennessee Infantry, bravery at Battle of Big Black River, 7; renamed from 81st Tennessee, 14; census in February 1863, 136; muster for March and April of 1863, 223; Federal troops charge their position at battle of Big Black River, 295-96; casualties from charge, 296-97; break and run after Federals breach defenses, 297-98; Rose issues order to fall back across Big Black River, 299; capture of regimental colors by Federals, 302; losses from casualties and capture of troops at Big Black River, 305, 311; position in fortifications at Vicksburg during siege, 319; surrender at Vicksburg and troop count, 465

62nd Tennessee Infantry, renamed from 80th Tennessee, 14; departure from Sweetwater, Tennessee, for Mobile, 17; praise by generals Pemberton and S. D. Lee for valor at Chickasaw Bluffs, 51; census of Company I at end of 1862, 57; census in February 1863, 136; casualties from tornado of March 28, 1863, 169; muster for March and April of 1863, 223; honored by Gen. Pemberton for their part in December 29, 1862, battle at Chickasaw Bluffs, 258; position at Big Black River battlefield, 288; Federal troops charge their position at battle of Big Black River, 295-96; break and run after Federals breach defenses, 297-98; losses at Big Black River, 307n, 311; escape from Big Black River, 312; June 25, 1863, letter to Gen. Pemberton detailing officer controversy, 435-36;

Barton brigade's sortie captures 97
Federals, 346; rumors of activity of
Gen. Johnston's Army of Relief, 347;
May 25, word of transfer of prisoners
from Big Black River and situation in
Vicksburg fortifications, 349-50; May
27, sinking of Federal ironclad
Cincinnati and paltry results of Federals
siege of Vicksburg, 352-53; concludes
diary, expressing hope that it reaches his
family in Tennessee, 353; May 31,
fierce artillery bombardment, mortar
boat shelling, and sharpshooting, 363-
64; June 1, good morale among troops
in spite of deprivations, illnesses, and
trench life, 370; June 2, rumors of Gen.
Kirby-Smith's and Gen. Price's
movements, 373; news of Federals
fortifications at Big Black River in
anticipation of Gen. Johnston's arrival,
375; June 4, picket duty between
Confederate and Federal trenches, 378-
80; June 6, rumors of actions by Gen.
Johnston and other relief efforts while
Federals continue encirclement of
garrison, 384; June 7, sounds of fighting
upriver and increasing pressures on
defenders at Vicksburg, 386-87; June
12, reports many men sick in hospital
and muster for 31st regiment, 399; June
13, fifth Sunday in trenches, soldiers
talk of families, 400; June 15 artillery
battle, reports of Federal casualties in
Vicksburg campaign, and endurance of
war to prevent destruction of the South,
403-04; June 16, 30th day of siege, good
condition of 31st regiment, good
morale, and rumors of relief from Gen.
Johnston and others, 406-08; June 18,
death of Sgt. Hill, bloodshed of war,
and beating back three Federal assaults
the previous day, 412; June 19, skirmish
with Federals charging picket lines, 415;
June 20, obtains newspapers in town,
learns that printers are printing on
wallpaper, 417; June 20, heavy
cannonade and report of casualties, 419;
June 21 men bear up under siege
conditions, short rations, and no
communication from outside, 420; June
21 sortie against forward Federal rifle
pits, 421; June 22 attack takes Federal

rifle pits, 426; diary entry of June 22,
extolling Confederate troops and fight
for liberty, 429-30; sharpshooters of
31st company and their effectiveness,
439; June 28, says he's still among the
living, and reports visit to hospital, 444-
45; death of Lt. Stallcup from friendly
fire, 447; July 1, garrison either must
make great effort to escape or
surrender, 455; July 3, ceasefire between
infantry lines, 457-58; surrender of
Confederate garrison, 469-
Smith, Private George W., wound at battle
of Big Black River, 297
Smith, Private James L., death of, 410
Smith, Private Joe A., letter of April 28,
1863 to Carrie Stakely, 214; continues
letter with rumors of Federal troop
landings to the south of Vicksburg area,
217
snakes in Vicksburg area, 210
Snyder's Bluff, April 15, 1863, feint of
Federal troops under Sherman, 190-91
Snyder's Mill (near Vicksburg), 42
"Soldiers's Rest", at Vicksburg Cedar Hill
Cemetery, 8
Southern, Private John, celebration at West
Point, Georgia, Christmas Day 1862, 39
Spears, Captain James D., 401
speech and dialect of East Tennessee
soldiers, 10-12
Spradling, Robert, arrival at Vicksburg on
night of Jan. 1, 1863, 59; April 30, 1863,
report of Federals landing at Port
Gibson, 219; battle of Port Gibson and
arrival of Reynolds' brigade too late for
action, 229; May 2-3, retreating across
Big Black River, 232; skirmishing near
Big Black River, 238; 43rd Tennessee's
role in repulsing May 22nd assault of
Federals on Vicksburg, 338; casualties
from May 22 assault, 339; May 24,
sharpshooting and cannonading all day,
342; June 22 attack on Federal rifle pits,
427
Stakely, Captain Sam, 22, 24
Stakely, Carrie, letter from William S.
Brown of December 2, 1862, 21-23;
letter from Private Jimmy Caldwell on
December 7, 1862, 24-25
Stallcup, Lieutenant King, death from
friendly fire, 447, 448

up, 450-51; July 1, renewed shelling by
Federals and hope of relief gone, 453;
flag of truce and continued shelling
from Federal gunboats, 459-60;
surrender of garrison, 466-67; awaiting
parole, unbroken spirit of troops, 472-
73
Sweetwater, Tennessee, 14
Switzerland (Federal) gunboat, 164-66

Talley, Private J. W., 182
Taylor, General Henry H., 91
Taylor, General Thomas, report on
conditions of brigades defending
Vicksburg, 351-52
Tennessee troops at Vicksburg in early
1863, 72n
3rd Maryland battery, 233; May 31, 1863,
fierce artillery bombardment by
Federals, 364
3rd Tennessee Infantry, 4; Battle of First
Manassas, 4; in brigade under command
of Col. Reynolds, 5; formation by
Vaughn and early history of, 14,
Kentucky campaign and winter camp in
Tennessee in 1862, 22n; ordered to
Knoxville in winter of 1862, 24; ordered
from Big Creek Gap to join Reynolds'
brigade in Knoxville in preparation for
trip to Jackson, Mississippi, 32; arrival at
camp near Vicksburg, Jan. 7, 1863, 73;
volunteers take skiff to grounded
transport *City of Vicksburg* and set it
ablaze, 170; position in fortifications
during siege of Vicksburg, 316, 319
3rd Tennessee Infantry (Clack's), praise by
Confederate commanders for valor at
Chickasaw Bluffs in December 1862,
51; from lower middle Tennessee on
loan from Gen. Bragg and Army of
Tennessee, 71
31st Tennessee Infantry, 5; service aboard
gunboats and sinking of ironclad
Indianola, 6; Federal soldiers' comments
on sharpshooter after end of siege of
Vicksburg, 8; in East Tennessee during
winter of 1862, 13-14; Kentucky
campaign, 22n; orders to leave for
Kingston, Tennessee on December 8,
1862, 24; trip from Tennessee to
Vicksburg by rail, 33; at Jackson,
Mississippi in January 1863, 71; role in

sinking of Federal warship *Indianola*,
126n; arrival back at Camp Reynolds
after sinking of *Indianola*, 129; summary
by Col. Bradford of actions in capturing
Queen of the West and sinking the
Indianola, 130; Special Order by Col.
Bradford praising their actions in battle
with the *Indianola*, 134; moving camp
on March 3, 1863, 141-42; May 16,
defends Pemberton's supply train at
battle of Baker's Creek, 269; position in
fortifications during siege of Vicksburg,
316, 319; muster report of June 12, 399;
sharpshooters from regiment and their
effectiveness, 439; parole after
surrender at Vicksburg, 476
36th Tennessee Infantry, 2
Thomas, Captain James D., 292
Tibbs, Congressman William H., 89
Tilghman, General Lloyd, 233; joining
Gen. Pemberton's troops on move to
Gen. Johnston's encampment, 259;
death of, at Big Black Bridge, 280
Toland, Lieutenant John, 299, 431
Toole, Sam, May 9, 1863, reportedly taken
prisoner in fighting at Grand Gulf, 246;
not captured as previously reported, 250
Tracy, General Edward D., Alabama
brigade, 200, 225; death of Gen. Tracy
May 1, 1863, at battle of Port Gibson,
226
trench conditions for Confederates at
Vicksburg, June 1, 1863, filth of
clothing, body lice, soldiers becoming
weak and feeble from lying in trenches,
366; heat, vermin, disease, filth, and
odors in trenches, 394; soldiers picking
off body lice, 398; cannonading at night
makes it impossible to sleep, 400n;
excruciating monotony, exposure to all
weathers, no adequate food or water,
411
Tullahoma, Tennessee, 152
Tunnard, William, remarks on rustic speech
of troops from Arkansas, 11n; June 22
attack on Federal rifle pits, capture of
Federal Lt. Col. Camm, 428
Turner, Captain, 84
Turner, Captain Sterling, death on May 22,
1863, at Vicksburg fortifications, 334;
338
26th Tennessee, 16